Juvenile Delinquency

Juvenile Delinquency

Classic and Contemporary Readings

WILLIAM E. THOMPSON
East Texas State University

JACK E. BYNUM
Oklahoma State University

ALLYN AND BACON
Boston   London   Sydney   Toronto

Series Editor: Karen Hanson
Editorial-Production Service: York Production Services
Cover Administrator: Linda K. Dickinson
Manufacturing Buyer: Tamara Johnson

Library of Congress Cataloging-in-Publication Data

Juvenile delinquency: classic and contemporary readings/[edited by]
William E. Thompson, Jack E. Bynum.
    p. cm.
    ISBN 0-205-12231-0
    1.   Juvenile delinquency. I. Thompson, William E. (William Edwin), 1950- . II. Bynum, Jack E.
    HV9069.J794 1990
    364.3 '6— dc20
                                  89-39769
                                  CIP

Printed in the United States of America
10 9 8 7 6 5 4 3 2   94 93 92

To our wives Marilyn Thompson and Margaret Bynum;
and to our children
Brandon and Mica Thompson and
Jenny Lynn (Bynum) Hilton and Danny Bynum

Contents

Preface

JUVENILE DELINQUENCY is a social problem. Like any social problem, it is an extremely complex phenomenon which is not likely to be fully understood much less resolved through simplistic approaches, half-hearted efforts, and idealistic panacea-type programs. Social problems are rarely (if ever) eliminated. Rather, they are usually either exacerbated, relieved, diminished, or ignored. Often, as a "new" social problem emerges, "older" ones may wane in their publicly acknowledged significance. Juvenile delinquency is a major social problem which has captured national attention since the establishment of the first juvenile court in 1899.

The purpose of this anthology is to bring together in one volume representative classic studies, landmark contributions, and contemporary research in the field of sociology on the topic of juvenile delinquency. These readings represent an overview of major sociological contributions to the understanding of juvenile delinquency. These insights from the past and present can provide a solid foundation for the delinquency research and theory building of the future.

This book of readings approaches the social problem of juvenile delinquency from a sociological perspective. While there are a variety of specific theoretical approaches within the sociological perspective, they are all united by some meaningful common elements. For example, sociologists perceive, analyze, and explain human behavior as emerging as part and product of the society in which it occurs. Specifically, juvenile delinquency must be viewed within the context of family, neighborhood, school, peer group, and other social institutions and groups to which adolescents belong.

In keeping with the sociological perspective, this anthology is divided into an unfolding sequence of five major parts. Part One, The Definition, Measurement, and Magnitude of Juvenile Delinquency focuses upon the definition of delinquency and how society establishes norms for adolescent behavior, and consequently determines what is conforming and what is deviant for juveniles. The emphasis is on how society defines what is considered appropriate and inappropriate behavior for its youth. Selected articles also look at the different types of data used in delinquency research. Part Two, Explanations of Juvenile Delinquency includes some of the major theoretical sociological explanations of delinquency. While these different theories may cite a variety of specific causal variables as contributing to delinquency, they all emphasize the social nature of the problem. Part Three, The Social Context of Juvenile Delinquency emphasizes the social nature and group context of juvenile delinquency. The influence of family and peers are explored as important variables related to juvenile delinquency.

While most delinquency does not involve juvenile gangs, the gang emerges as an important focus of study for understanding the influence of social groups upon juvenile behavior. Part Four, Society Versus the Juvenile Delinquent introduces the concept of the social arena and explores the arenas in which delinquents are likely to be confronted for their behavior. Of special interest are the arenas of the juvenile court and the school. Finally, Part Five, Prevention and Control of Juvenile Delinquency discusses the concept of social control and how society reacts to delinquency and delinquents as it attempts to regulate juvenile behavior and prevent youthful law violators from becoming adult criminals.

Each of these five parts begins with an introduction which defines and explains some of the major concepts and ideas included in the readings which follow. The introduction is followed by a synopsis and discussion of what is considered to be a "classic" book on that particular aspect of juvenile delinquency. The major ideas of the book are outlined and its relative strengths and weaknesses are discussed from a sociological viewpoint. Each book synopsis is followed by a selection of readings which serve to enhance the understanding of juvenile delinquency from the sociological perspective. These articles were written by a very diverse group of social scientists who are noted and respected for their knowledge and expertise in the area of juvenile delinquency. The readings were selected because they are sociological in their approach, unique in their contributions, and raise a variety of interesting and controversial issues about the subject of juvenile delinquency.

The readings are then followed by a summary and discussion major concepts and ideas from the readings included in that particular part. In order to stimulate thought and discussion about the articles in each part, we have provided some questions for review and discussion about the articles in that section. We encourage the reader to approach these articles with an open and inquisitive mind.

This book of readings, like any sociological inquiry, raises a variety of questions. We hope it arouses sufficient interest and provides the intellectual curiosity and stimulation which leads to the pursuit of these questions, and ultimately, to a better understanding of the complex phenomenon of juvenile delinquency.

It is impossible to produce an anthology such as this without help and cooperation from a large number of people. We would like to thank the authors, journal editors, and publishers who permitted us to reproduce their works. We especially thank Travis Hirschi, Edwin Schur, and Anthony Platt who graciously provided us with biographical data. Additionally, we would like to thank Bill Barke, Sue Brody and the others at Allyn and Bacon—especially Karen Hanson for their fine work. Special thanks go to Brenda Scheibmeir for her assistance and to Virginia Cunningham for her invaluable aid throughout the entire project. We are indebted to those who participated in the review process for their helpful and insightful comments—especially Greg Sheets. And finally, we give our sincere thanks and heartfelt love to Marilyn, Brandon, and Mica Thompson and Margaret Bynum for their continued love, support, and encouragement.

W.E.T.

J.E.B.

Juvenile Delinquency

The Definition, Measurement, and Magnitude of Juvenile Delinquency

INTRODUCTION

IN ANY COLLECTION of research reports and journal articles from a spectrum of diverse sources and authorities, high priority must be given to logically ordering the unfolding contributions so as to maximize coverage and clarity for readers. For example, Part One begins with a detailed discussion of the 1967 *Task Force Report: Juvenile Delinquency and Youth Crime*. This landmark publication not only brought together the insights of many of the leading scholars of that time in the field and underscores the seriousness of juvenile crime in the United States, but also lays important groundwork for contemporary reports that later appear in this volume. The Task Force Report begins with working definitions of juvenile delinquency and status offenses and then addresses various dimensions of juvenile justice and institutional factors associated with the causes and controls of delinquency.

Ruth Shonle Cavan's 1961 address to the Midwest Sociological Society, "The Concepts of Tolerance and Contraculture as Applied to Delinquency," appropriately views juvenile delinquency from a sociological perspective. Cavan introduced a bell-shaped behavior continuum that hypothetically and simultaneously depicted the incidence of conforming and nonconforming behavior in relation to social norms or modal behavior. Juvenile delinquency—as with other forms of deviant behavior—is seen on the behavior continuum as underconformity to normative or modal expectations. On the other hand, rigid and inflexible overconformity to social norms—depicted at the opposite extreme of the bell-shaped behavior continuum—is perceived as another form of deviance.

A clear grasp of the magnitude of juvenile delinquency is also of early and logical importance in a book of this nature. Official data regarding the number and kinds of juvenile offenses committed each year in the United States are available from two sources. The Federal Bureau of Investigation collects arrest data from county, city, and state law enforcement agencies and issues annual *Uniform Crime Reports*. The National Center for Juvenile Justice gathers information concerning cases appearing before juvenile courts and also issues annual summaries. The third paper included in this section is an excerpt from the 1988 *Report to the Nation on Crime and Justice* which brings together data from the above official sources and compares juvenile delinquency with adult crime on arrest rates and the incidence of various crimes by age. Excerpts from another United States government publication rounds out our consideration of official delinquency statistics. *Juvenile Court Statistics, 1984*, succinctly describes the number and characteristics of delinquency and status offense cases disposed during 1984 by courts with juvenile jurisdiction. A general model of juvenile court processing is presented that should prove useful to the reader in understanding the various steps and alternative dispositions available in the adjudication of cases.

The weaknesses and limitations of officially collected delinquency data are identified and examined in two additional research reports. William Chambliss and Richard Nagasawa, in their article, "On the Validity of Official Statistics," compared self-reported delinquency involvement of white, black, and Japanese high school boys with arrest and court reported data for the three racial groups. They found very serious discrepancies between the official rates and percentages of referrals and percentages of deviant involvement reflected in self-report surveys when they controlled for race and social class. Chambliss and Nagasawa concluded that official statistics have little validity as indicators of actual delinquency in the population. A similar indictment was leveled at official data on juvenile delinquency by Maynard Erickson and Lamar Empey in their article, "Court Records, Undetected Delinquency and Decision-Making." Their surveys of self-reported offenses by juveniles reveal that while official sources of statistics are troubled with chronic methodological weaknesses that limit generalizations—such as their inability to include undetected, unreported, and unsolved delinquency—they are useful in measuring the more serious and most common offense categories. At the same time, self-report surveys do support the conclusion that huge numbers of youth are involved in delinquent behavior—especially the less critical status offenses.

The article by Michael Hindelang, Travis Hirschi, and Joseph Weis reviews the criticisms of both official measures of criminality and self-report instruments and concluded that the apparently contradictory results that seem to invalidate one or both approaches is largely illusory. In their "Correlates of Delinquency: The Illusions of Discrepancy between Self-Report and Official Measures," these authors contend that each approach measures a different domain or dimension of the delinquency phenomena. Hindelang, Hirschi, and Weis conclude that official data correctly reflects the demographic distribution of sex, race, and social class as correlates of delinquency while the efficacy of self-report studies lie in valid and reliable indicators of offending behavior.

Peter Applebome's article "Juvenile Crime: The Offenders are Younger and the Offenses More Serious," points to an apparent increase in serious crimes on the part of juveniles. It further emphasizes that the offenders in these serious cases are getting younger and younger. The article presents data from the FBI *Uniform Crime Reports*, along with personal observations from juvenile judges, attorneys, and law enforcement officers which substantiate Applebome's claim. The "Letter to the Editor" written by Barry Krisberg, President of the National Council on Crime and Delinquency, in response to Applebome's article, warns that one must be very careful in drawing conclusions that serious juvenile crime is increasing. He points to an apparent downward overall trend in serious delinquency, and contends that "get tough on crime" attitudes and policies may be responsible for the apparent rise in juvenile crime.

The final article in Part One is "Rediscovering Delinquency: Social History, Political Ideology and the Sociology of Law" by John Hagan and Jeffrey Leon. In this thought-provoking work, the authors apply a Marxian class conflict perspective to the social control of so-called "deviant youth." Citing the American experience with the Child Savers' Movement at the beginning of this century, and using Canadian delinquency legislation as an example, Hagan and Leon argue that the sudden focus on lower class, adolescent misbehavior as a "social problem" and the generation of oppressive laws for its control represent the vested interests of the dominant classes.

CLASSIC BOOK SYNOPSIS 1

Task Force on Juvenile Delinquency, the President's Commission on Law Enforcement and Administration of Justice.
Task Force Report: Juvenile Delinquency and Youth Crime. Washington, D.C.: United States Government Printing Office, 1967.

THE COMMISSION AND THE CONSULTANTS

In contrast to the classic book synopses that open the subsequent four parts of this volume, this selection is not the scholarly contribution of a single author. Rather, the Task Force Report is a collection of significant papers from a distinguished panel of authorities on the problem of juvenile delinquency.

Born of our national concern and the growing challenge of youth crime, in 1967 the President's Commission on Law Enforcement and Administration of Justice issued this in-depth report. Chaired by Attorney General Nicholas DeB. Katzenbach, the Commission's undertaking involved the collaboration of federal, state, local, and private agencies and groups, and the coordination of hundreds of expert consultants, advisors, and staff members. The centerpiece and chief product of the Commission's special Task Force on juvenile delinquency are the papers of thirty-two consultants—a virtual "who's who" in the fields of juvenile justice and delinquency prevention at that time—that comprise the Report. Their names and the substance of their contributions are identified in this synopsis.

THE CONTENTS

The Task Force Report opens with a detailed and critical analysis of "The Administration of Juvenile Justice—the Juvenile Court and Related Methods of Delinquency Control." In Chapter 1, besides an enlightening discussion of the historic development of the juvenile court in the United States and adjudication and dispositional processes by police, courts, and informal community agencies, a number of suggestions are made for improving the juvenile justice system. These suggestions include the expanded use of community agencies such as the Youth Service Bureau to divert those youth from the juvenile justice system who can be rehabilitated without the stigma associated with court processing. Another suggestion is the fair and uniform application of the principles of due process in cases involving minors. Chapter 1 also includes useful and typical definitions of *juvenile delinquent* and *person in need of supervision* (PINS), although age boundaries often vary from state to state:

(a)   "Juvenile delinquent" means a person over 7 and less than 16 years of age who does any act which, if done by an adult, would constitute a crime.

(b)   "Person in need of supervision" means a male less than 16 years of age and a female less than 18 years of age who is an habitual truant or who is incorrigible, ungovernable or habitually disobedient and beyond the lawful control of parents or other lawful authority (The New York Family Court Act, 1963, page 712. Cited on page 26 of *Task Force Report: Juvenile Delinquency and Youth Crime*, 1967).

Another issue of major concern to the Task Force on Juvenile Delinquency is the broad category of *status offenses*—conduct that is illegal only for children—such as truancy from school, drinking of alcoholic beverages, smoking, and violating curfew regulations. Chapter 1 addresses the bias and discrimination intrinsic in the societal rationale that adult authorities have the right and responsibility to regulate youthful behavior that is nonthreatening to the larger society—for the sake of "developing character" through conformity.

In response to the concerns of the Task Force outlined in Chapter 1, several scholarly papers, written by consultants, appear as appendices to the *Task Force Report*.

Appendix A, "In re Gault (Supreme Court, May 15, 1967)," is a decision through which the U.S. Supreme Court affirmed and applied the constitutional principle of the due process to the case of 15-year-old Gerald Gault who had been charged, indicted, and committed to an Arizona correctional facility for making lewd telephone calls. *Due Process* is the constitutional guarantee that Americans have certain fundamental legal rights, including the right to know the charges, to a jury trial, to have an attorney, and to cross-examine complainants. The U.S. Supreme Court, by overturning the lower court ruling in the case of Gerald Gault on grounds that he had not fully received these rights, also emphasized and extended the viability of due process to all juvenile offenders in this country.

Appendix B, "Survey of Juvenile Courts and Probation Services, 1966," by the Children's Bureau, U.S. Department of Health, Education, and Welfare, tabulates data collected by questionnaire from nearly half of the nation's juvenile courts. The reported findings reflect many of the practices discussed in Chapter 1, including percentage of delinquency cases in which a lawyer is present at intake, percentage receiving medical and psychological examinations, demographic characteristics of offenders (gender, race, and socioeconomic status of families), and adjudication and disposition procedures.

Two other appendices also deal with the juvenile court: Appendix C, "The Juvenile Court as an Institution" by Robert D. Vinter, and Appendix D, "The Juvenile Court—Quest and Realities" by Edwin M. Lemert. Vinter's paper points out the court's important relationships with other parts of the juvenile justice system and its dependence upon other community agencies. For example, the basic mandate of the juvenile court is defined by the state legislature; much financial support is provided by local government; and the judge usually occupies his position by consent of the local electorate (Vinter, 1967:84). It follows that the juvenile court may be subject to conflicting pressures and relationships that may weaken its stability and reduce operational effectiveness. Lemert's paper reviews several major issues involving juvenile court policy and function. For instance, he points to the need to delimit more narrowly the jurisdictional authority of the court—especially regarding the kinds of problems or cases that should be handled by the court. In addition, Lemert is concerned about the minimum age of juveniles who can be referred to the court and the damaging social stigma that can be imputed to youngsters experiencing juvenile court proceedings. Lemert (1967:91) placed the philosophy and function of the juvenile court in clear perspective in addressing these issues:

> In general, American courts created for children were given broad grants of power by legislature to protect and help children, depart from strict rules of legal procedure, and utilize kinds of evidence ordinarily excluded from criminal and civil adjudication.

Henry D. McKay authored two of the appendices expanding on Chapter 1 of the *Task Force Report*. In Appendix E, "Report on the Criminal Careers of Male Delinquents in Chicago," McKay summarized the findings from two investigations that traced the subsequent development of criminal behavior patterns in several hundred adults who, earlier in their lives, had been juvenile delinquents. Prominent among his findings are the following:

> ... 58.3 percent (of the subjects) were found to have been arrested as adults; ... Seventy-two percent of those boys in the sample who had delinquent brothers were arrested as adults, while only 56.5 percent of the boys without delinquent brothers were arrested as adults. . . . A high proportion of the boys committed from Chicago to the Illinois State Training School for Boys, and returned to Chicago, acquired subsequent records of law violations. . . . Careers developing in the direction of criminality during the juvenile years are not effectively redirected toward conformity to law by special institutions for treatment of the juvenile offender in Chicago, Cook County, and the State of Illinois (McKay, 1967:109-111; 113).

In Appendix F, "Note on Trends in Rates of Delinquency in Certain Areas in Chicago," McKay presents convincing evidence from juvenile court records supporting the thesis that high delinquency rates prevail in urban areas characterized by poverty, hopelessness, and social disorganization regardless of the race or ethnic background of the local inhabitants.

The last paper in the Task Force Report focusing directly on the administration of juvenile justice is Appendix G, "The Youthful Offender" by Milton Luger with the assistance of Elias B. Saltman. In their study, Luger and Saltman point to an understudied, in between age grouping by defining the youthful offenders as

> ... those individuals enmeshed in the judicial and correctional process through illegal activities on their part, who are older than their own State's children's or juvenile court's jurisdiction and who have not reached the age of 24 (Luger and Saltman, in *Task Force Report* 1967:119).

The authors make a case—reinforced by arrest data from FBI *Uniform Crime Reports*—that young adults in this age grouping generally possess unique characteristics such as their involvement in certain kinds of crime (such as murder and rape) far in excess of their proportional representation in the general population. In addition, Luger and Saltman contend that this age grouping is culturally perceived as a comparatively distinct entity. For example, they are usually accorded less occupational opportunity, adult responsibility, and social status than the next older age groupings. Having concluded that young offenders between the maximum age of juvenile court jurisdiction and age 24 do indeed possess distinctive characteristics and special needs, Luger and Saltman argue that society would be better served in the long run if rehabilitation programs utilized by the corrections system effectively targeted the need for self esteem prevalent among young offenders.

Chapter 2 of the Task Force Report—"Understanding and Preventing Juvenile Delinquency"—is the final section in traditional book chapter format. As with Chapter 1, Chapter 2 is the study and discussion vortex for a cluster of appendices by consultants who analyzed and expanded relevant dimensions of the delinquency prevention topic of Chapter 2. Operating on the premise that the best control of delinquency is prevention, in Chapter 2 the Commission offers a series of concrete recommendations designed to strike at the societal causes of delinquency:

1. Reduce unemployment and devise methods of providing minimum family income.
2. Reexamine and revise welfare regulations so that they contribute to keeping the family together.
3. Improve housing and recreation facilities.
4. Insure availability of family planning assistance.
5. Provide help in problems of domestic management and child care.
6. Make counseling and therapy easily obtainable.
7. Develop activities that involve the whole family together.

This sociological perspective is exemplified in the 296 pages of supporting appendices that focus, in turn, on the basic social institutions of the family, education, religion, economic order, and the larger community as contexts for understanding and preventing juvenile delinquency. For example, Appendix L, "Juvenile Delinquency and the Family ..." by Hyman Rodman and Paul Grams, presents evidence that the lack of parental affection and discipline is especially conducive to the development of illegal behavior by children and youth. Among their recommendations for rehabilitation and prevention are programs for enhancing the family's ability to control its children and intensive therapy for families manifesting a delinquency problem. Marvin Wolfgang's article in Appendix I, "The Culture of Youth," also involves the delinquent's family. He traces the emergence of an age-graded, youth subculture in the United States to the extended socialization and dependency status imposed on youth in a rapidly changing, industrialized society. This situation leads to a generally unfulfilled quest for power and participation by alienated youth. These conditions, in turn, can generate deviant and delinquent behavior in many young people as they conflict with the values of dominant adult society. This phenomenon is addressed in Part III of this book.

Appendix M. "Delinquency and the Schools" by Walter E. Schafer and Kenneth Polk, directly relates juvenile misconduct to the educational institution. After a useful discussion of the philosophical objectives of public school education, the authors apply sociological theory in explaining the career beginnings of delinquency in the schools. Schafer and Polk point out that if youngsters perceive formal education as favoring middle-class values and standards and as irrelevant and unrewarding, they will demonstrate their disapproval with illegal conduct. Schafer and Polk call for radical changes in educational philosophy and teaching techniques in order to improve student commitment to the educational process and decrease juvenile delinquency. These points and recommendations are echoed by Appendix N, from the Office of Education, U.S. Department of Health, Education, and Welfare. In Appendix J, "The Function of Social Definitions in the Development of Delinquent Careers," Carl Werthman offers an institutional synthesis by analyzing how family members, school teachers, and local police are used by lower class gang boys to exercise their autonomy and acquire a measure of recognition. In the absence of occupational titles that furnish social identity and status to adults, these youths have discovered that the challenge of established authority in the family, school, and on the streets is a situation of risk from which coveted identity and status may be acquired from their peers. In short, even a deviant identity is better than none.

The religious institution in delinquency prevention is represented by Appendix P, "The Role of Religion in Programs for the Prevention and Correction of Crime and Delinquency," by Joseph Fitzpatrick. After reviewing the social control function and potential of religion in society, Fitzpatrick presents a number of effective, religiously related programs of delinquency prevention and treatment. He concluded that a sense of religious identity lends strength and cohesion to communities—especially those of migrating ethnic/racial minorities subject to a degree of social disorganization. Therefore, respected religious leaders and church-based delinquency control programs can positively influence many youths in such communities.

In Appendix O, "Economic Factors in Delinquency," Ivar Berg moves from the failure of many youths to achieve the cultural value of "education as a preparation for the world of work" to their reduced life chances as an economic circumstance associated with delinquency. Among other measures to help low-income, delinquent youth, Berg calls for strenuous efforts to enlist the business community to provide more jobs, on-the-job training programs, and provisions for vocational education. Jackson Toby, in Appendix H, takes a somewhat different position—that affluence itself has been a causal factor in the worsening problem of adolescent crime in contemporary society. He suggests that the prevailing materialism of our industrial society and the very visible success of some in acquiring personal property have elicited a sense of rising expectations and relative deprivation in those who are less affluent.

> People steal (in more affluent countries), not because they are starving, but because they are envious, and they are more likely to be envious of the possessions of others in countries with rising standards of living (Toby, *Task Force Report*, 1967:132).

In our reordering of the scholarly contributions comprising the *Task Force Report on Juvenile Delinquency,* we have identified three papers that deal with narrower and often underemphasized aspects of delinquency prevention. Appendix Q, "Recreation and Delinquency," by Bertram M. Beck with the assistance of Deborah B. Beck, includes a review of the literature exploring the relationship between these two variables. They found two polar opinions with one group holding that many youngsters misbehave because they have nothing to do with their leisure time. A contrary viewpoint is that delinquency is often a form of play for many youths and thus offers tough competition for the comparatively tame and supervised activities offered at public playgrounds and recreational centers. The Becks call for a realistic revision of the recreational system as part of a holistic approach to upgrade all dimensions of the environment of inner city youths—familial, educational, physical, and social. In Appendix R, "Delinquency and Community Action in Nonmetropolitan Areas," Kenneth Polk points out that despite the high visibility of crime and delinquency in heavily populated urban areas, poverty and other negative social conditions are generating considerable delinquency in smaller communities and rural areas. He outlines a community action program that addresses the particular social organization and problems of youth in such areas as a means to mitigate juvenile delinquency. Don M. Gottfredson, in Appendix K, "Assessment and Prediction Methods in Crime and Delinquency," reminds us that "If we seek to control delinquent and criminal behavior, then first we will need to be able to predict it" (*Task Force Report*, 1967:171). The objective of Gottfredson's paper was to identify the problems and potentials of existing delinquency prediction methods. His review of the literature revealed that the absence of effective parental supervision of the child and family cohesiveness, parole and probation violation, teacher nominations of maladjusted or potentially troublesome youngsters, and The Minnesota Multiphasic Personality Inventory are somewhat promising in predicting future delinquent behavior in some youths, though additional systematic research needs to be done in this area.

The last two articles in the *Task Force Report* summarize the entire field of delinquency prevention and control. Appendix S, authored by Virginia M. Burns and Leonard W. Stern, emphasized the need for social institutions to adapt their services to youth populations most likely to become delinquent and to offer opportunities for youth to acquire meaningful social roles and identities. Finally, Burns and Stern expressed concern that the present juvenile justice process is often a labeling process that paradoxically reinforces a subsequent criminal career. An excerpt from this article is presented in Part Four of this book. Appendix T, by Stanton Wheeler, Leonard S. Cottrell, Jr., and Anne Romasco, covers much of the same ground and stresses "the need for better information on types of delinquency and on the effectiveness of preventive and corrective programs. . ." (*Task Force Report*, 1967:xii).

CONTRIBUTION AND CRITIQUE

It is always hazardous to designate a work as "classic." Differences of opinion and preference among reviewers regarding the importance of the topic or problem addressed, theoretical orientation, methodological approach, and data interpretations, can confound such a conclusion. By our definition, *classic* is applied only to those scholarly works that, over time and after continuous scrutiny, receive consensual acclaim as original and significant contributions and set the standard for future work in the field. Such a designation for the *Task Force Report on Juvenile Delinquency* should evoke little disagreement. The impeccable credentials of the consultants and authors and their assiduous treatment of the various dimensions of the delinquency problem resulted in an unparalleled, comprehensive, and authoritative sourcebook. There was nothing of this magnitude in the field prior to the *Task Force Report* and though over a score of years have passed since its publication, it is cited extensively in every current textbook on delinquency. Amazingly, though a collection of articles, the *Task Force Report* often has been viewed as a definitive statement on juvenile delinquency in the United States.

At the same time, it would be unrealistic to ignore certain limitations of the volume. The treatment of etiology—or theories of delinquency causation—and of juvenile gangs is nonsystematic, scattered and often redundant, even though knowledge in both of these areas was well developed by 1967. Some exceptions to this generality are in the articles by Werthman and by Schafer and Polk. This shortcoming could have been partially resolved by a topical index to the *Task Force Report on Juvenile Delinquency* that could have helped scholars bring together the scattered discussions on these and other critical subjects. A good index would have facilitated the pursuit of details from contributors on any subtopic without obscuring the unfolding, institutional foci of the Task Force. A less critical problem that also reduces the utility of this rich source of information on juvenile delinquency is the surprising variability and lack of consistency in format, footnotes, references, bibliographies, and summaries from article to article.

With the passage of time, the invaluable *Task Force Report* has become seriously outdated. A new generation of researchers, theorists, and writers have entered the field of juvenile delinquency. Extensive new data have been generated, the juvenile justice system continues to evolve, and innovative programs of delinquency prevention and treatment are being tested. In addition, within recent years, middle- and upper-class delinquency has received more public attention and a frightening new mutation of gang activity has emerged involving sophisticated drug trafficking, automatic weapons, and massive warfare in the streets between rival gangs and with the police. These events underscore the need for a new federally commissioned Task Force and the harnessing of expert consultants in the production of a second Report on Juvenile Delinquency.

The Concepts of Tolerance and Contraculture as Applied to Delinquency*

RUTH SHONLE CAVAN

IN DEFINING juvenile delinquency, laws are of little use. Usually laws are specific only in relation to serious adult offenses such as murder, assault, robbery, burglary, and so forth. Children are delinquent if they are found guilty in court of breaking any of the federal, state, or local laws designed to control adult behavior. Delinquency statistics, however, indicate that these serious offenses account for only a small proportion of the delinquencies of children. Most of the behavior that gets a child into trouble with the police and courts comes under a much less definite part of the law on juvenile delinquency. Examples are easy to find. The Illinois law defines as delinquent a child who is incorrigible or who is growing up in idleness, one who wanders about the streets in the nighttime without being on any lawful business, or one who is guilty of indecent

Source: Cavan, Ruth Shonle. "The Concepts of Tolerance and Contraculture as Applied to Delinquency." *Sociological Quarterly,* Vol. 2, 1961:243–258. Reprinted by permission of Jai Press.

*Presidential Address, Midwest Sociological Society, April 28, 1961. In addition to the titles cited in the notes, the reader's attention is directed to the following general references:

Marshall Clinard, *Sociology of Deviant Behavior* (New York: Rinehart, 1957), Chap. 1; Richard A. Cloward, "Illegitimate means, Anomie, and Deviant Behavior," *American Sociological Review,* 24:164–76 (1959); Albert K. Cohen, "The Study of Social Disorganization and Deviant Behavior," in Robert K. Merton, Leonard Broom, and Leonard S. Cottrell (eds.), *Sociology Today: Problems and Prospects* (New York: Basic Books, 1959) Chap. 21; Robert Dubin, "Deviant Behavior and Social Structure: Continuities in Social Theory," *American Sociological Review,* 24:147–76 (1959); Robert K. Merton, "Social Conformity, Deviation, and Opportunity Structures: A Comment on the Contributions of Dubin and Cloward," *American Sociological Review,* 24:177–89 (1959); Robert K. Merton, *Social Theory and Social Structure* (rev. ed., Glencoe, Ill.: Free Press, 1957); Talcott Parsons, *The Social System* (Glencoe, Ill.; Free Press, 1951).

or lascivious conduct. Laws in some other states are still more vague. New Mexico rests its definition on the word habitual. A delinquent child is one who, by habitually refusing to obey the reasonable and lawful commands of his parents or other persons of lawful authority, is deemed to be habitually uncontrolled, habitually disobedient, or habitually wayward; or who habitually is a truant from home or school; or who habitually so deports himself as to injure or endanger the morals, health, or welfare of himself or others. In these laws there is no definition of such words or phrases as incorrigible, habitual, indecent conduct, or in the nighttime. How much disobedience constitutes incorrigibility? How often may a child perform an act before it is considered habitual?

The federal Children's Bureau dodges all this by stating flatly that juvenile delinquency cases are those referred to courts for certain violations of laws or for conduct so seriously antisocial as to interfere with the rights of others or to menace the welfare of the delinquent himself or of the community.[1] This approach does not help much. Someone has to decide when the child has violated a law or when his conduct is antisocial. Parents, teachers, and police make the decisions. What guides them in deciding when a child's behavior justifies a court hearing? Is a court hearing the only measure of delinquency? Or are there gradations in delinquency? If so, where along the line of gradation does a child become so out of line that his behavior merits calling him a delinquent? If delinquent behavior has gradations, does good behavior also have gradations?

This paper is an attempt to assign misbehavior to a place in the total social structure, and to determine when misbehavior should be termed delinquency. The Children's Bureau definition is tentatively used: behavior that interferes with the rights of others, or menaces the welfare of the delinquent or the welfare of the community. I am concerned chiefly with the last, construed to mean the effective functioning of the social organization.

THE BEHAVIOR CONTINUUM

A word now about Figure 1.1. The figure represents the social structure, the framework of which consists of the institutions and less formal but fairly permanent organizations that, operating together, carry on the functions of the society. Area D represents the central or dominant part of the social structure, where institutions are found that set the formal standards for behavior and exert the formal means of control. The base line represents the extent of deviations from the central social norms. According to this hypothetical formulation, behavior falls into a continuum from condemnable behavior (area A) through decreasing degrees of disapproved behavior to the central area D and then through increasing degrees of good behavior to near perfection in area G.

[1] *Juvenile Court Statistics*, 1957, Statistical Series No. 52 (Washington, D.C.: Children's Bureau, 1959), p. 4.

FIGURE 1.1 Hypothetical Formulation of Behavior Continuum

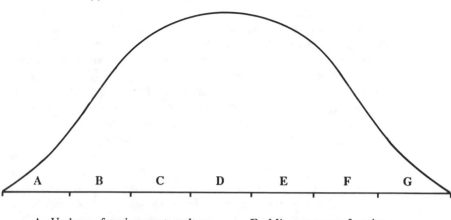

A. Underconforming contraculture
B. Extreme underconformity
C. Minor underconformity
D. Normal conformity

E. Minor overconformity
F. Extreme overconformity
G. Overconforming conformity

The area above the line represents the volume of behavior—or more concretely the number of people—that falls into the area controlled by the norms and into successive segments of deviation. There is sufficient evidence, that I will not quote, to support a bell-shaped curve.[2]

Even though we know that behavior falls into a continuum, nevertheless we tend to think in terms of dichotomies. We have the sinner and the saint, the devil and the angel, the alcoholic and the tee-totaller, the criminal and the upright citizen, the juvenile delinquent and the model child. We tend to think in terms of black and white, whereas between these two rare extremes are many shades of gray. For instance, one might set up such a series as pitch black, charcoal gray, slate gray, tattletale gray, dingy white, off white, and lily white. In this series of seven, the modal term (area *D*) is not white but tattletale gray. (This term is borrowed from the advertisements of a few years ago in which the sheets flapping on the line were tattletale gray because the housewife had not used the right kind of laundry soap.) Observed behavior falls into similar gradations. The child may break into a store at night and steal (black); deliberately pick up valuables during store hours; occasionally pick up things as opportunity arises; pilfer small objects (tattletale gray); be meticulous about not taking things; remonstrate with others who steal; or report other children to teachers or police for even minor pilfering (lily white).

---

[2] Floyd H. Allport, "The J-Curve Hypothesis of Conforming Behavior," *Journal of Social Psychology,* 5:141-83 (1934; R. T. LaPiere, and P. R. Farnsworth, *Social Psychology* (McGraw-Hill: New York, 1936), p. 400.

SOCIAL NORMS AND MODAL BEHAVIOR

To avoid confusion, certain terms require clarification. The formal standards that dominate area D are social norms. They are related to but not identical with values. Values are ideals or ultimate goals, perhaps never attained. They are abstractions. Social norms are the specific formulations to implement the values in practical, attainable form. They constitute the expectations of society and often are stated in terms implying that exact conformity is expected. However, a third level may be identified, the working plans or modal behavior of the majority of people.

For adequate functioning of society a balance must be maintained between the rigid social norms and the more flexible modal behavior. Complete conformity to the social norms, always, by everyone, is rarely demanded. A concession is made to human nature itself—to the difficulty of always observing rules, or always suppressing impulses, or always standing at attention. Some of these concessions have been institutionalized in the familiar swing back and forth between consecration and carnival. After the religious rites at Christmas we have our modern New Year's Eve; and Mardi Gras precedes Lenten abstinence. Concessions are often made in areas of behavior not vital to the main social functions. Other concessions are made to certain groups, especially the young and the very old. The behavior in the central area D therefore is not strict conformity to social norms, but permits some deviations. D is an area of flexibility or tolerance, but only to the extent that the social organization itself is not threatened.

Normally, children are taught to accept the social norms and to confine their behavior to the area of tolerance. Most people find in this area a satisfactory way of life. Their behavior is reasonably well restrained and predictable. The society functions adequately.

UNDERCONFORMITY AND OVERCONFORMITY

In the illustration of the continuum given above, pilfering of small objects was given as the modal type of behavior falling within the area of tolerance although not rigidly conforming to the social norm of honesty. With this formulation, both more serious forms of stealing and meticulous avoidance of taking things are deviations from the social norms and the modal behavior. There is deviation in the nature of underconformity to the social norms, shown to the left on Figure 1.1, and deviation in the nature of overconformity to the social norms, shown to the right. Underconformity is an exaggeration of the tolerance allowed by the modal norms; for example, if the modal behavior permits a small amount of pilfering of candy and comic books in the corner store, the underconformer expands the tolerance to include stealing of more valuable objects. Overconformity is an exaggeration of the strict observance of formal social norms. Honesty may be exaggerated to the point where a person would not keep even a pencil that he found nor use an article belonging to someone else even in an emergency.

Either underconformity or overconformity that exceeds the limits of tolerance poses a threat to the operation of the social organization. Overconformity, as a threatening type of deviation, has often been omitted from the formulations of sociologists or has been only casually mentioned. It is true that overconformity usually does not constitute delinquency or crime in the same degree as underconformity. However, it should be included in any discussion providing a complete picture of the social structure, of which delinquency and crime are one kind of deviation and overconformity the opposite kind.

The issue with reference to overconformity has sometimes been obscured by the tendency to think of the social norms not as our workable expectations of behavior but as ideal or perfect standards. An example may be drawn from the introductory text by Lundberg, Schrag, and Larsen.[3] These authors establish the institutional expectations and the area of tolerance in the middle, with most people fitting their behavior into this area. They also show disapproved behavior to the left, as is done in Figure 1.1. However, to the right they show approved deviations, whereas Figure 1.1 and Table 1.1 define these deviations as disapproved and a threat to area D. According to Lundberg, *et al.*, approved deviations exceed the standard set by the group, and include at the extreme some 2 or 3 per cent of people who are given public recognition for their overconformity. According to this formulation, the ideal standards for behavior would be at the extreme right, would constitute virtual perfection, and, practically, would be attained by almost no one. Everyone except the 2 or 3 percent would be deviants.

Research studies of juvenile delinquents sometimes ignore the central area of modal behavior and compare delinquent children (area A) with near-perfect children (area G). Sheldon .and Eleanor Glueck in their much discussed book, *Unraveling Juvenile Delinquency*, make such a comparison.[4] They matched each of 500 correctional-school boys with a boy of the same age, intelligence, and social background, whose behavior was exemplary. Not only were these control boys without any police, court, or correctional-school record, but 74 per cent were without any known delinquency of even a minor nature. The Gluecks had difficulty in finding 500 such overly good boys, and eventually had to include a few boys guilty of such misbehavior as smoking in their early years, hopping trucks, once or twice swiping much desired articles in five-and-ten-cent stores, crap shooting, sneaking into movies, occasional truancy, being stubborn to their mothers, and a very occasional occurrence of staying out late at night, using vile language, drinking, running away from home, and bunking out. Some of the deficiencies were very trivial and had occurred when the boy was seven or eight years old. The Gluecks then were comparing boys from area A—the most seriously underconforming—with boys from area G—the most seriously over conforming. This selection may account for the fact that, whereas the delinquents tended to be active, aggressive, impulsive, and rebellious, the control group tended to be neurotic, fearful of failure or defeat, and submissive to authority. The middle group of boys with normal conformity or D-type behavior, who live within the tolerance limits

[3] George A. Lundberg, Clarence C. Schrag, and Otto N. Larsen, *Sociology,* rev. ed. (Harper: New York, 1958), p. 349.
  [4] Sheldon and Eleanor Glueck, *Unraveling Juvenile Delinquency* (Cambridge, Mass.: Harvard University Press, 1950), pp. 23-39, Chap. 21.

TABLE 1.1 Characteristics of stages of continuity in behavior.

	A *Delinquent Contraculture*	B *Extreme Under-conformity*	C *Minor Under-conformity*	D *Normal Conformity*	E *Minor Over-conformity*	F *Extreme Over-conformity*	G *Overconforming Contraculture*
Public attitude	Condemnation; "hard core"	Disapproval	Toleration without approval	Tolerance with approval	Toleration without approval	Disapproval	Condemnation
Public reaction	Rejection; school expulsion; commitment to correctional school	Police warnings; school suspension; referral to social agency	Disciplinary action by school or parent	Indifference; acceptance; mild reproofs	Ignoring	Ostracizing	Rejection
Child's attitude toward public	Rejection of values of D	Wavering between acceptance and rejection of D values	Acceptance of values of D; feelings of guilt	Acceptance of values of D; no guilt feelings	No deviation in personal conduct	Criticism of D behavior in others	Rejection of D values
Child's self-concept	As delinquent, outlaw	Confused, marginal to C and A	As misbehaving nondelinquent	As a conforming nondelinquent	As a true conformer	Better than others	His way is the only right way
Examples	Armed robbery; burglary	Larceny of valuables	"Borrowing" and keeping; pilfering	Minor pilfering; unauthorized borrowing	Borrowing only with permission	Extreme care not to use other's possessions; criticism of others	Report even minor pilfering to teacher or police
	Rape; serious sex deviations	Promiscuity; minor sex deviations	Extensive normal sex relations	Minor normal sex relations; petting	Normal, only in marriage; no petting	Restrained, even in marriage	Celibacy as a philosophy
	Drug addiction	Occasional use of drugs	Smoking of marijuana	Smoking tobacco	No smoking; use of coffee or tea	No stimulating drinks, even though mild	Opposition to use by others

of the community, is completely ignored. In the Glueck study the control group is fully as deviant as the delinquent group, but in the opposite direction. Actually, it seems very doubtful whether so much admiration is really accorded the overconforming group as some sociologists and researchers state or imply. The good behavior and achievements that are rewarded by society seem much more likely to be in area *D* or *E* than in area *F* or *G*. For example, consider the descriptive terms and epithets that are applied to youths whose behavior falls into the different areas. Boys in area *A* are often referred to as little savages, hoodlums, punks, bums, or gangsters—not very complimentary terms. But boys in area *G* also are not complimented; they are often referred to as sissies, goody-goods, teacher's pet, drips, brains, fraidy-cats, wet blankets, or squares. Adults and youth alike admire the boys in area *D*, who are essentially conforming but not rigidly so. This area *D* youth is "all boy," or all-American boy; he can take care of himself; he is ambitious; he can hold his own with the best of them; he is a good sport. A little later, in college, he makes a "gentleman's C." He may occasionally borrow Table 1.1 small things that he needs and forget to return them, truant off and on but no enough to damage his school record, cheat on tests in subjects that he doesn't like, mark up the walks and walls of a rival high school, do some property damage under the stress of excitement, outwork and outsmart his rivals, lie for his own advantage, and occasionally sass his parents and neglect his home chores. But he stays within the tolerance limits; he is developing, even in misbehavior, traits that will help him fit into the adult competitive *D* pattern of behavior; he is moving toward the social expectations for his future as an adult.

AREAS C AND E

Let us look at areas *C* and *E*, representing minor deviations from the social norms and the modal behavior of area *D*. Minor deviations only are involved, whether they are under- or overconforming. Parents, teachers, employers, and other adults keep a wary eye out for these deviations. They are not a serious threat to the social organization but might become so if they increased in frequency or seriousness. The general attitude is toleration without approval, as indicated in Table 1.1 after "public attitude." Efforts to rectify or prevent these deviations usually are handled by parents or school officials. More attention is given to the underconformers than the overconformers. However, overconformers are admonished not to interfere with other people's fun, and are urged to get into the swing of things, to enjoy themselves, and to let themselves go in normal fashion.

The youth who falls into one of these two areas is regarded as a member of the social institutions and groups that control area *D*. He is "one of ours," erring a little, but to be brought back into the groups, disciplined if need be, and forgiven.[5]

---

[5] This analysis was drawn from Solomon Kobrin. "Problems in the Development of the Image of the Delinquent in Mass Society," paper presented at the annual meeting of the Illinois Academy of Criminology, Chicago, May 6, 1960.

The youth in areas C and E accepts the standards of area D. He identifies himself with groups in area D, and would be lost without them. He feels guilty about not meeting the expectations of groups in area D and tends to rationalize his shortcomings. In the C area the boy agrees that stealing is wrong and insists he meant to return the property he took; he is contrite and filled with good intentions. He thinks of himself as nondelinquent.[6] The overly conscientious youth in area E also feels guilty because he is not measuring up to the expectations of area D. He also rationalizes: he doesn't join the boys on Saturday night because he doesn't want to worry his parents; he needs the time to study, and so on.

AREAS B AND F

Behavior in areas B and F is definitely disapproved according to the social norms and the modal behavior patterns of area D. B- and F-type behaviors are a threat to the smooth operation of the social organization. The chronic truant of area B interferes with the effective operation of the school; but the boy who always is perfectly prepared or who is always on hand after school to do the schoolroom chores is also a hindrance in a school that wishes to draw all boys into participation. He may of course be temporarily rewarded by appreciation from an overworked teacher who welcomes his help even though it is at the expense of the boy's participation with other boys in nonschool activities.

The underconformers in area B are made to feel that they are violators of the social norms; but they are not abandoned by representatives of area D.[7] Police warn or arrest but do not necessarily refer boys to the juvenile court. The school may suspend disorderly boys but does not expel them. Parents inflict severe penalties. These disapproved underconformers are made to feel that they are on the outer margin of area C and in danger of losing their membership in conforming groups. One more misstep and they are out.

Youth in overconforming area F are handled somewhat differently. The attitude toward them is one of impatience, sometimes of scorn. They too are made to feel that they are on the outer margin of acceptability. They are socially ostracized, ignored in invitations to parties, and excluded by youth from membership in many groups because they would hamper activities. If adults take any action it is in the nature of trying to stimulate them to normal youth activities, or in some cases referring them to psychiatric clinics for diagnosis and treatment of their extremely overconforming behavior.

[6] William W. Wattenberg. "Ten-Year Old Boys in Trouble," *Child Development*, 28:43-46 (1957); Wattenberg and F. Quiroz. "Follow-up Study of Ten-Year Old Boys with Police Records," *Journal of Consulting Psychology*, 17:309-13 (1953): Wattenberg, "Eleven-Year-Old Boys in Trouble," *Journal of Educational Psychology*, 444:409-17 (1953); Wattenberg, "Normal Rebellion—or Real Delinquency?" *Child Study*, 34:15-20 (Fall, 1957).

[7] Stanley Schachter, "Deviation, Rejection, and Communication," *Journal of Abnormal and Social Psychology*, 46:190-207 (April, 1951). In an experiment with small groups, the dissenter at first is the object of increased interaction in the effort to restore him to consensus; when this fails, he is rejected.

Youth themselves in either area *B* or *F* feel themselves to be in a marginal position, neither in nor out of the normal social organization. They waver between accepting and adjusting to modal behavior and social norms of the *D* area, and abandoning these norms altogether. They are in contrast to youth in areas *C* and *E* with slightly deviating behavior who feel that they are wanted by groups in area *D*. The more seriously nonconforming youth in areas *B* and *F* feel alternately wanted and rejected by the conforming groups in area *D*. The youth is in an anomalous position and often feels isolated from all groups. He may become involved in a spiral type of interaction in which each move on the part of the representative of area *D* calls for a countermove on his part. If the youth perceives the approach to him as friendly he may respond with friendliness and a spiral will be set up that carries him back into conforming groups. But if he perceives the approach of conforming groups as hostile and rejective, he will respond in kind and the process of alienation will increase until he breaks off all contacts with the various conforming groups. Underconformers show their hostility by stealing, vandalism, and attacks of various sorts. Overconformers show hostility by vociferous criticism of conforming groups.

Areas *B* and *F* are the ones where reclamation of youth must occur if it is to take place at all. Much of what is done with nonconformers is punitive and tends to push a youth further along in the process of alienation from conforming groups. The reverse process might pull him back into conformity. He should be made to feel that he is not a threat to society or permanently outside the approved area of behavior, unworthy of association, even though he has seriously transgressed the codes or social normal.

AREAS A AND G

Areas *A* and *G* differ from the ones already considered in that they do not represent simply deviation from the central modal behavior and social norms, but rather detachment from social norms and opposition to them. In full development, areas *A* and *G* are contracultures, one of which is built up around disregard for the social norms, the other around overcompliance with the norms.

The term "contraculture" is new in sociology and calls for clarification. It is a replacement for the term subculture when applied to sharply deviating types of behavior. The term subculture refers to a body of beliefs and behavior that differs to some extent from the main culture but is not in conflict with it in destructive fashion. The term contraculture has been proposed by J. Milton Yinger to signify certain qualities of detached groups.[8] According to Yinger's analysis, the contraculture has developed values and modes of behavior that are in conflict with the prevailing social norms (area *D*). The values and behavior of the contraculture are not only different from but are opposed to the social norms.

The logical end result is that people who accept the contraculture tend to organize into small contra-organizations with their own social norms, hierarchy of status

[8] J. Milton Yinger, "Contraculture and Subculture," *American Sociological Review*, 25:625-35 (1960). Albert K. Cohen used the term "delinquent subculture" for essentially the same type of behavior as found in a contraculture.—*Delinquent Boy* (Glencoe, Ill.: Free Press, 1955).

positions, roles, and methods of control. A contracultural organization is not only a threat to the social norms but an active disintegrative element in the total social structure. Youth in areas *B* and *F* who are rejected by socially conforming groups may in turn reject these groups and pass into the appropriate contraculture. They are then no longer responsive to either the social norms or the efforts of members of area *D* to reclaim them.

Let us consider area *A*, extreme underconformity. Youth in this area are condemned not only in terms of their behavior but as persons. They are referred to as the "hard core" or "real" delinquents. They are physically exiled at least for a period of time. The school may expel them permanently, the judge may commit them to a correctional school or a prison. Occasionally such a youth may receive the death sentence.

The delinquent youth in the delinquent contraculture for his part rejects the conforming groups of society. He no longer measures his behavior against the expectations of area *D*. His standard of measurement is the small, more restricted, less demanding standard of the delinquent contraculture. Here he may be applauded for stealing, chronic truancy, or fighting. Toward groups in area *D* he is indifferent, hostile, or vengeful.

The effort to draw members of the delinquent contraculture back into area *D* is often doomed to failure. The street workers in New York City and other large cities, who have been successful in re-establishing approved social behavior in many street clubs or gangs, note that they cannot influence the hard-core delinquents who are thoroughly incorporated into a delinquent or youthful criminal gang. The street workers, who represent the values and norms of area *D*, are to the members of the contraculture outsiders and enemies who threaten the little structure of the contraculture.[9] If the street workers or other adults were able to influence individual members of the contraculture, the youth would again have to traverse the disorganizing experiences of area *B* before he could reach the relative security of area *C*. He would meet the scorn and rejection of his own gang-mates without having assurance that members of area *C* or *D* would accept him.

What of the overconforming contraculture? Criticism, ostracism, and rejection of youth in area *F* also drive many of them into withdrawal into small closed groups with their own social organization. Many enter already formed adult contracultures that have values and customs opposed to those of the central culture. As examples we have conscientious objection to war, refusal to salute the flag, rejection of medical care when ill or for ill children, refusal to have children vaccinated, refusal to send children to school for the number of years required by law, celibacy, and community ownership of property. Each of these practices is an exaggeration of some value or social norm contained in the general culture. Each is socially disapproved according to the norms of area *D* or is illegal. They are attacks on the general social values and norms, and if they were to spread throughout the nation they would undermine the social structure seriously. Some overconforming contracultures are content to withdraw into isolation; some attack the general social norms through propaganda or legislation. Others,

---

[9] *Reaching the Fighting Gang* (New York: New York City Youth Board, 1960).

however, are more militant and occasionally some members physically attack members or symbols of the general culture. (Carrie Nation, smashing the windows of saloons, might be an example of a member of a militant overconforming contraculture.)

FURTHER APPLICATIONS TO JUVENILE DELINQUENCY

This analysis of deviancy in the social organization clarifies several problems connected with juvenile delinquency. Three of these will be discussed.

1. The relation of public attitudes to social class.[10] Each social class or other large subcultural group has its own definition of what behavior falls into the area of tolerance, what is disapproved mildly or seriously, and what is condemned. Even when these groups share a basic culture and verbally accept the social norms, their concepts of approved and disapproved behavior may differ. The difference between middle- and lower-class definitions of behavior is especially pertinent, since most school officers and judges represent the middle class and most seriously misbehaving youth come from the lower class. Figure 1.2 is an attempt to indicate the difference between lower-class and middle-class judgments of what may and may not be tolerated. The behavior that the lower class would regard as falling in area D, to be accepted with tolerance, might be placed by the middle class in area C (barely tolerated behavior), or even in area B. Lower-class parents, other adults, and children might regard certain behavior as acceptable, whereas teachers and judges might regard it as unacceptable or reprehensible. An example is the case of the father whose son was in a correctional school for taking a car for joy riding. The father said, "Of course, he took a few cars, but he did not strip them; he just wanted to use them. He is not a bad boy." But in the eyes of the judge, the boy had stolen the cars. This shifting of the class judgments on behavior is especially interesting at the left-hand extreme. The middle class tends to regard certain acts as type A, condemned behavior, that the lower class would regard as either B or A. This gives a wide range of everyday lower-class behavior that receives middle-class condemnation.

At the overconforming end of the scale the situation is reversed. Behavior that the middle class regards as acceptable and approved (type D), the lower class might regard as overconforming type E behavior. The lower class would perhaps regard behavior that is either F or G by middle-class standards as all extremely overconforming.

These shifts can be illustrated briefly by sexual attitudes and behavior in the two social classes. The casual sex relations of boys and girls that are regarded as natural and normal in some lower-class groups are regarded as underconformity and delinquency by middle-class standards. On the other hand the petting that some middle-class groups regard as an acceptable substitute for intercourse, the lower class would regard as prudish overconformity. At the extreme left, however, the two classes would tend to

[10] Marshall Clinard, "Areas for Research in Deviant Behavior," *Sociology and Social Research,* 42:415-19 (1958). Among areas for research, Clinard suggests differences among social classes.

FIGURE 1.2 Discrepancies between lower-class and middle-class evaluations of identical behavior

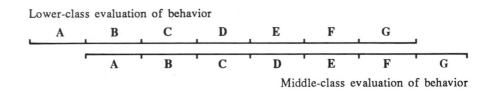

agree in condemning serious sex deviations, forcible rape, incest, exploitation of little children, and prostitution. At the extreme right, also, there would tend to be agreement, since both classes would probably look with disfavor on universal advocacy of celibacy, for example, as practiced by the Shakers. The argument would not apply to religious organizations where celibacy affects only a small portion of the total religious subculture. Such differences in attitudes of the two social classes lead to misunderstandings. Mishandling of the deviants of one social class by authorities in the other class almost automatically follows from such differences in judgment of the same behavior.

2. The evaluation of the behavior continuum is important in the expectations of behavior for delinquent youth on probation or parole. Usually probation or parole entails laying upon the youth a number of stringent restrictions on behavior. The penalty for disobedience often is commitment or return to correctional school. Such conditions as the following are typical: obedience to parents; regular school attendance; return home at an early hour of the evening, sometimes with the hour specified; and avoidance of disreputable companions and places. At least some of these requirements are overconforming by lower-class standards and virtually impossible for the youth to follow if he is to remain in the lower-class community and not be isolated from his natural social groups. The result is disregard for the requirements and deception on the part of the youth. Probation and parole might more often be successful if the youth were required to meet reasonably conforming lower-class standards.

3. The third point that may be clarified by the behavior continuum is the often repeated statement that all boys are delinquent but only poor boys are pulled into court or committed to correctional schools. It is true, according to several studies, that much delinquent behavior is overlooked and that most middle-class boys and girls at some time have behaved in such a way that they might have been brought into juvenile court. A recent study by Short and Nye compares misbehavior of high school students with that of correctional school students.[11] Some boys and girls in both groups had committed each of a long list of delinquencies. But it was apparent that the correctional

---

[11] James F. Short, Jr., and F. Ivan Nye, "Extent of Unrecorded Juvenile Delinquency, Tentative Conclusions," *Journal of Criminal Law, Criminology and Police Science,* 49:296-309 (1958).

school-boys and girls far outstripped the high-school students in the seriousness of their acts and the frequency with which they had committed them. For example, half of high-school boys but almost 100 per cent of correctional-school boys had skipped school; a fourth of high-school boys but 85 per cent of correctional school boys had skipped school more than once or twice. Or, take a more serious offense, the theft of something worth fifty dollars or more. Five per cent of high-school boys compared with 90 per cent of correctional-school boys had taken things of this value. Almost no high-school boys compared with almost half of the correctional-school boys had committed this offense more than once or twice. An examination of the entire set of data leads to the conclusion that the high-school students had confined their delinquencies to acts (within the area of tolerance of the community, where-as the correctional-school boys were guilty of behavior of types *B* or *A*, highly disapproved and regarded as threatening to the social organization.

In conclusion, this paper has attempted to state a hypothesis whereby behavior may be placed in a continuum running from an underconforming contraculture through various degrees of disapproved behavior to normal conformity and then through stages of overconforming behavior to an overconforming contraculture. The reaction of the normally conforming segment of the population to deviations varies in severity according to the threat posed to the social norms by either under- or overconformity. Minor deviants usually are drawn back into conformity. Serious deviants often are treated so severely that they are alienated and withdraw into a contraculture.

___ARTICLE 2___
What is Crime?

CRIMES ARE DEFINED BY LAW

In this report we define crime as all behaviors and acts for which a society provides formally sanctioned punishment. In the United States what is criminal is specified in the written law, primarily State statutes. What is included in the definition of crime varies among Federal, State, and local jurisdictions.

Criminologists devote a great deal of attention to defining crime in both general and specific terms. This definitional process is the first step toward the goal of obtaining accurate crime statistics.

To provide additional perspectives on crime it is sometimes viewed in ways other than in the standard legal definitions. Such alternatives define crime in terms of the type of victim (child abuse), the type of offender (white-collar crime), the object of the crime (property crime), or the method of criminal activity (organized crime). Such definitions usually cover one or more of the standard legal definitions. For example, organized crime may include fraud, extortion, assault, or homicide.

WHAT IS CONSIDERED CRIMINAL
BY SOCIETY CHANGES OVER TIME

Some types of events such as murder, robbery, and burglary have been defined as crimes for centuries. Such crimes are part of the common law definition of crime. Other types of conduct traditionally have not been viewed as crimes. As social values and mores change, society has codified some conduct as criminal while decriminalizing other conduct. The recent movement toward increased "criminalization" of drunk driving is an example of such change.

New technology also results in new types of conduct not anticipated by the law.

Source: Report to the Nation on Crime and Justice (2nd ed.). U.S. Dept. of Justice, Bureau of Justice Statistices, NCJ-105506, Washington, D.C.: U.S. Government Printing Office, March 1988:2-3; 42-43; 58-59; 78-80; 95; 110. Reprinted by permission

Changes in the law may be needed to define and sanction these types of conduct. For example, the introduction of computers has added to the criminal codes in many States so that acts such as the destruction of programs or data could be defined as crimes.

WHAT ARE SOME OTHER COMMON CRIMES IN THE UNITED STATES?

Drug abuse violations—Offenses relating to growing, manufacturing, making, possessing, using, selling, or distributing narcotic and dangerous nonnarcotic drugs. A distinction is made between possession and sale/manufacturing.

Sex offenses—In current statistical usage, the name of a broad category of varying content, usually consisting of all offenses having a sexual element except for forcible rape and commercial sex offenses, which are defined separately.

Fraud offenses—The crime type comprising offenses sharing the elements of practice of deceit or intentional misrepresentation of fact, with the intent of unlawfully depriving a person of his or her property or legal rights.

Drunkenness—Public intoxication, except "driving under the influence."

Disturbing the peace—Unlawful interruption of the peace, quiet, or order of a community, including offenses called "disorderly conduct," "vagrancy," loitering," "unlawful assembly," and "riot."

Driving under the influence—Driving or operating any vehicle or common carrier while drunk or under the influence of liquor or drugs.

Liquor law offenses—State or local liquor law violations, except drunkenness and driving under the influence. Federal violations are excluded.

Gambling—Unlawful staking or wagering of money or other thing of value on a game of chance or on an uncertain event.

Kidnapping—Transportation or confinement of a person without authority of law and without his or her consent, or without the consent of his or her guardian, if a minor.

Vandalism—Destroying or damaging, or attempting to destroy or damage, the property of another without his or her consent, or public property, except by burning, which is arson.

Public order offenses—Violations of the peace or order of the community or threats to the public health through unacceptable public conduct, interference with governmental authority or violation of civil rights or liberties. Weapons offenses, bribery, escape, and tax law violations, for example, are included in this category.

HOW DO VIOLENT CRIMES DIFFER FROM PROPERTY CRIMES?

The outcome of a criminal event determines if it is a property crime or a violent crime. Violent crime refers to events such as homicide, rape, and assault that may result in injury to a person. Robbery is also considered a violent crime because it involves the use or threat of force against a person.

Property crimes are unlawful acts with the intent of gaining property but which do not involve the use or threat of force against an individual. Larceny and motor vehicle theft are examples of property crimes.

In the National Crime Survey a distinction is also made between crimes against persons (violent crimes and personal larceny) and crimes against households (property crimes, including household larceny).

HOW DO FELONIES DIFFER FROM MISDEMEANORS?

Criminal offenses are also classified according to how they are handled by the criminal justice system. Most jurisdictions recognize two classes of offenses: felonies and misdemeanors.

Felonies are not distinguished from misdemeanors in the same way in all jurisdictions, but most States define felonies as offenses punishable by a year or more in a State prison. The most serious crimes are never "misdemeanors" and the most minor offenses are never "felonies." . . .

WHAT IS THE RELATIONSHIP BETWEEN AGE AND CRIME?

Young people make up the largest proportion of offenders entering the criminal justice system

In 1985—
- Two-thirds of all arrests and three-quarters of all UCR index arrests were of persons under age 30.
- Arrests of youths under age 21 made up half of all UCR Index property crime arrests and almost a third of all violent crime arrests.
- Arrests of juveniles (persons under age 18) made up 17% of all arrests and 31% of all UCR Index arrests.
- During 1976-85, the number of arrests of juveniles (persons under age 18) fell by 18%, reflecting the decline in the size of that age group and a 15% drop in their arrest rate.

Participation in crime declines with age

Arrest data show that the intensity of criminal behavior slackens after the teens, and it continues to decline with age. Arrests, however, are only a general indicator of criminal activity. The greater likelihood of arrests for young people may result partly from their lack of experience in offending and also from their involvement in the types of crimes

TABLE 2.1 What are the characteristics of some serious crimes?

Crime	Definition	Facts
Homicide	Causing the death of another person without legal justification or excuse, including UCR crimes of murder and nonnegligent manslaughter and negligent manslaughter.	• Murder and nonnegligent manslaughter occur less often than other violent UCR Index crimes. • 58% of the known murderers were relatives or acquaintances of the victim. • 20% of all murders in 1985 occurred or were suspected to have occurred as the result of some felonious activity.
Rape	Unlawful sexual intercourse with a female, by force or without legal or factual consent.	• Most rapes involve a lone offender and a lone victim. • About 32% of the rapes recorded by NCS in 1985 were committed in or near the victim's home. • 73% of the rapes occurred at night, between 6 p.m. and 6 a.m. • 58% of the victims of rape were under 25 years old.
Robbery	The unlawful taking or attempted taking of property that is in the immediate possession of another, by force or threat of force.	• Robbery is the violent crime that most often involves more than one offender (in almost half of all cases in 1985). • About half of all robberies reported by NCS in 1985 involved the use of a weapon.
Assault	Unlawful intentional inflicting, or attempted inflicting, of injury upon the person of another. Aggravated assault is the unlawful intentional inflicting of serious bodily injury or unlawful threat or attempt to inflict bodily injury or death by means of a deadly or dangerous weapon with or without actual infliction of injury. Simple assault is the unlawful intentional inflicting of less than serious bodily injury without a deadly or dangerous weapon or an attempt or threat to inflict bodily injury without a deadly or dangerous weapon.	• Simple assault occurs more frequently than aggravated assault. • Most assaults involve one victim and one offender.
Burglary	Unlawful entry of any fixed structure, vehicle, or vessel used for regular residence, industry, or business, with or without force, with the intent to commit a felony or larceny.	• Residential property was targeted in 2 out of every 3 reported burglaries; nonresidential property accounted for the remaining third. • In 1985, 42% of all residential burglaries occurred without forced entry. • About 37% of the no-force burglaries were known to have occurred during the day between 6 a.m. and 6 p.m.
Larceny-theft	Unlawful taking or attempted taking property other than a motor vehicle from the possession of another, by stealth, without force and without deceit, with intent to permanently deprive the owner of the property.	• Less than 5% of all personal larcenies involve contact between the victim and offender. • Pocket picking and purse snatching most frequently occur inside nonresidential buildings or on street locations. • Unlike most other crimes, pocket picking and purse snatching affect the elderly about as much as other age groups.
Motor vehicle theft	Unlawful taking or attempted taking of a self-propelled road vehicle owned by another, with the intent of depriving him or her of it, permanently or temporarily.	• Motor vehicle theft is relatively well reported to the police. In 1985 89% of all completed thefts were reported. • The stolen property is more likely to be recovered in this crime than in other property crimes.
Arson	The intentional damaging or destruction or attempted damaging or destruction by means of fire or explosion of property without the consent of the owner, or of one's own property or that of another by fire or explosives with or without the intent to defraud.	• Single-family residences were the most frequent targets of arson. • 16% of all structures where arson occurred were not in use.

Sources: BJS Dictionary of criminal justice data terminology, 2nd edition. 1981 BJS Criminal victimization in the U.S., 1985. FBI Crime in the United States 1985.

TABLE 2.2   Serious crime arrest rates are highest in young age groups

---

Arrest rate per 100,000 age-eligible populations

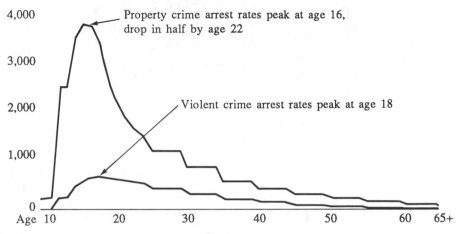

Source: FBI Uniform Crime Reports 3-year averages. 1983-85.

---

for which apprehension is more likely (for example, purse snatching vs. fraud). Moreover, because youths often commit crime in groups, the resolution of a single crime may lead to several arrests.

The decline in crime participation with age may also result from the incapacitation of many offenders. When repeat offenders are apprehended, they serve increasingly longer sentences, thus incapacitating them for long periods as they grow older. Moreover, a RAND Corporation study of habitual offenders shows that the success of habitual offenders in avoiding apprehension declined as their criminal careers progressed. Even though offense rates declined over time, the probabilities of arrest, conviction, and incarceration per offense all tended to increase. Recidivism data also show that the rates of returning to prison tend to be lower for older than for younger prisoners. Older prisoners who do return do so after a longer period of freedom than do younger prisoners.

Different age groups are arrested and incarcerated for different types of crimes

- Juveniles under age 18 have a higher likelihood of being arrested for robbery and UCR Index property crimes than any other age group.
- Persons between ages 18 and 34 are the most likely to be arrested for violent crimes.
- The proportion of each group arrested for public order crimes increases with age.

TABLE 2.3 Arrest rate trends vary by age group

Between 1961 and 1881—
• The most dramatic increases in arrest rates were for persons age 18 to 20.
• Smaller increases in arrest rates occurred for persons age 21 to 24 and age 25 to 29.

• For persons age 35 and older. arrest rates declined.
• Persons age 18 to 20 had the highest arrest rates followed by those age 21 to 24.
• Persons age 50 or older had the lowest arrest rates.

Arrests per 100,000 age-eligible population

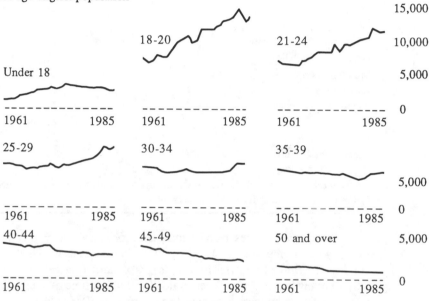

Source: FBI Uniform Crime Reports. 1961-85, unpublished data.

• Among jail and prison inmates, property crimes, particularly burglary and public order crimes, are more common among younger inmates.
• Violent crimes were more prevalent among older inmates admitted to prison in 1982 but showed little variation among jail inmates of different ages.
• Drug crimes were more prevalent among inmates age 25 to 44 in both prisons and jails.

Many older prison inmates had never been to prison before

Of all persons admitted to prison after age 40, nearly half were in prison for the first time.

TABLE 2.4   Average age at arrest varies by type of crime

Most Serious charge	Average age at arrest in 1985
Gambling	37 years
Murder	30
Sex Offenses	30
Fraud	30
Embezzlement	29
Aggravated assault	29
Forcible rape	28
Weapons	28
Forgery and Counterfeiting	27
Drug abuse violations	26
Stolen property	25
Larceny/theft	25
Arson	24
Robbery	24
Burglary	22
Motor vehicle theft	22

Source: Age-specific arrest rates and race-specific arrest rates for selected offenses 1965-85. FBI Uniform Crime Reporting Program December 1986

Inmates whose most recent admission to prison was at or after age 40 were more likely to be serving time for a violent crime than inmates who had the longest, most continuous criminal careers. The seriousness of their offenses alone probably explains why so many inmates were incarcerated for the first time at or after age 40.

Persons who were returning to prison at or after age 40 generally had prior criminal records rather than a current violent conviction. Given their records, these returnees did not have to commit a violent crime to bring them back to prison.

The average age of arrestees for most crimes remained fairly constant from 1965 to 1985

Some exceptions are that the average age of persons arrested for—
- murder declined
- forcible rape increased
- fraud declined
- embezzlement declined
- larceny/theft increased
- motor vehicle theft increased

The greatest increase in average age was for persons arrested for arson.

Historically, studies have shown property crimes to be more typical of youths than of older offenders

In a historical assessment of offending patterns, Cline reviewed several studies. These studies indicated a change from property to violent crimes as adolescents moved into adulthood.

Adults commit more serious crimes than juveniles

In a study of delinquency over time in England, Langan and Farrington examined the relationship between age of offenders and the value of the property they stole. The study found that crimes committed by adults were much more serious when measured in terms of value of stolen property than those committed by juveniles. Findings showed that the average amount stolen increased with age. . . .

The juvenile justice system

The processing of juvenile offenders is not entirely dissimilar to adult criminal processing, but there are crucial differences in the procedures. Many juveniles are referred to juvenile courts by law enforcement officers, but many others are referred by school officials, social services agencies, neighbors, and even parents, for behavior or conditions that are determined to require intervention by the formal system for social control.

When juveniles are referred to the juvenile courts, their *intake* departments, or prosecuting attorneys, determine whether sufficient grounds exist to warrant filing a petition that requests an *adjudicatory hearing* or a request to transfer jurisdiction to criminal court. In some States and at the Federal level prosecutors under certain circumstances may file criminal charges against juveniles directly in criminal courts.

The court with jurisdiction over juvenile matters may reject the petition or the juveniles may be diverted to other agencies or programs in lieu of further court processing. Examples of diversion programs include individual or group counseling or referral to educational and recreational programs.

If a petition for an adjudicatory hearing is accepted, the juvenile may be brought before a court quite unlike the court with jurisdiction over adult offenders. In disposing of cases juvenile courts usually have far more discretion than adult courts. In addition to such options as probation, commitment to correctional institutions, restitution, or fines, State laws grant juvenile courts the power to order removal of children from their homes to foster homes or treatment facilities. Juvenile courts also may order participation in special programs aimed at shoplifting prevention, drug counseling, or driver education. They also may order referral to criminal court for trial as adults.

Despite the considerable discretion associated with juvenile court proceedings, juveniles are afforded many of the due-process safeguards associated with adult criminal trials. Sixteen States permit the use of juries in juvenile courts; however, in light of the U.S. Supreme Court's holding that juries are not essential to juvenile hearings, most States do not make provisions for juries in juvenile courts.

CASES INVOLVING JUVENILES ARE HANDLED MUCH DIFFERENTLY THAN ADULT CASES

The juvenile court and a separate process for handling juveniles resulted from reform movements of the late 19th century

Until that time juveniles who committed crimes were processed through the criminal courts. In 1899 Illinois established the first juvenile court based on the concepts that a juvenile was a salvageable human being who needed treatment rather than punishment and that the juvenile court was to protect the child from the stigma of criminal proceedings. Delinquency and other situations such as neglect and adoption were deemed to warrant the court's intervention on the child's behalf. The juvenile court also handled "status offenses" (such as truancy, running away, and incorrigibility), which are not applicable to adults.

While the juvenile courts and the handling of juveniles remain separated from criminal processing, the concepts on which they are based have changed. Today, juvenile courts usually consider an element of personal responsibility when making decisions about juvenile offenders.

Juvenile courts may retain jurisdiction until a juvenile becomes legally an adult (at age 21 or less in most States). This limit sets a cap on the length of time juveniles may be institutionalized that is often much less than that for adults who commit similar offenses. Some jurisdictions transfer the cases of juveniles accused of serious offenses or with long criminal histories to criminal court so that the length of the sanction cannot be abridged.

Juvenile courts are very different from criminal courts

The language used in juvenile courts is less harsh. For example juvenile courts—
- accept "petitions" of "delinquency" rather than criminal complaints
- conduct "hearings," not trials
- "adjudicate" juveniles to be "delinquent" rather than find them guilty of a crime
- order one of a number of available "dispositions" rather than sentences.

Arrest is not the only means of referring juveniles to the courts

While adults may begin criminal justice processing only through arrest, summons, or citation, juveniles may be referred to court by law enforcement agencies, parents, schools, victims, probation officers, or other sources.

Law enforcement agencies refer three-quarters of the juvenile cases, and they are most likely to be the referral source in cases involving curfew violations, drug offenses, and property crimes. Other referral sources are most likely in cases involving status offenses (truancy, ungovernability, and running away).

TABLE 2.5   Most referrals to juvenile court are for property crimes, but 17% are for status offenses

Reasons for referrals to juvenile courts

11%	Crimes against persons	
	Criminal homicide	1 %
	Forcible rape	2
	Robbery	17
	Aggravated assault	20
	Simple assault	59
		100 %
46%	Crimes against property	
	Burglary	25 %
	Larceny	47
	Motor vehicle theft	5
	Arson	1
	Vandalism and trespassing	19
	Stolen proprty offenses	3
		100 %
5%	Drug offenses	100 %
21%	Offenses against public order	
	Weapons offenses	6 %
	Sex offenses	6
	Drunkenness and disorderly conduct	23
	Contempt, probation, and parole violations	21
	Other	44
		100 %
17%	Status offenses	
	Running away	28 %
	Truancy and curfew violations	21
	Ungovernability	28
	Liquor violations	23
		100 %

Note: Percents may not add to 100 because of rounding.

Source: Delinquency in the United States 1983. National Center for Juvenile Justice, July 1986.

"Intake" is the first step in the processing of juveniles

At intake, decisions are made about whether to begin formal proceedings. Intake is most frequently performed by the juvenile court or an executive branch intake unit, but increasingly prosecutors are becoming involved. In addition to beginning formal court proceedings, officials at intake may refer the juvenile for psychiatric evaluation, informal probation, or counseling, or, if appropriate, they may close the case altogether.

For a case involving a juvenile to proceed to a court adjudication, the intake unit must file a petition with the court

Intake units handle most cases informally without a petition. The National Center for Juvenile Justice estimates that more than half of all juvenile cases disposed of at intake are handled informally without a petition and are dismissed and/or referred to a social service agency.

Initial juvenile detention decisions are usually made by the intake staff

Prior to holding an adjudicatory hearing, juveniles may be released in the custody of their parents, put in protective custody (usually in foster homes or runaway shelters), or admitted to detention facilities. In most States juveniles are not eligible for bail, unlike adults.

Relatively few juveniles are detained prior to court appearance

One juvenile case in five involved secure detention prior to adjudication in 1983. Status offenders were least likely to be detained. The proportion of status offenders detained has declined from 40% in 1975 to 11% in 1983.

UNDER CERTAIN CIRCUMSTANCES, JUVENILES MAY BE TRIED IN CRIMINAL COURTS

All states allow juveniles to be tried as adults in criminal courts

Juveniles are referred to criminal courts in one of three ways—
- Concurrent jurisdiction—the prosecutor has the discretion of filing charges for certain offenses in either juvenile or criminal courts
- Excluded offenses—the legislature excludes from juvenile court jurisdiction certain offenses usually either very minor, such as traffic or fishing violations, or very serious, such as murder or rape
- Judicial waiver—the juvenile court waives its jurisdiction and transfers the case to criminal court (the procedure is also known as "binding over" or "certifying" juvenile cases to criminal courts).

TABLE 2.6   Age at which criminal courts gain jurisdiction of young offenders ranges from 16 to 19

Age of offender when under criminal court jurisdiction	State
16 years	Connecticut, New York, North Carolina
17	Georgia, Illinois, Louisiana, Massachusetts, Missouri, South Carolina, Texas
18	Alabama, Alaska, Arizona, Arkansas, California, Colorado, Delaware, District of Columbia, Florida, Hawaii, Idaho, Indiana, Iowa, Kansas, Kentucky, Maine, Maryland, Michigan, Minnesota, Mississippi, Montana, Nebraska, Nevada, New Hampshire, New Jersey, New Mexico, North Dakota, Ohio, Oklahoma, Oregon, Pennsylvania, Rhode Island, South Dakota, Tennessee, Utah, Vermont, Virginia, Washington, West Virginia, Wisconsin, Federal districts
19	Wyoming

Source: "Upper age of juvenile court jurisdiction statutes analysis." Linda A. Szymanski National Center for Juvenile Justice, March 1987

12 states authorize prosecutors to file cases in the juvenile or criminal courts at their discretion

This procedure, known as concurrent jurisdiction, may be limited to certain offenses or to juveniles of a certain age. Four States provide concurrent jurisdiction over juveniles charged with traffic violations. Georgia, Nebraska, and Wyoming have concurrent criminal jurisdiction statutes.

As of 1987, 36 States excluded certain offenses from juvenile court jurisdictions

Eighteen States excluded only traffic, watercraft, fish, or game violations. Another 13 States excluded serious offenses; the other 5 excluded serious offenses and some minor offenses. The serious offenses most often excluded are capital crimes such as murder, but several States exclude juveniles previously convicted in criminal courts.

48 States, the District of Columbia, and the Federal Government have judicial waiver provisions

A small proportion of juvenile cases are referred to criminal court

Recent studies found that most juveniles referred to criminal court were age 17 and were charged with property offenses. However, juveniles charged with violent offenses or with serious prior offense histories were more likely to be adjudicated in criminal court. Waiver of juveniles to criminal court is less likely where court jurisdiction extends for several years beyond the juvenile's 18th birthday.

Juveniles tried as adults have a very high conviction rate, but most receive sentences of probation or fines

More than 90% of the judicial waiver or concurrent jurisdiction cases in Hamparian's study resulted in guilty verdicts, and more than half the convictions led to fines or

TABLE 2.7 Youngest age at which juvenile may be transferred to criminal court by judicial waiver

Age	States
No specific	Alaska, Arizona, Arkansas, Delaware, Florida, Indiana, Kentucky, Maine, Maryland, New Hampshire, New Jersey, Oklahoma, South Dakota, West Virginia, Wyoming, Federal districts
10 years	Vermont
12	Montana
13	Georgia, Illinois, Mississippi
14	Alabama, Colorado, Connecticut, Idaho, Iowa, Massachusetts, Minnesota, Missouri, North Carolina, North Dakota, Pennsylvania, South Carolina, Tennessee, Utah
15	District of Columbia, Louisiana, Michigan, New Mexico, Ohio, Oregon, Texas, Virginia
16	California, Hawaii, Kansas, Nevada, Rhode Island, Washington, Wisconsin

Note: Many judicial waiver statutes also specify offenses that are waivable. This chart lists the States by the youngest age for which judicial waiver may be sought without regard to offense

Source: "Waiver/transfer/certification of juveniles to criminal court Age restrictions Crime restrictions." Linda A. Szymanski National Center for Juvenile Justice, February 1987

probation. Sentences to probation often occur because the criminal courts view juveniles as first offenders regardless of their prior juvenile record. However, serious violent juvenile offenders are more likely to be institutionalized. In a study of 12 jurisdictions with Habitual Serious or Violent Juvenile Offender Programs, 63% of those convicted were sentenced to prison and 14% to jail. The average prison sentence was 6.8 years.

Correctional activities for juveniles tried as adults in most states occur within the criminal justice system

In 1978, in more than half the States, youths convicted as adults and given an incarcerative sentence could only be placed in adult corrections facilities. In 18 jurisdictions, youths convicted as adults could be placed in either adult or juvenile corrections facilities, but sometimes this discretion was limited by special circumstances. Only 6 jurisdictions restricted placements of juveniles convicted as adults to State juvenile corrections institutions. Generally, youths sentenced in this manner will be transferred to adult facilities to serve the remainder of their sentence on reaching majority. . . .

JUVENILES RECEIVE DISPOSITIONS RATHER THAN SENTENCES

Juvenile court dispositions tend to be indeterminate

The dispositions of juveniles adjudicated to be delinquent extend until the juvenile legally becomes an adult (21 years of age in most states) or until the offending behavior has been corrected, whichever is sooner.

Of the 45 States and the District of Columbia that authorize indeterminate periods of confinement—
- 32 grant releasing authority to the State juvenile corrections agency
- 6 delegate it to juvenile paroling agencies
- 5 place such authority with the committing judges
- 3 have dual or overlapping jurisdiction

Most juvenile cases are disposed of informally

In 1982 about 54% of all cases referred to juvenile courts by the police and other agencies were handled informally without the filing of a petition. About 20% of all cases involved some detention prior to disposition.

Of about 600,000 cases in which petitions were filed, 64% resulted in formal adjudication. Of these, 61% resulted in some form of probation, and 29% resulted in an out-of-home placement.

The juvenile justice system is also undergoing changes in the degree of discretion permitted in confinement decisions

Determinate dispositions are now used in six States, but they do not apply to all offenses or offenders. In most cases they apply only to specified felony cases or to the juveniles with prior adjudications for serious delinquencies.

California imposes determinate periods of confinement for delinquents committed to State agencies based on the standards and guidelines of its paroling agency. Four States have similar procedures, administered by the State agencies responsible for operating their juvenile corrections facilities.

As of 1981 eight States had serious-delinquent statutes requiring that juveniles who are either serious, violent, repeat, or habitual offenders be adjudicated and committed in a manner that differs from the adjudication of other delinquents. Such laws require minimum lengths of commitment, prescribe a fixed range of time for commitment, or mandate a minimum length of stay in a type of placement, such as a secure institution.

Dispositions for serious juvenile offenders tend to look like those for adults

Aggregate statistics on juvenile court dispositions do not provide an accurate picture of what happens to the more serious offenders because many of the cases coming before juvenile courts involve minor criminal or status offenses. These minor cases are more likely to be handled informally by the juvenile court.

An analysis of California cases involving older juveniles and young adults charged by the police with robbery or burglary revealed more similarities in their disposition patterns than the aggregate juvenile court statistics would suggest. For both types of offenses, juvenile petitions were filed and settled formally in court about as often as were complaints filed and convictions obtained in the cases against adults. The juveniles charged with the more serious offenses and those with the more extensive prior records were the most likely to have their cases reach adjudication. At the upper limits of offense and prior record severity, juveniles were committed to secure institutions about as frequently as were young adults with comparable records.

The outcomes of juvenile and adult proceedings are similar, but some options are not available in juvenile court

For example, juvenile courts cannot order the death penalty, life terms, or terms that could exceed the maximum jurisdiction of the court itself. In Arizona the State Supreme Court held that, despite statutory jurisdiction of the juvenile courts to age 21, delinquents could not be held in State juvenile corrections facilities beyond age 18.

Yet, juvenile courts may go further than criminal courts in regulating the lifestyles of juvenile offenders placed in the community under probation supervision.

TABLE **2.8**   Most juveniles committed to juvenile facilities are delinquents

		Percent of juveniles
Total	100%	
Delinquents		74
Nondelinquents		
	Status offenders	12
	Nonoffenders (dependency neglect, abuse, etc.)	14

Source: BJS Children in Custody 1985. unpublished data

For example, the court may order them to—
- live in certain locations
- attend school
- participate in programs intended to improve their behavior.

The National Center for Juvenile Justice estimates that almost 70% of the juveniles whose cases are not waived or dismissed are put on probation; about 10% are committed to an institution. . . .

JUVENILE OFFENDERS ARE HOUSED IN MANY KINDS OF FACILITIES

More than 83,000 juveniles were in custody during 1984

They were held in 3,036 public and private juvenile custody facilities that were in operation in 1984. Such facilities include detention centers, training schools, reception or diagnostic centers, shelters, ranches, forestry camps or farms, halfway houses, and group homes.

The range of facilities and programs; the housing of delinquents, status offenders, voluntary admissions, and dependent and neglected children in the same facilities; and the participation of both the public and private sectors clearly distinguishes juvenile corrections from adult corrections.

Most juveniles in custody were being detained or were committed for a criminal offense

Of the 83,402 juveniles held in public and private facilities—
- 11% were being held for a violent offense of murder, forcible rape, robbery, or aggravated assault

- 23% were being held for the property crimes of burglary, arson, larceny-theft, or motor vehicle theft
- 4% were being held for alcohol or drug offenses.

Of the 25,451 nondelinquents held in juvenile facilities—

- 35% were status offenders
- 36% were being held for other reasons such as dependency, neglect, and abuse
- 28% were admitted voluntarily.

Public and private facilities generally hold different types of juveniles

Almost all (93%) of the juveniles in public facilities either are—

- detained pending adjudication
- have been committed after a finding of delinquency for a criminal offense (about a third of the juveniles in private facilities are in this classification).

Juvenile facilities are classified by the term of stay and type of environment

Term of stay

- Short-term—facilities that hold juveniles awaiting adjudication or other disposition.

TABLE 2.9   Most juvenile facilities are small; 80% are designed to house 40 residents or less

	Number of facilities		
Design capacity*	*Public and private combined*	*Public*	*Private*
Total	3,036	1,040	1,996
Less than 10 residents	1,053	141	912
10-20	913	326	638
21-40	464	226	207
41-99	387	174	193
100-199	146	114	32
200 and over	73	59	14

*The number of residents a facility is constructed to hold without double bunking in single rooms or using areas not designed as sleeping quarters to house residents.

Source: Children in Custody: Public juvenile facilities, 1985, BJS Bulletin, October 1986, and Children in Custody, 1985. unpublished data.

TABLE 2.10   What is the staffing ratio of juvenile facilities?

	Number of residents per 10 staff members	
	Public	Private
All staff	9	8
Part-time	38	30
Full-time	11	12
Staff function		
Treatment/education	49	40
Youth supervision	22	24
Other	43	41

Source: BJS Children in custody 1982/83 Census of Juvenile Detention and Correctional Facilities.

- Long-term—facilities that hold juveniles already adjudicated and committed to custody.

In 1985, 46% of public facilities and 9% of private facilities were short-term; 54% of public facilities and 91% of private facilities were long-term.

Type of environment
- Institutional—environments impose greater restraints on residents movements and limit access to the community. Most detention or diagnostic centers, training schools, and ranches are classified as having institutional environments.
- Open—environments allow greater movement of residents within the facilities and more access to the community. Facilities with open environments mainly include shelters, halfway houses, group homes, and ranches, forestry camps, or farms.

Most public facilities (65%) have institutional environments, but most private facilities (86%) have open environments.

Most juvenile facilities are private, but about three-fifths of the juveniles are held in public facilities

Private facilities usually have open environments and are used for long-term custody. About 30% of all juveniles in custody are held in such facilities. Public facilities generally have institutional environments and are used for both short- and long-term custody. About 30% of all juveniles held are in long-term institutional public facilities; another 18% are in short-term institutional public facilities.

BASIC SOURCES

U.S. DEPARTMENT OF JUSTICE
Bureau of Justice Statistics:
BJS Bulletin—
Jail inmates, 1983, NCJ-99175. November 1985
BJS Special Reports—
Criminal defense systems: A national survey, NCJ-94630, August 1984
Pretrial release and misconduct: Federal offenses and offenders, NCJ-96132, January 1985
BJS Reports—
Boland, Barbara, with Ronald Sones, INSLAW, Inc., *Prosecution of felony arrests, 1981*, NCJ-101380, September 1986
State court organization 1980, NCJ-76711, May 1982
Spangenberg, Robert L., et al. of Abt Associates, Inc., *National criminal defense systems study*, NCJ-94702, September 1986
National Institute of Justice:
Emerson, Deborah, *Grand jury reform: A review of key issues*, NCJ-87645, January 1983
Emerson, D., and N. Ames, *The role of the grand jury and the preliminary hearing in pretrial screening*, GPO-01230-2, May 1984
Gottlieb, Barbara, *Public danger as a factor in pretrial release: A comparative analysis of State laws*, GPO-01245-1, July 1985
Jacoby, J. n, *Pretrial screening projects*, January 1976
McDonald, William F., *Police-prosecutor relations in the United States,* executive summary, NCJ-77829, July 1982
"The effects of the exclusionary rule: A study in California." *Criminal Justice Research Report*, GPO-01187-0. December 1982
Toborg, M.A., *Pretrial release: A national evaluation of practice and outcomes*, 1981
Whitcomb, Debra, Bonnie P. Lewin, and Margaret J. Levine, *Citation release,* issues and practices, March 1984

OTHER SOURCES
Brosi, Kathleen B., *A cross-city comparison of felony case processing* (Washington: Institute for Law and Social Research, April 1979)
Delinquency in the United States 1983 (Pittsburgh: National Center for Juvenile Justice, July 1986)
Gaynes, Elizabeth, *Topology of State laws which permit the consideration of danger in the pretrial release decision* (Washington: Pretrial Services Resource Center, May 1982)
Gettinger, Stephen, "Has the bail reform movement stalled?" *Corrections magazine* (February 1980), 4 (1):26–35
Hamparian, Donna M., Linda K. Estep, Susan M. Muntean, Ramon R. Prestino, Robert G. Swisher, Paul L. Wallace, and Joseph L. White, *Youth in adult courts: Between two worlds* (Columbus, Ohio: The Academy for Contemporary Problems, 1982)
Jacoby, Joan E., *The American prosecutor: A search for identity* (Lexington, Mass.: Lexington Books, 1980)
Johnson, Elmer H., *Crime, correction and society,* 3rd edition (Homewood, Ill.: The Dorsey Press, 1974)
Nissman, David M., and Ed Hagen, *The prosecution function* (Lexington, Mass.: Lexington Books, 1982)
Pryor, Donald E., and Walter F. Smith, "Significant research findings concerning pretrial

release." *Pretrial issues* (Washington: Pretrial Services Resource Center, February 1982) 4(1)

Reed, Sue Titus, *Crime and criminology,* 4th edition (New York: CBS College Publishing, 1985)

Rossum, Ralph A., *The politics of the criminal justice system* (New York: Marcel Dekker, Inc., 1978)

Szymanski, Linda A., "Concurrent jurisdiction statutes found in State juvenile codes" (Pittsburgh: national Center for Juvenile Justice, June 1987)

Szymanski, Linda A., "Statutory exclusion of crimes from juvenile court jurisdiction" (Pittsburgh: National Center for Juvenile Justice, February 1987)

Szymanski, Linda A., "Upper age of juvenile courts jurisdiction statutes analysis" (Pittsburgh: National Center for Juvenile Justice, March 1987)

Toborg, M. A., et al., *Public danger as a factor in pretrial release,* draft report, February 1986

NOTES

[1] BJS *Justice agencies in the United States 1986,* forthcoming.

[2] K. M. Williams, *The role of the victim in the prosecution of violent crimes* (Washington: institute for Law and Social Research, 1978).

[3] *Arrest convictability as a measure of police performance,* final report (Washington: Institute for Law and Social Research, 1980).

[4] "Pretrial program directory" (Washington: National Association of Pretrial Services Agencies, July 1986.)

[5] Wayne Thomas, *Bail reform in America,* (Berkeley, Calif.: University of California Press, 1976)....

Procedures for the Development of National Estimates of Delinquency and Status Offense Cases

THIS SECTION describes the data and the statistical procedures employed to develop national estimates of the number and characteristics of delinquency and status offense cases disposed by juvenile courts in 1984.

DATA

The Juvenile Court Statistics series utilizes data provided to the National Juvenile Court Data Archive by state and county agencies responsible for the collection and/or dissemination of information on the processing of youth through the juvenile courts. These data are not the result of a census or scientifically designed (probability) sampling procedure. They are also not the result of a uniform data collection effort. The national estimates were developed by utilizing data from all courts who were willing and able to provide data for this work. The data were generated by state and local juvenile court information systems designed to meet their own informational needs. So the accuracy of the data was vital to those who recorded the information because the data were used in the daily operations of the courts as well as for planning and evaluation. The use of available data has its strengths and weaknesses. Therefore, to

Source: Juvenile Court Statistics, 1984. Pittsburgh: National Center for Juvenile Justice, Research Div. of National Council of Juvenile and Family Court Judges, National Institute of Juvenile Justice and Delinquency Prevention August, 1987:71–75; 13–15; 85–90. Reprinted by permission.

properly assess the validity of the national estimates found in this report, critical readers must balance the benefits and disadvantages of using available data from a large sample of courts to meet national reporting needs.

The data used in this report fall into one of two general categories: case-level data and court-level aggregate statistics. Case-level data are generated by courts with automated client tracking/management information systems or automated reporting systems. These data describe in detail the characteristics of each case handled by the court and usually contain information on the age and sex of the youth referred, the date and source of referral, the offense(s) charged, whether or not the youth was detained, whether or not the case was petitioned, the date of disposition, and the disposition of the case. The nonautomated court-level aggregate statistics were either abstracted from annual reports or supplied on request by local and state agencies. These figures report the number of petitioned and nonpetitioned cases handled by a court in a defined time period (e.g., calendar year, fiscal year).

The structure of each case-level data set (e.g., the definition of data elements, their codes, and interrelationships) was unique, having been designed to meet the informational needs and demands of the state or local jurisdiction. These disparate data sets were combined by converting (recoding) each into a common national data format, a process which required an intimate understanding of the development, structure, and content of each data set. This process consumed more time and energy than any other aspect of the project. Code books and operation manuals were studied, interviews were conducted with the data suppliers, and diagnostic analyses of each data file were reviewed. Even though there were some instances when coding decisions were made on less than complete information, the vast majority of cases were recorded into the standardized national format using sufficient information to assure confidence in the recoding decisions. The combination of these converted data sets formed the national case-level data base.

Of course case-level data can be aggregated to produce court-level statistics, but only case-level data can yield the detailed descriptions of juvenile court cases found in this statistical series. Court-level summaries of these case-level data sets combined with data from those courts which only reported court-level aggregate statistics formed the national court-level aggregate data set. In all, juvenile courts with jurisdiction over 96 percent of the youth population reported either case-level or aggregate data on their delinquency and status offense cases.

However, not all of the reported information could be incorporated in the national estimates. Each data set contributed to the archive was studied to determine its structural characteristics (e.g., unit of count and coding rules) and its consistency with data previously supplied by the same source. To be used in this report the data had to be compatible with the report's unit of count, *a case disposed,* and had to represent the complete reporting of delinquency and status offense cases handled with or without the filing of a petition in calendar year 1984. Of the case-level data files contributed to the Archive describing 1984 juvenile court activity, data from 1,040 jurisdictions in 20 states (Arizona, California, Connecticut, Florida, Hawaii, Iowa, Maryland, Minnesota, Mississippi, Missouri, Nebraska, New York, North Dakota, Ohio, Pennsylvania, South Dakota, Tennessee, Utah, Virginia, and Wisconsin) containing individual records on

538,000 cases met these criteria. Five hundred and sixty jurisdictions in these and nine other states (Alabama, District of Columbia, Georgia, Idaho, Illinois, New Mexico, South Carolina, Texas, and Vermont) reported compatible court-level aggregate statistics on an additional 220,000 cases. In other words, detailed case-level data were available from 1,040 jurisdictions containing 44 percent of the nation's youth population at risk. And 560 jurisdictions covering an additional 17 percent of the population at risk provided only court-level data. In all, court-level statistics (including aggregated case-level data) compatible with the reporting requirements of this series were available from 1,600 jurisdictions containing 61 percent of the nation's youth population at risk. These court-level data were the basis for the estimate of the total number of cases disposed in 1984 across the country. With the 1984 national caseload estimate in hand, national estimates of case characteristics were developed based on the contents of the detailed case-level data.

YOUTH POPULATION AT RISK

The number of juvenile court cases in a community has been shown to be highly related to the number of youth in the community that are under the jurisdiction of the juvenile court. Consequently, a critical element of the national estimation procedure was the development of a measure of the youth population at risk for juvenile court referral. A survey of the case-level data showed that very few delinquency or status offense cases involved youth below the age of 10. Therefore, the lower age limit of youth population at risk of juvenile court involvement was set at 10 years of age. Every state in the nation defines an upper age limit of original juvenile court delinquency jurisdiction.[1] While there are numerous exceptions to this age criterion (e.g., youthful offender legislation, concurrent jurisdiction statutes, and extended jurisdiction provisions), it was decided that the upper age of original juvenile court jurisdiction would be the best upper limit for the youth population at risk. Therefore, in a New York county where the upper age of juvenile court jurisdiction was 15, the youth population at risk equaled the number of youth 10 through 15 years of age residing in that county; in California where the upper age of juvenile court jurisdiction was 17, the youth population at risk equaled the number of youth 10 through 17 years of age.

While a juvenile court is likely to handle a few cases involving youth who are above or below the age limits of their youth population at risk, it was decided that the youth population at risk was the best indicator of the segment of the total population that generates juvenile court activity. Of course, juvenile court cases involving youth outside the population at risk age limits were retained for analysis purposes. The decision to exclude these youth from the population at risk calculations enabled the case rate statistic (which is an integral part of the national estimation procedure) to be more sensitive to variations across jurisdictions. In calculating case rates the number

[1] In 1984 the juvenile courts in 38 states and the District of Columbia had original jurisdiction (with minor exceptions) over all youth 17 years of age and below, in eight states (Georgia, Illinois, Louisiana, Massachusetts, Michigan, Missouri, South Carolina, and Texas) age 16 and below, in three states (Connecticut, New York, and North Carolina) age 15 and below, and in Wyoming age 18 and below.

of cases (involving youth of all ages) is divided by the youth population at risk. To include youth under 10 and above the upper age of jurisdiction in the population at risk calculations would cause the overall case rates to be less sensitive to changes or variations. Although including the small number of cases involving juveniles outside of the population at risk age range into the rate calculation will have some impact, its effect is minimal.

Data from the U.S. Bureau of the Census were used to develop youth population at risk figures for each county in the country. The U.S. Bureau of the Census reported county-level age group estimates in five-year groupings for July 1, 1984 on a machine-readable data file entitled County Population Estimates *(Experimental) by Age, Sex, and Race: 1980–1982–1984* and the national individual age group estimates for July 1, 1984 in *Current Population Reports, Population Estimates and Projections, Series P-225, No. 985: Estimates of the Population of the United States by Age, Sex, and Race: 1980 to 1985.* Using these data sets, estimates of the 1984 county-level youth population at risk figures were generated as follows. The 1984 county-level age groups estimates (0–4, 5–9, 10–14, and 15–19) were divided into individual age group estimates by assuming that the proportions at each individual age group within the county were equivalent to the national proportions reported in the P-25 series for 1984. With individual age group population estimates for each county and knowing the upper age of original juvenile court jurisdiction for each state, youth population at risk estimates were developed for each county nationwide.

DIFFERENCES BETWEEN NATIONAL AND SAMPLE YOUTH POPULATION AT RISK

Analyses were conducted to compare the demographic characteristics of the nation's 1984 youth population at risk with both the case-level data sample (1,040 jurisdictions) and the court-level data sample (1,600 jurisdictions). Both samples had proportions of males (51.2 percent) and females (48.8 percent) identical to those found in nation's youth population at risk. The age distribution of the court-level data sample was nearly identical to the nation's youth population. Nationally, 79.4 percent of juveniles were below 16 years of age, 12.0 percent were age 16, and 8.6 percent were older than 16. In the court-level sample, 79.8 percent were younger than 16, 11.8 percent were 16, and 8.4 were older than 16. The case-level sample had a slightly greater proportion of older youth (78.5 percent were under 16, 11.0 percent were 16, and 10.5 percent were over 16). Racial comparisons yielded similar results. Nationally, 81.8 percent of youth were white and 18.2 percent were nonwhite. Both samples had slightly larger proportions of nonwhites (18.7 percent in the case-level sample and 19.8 in the court-level sample).

Analyses were also performed which compared the relative mix of small and large counties in the two samples with that of the nation. The nation's 3,081 counties. . . were divided into four quartiles. The first quartile contained the 2,516 smallest counties, the second the next 411, the third the next 117, and the fourth contained the 37 largest counties in the country. Each group of counties contained 25 percent of the nation's 1984 youth population at risk. Using these county groupings, the proportion of youth at risk in each sample was determined. Both samples contained a larger proportion of youth from the larger counties. The court-level sample's smallest counties contained 20.1 percent of the juveniles in the sample. The second group of counties has 22.5 percent of youth at risk, the third group had 23.5 percent, and the fourth group of largest counties contained 33.9 percent. The case-level sample had 17.4 percent of its youth in the first group of counties, 20.7 percent in the second group, 25.9 percent in the third group, and 35.9 percent in the fourth group.

These analyses show that compared to the nation's youth population at risk the samples are slightly over representative of nonwhites and the detailed case-level sample had a somewhat higher proportion of older youth. Overall, though, the samples are quite representative of the country's youth population. Although the samples were drawn somewhat disproportionately from large counties, by controlling for county size in the estimation procedure the impact of this difference is diminished. The estimation procedure also controlled for age, and will in the future (beginning with in the *Juvenile Court Statistics 1985 report*) control for race.[2]

THE ESTIMATION PROCEDURE

A procedure was designed to develop national estimates of the number and the characteristics of delinquency and status offense cases disposed by juvenile courts in 1984 from the large nonprobability sample of case-level data and court-level aggregate statistics. Over the years different techniques for developing national estimates of court activity from a nonprobability sample have been tested. The current approach assumes that the dynamics which produce the volume and characteristics of juvenile court cases in reporting counties were shared by other nonreporting counties with similar characteristics that have been shown to be related to the rate of cases handled by juvenile courts. County was selected as the unit of aggregation because most juvenile court jurisdictions were concurrent with county boundaries, most juvenile court data report the county in which the case was handled, and because youth population estimates developed by the U.S. Bureau of Census were reported by county.[3]

To group counties into clusters which share characteristics relating to juvenile court case rate, a wide variety of county characteristics were studied to assess their

---

[2] A technical report detailing the revised estimation procedure will be prepared as a companion document to the *Juvenile Court Statistics 1985* report.

[3] Florida's data was the only information used in this report which could not be aggregated by county. These data were collected by the Florida Department of Health and Rehabilitative Services (HRS) which identified the HRS district in which the case was handled. Florida's juvenile courts (which were not county based, but organized into 20 multi-county district courts) did not collect case-level information. In order to utilize the quality data collected by HRS, the aggregation criterion was relaxed to include the 11 HRS districts. In 1984 there were 3,137 counties in the United States. By replacing Florida's 67 counties with the 11 HRS districts, the total number of aggregation units, or "counties," for this report became 3,081. Therefore, while the report uses the term "county" to describe the aggregation unit, the reader should be aware of the complications introduced by the use of Florida's HRS data.

relationship with the county's rate of juvenile court referrals. Of the more than 100 county characteristics studied, including population, sociological, economic and governmental factors, two emerged as the most predictive of juvenile court case rate: size of the youth population and the percentage of persons living in the county classified as urban residents. Further study showed that these two factors were highly correlated. Therefore, the decision was made to cluster counties on the basis of the size of their youth populations. The boundaries of each cluster on the population dimension were drawn to minimize the population range while insuring that each cluster contained a sufficient number of reporting jurisdictions to generate stable estimates. As a result each county in the country was placed in one of ten population clusters on the basis of the estimated number of 10- through 17-year-olds residing in the county.

The estimation procedure also controlled for variations in upper ages of original juvenile court jurisdiction within the population-based cluster by developing separate estimates for each of three age groups: youth age 15 and below, youth age 16, and youth age 17 and above. These three age groups were selected to correspond with the variations in the upper age of original juvenile court jurisdiction. By developing estimates for age groups within population clusters, the procedure not only compensated for the expected large variations in overall case rates among courts with divergent upper ages of original jurisdiction, but also for the fact that offense profiles and treatment patterns vary with the age of the youth and the size county in which the case is heard.

The estimation procedure developed independent estimates of the number of petitioned and nonpetitioned cases handled by the courts in each cluster. While most information systems reported data on each delinquency and status offense case disposed by their juvenile court system, some systems reported only cases handled formally through the filing of a petition. Therefore, to take advantage of all available data, estimating samples for petitioned and nonpetitioned cases were constructed separately.

... Counties were placed in one of ten clusters based on the size of their youth population age 10 through 17. Within each cluster, counties reporting petitioned and those reporting nonpetitioned court-level and case-level data consistent with this series' reporting requirements were identified. To develop estimates of the number of cases disposed by juvenile courts in each cluster, cluster-specific age group case rates were developed using data from reporting jurisdictions within the cluster. For example, Table A-1 shows that 68 of the 368 counties in Cluster 5 reported court-level aggregate statistics and another 101 counties reported individual case-level data (which could be analyzed to produce court-level aggregate counts) describing the number of petitioned cases processed by their juvenile courts in 1984. Estimates of the proportion of cases falling into each age group were developed by assuming that the proportions were equivalent to those observed in the jurisdictions reporting case-level data. Therefore, data from counties reporting aggregate caseload figures were partitioned into three age groups by assuming that their age distributions were the same as those reporting case-level data in their cluster. Using this procedure it was estimated that of the 14,153 petitioned cases reported by courts in the fifth cluster, 7,838 involved youth referred at age 15 or below, 3,259 involved youth referred at age 16, and 3,056 involved youth referred at age 17 or above.

Youth population at risk estimates were compiled for the reporting jurisdictions in a cluster and for the entire cluster. In Cluster 5 it was estimated that there were 626,000 youth 10 through 15 years of age in the reporting jurisdictions and 1,361,100 in the entire cluster. Given that the 10- through 15-year-old population in reporting jurisdictions generated 7,838 cases, the Cluster 5 case rate of 10- through 15-year-olds (number of cases disposed for each 1,000 youth in the age group) was estimated to be 12.5, or 7,838 cases divided by 626 thousand youth. Using the basic assumption that the reporting jurisdictions within the cluster are representative of the entire cluster, estimates of the total number of cases involving youth age 15 or below were calculated by multiplying the reporting sample's case rate by the total number of 10- through 15-year-old youth in the cluster. Using this procedure it was estimated that Cluster 5 courts handled 17,000 cases (i.e., 12.5 cases/1,000 youth times 1,361,100 youth in the cluster) involving youth referred at age 15 or below in 1984. This procedure was repeated for each of the other age groups and for each of the other clusters.

Having developed estimates of the total number of cases processed in each cluster, estimates of their characteristics were developed using the same underlying assumptions. Continuing with the example, . . . in Cluster 5 case-level data were reported on 5,574 petitioned cases involving youth age 15 or below. Therefore, for these cases to represent their age group for the entire cluster, each was weighted for all analyses by a weight equal to the estimated total number of petitioned cases in the cluster-age group (17,000) divided by the number of detailed case records from reporting jurisdictions (5,574). Each detailed case record involving a youth age 15 or below whose case was petitioned to court from a jurisdiction in Cluster 5 was given a weight of 3.05 (e.g., 17,040/5,574). Weights for the small number of cases with unknown ages at referral were set equal to the average weights of the other cases in the county. . .

A MODEL OF COURT PROCESSING

Although case processing procedures are not uniform across courts, cases generally proceed along the following path. Cases referred to juvenile courts are screened by an intake department.[4] The intake officer (or the prosecutor) may decide to dismiss the case for lack of legal sufficiency or to resolve the matter informally (e.g., by voluntary referral to a social agency for counseling; through informal probation; or, if the youth consents, by collecting fines by some form of restitution agreement). If there is sufficient evidence to proceed, intake may decide to recommend to the prosecutor that the case be handled formally, through the filing of a petition, and place the case on the court calendar for an adjudicatory or waiver hearing. If an adjudication hearing is held, the case could be dismissed, continued in contemplation of dismissal, or the youth

---

[4] Although in most states intake screening is a court function, in some states intake screening is performed by a state department of social services or the local prosecutor. In these jurisdictions, even though the intake unit may not technically be a part of the judicial branch of government, the referral of a case to the intake screening unit was considered for the purposes of this report to be the point of entry into the juvenile court system.

could be adjudicated delinquent or in need of supervision (status offender) and the case then proceeds to a dispositional hearing. During the dispositional phase of court processing, the judge, after reviewing the probation officer's report and dispositional recommendations, determines the most appropriate sanction. The range of options available to courts varies from jurisdiction to jurisdiction, but could include commitment to an institution for delinquents; placement in a group or foster home, or other residential treatment facility; probation; referral to an outside agency, day treatment or mental health program; or imposition of a fine or restitution order. If a waiver hearing is requested, the juvenile court judge is asked to decide whether or not the case should be waived to criminal court for prosecution.

CASE FLOW CHARACTERISTICS

Each year from 1975 through 1984 more than one half of all cases disposed by juvenile courts were handled informally (see Table 3.1). In 1984, 56 percent of all cases disposed were handled informally, without the filing of a petition, generally at the intake level. Nearly 3 out of 5 of these nonpetitioned cases were released, which includes those cases that received in outright dismissal, those cases held open in contemplation of dismissal, and those cases in which the youth was counselled and then released. One in 5 were placed on some form of voluntary probation and 1 in 7 were referred to an outside agency for service. In a very small number of nonpetitioned cases youth were either voluntarily placed out of their homes or returned to a previously ordered placement.

TABLE 3.1   Percentage and rate of cases disposed with and without the filing of a petition from 1975 through 1984

Year	Petitioned Cases		Nonpetitioned Cases	
	Percent	Case Rate*	Percent	Case Rate*
1975	47%	21.3	53%	23.9
1976	45%	20.3	55%	25.2
1977	47%	21.2	53%	24.0
1978	50%	22.6	50%	22.7
1979	46%	20.6	54%	24.5
1980	43%	20.4	57%	26.8
1981	47%	22.5	53%	25.5
1982	46%	21.8	54%	25.4
1983	46%	21.3	54%	25.1
1984	44%	21.5	56%	27.4

* Case rate is defined as the number of cases disposed annually for every 1,000 youth at risk

In 1984, 44 percent of all cases disposed were processed formally, through the filing of a petition, and scheduled for an adjudicatory or waiver hearing. As Figure 4 shows, 37 percent of petitioned cases were not adjudicated. Of these cases, 57 percent were released, 19 percent agreed to a form of informal/voluntary probation, 7 percent were referred to another agency for service, 4 percent (more than 9,000 cases) were waived to criminal court, and a small number were placed out of their homes. It is estimated that 63 percent of all petitioned cases resulted in a ruling of adjudication. Of those cases that were adjudicated, the majority (55 percent) were placed on formal probation and 29 percent were placed out of the home in a residential facility. The 4 percent that were released included those cases in which the disposition was suspended and those in which the youth's actions or sanctions imposed before the dispositional hearing were sufficient to satisfy the court. In 1 percent of the adjudicated cases youth were turned over to other agencies (e.g., drug treatment programs) for service.[5] . . .

. . . At times the court (i.e., the intake worker or the judge) orders a youth detained to protect the community when there is an expectation of future criminal activity by the youth, to protect the youth when parents or guardians cannot be located or when the youth is in immediate need of services, or to guarantee appearance at court hearings. Therefore, in many cases the same reasons for detaining a youth may also affect how the case is handled throughout the juvenile court process. Within each offense category, detained youth were twice as likely to be petitioned as youth who were not detained. In some jurisdictions, a petition must be filed on a case before the youth can be detained. In others the youth may be detained while the decision to petition is being considered. In 1984 a petition was filed in 74 percent of the cases nationally which involved secure detention in a restrictive facility under court authority. In comparison, petitions were filed in only 40 percent of the cases which were not detained. Youth who were detained were more than twice as likely to be adjudicated as those not detained. In 1984, 58 percent of all youth detained were adjudicated, compared to only 21 percent of those not securely detained. Therefore, in the majority of cases, detention was ordered for those youth who would eventually be formally placed under the supervision of the court. From these data it appears that the decision to securely detain a youth was, in the majority of cases, based on criteria which were also likely to lead to formal processing and adjudication. . . .

GLOSSARY OF TERMS

ADJUDICATED: Judicially determined to be a delinquent, status offender or dependent.

CASE RATE: The number of cases disposed per 1,000 youth (see Delinquency Child Population and Dependency Child Population).

[5] Some cases received dispositions coded into the "Other" category. Cases that fell into this dispositional category were primarily cases originally coded as receiving an "Unspecified" or "Other" disposition or which were coded into a category that was so broad that it could potentially include a wide range of dispositional alternatives. In addition, dispositions which were placed into this category because they were relatively uncommon included fines, restitution, and other short-term punitive orders (e.g., suspension of driver's license).

DELINQUENCY: Acts or conduct in violation of criminal law.

DELINQUENCY CHILD POPULATION: The number of children from age 10 through the upper age of jurisdiction. In all states the upper age of jurisdiction is defined by statute. In most states individuals are considered adults when they reach their 18th birthday. Therefore, for these states, the delinquency child population would equal the number of children who are 10 through 17 years of age living within the geographical area serviced by the court.

DELINQUENT ACT: An act committed by a juvenile for which an adult could be prosecuted in a criminal court, but when committed by a juvenile is within the jurisdiction of the juvenile court. *Delinquent acts* include *crimes against persons, crimes against property, drug offenses,* and *crimes against public order,* as defined under *Reason for Referral*, when such acts are committed by juveniles.

DEPENDENCY CASE: Those cases covering neglect or inadequate care on the part of the parents or guardians such as lack of adequate care or support resulting from death, absence, or physical or mental incapacity of the parents; abandonment or desertion; abuse or cruel treatment; and improper or inadequate conditions in the home.

DEPENDENCY CHILD POPULATION :   The number of children at or below the upper age of jurisdiction.

DISPOSITION :   Definite action taken or a treatment plan decided upon or initiated regarding a particular case. Case dispositions are coded into the following categories:

> **Transfer to Criminal Court/Waive**—Cases which were waived or transferred to a criminal court as the result of a waiver or transfer hearing.
>
> **Release**— Cases dismissed (including those warned, counselled, and released) with no further disposition anticipated.
>
> **Refer**—Cases that were referred outside the court for services with minimal or no further court involvement anticipated.
>
> **Probation**—Cases in which youth were placed on informal/voluntary or formal/court-ordered probation or supervision.
>
> **Placement**—Cases in which youth were placed out of the home in a residential facility housing delinquent or status offenders.
>
> **Other**—A variety of miscellaneous dispositions not included above. This category includes such dispositions as fine and restitution and those dispositions coded as *Other* in the original data.

JUVENILE COURT: Any court which has jurisdiction over matters involving juveniles.

MANNER OF HANDLING: A general classification of case processing within the court system. Petitioned cases are those that appear on the official court calendar for adjudication by the judge or referee as a result of the filing of a petition, affidavit, or other legal instrument used to initiate court action. Nonpetitioned cases are those cases which duty authorized court personnel screen for adjustment prior to the filing of a formal petition or affidavit. Such personnel include judges, referees, probation officers, other officers of the court and/or an agency statutorily designated to conduct petition screening for the juvenile court. The "nonpetition" category includes cases which were petitioned, but the petition was dropped or withdrawn prior to scheduling a formal hearing.

PETITION: A document filed in juvenile court alleging that a juvenile is delinquent, a status offender, or dependent and asking that the court assume jurisdiction over the juvenile or asking that an alleged delinquent be transferred to criminal court for prosecution as an adult.

RACE: The race of the youth referred as determined by the youth or by court personnel. **Note:** Coding of race and ethnicity is based upon OMB Revised Exhibit F, Circular No. A-46, Race and Ethnic Standards for Federal Statistics and Administrative Reporting. This exhibit provides standard classifications for recordkeeping, collection, and presentation of data on race and ethnicity in Federal program administrative reporting and statistical activities. These classifications should not be interpreted as being scientific or anthropological in nature. They were developed in response to needs expressed by both the executive branch and the Congress to provide for the collection and use of compatible, nonduplicated, exchangeable racial and ethnic data by Federal agencies.

White—A person having origins in any of the original peoples of Europe, North Africa, or the Middle East.

Black—A person having origins in any of the black racial groups of Africa.

Other—A person having origins in any of the original peoples of North America, the Far East, Southeast Asia, the Indian Subcontinent, or the Pacific Islands.

In the Data Briefs chapter, the ethnic categories of Hispanic and NonHispanic are at times incorporated into racial categories. The ethnic group "Hispanic" is defined as persons of Mexican, Puerto Rican, Cuban, Central or South American, or other Spanish cultures or origin, regardless of race.

REASON FOR REFERRAL: The most serious offense for which the youth was referred to court intake. Attempts to commit an offense were included under that offense except attempted murder, which was included in the aggravated assault category.

crimes against persons—This category includes *criminal homicide, forcible rape, robbery, aggravated assault, simple assault, and other person offenses* as defined below.

1. Criminal Homicide—Causing the death of another person without legal justification or excuse. *Criminal homicide* is a summary category, not a single codified offense. The term, in law, embraces all homicides where the perpetrator intentionally killed someone without legal justification, or accidentally killed someone as a consequence of reckless or grossly negligent conduct. It includes all conduct encompassed by the terms *murder, nonnegligent (voluntary) manslaughter, negligent (involuntary) manslaughter, and vehicular manslaughter.* The term is broader than the Index Crime category used in the FBI Uniform Crime Reports in which *murder* and *nonnegligent manslaughter* does not include *negligent manslaughter* or *vehicular manslaughter.*

2. Forcible Rape—Sexual intercourse or attempted sexual intercourse with a female against her will by force or threat of force. The term is used in the same sense as in the UCR Crime Index. (Some states have enacted gender neutral rape or sexual assault statutes which prohibit forced sexual penetration of either sex. Data reported by such states does not distinguish between *forcible rape* of females as defined above and other sexual assaults.)

3. Robbery—Unlawful taking or attempted taking of property that is in the immediate possession of another by force or the threat of force. The term is used in the same sense as in the UCR Crime Index.

4. Assault—Unlawful intentional inflicting, or attempted or threatened inflicting, of injury upon the person of another.

> **a. Aggravated Assault**—Unlawful intentional inflicting of serious bodily injury, or unlawful threat or attempt to inflict bodily injury or death by means of a deadly or dangerous weapon with or without actual infliction of any injury. The term is used in the same sense as in the UCR Crime Index. It includes conduct included under the statutory names *aggravated assault and battery, aggravated battery, assault with intent to kill, assault with intent to commit murder or manslaughter, atrocious assault, attempted murder, felonious assault and assault with a deadly weapon.*
>
> **b. Simple Assault**—Unlawful intentional inflicting, or attempted or threatened inflicting, of less than serious bodily injury without a deadly or dangerous weapon. The term is used in the same sense as in UCR reporting. *Simple assault* is often not distinctly named in statutes since it consists of all assaults not explicitly named and defined as serious.

5. Other Offenses Against Persons—This category includes kidnapping, custody interference, unlawful restraint, false imprisonment, reckless endangerment, harassment, etc., and attempts to commit any such acts.

crimes against property: This category includes *burglary, larceny, motor vehicle theft, arson, vandalism, stolen property offenses, trespassing, and other property offenses* as defined below.

1. Burglary—Unlawful entry or attempted entry of any fixed structure, vehicle or vessel used for regular residence, industry, or business, with or without force, with intent to commit a felony or larceny. The term is used in the same sense as in the UCR Crime Index.

2. Larceny—Unlawful taking or attempted taking of property (other than a motor vehicle) from the possession of another, by stealth, without force and without deceit, with intent to permanently deprive the owner of the property. This term is used in the same sense as in the UCR Crime Index. It includes shoplifting and pursesnatching without force.

3. Motor Vehicle Theft—Unlawful taking, or attempted taking, of a self-propelled road vehicle owned by another, with the intent to deprive him of it permanently or temporarily. The term is used in the same sense as in the UCR Crime Index. It includes *joyriding* or *unauthorized use of a motor vehicle* as well as *grand theft auto.*

4. Arson—Intentional damaging or destruction by means of fire or explosion of the property of another without his consent, or of any property with intent to defraud, or attempting the above acts.

5. Vandalism—Destroying or damaging, or attempting to destroy or damage, the property of another without his consent, or public property, except by burning.

6. Stolen Property Offenses—Unlawfully and knowingly receiving, buying, or possessing stolen property, or attempting any of the above. The term is used in the same sense as the UCR category *stolen property; buying, receiving, possessing.*

7. Trespassing—Unlawful entry or attempted entry of the property of another with the intent to commit a misdemeanor, other than larceny, or without intent to commit a crime.

8. Other Property Offenses—This category includes extortion and all fraud offenses, such as forgery, counterfeiting, embezzlement, check or credit card fraud, and attempts to commit any such offenses.

drug law violations: Unlawful sale, purchase, distribution, manufacture, cultivation, transport, possession, or use of a controlled or prohibited substance or drug, or drug paraphernalia, or attempt to commit these acts. Sniffing of glue, paint, gasoline and other inhalants and possession of paraphernalia are also included; hence, the term is broader than the UCR category *drug abuse violations.*

offenses against public order: This category includes *weapons offenses; sex offenses other than forcible rape; drunkenness; disorderly conduct; contempt, probation and parole violations;* and *other offenses against public order* as defined below.

1. Weapons Offenses—Unlawful sale, distribution, manufacture, alteration, transportation, possession, or use of a deadly or dangerous weapon, or accessory, or attempt to commit any of these acts. The term is used in the same sense as the UCR category *weapons; carrying, possessing, etc.*

2. Sex Offenses—All offenses having a sexual element, except forcible rape. The term combines the meaning of the UCR categories *prostitution and commercialized vice* and *sex offenses.* It includes all offenses such as *statutory rape, indecent exposure, sodomy, prostitution, solicitation, pimping, child molesting, lewdness, fornication, incest, adultery, etc.*

3. Drunkenness—Being in a public place while intoxicated through consumption of alcohol, or intake or a controlled substance or drug. It does not include driving under the influence. The term is used in the same sense as the UCR category of the same name. (Some states treat public drunkenness of juveniles as a status offense, rather than delinquency; hence, some of these offenses may appear under the status offense code *liquor law violations.* Where a person who is publicly intoxicated performs acts which cause a disturbance, he or she may be charged with *disorderly conduct.*)

4. Disorderly Conduct—Unlawful interruption of the peace, quiet, or order of a community, including offenses called *disturbing the peace, vagrancy loitering, unlawful assembly, and riot.*

5. Contempt, Probation and Parole Violations—This category includes intentionally obstructing a court in the administration of justice, acting in a way calculated to lessen the authority or dignity of the court, failing to obey the lawful order of a court, and violations of probation or parole other than *technical violations* which do not consist of the commission of a crime or are not prosecuted as such.

6. Other Offenses Against Public Order—This category includes other offenses against government administration or regulation, e.g. *escape from confinement, bribery, perjury, obstructing justice, gambling, fish and game violations, hitchhiking, health violations, false fire alarms, immigration violations, etc.*

status offenses: Acts or conduct which are offenses only when committed or engaged in by a juvenile, and which can be adjudicated only by a juvenile court. Although state statutes defining status offenses vary (and some states may classify cases involving these offenses as dependency cases), for the purposes of this report the following types of offenses were classified by NJCDA as status offenses:

1. Running Away—Leaving the custody and home of parents, guardians, or custodians without permission and failing to return within a reasonable length of time, in violation of a statute regulating the conduct of youth.

2. Truancy—Violation of a compulsory school attendance law.

3. Curfew Violations—Being found in a public place after a specified hour of the evening, usually established in a local ordinance applying only to persons under a specified age.

4. Ungovernability—Being beyond the control of parents, guardians, or custodians, or disobedient of parental authority, referred to in various juvenile codes as *unmanageable, incorrigible, unruly, etc*.

5. Liquor Law Violations—Violation of laws regulating the possession, purchase or consumption of liquor by minors. Some states or counties may include all liquor law violations, including acts which would be offenses if committed by adults.

dependency offenses: Those actions which come to the attention of a juvenile court involving neglect or inadequate care on the part of the parents or guardians, such as lack of adequate care or support resulting from death, absence, or physical or mental incapacity of the parents; abandonment or desertion; abuse or cruel treatment; and improper or inadequate conditions in the home.

In the Data Briefs chapter, offenses are also grouped into categories commonly used in the FBI Uniform Crime Reports (UCR). These groupings are:

index violent offenses: The offenses of murder/nonnegligent manslaughter, forcible rape, robbery, and aggravated assault.

index property offenses: The offenses of burglary, larceny-theft, motor vehicle theft, and arson.

nonindex offenses: In the FBI UCR, nonindex offenses include all offenses not contained within the two Crime Index categories above. However, for this work status offenses are reported in their own category and are not included within the report's nonindex crime category.

SECURE DETENTION: This variable indicates whether a youth was placed in a restrictive facility between referral to court intake and case disposition.

SOURCE OF REFERRAL: The agency or individual filing a complaint with intake (which initiates court processing).

> **Law Enforcement Agency**—Includes metropolitan police, state police, park police, sheriffs, constables, police assigned to the juvenile court for special duty, and all others performing a police function with the exception of probation officers and officers of the court.

> **Other**—Includes the youth's own parents, foster parents, adoptives parents, stepparents, grandparents, aunts, uncles, other legal guardians, counselors, teachers, principals, attendance officers, social agencies, district attorneys, probation officers, victims, other private citizens and a variety of miscellaneous sources of referral, which are often only defined by the code *other* in the data.

> In the Data Briefs chapter, cases referred by school personnel (teachers, principals, attendance officers, etc.) are presented separately.

STATUS OFFENSE: Behavior which is considered an offense only when committed by a juvenile (for example, running away from home). *See Reason for Referral.*

UNIT OF COUNT: Throughout this report the unit of count is a case disposed by a court with juvenile jurisdiction during the year 1984. The term *disposed* means that some definite action was taken or some treatment plan was decided upon or initiated. Each *case* represents a youth referred to the juvenile court during the year for a new referral for one or more of the reasons described in the Reason for Referral variable. Within this definition it is possible for a youth to be involved in more than one case within the calendar year.

UPPER AGE OF JURISDICTION: The oldest age at which a juvenile court has original jurisdiction over an individual for law-violating behavior. In 1984 in three states (Connecticut, New York, and North Carolina) the upper age of jurisdiction was 15, in eight states (Georgia, Illinois, Louisiana, Massachusetts, Michigan, Missouri, South Carolina, and Texas) the upper age of jurisdiction was 16, in Wyoming it was 18, and in the remaining 38 states and the District of Columbia the upper age of jurisdiction was 17.

YOUTH POPULATION AT RISK: See *Delinquency Child Population.*

ARTICLE 4

On the Validity of Official Statistics

A Comparative Study of White, Black, and Japanese High-School Boys

WILLIAM J. CHAMBLISS
RICHARD H. NAGASAWA

A continuing debate in the sociology of deviance is the degree to which official statistics are representative of the distribution and rate of deviance in the society. Some argue that official statistics are totally meaningless as indices of deviance rates; others maintain that although official statistics are distorted, they nonetheless indicate important trends and distributions of real rates of deviance. Official and unofficial delinquency rates of black, white, and Japanese youths in a large metropolitan area were analyzed. Our conclusion is that official statistics are so misleading that they are virtually useless as indicators of actual deviance in the population. It is suggested that the visibility of the offenses, the bias of the policing agencies, and the demeanor of the youth account for the rate and distribution of delinquency among the three groups and that official rates are a complete distortion of the actual incidence.

Source: Chambliss, William J. and Richard H. Nagasawa, "On the Validity of Official Statistics: A Comparative Study of White, Black, and Japanese High-School Boys." Journal of Research in Crime and Delinquency, Vol. 6 (January) 1969:71-77. Reprinted by permission of Sage Publications, Inc.

AN OLD AND CONTINUING DEBATE in the sociology of deviant behavior concerns the degree to which official statistics accurately depict the frequency and distribution of actual rates of deviance. That official reports of deviant behavior by agencies such as the police, courts, and prisons provide a biased picture is generally acknowledged. The debate, however, centers on whether the bias is sufficiently distorted to render the official statistics essentially useless or whether it is systematically consistent with the actual trend. Cressey offers what is probably the dominant point of view when he argues that, although official statistics are biased, they present an essentially accurate picture.[1] For example, he and others who share this opinion would argue that the biases of the official agencies probably lead to an overzealous tendency to arrest and process Negroes, which distorts their crime rate. However, Cressey would maintain, the distortion is not sufficient to account totally for the Negroes' consistently higher crime rate. Thus, the Negro population is seen as having a "real" crime rate higher than whites, but one that is not as much higher as official statistics suggest. Gold's study of white youths in Flint, Mich., attempts to demonstrate that lower-class youths in general do engage more extensively and more seriously in delinquency. These data are interpreted as support for the allegation that official delinquency represents "real" delinquency accurately.[2]

Difficulties arise with this position, of course, and the research used to support the contention fails to validate the hypothesis adequately. Gold's study, for example, determined involvement in delinquency from responses to interview questions of such a nature that they necessarily increased the likelihood that lower-class youths would respond as being "more delinquent" than middle-class youths. Typically, the offenses of lower-class youths involve the kinds of activities that Gold looked for and defined as delinquent, whereas the typical middle-class offenses were not mentioned. Furthermore, respondents were asked whether or not they had been truant—a term likely to be applied to the absences from school of lower-class youths but not to those of middle-class youths—thus biasing the responses in favor of more delinquency among lower-class respondents.[3]

Recognition of these difficulties has led some researchers to conclude that differences in involvement in delinquency are simply a function of systematic biases in the recording procedures that are not in any way indicative of differences in involvement in illegal behavior. Cicourel and Kitsuse, for example, have expressed the view that official reports tell us virtually nothing about the "real" distribution and frequency of deviant acts but only indicate something about the end product of the activities of the agencies responsible for defining people as deviant.[4]

[1] Donald R. Cressey, "The State of Criminal Statistics," *NPPA Journal,* July 1957, pp. 230-41

[2] Martin Gold, *Status Forces in Delinquent Boys* (Ann Arbor, Mich.: Institute for Social Research

[3] For a detailed analysis of social class differences in delinquency and societal responses to those differences, see William J. Chambliss, "Two Gangs," *Transaction* (in press).

[4] John I. Kitsuse and Aaron V. Cicourel, "A Note on the Use of Official Statistics," *Social Problems,* Autumn 1963, pp. 131-39.

METHOD

The empirical data for this study were gathered from two sources: (1) questionnaire responses of boys enrolled at a high school located in the central, lower-class, high-delinquency area of a metropolis and (2) official records of the juvenile court of the metropolis. The high-school student body was drawn largely from families in the lower socio-economic stratum, though not exclusively from those engaged in low-status occupations. The type of father's occupation by racial groups is presented in Table 4.1, which shows that the distribution of father's employment varies widely from gardeners on one hand to professional groups on the other, with various gradients in between.

The sample consisted of male high-school students between thirteen and eighteen years of age. Subjects were included from the three major racial groups represented at the school—white, Negro, and Japanese. Random samples of white and Negro subjects were obtained, while all the male Japanese pupils in attendance during the period of the study were selected. As the design called for only the three groups, those students who fell in the "other" category—Indian, Filipino, Chinese, etc.—were eliminated from the sample.

Questionnaires were administered to 226 male pupils, of whom 201 responded. The questionnaire was administered in small groups of less than twenty students during their study hour.[5] For those without registration free periods, arrangements were made to have them return after school.

FINDINGS

By comparing the relative frequency of involvement in delinquency as reported by the students in the three racial groups with the official—i.e., court reported—race-specific delinquency rates, we can obtain some measure of the degree to which official reports accurately reflect the "real" distribution of delinquency by racial groups.[6] Table 4.2 presents this comparison. These data indicate that the discrepancy between self-reported and official rates of delinquency involvement is large enough to preclude any reasonable statement about what one distribution should look like when given knowledge of the other. The Negroes have a substantially higher official rate, but the whites have a slightly higher self-reported rate. The Japanese have the lowest rate for both official and self-reported involvement, but the discrepancy between the two is so great as to render prediction of one rate from the other virtually meaningless.

The same general picture also appears from a comparison of students' self-reported delinquency and the high-school counselor's recorded misconduct of students. Table 4.3 reports the number and race of students referred to the counselor for misconduct. The percentage of teacher referrals for Negro youths is roughly three times

---

[5] In an attempt to preserve the anonymity of the respondents, only code numbers were placed on the questionnaires. Names of the students were attached to the questionnaire on a slip of paper which the respondents were instructed to remove and dispose of.

[6] Self-reported delinquency is, of course, subject to considerable distortion. Nonetheless, it is safe to assume that it depicts the actual behavior of the respondents more accurately than does the official

TABLE 4.1 Frequency distribution: type of father's occupation, by racial groups

Father's Occupation	White	Negro	Japanese	Total
Owner of Business; Executive	13	3	6	22
Professional	15	6	7	28
Office Worker; Salesman	7	7	10	24
Skilled Worker	11	19	15	45
Semi-skilled	7	21	6	34
Unskilled	5	14	10	29
Farmer; Rancher; Fisherman	0	0	2	2
Gardner	0	2	9	11
Total	58	72	65	195 *

that of the other two groups. While the Japanese youths are the least deviant as judged by both court-reported and self-reported delinquency, they are just as deviant as white (but not Negro) youths as judged by school misconduct. The white youths are notably less deviant than Negro youths by court-reported and counsel-or-reported misconduct but do not differ markedly by self-reports.

Table 4.4 shows teacher referrals and self-reports by social class and race. It can be seen that the lower-class youths are more prone to teacher referrals than their counterparts in the middle class. Self-reported delinquency involvement between the two class levels does not differ to any significant extent. According to self-reports, deviant behavior occurs equally in the different social class positions, but the middle-class youths seem less likely to be referred by teachers for misconduct in school than

TABLE 4.2 Comparison of arrests (for 1963) and self-reported delinquency involvement, by racial groups[a]

Racial Group	Per Cent Arrested	Per Cent Self-reporting High Delinquency Involved[b]
White	11	53
Negro	36	52
Japanese	2	36

[a] Based on data from Richard H. Nagasawa, *Delinquency and Non-Delinquency, A Study of Status Problems and Perceived Opportunity*, unpublished M.A. thesis, University of Washington, 1965, p. 35.

[b] A self-reported delinquency scale was developed and the respondents were divided so that 50 per cent of the sample was categorized as having high and 50 per cent as having low delinquent involvement.

TABLE 4.3 Racial grouping and teacher referrals

Racial Groups	Per Cent Referred to Counselor	n
White	21	58
Negro	60	72
Japanese	22	65

lower-class youths, except for Negroes, where middle-class youths are *more likely* to be referred for misconduct than lower-class youths. But even for lower-class Negro youths there is a 50-50 chance that they will be referred to a counselor for misconduct. One other tendency should be noted: middle-class Japanese boys are *more* likely to report deviant acts than those in the lower class but are *less* likely to be referred by teachers for misconduct in school.

In summary, our findings show that official records (court and counselor) of deviant behavior are low for white and Japanese boys and consistently high for Negro boys. However, the self-reported involvement in deviant behavior presents a picture of fairly similar involvement rates for all three groups.

Judging from these data, we must conclude that the notion that official statistics provide reliable indices of either actual or relative involvement in delinquent acts by racial groups is wrong. On the contrary, the data suggest that official and self-reported delinquency are sociologically distinct events. This conclusion thus supports the recent emphasis in sociological literature on studying the statistics-creating agencies rather than the persons labeled as deviant if we are to understand how some persons and groups come to be defined as deviant while others escape these designations.[7]

TABLE 4.4 Teacher referrals and self-reports by social class and race: percent of deviants

Racial Group	Middle Class		Lower Class	
	Teacher Referrals	Self-Reports	Teacher Referrals	Self-Reports
White	18%	50%	22%	59%
Negro	77%	59%	54%	52%
Japanese	17%	43%	24%	33%

[7] Kitsuse and Cicourel, *supra* note 4; Howard S. Becker, *Outsiders* (Glencoe, Ill.: Free Press, 1963); Edwin M. Lembert, *Social Pathology* (New York: McGraw-Hill, 1951); Frank Tannenbaum, *Crime and the Community* (New York: Columbia University Press, 1938),

INTERPRETATION

What are we to make of the fact that official and self-reported rates of delinquency involvement diverge as substantially as is suggested by this comparison of Negro, white, and Japanese delinquency rates? If the actual involvement in delinquency (as measured by self-reported delinquency) does not predict official rates, then what does? We believe that what actually accounts for the shape of the official rates is the interplay of certain characteristics of the culture of the different racial groups with features of the organizations that have principal responsibility for processing persons who deviate.

The operation of three interlocking variables accounts for the fact that the official rates of deviance are at odds with the self-reported rates. These variables are (1) the bias of the official agencies, (2) the visibility of the offenses, and (3) the demeanor of the youth when confronted with representative adult authority.[8]

Bias

Few residents of the metropolis seemed to doubt the prevailing view that the Japanese have an extremely low rate of crime and delinquency. Teachers, counselors, police, and other law enforcement officials interviewed by the authors completely agreed with this opinion. One might wonder at such a perspective, as gambling and prostitution are fairly wide-spread in the Japanese community; nevertheless, the view persisted.[9]

By the same token, most people with whom we talked—and especially law enforcement officials—were equally convinced that the Negroes (including the Negro youth) were the group most vulnerable to criminal and delinquent behavior. The white community was generally seen as being substantially more involved than the Japanese though not so involved as the Negro. White involvement, of course, was regarded as circumscribed pretty much by residence in "bad" neighborhoods.

Visibility

The views expressed by the police were of a self-fulfilling nature. The delinquent acts of the Japanese youths were not very likely to be seen since no one was looking for them. When they were seen (one is tempted to say *"inadvertently seen"*), the perceiver tended to dismiss the observation as a rare event.[10] Because of the bias of the officials, then, the transgressions of the Japanese youths were invisible.

Negro youths, by contrast, were scrutinized closely and whenever they did transgress the law, were much more likely to be seen than the Japanese youths.

[8] We can provide only a brief discussion of these variables here. A more detailed discussion appears in William J. Chambliss, "Two Gangs," *supra* note 3. The role of "demeanor" is articulated in Irving Piliavin and Scott Briar, "Police Encounters with Juveniles," *American Journal of Sociology*, September 1964, pp. 206-14.

[9] In a study conducted by the Atlantic Street Center, of the ninety-seven Japanese and Chinese boys in the sample, 5 per cent had police arrest records but none actually reached the court stage.

[10] For the most part, the Japanese community has been able to exert social control over its young members by means of community-sponsored agencies. In fact, such controls have extended into curbing information about Japanese delinquency to official agencies.

The whites were watched, though not so closely as the Negroes, and their transgressions were observed accordingly.

Demeanor

Part of the Japanese culture is to show respect for one's elders and for others in positions of authority. To be polite—and, when appropriate, contrite—is a manner of self-presentation fully institutionalized among the Japanese-Americans, especially those living in relatively homogeneous Japanese-American communities such as the one in the metropolis studied. Not surprisingly, when Japanese youths meet law enforcers, the bias with which the law enforcer approaches the encounter is likely to be sustained to the fullest. No youth so polite, neat, and middle class in demeanor could be involved in any very serious delinquency.

Negro culture is almost a polar extreme in its emphasis. Coolness, indifference, and a tough exterior are prized possessions of the Negro youth. When youths who operate in this world are confronted with an accuser, their response is likely to do more to convince him of their guilt and their problem than to allay his qualms about the seriousness of their suspected or known delinquent behavior.

The posture likely to be taken by lower-class white youths in their community is less clearly hostile to authority than that of the Negro youths. But they are nonetheless considerably more hostile in their demeanor than are the Japanese adolescents.

For each of these variables—visibility, bias, demeanor—the official response is likely to favor strongly the Japanese youth, give the benefit of the doubt to the white youth, and create an atmosphere of suspicion and caution toward the Negro Youth.

CONCLUSIONS

The official rate of delinquency for each of the three racial groups can be predicted with considerable accuracy by knowing the bias of the official agencies, the visibility of each group's acts of deviance, and the demeanor of the youth when confronted by adult authority. By contrast, the official delinquency rate could not be predicted at all well by knowing only the self-reported delinquency in the three groups.

The findings of this study thus lend support to the argument that official statistics may tell us a good deal about the activities of agencies responsible for generating statistics, but they tell us very little about the distribution of criminal or delinquent activities in the population. More important, the results of this survey enable us to characterize the particular features of rule enforcement and rule-enforcement agencies that lead to a continuous, agency perpetuated agreement between the official agencies' and the community's view of deviance in the society. The data suggest that a shift in perspective by the official agencies, a shift in the visibility of offenses, or a shift in the general demeanor of cultural groups will alter the official rates of deviance without actually reflecting any change in the propensity of different groups to engage in deviant acts.

ARTICLE 5

Court Records, Undetected Delinquency and Decision-Making

MAYNARD L. ERICKSON
LAMAR T. EMPEY*

THERE IS almost universal dissatisfaction with the accuracy of official records on delinquency.[1] Yet, at present, there are few realistic alternatives. Official records must be used, not only to provide statistical information on delinquent trends, but to act as an information base on the qualitative characteristics (i.e., delinquent types) of

Source: Erickson, Maynard L. and Lamar T. Empey, "Court Records, Undetected Delinquency and Decision-Making." *Journal of Criminal Law, Criminology and Police Science,* Vol. 54 (December) 1963:456–469. Reprinted by special permission of Northwestern University School of Law.

*Mr Erickson is Research Director of the Provo Experiment in Delinquency Rehabilitation, Brigham Young University. Mr. Empey is Director of the Provo Experiment.

Greatful acknowledgement is expressed by the authors to Monroe J. Paxman for his cooperation and support and to the Ford Foundation for the grant under which this research was conducted. Appreciation is also extended to Stanton Wheeler, Peter Garabedian, and James Short for their helpful criticisms.

[1]Discussions and criticisms are legion. A sample might include: Cressey, *The State of Criminal Statistics,* 3 NAT'L PROBATION & PAROLE ASS'N J. 230 (1957); McQueen, *A Comparative Prospective on Juvenile Delinquency,* in A SYMPOSIUM ON DELINQUENCY: PATTERNS, CAUSES AND CURES 1-21 (1960); Sellin, *The Basis of a Crime Index,* 22 J. CRIM. L. & C. 3335 (1931); SUTHERLAND, PRINCIPLES OF CRIMINOLOGY 29-30 (1947); TAFT, CRIMINOLOGY 61-65 (1956); and Van Vechten, *Differential Criminal Case Mortality in Selected Jurisdictions,* 7 AM. SOC. REV. 833 (1942).

On the other hand, Perlman and Schwartz, noting a high degree of agreement in trends between police and court records of juveniles, feel the two are subject to common determining factors. See Perlman, *The Meaning of Juvenile Delinquency Statistics,* 13 Fed. Prob. 63 (Sept. 1949). See also Perlman, *Reporting Juvenile Delinquency,* 3 NAT'L PROBATION & PAROLE ASS'N J. 242 (1957); and Schwartz, *Statistics of Juvenile Delinquency in the United States,* 261 ANNALS 9 (1949).

offenders. It is this base upon which many important practical and theoretical decisions are presently dependent. A host of provocative problems relative to each of these uses merits serious attention. Two are discussed below.

The first has to do with the currently increasing emphasis on preventing delinquency.[2] If prevention is to be successful, it must forestall delinquent behavior before it becomes a matter of official record. But how much is known about the whole body of delinquent acts which do not become a matter of official concern? How accurately do official statistics reveal the *actual* extent and types of offenses committed? Answers to these questions are needed before revisions in control strategies can proceed rationally toward desired goals.

At present most control decisions are without the benefit of answers to important questions. Most people are left in quandary as to whether official records understate or overstate the problem. For example, as a result of finding a vast number of undetected violations in their study, Murphy, Shirley and Witmer concluded that "even a moderate increase in the amount of attention paid to [them] by law-enforcement authorities could create a semblance of a 'delinquency wave' without there being the slightest change in adolescent behavior."[3]

Therefore, perhaps even more basic than deciding what should be done, we need more information in deciding whether, to what extent, or along what dimensions anything needs to be done. A greater knowledge of the nature of *undetected offenses* among the adolescent population might be important in determining prevention (and treatment) strategies.

A second problem has to do with the research on delinquency. Few authorities would dispute the value of using legal norms, in contrast to diffuse moral or extralegal concepts, to define a delinquent act. But the extension of this use to practical purpose often results in the development of extreme, either-or dichotomies: delinquent or nondelinquent, institutionalized or noninstitutionalized.

It is an obvious oversimplification to believe in the validity of such dichotomies. Delinquent behavior is not an attribute—something which one either is or is not, such as male or female, plant or animal. It is "a more or less thing,"[4] possibly distributed along one or more continua.

Even so, many sophisticated efforts to develop specific criminal or delinquent typologies based on this premise must still depend on the either-or nature of official records as the major criterion for selecting samples for study.

Once this is done, analyses tend to proceed in one of two directions: (1) either to rely further upon official records for specific information on such things as offense patterns; or (2) to reject as unimportant the official offense pattern in favor of

[2] A good example is President Kennedy's creation of the President's Committee on Juvenile Delinquency and Youth Crime; see Executive Order 10940, and THE FEDERAL DELINQUENCY PROGRAM OBJECTIVE AND OPERATION UNDER THE PRESIDENT'S COMMITTEE OF JUVENILE DELINQUENCY AND YOUTH OFFENSES CONTROL ACT OF 1961 (1962).

[3] Murphy, Shirley & Witmer. *The Incidence of Hidden Delinquency*, 16 AM. J. ORTHOPSYCHIATRY 696 (1946). See also, PORTERFIELD, YOUTH IN TROUBLE (1946; and a summary of studies in COHEN , DELINQUENT BOYS: THE CULTURE OF THE GANG 36-44 (1955).

[4] Short, *The Sociocultural Context of Delinquency*, 6 CRIME & DELINQUENCY 365, 366 (1960).

psychological, cultural, or interactional factors.[5] This latter action is usually taken on the premise that the delinquent act is merely a symptom of some more basic cause and that to understand or perhaps remove the cause is what is important. But, in either case, the paradox remains: the court record serves as the basic criterion for sample selection.[6] Any strong bias in it will likely color what is found. Thus, it may be that refined analyses based upon official samples are based also upon a rather questionable foundation.

So long as samples are selected on this basis, there is a possibility that important information is being excluded. What of the possibility, for example, that there are patterns of delinquent activity which are etiologically distinct?[7] What of the possibility that the search for different configurations of variables has been inadequate because of the incompleteness of official records of delinquent activity? Even further, what of the possibility that official records do not even reveal the pattern of offenses which most commonly characterizes an offender?

The fact that many studies have found age and sex to be more highly correlated with delinquency than a host of other supposedly more important etiological variables,[8] suggests the need to explore these questions. The addition of information on the actual, not official, amount and type of delinquency in which an individual has been involved might be an aid in filling many of the gaps which exist. One important gap would have to do with the extent to which, and under what circumstances, the delinquent offense pattern should be treated as an *independent* rather than as a dependent variable. What might be revealed if it were viewed as a variable which helps to explain rather than one which always explained by other factors?

THE PRESENT RESEARCH

This research is a modest attempt to provide some information on the questions just raised:

1. What is revealed about the total volume of delinquency when undetected offenses are enumerated? What offenses are most common?
2. To what degree do violations go undetected? To what extent do they go unacted upon in the courts?[9]

[5] For excellent summaries and bibliographies on typological developments in criminology, see: Gibbons & Garrity, *Some Suggestions for the Development of Etiological and Treatment Theory in Criminology,* 38 SOCIAL FORCES 51 (1960); Grant, *Inquiries Concerning Kinds of Treatment for Kinds of Delinquents,* CALIFORNIA BOARD OF CORRECTIONS MONOGRAPH No. 2 at 5 (1961).

[6] For example, such diverse typologies as those produced by Clyde Sullivan, Douglas and Marguerite Grant, in *The Development of Interpersonal Maturity, Applications to Delinquency,* 20 PHYCHIATRY 373 (1957), and Gresham Sykes, in THE SOCIETY OF CAPTIVES (1958), must still rely upon official definition for their basic samples of offenders.

[7] This question has been raised in Gibbons & Garrity, *supra* note 5, at 51; Short, *supra* note 4, at 366.

[8] Short, "The Study of Juvenile Delinquency by Reported Behavior—An Experiment in Method and Preliminary Findings" at 12 (unpublished paper read at the annual meeting of the American Sociological Association, 1955).

[9] For studies dealing with the problem of undetected delinquency, see: Murphy, Shirley & Witmer, *supra* note 3; Wallerstein & Wyle, *Our Law-Abiding-Lawbreakers,* 25 Fed. Prob. 110 (April 1947); Wilson,

3. Do non-official delinquents—young people that have never been convicted—commit delinquencies equal in number and seriousness to those committed by officially designated offenders?[10]
4. How useful are traditional dichotomies—delinquent or nondelinquent, institutionalized or non-institutionalized—in distinguishing groups of offenders from one another?
5. How valid are court records as an index of the total volume and types of offenses in which individuals are most commonly involved?

In seeking answers to such questions as these, this research sought: (1) to examine reported law-breaking across an adolescent continuum extending from those who had never been officially declared delinquent, through those who had appeared in court once, to those who were "persistent" offenders; and (2) to question adolescent respondents across the whole spectrum of legal norms for which they might have taken to court. In all they were asked about 22 violations.[11]

The Sample

The sample included only males, ages 15-17 years. It was made up of four subsamples:

1. A subsample of 50 randomly selected high school boys who had never been to court.
2. A subsample of 30 randomly selected boys who had been to court once.[12]
3. A subsample of 50 randomly selected, repeat offenders who were on probation. The respondents in this sample were assigned to a special community treatment program. If the program had not existed, 32 percent of these offenders would have been incarcerated, and 68 percent on regular probation.[13]
4. A subsample of 50 randomly selected, incarcerated offenders. Subsamples 1, 2, and 3 were drawn from the same community population. Subsample 4 was drawn from a statewide population of incarcerated offenders.

[10] Porterfield's work, *op. cit. supra* note 3, throws some light on this question; however, the evidence is not conclusive.

[11] Unfortunately, no data on sex violations can be presented. Two things stood in the way. The first was a general policy of high school administrators against questions on sex. The second had to do with possible negative reactions by parents against questions because of the brutal sex slaying of an 11-year-old girl and several attacks on women which occurred at the very time we began our study. For these reasons we did not attempt to gather these data for fear they might endanger the whole study.

[12] Since this study was part of a larger study comparing persistent delinquents—incarcerated and unincarcerated—with nondelinquent high school students, data were not collected initially from one-time offenders. Consequently, they had to be collected especially for this group. However, time and budgetary considerations required that the sample of one-time offenders be limited to 30.

[13] They are assignees to the Provo Experiment in Delinquency Rehabilitation. All assignees are, by design, persistent offenders. Assignment is made on a random basis and includes both offenders who might otherwise be left on regular probation and offenders who might otherwise be incarcerated in the State Industrial School. See Empey & Rabow, *The Provo Experiment in Delinquency Rehabilitation,* 26 Am. Soc. Rev. 693 (1961).

It was necessary to keep the number of respondents relatively small because each respondent was questioned at length about the whole spectrum of legal norms for which he might have been taken to court—22 different violations in all. As will be seen, this questioning resulted in the accumulation of a large mass of data which turned out to be expensive and difficult to handle.

Data Collection

All respondents were contacted in person by the authors. The study was explained to them and they were asked to participate. There were no refusals. Data were gathered by means of a detailed interview which was conducted as follows:

First, each of the 22 offenses was described in detail. For example, under the section regarding breaking and entering, it is not enough to ask a boy, "Have you ever broken into a place illegally?" He wants to know what constitutes "a place" : a car, a barn in the country, an unlocked garage? All of these had to be defined.

Second, after the act was defined, the respondent was asked if he ever committed the offense. In judging his response, attention was paid to non-verbal cue—blushes, long pauses, nervousness—as well as to verbal cues. These cues served as guidelines to further questions, probes and reassurances.

Third, if the respondent admitted having committed the offense, he was asked how many times he had done so. Again, considerable time and effort were spent in obtaining an estimate, the idea being that the greater accuracy could be obtained by this means than by fitting answers to a predetermined code or having him respond to such general categories as "none," "a few times" or "a great many times." In the case of habitual offenders, however, it was necessary on some offenses to have them estimate a range—15-20 times, 200-250 times—rather than a specific number.

Finally, the respondent was asked if he had ever been caught, arrested, or to court for each type of offense. If so, he was asked how many times this had occurred.

Methodological Problems

Beside the methodological problems inherent in any reported data, there are others peculiar to the nature of this type of study.[14] Perhaps the most important has to do with the method of obtaining data. An extended pilot study[15] and pretests, using both interviews and questionnaires, suggested that interviews could provide more complete and reliable data. Two main considerations let to this conclusion.

The first had to do with the lack of literacy skills among persistent delinquents. Two 15-year-olds in this study could neither read nor write; others had great trouble

---

[14] See Short, *supra* note 8; and Short & Nye, *Reported Behavior as a Criterion of Deviant Behavior*, 5 SOCIAL PROBLEMS 210 (Winter 1957-1958).

[15] Erickson, "An Experiment To Determine the Plausibility of Developing an Empirical Means of Differentiating Between Delinquents and Nondelinquents Without Consideration to Involvement in Legal Process," (unpublished Masters Thesis, Brigham Young University, 1960).

with simple instructions and questions. In our opinion, therefore, an interview was the only alternative for the delinquent subsamples.

Second, in addition to the need for comparable data, our pilot studies indicated that high school samples had trouble understanding specific questions and supplying the data wanted. Therefore, the value of using an interview for this group, as for delinquents, seemed to outweigh the virtues of an anonymous questionnaire.

We did not find the confrontation of an interview to be generally harmful. By using only three skilled interviewers, it became possible to anticipate recurring difficulties and to deal more effectively with them. These interviewers encountered two types of problems.

The first was the resistance on the part of high school students to revealing offenses. Patience, skepticism regarding replies, probes, and reassurances seemed to encourage candor. The second was a memory problem. Habitual offenders were not so reluctant to admit offenses, but they had often committed them so frequently that they could make an easy estimate neither as to number nor the age at which they began Probes and extended discussions helped considerably here in settling upon a reasonable estimate.

One possible problem regarding the validity of these data has to do with the perceptions of respondents regarding the "social desirability" of answering questions according to social expectation. What is each respondent's reference group? How does he perceive the interviewer? Are his responses biased by special perceptions of each?

For example, if among delinquents, it is desirable to exhibit extensive delinquent behavior, then, at least up to a certain point, the less delinquent an individual is, the more likely he may be to inflate his own actual violations. The converse might also be true for the conventional boy. Actually, as will be seen later, our findings tended to question the premise that social expectation influences boys' answers (or at least they failed to establish its validity). Nondelinquents reported so much delinquent behavior that it became difficult to assess the extent to which official delinquents, by contrast, might have inflated their own illegal behavior.

By way of determining validity, the names of all respondents were run through court records. None of those who had been to court failed to say so in the interview, nor did anyone fail to describe the offense(s) for which he was charged.

Few responses were so distorted as to be questionable. For example, no one maintained complete detachment from lawbreaking; no one admitted having committed all offenses. These findings tended to parallel the experience of Short and Nye in this regard.[16]

FINDINGS

1. *What is revealed about the total volume of delinquency when undetected offenses are enumerated? What offenses are most common?*

The number of violations which respondents admitted having committed was tre-

[16] Short & Nye, *supra* note 14, at 221.

TABLE 5.1 Extent of violations and percent undetected and unacted upon

| | | Subsamples | | | | | | | | | | | | | | |
| | | Entire Adolescent Sample[1] | | | Non Delinquent[2] | | | One Time Offenders[3] | | | Delinquents Community[4] | | | Delinquents Incarcerated[5] | | |
Offense	Rank	Total Offenses	% Unde-tected	% Unacted Upon	Total Offenses	% Unde-tected	% Unacted Upon	Total Offenses	% Unde-tected	% Unacted Upon	Total Offenses	% Unde-tected	% Unacted Upon	Total Offenses	% Unde-tected	% Unacted Upon
Traffic Offenses	1															
Driving Without License		11,796	98.9	99.7	1,845	99.6	100.0	512	98.7	98.7	2,386	98.0	99.1	7,053	99.1	99.9
Traffic Viol. (not lic.)		12,150	98.2	99.3	2,040	98.3	99.9	2,142	98.4	98.7	3,068	96.8	98.4	4,900	99.0	98.8
Total		23,946	98.6	99.5	3,885	98.9	100.0	2,654	98.4	98.6	5,454	97.3	98.7	11,953	99.0	99.8
Theft	2															
Articles less than $2		15,175	97.1	99.8	966	91.7	100.0	1,738	96.5	99.6	7,886	98.6	99.8	4,585	95.6	99.8
Articles worth $2 to $5		7,396	97.1	99.1	60	83.3	100.0	80	93.8	95.8	4,671	98.5	99.2	2,585	94.8	99.1
Articles more than $50		294	71.0	92.8	1	100.0	100.0	2	100.0	100.0	90	66.7	91.1	201	72.6	93.5
Auto Theft		822	88.9	95.5	4	100.0	100.0	0	0.0	0.0	169	84.6	93.5	649	90.0	96.0
Forgery		512	93.4	97.5	0	0.0	0.0	0	0.0	0.0	60	70.0	90.0	452	96.5	98.5
Total		24,199	96.3	99.3	1,031	91.3	100.0	1,820	96.3	99.4	12,876	98.0	99.4	8,472	94.5	99.0
Alcohol and Narcotics	3															
Buying Beer or Liquor		8,890	99.6	99.9	18	100.0	100.0	57	94.1	100.0	1,453	99.6	100.0	7,362	99.6	99.9
Drinking Beer or Liquor		12,808	98.8	99.8	219	100.0	100.0	270	100.0	100.0	4,173	9.0	99.7	8,146	98.6	99.8
Selling Narcotics		1	100.0	100.0	0	0.0	0.0	0	0.0	0.0	0	0.0	0.0	1	100.0	100.0
Using Narcotics		74	100.0	100.0	0	0.0	0.0	0	0.0	0.0	3	100.0	100.0	71	100.0	100.0
Total		21,773	99.1	99.9	237	100.0	100.0	327	99.0	100.0	5,629	99.1	99.8	15,580	99.1	99.9
Open Defiance of Authority	4															
Defying Parents		8,142	99.7	99.9	138	100.0*	100.0	128	100.0*	100.0	4,804	99.7*	99.9	3,072	99.8*	99.9
Defying Others		6,497	99.4	99.7	124	100.0*	100.0	170	100.0*	100.0	1,478	99.3*	99.3	4,725	99.5*	99.9
Total		14,639	99.5	99.9	262	100.0*	100.0	298	100.0*	100.0	6,282	99.6*	99.8	7,797	99.6*	99.9

TABLE 5.1 Extent of violations and percent undetected and unacted upon (Cont.)

| Offense | Rank | Entire Adolescent Sample[1] | | | Subsamples | | | | | | | | | | | |
| | | | | | Non Delinquent[2] | | | One Time Offenders[3] | | | Delinquents Community[4] | | | Delinquents Incarcerated[5] | | |
		Total Offenses	% Undetected	% Unacted Upon	Total Offenses	% Undetected	% Unacted Upon	Total Offenses	% Undetected	% Unacted Upon	Total Offenses	% Undetected	% Unacted Upon	Total Offenses	% Undetected	% Unacted Upon
Property Violations	5															
Breaking and Entering		1,622	85.6	94.4	67	94.0	100.0	102	98.4	100.0	527	84.4	93.5	926	84.9	94.2
Destroying Property		10,645	98.5	99.7	477	97.1	100.0	800	98.5	99.7	4,297	98.7	99.6	4,441	98.7	99.4
Setting Fires (Arson)		11	40.0	90.0	2	0.0	0.0	2	100.0	100.0	0	0.0	0.0	7	100.0	100.0
Total		12,278	96.8	99.0	546	96.7	100.0	904	96.5	9.6	5,454	97.3	99.0	5,374	96.4	98.5
Retreatist Activities	6															
Running Away from Home		578	86.8	94.7	19	100.0	100.0	19	100.0	100.0	103	75.0	87.4	437	89.0	96.1
Skipping School		9,375	93.9	99.8	377	94.7	100.0	698	93.1	100.0	3,478	93.2	99.8	4,822	94.4	99.8
Total		9,953	93.5	99.5	396	94.9	100.0	717	93.2	100.0	3,581	92.6	99.5	5,259	94.0	99.5
Offenses Against Person	7															
Armed Robbery		46	80.4	91.3	0	0.0	0.0	0	0.0	0.0	22	68.2	90.9	24	91.7	91.7
Fighting, Assault		8,980	99.7	99.9	354	100.0*	100.0	103	100.0*	100.0	2,207	99.9*	99.8	6,316	99.6*	99.9
Total		9,026	99.6	99.9	354	100.0*	100.0	103	100.0*	100.0	2,229	99.6*	99.7	6,340	99.5*	99.9
Others	8															
Gambling (habitually)		6,571	99.9	99.8	1,185	100.0	100.0	2,400	100.0	100.0	1,186	99.3	99.5	2,800	99.9	100.0
Smoking (habitually)		86	87.1	91.8	1	...*	100.0	3	50.0	100.0	39	...*	94.9	43	...*	88.4

[1]Number of Respondents = 180, except on Arson (N = 136) and Gambling (N = 171).

[2]N = 50.

[3]Actual N = 30. However, figures in this column have been inflated as though N = 50. This was done to make frequencies comparable with other subsamples.

[4]N = 50, except on Arson (N = 15) and Gambling (N = 41).

[5]N = 50, except on Arson (N-41).

*Because of their nature, these offenses almost never remain undetected by someone in authority. Thus, these figures refer to per cent *unarrested*, rather than *undetected*.

analysis. A comprehensive table, Table 5.1, was prepared for use throughout the paper. The reader's patience is requested in referring to it.

The first two columns of Table 5.1 deal with the total volume of reported delinquency. These columns rank types of offenses in terms of the total frequency with which they were reported by all four samples. The frequencies reported for one-time offenders (N = 30) has been inflated by two-fifths in order to make them comparable to the other subsamples (N = 50). This inflation is also reflected in the *totals column* of Table 5.1 for the entire sample.[17] (Many other refinements and differences among subsamples in this comprehensive table will be discussed later.)

Three types of offenses were most common: theft (24,199)—especially of articles worth less than $2 (15,175)—traffic (23,946), and the purchase and drinking of alcohol (21,698).

Grouped somewhat below these three were open defiance of authority—parents and others—(14,639); violations of property, including breaking and entering (12,278); retreatist activities such as running away (9,953); offenses against person (9,026); and finally such offenses as gambling (6,571). In the case of smoking, the total number of respondents who smoke habitually, rather than the estimated number of times all have smoked, was obtained. Of the 200, 86 reported smoking habitually.

2. *To what degree do violations go undetected? To what extent do they go unacted upon in the courts?*

The reader is again referred to in Table 5.1 where, along with the volume of delinquent violations, the percentage of each of those violations which went (1) *undetected* and (2) *unacted upon* in court is presented.

With regard to detection, respondents were asked after each reported violation to tell whether they had been *caught by anyone*: parents police, or others. With regard to court action, they were asked to report *any* appearance, *formal or informal,* before *any* officer of the court: judge, referee, or probation officer. (It was this question which served as an outside check on reliability. As noted above, respondents were generally very accurate.)

More than nine times out of ten—almost ten times out of ten—most offenses go *undetected* and *unacted upon.* This is especially true with respect to so-called minor violations: traffic offenses, theft of articles worth less than $50, buying and drinking liquor, destroying property, skipping school, and so on.

As might be expected, the picture changes with respect to more serious violations—theft of articles worth more than $50, auto theft, breaking and entering, forgery, and so on. Fewer of these offenses went undetected and unacted upon . Yet, even in these cases, eight out of ten reported that their violations went undetected and nine out of ten did not result in court action.

[17] It is impossible to assess any increase in error which might have resulted from this inflation. If there is bias in the sample of 30, it will have been magnified. See HANSEN, HURWITZ & MADOW, SAMPLE SURVEY METHOD AND THEORY (1953). Insofar as sample size, *per se,* is concerned, error would not have been significantly decreased had the sample of 30 been increased by 50. Both (N= 30) and (N = 50) are very small portions of the total population of one time offenders.

3. *Do nonofficial delinquents—young people who have never been convicted— commit delinquencies equal in number and seriousness to those committed by officially designated offenders?*

The answer to this question illustrates the extreme importance of distinguishing between the *frequency* with which a given norm or set of norms is violated by two different samples and the proportion of respondents in each sample who report having violated them. The distinction helps to avoid the pitfall of concluding that, because large *proportions* of two different samples—i.e., students and institutionalized delinquents—have committed various offenses, the samples are equally delinquent in terms of total volume. Because of early studies, this impression regarding the total volume of delinquency in different samples has become almost traditional, even though it was not embraced by the authors of these studies.[18] The fact is that the *frequency,* as well as the types of offenses, with which individuals violated certain statutes turns out to be vitally important.

By way of example, consider Table 5.2. It presents the *proportions* of respondents in the four different samples who reported committing various offenses. On some offenses —theft of articles worth less than $2, traffic violations, and destroying property—there is little to choose among the four samples. Most young people in each sample reported having committed them.

The proportions of all 180 boys who reported committing various offenses were as follows: petty theft (93%), gambling (85%), driving without a license (84%), skipping school (83%) destroying property (80%), other traffic offenses (77%), drinking (74%), fighting (70%), defying others (64%), and thefts of from $2 to $50 (59%).

However, it would be premature and superficial to conclude that, because large *proportions* of the entire sample have committed these offenses, the subsamples are equally delinquent. On only two offenses—gambling and traffic—did the proportions of nodelinquents exceed those of the delinquent subsamples. (However, the proportions for the nondelinquents and one-time offenders were very much the same.)

Furthermore, a re-examination of Table 5.1 reveals that the *frequency* with which official offenders violate the law is in excess of the *frequency* with which non-official offenders violate it. (Again, however, non-official and one-time offenders differ very little. More will be said on them later.) The chief distinctions were between non- and one-time offenders, on the one hand, and the two subsamples of persistent offenders on the other.

If non- and one-time offenders are combined—because of their similarity—the cumulative violations of persistent offenders exceed their violations by thousands: thefts, excluding forgery (20,836 vs. 2,851); violations of property (10,828 vs. 1,450); violations of person (8,569 vs. 457); and violations involving the purchase and drinking of alcohol (21,134 vs. 564).

In addition, as shown in Table 5.2, far smaller proportions of non- and one-time offenders committed offenses of a "serious" nature than did persistent offenders: theft of articles worth more than $50 (2% vs. 50%), auto theft (2% vs. 52%), forgery (0% vs 25%), and armed robbery (0% vs. 9 %).

[18] See PORTERFIELD, *op. cit. supra* note 3.

TABLE 5.2 Proportion of respondents committing offenses

Offense	Rank	Per Cent of Total[1]	Subsamples			
			Non-Delinquents[2]	One-Time Offenders[3]	Delinquents Community[4]	Delinquents Incarcerated[5]
Theft	1					
Less than $2		93	92	98	96	86
Worth $2 to $50		59	22	36	78	90
More than $50		26	2	2	46	54
Auto Theft		29	2	2	54	60
Forgery		13	0	0	16	34
Others	2					
Gambling		85	90	100	56	72
Smoking (habitually)		42	2	4	76	86
Traffic Offenses	2					
Driving Without License		84	72	78	94	92
Traffic Viol. (not lic.)		77	84	84	72	66
Retreatist Activities	4					
Running Away from Home		38	22	24	46	60
Skipping School		83	66	68	96	100
Property Violations	5					
Breaking and Entering		59	32	46	74	84
Destroying Property		80	66	84	86	84
Setting Fires (Arson)		6	2	2	0	8
Alcohol and Narcotics	6					
Buying Beer or Liquor		29	4	8	46	58
Drinking Beer or Liquor		74	52	66	84	94
Selling Narcotics		0.5	0	0	0	2
Using Narcotics		4	0	0	2	12
Offenses Against Person	7					
Armed Robbery		5	0	0	4	14
Fighting, Assault		70	52	60	82	86
Open Defiance of Authority	8					
Defying Parents		53	40	44	64	64
Defying Others		64	52	54	72	78

[1]Number of Respondents = 200, except on Arson (N = 156) and Gambling (N = 191).
[2]N = 50.
[3]N = 30.
[4]N = 50, except on Arson (N = 15) and Gambling (N = 41).
[5]N = 50, except on Arson (N = 41).

The significance of these data, then, seems to be that one should guard against the use of *proportions* of total populations as a measure of delinquent involvement without also taking into account the *frequency* with which these proportions commit violations. Although in two cases proportionately fewer of the delinquent samples had committed certain violations, those who had committed them did so with much greater *frequency* than official nondelinquent samples.

How useful are traditional dichotomies—delinquent or nondelinquent, institutionalized or noninstitutionalized— in distinguishing groups offenders one from another?

A series of tests was run, beginning on the nondelinquent end of the continuum, to discover where, if any, there were discriminating dichotomies on the volume of delinquent offenses, either between delinquent and nondelinquent subsamples or between institutionalized and noninstitutionalized offenders.

Chi Square was used as a test of significance. This test examines the possibility that any difference between groups could have occurred by chance. If differences are so great as to suggest that factors other than chance are responsible, it then suggests the confidence one might have in making that assumption.

To lend further refinement, a measure of association (T) was used to indicate the degree of relationship, when any difference was significant,[19] between official status and total volume of delinquency. For example, if Chi Square indicated that a delinquent and a nondelinquent sample differed significantly on a given offense, the measure of association (T) suggests the power of that offense to distinguish between these two samples.

An effort was made to increase the validity of all comparisons by diminishing the impact of the large number of offenses committed by a few individuals. Thus, instead of making a gross comparison between two samples on the total number of times an offense was committed, respondents in each sample were ordered according to the number of times they reported committing an offense (i.e., 1-3 times, 4-6 times, etc.). Comparisons were then made between the number of respondents from each sample found in each category.

The wisdom of doing this can be illustrated by examining Table 5.1. persistent delinquents in the community reported having committed more petty theft than institutionalized offenders, while the reverse is true for auto theft. But these differences were largely due to the excessive activities of a few individuals. By taking them into account, the tests could more accurately reflect real, overall differences. If we had not accounted for them, excessively large differences between samples might have been suggested when, in fact, they did not exist.

Official Nondelinquents vs. Official One-time Offenders. The first comparison was between the subsamples of 50 high school boys who had no court record and the 30 one-time offenders.[20] In this particular comparison, only one significant difference past the .05 level of confidence was found; the offense was *destruction of property*. Official offenders were more likely to have been involved.

[19] HAGOOD & PRICE, STATISTICS FOR SOCIOLOGISTS 370-71 (1952).

[20] This and other comparisons have the serious weakness of dealing with only a limited number of boys. But, at the same time, two things must be recalled: (1) that such comparisons involve an enumeration of violations which, in most cases, was very large; and (2) that it was necessary to limit the number of respondents because of the time and money involved in gathering and analyzing data on such a large number of violations.

Comparisons on such offenses as stealing articles worth more than $50, auto theft, armed robbery, forgery, etc., were meaningless because they were seldom, if ever, reported by either group. This in itself tells us much about the similarity of these two groups.

This dichotomy, then—official nondelinquent vs. one-time offenders—did not prove to be discriminating.

Official One-time vs. Persistent Offenders. The second comparison was between one-time offenders and the subsample of 50 boys who were non-incarcerated persistent offenders. Differences between these two on most offenses were marked.

Persistent offenders were significantly—that is, 99 times out of 100—more inclined than one-time offenders, as a group, to have stolen expensive and inexpensive items, skipped school, defied parents, bought and drunk liquor, smoked regularly, stolen autos, fought, and driven without a license. There was also a significant difference past the .05 level with regard to forgery.

They did not differ significantly from one-time offenders on such things as running away from home, breaking and entering, destroying property, or committing most types of traffic violations. They could not be compared on such offenses as armed robbery, arson, or selling and using narcotics because of the small number of violations by both groups, but especially by one-time offenders.

This dichotomy, then—*one time* vs. *persistent* offenders in the community—was generally discriminating.

Institutionalized vs. Noninstitutionalized Offenders. The final comparisons had to do with the institutionalized vs. the noninstitutionalized dichotomy. First, the sample of institutionalized offenders (Subsample 4) was compared with those noninstitutionalized offenders who had been to court *once* (Subsample 2). As might be expected, differences were significant on virtually all offenses. The samples seemed to represent two different populations because of the much heavier involvement of the institutionalized offenders (Subsample 4) in delinquency.

Second, institutionalized offenders (Subsample 4) were compared with the subsample of persistent offenders who had not been institutionalized (Subsample 3). The two did not differ significantly.

Persistent institutionalized offenders as a group reported having committed more traffic offenses, forgeries, auto thefts, offenses involving alcohol, and fights than persistent noninstitutionalized offenders. The latter, meanwhile, reported considerably more petty thefts, thefts of items worth up to $50, defying parents and destruction of property. But these differences were due largely to a few extreme individuals. Consequently, as explained earlier, when tests of significance took this fact into account, the modal behavior of boys in the two samples tended to be very much the same.

Consequently, the only significant difference between these two subsamples was on habitual smoking; more boys in the reformatory smoked regularly. Otherwise, the two samples might be taken as representative of the same population insofar as the modal volume and nature of their offenses were concerned.

The significance of this finding is diluted somewhat by the fact that only two-thirds of the noninstitutionalized group (Subsample 3) would have been on probation (and free in the community) had they not been attending a special rehabilitative program. Nevertheless, the findings strongly support the idea that a dichotomy which

TABLE 5.3   Comparison of official non- and one-time offenders with persistent offenders

Offense	Probability that Differences Could be Due to Chance	Degree of Association Between Volume and Official Classification
Theft		
Articles less than $2	.001	.28
Articles worth $2 to $50	.001	.46
Articles more than $50	.001	.45
Auto Theft	.001	.45
Forgery	.001	.31
Property Violations		
Breaking and Entering	.001	.34
Destroying Property	.001	.24
Setting Fires (Arson)	*	
Offenses Against Person		
Armed Robbery	*	
Fighting, Assault	.001	.41
Open Defiance of Authority		
Defying Parents	.001	.27
Defying Others	.001	.34
Retreatist Activities		
Running Away from Home	.001	.32
Skipping School	.001	.50
Traffic Offenses		
Driving Without License	.001	.36
Traffic Viol. (not Lic.)	.05	.17
Alcohol and Narcotics		
Buying Beer or Liquor	.001	.40
Drinking Beer or Liquor	.001	.42
Selling Narcotics	*	
Using Narcotics	*	
Others		
Gambling	.001	.29
Smoking (habitually)	.001	.78

* Offense not committed enough times to test differences

ized offenders may not be valid. *Persistency* rather than institutionalization seems to be the more important variable in distinguishing groups. In this study, for example, the clearest distinction among official offenders was between *one-time* offenders, on one hand, and persistent offenders—whether institutionalized or noninstitutionalized—on the other.

This finding suggests that where persistent offenders are involved, the decision to incarcerate one group and to leave the other in the community may be highly subjective. Factors other than the extent and seriousness of these offenses seem to subjective. Factors other than the extent and seriousness of these offenses seem to determine whether they are incarcerated or not.

Because of the significance of this finding, both samples of persistent offenders were combined and compared with the two subsamples on the nondelinquent end of the continuum (Subsamples 1 and 2, the official nondelinquents and one-time offenders) which likewise had been found not to differ. By combining samples in this way, comparisons could be made more reliable because of larger numbers with which to work. The results are displayed in Table 5.3.

Differences were strong and striking. On virtually all offenses, the chances were less than one in a thousand that they could have occurred by chance (see Table 5.3). Furthermore, all relationships were positive as indicated by the measures of association (T). This means that persistent offenders report having committed more of virtually every offense. Those offenses which best distinguished them from official non- or one-time offenders were smoking regularly (T= .78), skipping school (T = .50), theft of articles worth \$2 to \$50 (T = .46), theft of articles worth more than \$50 (T = .45), auto theft (T = .45), and drinking alcohol (T = .42).

This finding re-emphasizes the idea that the old dichotomies may be misleading. Persistency is the most distinguishing variable.

To what extent this finding may be generalized is hard to say. Many of the most significant differences—smoking regularly, all kinds of theft, drinking, fighting, and skipping school—are associated with behavior often thought to be more characteristic of the lower than middle class. Other offense patterns may have been characteristic of their setting in a Mormon subculture. However, such offenses as auto theft, forgery, breaking and entering, or stealing items worth more than \$50 were also highly discriminating between these two samples and are likely to draw strong official reaction anywhere.

The implication of these findings for both practice and research seems to be that the unqualified use of traditional dichotomies—i.e., delinquent vs. nondelinquent or institutionalized vs. non-institutionalized—may be unreliable. A further examination of undetected offenses on other population, to test the validity of these dichotomies, might be an important prerequisite to their future use as an important source of data.

5. *How valid are court records as an index of the total volume and types of offenses which are committed?*

Court Records as an Index Volume. Evidence presented earlier indicated that the great majority of all delinquent offenses remain undetected and unacted upon. It might be concluded, therefore, that official records do not accurately reflect the total volume of delinquency. However, this might not be true.

It may be that official records are useful in reflecting volume by (1) distinguishing between those who have been heavily delinquent from those who have not; and/or (2) reflecting a tiny but consistently accurate portion of all offenses.

One method of treating these possibilities is to calculate the correlation between the actual number of court appearances for a given population and the number of violations it reports having committed. This calculation was made.

A coefficient of correlation was calculated for all 180 respondents. To do this and still maintain specificity, court appearances were broken into 9 categories—never been

TABLE 5.4   Correlation coefficient between court appearances and reported Number of violations

Offense	Correlation	Percentage of Variation Explained
Misdemeanors		
A. Taken Singly		
Skipping School	.17	.03
Theft (less than $2)	.19	.04
Theft ($2 to $50)	.20	.04
Traffic Violations (all types)	.18	.03
B. Combined	.15	.02
Felonies*		
A. Taken Singly		
Theft (more than $50)	.25	.06
Auto Theft	.43	.18
Breaking and Entering	.40	.15
Forgery	.05	.003
B. Combined	.29	.08

* Armed robbery, arson and the selling and use of narcotics were not included because the number reporting such violations was small.

to court, been to court one time, two times, three times. . . nine or more times. The total number of reported violations was broken into 11 categories—never, 1-50, 51-100, 101-150 . . . 501 or more. The degree of association between these two variables was then calculated.

A correlation of .51 was obtained. This coefficient is statistically significant, indicating the existence of a relationship between appearing in court and the total number of violations one has committed; that is, the greater the number of reported violations, the greater likelihood that an individual will have appeared in court.

On one hand, this coefficient leaves much to be desired in terms of accurate predictability. A coefficient of .51 means that 26 percent of the variation in the number of court appearances among the 180 respondents could be associated with variations in the number of delinquent offenses they reported having committed.

When only 26 percent of the variation in violation rates, using specific categories, is explained in terms of court appearances, the ability of these appearances to supply a good index of the actual number of violations may be highly questionable.

To further illustrate this point we found a correlation of .56 between dropping out of school and the number of reported violations. This suggested that whether or not individuals had dropped out of school was as accurate or possibly more accurate a predictor of reported violations than court records. (For those respondents incarcerated in the Utah State Industrial School, this meant dropping out of school prior to incarceration, not because of incarceration.)

One would not expect official delinquency rates to be an exact match of the volume of delinquency. Seriousness is also very important. Society demands that stronger measures be taken for serious violations.

In order to examine its significance, correlation coefficients were run between court appearances and a series of single violations, extending all the way from misdemeanors to felonies. The results are displayed in Table 5.4.

As might be expected, reported felonies correlated more highly with court appearances than did reported misdemeanors. However, taken singly, the correlation between any one of the felonies (theft of articles worth more than $50, auto theft, breaking and entering, and forgery)[21] was not so high as that between the total *volume* of violations and court appearance.

Furthermore, even though the total number of reported violations for the four felonies, when they were combined and then correlated with court appearances, produced a higher coefficient (.29) than did the combined misdemeanors (.15); this correlation (.29) was considerably lower than the correlation (.51) between the total volume of offenses and court appearance.

This finding raises questions regarding the traditional assumption that the court record is a better index of serious violations than it is of the total number of offenses an individual has omitted. One might speculate, however that the finding is due to the inaccuracy of reported data. But if one were to discard these reported data as inaccurate, he would have to ignore the fact that, except for seriousness, these findings met other assumptions rather consistently regarding distinctions between persistent and nonpersistent offenders, as to both frequency and seriousness. And they also seemed capable of making more precise distinctions in the direction of theoretical expectations among various dichotomies than court records.

Thus, these findings also raise important questions regarding the accuracy of official records as an index of volume and seriousness. But it is difficult either to assess the amount of combined error inherent in these court and reported data or to generalize from this to other police and court jurisdictions.

Court Records and Types of Offenses. One of the major problems raised in the introduction had reference to the adequacy of official records for the purpose of conducting typological research. There are at least two different levels of complication.

The first has to do with the validity of the official dichotomies—delinquent or nondelinquent, institutionalized or noninstitutionalized—which are used as the major criteria for distinguishing groups and setting up research samples. The foregoing analysis has already suggested some possible difficulties. It suggests that important qualifications may be needed.

The second level of complication comes in specific attempts to establish delinquent typologies based not only upon basic dichotomies but upon the offense patterns which are revealed by court records. To be accurate, these records would have to reflect reliably an individual's major offense pattern, with respect to both number and seriousness. Some test of their ability to do so was made.

---

[21] Armed robbery, arson, and the selling and use of narcotics were not included in this analysis because the number reporting such violations was small.

The first part of the analysis was concerned with volume. It sought to determine how well the court record reflected, without special regard to seriousness, the offense which each respondent reported having committed *most often*. The court record proved to be a fair index for offenders who had been to court only once. Sixteen of 30, half of them, had appeared in court for the types of offenses they reported having committed most often.

But this was not the case for the more persistent offenders. The more delinquent they tended to be, the less predictive the court record was of their most commonly reported violations. For example, only 26 of the 100 official, persistent delinquents had appeared in court more often for their major areas of offense than for other offenses. Nineteen of the 100 had *never* appeared in court for their reported major areas of offense. Thus, if these reported data are valid, the court record for this latter group would not give any clues as to the types of offenses they reported having committed most frequently.

In between these two extremes were 55 other boys, all of whom had been to court for their major patterns of offense, but they had also been there equally as often for other offenses. Consequently, even for them court records would fail to provide a clear picture of the most commonly reported offense patterns.

With regard to seriousness, the foregoing analysis has already suggested that court records may be a relatively poor index of the total number of *serious* violations. But what of individual offenders rather than their total offenses? How well does the court record eventually select boys who report having committed *serious* violations?

Answers to such questions are important. Although an offender may have a long record of petty violations, his commission of a serious offense, such as breaking and entering, will more likely type him as a burglar than a petty thief.

In order to examine this dimension, a crude "seriousness" classification was established. Five judges and five chief probation officers from Utah's six juvenile judicial districts[22] were asked to rank 25 offenses according to seriousness. The first ten of these offenses were then selected to serve as the serious criterion. They were:

1.	Rape[23]	6.	Breaking and entering
2.	Selling narcotics	7.	Forgery
3.	Arson	8.	Auto theft
4.	Using narcotics	9.	Homosexuality[23]
5.	Armed robbery	10.	Theft of items worth more than $50

Two specific questions were examined: (1) How accurate is the court record in reflecting the most *serious* offense each respondent has committed (in terms of the hierarchy of eight serious violations)? (2) How accurate is the court record in reflecting each offender's most frequently committed *serious* violation?

---

[22] Utah has one of the two State Juvenile Court Systems in the United States. Connecticut has the other. Judges are appointed for six-year terms; they must be members of the bar. Chief probation officers are selected on the basis of a state merit system examination and training and experience in correctional work.

[23] It will be recalled that data on rape and homosexuality are not presented in this paper. Therefore, the seriousness classification includes the eight remaining offenses.

For a relatively large group, the court record could supply no information regarding these questions. This group was comprised primarily of the official nondelinquents and one-time offenders. Twenty-three of the 50 nondelinquents (46%) and 14 of the 30 one-time offenders (47%) had committed one or more of the serious violations, but none had ever been to court for any of them. (The close similarity between the nondelinquents and one-time offenders in this study is again illustrated.)

By contrast, a much higher proportion of the two most delinquent samples had not only committed serious offenses—i.e., 88 of 100—but had also been to court for committing them—i.e., 77 of the 88 (or 88%).

Upon reading such information one might conclude that official records are likely biased against persistent offenders. It should be recalled from Table 5.1, however, that respondents in the two most delinquent samples reported having committed many more serious offenses than the less delinquent subsamples. Court records, therefore, may simply reflect the greater probability of being caught because of excessive violations.

For this group of 77 persistent offenders who had been to court, the court record was accurate for 65 percent of them in reflecting the most serious offense they had committed. It said nothing of the remaining 35 percent. If, therefore, the premise is accepted that an offender would likely be typed on the basis of his most serious known offense, the court record would be accurate approximately two-thirds of the time for this select group. This is encouraging in some ways because it is persistent offenders with whom officials and researchers have been most concerned.

On the other hand, the large proportion of juveniles whose serious offenses remained undetected might easily have been typed in the same way had they been apprehended. Yet without official action, many of them apparently make a reasonable, conventional adjustment.

A second qualification has to do with the ability of the court record to reflect not only an individual's most *serious* violation, but the type(s) of *serious* violation(s) he commits most frequently. Another premise might be that an individual should be typed on the basis of frequency of seriousness rather than extremity of seriousness. For example, it may be preferable to type an individual as an auto thief for having been to court three times for auto theft than to type him as an armed robber for having been to court once for armed robbery.

The court records were somewhat less accurate in this regard. About half (39) of the 77 persistent offenders who had appeared in court for serious violations had appeared there more often for the types of *serious* violations they reported committing most often than for any other *serious* violation. However, the picture for this group of 39 was muddied somewhat because 52 percent of them had appeared in court just as often, or more often, for other offenses not considered serious.

For the other half of the 77 offenders who had not been to court more often for their most common serious violation, 20 (26%) had *never* been to court for their most common *serious* offense. And 18 (23%) had been to court just as often for the other *serious* offenses. In these cases , the court record would not be an accurate means for typing an individual according to *serious* offense.

CONCLUSION

In conclusion, official records seemed more accurate in reflecting an individual's single most *serious* violation than the pattern of offenses, either *serious* or *nonserious*, which he most commonly commits.

On the surface, these findings may seem more encouraging from the treatment and control, than the research, standpoints. That is, court records, when compared with reported behavior, did distinguish persistent offenders (with whom officials are most concerned) from one-time offenders or nondelinquents, in terms of both number and seriousness of violation. Furthermore, they seemed quite efficient in indicating the most *serious* violations which persistent offenders had committed.

However, a great deal of refined information regarding types of offenders is needed if treatment and control strategies are to be effective. And, even though such information may be most needed for the persistent offender, it cannot be supplied, even for him, until more is known about two things: (1) about any differences or similarities between him and those juveniles who, if they were apprehended, might be typed the same way; and (2) about the offense patterns of him and others who, though they are apprehended, often remain largely unincorporated into the official record. Varying degrees of such information are needed no matter what theoretical orientation one takes towards developing typologies for treatment and control purposes.

Obviously, the findings which led to these conclusions must be qualified because of the data from which they were derived and the methodological problems inherent in obtaining them. Yet, even if they are only partially correct, they indicate one possible reason why we have encountered so much difficulty in pinpointing important etiological and treatment variables.

If different patterns of delinquency have important significance for the administration of justice, for prevention and treatment strategies, and for research purposes, data which could be used to supplement official records seem needed. At least it would seem important to explore the possibility that reported data on undetected offenses might be helpful in understanding delinquency.

The methods for obtaining such data need not be greatly different from those which are used in a variety of other areas, clinical and scientific. Possible legal and constitutional questions would have to be explored. Yet, we are not without precedent in the clinical field where the communication of important information is privileged.

Furthermore, reported data might also open avenues to more detailed examination of the circumstances surrounding the commission of delinquent acts: Who is present? How are the acts carried out? What social and psychological variables seem to be operating? And then attempts might be made to relate such questions to court, control, and research strategies.

Correlates of Delinquency
The Illusion of Discrepancy Between Self-Report and Official Measures

MICHAEL J. HINDELANG
TRAVIS HIRSCHI
JOSEPH WEIS

This paper reviews the research literature concerning the extent to which studies of delinquency that use official records produce results compatible with studies of delinquency that use self-reports of adolescents. Particular attention is given to sex, race, and social class as correlates of delinquency. The notice that official and self-report methods produce discrepant results with respect to sex, race, and class is largely illusory. In reaching conclusions of discrepancy several techniques have been used in the literature: the most general is the assumption that self-report and official data tap the same domain of behavior. When the domain limitations of self-reports are recognized (and other illusory techniques are abandoned) the conclusion of general consistency between self-reports and official correlates for sex, race, and class emerges. This consistency and other evidence from victimization surveys, studies of the reliability and validity of self-reports, and studies of biases in criminal justice processing, suggest that both official data and self-reports provide valid indicators of the demographic characteristics of offenders within the domain of behavior effectively tapped by each method.

Source: Hindelang, Michael J., Travis Hirschi, and Joseph Weis, "Correlates of Delinquency: The Illusion of Discrepancy Between Self-Report and Offical Measures." *American Sociological Review,* Vol. 44 (December) 1979:995-1014. Reprinted by permission of the American Sociological Association and the authors.

FOR 160 YEARS scholars have attempted to solve the crime measurement problem by cataloging sources of possible error in existing techniques by deriving the facts about crime from theories of criminality and by simply accepting observed results at face value. About twenty years ago, a new dimension was added to this enterprise. Following preliminary and unsystematic work by Porterfield (1946) and Wallerstein and Wyle (1947) Short and Nye (1957) introduced the self-report method of measuring delinquent behavior. This new method produced results apparently contrary to those produced by established methods. Consequently, it did not settle the measurement issue. On the contrary, scholars could then catalog sources of error in either of two techniques: they could derive either of two sets of facts from criminological theory; and they could accept either of two sets of facts at face value. In short, the basic results of criminological research remained open to dispute. No simple conclusion about demographic correlates or causes of crime could command acceptance by more than a portion of interested scholars. And so it remains today.

Whatever approach one takes to a criminological issue, its vulnerability to the measurement question quickly surfaces. A recent example is the apparently definitive paper by Tittle, Villemez, and Smith (1978). Drawing on 35 studies and 363 separate estimates of the class/crime relation, Tittle et al. conclude that the assumed negative correlation between social class and criminality is a "myth." They also conclude that the discrepancy between self-report and official results in years prior to 1964 probably reflects class-linked biases in official processing. Given the history of the field we may safely assume that both of these conclusions will provide little more than a starting point for future debate.[1] As long as there is disagreement on the methodological and statistical underpinnings of such conclusions, assessments of the empirical evidence however thorough, will continue to produce ambiguous results.

In this paper we argue that the invention of self-report procedures could have resolved the crime measurement problem by showing consistency in results across methods. We argue further that it did not resolve the crime measurement problem because of continued misinterpretation of self-report findings. Such misinterpretation may be traced to a variety of techniques all of which create the illusion[2] of discrepancy between the correlates of official and self-reported delinquency when, in general, no such discrepancy has been demonstrated. These arguments will be illustrated by using sex, race, and social class as examples.

ORIGINS OF THE SELF-REPORT METHOD

In historical context, the self-report method may be seen as a device for studying delinquency in "nondelinquent" populations where all "official"[3] measures of delin-

---

[1] In May, 1979, Elliott and Ageton (1979:25) reported that results from their normal self-report survey show that "lower class youth are found disproportionately among high frequency offenders." Elliott and Ageton cite Tittle, et al. (1978).

[2] We do not use the word illusion as synonymous in any way with deception. Rather, we use it to refer to the appearance of inconsistency where it need not or does not exist.

[3] Most of the data in this paper using official measures of delinquency are data on arrests of contacts

quency (e.g. police records, court records, and incarceration) were too stringent to reveal adequate variation. Given this purpose, those constructing self-report instruments could not reasonably include offenses like homicide and rape for which observed variance in a small general population sample would have to be treated as error rather than true variance.[4] In fact, the requirement that items produce meaningful variation further skewed self-report instruments toward behavior occurring *frequently* in "nondelinquent" samples. Although perfectly reasonable from a statistical perspective, such items are almost by definition outside the domain of behavior that elicits official attention.

Early attempts to produce cumulative, unidimensional (Guttman) scales eliminated the very infrequent (and generally more serious) offenses from this already skewed pool. The final Short/Nye (1957) scale items are:

> Driven a car without a driver's license or permit.
> Skipped school without a legitimate excuse.
> Defied parents' authority (to their face).
> Taken little things (worth less than $2) that did not belong to you.
> Bought or drank beer, wine or liquor (including drinking at home).
> Purposely destroyed public or private property that did not belong to you.
> Had sex relations with a person of the opposite sex.

Although they scaled by Guttman criteria, four additional items had to be eliminated by Short and Nye because they were committed too infrequently by their noninstitutional respondents:

> Taken things of medium value (between $2 and $50).
> Taken things of large value (over $50).
> Used or sold narcotic drugs.

In rankings of offense seriousness by samples of the general population, the seven Short/Nye items retained are virtually off the scale; in one study they do no better than 125th in a list of 140 items (Rossi et al., 1974).[5] Such offenses, which constitute the care of self-report items widely used into the early 1970s (Hindelang, 1971; Hirschi, 1969), are largely outside the domain even of police contacts (e.g., Wolfgang et al., 1972: Table 5.3). In recent research, there has been a movement toward the inclusion of more serious items, but even current instruments as a whole are dominated by nonserious delinquent offenses (Elliot and Ageton, 1979; Farrington, 1973; Gold and Reimer, 1975; Berger and Simon, 1974).

---

drawn from police files. Occasionally, data relating to court records or incarceraton are also referred to as "official" delinquency data.

[4] For example, Porterfield's (1946:41) results showing one murder in his sample of 200 college men strain credibility. Subsequent self-report researchers have excluded the homicide item and have uncovered no murderers in their samples.

[5] Breaking a plate glass window in a shop ranked 125th, theft of a book from a store ranked 129th, and repeated truancy ranked 136th. As described in the Rossi et al. (1974) study, these offenses are more serious than the typical offense implicitly described in parallel self-report items.

Even apparently serious items in current self-report instruments turn out on inspection to allow the respondent to report behavior that would be hard to construe as serious delinquency. Gold (1970:25), for example, used a probe technique to screen out nonchargeable offenses. The remaining chargeable offenses were then scored for frequency (F) and seriousness (S). One respondent, *among the 10% most delinquent in Gold's sample,* had scores of F=12 and S=10. Gold (1970:30) summarizes this youth's delinquent activities.

> ...[at age 12] he and a friend had knocked down a tent in a neighbor boy's back yard— the aftermath of an earlier mud-throwing fight.
>
> That winter, he had shoplifted gum a few times from a neighborhood store.
>
> On turning 13, he had begun to lie regularly about his age to cashiers at movie theaters.
>
> In June, 1961, he had shoplifted a cartridge belt from a hardware store and later given it to a friend.
>
> The month after, he had taken an address book from a department store.
>
> In the summer of 1961, he and a friend had helped themselves to several beers from his friend's refrigerator.
>
> In late August, 1961, he and another friend had twice raided an orchard not far from R's home, taking ripe pears and unripe apples and grapes. They ate the first, and threw the rest at various targets.
>
> September, 1961, he had lifted a hunting knife from a sporting-goods store just for something to do. "We took it back the next day, snuck it back in."
>
> He regularly carried a hunting knife under his jacket "for protection" when he went collecting Friday nights on his paper route.

All subsequent discussion of self-report results should be interpreted with Gold's serious delinquent in mind: "more serious" refers to the upper part of a very limited seriousness range. When the reader encounters a statement such as "class is uncorrelated with delinquency," it is safe to assume that as delinquency has been measured by self-reports, the level does not generally exceed that illustrated by Gold's case history of one of his most delinquent boys. Regardless of how often it is said that self-reports measure primarily trivial offenses (e.g., Gold, 1966), it is easy to forget that they do. Self-report offenses are routinely treated as equivalent to official offenses in comparing correlates of delinquency (e.g., Tittle et al., 1978; Elliott and Voss, 1974). When the results using the two criteria are inconsistent, it seems to follow that one or both measurement procedures is faulty. An alternative interpretation remains: it may be simply inappropriate to compare the correlates of trivial and serious offenses. In fact, the most general technique for creating the illusion of discrepancy between self-reports and official statistics is to imply or state that both tap the same domain of "chargeable" offenses.[6]

The domain of delinquent offenses has two critical components relevant to comparison of methods. The first relates to behavioral content or type of offense. In

---

[6]Actually, self-report results are often argued by self-report researchers to measure delinquent *behavior,* while official data are said to measure the actions of officials. This suggests that despite their obvious domain limitations, self-report results are superior to official results, because they alone tap the appropriate domain.

Uniform Crime Report (UCR) arrest data, the most commonly used distinction is between violent and property offenses (a distinction that produces important differences in demographic correlates): in self-reports, distinctions often relate to offense types such as theft, property damage, drugs, school offenses, and violence. The second relates to seriousness, both within (e.g., amount of theft) and across (e.g., school versus violent) offense types. Seriousness is often judged on the basis of harm to the victim or potential adverse consequences to the offender (e.g., in the penal code). These methods of assessing seriousness generally produce highly consistent results across population sub-groups (Sellin and Wolfgang, 1964; Rossi et al., 1974). The consequence of a failure to take such domain considerations into account is an undifferentiated comparison of self-report and official results.

The trivial items in self-report scales swamp more serious items when, as is common, global simple sum scales are used. To the extent that the correlates of serious items differ from the correlates of trivial items, global scales will reflect the correlates of trivial delinquency. Similarly, to the extent that the correlates of certain types of delinquency differ, global scales will mask these differences.

CONTENT, SCORING, AND CORRELATES OF SELF-REPORTS

Sex

When one decomposes self-report instruments and examines the correlations of individual items with external variables, one is immediately struck by the variation in the results. Sex differences in self-report data are highly contingent on item content. If we take into account the content and the limited seriousness tapped by self-report items, the pattern of this variation resembles patterns in official data. Variation in these differences is illustrated in Table 6.1 where commonly used self-report items are shown. Significantly, the lowest mean sex ratio in the table is for running away (.96); this ratio in UCR arrest data on juveniles has hovered around 1.0 for the years covered by these data.[7] Another possible comparison is for "beat up/assault." As Table 6.1 shows, the mean sex ratio in self-report studies is 3.6, which is similar to that for "other assault" in the UCR (e.g., 1968=5.0; 1972=3.5). Significantly, precise comparisons of standard self-report items with other UCR offenses are not possible. However, those items even crudely comparable to UCR categories produce roughly comparable results. For example, the sex ratio for the self-report offenses of theft of items worth more than $2 is about 3.3 and that for larceny-theft in UCR data on juveniles has fallen from 4.7 in 1964 to 2.5 in 1976. When a violence component is added to the theft (strong-arm), the self-report mean sex ratio is 4.5, whereas the sex ratio for robbery in UCR data has not been lower than 12 in recent years. Self-report "strong-arm" offenses are not equivalent to UCR robbery offenses; however, given the progression in the size

---

[7] Where possible from published self-report literature, we have used prevalence ratios; some of our ratios are, however, based on incidence data. UCR data reflect the incidence of arrest.

TABLE 6.1 Sex ratios for commonly used self-report items, ranked by magnitude of mean sex ratio

	Range	Mean	Median	Number of Samples[a]
Runaway	.35 - 1.43	.96	1.00	13
Drink	.85 - 1.75	1.28	1.28	20
Truancy	1.06 - 1.91	1.34	1.28	12
Theft LT $2	1.16 - 2.05	1.63	1.75	12
Drive without license	1.08 - 3.32	1.73	1.50	8
Sex relations	1.51 - 83.86[b]	2.76	2.86	7
Theft $2-$50	1.48 - 5.03	2.79	2.70	12
Damage/destroy property	1.71 - 5.15	3.13	2.92	14
Take car	1.48 - 13.26[c]	3.27	3.37	15[c]
Gang fight	.92 - 4.60	3.61	3.28	11
Beat up/assault	1.17 - 6.50	3.64	3.61	10
Theft GT $50	1.43 - 6.60	3.86	3.68	11
Strong arm	1.00 - 8.00	4.54	2.87	10

[a]The samples on which this table is based are reported in: Akers (1964); Columbano (1974); Elliott and Voss (1974); Hirschi (1969); Kratcoski and Kratcoski (1975); Short and Nye (1958); Walberg et al. (1974); Gold and Reimer (1975); Gold (1970); Hindelang (1971); Wechsler and Thum (1973); Slocum and Stone (1963). Where the published data were reported by age group, race, or geographic region we have computed more than one ratio.
[b]The mean value excludes an extreme outlier of 83.36 (Porterfield, 1946).
[c]The mean value excludes an extreme outlier of 13.26 (Walberg et al., 1974).

of the mean sex ratios shown in Table 6.1 as the items move from theft of less than $2, to theft of $2–$50, to theft of more than $50, to strong-arm, it seems reasonable to suppose that if self-report items picked up serious robberies the sex ratio would move toward that in the UCR.*

Sex ratios on the order of 2:1 (or less) are frequently found for global self-reported delinquency scales (see Table 6.2). These are often compared with official data that show a ratio on the order of 4 or 5 to 1. Since the magnitude of the sex ratio depends upon the frequency and seriousness cutting points used in self-report research, and since officials also take such considerations into account in deciding whether to process offenders—both frequency (prior record) and seriousness are factors affecting official decision (Wolfgang et al., 1972 chap. 13)—it is misleading to compare self-report and official results ignoring such considerations (see Reiss, 1975).

*We should note here that as seriousness increases, the proportion of general adolescent respondents reporting involvement generally diverges from .5; hence the variance of more serious items is typically smaller than that for less serious items. The result is that ratios tend to increase somewhat with skewness, even though *absolute* percentage differences in self-report involvement (e.g., between sexes) may be similar for less serious and more serious items. However, in these data, the odds ratios for less serious and more serious items are different, indicating differential effects by seriousness level. Such differences are reflected in our simple ratio.

TABLE 6.2   Sex ratios in indexes of self-reported delinquency

	Ratio	*Study*
Any delinquency (Index F)	1.64	Gold (1970
"High" delinquency (Index F)	11.40	
Any seriousness (Index S)	2.38	
"Very high" seriousness (Index S)	12.00	
Any delinquency (%)	1.03	Elliott and Voss (1974)
Nonserious offenses (X). Jr. High	1.48	
Nonserious offenses (X). Sr. High	1.58	
Serious offenses (X). Jr. High	2.66	
Serious offenses (X). Sr. High	2.89	
Scale scores, 8 Nye/Short items (X)	2.11	Akers (1964)
Any theft (%)	1.94	Dentler and Moore (1961)
High theft (%)	2.26	
"Significant" delinquency (X) 1967	1.97	Gold and Reimer (1975)
1972	1.47	
Seriousness scale (X) 1967	2.77	
1972	2.82	
1 or more recent acts (%)	1.72	Hindelang (1973)
3 or more recent acts (%)	3.88	
5 or more recent acts (%)	6.00	

The content, seriousness, and frequency considerations that help to account for apparent discrepancies between self-report and official results with respect to sex need also be examined for race, the correlate that consistently produces the largest discrepancy between self-report and official results.

Race

An abundance of studies use official data to compare blacks and whites (e.g., Eaton and Polk, 1961; Wolfgang et al., 1972; Kelley, 1977). All show marked racial differences, with blacks substantially overrepresented among offenders. While self-report research has not often attended to race—in part, because self-report samples tend either to be drawn from small town white populations or to be nationally representative, in which case there are too few blacks for meaningful comparisons—existing data raise serious questions about the compatibility of official and self-report results. In fact, until very recently the range of sex-specific black to white ratios found in self-report samples did not overlap with the range of ratios found in official data. In general, self-report studies simply have not found substantial racial differences (Chambliss and Nagasawa, 1969; Epps, 1967; Gold, 1966; Gould, 1969; Hirschi, 1969; Lively et al., 1962; Williams and Gold, 1972; Gold and Reimer, 1975).

The hypothesis that blacks are no more likely to engage in illegal behavior than whites but are discriminated against by the police may be plausible, but the small or nonexistent racial biases shown in studies of differential selection (e.g., Wolfgang et al., 1972; Table 13.5) simply cannot account for the large racial differences in offending suggested by official data (e.g., Wolfgang et al., 1972: Table 5.3). Furthermore, an independent third source of data, reports of victims on the race of offenders in victimization surveys, produces results that parallel official data for common-law personal crimes (Hindelang, 1978).

How, then, can we account for the "inconsistency" of self-reports with official and victimization data? We hypothesize that this discrepancy, like the apparent sex discrepancy, is attributable to the great weight that self-report instruments give to minor offenses. Consistent with this hypothesis, although Hirschi (1969) reports no significant relation between total self-reported delinquency and race, examination of the race differences in three individual theft items shows progressively greater black involvement as the seriousness increases. For theft of items worth less than $2, theft of items worth $2–$50, and theft of items worth more than $50, the black to white prevalence ratios are .9, 1.24 and 1.75 respectively. However, because the percentages of all respondents reporting involvement in the acts are 51, 21, and 9, respectively, the simple sum scale is dominated by the least serious item, when only the two more serious items, in which blacks report more involvement, are likely to come to the attention of the police.[9] Compatible findings are reported by Williams and Gold (1972) and Elliott and Voss (1974), where slightly larger racial differences are found in offenses they classify as serious.

Data clearly indicating that self-report items approaching the seriousness of offenses in police records (particularly violent offenses) reveal racial differences are provided by Berger and Simon's (1974) study of more than 3,100 adolescents in Illinois. Using factor analysis, they created homogeneous subscales before making racial comparisons; fortunately, this procedure had the consequence of separating the more serious items from the rest of the set. Their normal deviance factor, containing such items as "cheating on exams," "skipping school," and "drinking," showed a very high proportion of all respondents reporting involvement, with a general tendency for whites to report slightly greater involvement than blacks. The theft scale, made up of standard self-report items such as "property damage," "theft of little things," and "keeping or using stolen goods" revealed no racial differences. In contrast, their violence scale, which includes items such as "used a weapon," "been in a gang fight," and "strong-armed robbery," produced consistent black/white differences. Among males, the ratio of black to white percentages is about 2:1; and among females the ratios tend to be higher (nearly 3:1) than the male ratios, a finding consistent with official data (Berger and Simon, 1974:151).

---

[9] See Gottfredson and Hindelang (1976) regarding the association between the victim's likelihood of reporting an event to the police and the value of stolen property.

If the general argument that blacks and whites differ in *serious* delinquent behavior but are more similar in less serious forms of delinquent behavior is correct, then this phenomenon should be reflected, at least to some extent, in official data as well. Table 6.3 presents data from UCR arrests for 1976. This table shows the ratio of black arrest rates to white arrest rates for selected UCR crimes.

Consistent with the argument outlined above, the ratio of black to white arrest rates is much larger for the more serious index offenses (3.49:1) than for the less serious nonindex offenses (1.71:1). Noteworthy is the finding that among index offenses the ratio for violent crimes is substantially larger than that for property crimes (9.08:1 vs. 3.14:1). Not only are the former more serious, but they also have a clearance rate two and one-half times greater than the latter. Thus, assuming these arrest data by race are proportional to offending behavior by race, black youths are probabilistically more likely than white youths to be arrested, simply because violent crimes have higher clearance rates than do property crimes.

Other arrest data shown in Table 6.3 provide support for our hypothesis that the general failure of self-report studies to parallel official data on race may be attributable to the more trivial nature of self-report than official items. Comparing the ratios for aggravated and "other" assaults it can be seen that, relative to whites, blacks are slightly more often arrested for the former (more serious) offense than the latter (5.69 vs. 4.47); similarly, comparing black to white arrest rate ratios for rape and "other" sex offenses, blacks are arrested relatively more often for the more serious rape offenses than for "other" sex offenses (9.64 vs. 3.22).

In Table 6.3, it is also possible to examine items commonly found in self-report instruments—vandalism, drunkenness, driving under the influence, and running away.

TABLE 6.3 Ratio of black to white arrest rates of persons under 18 years of age, for selected offenses, United States, 1976 [a]

Index Offenses	3.49
Violent	9.08
Property	3.14
Nonindex offenses	1.71
Aggravated assault	5.69
Other assault	4.47
Forcible rape	9.64
Other sex offenses (excludes forcible rape and prostitution)	3.22
Vandalism	1.23
Driving under the influence	.29
Drunkenness	.56
Runaways	.94

[a]The ratios in this table were derived by taking the black to white raw arrest ratios and adjusting them by the black to white ratios for the general population (1:8).
Source: Kelley (1977: Table 35).

TABLE 6.4   Perceived race of offender in national crime survey victimizations, in which offenders were perceived to be under 18 years of age, by seriousness level, United States, 1976[a]

| | Perceived Race of Offender | | |
Seriousness[b]	White	Black	Total
1	(588,126) 50%	(589,480) 50%	(1,177,606) 100%
2	(626,849) 53%	(546,245) 47%	(1,173,094) 100%
3	(457,178) 53%	(410,203) 47%	(867,381) 100%
4	(89,263) 33%	(178,667) 67%	(267.930) 100%
Total	(1,761,415) 51%	(1,724,594) 49%	(3,486,009) 100%

[a]Includes only offenders perceived to be under 18 years of age. Each incident is weighted according to the number of offenders involved. Excluded offenders of "other" races, groups of offenders of mixed races, and incidents in which offender characteristics were unknown to the victim.
[b]Sellin-Wolfgang seriousness weights were recoded as follows: 0-1 = 1; 2-3 = 2; 4-5 = 3; 6 or more = 4. See Sellin and

For these petty offenses, the black/white ratios are much smaller (or in most cases reversed, 1.23, .29, .56, and .94, respectively) than those for violent or property index offenses. The overall pattern of findings in Table 6.3 is therefore compatible with the hypothesis that the general failure of self-report studies to find the overrepresentation of blacks relative to whites in official data is attributable in large part to an overabundance in current self-report instruments of items tapping less serious, more numerous offenses.

Data available from the national victimization survey being conducted by the Bureau of the Census for the Law Enforcement Assistance Administration also shed light on the relationship between the seriousness of the offense and the race of the offender. In these surveys, about 130,000 persons are interviewed twice a year regarding the personal crimes of rape, robbery, assault, and larceny from the person. Although these offenses are generally much more serious than those elicited by self-report instruments, there is a wide range of seriousness in the incidents reported to survey interviewers.[10]

The data in Table 6.4 from the national survey for 1976 include only victimizations in which the offender was reported by the victim to have been under 18 years of age. Victimizations have been scored for seriousness using the Sellin-Wolfgang (1964) method, and weighted to be representative of the United States as a whole. Attending first to the total row in Table 6.4, it can be seen that black offenders account for almost

[10] For example, it has been found that about half of the incidents reported involved neither injury nor financial loss to the victim—i.e., they were attempts (Hindelang, et al., 1978: chap. 2). Nonetheless, even these *relatively* minor events fall within UCR definitions. Similar to the problem faced by self-report instruments, each offense category contains a variety of offenses that are heterogeneous with respect to seriousness. Thus, a strict test of our hypothesis would require that self-report instruments specify rather carefully the behavior included even within a serious offense category (e.g., robbery).

half of the personal victimizations reported to survey interviewers. When it is recalled that blacks in the United States account for less than 15% of the juvenile population, it is clear that, for these offenses, black youths are substantially overrepresented among offenders in relation to their representation in the general population. Despite the heterogeneity of these events with respect to seriousness, they are on the whole considerably more serious than the events typically elicited by self-report instruments (most meet the Uniform Crime Report criteria for Part I offenses). For the less serious victimizations, blacks account for about the same percentage of all offenders as do whites. More important, however, for the most serious victimizations—those most likely to be reported to the police (Gottfredson and Hindelang, 1979)—blacks account for two-thirds of the offenders. Once again, these data are congruent with the hypothesis that self-reports fail to find racial differences in large part because self-report instruments generally do not pick up the most serious kinds of street crime. The compatibility of victimization survey results and UCR arrest data (Hindelang, 1978) severely damages the hypothesis that arrest data merely reflect racial biases inherent in police practices.

Up to this point, we have shown that various sources of data on delinquency are consistent when attention is given to obvious differences in content. As noted, it would be unreasonable to expect greater correspondence for sex and race than that actually observed, owing to domain limitations of self-report instruments used to date. With this background, we turn to social class, where an abundance of "illusions of discrepancy" may be found.

Social Class

Unlike sex and race, social class data are not available for either UCR arrestees or for offenders in victimization surveys. Thus, if understanding the relationship of social class to serious offending is our aim, data limitations are much more severe for social class than for sex or race.

Until publication of "The Myth of Social Class and Criminality" (Tittle et al., 1978), the dominant view in the field was that summarized by Gordon (1976:201): "One of the most thoroughly documented known crime and delinquency relationships is that with socioeconomic status."[11] Tittle et al. (1978) take strong exception to this position for data from recent years. They note that self-reports have always shown a near-zero relationship with social class while studies using official statistics have shown moderate to strong inverse associations with class in the pre-1964 period. This leads them to the conclusion that there must have been class-linked biases in criminal justice processing in the earlier period. This suggestion (and data supporting it) is not new. Indeed, the first study suggested comparing the SES-delinquency relationship for self-report and official criteria (Short and Nye, 1957).

Short and Nye compared the social class distributions of high school and training

[11] In support of this statement Gordon lists 23 studies published in the three previous decades, including many of the better-known works in the field. Close inspection reveals that only four of these are American studies that allow estimation of individual-level relations; only two of these permit direct comparisons between self-reports and official data with respect to the SES-delinquency relationship.

school boys. The resultant 2 x 4 table (training school vs. high school by four social class categories) produced a contingency coefficient of .45. Among the high school boys, the contingency coefficient between social class and *self-reported* delinquency (a dichotomized global scale) was .10, a nonsignificant relation (p = .3). This shift in the contingency coefficient from .45 to .10, when the criterion became *self-reported* rather than official delinquency (i.e., institutionalization), had significant implications for criminological research and theory.

On the level of *theory,* these results provided fuel to the then nascent labelling and conflict approaches to delinquency. They did much to quicken interest in *research* on official processing of offenders. More important for present purposes, they established the expectation that *valid* self-report procedures will often produce results contrary to official data. Ironically, the Short/Nye data do not support this expectation when the contingency coefficient (or any other marginally dependent measure of association) is used appropriately as the criterion. On the contrary, the self-report and official results show remarkable consistency with respect to estimates of the class-delinquency association in the general adolescent population.

This fact was overlooked because of two factors that contributed to the illusion of discrepancy between official and self-report results. The first, discussed in another context by Tittle et al. (1978), was the implicit comparison of the Short/Nye self-report results with previously established ecological-level[12] class delinquency relations, which often ran as high as –.7 or –.8, depending on the indicator of class (e.g., Shaw and McKay, 1942). A greater ecological than individual level association is expected even when precisely the same delinquency measure is used, simply as a function of the aggregation of individual level data. Hence, a similar discrepancy when *different* criterion measures are used need say nothing about the compatibility of the measures. Second, the contingency coefficient used by Short and Nye substantially overestimated the magnitude of the relation between SES and delinquency by using the official criterion (institutionalization). Because C is marginally dependent, it is misleading to compare an association based on the general high school population with an association based on an unweighted aggregation of institutionalized and general population adolescents. In the table that produced a contingency coefficient of .45, the institution-alized boys (N = 146) constituted almost 15% of the total. This table (Short and Nye, 1957: Table 1) misleadingly suggests that 39% of all lower class boys, and even 5% of the highest class, were in a training school.

A reasonable estimate of the prevalence of institutionalization in training schools by age 18 is approximately 1% for white males (Gordon, 1976: Table 2). At any given time the proportion of the general adolescent population in training schools is much less than 1%. For illustrative purposes, we recalculated the contingency coefficient in the Short/Nye data allowing the training school population to be 1% of the total sample. Under these conditions, the coefficient drops from .45 to .11, which leaves class no better able to predict official than self-reported delinquency (C = .10) by this criterion.[13]

---

[12] See Nye et al. (1958) for a list of empirical studies dominated by ecological research.

[13] For those concerned with the modifiability of measures of association as a result of manipulating the marginals, it is important to note that our secondary analysis of the raw data from this study revealed that the relation between class and *self-reported* official delinquency (measured by "Have you ever been arrested

Two additional studies are often cited as evidence of discrepancy in the association of social class with self-reports as compared to official data. Williams and Gold (1972) present data collected by Gold in 1967. In their paper they utilize a major device for creating the illusion of discrepancy: despite the fact that the official and self-report data are consistent, they treat them as discrepant. Williams and Gold make an apparently important distinction between "delinquent behavior" (as measured in self-reports) and "official delinquency." In justifying such a distinction they focus on the SES-delinquency relation.

> The often cited finding of official delinquency as a lower-class phenomenon is a product of the above mentioned filtering process. This finding, *which is by our definition quite valid,* now takes on new meaning: official identification of and response to delinquent behavior shows a strong relationship to lower-status juveniles. However, it does not necessarily mean that lower status youths are involved in more delinquent behavior than any other social status group. (Williams and Gold 1972:210, emphasis added)

The premise of Williams and Gold's (1972: e.g., 210, 211, 217) article states that official and self-report data produce different results. Throughout their discussion, they use class to illustrate differences between the correlates of official delinquency and delinquent behavior. Nevertheless, they actually report, virtually without comment, a gamma of −.02 (1972:225) for occupational prestige and frequency of police records, and, for the same white male group, gammas of .05 (frequency) and .12 (seriousness) for occupational prestige and self-reported delinquency. Neither the frequency of self-reported delinquency nor the frequency of police records was significantly correlated with social status among white males.[14] Contrary to the thrust of Williams and Gold's discussion and the title of their paper, the SES-delinquency correlations for males in the 1967 National Survey of Youth do not depend on the method of measurement.

The presentation format used by Elliott and Voss (1974: Table 4–7) illustrates yet another analytic technique that has fed the illusion of discrepancy: a failure to disaggregate data properly in order to examine potentially confounded effects. Elliott and Voss present data on police contacts per 100 self-reported delinquent behaviors that show market differences by class status. For example, in the highest of five SES classes there were 1.692 police contacts per hundred self-reported offenses compared to 7.382 in the lowest category, a finding apparently strongly supportive of the discrepancy position. That is, in the absence of differential self-report measurement error by class and differential selection by the police, these ratios would be expected to be identical across classes. However, these data are problematic because the Elliott/Voss table (1974: Table 4-7) is not disaggregated by either sex or ethnicity (closely

---

and convicted...?") in the Short/Nye data (C = .06) is even smaller than our .11 estimate of the relation between official delinquency and class. To the extent that researchers accept self-reports of delinquent behavior as reliable and valid, it follows that self-reports of official records are at least as reliable and valid.

[14] The values shown for the Gold subjects in our Table 5, discussed below, differ from these coefficients primarily because the latter are based on a trichotomy for class and grouped data on the F scale.

associated with delinquency and/or social class).[15] Reanalysis of the Elliott and Voss raw data shows, in fact, that ethnicity and sex were confounding the relationship between social class and these ratios.[16] One-way analysis of variance of the ratios by social class within homogeneous sex-ethnicity groups reveals no significant effect of social class on these police-selection ratios. Again, the illusion of discrepancy turns out to be just that.

The recent systematic and thorough review by Tittle et al. (1978) concludes, in part, that a discrepancy between self-report and official results is evident. Unfortunately, their analysis suffers from shortcomings that compromise its conclusions. Not only do the authors accept self-report results at face value and assume that their domain is comparable to that in official data, which we have argued here is inappropriate, but they also use an analytic technique which can produce the illusion of discrepancy when none necessarily exists. In their secondary analysis of the published literature. Tittle et al. use regression analysis to account for variation in the magnitude of the class/crime association (gammas) as a function of such variables as the nature of the crime criterion (self-report vs. official), year of data collection, and sample size. Rather than making direct comparisons of self-report and official results, when both were available in a single study. Tittle et al. rely upon statistical adjustment to control for the effects of other variables:

> Given instances using two samples of exactly the same type and size, drawn from precisely the same areas in a given year and employing the same number of defined social classes, the equation shows that we may expect the study employing official statistics to produce a gamma showing a .10 greater negative association for the same relationship than an instance employing self-report data (Tittle et al., 1978:649).

This conclusion suggests much more precise control of the dimensions in the regression equation than is in fact possible. Most self-report studies have been conducted in the period (post-1970) when official studies had virtually ceased (Tittle et al., 1978: Table 6.3). Nonetheless, some direct comparisons are possible. All American studies allowing such comparisons are shown in Table 6.5.

The oldest data in Table 6.5, collected in 1957 by Reiss and Rhodes (1961), show identical asymmetric Somers's d's (–.16) using the self-report or the official criterion to assess the class/delinquency association.[17] In contrast, the Tittle et al. comparison for this period (1950–59)—based on three studies using a self-report criterion and seven using an official criterion—showed very divergent mean gammas of –.04 and –.43 for

---

[15] A small number of adolescents with extreme scores on the numerator and/or the denominator of these ratios may have disproportionately affected the mean ratios presented by Elliott and Voss (1974).

[16] Unfortunately, the original investigators provided us with data regarding official delinquency records only for part of the period covered by their study. These data include about 50% of the official delinquencies recorded for the full period of the original study.

[17] In r x 2 tables where the independent variable is the dichotomy neither gamma nor Somers's asymmetric d is marginally dependent. In 3 x 3 and larger tables both gamma and asymmetric Somers's d are marginally dependent (Somers, 1962:808). Gamma has the disadvantage of being based upwards by small cell counts which often result from severe skewness. Somers's d is less sensitive to small counts in some cells.

TABLE 6.5 Percent with police record of delinquency and percent with self reported delinquency[a], across social class (secondary analyses of raw data)

Study	Date of Data Collection	Sample Subgroup	Social Class Indicators		Second Class Groups			Gamma	Asymmetric Somers's d
					Blue Collar / Low	White Collar / Medium	High		
Reiss and Rhodes	1957	White males (n = 7963)	Father's occupation	Official	6 (4,661)	3 (3,302)			
				Self report (2 or random sample)	10 (98)	5 (98)			
Elliott and Voss	1963–1967	White males (n = 974)	Hollingshead	Period I: Non-serious Official					
				(1 or more)	16	12	13	.04	.01
				Self-report					
				(5 or more)	34	27	26	.04	.03
				Serious Official					
				(1 or more)	6	5	4	.09	.01
				Self-report					
				(2 or more)	28	24	21	.12	.07
					(131)	(389)	(454)		
				Period II: Non-serious Official					
				(1 or more)	7	10	8	.04	.01
				Self-report					
				(8 or more)	36	26	27	.04	.03
				Serious Official					
				(1 or more)	4	2	2	.05	.00
				Self-report					
				(3 or more)	28	23	27	.01	.00
					(105)	(346)	(412)		

TABLE 6.5 Percent with police record of delinquency and percent with self reported delinquency[a], across social class (secondary analyses of raw data) (Cont.)

Study	Date of Data Collection	Sample Subgroup	Social Class Indicators	Second Class Groups			Gamma	Asymmetric Somers's d
		Mexican American males (n = 178)	**Period I: Non-serious Official**					
			(1 or more)	27	19	12	.28	.09
			(1 or more)	27	19	12	.28	.09
			Self-report					
			(5 or more)	35	31	31	.05	.04
			Serious Official					
			(1 or more)	9	80		(−.39)	−.05
			Self-report					
			(2 or more)	38	28	16	−.26	−.16
				(66)	(80)	(32)		
			Period II: Non-serious Official					
			(1 or more)	14	12	6	−.19	−.04
			Self-report					
			(8 or more)	19	27	39	.25	.20
			Serious Official					
			(1 or more)	3	2	0	.38	.02
			Self-report					
			(3 or more)	21	24	16	.03	.02
				(58)	(70)	(31)		
		Black males (n = 89)	**Period I: Non-serious Official**					
			(1 or more)	14	21	13	.04	.01
			Self-report					
			(5 or more)	29	37	44	.14	.10
			Serious Official					
			(1 or more)	20	13	12	−.21	−.05
			Self-report					
			(2 or more)	26	26	25	−.02	−.01
				(35)	(38)	(16)		

TABLE 6.5 Percent with police record of delinquency and percent with self reported delinquency[a], across social class (secondary analyses of raw data) (Cont.)

Study	Date of Data Collection	Sample Subgroup	Social Class Indicators	Delinquency Measure	Second Class Groups			Gamma	Asymmetric Somers's d
				Period I: Non-serious Official					
				(1 or more)	23	24	29	.18	.15
				Self-report (5 or more)	11	8	12	-.03	-.01
				Serious Official (1 or more)	26	30	36	.01	.00
				Self-report (3 or more)	(31)	(33)	(14)		
Hirschi[b]	1964	White males (n = 1430)	Father's occupation	Official (1 or more)	29	28	20	-.16	-.06
				Self-report (3 or more)	27	24	21	-.03	-.02
					(375)	(463)	(501)		
		Black males (n = 720)		Official (1 or more)	55	51	44	-.14	-.07
				Self-report (3 or more)	28	30	26	-.01	-.01
					(412)	(187)	(121)		
Gold[c]	1967	White males (n = 357)	Father's occupation	Official (1 or more)	5	6	6	.09	.01
				Self-report frequency	36	35	29	-.02	-.01

[a] Self-reported delinquency cut-off points were selected to be as close as possible to the 75th percentile on the delinquency distribution. Measures of association shown are based on the full tables (usually 3x4).

[b] Reiss and Rhodes (19612: Table i), excluding truancy and traffic offenses.

[c] Derived from Reiss and Rhodes (1962:732).

the self-report and official criteria, respectively. (In terms of gammas, the Reiss and Rhodes coefficients for self-report and official data are –.36 and –.33 again virtually identical.)

Most of the data in our Table 6.5 are from the period (1960–69) in which the Tittle et al. comparisons show the mean official gamma to be –.22 and the mean self-report gamma to be –.11. Our direct comparison of results shows that the two criteria produce very similar associations. In this period, the mean official Somers's d is –.02 (mean gamma = –.11) and the mean self-report Somers's d is .01 (mean gamma = .00).[18] In both the Tittle et al. indirect comparisons and in our own direct comparisons, the differences in the size of the class-crime association using the official and the self-report criterion are slight for the 1960–69 period; in the 1950–59 period, however, the large discrepancy reported by Tittle et al. is not replicated using direct comparisons. Owing particularly to official/self-report differences in the domains tapped, these comparisons must be viewed as extremely crude. In light of this and the general consistency shown in Table 6.5, conclusions of discrepancy between the two measures are at best weak.

Our earlier admonition that omnibus scale comparisons can be misleading should not be ignored. Unfortunately, however, the fact is that with respect to social class, adequate data for making offense-specific comparisons among the social classes are simply unavailable. There is no published source of police data that is large enough to permit class comparisons of the kind shown for race in Table 6.3: there is no source of self-report data that permits reliable interclass comparisons for categories of serious crime. For example, Williams and Gold's (1972) data represented in the Tittle et al. table and in our Table 6.5 have both official and self-report data from the mid to late 1960s. However, in this sample of 847 respondents, only 4% or 34 males and females had police records. In the Elliott and Voss sample of 2,617 respondents, although 26% had records of offenses more serious than traffic infractions, nearly nine out of ten of these were for petty theft, running away, vandalism, truancy, and liquor offenses. In light of the variations by offense in the magnitude of sex and race relationships in both sources of data, omnibus comparisons are far too crude to permit confident conclusions that discrepancy exists.

In sum, although illusions of discrepancy abound, we are hard-pressed to locate persuasive evidence that self-report and official methods produce discrepant results. Our conclusion is consistent with studies of the psychometric properties of self-report measures of delinquency. In terms of reliability, many studies indicate that rest/retest or split-half measures of the reliability of self-reports are on the order of .9 (Kulik, Stein, and Sarbin, 1968: Dentler and Monroe, 1961: Elmhorn, 1965). Although validity is inherently more difficult to establish, a variety of approaches to this question have produced generally consistent results. Studies using the nominated or known group method (Nye, 1958; Erickson and Empey, 1963), concurrent checks of official records (Hardt and Peterson-Hardt, 1977; Elliott and Voss, 1974; Farrington, 1973; Erickson, 1972; Kulik, Stein and Sarbin, 1968) and reports of informants (Gold, 1970), have

[18] Interestingly enough, in the 1960–69 period the gammas from our direct comparisons in studies where both self-report and official data are available are smaller than those reported by Tittle et al., which illustrates once again that the magnitude of the association between class and delinquency is sufficiently

found self-reports to have considerable validity.[19] Thus, in terms of the standard criteria of reliability and validity, self-report measures of delinquency are not obviously defective *within the domain of content they tap.*

If the domain limitations of self-reports may be safely ignored, if the results for a sample of individuals may be compared with results from areal units or with improperly weighted aggregates, if standard disaggregation procedures may be ignored in analysis, and if assertions contrary to data presented are accepted, then, and only then, it seems to us, is the conclusion of discrepancy between self-report and official results warranted. Since these procedures are not acceptable, we believe the conclusion of discrepancy is not justified by currently available evidence.

In short, we believe the evidence on the crime measurement issue is now sufficient to allow resolution of many of the apparent inconsistencies among various measures of criminality. This evidence suggests to us that: (1) official measures of criminality provide valid indications of the demographic distribution of criminal behavior; (2) self-report instruments typically tap a domain of behavior virtually outside the domain of official data; (3) within the domain they tap, self-report measures provide reliable and valid indicators of offending behavior; (4) the self-report *method* is capable of dealing with behavior within the domain of official data; and (5) in practice, self-report samples have been inadequate for confident conclusions concerning the correlates of offending behavior comparable in seriousness to that represented in official data.

IMPLICATIONS

The reaction to essentially illusory "inconsistencies" between the correlates of self-report and police data has taken one of two general forms: either self-report methodology has been rejected, or sex, class, race, and other biases have been imputed to criminal justice system representatives. The first of these reactions is inconsistent with evidence of the basic reliability and validity of the self-reported method. But as long as discrepancy is accepted, the conclusion that self-reports are reasonably reliable and valid will merely shift attention to official data as the probable source of discrepancy. Of course, the hypothesis that the procedures producing official data are biased against the less powerful segments of society antedates self-report research (e.g., Bonger, 1916). It seems fair to say, however, that the major impetus behind empirical studies of the differential selection of delinquents by officials has been the lack of a substantial relationship between social class and race on the one hand and self-report measures of delinquency on the other. Interestingly enough, studies of the administration of juvenile justice have failed to locate sufficient bias against powerless groups in official processing to account for their higher rates of criminality. Once the seriousness of the instant offense and prior record of the offender are taken into account, apparent class

---

[19] The polygraph study of Clark and Tiffet (1966) is often cited as evidence of validity. We are in essential agreement with De Fleur (1967) that because of its design, this study provides evidence only about reliability.

bias plays only a relatively minor role in the generation of official data (Wolfgang et al., 1972, Table 13.5; Cohen, 1975; Terry, 1967; Hohenstein, 1969). Our earlier analyses suggested that no class bias should have been expected, since direct comparisons reveal little or no self-report/official discrepancy, and the bias uncovered by processing studies is not sufficiently strong to account for differences found in official data for race and sex.[20]

Consistent with these findings, comparisons of UCR arrest data with victimization data for race and sex (Hindelang, 1978; 1979) have shown remarkable consistency. As noted above, because official data are inadequate for making reliable estimates of the substantive class-official data relation, it is premature to conclude that there is no relationship, except for those minor offenses measured reliably in typical (i.e., Short/Nye type) self-report scales. For offenses that are likely to result in deprivation of liberty (i.e., UCR index level offenses) the class-crime relationship simply has not been examined adequately. If class-linked criminal justice system biases are relatively small for serious common-law offending, the heavy over-representation of poor and uneducated persons in jails and prisons (e.g., LEAA, 1977:20), probably reflects a class-serious offending association for UCR index crimes. Our previous discussion suggests that, in principle, properly constructed self-report instruments should be capable of confirming this association if it is actually present. However, the research problem is more complex than this solution suggests.

Let us assume that the most serious offenders, say those involved in UCR index offenses, are in fact disproportionately poor and uneducated as the prison population data suggest. Would a properly constituted self-report instrument (or even an examination of police records for the general population) be expected to substantiate this class difference in illegal behavior? If the research design were similar to that typically employed in self-report surveys, there is good reason to believe that the results would be problematic. In the Wolfgang, Figlio, and Sellin (1972: Table G1.1) cohort data, the prevalence (from age 7 through age 17) of contact with the police for at least one index offense was 8.62% for white males and 20.43% for nonwhite males. Weighted to the racial distribution for the United States, the prevalence of contact with the police (through age 17) for an index offense is about 10% for (urban) males. If we assume that one out of two index offenders does not have any police contacts for index offenses during adolescence, the prevalence of at least one index offense would be about 20%.[21] However, since this 20% figure is for all of adolescence and the typical self-report survey has a one-year reference period, an ideal self-report survey would have to be sensitive to class differences around an annual population prevalence rate of 2 or 3%. Thus, if the lower class index offense prevalence rate were double that of the middle

---

[20] The Piliavin and Briar (1964) study is often cited as showing racial biases operating through demeanor. However, what is almost always ignored is the fact that in this study of sixty-six youth, neither the seriousness of the offense nor the prior record of the juvenile was controlled because N's were too small for reliable estimates. Piliavin and Briar (1964:209–12) state, however, that for serious personal crimes and for offenders with prior records, demeanor was much less significant.

[21] It is important to note that 37% of those coming into contact with the police for index offenses were not arrested (Wolfgang et al., 1972: Table 13.1). Hence more than one-third of the index contacts *recorded* by the police were judged (by their release of the juvenile) to be insufficiently serious to warrant arrest.

class rate, the study would have to be sensitive to rate differences of two or three percentage points.

Given such skewness in the distribution of a dependent variable, what kind of self-report study is required to find appreciable class differences? First, the sample selected must generate enough self-reported delinquency for reliable measurement of serious crime. This can be done in one of two ways; either the sample size must be extremely large or the sample must be stratified by variables known to be correlated with serious delinquent behavior. If the extremely large sample route is taken, perhaps the best analogue to sample size requirements is the sample size required to measure reliably criminal victimizations suffered by Americans. (As noted above, the Census Bureau conducts interviews with more than 130,000 persons twice per year.) The largest nationwide self-reported delinquency study published to date is Gold's National Survey of Youth, which conducted interviews with 1,395 11 to 18 year old males and females, 182 of whom were black. In estimating the distribution of delinquency by social class for 13 to 16 year old males, Gold had 115 or fewer males in each of his three social class cells. If delinquency of the UCR index-type is of interest, these numbers are inadequate for reliably distinguishing class effects. Even in studies that include examination of police records for general population samples, the proportion of *police-recorded* offenses of UCR index seriousness is so small that the task of finding reliable class differences would require much larger sample sizes than those typically used.

An alternative to such extremely large samples is to sample probabilistically within strata known to differ sharply on self-reported delinquency—for example, subjects with and without court records of serious delinquency. To the extent that the stratification variable is related to serious self-reported delinquency, the absolute sample size required to measure the dependent variable reliably will be reduced. By knowing the proportion of respondents falling into each stratum, in the population as a whole, the data can be weighted to produce unbiased estimates of population parameters.[22]

Second, regardless of sampling method, if the population estimate of the class-crime association is summarized by a measure of association that is affected by the marginal distribution of the dependent variable, the tremendous skew of index-level offending in the general population would reduce to near zero even very large differences across classes in *rates* of offending. Third, when we add the problem of nonresponse, it seems unlikely that serious offenders will be as cooperative as nonoffenders. For example, there is strong evidence that those known to have police records are less likely to participate in such surveys than those without police records (e.g., Hirschi, 1969: Table 5).

Thus, for all of these reasons, the substantive limits of conclusions regarding the consistency of self-report and official delinquency measures with respect to class are clear. At present, data on the most serious portion of the distribution of delinquent *behavior* are insufficient to allow class comparisons and hence confident substantive

---

[22] Parenthetically, it is important to note that this design will improve sampling efficiency and will be appropriate even if there are biases involved in labelling persons as court delinquents. As long as court records are related to delinquent behavior, stratifying on court records will improve sampling efficiency.

conclusions. However, if we move to the point of incarceration where social class data on serious offenders are available, we find the substantial class differences assumed by traditional sociological theories. At the other (non-serious) extreme, there do not appear to be class differences in adolescent behavior for the relatively minor offenses that make up the great bulk of what is collected in self-report studies and recorded in local police files.[23]

The "trivial content" objection to the self-report method has had little impact on the revision of self-report instruments or sampling procedures. Although self-report instruments have gradually come to include somewhat more serious items, they are still dominated by less serious items. As shown above, even within the restricted seriousness range available in extant self-report studies, there is plentiful evidence that seriousness and item content affect self-report results. With respect to sex, these dimensions appear to account for much of the apparent discrepancy between official and self-report findings. Similarly, with respect to race, both self-report and victimization data suggest an overinvolvement of blacks in more serious offenses; some self-report (e.g., Berger and Simon, 1974) and virtually all official data suggest strong race effects for violent offenses. Thus, explicit attention to seriousness and content differences across methods must precede comparisons of their results. In the absence of sharply increased sample sizes or more efficient designs, however, the inclusion of more serious items in self-report instruments will not solve the problem of reliably measuring index offenses with the self-report technique.[24]

In historical perspective, it can be seen that students of crime have focused their attention on at least three measures of youthful misconduct: the Uniform Crime Reports index offenses, local police and court data, and self-report offenses. Because these data are all taken to be measures of delinquent behavior, it is easy to assume that they should produce similar findings without further adjustment for obvious differences among them. Close examination reveals that this assumption is unfounded. These measures are rarely available on the same subjects and the overlap in their content is often minimal. Wholesale comparisons of results using these three measures are therefore inappropriate and, in themselves, say little or nothing about the extent of criminal justice system biases or the adequacy of the self-report method.

REFERENCES

Akers, Ronald. (1964). "Socio-economic status and delinquent behavior: a retest." Journal of Research in Crime and Delinquency 1:38–46.

Berger, Alan S. and William Simon. (1974). "Black families and the Moynihan report: a research evaluation." Social Problems 22:146–61.

[23] Even at the court level, most researchers are surprised at the triviality of the offenses described in official accounts of juvenile misconduct. Such descriptions are consistent with Gordon's prevalence estimates reported above (see also note 21).

[24] Recently, Elliott and Ageton (1979) have subjected some of these hypotheses to empirical test with their National Youth Survey data. Unfortunately their instrument and research design (e.g., failure to draw a sufficiently large sample and failure to stratify disproportionately enough on key variables) do not allow definitive resolution of most of the issues raised in our paper.

Bonger, Wilhelm. (1916). Criminality and Economic Conditions. Trans. H.P. Horton. Boston: Little, Brown.

Chambliss, William J. and Richard H. Nagasawa. (1969). "On the validity of official statistics: a comparative study of white, black, and Japanese high-school boys." Journal of Research in Crime and Delinquency 6:71–7.

Clark, John P. and Larry L. Tifft. (1966). "Polygraph and interview validation of self-reported delinquent behavior." American Sociological Review 31:516–23.

Cohen, Lawrence. (1975). "Juvenile dispositions: social and legal factors related to the processing of Denver delinquency cases," Analytic Report SDAR-4. U.S. Department of Justice, Law Enforcement Assistance Administration, National Criminal Justice Information and Statistics Service.

De Fleur, Lois B. (1967). "On polygraph and interview validation." American Sociological Review 31:114–5.

Dentler, Robert A. and Lawrence J. Monroe. (1961). "Social correlates of early adolescent theft." American Sociological Review 26:733–43.

Eaton, Joseph W. and Kenneth Polk. (1961). Measuring Delinquency. Pittsburgh: University of Pittsburgh Press.

Elliott, Delbert S. and Suzanne Ageton. (1979). "Reconciling race and class differences in self-reported and official estimates of delinquency." Behavioral Research Institute. Mimeo.

Elliott, Delbert S. and Harwin L. Voss. (1974). Delinquency and Dropout. Lexington, Ma.: Heath.

Elmhorn, Kerstin. (1965). "Study in self-reported delinquency among school children in Stockholm," Pp. 117–46 in K.O. Christiansen (ed.). Scandinavian Studies in Criminology, Vol. 1. London: Tavistock.

Epps, E.G. (1967). "Socio-economic status, race, level of aspiration, and juvenile delinquency: a limited empirical test of Merton's conception of deviation." Phylon 28:16–27.

Erickson, Maynard L. (1972). "The changing relation between official and self-reported measures of delinquency: an exploratory descriptive study." Journal of Criminal Law, Criminology and Police Science 63:388–95.

Erickson, Maynard L. and LeMar T. Empey. (1963). "Court records, undetected delinquency, and decision-making." Journal of Criminal Law, Criminology and Police Science 54:456–69.

Farrington, David P. (1973). "Self-reports of deviant behavior: predictive and stable?" Journal of Criminal Law and Criminology 64:99–110.

Gold, Martin. (1966). "Undetected delinquent behavior," Journal of Research in Crime and Delinquency 3:27–46.

——— (1970). Delinquent Behavior in an American City. Belmont, Calif.: Brooks/Cole.

Gold, Martin and David J. Reimer. (1975). "Changing patterns of delinquent behavior among Americans 13 through 16 years old: 1967–1972." Crime and Delinquency Literature 7:483–517.

Gordon, Robert A. (1976). "Prevalence: the rare datum in delinquency measurement and its implications for the theory of delinquency." Pp. 201–84 in Malcolm W. Klein (ed.). The Juvenile Justice System. Beverly Hills: Sage.

Gottfredson, Michael and Michael Hindelang. (1979). "A study of the behavior of law." American Sociological Review 43:3–18.

Gould, Leroy C. (1969). "Who defines delinquency: a comparison of self-reported and officially reported indices of delinquency for three racial groups." Social Problems 16:325–36.

Hardt, Robert and Sandra Peterson-Hardt. (1977). "On determining the quality of the delinquency self-report method." Journal of Research in Crime and Delinquency 14:247–61.

Hindelang, Michael J. (1971). "Age, sex, and the versatility of delinquent involvement." Social Problems 18:522–35.

(1973). "Causes of delinquency: a partial replication and extension." Social Problems 20:471–87.

(1976). Criminal Victimization in Eight American Cities. Cambridge: Ballinger.

(1978). "Race and involvement in common law personal crimes." American Sociological Review 43:93–109.

(1979). "Sex and involvement in criminal activity." Social Problems. In press.

Hindelang, Michael J. and Michael R. Gottfredson. (1976). "The victim's decision not to invoke the criminal justice process." Pp. 57–78 in William McDonald (ed.). Criminal Justice and the Victim. Beverly Hills: Sage.

Hindelang, Michael J., Michael R. Gottfredson and James Garafalo. (1978). Victims of Personal Crime. An Empirical Foundation for a Theory of Persona: Victimization. Cambridge: Ballinger.

Hirschi, Travis. (1969). Causes of Delinquency. Berkeley University of California Press.

Hirschi, Travis, Michael J. Hindelang, and Joseph G. Weis. (Forthcoming). The Measurement of Delinquency by the Self-Report Method. Cambridge, Ma., Oelgeschlager, Gunn, and Hain.

Hohenstein, William F. (1969). "Factors influencing the police disposition of juvenile offenders." Pp. 138–49 in Thorsten Sellin and Marvin E. Wolfgang (eds.). Delinquency Selected Studies, New York: Wiley.

Kelley, Clarence. (1977). Crime in the United States—Uniform Crime Reports—1976. Washington, D.C.: U.S. Government Printing Office.

Kratcoski, Peter C. and John E. Kratcoski. (1975). "Changing patterns in the delinquent activities of boys and girls, a self-reported delinquency analysis." Adolescence 10:83–91.

Kulik, James A., K.B. Stein and T.R. Sarbin. (1968). "Disclosure of delinquent behavior under conditions of anonymity and non-anonymity," Journal of Consulting and Clinical Psychology 32:506–9.

Law Enforcement Assistance Administration. (1977). Survey of Inmates and Local Jails, 1972, Washington, D.C.; Pre-Publication Report.

Lively, E.L., Simon Dinitz and Walter Reckless. (1962). "Self concepts as a predictor of juvenile delinquency." American Journal of Ortho-psychiatry 32:159–68.

Nye, F. Ivan. (1958). Family Relationships and Delinquent Behavior, New York: Wiley.

Nye, F. Ivan, James F. Short and Virgil Olson. (1958). "Socio-economic status and delinquent behavior." American Journal of Sociology 63:381–9.

Piliavin, Irving and Scott Briar. (1964). "Police encounters with juveniles," American Journal of Sociology 70:206–14.

Porterfield, Austin. (1946). Youth in Trouble, Fort Worth. Leo Potishman Foundation.

Reiss, Albert J. (1975). "Inappropriate theories and inadequate methods as policy plagues self-reported delinquency and the law." Pp. 211–22 in N.J. Demerath, Ill, Otto Larsen, and Karl F. Schuessler (eds.). Social Policy and Sociology, New York: Academic Press.

Reiss, Albert J. and Albert L. Rhodes. (1961). "The distribution of juvenile delinquency in the social class structure." American Sociological Review 26:720–32.

Rossi, Peter, Emily Waite, Christine E. Bose, and Richard E. Berk. (1974). "The seriousness of crimes normative structure and individual differences," American Sociological Review 39:224–37.

Sellin, Thorsten and Marvin Wolfgang. (1964). The Measurement of Delinquency, New York: Wiley.

Shaw, Clifford R. and Henry D. McKay. (1942). Juvenile Delinquency and Urban Areas, Chicago: University of Chicago Press.

Short, James F., Jr. and F. Ivan Nye. (1957). "Reported behavior as a criterion of deviant behavior." Social Problems 5:207–13.

Slocum, Walter L. and Carol L. Stone. (1963). "Family culture patterns and delinquent-type behavior." Marriage and Family Living 25:202–03.

Somers, Robert. (1962). "A new asymmetric measure of association for ordinal variables." American Sociological Review 27:799–811.

Terry, Robert. (1967). "The screening of juvenile offenders." Journal of Criminal Law, Criminology, and Police Science 58:173–81.

Tittle, Charles R. (1976). "Labelling and crime an empirical evaluation." Pp. 157–80 in Walter Gove (ed.). The Labelling of Deviance: Evaluation of a Perspective, New York: Halsted.

Tittle, Charles R., Wayne J. Villemez, and Douglas A. Smith. (1978). "The myth of social class and criminality: an empirical assessment of the empirical evidence." American Sociological Review 43:643–56.

Walberg, Herbert J., Elaine Gee Yeh, and Stephanie Mooney Paton. (1974). "Family background, ethnicity, and urban delinquency." Journal of Research in Crime and Delinquency 11:30–7.

Wallerstein, James S. and Clement J. Wyle. (1947). "Our law-abiding law-breakers," Probation 25:107–12.

Wechsler, Henry and Denise Thum. (1973). "Teen-age drinking, drug use, and social correlates." Quarterly Journal of Studies on Alcohol 34:1220–7.

Williams, Jay R. and Martin Gold. (1972). "From delinquent behavior to official delinquency." Social Problems 20:209–29.

Wolfgang, Marvin, Robert Figlio, and Thorsten Sellin. (1972). Delinquency in a Birth Cohort. Chicago: University of Chicago Press.

Juvenile Crime

The Offenders are Younger and the Offenses More Serious

PETER APPLEBOME

Fort Worth—After the judge read the jury's verdict last week, the defendant looked up for an explanation to his attorney, who told him softly, "We lost."

With that, the 10-year-old boy in the blue and gray athletic jacket buried his head in his hands and began to cry. He had just been found guilty of delinquent conduct in the stabbing and beating of a 101-year-old woman in December.

The woman, a neighbor, had identified the boy as her assailant while testifying from her wheelchair in a two-day trial in juvenile court here. A jury trial, which is not usually held in juvenile cases, was conducted in open court at the request of the boy's attorney.

It was a jarring scene, but similar ones seem to be occurring with increasing frequency, according to juvenile experts around the country. They say younger children are becoming involved more often in serious criminal activity usually associated with older youths or adults.

Source: Applebome, Peter, "Juvenile Crime: The Offenders are Younger and the Offenses More Serious," *New York Times*, p. 16. February 3, 1987. Copyright © 1987 by The New York Times Company. Reprinted by permission. Letter to the Editor reprinted by permission of N.Y. Times and Barry Krisberg.

WARY OF GENERALIZATIONS

Figures in juvenile crime can be elusive because much of the crime involving young children is not handled through conventional judicial channels.

Some officials say that serious crime by preteen-agers remains a minor part of the juvenile crime picture, and for that reason they are wary of generalizations about major changes in the nature of juvenile crime.

But interviews with juvenile justice officials around the country indicate that the age at which youngsters are committing serious crimes is declining steadily, and that cases that seemed like bizarre anomalies a few years ago are now becoming more common.

Crime figures compiled by the Federal Bureau of Investigation, based on reports from 11,249 agencies in 1985, reported that youths 15 years old and younger were responsible for 381 cases of murder and non-negligent manslaughter, 18,021 aggravated assaults, 13,899 robberies and 2,645 rapes. Children 12 and under were responsible for 21 of the killings, 436 of the rapes, 3,545 aggravated assaults and 1,735 robberies, the F.B.I. said.

INCREASE IN YOUNGER CRIMINALS

Officials at the National Center for Juvenile Justice, a private, nonprofit research organization in Pittsburgh, said that from 1978 to 1983 the fastest-growing areas in juvenile crime were the youngest age groups. The rate of referrals to juvenile courts rose 38 percent for 12-year-olds, 37 percent for 13-year-olds, 22 percent for 11-year-olds and 15 percent for 10-year-olds, the youngest age for which figures were available.

"Without question, all the biggest increases are in the younger ages," said Hunter Hurst, director of the center. "Once you pass 13, all the increases begin to drop."

Explanations range from increasing drug and gang activities in elementary schools, including criminal activity involving a highly potent form of cocaine, crack, to the high level of violence in the society as a whole and to increasing stress on families, particularly in poor urban areas.

Many experts say that as crime becomes more prevalent among younger teen-agers, a trickle-down effect among younger children is almost inevitable.

"Not only is the age dropping at which kids are getting involved in crime, but violent crimes are being committed by younger and younger kids," said Daniel P. Dawson, chief of the juvenile division for the Ninth Circuit State Attorney's office in Orlando, Florida.

"Four or five years ago, even two or three years ago, it was very unusual to see a child younger than 12 or 13 in the system, particularly with multiple charges," he said. "Now you see kids aged 7, 8 or 9 come in with a whole string of burglaries."

Officials in the New York City area say the overall rate of juvenile crime has been decreasing for several years, and some lawyers question whether there is any documentable increase in crimes by children.

CHILD ABUSE UP IN NEW YORK

"Younger kids are more likely to be the victims than the offenders," said Janet Fink, assistant attorney in charge of the juvenile rights division of the Legal Aid Society. "It's partly a result of demographics, but in New York City the juvenile delinquency rate is down in sharp contrast to cases of child abuse and neglect, which have gone off the charts."

But judges and police officials say that while the overall number of youthful offenders may not be rising, there is no question that the severity of the crimes is increasing.

James A. Payne, chief of Family Court for New York City's Law Department, said that in 1985 the court heard 4.2 percent fewer cases than in 1984, but there was a 7.3 percent increase in serious crimes.

"A 10-year-old is now like a 13-year-old used to be," Sgt. Richard J. Paraboschi of the Newark Police Department's Youth Aid Bureau. "And the 16-year-olds are going on 40."

GUNS MAKE A DIFFERENCE

Sergeant Paraboschi said one of the biggest changes in recent years has been the dramatic increase in the number of children involved in gun incidents. Judges see the same trend.

"When I was first on the bench in 1978, if I had one gun case a year it was a lot," said Justice Richard Huttner of the State Supreme court in Brooklyn. "Now from what I hear it's not unusual to have one or two in a week."

Justice Huttner, a former head of New York City's Family Court, added: "I don't think we see more young kids than we did, but they used to be kids arrested for stealing Twinkies from a grocery store. Now it's different. An 11- or 12-year-old is not big enough to rob most people, but with a gun it's a different story."

Judge Tom Rickhoff of San Antonio District Court, who hears only juvenile cases, said he was struck by the alarming increase in young children who have already veered toward persistent criminal behavior.

'EXCEPTIONALLY DANGEROUS PEOPLE'

"When you see a 10-year-old in your court you almost want to reach out and pat them and tell them they'll be all right, but these are exceptionally dangerous people," Judge Rickhoff said.

"I see more and more children of parents who are mentally ill or on drugs," he added. "Some of them are kids who've dropped out of school in the fourth or fifth grades. If you drop out in the fourth or fifth grade, you're dead in the United States."

Some recent cases range from a 10-year-old baby sitter in California who strangled a child she was taking care of to a recent incident in Queens in which a 12-year-old faced 27 charges, including first-degree rape, robbery, aggravated assault and grand larceny, in a case that also involved another 12-year-old and an adult.

Of particular worry nationwide is the increasing drug use in elementary schools, especially the use of crack and of such inhalants as paint or glue. Officials say that although the national incidence of drug use is decreasing, its use by children is increasing dramatically.

"Drug use used to be a decision of adolescence," said Mr. Hurst of the juvenile justice center in Pittsburgh. "Now it's a fourth-grade decision."

Mr. Payne of New York's Family Court said drug use was part of the reason for a marked increase in violent activity by younger juveniles in recent years. Drugs accounted for 4.2 percent of all juvenile arrests in 1985 and 6.8 percent last year, he said.

"We've had almost a 50 percent increase in drug crime," Mr. Payne continued. "Crack is the main reason. We are seeing kids as young as 10 or 11. They can make $800 a week. They only stay in school because that's where their constituency is."

In other areas of the country gangs are blamed for a major impact on juvenile crime. Officials in California say the average age of gang members is steadily dropping as older children bring in younger ones.

"We have a great number of gang children," said Ron W. Hayes, deputy director of Prevention and Community Corrections for the California Department of the Youth Authority. "There are about 500 gangs and about 50,000 members. You put drugs and gang behavior together and you get violent behavior."

IMPLICATIONS ARE TROUBLING

Officials say the implications of a lowering of juvenile crime ages are extremely troubling.

One problem, officials say, is that the juvenile justice system is poorly equipped to deal with young children committing serious crimes. Beyond that, any lowering of the age at which young people begin to commit crimes has ominous implications for the overall crime rate.

"We've considered the prime criminal activity years to be from 16 or 17 to 22 or 23," said Mr. Dawson, the Ninth Circuit State Attorney's official in Orlando. "Now we're seeing increases in crime not because of population shifts in that age group, but because there's more crime involving young kids. If you expand that bell curve in which you see the most crime down to 13 or 14, the total crime rate is going to skyrocket."

One aspect of juvenile crime that is being treated with increasing concern is the racial issue. The nation's crime rate has dropped since the 1970's, primarily because there are fewer youths in the prime criminal ages.

Demographers say that the trends are now becoming more worrisome, and that the bulk of the increase among juveniles will involve those who are members of minority groups.

In 1965, 50 percent of the inmates of youth facilities operated by the California State Youth Authority were white, 19.7 percent were Hispanic and 28 percent were black. In 1986 25.3 percent of the inmates were white, 32 percent were Hispanic and 39 percent were black.

"There has been a rise in the crime rate," said Dr. Alfred Blumstein, dean of the School of Urban and Political Affairs at Carnegie-Mellon University in Pittsburgh. "And it comes at a time when there should be a decline."

CHANGES IN JUVENILE LAWS

"What we may be seeing is a disproportionate number of children who are coming from the underclass, which has had higher fertility rates than the middle class," Dr. Blumstein continued. "We may be seeing the children of the middle class baby boom and the grandchildren of the underclass."

The juvenile justice system has been trying for years to cope with the steady drop in the age of criminal activity, and officials say the nation is slowly changing the way it looks at juvenile offenders. In New York for example, the Juvenile Offender Law of 1978 made it possible for 14- and 15-year-olds charged with serious felonies and 13-year-olds charged with murder to be tried in adult courts.

Rolan Henley was one of the jurors in the case of the 10-year-old boy charged with delinquent conduct in the attack on the 101-year-old Forth Worth woman. The boy, whose mother and father have served prison terms, faces sentencing this week that could include placement in state youth facilities until he is 21.

Asked why the jury deliberated for two hours, Mr. Henley replied, "I just wanted to be fair to the man."

A Downward Trend for Juvenile Crime

To the Editor:

An old and popular myth is that today's young people are worse than those of previous generations. It was reinforced by your Feb. 3 article on juvenile crime in the United States, which concludes that offenders are younger and the offenses more serious. You presented interesting statistics, but other pertinent facts support different conclusions.

Most important, arrests of juveniles declined steadily from the mid-1970's until 1984, when the Federal Bureau of Investigation reported the first modest increase in juvenile arrests in more than 10 years. Juvenile arrests for serious crimes in 1985 were 21 percent less than in 1976. This drop was primarily due to the declining number of teenagers in the U.S. The arrest rate per 100,000 youths makes the 1985 juvenile-crime rate quite similar to that of 1976.

The data show little change in the number of arrests of those younger than 15 (the focus of the alleged crime wave). For example, their 1985 arrest rates for murder, robbery and aggravated assault were similar to rates a decade ago. Arrest rates of children for burglary in 1985 were way down, compared with 1976.

The one area of increase was for the crime of rape. Between 1976 and 1985, arrests of juveniles and adults for rape climbed dramatically. Some of this increase may be attributed to the greater likelihood of victims to report rape and more aggressive law-enforcement efforts.

Court-referral data are highly dependent on juvenile-justice policies. Thus, if there are fewer community programs, more arrested youths will be sent to court. These data are more an indicator of public policies attempting to "get tough" with lawbreakers.

Indeed, in the last decade, as juvenile arrests have dropped, the number of incarcerated youths has increased dramatically. The juvenile-justice system has become more restrictive, formal and oriented toward punishment than rehabilitation. Research evidence strongly indicates that expanded incarceration of juveniles does not protect public safety and may actually increase rates of serious youth crime.

Barry Krisberg
President, National Council
on Crime and Delinquency
San Francisco, Feb. 5, 1987

ARTICLE **8**

Rediscovering Delinquency

Social History, Political Ideology and the Sociology of Law*

JOHN HAGAN
JEFFREY LEON

This paper examines a Marxian social historical approach to the study of legal evolution. The emergence of the Marxian perspective and the logic of its premises are reviewed. Using Canadian delinquency legislation as an historical example, it is found that the Marxian perspective assumes a great deal that is unconfirmed (e.g., that this legislation serves the teleologically inferred "basic interests" of an ambiguously identified "ruling class"), asserts other things that are wrong or misleading (that this legislation increased imprisonment, "invented" new categories of youthful misbehavior, created a "specialized labor market" and increased "industrial discipline"), and ignores much that an organizational analysis helps to reveal (that the emergence of probation work as an organizational concern was the prime factor in the development of Canadian delinquency legislation). Implications of these findings are considered.

IT IS NOW COMMON to begin sociological discussions of deviance by reaffirming the shift, in the 1960s, from studying the antecedents of rule-breaking behavior to a concern with the origins of legal norms and the statuses that may or may not follow their violation. Equally noteworthy, however, is an increasingly apparent shift from studying the entrepreneurial and organizational origins of legal norms

* Authorship is alphabetized and does not reflect seniority or priority; the authors share equal responsibility for this paper.

Source: Hagan, John and Jeffrey Leon, "Rediscovering Delinquency: Social History, Political Ideology and the Sociology of Law." *American Sociological Review,* Vol. 42 (August) 1977:587–598. Reprinted by permission of the American Sociological Association and the authors.

(e.g., Becker, 1963; Gusfield, 1963; Lemert, 1970; Dickson, 1968) and their enforcement (e.g., Wheeler, 1968; Reiss, 1971; Blumberg, 1967), to a more monotheistic focus in the 1970s on class conflict as the independent variable of concern (Taylor et al., 1973; Quinney, 1975a; Chambliss, 1973; Platt, 1975).

Several recent papers have questioned the accuracy of class conflict propositions about normative dissensus (Rossi et al., 1974) and the enforcement process (Hagan, 1974; Chiricos and Waldo, 1976). These studies have helped stimulate a clarification and reformulation of propositions (Turk, 1976). At the same time, however, the presumed strength of a Marxian conflict perspective continues to be a class-based, social historical approach to the study of legal evolution (Platt, 1973:30; Chambliss, 1974:8; Taylor et al., 1973:266). This paper reviews recent developments in the sociology of law and critically examines the theoretical and empirical usefulness of the class conflict approach, using the origins of juvenile delinquency legislation in Canada as its data.

CONFLICT, CONSENSUS, AND THE SOCIOLOGY OF LAW

It is still less than a decade since most sociologists adopted a rather agnostic view of the "conflict-consensus debate." (For discussion of this debate see Chambliss and Seidman, 1973; Hills, 1971; Chambliss, 1973; Hagan, 1977.) Chambliss (1969:8) expressed a common view when he reasoned that "a resolution of this debate...would be premature"; that "in many cases there is no conflict..."; and that "the influence of interest groups...is but one aspect of the processes which determine the emergence and focus of the legal norms" (Chambliss, 1969:10). However, two years later, Chambliss (Chambliss and Seidman, 1971:19) finds the literature far more conclusive: "Indeed, the empirical studies...make it quite clear that the value-consensus model is...incapable of accounting for the shape and character of the legal system...."

Similarly, Quinney's (1969:1970) early work contained pluralistic themes and a restrained optimism about legal change. Perhaps nostalgically, Quinney (1969:5) noted that criminal prosecutions emerged in Athens, in the sixth century B.C., and that "this step protected...the lower class of Athens from aggression by the rich and powerful." Furthermore, Quinney (1970:41) conceded that "groups...similar in power may well check each others' interests..." and that "interest groups receive their individual claims in return for allowing other groups to press for their interests." At this stage, he was a reformed pluralist, denying the assumption that a diversity of interests typically is resolved through compromise, but acknowledging that a plurality of interests operate, and clinging to the Poundian hope that "the public interest may become an ideal fulfilled..." (Quinney, 1970:42; cf. Pound, 1943).

The "New Criminologists" (Taylor et al., 1973:265–6) responded by arguing that "the view of law as...in the hands of 'powerful interest groups,' does not take us far enough...." Quinney (1975b:193) soon agreed that "from the evidence of radical scholarship, government and business are inseparable." Thus, "whilst pluralists may suggest that there are diverse and conflicting interests among groups in the upper class, what is ignored is the fact that members of the ruling class work within a common framework..." (Quinney, 1975:194). Taylor et al. (1975:3) endorse Quinney's new position as a "move to a Marxist economism."

The key proposition in this new Marxian perspective on law creation is that "The criminal law is...first and foremost a reflection of the interests and ideologies of the governing class..." (Chambliss, 1974:37; see also Quinney, 1975b:192), Chambliss (1974:37) comes closest to identifying this "ruling class," but is ultimately unable to decide "whether that class is private industry or state bureaucracy." Instead, he offers the contradictory conclusion that "government bureaucracies may, in the last analysis, be controlled by those who influence the society's economic resources..., but they also have a life and a force of their own..." (1974:27). Assuming these two possibilities were not mutually exclusive, which they are, undermining the notion of a *single* ruling class, some significant questions would remain unanswered. For example, how much of private industry and state bureaucracy is to be included within the "ruling class"? How diverse and extensive can these groupings be and still be considered a single "ruling class"? To what extent is there conflict within and between private industries and state bureaucracies? And, under what conditions do various industrial or bureaucratic groups prevail?

Quinney's response to such questions is to argue that "in contrast to pluralist theory, radical theory notes that the *basic interests,* in spite of *concrete differences,* place the elite into a distinct ruling class" (1975b:194, emphasis added). A difficulty with this argument is that "basic interests" are not identified with sufficient specificity to allow a predictive test of legal control strategies presumed to follow from these interests. Thus, one "Marxist criminologist" includes "direct release" as evidence of an "integrative control" used to perpetuate "state capitalism" (Spitzer, 1975:647–9). Unfortunately, this type of conceptualization encourages tautologous theorizing and, in a manner similar to functionalist formulations of the past, engages the fallacy of affirming the consequences. Thus, discussions of "interests served," like those of "functions performed," characteristically are retrospective in form, reasoning teleologically from selected consequences to presumed motivations (cf. Rock, 1974:598; Hirst, 1972).

A different type of evidence sometimes offered in support of class conflict propositions consists of information on the backgrounds and contacts of persons active in lawmaking. For example, Chambliss (1974:21) regards the fact that "legislatures, appellate court judges, and committee members are drawn largely from upper-class members of society..." as evidence of what Schattschneider (1960) calls the "mobilization of bias." However, since the membership of a class itself can be in conflict and since membership in one class need not exclude the possibility of siding with another (Mintz et al., 1976:316, 317), the use of this "guilt by membership" argument often amounts to a genetic fallacy and the tendency to argue *ad hominem.*

Finally, Chambliss and Quinney give little empirical attention to the actual level of conflict, consensus or apathy that may accompany the operation of interests, ignoring that the pursuit of these interests may occur with the explicit or tacit support of those affected (Hopkins, 1975:616). The issue is whether "class interests" operate as causes or whether, in many instances, the association with assumed effects may be spurious.

Where the active pursuit of class interests can be tested for its influence in the presence or absence of consensus, a scientific purpose can be served. It is, however, the recent extension of the Marxian perspective beyond its scientific base that concerns us. Quinney (1973:594) argues that "ideas are to be put at the service of the community..., and we ourselves must engage in people's struggles." Our concern is that this ideological mission is based on a perspective that is (1) prone to logical errors, (2) largely unconfirmed, (3) often unconfirmable and (4) possible quite frequently false.

THE SOCIAL HISTORY OF AMERICAN DELINQUENCY LEGISLATION

The patterns observed in the development of a Marxist theory of law creation are repeated in Anthony Platt's analysis of the origins of American juvenile delinquency legislation. Platt's original work, *The Child Savers,* is grounded in a theoretical tradition (Ranulf, 1938; Gusfield, 1963; cf. Platt, 1969:3,7) that focused on middle-class interests: "Child-saving may be understood as a crusade which served symbolic and ceremonial functions for native, middle-class Americans" (Platt, 1969:98). The culmination of this "symbolic crusade" was the Illinois Juvenile Court Act of 1899, and Platt adopted a partially pluralist stance in explaining that "its success was due in large measure to the fact that it was *widely* sponsored and in turn satisfied *diverse* interest groups" (1969:134, emphasis added). At this point, Platt's most pressing concerns were that "the juvenile court system... 'invented' new categories of youthful deviance..." (1969:145), that the child-savers "recommended increased imprisonment..." (1969:135), and therefore that " 'delinquents' were increasingly committed to institutions..." (1969:145).

Four years later, Platt (1973:26) argues that "ideology is healthy and should be made explicit," and concludes that "the problem with *The Child Savers* is that...[it] focuses too much attention on the middle-class reformers...." Platt reasons anew that the impetus for delinquency legislation flowed from close and compromising links between members of the middle and upper classes (1974:369), and that "the juvenile court system was part of a general movement directed towards developing a specialized labor market and industrial discipline under corporate capitalism by creating new programs of adjudication and control..." (1974:377).

Evidence for this new, class-interested Marxian theory is the same as that presented in Platt's (1969:ch.3) original account and is similar in type to that proposed by Chambliss and Quinney. Descriptions of a "new penology" are offered, but no evidence is provided that passage of juvenile court legislation resulted in an increase in the number of juveniles incarcerated, that the industrial elite benefited significantly as a result of this incarceration, or that the "ruling class" played any direct role in the passage of this legislation. Instead, the primary evidence presented engages a genetic fallacy of the type we previously associated with the "mobilization of bias" argument. Thus, the main body of information consists of a cataloguing of the class backgrounds and backings of persons involved in the child-saving movement. Platt (1969:367–8) concludes that this movement "would not have been capable of achieving significant reforms without the financial and political support of the wealthy and powerful" and that "Even the more radically-minded childsavers came from upper-class backgrounds." What is lacking in this account is any concrete evidence that this sponsorship was a *causal* factor that operated independently of widespread support for the ensuing legislation.

Summarizing, Platt's primary concerns are that links between middle-class reformers and upper-class sponsors resulted in the wealthy and powerful using the passage of American delinquency legislation to "invent" new forms of youthful misbehavior and increase imprisonment, all in the larger interest of "developing a specialized labor market and industrial discipline under corporate capitalism." Alternatively, we have argued that this Marxian perspective on the origins of American delinquency legislation is either unconfirmed or unconfirmable, plagued by logical errors and, therefore, quite possibly false. In the following section, these conclusions are tested anew with historical information on the origins of Canadian delinquency legislation.

THE SOCIAL HISTORY OF CANADIAN DELINQUENCY LEGISLATION

This part of our analysis is based on historical data drawn from a variety of sources: historical accounts written by participants in, and observers of the child-saving movement; personal correspondence and accounts drawn from the archives of leading advocates of delinquency legislation; proceedings of conferences concerned with child welfare; reports of government commissions; legislative debates; and statistics drawn from the Toronto Juvenile Court. Particular attention is given to an extensive correspondence between the two leading advocates of delinquency legislation in Canada: J.J. Kelso and W.L. Scott.

Our analysis focuses on entrepreneurial interests and activities leading to the emergence of the juvenile court, the organizational development of this court, and the objective consequences of this process (Becker, 1963; Dickson, 1968). Of particular concern is the manner in which the entrepreneurial interests of individuals are aggregated and polarized into organizational issues (Lemert, 1970). Weber reminds us that these organizational issues can be directed to various ends: "bureaucracy as such is a precision instrument which can put itself at the disposal of quite varied—purely political as well as purely economic, or any other sort—of interests..." (Gerth and Mills, 1946:231). Thus, Platt's Marxian position is only one among the possibilities entertained by Weber. With this in mind, we will consider first the link proposed by Platt between class interests in social control and the coercive consequence of increased juvenile imprisonment.

Data available for the City of Toronto[1] do not support Platt's position. In the year preceding juvenile court operations, 123 juveniles were sent to industrial schools; 71 were sent to such schools in the first year of juvenile court proceedings (City of Toronto, 1912:14). More detailed information on other forms of institutionalization (including a working-boys home, two hospitals and a training school) is available from the court reports of succeeding years (see Table 8.1). Here again, no consistent pattern of increase is apparent and at no time during the forty-year period does the *total* institutionalized population exceed the number sent to industrial school alone in the year before court operations began.[2] In the following historical discussion, we will see that the inaccuracy of Platt's position derives from a misrepresentation of legal developments that preceded delinquency legislation in Canada. Furthermore, we will find little evidence, either in personal correspondence or in public documents, that members of the industrial elite expressed an active economic interest in the passage of delinquency legislation. The activities of other individuals and interest groups, particularly those involved with the probation movement (cf. Schultz, 1973), will be considered, but the involvement of the "ruling class" seems to have been peripheral at most. We discuss three periods that preceded the passage of delinquency legislation: an initial period in which lengthy stays in reformatories replaced sentences spent in common gaols; a second period during which treatment-focused industrial schools began to replace reformatories; and a third period when organized probation emerged as a new treatment strategy influential in the development of delinquency legislation.

The child-savers focused first on juveniles convicted as criminals. Two acts were passed in 1857: *An Act for Establishing Prisons for Young Offenders and An Act for the More Speedy Trial and Punishment of Young Offenders*. The first directed the construction of "reformatory prisons," while the second provided for summary trial procedures and increased powers to discharge juveniles in order "to avoid the evils of their long imprisonment previously to trial." Thus, as early as 1857 in Canada, there were provisions for special institutions and trial procedures for juveniles.

In 1874, Ontario passed *An Act Respecting Industrial Schools*, intending to provide residential institutions that would be less severe than reformatories and to which "neglected, uncontrolled, and delinquent" children could be sent. Subsequent

---

[1] In the following, emphasis is placed on the development of a system of juvenile justice in Ottawa and Toronto, and the Province of Ontario, as well as on the federal level. Much of the federal legislation was anticipated and first implemented in Ontario, where many of the most influential child-savers lived. As a result of limitations in resources, the provisions of this Act allowed that it not take immediate effect in some cities and provinces, therefore, dates of implementation varied. Toronto was among the first Canadian cities to establish a Juvenile Court in 1912 (Ontario Law Reform Commission 1974).

[2] This finding is a consistent with less comprehensive figures reported by Scott (1906–1908) for Ottawa and in his correspondence with provincial officials in many other parts of Canada.

TABLE 8.1 City of Toronto juvenile and family court statistics, 1912, 1920, and in two year intervals to 1952

Year	1912	1920	1922	1924	1926	1928	1930	1932	1934	1936	1938	1940	1942	1944	1946	1948	1950	1952
Court Staff																		
Judges[b]	1	1	1	1	1	1	2	2	2	2	2	2	2	5	4	4	4	5
Probation Officers[c]	5	7	7	6	6	6	11	12	12	12	10	10	13	14	14	15	15	15
Clerical Staff	1	5	5	6	5	5	7	7	7	7	8	8	8	8	8	9	10	9
Psychiatrists & Psychologists	0	0	0	1	1	1	1	1	2	1	1	1	1	1	1	1	1	2
Other	0	0	0	0	1	1	2	2	2	2	2	2	2	2	2	2	2	3
Total	7	13	13	14	14	14	23	24	25	24	23	23	26	30	29	31	33	34
Probation Department Statistics																		
Interviews	-	2976	2814	3643	4651	10624	9984	9789	8547	9547	9895	11711	-	-	-	-	-	-
Occurrences	725	955	1753	1243	1636	1701	4127	4021	3962	4780	3415	3488	3800	4732	6574	-	-	-
Percent Referred to Court	20.7	7.9	6.0	4.5	2.9	1.8	2.7	1.1	3.2	5.3	6.8	10.2	13.1	13.0	10.3	-	-	-
Court Dispositions																		
Probation	769	733	731	877	350	207	304	538	425	629	488	486	544	415	316	387	418	345
Fines	202	77	92	245	228	94	28	28	13	15	29	31	80	111	30	14	17	18
Suspended Sentence & Adjournments[d]	387	679	764	971	1596	2105	1584	846	780	520	416	479	805	413	216	227	280	273
Institutionalized	85	78	43	61	34	49	71	30	44	46	53	50	85	120	67	71	72	97
Dismissed & Withdrawn	105	83	132	66	21	38	56	34	15	28	48	59	107	99	56	39	70	79
Other[e]	191	59	43	77	52	45	74	7	10	0	60	73	72	56	55	12	33	15
Total	1744	1709	1805	2297	2281	2538	2122	1483	1287	1238	1094	1178	1693	1214	740	750	890	827
Support Actions	-	-	-	-	-	-	756	586	510	435	411	689	880	1089	1349	1202	1167	1310

a. Juvenile court work began in 1912 in Toronto; reports were not issued from 1913-1919; reports ceased in 1952. Dashes indicate years for which specific types of data were not recorded.
b. Includes commissioners, judges and magistrates.
c. Includes probation officers, social investigators and social workers.
d. Includes commitments to industrial schools, Working Boys Home, Orillia Hospital, Ontario Hospital and training schools.
e. Includes cases pending, remanded, wards of Children's Aid Society, home placements and transfers to higher courts.

to this legislation. J.J. Kelso, a crusading news reporter who later became Ontario's Superintendent of Neglected and Dependent Children, emerged as a key "moral entrepreneur" (cf. Becker, 1963) in the Canadian child-saving movement. In 1887, Kelso brought together the Toronto Humane Society for "better laws, better methods, [and] the development of the humane spirit in all affairs of life" (Kelso, 1911:17; Hodgins, 1888).

Generally consistent with such principles, Ontario passed *An Act for the Protection and Reformation of Neglected Children* the following year. Provisions of this act allowed that "the Lieutenant-Governor may...appoint...commissioners...to hear and determine complaints against juvenile offenders..." and that "their cases be disposed of...separately from other offenders...." However, this act also authorized the courts to commit neglected children to industrial schools. Kelso consistently tempered this approach by arguing that "the aim...is not to steal children from their parents..., but by every available means to make the home and family all it ought to be" (Province of Ontario, 1895). It took Kelso several years to translate these views into law.

In 1890, two additional statutes were enacted in Ontario *(An Act Respecting the Custody of Juvenile Offenders and An Act Respecting the Commitment of Persons of Tender Years),* each of which further restricted the use of reformatories and expanded the use of industrial schools for selected children. In 1891, a Commission of Inquiry into the Prison and Reformatory System of Ontario (Province of Ontario, 1891) completed a report that seemed to forecast the shape of things to come. In addition to dealing with institutional reforms, the Commission recommended that magistrates grant discharges to first offenders convicted of trivial offenses and that various powers be given to probation officers.

Later the same year, the Commission's chairman and one of its most prominent members joined Kelso in Toronto to organize a public meeting at which the Children's Aid Society and Fresh Air Fund was founded, with Kelso as President. A letter announcing the goals of this meeting signaled a growing interest in an important organizational innovation: "The appointment of a probation officer to ascertain and submit to the court full particulars of each child brought up for trial, and to act in the capacity of the child's next friend" (see Kelso, 1911:69).

As reform efforts gathered momentum, a theme of professionalism emerged: "What is needed," wrote Kelso (n.d.(a):20), "is personal service, the complete organization of charitable forces, harmony of action, and the appointment of trained and experienced workers...." Gradually, persons involved in the movement seemed to develop an interest in their own positions in an emerging bureaucracy. The influence of this emerging interest group on the legislative process is suggested in Kelso's comment to the Sixth Canadian Conference of Charities and Corrections that "we have as much if not more law than we can assimilate, and the governments are ready to give new measures whenever they are asked to do so..." (Proceedings, 1903–1909:21).

The legislation of this period was particularly useful in setting the organizational base for probation work. The first *Criminal Code of Canada* was passed in 1892, providing for separate trials of persons under sixteen where it was "expedient and practicable" to do so; and, in 1893, at the urging of Kelso and others, the Ontario legislature enacted a comprehensive *Children's Protection Act* giving explicit recognition and authority to Children's Aid Societies. The latter act specifically stipulated that it was the duty of the court to notify the Executive Officer of the Children's Aid Society (if one existed in the county) prior to initiating proceedings against a boy under twelve or a girl under thirteen; this officer was then to investigate the charges, inquire into the child's family environment, and report back to the court with his findings. These procedures were reaffirmed in the following year with a federal *Act Respecting Arrest, Trial and Imprisonment of Youthful Offenders.*

In a short Commons debate of this act, the Minister of Justice and Attorney General noted that "a great many magistrates from motives of humanity" were already conducting separate trials for juveniles (Canada, 1894, June 24:4940–1). A magistrate in the Toronto Police Court later confirmed this, noting that "in 1892 we instituted the Children's Court....We set apart a small room in the lower part of City Hall..., and I was accustomed to go down to that room to try all charges against children..." (Denison, 1920:254). These developments, and Kelso's role in them, became the basis for claims that the juvenile court had a Toronto origin and was therefore a "Canadian enterprise" that had been appropriated by "American social workers." [3] Thus, Kelso later expressed his concern to Scott that "our Ontario work should not be overlooked as I advocated the Children's Court here twenty years ago, gave addresses in Chicago and elsewhere in favor of it and got the law (the Children's Protection Act) passed here in 1893" (Scott, 1906–1908: 12/27/1906; 7/4, 8/1907). One address to which Kelso refers was given in Chicago on October 11, 1893 (Proceedings, 1893; see, also, 1895). Kelso notes that "Judge Hurd consulted with me as to the drafting of the Juvenile Court following my address,"[4] and that a much discussed extract from this speech appeared in the *Chicago Tribune* the following day (cf. Flexner and Baldwin, 1914:3–4). Kelso's view was that "...of course, the Denver and Chicago courts have far outstripped us but at the same time we gave them the inspiration that led to their present success (Scott, 1906–1908: 12/27/1906).

In 1903, a subsection was added to the Ontario *Children's Protection Act*, specifying that without being convicted of a provincial offense, persons under sixteen could be placed by a judge under the care of a probation officer, who would report periodically "concerning the progress and welfare of the child." The idea of a probation *system* "to help the children before they become criminally disposed" was increasingly discussed (Kelso, 1907:107). Kelso gave this top priority: "We want to bring about what is called the Probation System, following the children up from their first offense..." (Proceedings, 1903:21). The assumption behind this proposal

---

[3] For example, these claims are made in a 1933 Toronto newspaper article titled "Juvenile Court had Toronto Origin" (see Hagan, 1977:21). These claims (as contrasted, for example, with those made for New York and Massachusetts) are less important for their factual accuracy than for their indication of close connections between Canadian and American child-saving efforts.

[4] This comment is found in Kelso's (n.d.(b):19) handwriting at the bottom of a page of an article by Hurly on "The History of the Illinois Juvenile Court Law."

was that imprisonment frequently could be avoided: "Whenever there is an offense there is a cause behind it and our children's court and probation system should be able to reach that cause and...remove it for the safety and protection of the children in the home" (Department of Neglected and Dependent Children, 1907:15).

To this point, we have focused on J.J. Kelso as the central "moral entrepreneur" in the advocacy of probation and delinquency legislation. However, he was joined in this pursuit by a "professional" (cf. Becker, 1963:152) counterpart, W.L. Scott, Local Master for the Supreme Court of Ontario and President of the Ottawa Children's Aid Society. Kelso and Scott vocalized three primary concerns. First, additional funds were needed to elevate "philanthropic work to the status of a profession and to encourage University graduates to become specialists in social and moral reform work" (Proceedings, 1907:8). Second, it was claimed that probation officers were now hampered in their work by a lack of "legislative recognition" (Scott, 1906–1908:1/2/1907). and, third, there was a perceived need for special judges: "The Children's Court should undoubtedly be...conducted by specially selected persons..." (Kelso, 1908:164).

Drafted by Scott and others in response to these concerns, the federal *Juvenile Delinquents Act* was introduced first in the Speech from the Throne in 1906, reintroduced to the Senate in 1907 and eventually passed in 1908. A "juvenile delinquent" was defined broadly by this act as any child under sixteen who violated any federal or provincial statute, or municipal by-law, or who was liable by any other act to committal to an industrial school or juvenile reformatory. Thus, this act consolidated various previously illegal behaviors into a new category called "delinquency," but it did not add any behaviors to those already specified under existing statutes and by-laws. It would be misleading to conclude, as Platt does for the United States, that Canadian delinquency legislation " 'invented' new categories of youthful misbehavior."[5]

The act did, however, give juvenile courts exclusive primary jurisdiction in cases of delinquency. It also provided for the formation of a voluntary Juvenile Court Committee to consult with and advise probation officers, or to appoint an officer where remuneration was available and an officer was not already appointed under provincial authority. Furthermore, probation officers were assigned powers of a constable, with their duties including: conducting investigations, being present

---

[5] Sixteen years later, *An Act to Amend the Juvenile Delinquents Act, 1924*, proposed the addition of an omnibus clause—"or who is guilty of sexual immorality or any other form of vice"—to the definition of a juvenile delinquent. However, by this time, such omnibus clauses had been a part of legal definitions of neglect for more than thirty years. It is sometimes argued that such clauses define as delinquent behaviors that are most common among underclass youth. However, this alone cannot count as support for a Marxian class conflict perspective, since the underclass may agree with such legal definitions. The latter possibility is supported by the finding of Black and Reiss (1970) that black complainants are more likely than whites to insist on the arrest of blacks accused of delinquency. Perhaps most significantly, however, the same Marxian theorists (e.g., Liazos, 1974) who claim underclass behaviors are defined differentially by law as delinquent, also cite self-report studies reporting an absence of relationship between social class and delinquent behavior. Probably the safest conclusion is that vague statutory clauses like those defining delinquency depend most heavily for their consequences on the discretion of those who must interpret and enforce them: citizens, the police and prosecutors.

and representing the interests of the child in court, furnishing the court with such assistance and information as required, and taking charge of any child before or after trial, as directed by the court.

Discussions of these and other provisions of the act mainly involved two groups. The ultimately successful group included those who advocated treatment and prevention through probation and a special court; they distributed copies of the bill, circulated petitions, and invited such speakers as Judge Lindsay, of the Denver Juvenile Court, and Mrs. Schoff, of the Philadelphia Mother's Union, to address various gatherings. The opposition included police officers and magistrates who already assumed organizational responsibilities for children and who, therefore, had a very immediate interest to protect (see Scott 1906–1908:3/7, 3/15/1907). This group advocated a more "punitive" approach to delinquency. Particularly vehement in this view were several police officials, including Inspector Archibald and Police Magistrates Denison and Kingsford, associated with the Toronto Children's Court. The debate was often bitter, with Archibald, in a report circulated to gain support for the police position, charging that the new proposals:

> work upon the sympathies of philanthropic men and women for the purpose of introducing a jelly-fish and abortive system of law enforcement, whereby the judge or magistrate is expected to come down to the level of the incorrigible street Arab and assume an attitude absolutely repulsive to British subjects. The idea seems to be that by profuse use of slang phraseology he should place himself in a position to kiss and coddle a class of perverts and delinquents who require the most rigid disciplinary and corrective methods to ensure the possibility of their reformation. (Archibald, 1907:5)

In response, Scott (1906–1908:3/19/1907) labeled Archibald a "person of very limited intelligence," while Kelso (Scott 1906–1908:5/14/1907) called him "self-opinionated" and opposed to those who failed to treat him with "deference." Scott (5/2/1907) concluded that the members of the Toronto Police Department felt the new proposals were intended to supplant them and were therefore a reflection on their past work. Moreover, Archibald's particularly negative attitude was said to be based on the fact that he "had prepared all the legislation on the subject during the last forty years and...is apparently deeply offended that anyone else should have usurped this prerogative" (Scott, 1906–1908 4/16/1907).

Scott (1908:894) went on to campaign successfully for the *Juvenile Delinquents Act*, emphasizing in his arguments "that probation is the only effective method for dealing with young offenders." Thus, when the bill was reintroduced to the Senate in May, 1908, Senator Coffey referred to "the difference of view as to the means and methods whereby the best results may be achieved," and explicitly dismissed the position of Inspector Archibald as being characterized by an outmoded "spirit of rigidity and severity" (Canada, 1907–8:975–7). Although some objections were raised in the House of Commons by those concerned with the legal rights of children, the temper of the ensuing debate probably is summarized best by one member of Parliament who observed that the act "is to be laughed through as a joke." (Canada, 1907–8:1240–1). The legislation was passed, but this did not end the organizational search for support. The following years brought a succession of minor revisions and extensions of the original legislation, concerted efforts to secure appropriate provincial legislation creating the newly authorized juvenile courts, and continued efforts to obtain sufficient funds from various levels of government to employ probation officers (Proceedings, 1909; Scott, 1952).

The consequences of the entrepreneurial activities we have described are illustrated in the statistical records of the Toronto Juvenile and Family Court (see Table 8.1). Probation officers in this court predominated in both their number and scale of activities. Thus, while the number of *official* occurrences recorded by the Juvenile Court actually was lower in 1952 than in 1912, during this period the number of probation officers increased from 4 to 14, and the number of occurrences handled *unofficially* by probation officers escalated more than 900 percent, from 735 to 6,574 cases. The Probation Department apparently did this in a manner the Toronto Police Department seemed initially to fear, that is, by attracting their own new cases and refusing to refer them either to the police or court. Thus, the Probation Department publically proclaimed that "it is our aim, as far as possible, to settle through the Probation Department all difficulties without making them court cases" (City of Toronto, 1920:5), while also annually advising that "we again, as many times before, earnestly solicit those having problems of various kinds, within the jurisdiction of the Court, coming and allowing us to assist before these problems become too acute so as to require official action" (City of Toronto, 1933:9). Specifically, the Probation Department offered social and clinical investigations in all such cases, leading to dramatic increases in the number of interviews counted annually into the Court Reports. This aspect of the court's work was augmented in 1929 with increased jurisdiction over family matters, followed by increasing rates of court referrals and support actions in succeeding years. In this way, *the social work of the Probation Department steadily increased, without simultaneous increases in the number of adolescents institutionalized or placed on probation*. Thus, in those years when official delinquency actually declined, the Probation Department was quick to observe optimistically "that while we had a decrease in delinquency...we had an increase of the numbers who came of their own free will to get help. If it is safe to draw an observation from this fact, it would be reasonable to assume that the non-official effort of the court is reducing its official acts" (City of Toronto, 1933:9). This conclusion was, of course, self-serving; the long term effect on children of this increase in non-official activity remains unclear.

DISCUSSION AND CONCLUSIONS

The conflict that surrounded the *Juvenile Delinquents Act* in Canada was less about normative definition than about the organizational arrangements under which violators of the norm would be processed. More specifically, it was supporters of the police and advocates of probation who quarreled most about the organizational procedures to be followed. J.J. Kelso, a moral entrepreneur who rose from news reporter to a high position in the child-care bureaucracy, collaborated with W.L.

Scott, a professional counterpart and philanthropist who occupied an administrative position in the Ontario Supreme Court, to engineer a legislative movement whose organizational goal became the prevention of delinquency through juvenile probation work. Opposition came from representatives of existing police organizational interests whose more punitive philosophy was reflected in writing prior legislation and their current activities in handling juveniles. Advocates of probation prevailed in the passage of delinquency legislation in 1908, and the consequences of these efforts became apparent in the organizational composition and activities of the new Juvenile Court in Toronto: the handling of *unofficial* occurrences by probation officers dramatically increased, while the level of *official activity* showed some signs of decline.

Whether the eventual success of advocates of probation served the basic interests of the ruling elite is unknown, and probably unknowable, for the various reasons discussed above; however, little influence of the industrial elite was revealed in the personal correspondence and public documents of the key proponents of this legislation. Moreover, in contrast to Platt's account of the passage of delinquency legislation in the United States, no evidence was found in the Canadian data that institutionalization increased as a result of such legislation, or that this legislation was useful in developing a "specialized labor market" or "industrial discipline."

Part of Platt's (1974:389) argument procedes from a basic Marxian assumption that "as the contradictions (of capitalism) become more apparent and the control system more unsuccessful, the methods of coercion become similarly more explicit and more desperate. "It is apparently for this reason that Platt places such great emphasis on the role of the "New Penology" in the emergence of delinquency legislation. In contrast, the argument of this paper is that it was an emphasis on probation work, and not imprisonment, that led to this new legislation substantially changed the operation of the juvenile and criminal court, probably with consequences both good and bad, intended and unintended (cf. Hagan, 1975), the overall effect was not to intensify a formal and explicit system of coercion, but rather to reinforce and increasingly intervene in informal systems of social control, particularly the family. These findings raise the possibility that assumed contradictions in the economic sphere may have only marginal significance for the juvenile justice system, or that these assumed contradictions need not necessarily lead to more explicit methods of social coercion. In any case, this paper provides a considerably different account of the origin of delinquency legislation than is offered by Platt, and it is an account which encourages a reconsideration of the conditions under which this version of a Marxian, class conflict perspective can be usefully applied.

REFERENCES

Archibald D. (1907). Report on the Treatment of Neglected Children in Toronto, Toronto: Arcade.

Becker, Howard. (1963). Outsiders, New York: Free Press.

Black, Donald and Albert Reiss. (1970). "Police control of juveniles," American Sociological Review 25:63-77.

Blumberg, Abraham. (1967). Criminal Justice. Chicago: Quadrangle Books

Canada

    (1894). Commons Debates Ottawa: Queen's Printer.

    (1907). Senate Debates, Ottowa: Queen's Printer

    (1908).

Chambliss, William. (1969). Crime and the Legal Process, New York McGraw-Hill.

    (1973). "Functional and conflict theories of crime." MSS Modular Publications 17:1-23.

    (1974). "The state, the law and the definition of 7-42 in Daniel Glaser (ed.), Handbook of Criminology, Indianapolis: Bobbs-Merrill.

Chambliss, William and Robert Seidman. (1971). Law, Order and Power, Reading, Ma.: Addison-Wesley.

Chiricos, Theodore and Gordon Waldo. (1976). "Socioeconomic status and criminal sentencing: an empirical assessment of a conflict proposition." American Sociological Review 40:753-72.

City of Toronto. (1912–1952). Annual Reports of the Juvenile Courts of the City of Toronto, Toronto.

Denison, G.T. (1920). Recollections of a Police Magistrate. Toronto: Musson.

Department of Neglected and Dependent Children. (1907). Fourteenth Report of the Department of Neglected Children. Toronto: Warwick.

Dickson, Donald. (1968). "Bureaucracy and morality: an organizational perspective on a moral crusade." Social Problems 16:143-56.

Flenner, Bernard and Roger Baldwin. (1914). Juvenile Courts and Probation, New York: Century.

Gerth, H. and C.W. Mills. (1946). From Max Weber, New York: Oxford University Press.

Gusfield, Joseph. (1963). Symbolic Crusade, Urbana: University of Illinois Press.

Hagan, John. (1974). "Extra-legal attributes and criminal sentencing: an assessment of a sociological viewpoint." Law and Society Review 8:357-83.

    (1975). "The social and legal construction of criminal justice a study of the pre-sentencing process." Social Problems 22:620-37.

    (1977). The Disreputable Pleasures. Toronto: McGraw-Hill Ryerson.

Hills, Stuart. (1971). Crime, Power and Morality. Toronto: Chandler.

Hirst, P.Q. (1972). "Marx and Engels on law, crime and morality." Economy and Society 1:28-56.

Hodgins, J.G. (ed.) . (1888). Aims and Objects of the Toronto Humane Society, Toronto: Briggs.

Hopkins, Andrew. (1975). "On the sociology of criminal law." Social Problems 22:608-19.

Kelso, J.J. (1907). "Delinquent children: some improved methods whereby they may be prevented from following a criminal career." Canadian Law Review 6:106-10.

    (1908). "Children's court." Canadian Law Times and Review 26:163-6.

    (1909). Helping Erring Children, Toronto: Warwick.

    (1911). Early History of the Humane and Children's Aid Movement in Ontario, 1886-1893. Ontario: King's Printer.

    n.d.(a). "Can slums beabolished or must we continue to pay the penalty," Toronto.

    n.d.(b). J.J. Kelso Papers. Ottawa: Public Archives.

Lemert, Edwin. (1970). Social Action and Legal Change, Chicago: Aldine.

Liazos, Alexander. (1974). "Class oppression: the function of juvenile justice," Insurgent Sociological Inquiry 5:2-24.

Ontario Law Reform Commission. (1974). Report on Family Law, Part V, Family Courts, Toronto: Queen's Printer.

Platt, Anthony. (1969). The Child Saves, Chicago: University of Chicago Press.
   (1973). "Dialogue with Anthony Platt." Issues in Criminology 8:19-33.
   (1974). "The triumph of benevolence: the origins of the juvenile justice system in the United States." Pp. 356-89 in Richard Quinney (ed.), Criminal Justice in America, Boston: Little, Brown.
   (1975). "Prospects for a radical criminology in the U.S.A." Pp. 95-112 in Ian Taylor, Paul Walton and Jock Young (eds.), Critical Criminology. London: Routledge and Kegan Paul.

Pound, Roscoe. (1943). "A survey of social interests," Harvard Law Review 57:1-39.

Proceedings. (1893). Proceedings of the Waif-Saving Congress. Chicago, Illinois
   (1895). Proceedings of the 22nd National Conference of Charities and Corrections. New Haven, Connecticut.
   (1903–1909). Proceedings of the Canadian Conference of Charities and Corrections, Ottowa, Ontario.

Province of Ontario. (1891). Report of the Commissioners Appointed to Enquire into the Prison and Reformatory System in Ontario.
   (1895). Annual Report of the Superintendent of Neglected and Dependent Children.

Quinney, Richard.. (1969). Crime and Justice in Society, Boston: Little, Brown.
   (1970). The Social Reality of Crime, Boston: Little, Brown.
   (1973). Review of the "New Criminology." Sociological Quarterly 14: 589-9.
   (1975a). Criminology, Boston: Little, Brown.
   (1975b). "Crime control in capitalist society: a critical philosophy." Pp. 181-212 in Ian Taylor, Paul Walton and Jock Young (eds.) Critical Criminology, London: Routledge and Kegan Paul.

Ranulf, Svend. (1983). Moral Indignation and Middle Class Psychology. Copenhagen: Levin and Monksgard.

Reiss, Albert. (1971). The Police and the Public. New haven: Yale University Press.

Rock, Paul. (1974). "Comment on Mugford," Sociological Quarterly 15:597-8.

Rossi, Peter, Emily Waite, Christine Bose and Richard Berk. (1974). "The seriousness of crimes: normative structure and individual differences." American Sociological Review 39:224-37.

Schattschneider, E.E. (1960). The Semi-Sovereign People. New York: Holt, Rinehart and Winston.

Schultz, J.L. (1973). "The cycle of juvenile court history." Crime and Delinquency 19:457-76.

Scott, W.L. (1906). W.L. Scott Papers. Ottawa: Public Archives
   (1908). "The *Juvenile Delinquents Act*." Canadian Law Times and Review 28:892-904.
   (1952). The Juvenile Court in Law. Ottawa: Canadian Welfare Council.

Spitzer, Steven. (1975). "Toward a Marxian theory of deviance." Social Problems 22:638-51.

Taylor, Ian, Paul Walton and Jock Young. (1973). The New Criminology. London: Routledge and Kegan Paul.
   (1975). Critical Criminology. London: Routledge and Keagan Paul.

Turk, Austin. (1976). "Law, conflict, and order: from theorizing to theories." Canadian Review of Sociology and Anthropology: In press.

Wheeler, Stanton (ed.). (1968). Controlling Delinquents. New York: Wiley.

Summary and Discussion

PART ONE defines juvenile delinquency, explains how data on delinquency are collected, and explores some of the relative strengths and weaknesses of official and unofficial delinquency data. We began with a synopsis of the 1967 *Task Force Report: Juvenile Delinquency and Youth Crime* because it serves as a pivotal work in the study of juvenile delinquency since it summarized much of the previous work in the field and laid important groundwork for future contributions. The Task Force was comprised of some of the most prominent sociological and criminological researchers of the twentieth century. Through a series of reports, these scholars defined and explained delinquency, outlined the seriousness of its consequences, and offered suggestions for reducing its negative impact on individuals, families, and society.

The first article, "The Concepts of Tolerance and Contraculture as Applied to Delinquency" by Ruth Shonle Cavan, presents an overview of conforming and non-conforming behavior. Through the use of a hypothetical model, Cavan plots the incidence of behavior ranging from an underconforming contraculture to overconformity. She points out how minor delinquents are more easily brought back into conformity, or modal behavior, than those at the two polar extremes.

The two readings in Part One, "What is Crime?" and "Procedures for the Development of National Estimates of Delinquency and Status Offense Cases," deal with official data. These official data come from two different sources. "What is Crime?" is excerpted from *Report to the Nation on Crime and Justice,* a report using data collected and compiled by the Federal Bureau of Investigation and published by the United States Department of Justice. This report primarily focuses on adult crime, but includes a statistical description of law violating behavior by youths under the age of eighteen. In fact, as indicated in that report, arrest rates for property crimes actually peak at age sixteen—an age at which most states consider the offender to be a juvenile. This report also discusses the differential handling of juvenile cases as compared to adult criminal proceedings.

When law violators are processed through the justice system as juveniles rather than adults, the most comprehensive source of official data is prepared by the National Council of Juvenile and Family Court Judges and published periodically as *Juvenile Court Statistics*. Data in this volume represent estimates based on actual reports of caseloads from juvenile courts across the country who voluntarily submit records of their activities.

Both of these sources of official data on delinquency suffer some serious short-comings. For example, the article by William Chambliss and Richard Nagasawa suggests that the official statistics were so misleading that they were virtually useless in analyzing the actual delinquency committed by the white, black, and Japanese boys in their study. This article represents a common complaint against official data in that selective law enforcement, differential visibility of types of offenses and offenders, and other extralegal factors involved in the collection and reporting, seriously underrepresent the actual amount of delinquency taking place and distort the extent to which lowerclass youths are involved in delinquent activities.

Maynard Erickson and LaMar Empey further explicated the problems of official data in their article "Court Records, Undetected Delinquency and Decision-Making." They concluded that rather than official statistics representing the *actual* extent of juvenile delinquency, official records are more likely to represent an individual's single most serious offense.

Self-report data on delinquency and other unofficial sources such as victimization studies, tend to show that a large amount of juvenile delinquency goes undetected and officially unreported. Therefore, actual rates of juvenile delinquency, especially in the category of less serious status offenses, far exceed the estimates derived from official data. Unofficial data also suffer noteworthy limitations. For example, some juveniles may exaggerate the extent of their delinquent involvement, thus inflating self-report data. Others, fearing some type of reprisal, may be reluctant to admit to their participation in delinquency which has gone officially undetected. More seriously, self-report studies tend to involve small and unrepresentative samples from which it is difficult to generalize.

In a very important article, Michael Hindelang, Travis Hirschi, and Joseph Weis address this apparent discrepancy between official records and self-report data. While they acknowledge that there are significant differences in rates of delinquency when self-report data are compared to official data, they somewhat resolve the dilemma posed by this discrepancy by pointing out that each type of data measures a *different* type of delinquency. Therefore, both official data and self-reports are useful measures of delinquency. They are simply measuring different things. Official data tend to focus on more serious delinquency—those acts which would have been defined as crimes if committed by adults— whereas self-report studies, on the other hand, tend to focus on the less serious status offenses such as running away, truancy, smoking, and sexual promiscuity. All of these sources of delinquency data underscore the magnitude and seriousness of juvenile delinquency as a major social problem.

The issue of serious juvenile crime is pursued in Peter Applebome's article "Juvenile Crime: The offenders are Younger and the Offenses More Serious." Applebome cites both official and unofficial data which seemingly indicate an upswing in serious crimes committed by juveniles. Most disturbing, is the evidence that serious juvenile delinquency is no longer the domain of older offenders in their late teens, but is increasingly being committed by youths barely entering adolescence. Applebome attributes much of this rise in young juvenile crime to the increased availability of guns and illegal drugs to adolescents. Barry Krisberg who is the President of the National Council on Crime and Delinquency seriously questioned Applebome's thesis in a "Letter to the Editor" written in response to the article. Krisberg contends that serious juvenile crime is not dramatically increasing. Instead, he points to an overall decline in juvenile arrests from the mid-1970s to 1984 except in the case of rape. Krisberg attributes much of the decrease in juvenile arrests during that period to the demographic fact that there were declining numbers of teenagers in the United States. Finally, Krisberg points out that juvenile justice policies importantly affect arrest and incarceration rates and may not accurately reflect the extent of juvenile crime. The final article in Part One departs in theme from the others somewhat, but provides a thought provoking analysis of the sociological aspects of defining delinquency. Contrasting the development of delinquency legislation in Canada to its development in America as outlined by Anthony Platt (see Part Four for a synopsis of Platt's classic work *The Child Savers: The Invention of Delinquency)*, John Hagan and Jeffrey Leon emphasize the social, economic, and political dimensions to the process of defining juvenile delinquency. This article serves as an appropriate transition to Part Two—which explores

PART ONE

Questions for Review and Discussion

1. Based on your reading of the synopsis of the *Task Force Report: Juvenile Delinquency and Youth Crime,* what is the difference between adult crime and juvenile delinquency?

2. Identify and discuss the recommendations made by the President's Commission on Law Enforcement and Administration of Justice to prevent juvenile delinquency by striking at its societal causes.

3. In "The Concepts of Tolerance and Contraculture as Applied to Delinquency," Ruth Shonle Cavan presents a bell-shaped behavior continuum that depicts conforming and deviant behavioral modes in relation to socially acceptable behavior. Explain Cavan's model.

4. The excerpt in this section form the *Report to the Nation on Crime and Justice* shows that arrest rates vary by age groups. Why does participation in crime decline with age?

5. With information derived from the *Juvenile Court Statistics, 1984,* trace the processing of a hypothetical case of delinquency through a juvenile court.

6. Based on your reading of the article by William Chambliss and Richard Nagasawa, critique the validity of official statistics on juvenile delinquency.

7. Outline the methodology used by Maynard Erickson and Lamar Empey in their self-report surveys as described in their article "Court Records, Undetected Delinquency and Decision Making." What advantages do such surveys have over juvenile court records?

8. How did Michael Hindelang, Travis Hirschi, and Joseph Weis, in their article "Correlates of Delinquency," harmonize and synthesize the contributions of self-report and official measures of juvenile delinquency?

9. What evidence does Peter Applebome present to support his thesis in "Juvenile Crime: The Offenders are Younger and the Offenses More Serious?" Do you think that Applebome is correct or do you think that Barry Krisberg's response negates much of Applebome's contention?

10. What is the theoretical argument advanced by John Hagan and Jeffrey Leon in "Rediscovering Delinquency: Social History, Political Ideology, and the Sociology of Law"? How does their argument differ from that of Anthony Platt's in *The Child Savers?*

Explanations of Juvenile Delinquency

INTRODUCTION

The term *theory* is commonly used to mean "an educated guess or even an intuitive, subjective explanation of why a phenomenon occurs or why people act like they do." However, to the scientist, a theory is a carefully structured statement explaining the causal relationship between systematically established facts and variables. Sociologists have attempted to apply this general scientific principle of theory building in generating explanations for all sorts of human behavior—including juvenile delinquency. At the same time, sociologists' pursuit of etiological explanations generally conform to their unique and traditional sociological perspective or viewpoint that human behavior is best understood and interpreted in its social context. Thus, sociological theorists have traced delinquency to the negative impacts on young people of lower-class poverty, community disorganization, adult role models in crime, and a wide variety of other societal variables. Part II is a collection of some of the most important and influential of these sociological explanations of juvenile delinquency.

We begin with a synopsis of Travis Hirschi's classic book *Causes of Delinquency*. In this volume, Hirschi first reviews and critiques much of the existing sociological theory of juvenile delinquency before developing his own variation of control theory as a well thought-out explanation of this form of youthful misconduct. His objective was to compare the ethical development of those juveniles who violate the laws of society and those who conform. Hirschi introduced the concept of the *social bond* to describe the natural attachment experienced by most children to the basic values and behavioral expectations of the larger society as reflected by parents, teachers, and other

137

conforming models and mentors. Supported by considerable empirical evidence, Hirschi argued that if the social bond is firmly intact for an individual, there will be no delinquency pattern. Conversely, if the social bond is weak, juvenile delinquency can be anticipated.

A more contemporary article by William Thompson, Jim Mitchell, and Richard Dodder is "An Empirical Test of Hirschi's Control Theory of Delinquency" (1984). This research study included the variable of delinquent companions with Hirschi's causal scheme involving a weakened bond or attachment to conventional attitudes and norms. Thompson and his associates found that delinquent companions are far more influential in causing an individual to participate in delinquent behavior than the weakened quality of the social bond.

A major breakthrough in the construction of a general theory of deviant behavior, with strong applications for juvenile delinquency, is the 1938 social strain theory of Robert Merton. In his "Social Structure and Anomie," Merton pointed to a pervasive sense of disappointment and strain that afflicts many lower-class Americans who grimly recognize that they will not be able to achieve the culturally endorsed goals of material and social success via the traditional and culturally approved means of honesty, education, and hard work. Many of these individuals, in their anomic frustration over their lack of realistic opportunity to achieve, may adapt or cope through deviant or delinquent means in an effort to reach the idealized success goals.

Walter Miller viewed the primary cause of delinquency as resulting from the transmission of cultural values which promote and support delinquent behavior. In his article "Lower Class Culture as a Generating Milieu of Gang Delinquency," Miller identifies six focal concerns of lower-class culture which he believes lead to delinquency, especially gang delinquency among lower-class boys.

Another promising and popular explanation of criminal and delinquent behavior was presented in 1943 by Edwin Sutherland and Donald Cressey who emphasized socialization or the social learning process as the original source of values, beliefs, and attitudes conducive to illegal conduct. Just as most people *learn* to conform to societal standards through the association and influence of those who are favorable to law abiding behavior, others *learn* to deviate from social norms through their primary contact with criminalistic elements. Thus, Sutherland and Cressey appropriately named their explanation the "Theory of Differential Association."

Support for Sutherland's theory is offered in a recent study by James Orcutt who empirically tested deviance and delinquency with his "Differential Association and Marijuana Use: A Closer Look at Sutherland (With a Little Help from Becker)." This 1987 study, utilizing a carefully designed research strategy, not only reinforced Sutherland's original formulation, but constitutes a formidable denial of the charges by some critics that Differential Association Theory is untestable and has been rendered obsolete by other theories.

Frank Tannenbaum, in his 1938 "Point of View: Dramatization of Evil," is credited as one of the earliest and most effective proponents of "tagging" or Labeling Theory of Delinquency. Tannenbaum focused on the societal reaction to perceived acts of deviance and delinquency that can assign a negative social identity to targeted individuals. It follows that imputation of a stigmatized delinquent role to a person can drastically alter his or her personal identity and desire to conform to societal expectations. Thus, paradoxically, the labeling process itself is a social force capable of eliciting subsequent deviant behavior by the person so labeled.

Walter Reckless, in his 1961 article, "A New Theory of Delinquency and Crime," contributed his well-known Containment Theory. By concentrating on society's control system that regulates human conduct, Reckless accounted for both conformity and deviance. He conceptualized the control system as comprised of two lines of defense against antisocial behavior—the inner self-control exercised by each individual in resisting serious deviance and the external, societal control of social norms and law-enforcement agencies that can be imposed on those persons whose inner control system is too weak to resist transgression.

Another social control approach to accounting for juvenile crime was formulated by Gresham Sykes and David Matza in the "Techniques of Neutralization: A Theory of Delinquency." They contended that some juveniles are able to justify their misbehavior by employing a convenient set of rationalizations that temporarily neutralize personal responsibility to their victims and to the normative system of society. Thus, these youngsters are able to intermittently "drift" into a delinquent mode.

Terrence Thornberry, in "Toward an Interactional Theory of Delinquency," developed a new synthesized theoretical explanation of juvenile delinquency. Combining and extending elements from social control, social learning, and other theoretical constructs, Thornberry suggests that delinquency is an active part of a dynamic and developmental process and interaction with other social factors over time.

The concluding paper in this section is by James Short, Jr., who, while acknowledging the limitations often imposed by provincial scholarly disciplines and uncertain "grey areas" of knowledge regarding delinquency causation, explores the possible integration of theoretical levels of explanation. Short calls for a closer scrutiny of those areas where disciplinary subject matter overlaps. For example, biology and social experience *do* interact in producing much human behavior. Furthermore, Short suggests that the young gang is a "bridging concept . . . between social psychological and social structural explanations."

Travis Hirschi, *Causes of Delinquency.*
Berkeley: University of California Press, 1969.

THE AUTHOR

Travis Hirschi was born in Rockville, Utah in 1935. He attended the College of Southern Utah and the University of Utah, where he received a master's degree in sociology in 1958. Hirschi wrote his thesis on Durkheim's concept of anomie, an exercise that kindled his interest in social control theory.

Hirschi entered the University of California, Berkeley, where he was greatly influenced by sociological scholars including Erving Goffman, Albert Cohen, David Matza, John Lofland, Irving Piliavin, and Ruth Kornhauser. While a graduate student, Hirschi was allowed to add delinquency items to a questionnaire about to be administered to a large sample of students in Richmond, California. This study, the Richmond Youth Project, being conducted by Charles Y. Glock and Alan B. Wilson, was heavily influenced by the ideas of Richard Cloward and Lloyd Ohlin who authored *Delinquency and Opportunity.* The data produced by the Richmond Youth Project served as the basis for Hirschi's doctoral dissertation, which became published as *Causes of Delinquency*—a book sharply opposed to the strain theory advanced by Cloward and and Ohlin.

After receiving his Ph.D. at Berkeley in 1968, Hirschi taught at the University of Washington, the University of California at Davis, and the State University of New York at Albany (where he collaborated with Michael J. Hindelang on *Measuring Delinquency*). Hirschi has served as President of the American Society of Criminology, and was the recipient of its Edwin H. Sutherland Award in 1986. He currently is Professor of Sociology and Management and Policy at the University of Arizona, where he is working with Michael Gottfredson on what he describes as a large book with the tentative title *Crime and Criminality.*

THE BOOK

In *Causes of Delinquency,* Hirschi states and tests social control theory, or what is often called the "social bond" theory of delinquency. He states in the preface to his work that this theory "sees in the delinquent a person relatively free of the ultimate attachments, the aspirations, and the moral beliefs that bind most people to a life within the law."

In the Durkheimian tradition, social control theory assumes that delinquency occurs when an individual's bond to society is weakened or broken. Unlike the strain theories of delinquency which assume that youths want to conform, but due to social and structural constraints, must resort to deviant means for achieving success, control theory assumes that there is a natural propensity on the part of youths to violate the law. This assumption then focuses not upon the question "Why do some youths commit delinquency?," but upon the question "Why don't all youths commit delinquency?" The answer to this second question is the social bond. This bond to society is comprised of four elements: attachment, commitment, involvement, and belief.

Attachment is the extent to which an individual is sensitive to the opinions of others. It is the moral restraint that one exercises as a result of having internalized the norms of society. Hirschi refers to attachment as being the counterpart to the superego or conscience. *Commitment* refers to the extent to which an individual has stakes in conformity to societal norms. It involves the amount of risk an individual perceives in violating conventional behavior. In Hirschi's words, "If attachment to others is the counterpart of the superego or conscience, commitment is the counterpart to the ego or common sense" (p. 20). *Involvement* refers to the extent to which an individual is so busy doing conventional activities that he or she has little or no time or opportunity to commit delinquent acts. Thus, youths actively involved in sports, scouting, school activities and other conforming behavior are believed to be less likely to commit delinquent acts (if for no other reason, because there is little time left for delinquent activities). *Belief* relates to the extent to which an individual believes in the validity of norms and yet is able to rationalize violating them. As Sykes and Matza (1957) pointed out, delinquents typically do not have totally different value systems than other youths. Rather, they are more likely to view norms as flexible guidelines which they can bend or break in various situations.

THE SAMPLE AND THE DATA

The sample was drawn as part of the Richmond Youth Project in Costa County, California. The sample was stratified by race, sex, school, and grade and drawn from approximately 17,500 students entering public junior and senior high schools in the San Francisco and Oakland area. A total sample of 5,545 students was selected. Due to a variety of problems (e.g., failure of parents to give permission for the youth to participate, moving away from the area, absenteeism, or invalid data), approximately twelve percent of the sample was excluded from final data analysis. Data came from three sources: official school records, questionnaires completed by the students (administered over a three-day period in the classroom), and official police records. Thus, Hirschi effectively combined official delinquency data with self-report delinquency data.

FINDINGS AND CONCLUSIONS

Hirschi's study found the relationship between socioeconomic status and delinquent acts to be very small or nonexistent. While lower-class boys were more likely to be picked up by the police, they were not more likely to commit delinquent acts. Similarly, race was not a significant variable in the self-report data.

What emerged as the most strongly related variables to juvenile delinquency were the elements of the social bond, especially attachment to parents, school, and teachers. Those youths who expressed the strongest bond of affection for their parents were least likely to have been involved in delinquency. Hirschi concluded that children who perceive their parents as unaware of their activities and their whereabouts are most likely to become involved in delinquency. Conversely, children who have a strong attachment to their parents are likely to have their parents "psychologically present" when temptation to violate the law occurs. This bond greatly reduces the likelihood of their committing delinquent acts.

Attachment to school was also an important insulator against delinquency. Poor school performance coupled with a dislike for school was determined to be a strong motivator for delinquency. Likewise, an attachment to teachers was inversely related to delinquent activities. Hirschi proposed a causal chain in which academic incompetence is viewed as causing poor school performance which leads to disliking school. Disliking school, in turn, leads to the rejection of authority which finally leads to the commission of delinquent acts. Hirschi presented statistical data which indicated that his findings were consistent with this hypothesized causal chain.

Hirschi's data also supported the notion that commitment to conventional norms makes one less likely to become involved in delinquency. Those youths with commitment to education and those with high occupational aspirations also had the lowest rates of delinquency. Hirschi found his data to be at odds with the earlier theories of Merton (1957), Cohen (1955), Cloward and Ohlin (1960), and others who suggested that frustrated aspirations and social strain cause juvenile delinquency.

Involvement in conventional activities also appeared to be an insulator against delinquency. Those youths who had jobs, played sports, had hobbies, or were actively engaged in other socially conforming activities had lower rates of delinquency.

Finally, Hirschi concluded that as Sykes and Matza (1957) had contended, delinquent youths were most likely to be those whose belief in norms could be most readily rationalized. Although his data provided more ambiguous support on this variable than the other elements of the social bond, Hirschi concluded that youths who could most readily neutralize their deviance through one of the techniques suggested by Sykes and Matza—denial of responsibility, denial of injury, denial of a victim, condemnation of the condemners and by appealing to higher loyalties—were most likely to be involved in delinquency.

LIMITATIONS

Hirschi's work has become a classic in the juvenile delinquency literature for many reasons. It is a systematic scientific approach to test a theory of juvenile delinquency with empirical data. His combination of official delinquency reports with self-reported data was a methodological strength lacking in many delinquency studies. This work, like any scientific investigation, however, is not without some shortcomings.

One weakness relates to the sample. While Hirschi used a large stratified sample, it was geographically limited, and the generalizability of his findings may be questioned. Also, while Hirschi collected data from whites, blacks, males, and females, support for his theory seems to predominantly come from the data from white males.

A more serious problem regarding Hirschi's findings resides in the statistical methodologies used to test his hypotheses. The causal model proposed by Hirschi appears to be supported by his data. However, Hirschi used correlations rather than multivariate techniques such as multiple regression path analysis. Consequently, while Hirschi's variables are statistically related, no causal order can be assumed. Thus, while poor performance in school is linked to disliking school which is linked to rejection of authority and the commission of delinquency, there is no indication that those variables occur in a causal sequence—they would have the same correlations in the reverse order. One could just as reasonably assume that committing delinquent acts causes the rejection of authority which causes one to dislike school which ultimately leads to poor academic performance.

Finally, an apparent flaw in Hirschi's original version of control theory was that it assumed that delinquents also lack a meaningful attachment to peers. By his own admission, Hirschi underestimated the influence of delinquent friends and overestimated the significance of involvement in conventional activities. Subsequently, Hirschi has modified his theory to recognize the important influence of delinquent peers in the causal chain of delinquency. It appears that consistent with differential association theory (Sutherland and Cressey, 1966), having friends who commit delinquent acts is strongly related to delinquency.

Despite these few limitations of Hirschi's study, the contributions to delinquency understanding made by *Causes of Delinquency* should not be underestimated. Numerous studies have supported the contention that a strong social bond (especially to school and parents) is negatively related to delinquency. Hirschi's theory is sociologically strong, the elements of the social bond can be operationalized, and his theory can be scientifically tested. In short, Travis Hirschi's *Causes of Delinquency* truly stands as a classic in the field of juvenile delinquency study.

REFERENCES

Cloward, Richard A. and Lloyd E. Ohlin. (1960). *Delinquency and Opportunity*. New York: The Free Press.

Cohen, Albert K. (1955). *Delinquent Boys*. New York: The Free Press.

Merton, Robert K. (1957). *Social Theory and Social Structure*. New York: The Free Press.

Sutherland, Edwin H. and Donald R. Cressey. (1966). *Principles of Criminology* (7th Ed.). Philadelphia: Lippincott.

Sykes, Gresham M. and David Matza. (1957). "Techniques of Neutralization: A Theory of Delinquency." *American Sociological Review* 22:664-670.

ARTICLE 9

An Empirical Test of Hirschi's Control Theory of Delinquency

WILLIAM E. THOMPSON
JIM MITCHELL
RICHARD A. DODDER

Hirschi's control theory of delinquency (1969) contends that lack of attachment to peers, parents, and school leads to a lack of conventional attitudes, which ultimately leads to juvenile delinquency. In order to test this theory, data were collected from questionnaires administered to 724 students in four high schools and three juvenile correctional instructions in the Southwest. Findings from this study indicate that when subjected to path analysis, Hirschi's contention is only supported when the variable of delinquent companions is included; that is to say the extent of explained variation in delinquency is greatly enhanced when delinquent companions is introduced as an additional antecedent variable in Hirschi's causal scheme. In addition, the findings are more consistent with a social learning or differential association theory than the original theory proposed by Hirschi in Causes of Delinquency (1969).

An earlier version of this manuscript was presented at the Southwestern Sociological Association meetings in Ft. Worth, Texas, March 28-31, 1979.

Source: Thompson, William, Jim Mitchell and Richard A. Dodder, "An Empirical Test of Hirschi's Control Theory of Delinquency." *Deviant Behavior,* Vol. 5 1984:11-22. Reprinted by permission of Hemisphere Publishing Corporation.

HIRSCHI (1969:i) proposes a theoretical explanation in which the delinquent is viewed as "...a person relatively free of the intimate attachments, the aspirations, and the moral beliefs that bind most people to a life within the law." He contrasts strain, control, and cultural deviance perspectives emphasizing the basic incompatibility of their assumptions. Hirschi's (1969) findings indicate that for males, attachment to conventional peers, parents, and school is conducive to the development of conventional attitudes, forming a bond between the juvenile and society hence preventing delinquency. His analysis suggests a theoretical approach where the lack of attachment to family, school, and peers results in lack of conventional attitudes. The juvenile subsequently has low stakes in conformity which results in association with delinquent friends and commission of delinquent acts. Hirschi's ideas have been very influential, but their claim to validity rests almost entirely on his own research.

The purpose of this paper is to test Hirschi's approach through path analysis with more recent data. While Hirschi (1969) supports his theory for the causes of delinquency with empirical data, his method of analysis relied primarily on correlation. Correlations were found among the variables included within his model; and from them he imputed causation. In an attempt to test Hirschi's control theory, multiple regression analysis expressed in the form of path diagrams was used, which goes beyond correlational procedures (indicating relationship between pairs of variables) to controlling the effects of each variable in turn on the correlation in terms of a time ordered model with causal implications. Further, whereas Hirschi (1969) confined his empirical study to males, path models are presented for both males and females.

METHOD

To test the model derived from Hirschi's theory, data were collected from questionnaires administered to students in four high schools and three juvenile correctional institutions all in the same metropolitan area in the Southwest. The high schools varied from a small, rural school comprised predominantly of white students to a large, urban school with a substantial number of black students. The four high schools were chosen because of the diversity of their student populations. The correctional institutions selected consisted of one institution for boys, one for girls, and one coeducational. One of the institutions was privately financed, while the other two were state-supported. All students arriving at the institutions over an eight month period were included in the sample. By including students from both high schools and juvenile correctional institutions, the final sample of 724 subjects included a range of juveniles with varied self-reported delinquency experience and a variety of contacts with authorities ranging from no official contact to having committed at least one act which was serious enough to warrant being adjudicated to a correctional facility. This large, varied sample included 322 males and 402 females; 375 white females, 302 white males, 20 males and 27 females of other races. The demographic information that was collected indicated there were respondents from each social class,[1] with the largest group of subjects coming from primarily working and middle-class backgrounds (approximately 9% indicated their fathers to be unskilled workers, 23% semi-skilled, 28% skilled workers, 11% in service type occupations, 17% in lower management positions, 6% in professional occupations and high level management occupations, and 6% reported their fathers to have professional occupations requiring an advanced college degree).

A version of the Nye-Short (1958) self-report delinquency scale, modified to conform with local laws and to include more serious delinquent acts, was used to measure delinquency. The modified Nye-Short Self-Reported delinquency scale contains the following items:

Have You
1. Ever driven a car without a driver's license or permit (do not include driver's training)?
2. Ever drunk beer, wine, or liquor?
3. Ever purchased beer, wine, or liquor?
4. Ever defied parents' authority (for example: running away from home or hitting them)?
5. Ever forged a check?
6. Ever severely "beat up" or assaulted someone?
7. Ever been placed on school probation?
8. Ever vandalized (seriously damaged) property that did not belong to you?
9. Ever taken things (worth less than $20) that did not belong to you?
10. Ever taken a car without the owner's permission (other than that of your parents or friends' parents)?
11. Ever taken things (worth $20 or more) that did not belong to you?
12. Ever burglarized (broken into) a house or car to take things that did not belong to you?

Response Categories: 1=never, 2=1 or 2 times, 3=3 or 4 times, 4=5 or more times.

Subjects were asked how often they had engaged in 12 different delinquent acts, and a delinquency score was then determined by the sum of their responses to all 12 acts. In addition, each subject was asked how many, if any, companions were with them when the delinquent act was committed. Delinquent companions was then indexed by the sum of the number of companions present for all 12 acts. Consequently, the measurements of delinquency and of delinquent companions were not totally independent of each other. The delinquency scale, however, included a number of minor offenses such as drinking beer and taking something worth less than $20. Very few of the subjects indicated they had committed no delinquent acts (6.7%) and only a few had no delinquent companions (8.3%). In addition, some respondents also reported that

[1] Basis for social class categories were the categories of occupational prestige presented by Hollingshead and Redlich (1958). Taken from August Hollingshead and F. Redlich, *Social Class and Mental Illness: A Community Study,* New York: Wiley.

they had never committed specific acts, like burglarizing a home, but they had been with others who had.[2]

Ten items were constructed to measure Hirschi's concept of conventional attitudes (see Appendix 9.A). These ten items were factor analyzed with the principal axis method using unity in the diagonal.

Only one factor was generated, and all ten items loaded substantially on this factor. In fact, the lowest loading was .52 for the item concerned with going to college. In addition, this one factor identified 34.7% of the total variation of these items. The average correlation among the items was .24, generating an internal consistency coefficient, Kuder-Richardson (K-R 20) of .76. Consequently, subject's responses to the ten items were summed to index conventional attitudes.

Eighteen items were constructed to measure attachment. Five items were concerned with attachment to peers, seven items with parents, and six items with attachment to school. The same method of factor analysis was applied to these 18 items, and all the items loaded substantially on the first factor generated, with the lowest loading being .33 for the item concerned with parents' listening. This factor identified 23.6% of the variations of the 18 items. The average correlation among these items was .18, generating an internal consistency coefficient, K-R 20, 80. Three additional factors were generated having eigenvalues greater than unity. A varimax rotation of the four factors identified one factor on which all items loaded strongly which were concerned with attachment to parents, one factor which had strong loadings for the first four items concerned with attachment to school, and one factor contained the last two items about school. These results suggested that while the various kinds of attachment are somewhat distinct, they also relate quite well together. Consequently, subject's responses to the 18 items were summated to index the attachment variable. To enhance the consistency of data presentation, the primary statistical procedure used was path analysis.[3]

FINDINGS AND CONCLUSIONS

Correlation matrices of the variables under consideration for both males and females can be found in Table 9.1. The relationship between delinquent companions and delinquent acts for males is particularly striking (r=.71). Part of this correlation can perhaps be explained by the research procedure (i.e., the two measures were not completely independent), but it is still worthy of note. The relationship between these two variables is not nearly so pronounced among females (r=.48), although it is strong. In addition, both attachment and conventional attitudes related negatively and moder-

---

[2] Path analysis assumes that all variables included in a model are measured independently of each other. Unfortunately, since the number of delinquent companions and the extent of delinquent acts were not measured by completely separate items, some degree of correlation would be expected between these two variables as a result of the measurement. Thus, there is a need for caution in interpreting these results.

[3] For a thorough treatment of this form of graphic representation of multiple regression analysis through a path model, see Mueller, Schuessler, and Costner (1977:312-30), Pine (1977:354-73) or Land (1969).

TABLE 9.1 Correlation Matrices of Relevant Variables by Sex

	Delinquent Companions	Attachment	Conventional attitudes	Delinquent acts
	x=1.98	x=4.78	x=5.30	x=1.89
	s=1.18	s= .85	s=1.03	s=.60
Males [a]				
Delinquent companions		-.27	-.33	.71
Attachment			.64	-.29
Conventional attitudes				-.36
Delinquent acts				
	x=1.50	x=4.94	x=5.53	x=1.53
	s= .49	s= .88	s= .49	s= .45
Females [b]				
Delinquent companions		-.13	-.14	.48
Attachment			.55	-.26
Conventional attitudes				-.30
Delinquent acts				

[a] (with N=322, r .11 is significant at the p< .05 level)
[b] (with N=322, r .11 is significant at the p< .05 level)

ately to delinquent acts among males (r=-.29 and -.36 respectively) as well as among females (r=-.26 and -.30 respectively). Delinquent companions, also correlated negatively and moderately to attachment and to conventional attitudes among males (r=-.27 and -.33 respectively) but weakly among females (r=-.13 and -.14).

The results of the path analysis connecting attachment, conventional attitudes, and delinquent acts are presented for both males and females in Figure 9.1. Consistent with control theory, a negative, although very weak, path coefficient was found between attachment and delinquent acts (P=-.12 for males and -.13 for females). At the same time, a negative, low path coefficient was found between conventional attitudes and delinquent acts (P=-.28 for males and -.23 for females). In both cases, the path coefficients were weaker than the original correlations. Such is the case, of course, since attachment and conventional attitudes are substantively related (r and P=.64 for males and .55 for females). Furthermore, contrary to the expectations offered by Hirschi, attachment and conventional attitudes together explained only 13% of the variation in delinquent acts among males and 10% among females.

These same models are presented in Figure 9.2 except with the addition of delinquent companions as another causal variable. Delinquent companions is placed

FIGURE 9.1   Hirshi's proposed model

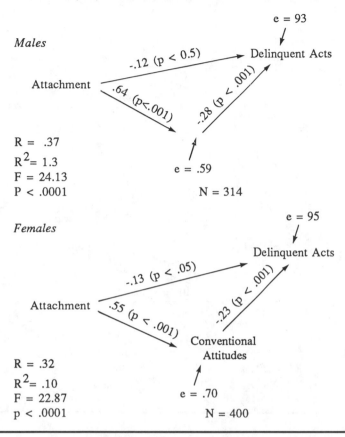

$R = .37$
$R^2 = 1.3$
$F = 24.13$
$P < .0001$

$N = 314$

$R = .32$
$R^2 = .10$
$F = 22.87$
$p < .0001$

$N = 400$

directly antecedent to delinquent acts since Hirschi wrote that low stakes in conformity result in association with delinquent friends and the commission of delinquent acts.[4] Since Hirschi believed that delinquent companions was not part of the causal process, however, whatever relationship might be found between delinquent companions and delinquent acts would be spurious and should disappear by controlling for the effects of attachment and conventional attitudes. As can be seen in Figure 9.2, for males, the direct relationship between delinquent companions and delinquent acts, while control-

[4] Hirschi reasoned that those who lack attachment to conventional others, particularly to parents, have not internalized conventional norms and are free from moral restraints. The essence of internalizing conventional attitudes (forming a conscience or superego) is in the attachment of youth to others. The more youth respect their parents and adults in general, the more they will accept the rules; the more they accept the rules, the more likely they are to obey the rules. Those who do not form attachment to their parents will not be capable of forming attachments to others (delinquent peers) either. Youth do not commit delinquency to conform to delinquent friends' expectations; they do so because they have not formed attachments and, subsequently, internalized conventional expectations.

FIGURE 9.2   Hirshi's model with delinquent companions added

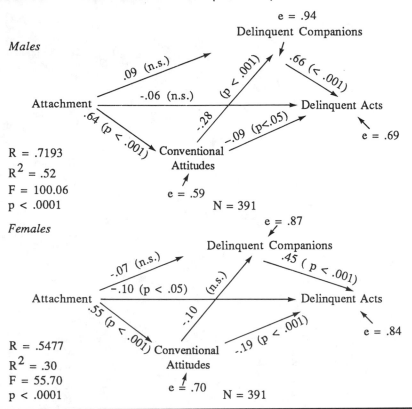

ling for conventional attitudes and attachment (P=.66), is only slightly less than the correlation between delinquent companions and delinquent acts (r=.71). Similarly for females, this path is only slightly less than the original correlation between delinquent companions and delinquent acts (P=.45 While r=.48). While the two path models appear to be quite consistent among males and females, delinquent companions appear to have a greater direct effect on delinquent acts for males.

In addition, the paths connecting delinquent acts with both attachment and conventional attitudes were even weaker when delinquent companions was added to the model for both males and females. For example, among males the path connecting attachment with delinquent acts while controlling only for conventional attitudes was -.12 (see Figure 9.1) but became -.06 when delinquent companions was also controlled (see Figure 9.2). This same kind of result was found for the remaining paths connecting delinquent acts to attachment and to conventional attitudes in Figure 9.1 compared to Figure 9.2.

Even the paths connecting attachment to delinquent companions (P=-.09 for males and -.07 for females) as well as those connecting conventional attitudes to delinquent companions (P=-.15 for males and -.10 for females) were in the correct direction, but weak. That is, the greater the attachment as well as the more conventional the attitudes, independently assessed, the fewer the delinquent companions; but these relationships were quite weak. With these weak paths, even the indirect effects that attachment or conventional attitudes might have on delinquent acts when mediated through delinquent companions are weak.

These findings seem to indicate that delinquent companions is fundamentally related to committing delinquent acts, regardless of the level of attachment or of conventional attitudes, for females and especially for males. When delinquent companions was included in the models, the levels of explained variation in delinquent acts raised dramatically for both males (from 13% to 52%) and for females (from 10% to 30%).

These findings which suggest that delinquent companions is an important additional variable to Hirschi's theory immediately prompt one to consider differential association theory as an alternative model for explaining delinquency. According to differential association (Cohen, 1955; Cloward and Ohlin, 1960; Sutherland and Cressey, 1974; Burgess and Akers, 1966), one important way that the delinquent learns to accept the appropriateness of delinquent acts is in greater interaction with others who are delinquent or support definitions favorable to delinquency. Assuming all behavior is socially learned, differential association offers a theoretical explanation for delinquency in which delinquent companions would be the primary antecedent variable. This theory implies a causal order based on the assumption that intimate associations cause persons to hold particular attitudes, which in turn, lead to norm-violating behavior. More specifically, learning definitions favorable to the violation of norms leads to more favorable views of and subsequent commission of delinquent acts. Thus, differential association would suggest that, of the variables in this study, the initial independent variable in a causal scheme explaining delinquency is association with delinquent companions—or at least with those from whom one learns definitions favorable to law violation.

Since this research project was not explicitly designed to test differential association theory, the research instrument did not contain the types of items that would be ideal to measure the intricate concepts contained within the differential association theory (e.g. the actual process of social learning, developing attitudes, or the history of past associations and their definitions acquired). However, the utilization of path analysis does allow for an alternative path model to be developed which would include the variable of delinquent companions in a time-ordered sequence which would more closely fit with the differential association perspective.[5] In other words, the role of delinquent companions seems to be a pivotal conceptualization in defferentiating between control theory as presented by Hirschi (1969) and differential association (Sutherland and Cressey, 1974; among others).

Figure 9.3 illustrates the path models from the differential association perspective for males and females. It should be noted for reasons of comparison with the model

---

[5] We used the measure of the number of delinquent friends which has been used extensively in the past as an index of association with definitions favorable to law violation (as well as measures of conventional attitudes which could index developing attitudes unfavorable to law violation).

FIGURE 9.3   Differential association

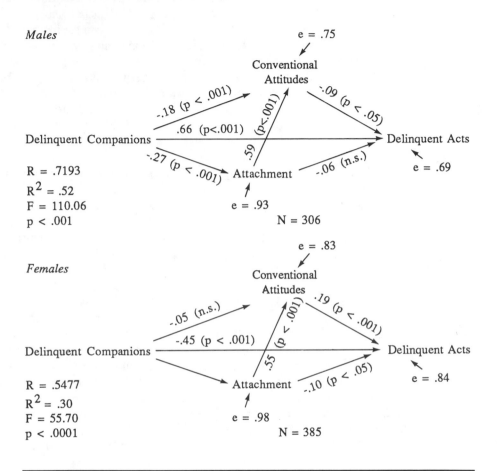

Males

Conventional
Attitudes

e = .75

-.18 (p < .001)

.66 (p<.001)

.59 (p<.001)

-.09 (p < .05)

Delinquent Companions   Delinquent Acts

-.27 (p < .001)   Attachment   -.06 (n.s.)

R = .7193
R^2 = .52
F = 110.06
p < .001

e = .93

e = .69

N = 306

Females

Conventional
Attitudes

e = .83

-.05 (n.s.)

-.45 (p < .001)

.55 (p < .001)

.19 (p < .001)

Delinquent Companions   Delinquent Acts

Attachment   -.10 (p < .05)

R = .5477
R^2 = .30
F = 55.70
p < .0001

e = .98

e = .84

N = 385

suggested by Hirschi (1969), that the model representing a differential association approach has ,as a component, a measure of general belief or conventional attitudes rather than the learning of specific definitions accompanying a variety of delinquent acts.

As shown in Figure 9.3, the pattern for males and females was consistent throughout, with delinquent companions exhibiting more of an impact with males than with females. This was demonstrated also by the levels of explained variation for the models representing males and females. the extent of explained variation, of course, was the same for the delinquent companions added since the dependent variable and the independent variables are the same. Individual path coefficients were changed, however, since the ordering of the independent variables was changed.

In Figure 9.3, the strongest path coefficients were still, of course, those between delinquent companions and delinquent acts. That is, the direct effects of both attachment and conventional attitudes (while controlling for the remaining variables in the model) upon delinquent acts were negligible, but the direct effect of delinquent companions with delinquent acts while controlling for both attachment and conventional attitudes was substantial (P=.66 for males and .45 for females). On the other hand, from the differential association perspective one might anticipate substantial negative relationships between delinquent companions and attachment to conventional society. The path coefficients connecting delinquent companions and attachment were low (r and P-.27 for males and-.13 for females) but in the correct direction. Similarly, delinquent companions was very weakly related to conventional attitudes (P=-.18 for males and -.05 for females) but also in the correct direction. Although the path coefficients are unimpressive, it could be conceptualized that having delinquent companions tended to lead to a lack of conventionally accepted attachments and, consequently, to unconventional attitudes; but the effect upon delinquent acts was then negligible. Similar to the results depicted in Figure 9.2, males could be considered to be more likely to commit delinquent acts in the company of others regardless of attachment or conventional attitudes.

SUMMARY

These data indicated a consistently strong relationship between delinquent acts and delinquent companions even after controlling the effects of other causal variables. Hirschi (1969) contended that attachments and conventional beliefs or attitudes deter delinquent acts. When attachments and conventional attitudes were considered, however, they had little effect on delinquent acts regardless of the causal ordering. Delinquent companions was consistently a more important variable in the case of males than females. Thus, the findings from these data suggest that while relationships may appear to exist between attachments and conventional attitudes with delinquent acts, these relationships diminish to the point of being virtually non-existent when the effect of delinquent companions is controlled. Therefore a more reasonable causal explanation for juvenile delinquency should focus on the possible influences of delinquent companions rather than on attachment or conventional attitudes.

Differential associations appears to provide an explanation for delinquency more consistent with the findings in this research than does the original control theory model proposed by Hirschi (1969). At least, the variable of delinquent companions emerges as more important than the control variables. Even Hirschi (1969:230-31) acknowledged he had somewhat underestimated the possible influence of delinquent peers, and his own data showed them to be important; but he still maintained that companions were not significant in understanding the causes of delinquency because delinquents, he believed, were unable to form meaningful attachments to others. "In the control model, the relationship between delinquent acts and delinquent companions is spurious" (Hirschi, 1969:153). The explanatory power of Hirschi's model was greatly enhanced, however, when delinquent companions were added to it. The relationship between delinquent companions and delinquent acts was revealed even more clearly when placed in the time order which would logically be derived from differential association theory.

This apparent support for differential association is not clear cut, however. According to differential association, delinquent peers would help one develop unconventional attitudes, which then could lead to delinquency. No meaningful relationship between unconventional attitudes and delinquency appeared in the differential association model nor between delinquent peers and unconventional attitudes.

Further, it should be understood that the use of multiple regression coefficients in a path analysis is controversial in regard to implying causality when the time-ordered sequence of variables is unclear. While its results are generally more acceptable as having causal implications than the correlation procedures initially used by Hirschi (1969), it is not a substitute for genuine longitudinal research which is sorely needed in the area of juvenile delinquency.

Thus, it is more accurate to conclude that these data clearly do not support Hirschi's theory than to claim support for the alternative theory of differential association. Judging from these data it appears that, contrary to Hirschi's theory, delinquent companions appears to be a very significant variable which ought to be included in a meaningful causal scheme of juvenile delinquency.

REFERENCES

Burgess, Robert L. and Ronald L. Akers. (1966). "A Differential Association - Reinforcement Theory of Criminal Behavior." Social Problems 14:128-147.

Cloward, Richard A. and Lloyd E. Ohlin. (1960). Delinquency and Opportunity. New York: Free Press.

Cohen, Albert K. (1955). Delinquent Boys: The Culture of the Gang. Glencoe, Illinois: Free Press.

Hirschi, Travis. (1969). Causes of Delinquency. Berkeley: University of California Press.

Land, Kenneth. (1969). "Principles of Path Analysis." Pp. 3-37 in Borgatta (ed.) Sociological Methodology. San Francisco: Jossey-Bass Inc.

Mueller, John K., Schuessler, Karl F. and Herbert L. Costner. (1977). Statistical Reasoning in Sociology. Boston: Houghton Mifflin Company.

Pine, Vanderlyn R. (1977). Introduction To Social Statistics. Englewood Cliffs, New Jersey: Prentice-Hall Inc.

Sutherland, Edwin H. and Donald R. Cressey. (1974). Criminology (9th Edition). Philadelphia: Lippincott.

APPENDIX 9.A   Scales of attachment and conventional attitudes by items.

	Factor loadings
Attachmnent to peers, parents, and school	
There are many people who call me their friend.	.37
My friends consult me when making decisions.	.37
My friends appreciate my accomplishments.	.53
* My friends are often too busy to listen to me.	.33
My friends accept me for myself.	.48
My parents praise me when I deserve it.	.49
I have a close relationship with my father.	.43
* Often my parents are too busy to listen to me.	.34
I follow rules established by my parents.	.52
My family offers meaningful roles to me.	.59
I have a close relationship with my mother.	.55
I am consulted in family decisions.	.60
The school has meaningful activities available to me.	.46
I follow the rules set up by the school.	.54
I complete assignments given to me by my teacher.	.55
I feel accepted by my teacher.	.59
I have a voice in school policies.	.41
I am supported by the school for my efforts.	.46

Conventional attitudes

We should respect the achievements of our forefathers.	.59
I meet the requirements if I want to go to college.	.52
The really worthwhile things in life require sacrifice.	.54
It is important to help in trying to improve things.	.62
It is important to save for the future.	.60
In order to be sucessful in life, one should obtain as much schooling as possible.	.56
It is desirable to show concern for those people less fortunate than myself.	.59
One should work hard for sucess and recognition or achievements	.66
It is best to do things according to the rules.	.62
One should be actively engaged in some kind of disciplined, productive activity.	.59

*This is an intentionally reversed item.

ARTICLE 10

Social Structure and Anomie

ROBERT K. MERTON

THERE PERSISTS a notable tendency in sociological theory to attribute the malfunctioning of social structure primarily to those of man's imperious biological drives which are not adequately restrained by social control. In this view, the social order is solely a device for "impulse management" and the "social processing" of tensions. These impulses which break through social control, be it noted, are held to be biologically derived. Nonconformity is assumed to be rooted in original nature.[1] Conformity is by implication the result of an utilitarian calculus or unreasoned conditioning. This point of view, whatever its other deficiencies, clearly begs one question. It provides no basis for determining the nonbiological conditions which induce deviations from prescribed patterns of conduct. In this paper, it will be suggested that certain phases of social structure generate the circumstances in which infringement of social codes constitutes a "normal" response.[2]

The conceptual scheme to be outlined is designed to provide a coherent, systematic approach to the study of sociocultural sources of deviant behavior. Our primary aim lies in discovering how some social structures *exert a definite pressure* upon certain persons in the society to engage in nonconformist rather than conformist

Source: Merton, Robert K. "Social Structure and Anomie." *American Sociological Review,* Vol. 3 (October) 1938: 672 – 682.

[1] E.g., Ernest Jones, *Social Aspects of Psychoanalysis,* 28, London, 1924. If the Freudian notion is a variety of the "original sin" dogma, then the interpretation advanced in this paper may be called the doctrine of "socially derived sin."

[2] "Normal" in the sense of a culturally oriented, if not approved, response. This statement does not deny the relevance of biological and personality differences which may be significantly involved in the *incidence* of deviate conduct. Our focus of interest is the social and cultural matrix; hence we abstract from other factors. It is in this sense, I take it, that James S. Plant speaks of the "normal reaction of normal people to abnormal conditions." See his *Personality and the Cultural Pattern,* 248, New York, 1937.

conduct. The many ramifications of the scheme cannot all be discussed; the problems mentioned outnumber those explicitly treated.

Among the elements of social and cultural structure, two are important for our purposes. These are analytically separable although they merge imperceptibly in concrete situations. The first consists of culturally defined goals, purposes, and interests. It comprises a frame of aspirational reference. These goals are more or less integrated and involve varying degrees of prestige and sentiment. They constitute a basic, but not the exclusive, component of what Linton aptly has called "designs for group living." Some of these cultural aspirations are related to the original drives of man, but they are not determined by them. The second phase of the social structure defines, regulates, and controls the acceptable modes of achieving these goals. Every social group invariably couples its scale of desired ends with moral or institutional regulation of permissible and required procedures for attaining these ends. These regulatory norms and moral imperatives do not necessarily coincide with technical or efficiency norms. Many procedures which from the standpoint of *particular individuals* would be most efficient in securing desired values, for example, illicit oil-stock schemes, theft, fraud, are ruled out of the institutional area of permitted conduct. The choice of expedients is limited by the institutional norms.

To say that these two elements, culture goals and institutional norms, operate jointly is not to say that the ranges of alternative behaviors and aims bear some constant relation to one another. The emphasis upon certain goals may vary independently of the degree of emphasis upon institutional means. There may develop a disproportionate, at times, a virtually exclusive, stress upon the value of specific goals, involving relatively slight concern with the institutionally appropriate modes of attaining these goals. The limiting case in this direction is reached when the range of alternative procedures is limited only by technical rather than institutional considerations. Any and all devices which promise attainment of the all important goal would be permitted in this hypothetical polar case.[3] This constitutes one type of cultural malintegration. A second polar type is found in groups where activities originally conceived as instrumental are transmuted into ends in themselves. The original purposes are forgotten, and ritualistic adherence to institutionally prescribed conduct becomes virtually obsessive.[4] Stability is largely ensured while change is flouted. The range of alternative

---

[3] Contemporary American culture has been said to tend in this direction. See André Siegfried, *America Comes of Age,* 26-37, New York, 1927. The alleged extreme(?) emphasis on the goals of monetary success and material prosperity leads to dominant concern with technological and social instruments designed to produce the desired result, inasmuch as institutional controls become of secondary importance. In such a situation, innovation flourishes as the *range of means* employed is broadened. In a sense, then, there occurs the paradoxical emergence of "materialists" from an "idealistic" orientation. Cf. Durkheim's analysis of the cultural conditions which predispose toward crime and innovation, both of which are aimed toward efficiency, not moral norms. Durkheim was one of the first to see that "contrairment aux idées courantes le criminal n´apparait plus comme un être radicalement insociable, comme une sorte d´element parasitaire, de corps étranger et inassimilable, introduit au sein de la société; c´est un agent régulier de la vie sociale." See les *Régles de la Méthode Sociologique,* 86-89, Paris, 1927.

[4] Such ritualism may be associated with a mythology which rationalizes these actions so that they appear to retain their status as means, but the dominant pressure is in the direction of strict ritualistic conformity, irrespective of such rationalizations. In this sense, ritual has proceeded farthest when such rationalizations are not even called forth.

behaviors is severely limited. There develops a tradition-bound, sacred society characterized by neophobia. The occupational psychosis of the bureaucrat may be cited as a case in point. Finally, there are the intermediate types of groups where a balance between culture goals and institutional means is maintained. These are the significantly integrated and relatively stable, though changing, groups.

An effective equilibrium between the two phases of the social structure is maintained as long as satisfactions accrue to individuals who conform to both constraints, viz., satisfactions from the achievement of the goals and satisfactions emerging directly from the institutionally canalized modes of striving to attain these ends. Success, in such equilibrated cases, is twofold. Success is reckoned in terms of the product and in terms of the process, in terms of the outcome and in terms of activities. Continuing satisfactions must derive from sheer *participation* in a competitive order as well as from eclipsing one's competitors if the order itself is to be sustained. The occasional sacrifices involved in institutionalized conduct must be compensated by socialized rewards. The distribution of statuses and roles through competition must be so organized that positive incentives for conformity to roles and adherence to status obligations are provided *for every position* within the distributive order. Aberrant conduct, therefore, may be viewed as a symptom of dissociation between culturally defined aspirations and socially structured means.

Of the types of groups which result from the independent variation of the two phases of the social structure, we shall be primarily concerned with the first, namely, that involving a disproportionate accent on goals. This statement must be recast in a proper perspective. In no group is there an absence of regulatory codes governing conduct, yet groups do vary in the degree to which these folkways, mores, and institutional controls are effectively integrated with the more diffuse goals which are part of the cultural matrix. Emotional convictions may cluster about the complex of socially acclaimed ends, meanwhile shifting their support from the culturally defined implementation of these ends. As we shall see, certain aspects of the social structure may generate countermores and antisocial behavior precisely because of differential emphases on goals and regulations. In the extreme case, the latter may be so vitiated by the goal emphasis that the range of behavior is limited only by considerations of technical expendiency. The sole significant question then becomes, which available means is most efficient in netting the socially approved value?[5] The technically most feasible procedure, whether legitimate or not, is preferred to the institutionally prescribed conduct. As this process continues, the integration of the society becomes tenuous and anomie ensues.

Thus, in competitive athletics, when the aim of victory is shorn of its institutional trappings and success in contests becomes construed as "winning the game" rather than

---

[5] In this connection, one may see the relevance of Elton Mayo's paraphrase of the title of Tawney's well-known book. "Actually the problem is *not that of the sickness of an acquisitive society; it is that of the acquisitiveness of a sick society.*" *Human Problems of an Industrial Civilization,* 153, New York, 1933. Mayo deals with the process through which wealth comes to be a symbol of social achievement. He sees this as arising from a state of anomie. We are considering the unintegrated monetary-success goal as an element in producing anomie. A complete analysis would involve both phases of this system of interdependent variables.

"wining through circumscribed modes of activity," a premium is implicitly set upon the use of illegitimate but technically efficient means. The star of the opposing football team is surreptitiously slugged; the wrestler furtively incapacitates his opponent through ingenious but illicit techniques; university alumni covertly subsidize "students" whose talents are largely confined to the athletic field. The emphasis on the goal has so attentuated the satisfactions deriving from sheer participation in the competitive activity that these satisfactions are virtually confined to a successful outcome. Through the same process, tension generated by the desire to win in a poker game is relieved by successfully dealing oneself four aces, or, when the cult of success has become completely dominant, by sagaciously shuffling the cards in a game of solitaire. The faint twinge of uneasiness in the last instance and the surreptitious nature of public delicts indicate clearly that the institutional rules of the game *are known* to those who evade them, but that the emotional supports of these rules are largely vitiated by cultural exaggeration of the success-goal.[6] They are microcosmic images of the social macrocosm.

Of course, this process is not restricted to the realm of sport. The process whereby exaltation of the end generates a *literal demoralization,* i.e., a deinstitutionalization, of the means is one which characterizes many[7] groups in which the two phases of the social structure are not highly integrated. The extreme emphasis upon the accumulation of wealth as a symbol of success[8] in our own society militates against the completely effective control of institutionally regulated modes of acquiring a fortune.[9] Fraud, corruption, vice, crime, in short, the entire catalogue of proscribed behavior, becomes increasingly common when the emphasis on the *culturally induced* success-goal becomes divorced from a coordinated institutional emphasis. This observation is of crucial theoretical importance in examining the doctrine that antisocial behavior most frequently derives from biological drives breaking through the restraints imposed by society. The difference is one between a strictly utilitarian interpretation which

[6] It is unlikely that interiorized norms are completely eliminated. Whatever residuum persists will induce personality tensions and conflict. The process involves a certain degree of ambivalence. A manifest rejection of the institutional norms is coupled with some latent retention of their emotional correlates. "Guilt feelings," "sense of sin," "pangs of conscience" are obvious manifestations of this unrelieved tension; symbolic adherence to the nominally repudiated values or rationalizations constitute a more subtle variety of tensional release.

[7] "Many," and not all, unintegrated groups, for the reason already mentioned. In groups where the primary emphasis shifts to institutional means, i.e., when the range of alternatives is very limited, the outcome is a type of ritualism rather than anomie.

[8] Money has several peculiarities which render it particularly apt to become a symbol of prestige divorced from institutional controls. As Simmel emphasized, money is highly abstract and impersonal. However acquired, through fraud or institutionally, it can be used to purchase the same goods and services. The anonymity of metropolitan culture, in conjunction with this peculiarity of money, permits wealth, the sources of which may be unknown to the community in which the plutocrat lives, to serve as a symbol of status.

[9] The emphasis upon wealth as a success symbol is possibly reflected in the use of the term "fortune" to refer to a stock of accumulated wealth. This meaning becomes common in the late sixteenth century (Spenser and Shakespeare). A similar usage of the Latin *fortuna* comes into prominence during the first century B.C. Both these periods were marked by the rise to prestige and power of the "bourgeoisie."

conceives man's ends as random and an analysis which finds these ends deriving from the basic values of the culture.[10]

Our analysis can scarcely stop at this juncture. We must turn to other aspects of the social structure if we are to deal with the social genesis of the varying rates and types of deviate behavior characteristic of different societies. Thus far, we have sketched three ideal types of social orders constituted by distinctive patterns of relations between culture ends and means. Turning from these types of *culture patterning,* we find five logically possible, alternative modes of adjustment or adaptation *by individuals* within the culture-bearing society or group.[11] These are schematically presented in the following table, where (+) signifies "acceptance," (-) signifies "elimination," and (±) signifies "rejection and substitution of new goals and standards."

		Culture goals	Institutionalized means
I.	Conformity	+	+
II.	Innovation	+	-
III.	Ritualism	-	+
IV.	Retreatism	-	-
V.	Rebellion[12]	±	±

Our discussion on the relation between these alternative responses and other phases of the social structure must be prefaced by the observation that persons may shift from one alternative to another as they engage in different social activities. These categories refer to role adjustments in specific situations, not to personality *in toto*. To treat the development of this process in various spheres of conduct would introduce a complexity unmanageable within the confines of this paper. For this reason, we shall be concerned primarily with economic activity in the broad sense, "the production, exchange, distribution, and consumption of goods and services" in our competitive society, wherein wealth has taken on a highly symbolic cast. Our task is to search out some of the factors which exert pressure upon individuals to engage in certain of these logically possible alternative responses. This choice, as we shall see, is far from random.

[10] See Kinglsey Davis, "Mental Hygiene and the Class Structure," *Psychiatry,* 1928, 1:esp. 62-63; Talcott Parsons, *The Structure of Social Action,* 59-60, New York, 1937.

[11] This is a level intermediate between the two planes distinguished by Edward Sapir; manely, culture patterns and personal habits systems. See his "Contribution of Psychiatry to an Understanding of Behavior in Society," *Amer. J. Sociol.,* 1937, 42:862-870.

[12] This fifth alternative is on a plane clearly different from that of the others. It represents a *transitional* response which seeks to *institutionalize* new procedures oriented toward revamped cultural goals shared by the members of the society. It thus involves efforts to *change* the existing structure rather than to perform accommodative actions *within* this structure, and introduces additional problems with which we are not at the moment concerned.

In every society, Adaptation I (conformity to both culture goals and means) is the most common and widely diffused. Were this not so, the stability and continuity of the society could not be maintained. The mesh of expectancies which constitutes every social order is sustained by the model behavior of its members falling within the first category. Conventional role behavior oriented toward the basic values of the group is the rule rather than the exception. It is this fact alone which permits us to speak of a human aggregate as comprising a group or society.

Conversely, Adaptation IV (rejection of goals and means) is the least common. Persons who "adjust" (or maladjust) in this fashion are, strictly speaking, *in* the society but not *of* it. Sociologically, these constitute the true "aliens." Not sharing the common frame of orientation, they can be included within the societal population merely in a fictional sense. In this category are *some* of the activities of psychotics, psychoneurotics, chronic autists, pariahs, outcasts, vagrants, vagabonds, tramps, chronic drunkards, and drug addicts.[13] These have relinquished, in certain spheres of activity, the culturally defined goals, involving complete aim-inhibition in the polar case, and their adjustments are not in accord with institutional norms. This is not to say that in some cases the source of their behavioral adjustments is not in part the very social structure which they have in effect repudiated nor that their very existence within a social area does not constitute a problem for the socialized population.

This mode of "adjustment" occurs, as far as structural sources are concerned, when both the culture goals and institutionalized procedures have been assimilated thoroughly by the individual and imbued with affect and high positive value, but where those institutionalized procedures which promise a measure of successful attainment of the goals are not available to the individual. In such instances, there results a twofold mental conflict insofar as the moral obligation for adopting institutional means conflicts with the pressure to resort to illegitimate means (which may attain the goal) and inasmuch as the individual is shut off from means which are both legitimate *and* effective. The competitive order is maintained, but the frustrated and handicapped individual who cannot cope with this order drops out. Defeatism, quietism, and resignation are manifested in escape mechanisms which ultimately lead the individual to "escape" from the requirements of the society. It is an expedient which arises from continued failure to attain the goal by legitimate measures and from an inability to adopt the illegitimate route because of internalized prohibitions and institutionalized compulsives, *during which process the supreme value of the success-goal has as yet not been renounced.* The conflict is resolved by eliminating *both* precipitating elements, the goals and means. The escape is complete, the conflict is eliminated, and the individual is associalized.

Be it noted that where frustration derives from the inaccessibility of effective institutional means for attaining economic or any other type of highly valued "success," that Adaptation II, III, and V (innovation, ritualism, and rebellion) are also

---

[13] Obviously, this is an elliptical statement. These individuals may maintain some orientation to the values of their particular differentiated groupings within the larger society or, in part, of the conventional society itself. Insofar as they do so, their conduct cannot be classified in the "passive rejection" category (IV). Nels Anderson's description of the behavior and attitudes of the bum, for example, can readily be recast in terms of our analytical scheme. See *The Hobo,* 93-98, *et passim,* Chicago, 1923.

possible. The result will be determined by the *particular* cultural background, involved. Inadequate socialization will result in the innovation response whereby the conflict and frustration are eliminated by relinquishing the institutional means and retaining the success-aspiration; an extreme assimilation of institutional demands will lead to ritualism wherein the goal is dropped as beyond one's reach but conformity to the mores persists; and rebellion occurs when emancipation from the reigning standards, due to frustration or to marginalist perspectives, leads to the attempt to introduce a "new social order."

Our major concern is with the illegitimacy adjustment. This involves the use of conventionally proscribed but frequently effective means of attaining at least the simulacrum of culturally defined success,—wealth, power, and the like. As we have seen, this adjustment occurs when the individual has assimilated the cultural emphasis on success without equally internalizing the morally prescribed norms governing means for its attainment. The question arises, Which phases of our social structure predispose toward this mode of adjustment? We may examine a concrete instance, effectively analyzed by Lohman,[14] which provides a clue to the answer. Lohman has shown that specialized areas of vice in the near north side of Chicago constitute a "normal" response to a situation where the cultural emphasis upon pecuniary success has been absorbed, but where there is little access to conventional and legitimate means for attaining such success. The conventional occupational opportunities of persons in this area are almost completely limited to manual labor. Given our cultural stigmatization of manual labor, and its correlate, the prestige of white collar work, it is clear that the result is a strain toward innovational practices. The limitation of opportunity to unskilled labor and the resultant low income cannot compete *in terms of conventional standards of achievement* with the high income from organized vice.

For our purposes, this situation involves two important features. First, such antisocial behavior is in a sense "called forth" by certain conventional values of the culture *and* by the class structure involving differential access to the approved opportunities for legitimate, prestige-bearing pursuit of the culture goals. The lack of high integration between the means-and-end elements of the cultural pattern and the particular class structure combine to favor a heightened frequency of antisocial conduct in such groups. The second consideration is of equal significance. Recourse to the first of the alternative responses, legitimate effort, is limited by the fact that actual advance toward desired success symbols through conventional channels is, despite our persisting open-class ideology,[15] relatively rare and difficult for those handicapped by little formal education and few economic resources. The dominant pressure of group

[14] Joseph D. Lohman, "The Participant Observer in Community Studies," *Amer. Sociol. Rev.*, 1937, 2:890-898.

[15] The shifting historical role of this ideology is a profitable subject for exploration. The "office-boy-to-president" stereotype was once in approximate accord with the facts. Such vertical mobility was probably more common then than now, when the class structure is more rigid. (See the following note.) The ideology largely persists, however, possibly because it still performs a useful function for maintaining the *status quo*. For insofar as it is accepted by the "masses," it constitutes a useful sop for those who might rebel against the entire structure, were this consoling hope removed. This ideology now serves to lessen the probability of Adaptation V. In short, the role of this notion has changed from that of an ideology, in Mannheim's sense.

standards of success is, therefore, on the gradual attenuation of legitimate, but by and large ineffective, strivings and the increasing use of illegitimate, but more or less effective, expedients of vice and crime. The cultural demands made on persons in this situation are incompatible. On the one hand, they are asked to orient their conduct toward the prospect of accumulating wealth and on the other, they are largely denied effective opportunities to do so institutionally. The consequences of such structural inconsistency are psychopathological personality, and/or antisocial conduct, and/or revolutionary activities. The equilibrium between culturally designated means and ends becomes highly unstable with the progressive emphasis on attaining the prestige-laden ends by any means whatsoever. Within this context, Capone represents the triumph of amoral intelligence over morally prescribed "failure," when the channels of vertical mobility are closed or narrowed[16] *in a society which places a high premium on economic affluence and social ascent for all its members.*[17]

This last qualification is of primary importance. It suggests that other phases of the social structure besides the extreme emphasis on pecuniary success must be considered if we are to understand the social sources of antisocial behavior. A high frequency of deviate behavior is not generated simply by "lack of opportunity" or by this exaggerated pecuniary emphasis. A comparatively rigidified class structure, a feudalistic or caste order, may limit such opportunities far beyond the point which obtains in our society today. It is only when a system of cultural values extols, virtually above all else, certain *common* symbols of success *for the population at large* while its social structure rigorously restricts or completely eliminates access to approved modes of acquiring these symbols *for a considerable part of the same population* that antisocial behavior ensues on a considerable scale. In other words, our egalitarian ideology denies by implication the existence of noncompeting groups and individuals in the pursuit of pecuniary success. The same body of success symbols is held to be desirable for all. These goals are held to *transcend class lines,* not to be bounded by

[16] There is a growing body of evidence, though none of it is clearly conclusive, to the effect that our class structure is becoming rigidified and that vertical mobility is declining. Taussig and Joslyn found that American business leaders are being *increasingly* recruited from the upper ranks of our society. The Lynds have also found a "diminished chance to get ahead." for the working classes in Middletown. Manifestly, these objective changes are not alone significant; the individual's subjective evaluation of the situation is a major determinant of the response. The extent to which this change in opportunity for social mobility has been recognized by the least advantaged classes is still conjectural, although the Lynds present some suggestive materials. The writer suggests that a case in point is the increasing frequency of cartoons which observe in a tragi-comic vein that "my old man says everybody can't be President. He says if ya can get three days a week steady on W.P.A. work ya ain't doin' so bad either." See F. W. Taussig and C. S. Joslyn, *American Business Leaders,* New York, 1932; R. S. and H.M. Lynd, *Middletown in Transition,* 67 ff., chap. 12, New York, 1937.

[17] The role of the Negro in this respect is of considerable theoretical interest. Certain elements of the Negro population have assimilated the dominant caste's values of pecuniary success and social advancement, but they also recognize that social ascent is at present restricted to their own caste almost exclusively. The pressures upon the Negro which would otherwise derive from the structural inconsistencies we have noticed are hence not identical with those upon lower class whites. See Kinglsey Davis, *op. cit.,* 63; John Dollard, *Caste and Class in a Southern Town,* 66 ff., New Haven, 1936; Donald Young, *American Minority Peoples,* 581, New York, 1932.

them, yet the actual social organization is such that there exist class differentials in the accessibility of these *common* success symbols. Frustration and thwarted aspiration lead to the search for avenues of escape from a culturally induced intolerable situation; or unrelieved ambition may eventuate in illicit attempts to acquire the dominant values.[18] The American stress on pecuniary success and ambitiousness for all thus invites exaggerated anxieties, hostilities, neuroses, and antisocial behavior.

This theoretical analysis may go far toward explaining the varying correlations between crime and poverty.[19] Poverty is not an isolated variable. It is one in a complex of interdependent social and cultural variables. When viewed in such a context, it represents quite different states of affairs. Poverty as such, and consequent limitation of opportunity, are not sufficient to induce a conspicuously high rate of criminal behavior. Even the often mentioned "poverty in the midst of plenty" will not necessarily lead to this result. Only insofar as poverty and associated disadvantages in competition for the culture values approved for *all* members of the society are linked with the assimilation of a cultural emphasis on monetary accumulation as a symbol of success is antisocial conduct a "normal" outcome. Thus, poverty is less highly correlated with crime in southeastern Europe than in the United States. The possibilities of vertical mobility in these European areas would seem to be fewer than in this country, so that neither poverty *per se* nor its association with limited opportunity is sufficient to account for the varying correlations. It is only when the full configuration is considered, poverty, limited opportunity, and a commonly shared system of success symbols, that we can explain the higher association between poverty and crime in our society than in others where rigidified class structure is coupled with *differential class symbols of achievement*.

In societies such as our own, then, the pressure of prestige-bearing success tends to eliminate the effective social constraint over means employed to this end. "The-end-justifies-the-means" doctrine becomes a guiding tenet for action when the cultural structure unduly exalts the end and the social organization unduly limits possible recourse to approved means. Otherwise put, this notion and associated behavior reflect a lack of cultural coordination. In international relations, the effects of this lack of integration are notoriously apparent. An emphasis upon national power is not readily coordinated with an inept organization of legitimate. i.e., internationally defined and accepted, means for attaining this goal. The result is a tendency toward the abrogation

[18] The psychical coordinates of these processes have been partly established by the experimental evidence concerning *Anspruchsniveaus* and levels of performance. See Kurt Lewin, *Vorsatz, Willie und Bedurfnis*, Berlin, 1926; N. F. Hoppe, "Erfolg und Misserfolg," *Psychol. Forschung*. 1930, 14:1-63; Jerome D. Frank, "Individual Differences in Certain Aspects of the Level of Aspiration," *Amer. J. Psychol.*, 1935, 47:119-128.

[19] Standard criminology texts summarize the data in this field. Our scheme of analysis may serve to resolve some of the theoretical contradictions which P. A. Sorkin indicates. For example, "not everywhere nor always do the poor show a greater proportion of crime . . . many poorer countries have had less crime than the richer countries. . . . The [economic] improvement in the second half of the nineteenth century, and the beginning of the twentieth, has not been followed by a decrease of crime." See his *Contemporary Sociological Theories*, 560-561, New York, 1928. The crucial point is, however, that poverty has varying social significance in different social structures, as we shall see. Hence, one would not expect a linear correlation between crime and poverty.

of international law, treaties become scraps of paper. "undeclared warfare" serves as a technical evasion, the bombing of civilian populations is rationalized,[20] just as the same societal situation induces the same sway of illegitimacy among individuals.

The social order we have described necessarily produces this "strain toward dissolution." The pressure of such an order is upon outdoing one's competitors. The choice of means within the ambit of institutional control will persist as long as the sentiments supporting a competitive system, i.e., deriving from the possibility of outranking competitors and hence enjoying the favorable response of others, are distributed throughout the entire system of activities and are not confined merely to the final result. A stable social structure demands a balanced distribution of affect among its various segments. When there occurs a shift of emphasis from the satisfactions deriving from competition itself to almost exclusive concern with successful competition, the resultant stress leads to the breakdown of the regulatory structure.[21] With the resulting attenuation of the institutional imperatives, there occurs an approximation of the situation erroneously held by utilitarians to be typical of society generally wherein calculations of advantage and fear of punishment are the sole regulating agencies. In such situations, as Hobbes observed, force and fraud come to constitute the sole virtues in view of their relative efficiency in attaining goals—which were for him of course, not culturally derived.

It should be apparent that the foregoing discussion is not pitched on a moralistic plane. Whatever the sentiments of the writer or reader concerning the ethical desirability of coordinating the means-and-goals phases of the social structure, one must agree that lack of such coordination leads to anomie. Insofar as one of the most general functions of social organization is to provide a basis for calculability and regularity of behavior, it is increasingly limited in effectiveness as these elements of the structure become dissociated. At the extreme, predictability virtually disappears and what may be properly termed cultural chaos or anomie intervenes.

This statement, being brief, is also incomplete. It has not included an exhaustive treatment of the various structural elements which predispose toward one rather than another of the alternative responses open to individuals; it has neglected, but not denied the relevance on the factors determining the specific incidence of these responses; it has not enumerated the various concrete responses which are constituted by combination of specific values of the analytical variables; it has omitted, or included only by implication, any consideration of the social functions performed by illicit responses; it has not tested the full explanatory power of the analytical scheme by examining a large number of group variations in the frequency of deviate and conformist behavior; it has not adequately dealt with rebellious conduct which seeks to refashion the social framework radically; it has not examined the relevance of cultural conflict for an analysis of culture-goal and institutional-means malintegration. It is suggested that these and related problems may be profitably analyzed by this scheme.

[20] See M. W. Royse, *Aerial Bombardment and the International Regulation of War*, New York, 1928.

[21] Since our primary concern is with the socio-cultural aspects of this problem, the psychological correlates have been only implicitly considered. See Karen Horney, *The Neurotic Personality of Our Time*, New York, 1937, for a psychological discussion of this process.

ARTICLE 11

Lower Class Culture as a Generating Milieu of Gang Delinquency

WALTER B. MILLER

THE ETIOLOGY OF DELINQUENCY has long been a controversial issue, and is particularly so at present. As new frames of reference for explaining human behavior have been added to traditional theories, some authors have adopted the practice of citing the major postulates of each school of thought as they pertain to delinquency, and going on to state that causality must be conceived in terms of the dynamic interaction of a complex combination of variables on many levels. The major sets of etiological factors currently adduced to explain delinquency are, in simplified terms, the physiological (delinquency results from organic pathology), the psychodynamic (delinquency is a "behavioral disorder" resulting primarily from emotional disturbance generated by a defective mother-child relationship), and the environmental (delinquency is the product of disruptive forces, "disorganization," in the actor's physical or social environment).

This paper selects one particular kind of "delinquency"[1]—law-violating acts committed by members of adolescent street corner groups in lower class communi-

Source: Miller, Walter B. "Lower Class Culture as a Generating Milieu of Gang Delinquency." *The Journal of Social Issues*, Vol. 14 (3) 1958: 5–19. Reprinted by permission of Plenum Publishing Corp.

[1] The complex issues involved in deriving a definition of "delinquency" cannot be discussed here. The term "delinquent" is used in this paper to characterize behavior or acts committed by individuals within specified age limits which if known to official authorities could result in legal action. The concept of a "delinquent" individual has little or no utility in the approach used here; rather specified types of *acts* which may be committed rarely or frequently by few or many individuals are characterized as "delinquent."

ties—and attempts to show that the dominant component of motivation underlying these acts consists in a directed attempt by the actor to adhere to forms of behavior, and to achieve standards of value as they are defined within that community. It takes as a premise that the motivation of behavior in this situation can be approached most productively by attempting to understand the nature of cultural forces impinging on the acting individual as they are perceived *by the actor himself*—although by no means only that segment of these forces of which the actor is consciously aware—rather than as they are perceived and evaluated from the reference position of another cultural system. In the case of "gang" delinquency, the cultural system which exerts the most direct influence on behavior is that of the lower class community itself—a long-established distinctively patterned tradition with an integrity of its own—rather than a so-called "delinquent subculture" which has arisen through conflict with middle class culture and is oriented to the deliberate violation of middle class norms.

The bulk of the substantive data on which the following material is based was collected in connection with a service-research project in the control of gang delinquency. During the service aspect of the project, which lasted for three years, seven trained social workers maintained contact with twenty-one corner group units in a "slum" district of a large eastern city for periods of time ranging from ten to thirty months. Groups were Negro and white, male and female, and in early, middle, and late adolescence. Over eight thousand pages of direct observational data on behavior patterns of group members and other community residents were collected; almost daily contact was maintained for a total time period of about thirteen worker years. Data include workers' contact reports, participant observation reports by the writer—a cultural anthropologist—and direct tape recordings of group activities and discussions.[2]

FOCAL CONCERNS OF LOWER CLASS CULTURE

There is a substantial segment of present-day American society whose way of life, values, and characteristic patterns of behavior are the product of a distinctive cultural system which may be termed "lower class". Evidence indicates that this cultural system is becoming increasingly distinctive, and that the size of the group which shares this tradition is increasing.[3] The lower class way of life, in common with that of all distinctive cultural groups, is characterized by a set of focal concerns—areas or issues

[2] A three year research project is being financed under National Institutes of Health Grant M-1414, and administered through the Boston University School of Social Work. The primary research effort has subjected all collected material to a uniform data-coding process. All information bearing on some seventy areas of behavior (behavior in reference to school, police, theft, assault, sex, collective athletics, etc.) is extracted from the records, recorded on coded data cards, and filed under relevant categories. Analysis of these data aims to ascertain the actual nature of customary behavior in these areas, and the extent to which the social work effort was able to effect behavioral changes.

[3] Between 40 and 60 per cent of all Americans are directly influenced by lower class vulture, with about 15 per cent, or twenty-five million, comprising the "hard-core" lower class group—defined primarily by its use of the "female-based" household as the basic form of child-rearing unit and of the "serial

TABLE 11.1   Focal Concerns of Lower Class Culture

Area	Perceived Alternatives (state, quality, condition)	
1. *Trouble:*	law-abiding behavior	law-violating behavior
2. *Toughness:*	physical prowess, skill: "masculinity" fearless, bravery, daring	weakness, ineptitude; effeminacy; timidity, cowardice, caution
3. *Smartness:*	ability to outsmart, dupe, "con": gaining money by "wits" shrewdness, adroitness in repartee	gullibility, "con-ability"; gaining money by hard work; slowness, dull-wittedness. verbal maladroitness
4. *Excitement:*	thrill; risk, danger; change, activity	boredom; "deadness," safeness; sameness, passivity
5. *Fate:*	favored by fortune, being "lucky"	ill-omened, being "unlucky"
6. *Autonomy:*	freedom from external constraint; freedom from superordinate authority; independence	presence of external constraint; presence of strong authority; dependency, being "cared for"

which command widespread and persistent attention and a high degree of emotional involvement. The specific concerns cited here, while by no means confined to the American lower classes, constitute a distinctive *patterning* of concerns which differs significantly, both in rank order and weighting from that of American middle class culture. The following table presents a highly schematic and simplified listing of six of the major concerns of lower class culture. Each is conceived as a "dimension" within which a fairly wide and varied range of alternative behavior patterns may be followed

---

monogamy" mating pattern as the primary form of marriage. The term "lower class culture" as used here refers most specifically to the way of life of the "hard core" group; systematic research in this area would probably reveal at least four to six major subtypes of lower class culture, for which the "concerns" presented here would be differently weighted, especially for those subtypes in which "law-abiding" behavior has a high overt valuation. It is impossible within the compass of this short paper to make the finer intracultural distinctions which a more accurate presentation would require.

by different individuals under different situations. They are listed roughly in order of the degree of *explicit* attention accorded, each, and in this sense represent a weighted ranking of concerns. The "perceived alternatives" represent polar positions which define certain parameters within each dimension. As will be explained in more detail, it is necessary in relating the influence of these "concerns" to the motivation of delinquent behavior to specify *which* of its aspects is oriented to, whether orientation is *overt* or *covert*, *positive* (conforming to or seeking the aspect), or *negative* (rejecting or seeking to avoid the aspect).

The concept "focal concern" is used here in preference to the concept "value" for several interrelated reasons: (1) It is more readily derivable from direct field observation. (2) It is descriptively neutral—permitting independent consideration of positive and negative valences as varying under different conditions, whereas "value" carries a built-in positive valence. (3) It makes possible more refined analysis of subcultural differences, since it reflects actual behavior, whereas "value" tends to wash out intracultural differences since it is colored by notions of the "official" ideal.

Trouble: Concern over "trouble" is a dominant feature of lower class culture. The concept has various shades of meaning; "trouble" in one of its aspects represents a situation or a kind of behavior which results in unwelcome or complicating involvement with official authorities or agencies of middle class society. "Getting into trouble" and "staying out of trouble" represent major issues for male and female, adults and children. For men "trouble" frequently involves fighting or sexual adventures while drinking: for women, sexual involvement with disadvantageous consequences. Expressed desire to avoid behavior which violates moral or legal norms is often based less on an explicit commitment to "official" moral or legal standards than on a desire to avoid "getting into trouble," e.g., the complicating consequences of the action.

The dominant concern over "trouble" involves a distinction of critical importance for the lower class community—that between "law -abiding" and "non law abiding" behavior. There is a high degree of sensitivity as to where each person stands in relation to these two classes of activity. Whereas in the middle class community a major dimension for evaluating a person's status is "achievement" and its external symbols, in the lower class, personal status is very frequently gauged along the law abiding -non law abiding dimension. A mother will evaluate the suitability of her daughter's boyfriend less on the basis of his achievement potential than on the basis of his innate "trouble" potential. This sensitive awareness of the opposition of "trouble-producing" and "non-trouble-producing" behavior represents both a major basis for deriving status distinctions, and an internalized conflict potential for the individual.

As in the case of other focal concerns, which of two perceived alternatives—"law-abiding" or "non law abiding"—is valued varies according to the individual and the circumstances; in many instances there is an overt commitment to the "law-abiding" alternative, but a convert commitment to the "non-law-abiding." In certain situations, "getting into trouble" is overtly recognized as prestige-conferring: for example, membership in certain adult and adolescent primary groupings ("gangs") is contingent on having demonstrated an explicit commitment to the law-violating alternative. It is most important to note that the choice between "law abiding" and "non law abiding" behavior is still a choice *within* lower class culture; the distinction between the policeman and the criminal, the outlaw and the sheriff, involves primarily this one dimension; in other respects they have a high community of interests. Not infrequently brothers raised in an identical cultural milieu will become police and criminals respectively.

For a substantial segment of the lower class population "getting into trouble" is not in itself overtly defined as prestige-conferring, but is implicitly recognized as a means to other valued ends, e.g., the covertly valued desire to be "cared for" and subject to external constraint, or the overtly valued state of excitement or risk. Very frequently "getting into trouble" is multi-functional, and achieves several sets of valued ends.

Toughness: The concept of 'toughness" in lower class culture represents a compound combination of qualities or states. Among its most important components are physical prowess, evidenced both by demonstrated possession of strength and endurance and athletic skill; "masculinity," symbolized by a distinctive complex of acts and avoidances (bodily tatooing: absence of sentimentality; nonconcern with "art" "literature," conceptualization of women as conquest objects, etc); and bravery in the face of physical threat. The model for the "tough guy"—hard, fearless, undemonstrative, skilled in physical combat—is represented by the movie gangster of the thirties, the "private eye," and the movie cowboy.

The genesis of the intense concern over "toughness" in lower class culture is probably related to the fact that a significant proportion of lower class males are reared in a predominantly female household, and lack of consistently present male figure with whom to identify and from whom to learn essential components of a "male" role. Since women serve as a primary object of identification during pre-adolescent years, the almost obsessive lower class concern with "masculinity" probably resembles a type of compulsive reaction-formation. A concern over homosexuality runs like a persistent thread through lower class culture. This is manifested by the institutionalized practice of baiting "queers," often accompanied by violent physical attacks, an expressed contempt for "softness" or frills, and the use of the local term for "homosexual" as a generalized pejorative epithet (e.g., higher class individuals or upwardly mobile peers are frequently characterized as "fags" or "queers"). The distinction between "overt" and "covert" orientation to aspects of an area of concern is especially important in regard to "toughness." A positive overt evaluation of behavior defined as "effeminate" would be out of the question for a lower class male; however, built into lower class culture is a range of devices which permit men to adopt behaviors and concerns which in other cultural milieux fall within the province of women, and at the same time to be defined as "tough" and manly. For example, lower class men can be professional short-order cooks in a diner and still be regarded as "tough." The highly intimate circumstances of the street corner gang involve the recurrent expression of strongly affectionate feelings towards other men. Such expressions, however, are disguised as their opposite, taking the form of ostensibly aggressive verbal and physical interaction (kidding, "ranking," roughhousing, etc.).

Smartness: "Smartness," as conceptualized in lower class culture, involves the capacity to outsmart, outfox, outwit, dupe, "take," "con" another or others, and the concomitant capacity to avoid being outwitted, "taken" or duped oneself. In its essence, smartness involves the capacity to achieve a valued entity—material goods, personal status—through a maximum use of mental agility and a minimum use of physical effort. This capacity has an extremely long tradition in lower class culture, and is highly valued. Lower class culture can be characterized as "non-intellectual" only if intellectualism is defined specifically in terms of control over a particular body of formally learned knowledge involving "culture" (art, literature, "good" music, etc.), a generalized perspective on the past and present conditions of our own and other societies, and other areas of knowledge imparted by formal education institutions. This particular type of mental attainment is, in general, overtly disvalued and frequently associated with effeminancy; "smartness" in the lower class sense, however, is highly valued.

The lower class child learns and practices the use of this skill in the street corner situation. Individuals continually practice duping and outwitting one another through recurrent card games and other forms of gambling, mutual exchanges of insults, and "testing" for mutual "conability". Those who demonstrate competence in this skill are accorded considerable prestige. Leadership roles in the corner group are frequently allocated according to demonstrated capacity in the two areas of "smartness" and "toughness"; the ideal leader combines both, but the "smart" leader is often accorded more prestige than the "tough" one—reflecting a general lower class respect for "brains" in the "smartness" sense.[4]

The model of the "smart" person is represented in popular media by the card shark, the professional gambler, the "con" artist, the promoter. A conceptual distinction is made between two kinds of people: "suckers," easy marks, "lushes," dupes, who work for their money and are legitimate targets of exploitation; and sharp operators, the "brainy" ones, who live by their wits and "getting" from the suckers by mental adroitness.

Involved in the syndrome of capacities related to "smartness" is a dominant emphasis in lower class culture on ingenious aggressive repartee. This skill learned and practiced in the context of the corner group, ranges in form from the widely prevalent semi-ritualized teasing, kidding, razzing, "ranking," so characteristic of male peer group interaction, to the highly ritualized type of mutual insult interchange known as "the dirty dozens," "the dozens," "playing house," and other terms. This highly patterned cultural form is practiced on its most advanced level in adult male Negro society, but less polished variants are found throughout lower class culture—practiced, for example, by white children, male and female, as young as four or five. In essence, "doin' the dozens" involves two antagonists who vie with each other in the exchange of increasingly inflammatory insults, with incestuous and perverted sexual relations with the mother a dominant theme. In this form of insult interchange, as well as on other less ritualized occasions for joking, semiserious, and serious mutual invective, a very high premium is placed on ingenuity, hair-trigger responsiveness, inventiveness, and the acute exercise of mental faculties.

Excitement: For many lower class individuals the rhythm of life fluctuates between periods of relatively routine or repetitive activity and sought situations of great

----

[4] The "brains-brawn" set of capacities are often paired in lower class folk lore or accounts of lower class life, e.g., "Brer Fox" and "Brer Bear" in the Uncle Remus stories, or George and Lennie in "Of Mice and Men."

emotional stimulation. Many of the most characteristic features of lower class life are related to the search for excitement or "thrill." Involved here are the highly prevalent use of alcohol by both sexes and the widespread use of gambling of all kinds—playing the numbers, betting on horse races, dice, cards. The quest for excitement finds what is perhaps its most vivid expression in the highly patterned practice of the recurrent "night on the town." This practice, designated by various terms in different areas ("honky-tonkin'"; "goin' out on the town"; "bar hoppin'"), involves a patterned set of activities in which alcohol, music, and sexual adventuring are major components . A group or individual sets out to "make the rounds" of various bars or night clubs. Drinking continues progressively throughout the evening. Men seek to "pick up" women, and women play the risky game of entertaining sexual advances. Fights between men involving women, gambling, and claims of physical prowess, in various combinations, are frequent consequences of a night of making the rounds. The explosive potential of this type of adventure with sex and aggression, frequently leading to "trouble," is semi-explicitly sought by the individual. Since there is always a good likelihood that being out on the town will eventuate in fights, etc., the practice involves elements of sought risk and desired danger.

Counterbalancing the "flirting with danger" aspect of the "excitement" concern is the prevalence in lower class culture of other well established patterns of activity which involve long periods of relative inaction, or passivity. The term "hanging out" in lower class culture refers to extended periods of standing around, often with peer mates, doing what is defined as "nothing," "shooting the breeze," etc. A definite periodicity exists in the pattern of activity relating to the two aspects of the "excite-ment" dimension. For many lower class individuals the venture into the high risk world of alcohol, sex, and fighting occurs regularly once a week, with interim periods devoted to accommodating to possible consequences of these periods, along with recurrent resolves not to become so involved again.

Fate: Related to the quest for excitement is the concern with fate, fortune, or luck. Here also a distinction is made between two states—being "lucky" or "in luck," and being unlucky or jinxed. Many lower class individuals feel that their lives are subject to a set of forces over which they have relatively little control. These are not directly equated with the supernatural forces of formally organized religion, but relate more to a concept of "destiny," or man as a pawn of magical powers. Not infrequently this often implicit world view is associated with a conception of the ultimate futility of directed effort towards a goal: if the cards are right, or the dice good to you, or if your lucky number comes up, things will go your way; if luck is against you, it's not worth trying. The concept of performing semi-magical rituals so that one's "luck will change" is prevalent; one hopes that as a result he will move from the state of being "unlucky" to that of being "lucky." The element of fantasy plays an important part in this area. Related to and complementing the notion that "only suckers work" (Smartness) is the idea that once things start going your way, relatively independent of your own effort, all good things will come to you. Achieving great material rewards (big cars, big houses, a roll of cash to flash in a fancy night club), valued in lower class as well as in other parts of American culture, is a recurrent theme in lower class fantasy and folk lore; the cocaine dreams of Willie the Weeper or Minnie the Moocher present the components of this fantasy in vivid detail.

The prevalence in the lower class community of many forms of gambling, mentioned in connection with the "excitement" dimension, is also relevant here. Through cards and pool which involve skill, and thus both "toughness" and "smartness"; or through race horse betting, involving "smartness"; or through playing the numbers, involving predominantly "luck," one may make a big killing with a minimum of directed and persistent effort within conventional occupational channels. Gambling in its many forms illustrates the fact that many of the persistent features of lower class culture are multi-functional—serving a range of desired ends at the same time. Describing some of the incentives behind gambling has involved mention of all of the focal concerns cited so far—Toughness, Smartness, and Excitement, in addition to Fate.

Autonomy: The extent and nature of control over the behavior of the individual—an important concern in most cultures—has a special significance and is distinctively patterned in lower class culture. The discrepancy between what is overtly valued and what is covertly sought is particularly striking in this area. On the overt level there is a strong and frequently expressed resentment of the idea of external controls, restrictions on behavior, and unjust or coercive authority. "No one's gonna push *me* around," or "I'm gonna tell him he can take the job and shove it . . ." are commonly expressed sentiments. Similar explicit attitudes are maintained to systems of behavior-restricting rules, insofar as these are perceived as representing the injunctions, and bearing the sanctions of superordinate authority. In addition, in lower class culture a close conceptual connection is made between "authority" and "nurturance." To be restrictively or firmly controlled is to be cared for. Thus the overtly negative evaluation of superordinate authority frequently extends as well to nurturance, care, or protection. The desire for personal independence is often expressed in such terms as "I don't need *nobody* to take care of me. I can take care of myself!" Actual patterns of behavior, however, reveal a marked discrepancy between expressed sentiment and what is covertly valued. Many lower class people appear to seek out highly restrictive social environments wherein stringent external controls are maintained over their behavior. Such institutions as the armed forces, the mental hospital, the disciplinary school, the prison or correctional institution, provide environments which incorporate a strict and detailed set of rules defining and limiting behavior, and reinforced by an authority system which controls and applies coercive sanctions for deviance from these rules. While under the jurisdiction of such systems, the lower class person generally expresses to his peers continual resentment of the coercive, unjust, and arbitrary exercise of authority. Having been released, or having escaped from these milieux, however, he will often act in such a way as to insure recommitment, or choose recommitment voluntarily after a temporary period of "freedom."

Lower class patients in mental hospitals will exercise considerable ingenuity to insure continued commitment while voicing the desire to get out; delinquent boys will frequently "run" from a correctional institution to activate efforts to return them; to be caught and returned means that one is cared for. Since "being controlled" is equated with "being cared for," attempts are frequently made to "test" the severity or strictness of the superordinate authority to see if it remains firm. If intended or executed rebellion produces swift and firm punitive sanctions, the individual is reassured, at the same time that he is complaining bitterly at the injustice of being caught and punished. Some environmental milieux, having been tested in this fashion for the "firmness" of their coercive sanctions, are rejected ostensibly for being too strict, actually for not being strict enough. This is frequently so in the case of "problematic" behavior by lower class youngsters in the public schools, which generally cannot command the coercive controls implicitly sought by the individual.

A similar discrepancy between what is overtly and covertly desired is found in the area of dependence-independence. The pose of tough rebellious independence often assumed by the lower class person frequently conceals powerful dependency cravings. These are manifested primarily by obliquely expressed resentment when "care" is not forthcoming rather than by expressed satisfaction when it is. The concern over autonomy-dependency is related both to "trouble" and "fate." Insofar as the lower class individual feels that his behavior is controlled by forces which often propel him into "trouble" in the face of an explicit determination to avoid it, there is an implied appeal to "save me from myself." A solution appears to lie in arranging things so that his behavior will be coercively restricted by an externally imposed set of controls strong enough to forcibly restrain his inexplicable inclination to get in trouble. The periodicity observed in connection with the "excitement" dimension is also relevant here; after involvement in trouble-producing behavior (assault, sexual adventure, a "drunk"), the individual will actively seek a locus of imposed control (his wife, prison, a restrictive job); after a given period of subjection to this control, resentment against it mounts, leading to a "break-away" and a search for involvement in further "trouble."

FOCAL CONCERNS OF THE LOWER CLASS ADOLESCENT STREET CORNER GROUP

The one-sex peer group is a highly prevalent and significant structural form in the lower class community. There is a strong probability that the prevalence and stability of this type of unit is directly related to the prevalence of a stabilized type of lower class child-rearing unit—the "female-based" household. This is a nuclear kin unit in which a male parent is either absent from the household, present only sporadically, or, when present, only minimally or inconsistently involved in the support and rearing of children. This unit usually consists of one or more females of child-bearing age and their offspring. The females are frequently related to one another by blood or marriage ties, and the unit often includes two or more generations of women, e.g., the mother and/or aunt of the principal child-bearing female.

The nature of social groupings in the lower class community may be clarified if we make the assumption that it is the *one-sex peer unit* rather than the two-parent family unit which represents the most significant relational unit for both sexes in lower class communities. Lower class society may be pictured as comprising a set of age-graded one-sex groups which constitute the major psychic focus and reference group for those over twelve or thirteen. Men and women of mating age leave these groups periodically to form temporary marital alliances, but these lack stability, and after varying periods of "trying out" the two-sex family arrangement, they gravitate back to the more "comfortable" one-sex grouping, whose members exert strong pressure on the individual *not* to disrupt the group by adopting a two-sex household pattern of life.[5] Membership in a stable and solidary peer unit is vital to the lower class individual precisely to the extent to which a range of essential functions—psychological, educational, and others, are not provided by the "family" unit.

The adolescent street corner group represents the adolescent variant of this lower class structural form. What has been called the "delinquent gang" is one subtype of this form, defined on the basis of frequency of participation in law-violating activity; this subtype should not be considered a legitimate unit of study per se, but rather as one particular variant of the adolescent street corner group. The "hanging" peer group is a unit of particular importance for the adolescent male. In many cases it is the most stable and solidary primary group he has ever belonged to; for boys reared in female-based households the corner group provides the first real opportunity to learn essential aspects of the male role in the context of peers facing similar problems of sex-role identification.

The form and functions of the adolescent corner group operate as a selective mechanism in recruiting members. The activity patterns of the group require a high level of intragroup solidarity; individual members must possess a good capacity for subordinating individual desires to general group interests as well as the capacity for intimate and persisting interaction. Thus highly "disturbed" individuals, or those who cannot tolerate consistently imposed sanctions on "deviant" behavior cannot remain accepted members; the group itself will extrude those whose behavior exceeds limits defined as "normal." This selective process produces a type of group whose members possess to an unusually high degree both the *capacity* and *motivation* to conform to perceived cultural norms, so that the nature of the system of norms and values oriented to is a particularly influential component of motivation.

Focal concerns of the male adolescent corner group are those of the general cultural milieu in which it functions. As would be expected, the relative weighting and importance of these concerns pattern somewhat differently for adolescents than for adults. The nature of this patterning centers around two additional "concerns" of particular importance to this group—concern with "belonging," and with "status." These may be conceptualized as being on a higher level of abstraction than concerns previously cited, since "status" and "belonging" are achieved *via* cited concern areas of Toughness, etc.

Belonging: Since the corner group fulfills essential functions for the individual,

---

[5] Further data on the female-based household unit (estimated as comprising about 15 per cent of all American "families") and the role of one-sex groupings in lower class culture are contained in Walter B. Miller," Implications of Urban Lower Class Culture for Social Work. *Social Service Review*, 1959, *33*, No. 3.

being a member in good standing of the group is of vital importance for its members. A continuing concern over who is "in" and who is not involves the citation and detailed discussion of highly refined criteria for "in-group" membership. The phrase "he hangs with us" means "he is accepted as a member in good standing by current consensus"; conversely, "he don't hang with us" means he is not so accepted. One achieves "belonging" primarily by demonstrating knowledge of and a determination to adhere to the system of standards and valued qualities defined by the group. One maintains membership by acting in conformity with valued aspects of Toughness, Smartness, Autonomy, etc. In those instances where conforming to norms of this reference group at the same time violates norms of other reference groups (e.g., middle class adults, institutional "officials"), immediate reference group norms are much more compelling since violation risks invoking the group's most powerful sanction: exclusion.

Status: In common with most adolescents in American society, the lower class corner group manifests a dominant concern with "status." What differentiates this type of group from others, however, is the particular set of criteria and weighting thereof by which "status" is defined. In general, status is achieved and maintained by demonstrated possession of the valued qualities of lower class culture—Toughness, Smartness, expressed resistance to authority, daring, etc. It is important to stress once more that the individual orients to these concerns *as they are defined within lower class society;* e.g., the status-conferring potential of "smartness" in the sense of scholastic achievement generally ranges from negligible to negative.

The concern with "status" is manifested in a variety of ways. Intra-group status is a continued concern, and is derived and tested constantly by means of a set of status-ranking activities; the intra-group "pecking order" is constantly at issue. One gains status within the group by demonstrated superiority in Toughness (physical prowess, bravery, skill in athletics and games such as pool and cards), Smartness (skill in repartee, capacity to "dupe" fellow group members), and the like. The term "ranking," used to refer to the pattern if intra-group aggressive repartee, indicates awareness of the fact that this is one device for establishing the intra-group status hierarchy.

The concern over status in the adolescent corner group involves in particular the component of "adultness," the intense desire to be seen as "grown-up," and a corresponding aversion to "kid-stuff." "Adult" status is defined less in terms of the assumption of "adult" responsibility than in terms of certain external symbols of adult status—a car, ready cash, and, in particular, a perceived "freedom" to drink, smoke, and gamble as one wishes and to come and go without external restrictions. The desire to be seen as "adult" is often a more significant component of much involvement in illegal drinking, gambling, and automobile driving than the explicit enjoyment of these acts as such.

The intensity of the corner group member's desire to be seen as "adult" is sufficiently great that he feels called upon to demonstrate qualities associated with adultness (Toughness, Smartness, Autonomy) to a much greater degree than a lower class adult. This means that he will seek out and utilize those avenues to these qualities which he perceives as available with greater intensity than an adult and less regard for the "legitimacy." In this sense the adolescent variant of lower class culture represents a maximization or an intensified manifestation of many of its most characteristic features.

Concern over status is also manifested in reference to other street corner groups. The term "rep" used in this regard is especially significant, and has broad connotations. In its most frequent and explicit connotation, "rep" refers to the "toughness" of the corner group as a whole relative to that of other groups; a "pecking order" also exists among the several corner groups in a give interactional area, and there is a common perception that the safety or security of the group and all its members depends on maintaining a solid "rep" for toughness vis-a-vis other groups. This motive is most frequently advanced as a reason for involvement in gang fights: "We *can't* chicken out on this; our rep would be shot!"; this implies that the group would be relegated to the bottom of the status ladder and become a helpless and recurrent target of external attack.

On the other hand, there is implicit in the concept of "rep" the recognition that "rep" has or may have a dual basis—corresponding to the two aspects of the "trouble" dimension. It is recognized that group as well as individual status can be based on both "law-abiding" and "law-violating" behavior. The situational resolution of the persisting conflict between the "law-abiding" and "law-violating" bases of status comprises a vital set of dynamics in determining whether a "delinquent" mode of behavior will be adopted by a group, under what circumstances, and how persistently. The determinants of this choice are evidently highly complex and fluid, and rest on a range of factors including the presence and perceptual immediacy of different community reference-group loci (e.g., professional criminals, police, clergy, teachers, settlement house workers), the personality structures and "needs" of group members, the presence in the community of social work, recreation, or educational programs which can facilitate utilization of the "law-abiding" basis of status, and so on.

What remains constant is the critical importance of "status" both for the members of the group as individuals and for the group as a whole insofar as members perceive their individual destinies as linked to the destiny of the group, and the fact that action geared to attain status is much more acutely oriented to the fact of status itself than to the legality or illegality, morality or immorality of the means used to achieve it.

LOWER CLASS CULTURE AND THE MOTIVATION OF DELINQUENT BEHAVIOR

The customary set of activities of the adolescent street corner group includes activities which are in violation of laws and ordinances of the legal code. Most of these center around assault and theft of various types (the gang fight; auto theft; assault on an individual; petty pilfering and shoplifting; "mugging"; pocketbook theft). Members of street corner gangs are well aware of the law-violating nature of these acts; they are not psychopaths, nor physically or mentally "defective"; in fact, since the corner group supports and enforces a rigorous set of standards which demand a high degree of fitness and personal competence, it tends to recruit from the most "able" members of the community.

Why, then, is the commission of crimes a customary feature of gang activity? The most general answer is that the commission of crimes by members of adolescent street corner groups is motivated primarily by the attempt to achieve ends, states, or conditions which are valued, and to avoid those that are disvalued within their most meaningful cultural milieu, through those culturally available avenues which appear as the most feasible means of attaining those ends.

The operation of these influences is well illustrated by the gang fight—a prevalent and characteristic type of corner group delinquency. This type of activity comprises a highly stylized and culturally patterned set of sequences. Although details vary under different circumstances, the following events are generally included. A member or several members of group A "trespass" on the claimed territory of group B. While there they commit an act or acts which group B defines as a violation of its rightful privileges, an affront to their honor, or a challenge to their "rep." Frequently this act involves advances to a girl associated with group B; it may occur at a dance or party; sometimes the mere act of "trespass" is seen as deliberate provocation. Members of group B then assault members of group A, if they are caught while still in B's territory. Assaulted members of group A return to their "home" territory and recount to members of their group details of the incident, stressing the insufficient nature of the provocation ("I just *looked* at her! Hardly even said anything!"), and the unfair circumstances of the assault ("About *twenty* guys jumped just the *two* of us!"). The highly colored account is acutely inflammatory; group A, perceiving its honor violated and its "rep" threatened, feels obligated to retaliate in force. Sessions of detailed planning now occur; allies are recruited if the size of group A and its potential allies appears to necessitate larger numbers; strategy is plotted, and messengers dispatched. Since the prospect of a gang fight is frightening to even the "toughest" group members, a constant rehearsal of the provocative incident or incidents and the essentially evil nature of the opponents accompany the planning process to bolster possibly weakening motivation to fight. The excursion into "enemy" territory sometimes results in a full scale fight: more often group B cannot be found, or the police appear and stop the fight, "tipped off" by an anonymous informant. When this occurs, group members express disgust and disappointment; secretly there is much relief; their honor has been avenged without incurring injury; often the anonymous tipster is a member of one of the involved groups.

The basic elements of this type of delinquency are sufficiently stabilized and recurrent as to constitute an essentially ritualized pattern, resembling both in structure and expressed motives for action classic forms such as the European "duel," the American Indian tribal war, and the Celtic clan feud. Although the arousing and "acting out" of individual aggressive emotions are inevitably involved in the gang fight, neither its form nor motivational dynamics can be adequately handled within a predominantly personality-focused frame of reference.

It would be possible to develop in considerable detail the processes by which the commission of a range of illegal acts is either explicitly supported by, implicitly demanded by, or not materially inhibited by factors relating to the focal concerns of lower class culture. In place of such a development, the following three statements condense in general terms the operation of these processes:

1. Following cultural practices which comprise essential elements of the total life pattern of lower class culture automatically violates certain legal norms.

2. In instances where alternate avenues to similar objectives are available, the non-law-abiding avenue frequently provides a relatively greater and more immediate return for a relatively smaller investment of energy.

3. The "demanded" response to certain situations recurrently engendered within lower class culture involves the commission of illegal acts.

The primary thesis of this paper is that the dominant component of the motivation of "delinquent behavior" engaged in by members of lower class corner groups involves a positive effort to achieve states, conditions, or qualities valued within the actor's most significant cultural milieu. If "conformity to immediate reference group values" is the major component of motivation of "delinquent" behavior by gang members, why is such behavior frequently referred to as negativistic, malicious, or rebellious? Albert Cohen, for example, in *Delinquent Boys* (Glencoe: Free Press, 1955) describes behavior which violates school rules as comprising elements of "active spite and malice, contempt and ridicule, challenge and defiance." He ascribes to the gang "keen delight in terrorizing 'good' children, and in general making themselves obnoxious to the virtuous." A recent national conference on social work with "hard-to-reach" groups characterized lower class corner groups as "youth groups in conflict with the culture of their (*sic*) communities." Such characterizations are obviously the result of taking the middle class community and its institutions as an implicit point of reference.

A large body of systematically inter-related attitudes, practices, behaviors, and values characteristic of lower class culture are designed to support and maintain the basic features of the lower class way of life. In areas where these differ from features of middle class culture, action oriented to the achievement and maintenance of the lower class system may violate norms of middle class culture and be perceived as deliberately non-conforming or malicious by an observer strongly cathected to middle class norms. This does not mean, however, that violation of the middle class norm is the dominant component of motivation; it is a by-product of action primarily oriented to the lower class system. The standards of lower class culture cannot be seen merely as a reverse function of middle class culture—as middle class standards "turned upside down"; lower class culture is a distinctive tradition many centuries old with an integrity of its own.

From the viewpoint of the acting individual, functioning within a field of well-structured cultural forces, the relative impact of "conforming" and "rejective" elements in the motivation of gang delinquency is weighted preponderantly on the conforming side. Rejective or rebellious elements are inevitably involved, but their influence during the actual commission of delinquent acts is relatively small compared to the influence of pressures to achieve what is valued by the actor's most immediate reference groups. Expressed awareness by the actor of the element of rebellion often represents only that aspect of motivation of which he is explicitly conscious; the deepest and most compelling components of motivation—adherence to highly meaningful group standards of Toughness, Smartness, Excitement, etc.—are often unconsciously patterned. No cultural pattern as well-established as the practice of illegal acts by members of lower class corner groups could persist if buttressed primarily by negative, hostile, or rejective motives; its principal motivational support, as in the case of any persisting cultural tradition, derives from a positive effort to achieve what is valued within that tradition, and to conform to its explicit and implicit norms.

A Sociological Theory of Criminal Behavior

EDWIN H. SUTHERLAND
DONALD R. CRESSEY

THE PROBLEM FOR CRIMINOLOGICAL THEORY

If criminology is to be scientific, the heterogeneous collection of multiple factors known to be associated with crime and criminality must be organized and integrated by means of explanatory theory which has the same characteristics as the scientific theory in other fields of study. That is, the conditions which are said to cause crime should be present when crime is present, and they should be absent when crime is absent. Such a theory or body of theory would stimulate, simplify, and give direction to criminological research, and it would provide a framework for understanding the significance of much of the knowledge acquired about crime and criminality in the past. Furthermore, it would be useful in minimizing crime rates, provided it could be "applied" in much the same way that the engineer "applies" the scientific theories of the physicist.

There are two complementary procedures which may be used to put order into criminological knowledge. The first is logical abstraction. Blacks, males, urban-dwellers, and young adults all have comparatively high crime rates. What do they have in common that results in these high crime rates? Research studies have shown that criminal behavior is associated, in greater or lesser degree, with such social and personal pathologies as poverty, bad housing, slum-residence, lack of recreational facilities, inadequate and demoralized families, mental retardation, emotional instability, and other traits and conditions. What do these conditions have in common which

Source: Sutherland, Edwin H. and Donald R. Cressey, in *Criminology* (10th Ed.) Philadelphia: J.B. Lippincott Co., 1978: 77–83. Reprinted by permission.

apparently produces excessive criminality? Research studies have also demonstrated that many persons with those pathological traits and conditions do not commit crimes and that persons in the upper socio-economic class frequently violate the law, although they are not in poverty, do not lack recreational facilities, and are not mentally retarded or emotionally unstable. Obviously, it is not the conditions or traits themselves which cause crime, for the conditions are sometimes present when criminality does not occur, and they also are sometimes absent when criminality does occur. A generalization about crime and criminal behavior can be reached by logically abstracting the conditions and processes which are common to the rich and the poor, the males and the females, the blacks and the whites, the urban- and the rural-dwellers, the young adults and the old adults, and the emotionally stable and the emotionally unstable who commit crimes.

In developing such generalizations, criminal behavior must be precisely defined and carefully distinguished from noncriminal behavior. Criminal behavior is human behavior, and has much in common with noncriminal behavior. An explanation of criminal behavior should be consistent with a general theory of other human behavior, but the conditions and processes said to produce crime and criminality should be specific. Many things which are necessary for behavior are not important to criminality. Respiration, for instance, is necessary for any behavior, but the respiratory process cannot be used in an explanation of criminal behavior, for it does not differentiate criminal behavior from noncriminal behavior.

The second procedure for putting order into criminological knowledge is differentiation of levels of analysis. The explanation or generalization must be limited, largely in terms of chronology, and in this way held at a particular level. For example, when Renaissance physicists stated the law of falling bodies, they were not concerned with the reasons why a body began to fall except as this might affect the initial momentum. Galileo did not study the "traits" of falling objects themselves, as Aristotle might have done. Instead, he noted the relationship of the body to its environment while it was falling freely or rolling down an inclined plane, and it made no difference to his generalization whether a body began to fall because it was dropped from the hand of an experimenter or because it rolled off the ledge of a bridge due to vibration caused by a passing vehicle. Also, a round object would roll off the bridge more readily than a square object, but this fact was not significant for the law of falling bodies. Such facts were considered as existing on a different level of explanation and were irrelevant to the problem of explaining the behavior of falling bodies.

Much of the confusion regarding crime and criminal behavior stems from a failure to define and hold constant the level at which they are explained. By analogy, many criminologists and others concerned with understanding and defining crime would attribute some degree of causal power to the "roundness" of the object in the above illustration. However, consideration of time sequences among the conditions associated with crime and criminality may lead to simplicity of statement. In the heterogeneous collection of factors associated with crime and criminal behavior, one factor often occurs prior to another (in much the way that "roundness" occurs prior to "vibration," and "vibration" occurs prior to "rolling off a bridge"), but a theoretical statement can be made without referring to those early factors. By holding the analysis at one level, the early factors are combined with or differentiated from later factors or conditions, thus reducing the number of variables which must be considered in a theory.

A motion picture made several years ago showed two boys engaged in a minor theft; they ran when they were discovered; one boy had longer legs, escaped, and became a priest; the other had shorter legs, was caught, committed to a reformatory, and became a gangster. In this comparison, the boy who became a criminal was differentiated from the one who did not become a criminal by the length of his legs. But "length of legs" need not be considered in a criminological theory because it is obvious that this condition does not determine criminality and has no necessary relation to criminality. In the illustration, the differential in the length of the boys' legs apparently was significant to subsequent criminality or noncriminality only to the degree that it determined the subsequent experiences and associations of the two boys. It is in these experiences and associations, then, that the mechanisms and processes which are important to criminality or noncriminality are to be found.

TWO TYPES OF EXPLANATIONS OF CRIMINAL BEHAVIOR

Scientific explanations of criminal behavior may be stated either in terms of the processes which are operating at the moment of the occurrence of crime or in terms of the processes operating in the earlier history of the criminal. In the first case, the explanation may be called "mechanistic," "situational," or "dynamic"; in the second, "historical" or "developmental." Both types of explanation are desirable. The mechanistic type of explanation has been favored by physical and biological scientists, and it probably could be the more efficient type of explanation of criminal behavior. As Gibbons said:

> In many cases, criminality may be a response to nothing more temporal than the provocations and attractions bound up in the immediate circumstances. It may be that, in some kinds of lawbreaking, understanding of the behavior may require detailed attention to the concatination of events immediately preceding it. Little or nothing may be added to this understanding from a close scrutiny of the early development of the person.[1]

However, criminological explanations of the mechanistic type have thus far been notably unsuccessful, perhaps largely because they have been formulated in connection with an attempt to isolate personal and social pathologies among criminals. Work from this point of view has, at least, resulted in the conclusion that the immediate determinants of criminal behavior lie in the person-situation complex.

The objective situation is important to criminality largely to the extent that it provides an opportunity for a criminal act. A thief may steal from a fruit stand when

[1] Don C. Gibbons, "Observations on the Study of Crime Causation," *American Journal of Sociology*, 77:262–78, 1971.

the owner is not in sight but refrain when the owner is in sight; a bank burglar may attack a bank which is poorly protected but refrain from attacking a well-protected bank. A corporation which manufactures automobiles seldom violates the pure food and drug laws, but a meat-packing corporation might violate these laws with great frequency. But in another sense, a psychological or sociological sense, the situation is not exclusive of the person, for the situation which is important is the situation as defined by the person who is involved. That is, some persons define a situation in which a fruit-stand owner is out of sight as a "crime-committing" situation, while others do not so define it. Furthermore, the events in the person-situation complex at the time a crime occurs cannot be separated from the prior life experiences of the criminal. This means that the situation is defined by the person in terms of the inclinations and abilities which he or she has acquired. For example, while a person could define a situation in such a manner that criminal behavior would be the inevitable result, past experiences would, for the most part, determine the way in which he or she defined the situation. An explanation of criminal behavior made in terms of these past experiences is a historical or developmental explanation.

The following paragraphs state such a developmental theory of criminal behavior on the assumption that a criminal act occurs when a situation appropriate for it, as defined by . . . the person, is present. The theory should be regarded as tentative, and it should be tested by all other factual information and theories which are applicable.

DEVELOPMENTAL EXPLANATION OF CRIMINAL BEHAVIOR

The following statements refer to the process by which a particular person comes to engage in criminal behavior:

1. *Criminal behavior is learned.* Negatively, this means that criminal behavior is not inherited, as such; also, the person who is not already trained in crime does not invent criminal behavior, just as a person does not make mechanical inventions unless he has had training in mechanics.

2. *Criminal behavior is learned in interaction with other persons in a process of communication.* This communication is verbal in many respects but includes also "the communication of gestures."

3. *The principal part of the learning of criminal behavior occurs within intimate personal groups.* Negatively, this means that the impersonal agencies of communication, such as movies and newspapers, play a relatively unimportant part in the genesis of criminal behavior.

4. *When criminal behavior is learned, the learning includes (a) techniques of committing the crime, which are sometimes very complicated, sometimes very simple; (b) the specific direction of motives, drives, rationalizations, and attitudes.*

5. *The specific direction of motives and drives is learned from definitions of the legal codes as favorable or unfavorable.* In some societies an individual is surrounded by persons who invariably define the legal codes as rules to be observed, while in others he is surrounded by persons whose definitions are favorable to the violation of the legal codes. In our American society these definitions are almost always mixed, with the consequence that we have culture conflict in relation to the legal codes.

6. *A person becomes delinquent because of an excess of definitions favorable to violation of law over definitions unfavorable to violation of law.* This is the principle of differential association. It refers to both criminal and anticriminal associations and has to do with counteracting forces. When persons become criminal, they do so because of contacts with criminal patterns and also because of isolation from anticriminal patterns. Any person inevitably assimilates the surrounding culture unless other patterns are in conflict; a southerner does not pronounce r because other southerners do not pronounce r. Negatively, this proposition of differential association means that associations which are neutral so far as crime is concerned have little or no effect on the genesis of criminal behavior. Much of the experience of a person is neutral in this sense, for instance, learning to brush one's teeth. This behavior has no negative or positive effect on criminal behavior except as it may be related to associations which are concerned with the legal codes. This neutral behavior is important especially as an occupier of the time of a child so that he or she is not in contact with criminal behavior during the time the child is so engaged in the neutral behavior.

7. *Differential associations may vary in frequency, duration, priority, and intensity.* This means that associations with criminal behavior and also associations with anticriminal behavior vary in those respects. Frequency and duration as modalities of associations are obvious and need no explanation. Priority is assumed to be important in the sense that lawful behavior developed in early childhood may persist throughout life, and also that delinquent behavior developed in early childhood may persist throughout life. This tendency, however, has not been adequately demonstrated, and priority seems to be important principally through its selective influence. Intensity is not precisely defined, but it has to do with such things as the prestige of the source of a criminal or anticriminal pattern and with emotional reactions related to the associations. In a precise description of the criminal behavior of a person, these modalities would be rated in quantitative form and a mathematical ratio would be reached. A formula in this sense has not been developed, and the development of such a formula would be extremely difficult.

8. *The process of learning criminal behavior by association with criminal and anticriminal patterns involves all of the mechanisms that are involved in any other learning.* Negatively, this means that the learning of criminal behavior is not restricted to the process of imitation. A person who is seduced, for instance, learns criminal behavior by association, but this process would not ordinarily be described as imitation.

9. *While criminal behavior is an expression of general needs and values, it is not explained by those general needs and values, since noncriminal behavior is an*

expression of the same needs and values. Thieves generally steal in order to secure money, but likewise honest laborers work in order to secure money. The attempts by many scholars to explain criminal behavior by general drives and values, such as the happiness principle, striving for social status, the money motive, or frustration, have been, and must continue to be, futile, since they explain lawful behavior as completely as they explain criminal behavior. They are similar to respiration, which is necessary for any behavior, but which does not differentiate criminal from noncriminal behavior.

It is not necessary, at this level of explanation, to explain why persons have the associations they have; this certainly involves a complex of many things. In an area where the delinquency rate is high, a boy who is sociable, gregarious, active, and athletic is very likely to come in contact with the other boys in the neighborhood, learn delinquent behavior patterns from them, and become a criminal; in the same neighborhood the psychopathic boy who is isolated, introverted, and inert may remain at home, not become acquainted with the other boys in the neighborhood, and not become delinquent. In another situation, the sociable, athletic, aggressive boy may become a member of a scout troop and not become involved in delinquent behavior. The person's associations are determined in a general context of social organization. A child is ordinarily reared in a family; the place of residence of the family is determined largely by family income; and the delinquency rate is in many respects related to the rental value of the houses. Many other aspects of social organization affect the associations of a person.

The preceding explanation of criminal behavior purports to explain the criminal and noncriminal behavior of individual persons. As indicated earlier, it is possible to state sociological theories of criminal behavior which explain the criminality of a community, nation, or other group. The problem, when thus stated, is to account for variations in crime rates, which involves a comparison of the crime rates of various groups or the crime rates of a particular group at different times. The explanation of a crime rate must be consistent with the explanation of the criminal behavior of the person, since the crime rate is a summary statement of the number of persons in the group who commit crimes and the frequency with which they commit crimes. One of the best explanations of crime rates from this point of view is that a high crime rate is due to social disorganization. The term *social disorganization* is not entirely satisfactory, and it seems preferable to substitute for it the term *differential social organization.* The postulate on which this theory is based, regardless of the name, is that crime is rooted in the social organization and is an expression of that social organization. A group may be organized for criminal behavior or organized against criminal behavior. Most communities are organized for both criminal and anticriminal behavior, and, in that sense the crime rate is an expression of the differential group organization. Differential group organization as an explanation of variations in crime rates is consistent with the differential association theory of the processes by which persons become criminals.

Differential Association and Marijuana Use
*A Closer Look at Sutherland (With a Little Help From Becker)**

JAMES D. ORCUTT

Based on Sutherland's differential association theory and Becker's early research on marijuana use, a contingency model estimating the exact probability of getting high on marijuana under various associational and motivational conditions is specified and tested. Data from surveys at two universities fit this model closely. Predicted first-order interactions and nonlinear effects of motivational balance and peer association are statistically significant and generate highly precise estimates of the probability of getting high. These results suggest that linear main-effects models employed in previous research on differential association processes do not adequately reflect the complex causal structure of Sutherland's theory. In addition, this study raises serious questions about claims that differential association theory is untestable and has been made outdated by social learning theory.

AFTER A LONG PERIOD of relative inattention, deviance researchers have recently shown renewed interest in Sutherland's (1947) differential association theory. In 1960, Cressey was able to draw upon a huge empirical and critical literature in his definitive

Source: Orcutt, James D. "Differential Association and Marijuana Use: A Closer Look at Sutherland (With a Little Help from Becker)." *Criminology* Vol. 25 (2) 1987: 341-358. Reprinted by permission of The American Society of Criminology.

    *Revised version of a paper presented at the 1984 annual meeting of The American Society of Criminology.

review of work on the theory to that date. Cressey's rather discouraging appraisal of the theory as an untestable "organizing principle" appeared to be borne out over the next two decades, which witnessed only occasional efforts to address research to Sutherland's explanation of deviant behavior (for example, Jensen, 1972; Krohn, 1974; Voss, 1964). However, in the past few years, several investigations have reopened the question of testability by providing impressive evidence for the explanatory power of Sutherland's central variables—differential primary group associations and favorable/unfavorable definitions of deviant behavior (Akers, Krohn, Lanza-Kaduce, and Radosevich, 1979; Jaquith, 1981; Johnson, 1979; Marcos, Bahr, and Johnson, 1986; Massey and Krohn, 1986; Matsueda, 1982). Based on multiple regression and structural equation analyses of survey data, these studies have found strong linear effects of differential association variables on delinquent behavior and psychoactive drug use among adolescents.

Yet, in certain crucial respects, these studies have left sociological knowledge about differential association theory in much the same state as Cressey found it in 1960. While the substantial variance explained in self-reported deviant behavior by direct and indirect effects of measures of differential association reconfirm the utility of Sutherland's framework as an "organizing principle," the main-effects models employed in these linear analyses fail to reflect or assess the elegant structure of causal contingencies specified by the theory. In this paper the author will first show that some precise and testable predictions of *non*additive and *non*linear effects of differential association and definitions on initiation of deviant behavior can be derived from Sutherland's theory. The author will then present an analysis of data on marijuana use that approximate several ideal conditions for a quantitative assessment of these derivations.

THE CAUSAL STRUCTURE OF DIFFERENTIAL ASSOCIATION THEORY

Sutherland's 1947 version of differential association theory is generally considered to be the most systematic and formalized explanation of deviant behavior in the literature. This is evidenced by DeFleur and Quinney's (1966) translation of the theory into a formal logical calculus based on set notation. Their analysis demonstrates that the theory is an internally consistent system of deductive statements about the necessary and sufficient conditions for the learning and performance of law-violating behavior.

The causal approach taken by Sutherland is made explicit in DeFleur and Quinney's (1966:7) verbal reformulation of the central assertion (Statement 6) of differential association theory:

> Overt criminal behavior has as its necessary and sufficient conditions a set of criminal motivations, attitudes, and techniques, the learning of which takes place when there is exposure to criminal norms in excess of exposure to corresponding anticriminal norms during symbolic interaction in primary groups.

This assertion follows from Sutherland's (1956:9) Statement 4, where the "end products" of criminal learning are partitioned into a *technical component* ("techniques of committing the crime, which are sometimes very complicated, sometimes very simple") and a *motivational component* ("the [specifically criminal] direction of motives, drives, rationalizations and attitudes"). As DeFleur and Quinney point out, the initiation of criminal behavior necessarily depends on the conjunction of both components—the learned ability and willingness to perform the deviant act. When either of these conditions is absent, no criminal behavior will result. The proximate causes that lie at the core of differential association theory, then, are articulated as joint contingencies rather than as additive determinants of deviant behavior.

Although DeFleur and Quinney's reformulation correctly calls attention to the nonadditivity of Sutherland's structure of necessary and sufficient causes, their implication (1966:7) that the technical and motivational components are mutually contingent on "exposure to criminal norms in excess of exposure to corresponding anticriminal norms" is more questionable. Whereas Sutherland (1956:9) explicitly stated that the "specific direction of [subjective] motives and drives is learned from [normative] definitions of the legal codes as favorable or unfavorable," he did *not* link the learning of techniques to this normative context. Instead, Sutherland's (1956:8–10) passing references to "the communication of gestures" and to the "process of imitation" indicate he recognized that criminal techniques could be acquired through nonverbal and observational modes of association. Furthermore, much less than requiring an "excess" of criminal exposure, the necessary skills for many deviant acts might be learned through contact with a single criminal pattern (for example, one close friend who smokes marijuana) or even through association with noncriminal patterns (for example, being taught to handle firearms or drive a car; Akers, 1985:48–49). In its simplest and most abstract form, the technical component of criminal learning can be conceptualized as a binary variable—either present or absent in a given case—which depends on the corresponding presence or absence of effective learning opportunities in one's interpersonal environment.

On the other hand, there is little doubt that Sutherland conceived of the "specific direction of motives and drives" as a net quotient or ratio variable, isomorphic to and dependent on the normative ratio of favorable and unfavorable definitions. In reference to the latter in his 1947 statement, Sutherland noted (1956:10) that an ideally precise and abstract description of relative exposure to criminal versus anticriminal patterns would "be stated in quantitative form and a mathematical ratio be reached." Elsewhere (1956:40), he argued that in certain cultural settings "like those of the criminal tribes of India" the net ratio of criminal to anticriminal definitions "may be presumed to be far above unity." Likewise, the subjective motives and drives of an individual socialized into such a culture would be "far above unity" and—given acquisition of necessary techniques—this individual's likelihood of performing a given criminal act would be a virtual certainty. Conversely, noncriminal behavior can be predicted with a high degree of confidence where the normative (and subjective) ratio of criminal to anticriminal definitions falls far below unity.

While these implications are well known, Sutherland also pointed to an important limiting condition of his ratio conception of normative definitions and subjective motivations that has rarely received serious attention (1956:40): " the [differential association] hypothesis becomes increasingly uncertain in its operation as the quotient approaches unity." That is, where neither criminal nor anticriminal definitions are in excess, the specific direction of subjective motives and drives should accordingly be uncertain or determinative. Therefore, the behavioral consequences of this neutral or balanced state of motivation should also be uncertain (assuming that the individual has at least acquired the necessary techniques). In effect, Sutherland's observation about the indeterminacy of the theory under these peculiar normative and subjective circumstances implies that *deviant and nondeviant outcomes will be equiprobable* for any given individual in this state of the differential association process.

In light of the practical difficulty of measuring a ratio of associations with behavior patterns and normative definitions that vary in "frequency, duration, priority, and intensity" (Statement 7), it is understandable that many researchers have concluded that Sutherland's theory is untestable, particularly at the level of quasi-mathematical precision described above. However, the methodological requirements for a more immediate focus on the contingent effects of the technical and motivational "end products" of differential association are less imposing. Specifically, an examination of these implications for individual deviant behavior requires empirical indicators of (1) the presence or absence of techniques necessary for performance of the deviant act and (2) the net balance of subjective motivations toward the act (for example, positive, negative, or neutral).

The remainder of this paper focuses on a form of illegal behavior that constitutes an especially suitable site for research on these components of the differential association process: marijuana use. Several recent investigations have shown that primary group associations and normative definitions explain a substantial proportion of the variation in the use of marijuana (Akers et al., 1979; Jaquith, 1981; Kandel, Kessler, and Margulies, 1978). However, a more precise specification of the immediate causal contingencies in differential association theory can be derived from an early study that never made reference to Sutherland's work—Becker's (1953) classic analysis of the process of "Becoming a Marijuana User."

SOME IMPLICATIONS OF BECKER'S RESEARCH

Becker's (1953, 1963) sequential description of stages of initiation into marijuana use parallels Sutherland's theoretical treatment of the differential association process in a number of respects. Becker observed, of course, that close personal contacts with more experienced users were necessary at each stage. More importantly, the very contingencies that lie at the core of Sutherland's causal structure—techniques and motivations—are central to Becker's account of marijuana use for pleasure. The technical component of learning is reflected in the first two stages of becoming a marijuana user. In addition to mastering the *physical* technique of smoking properly, the would-be user must also learn *perceptual* techniques that make it possible to recognize and categorize ambiguous symptoms of intoxication as a marijuana "high." Becker notes (1953:237) that novices may acquire these physical and perceptual skills directly through interaction with one or more experienced users or "through the more indirect means of observation and imitation." However, at least some contact with patterns of marijuana use is a necessary condition for becoming a technically competent user of the drug. Clearly, this implies that *the expected probability of getting high on marijuana is zero for individuals with no interpersonal associations with patterns of marijuana use.*

The motivational component of the differential association process is introduced in the third stage of Becker's sequential model (1953:239), in which the new user "must learn to enjoy the effects he has learned to experience." This is a two-sided accomplishment which typically involves (1953:241) not only "the favorable definition of the experience that one acquires from others" but also redefinition of sensations that are initially unpleasant or frightening. In accord with Sutherland, Becker's image here is one of conflicting moral definitions—positive definitions acquired through association with other users versus conventional, negative definitions of the act as harmful, dangerous, or immoral. These moral definitions bear upon and are reflected in the specific direction of the individual's motives and attitudes. A positive resolution of this state of normative conflict and motivational ambivalence is a necessary condition for continued use of marijuana for pleasure. Therefore, *the expected probability of getting high on marijuana approaches zero for individuals with a negative balance of motives and attitudes toward marijuana.* On the other hand, the extent to which novices who have become both able and willing to get high actually continue to exercise this option depends directly on the opportunities created by participation in drug-using groups and by relative insulation from nonusers (Becker, 1963:59–78; compare Sutherland, 1956:31–33). That is, *among individuals who have learned the techniques and with a positive balance of motives and attitudes, the expected probability of getting high approaches 100% as a direct function of the ratio of associations with users versus nonusers of marijuana.*

Although Becker's interactionist account of marijuana use as a socially constructed choice steadfastly avoids the deterministic cast of differential association theory, it provides some useful points of reference for a quantitative assessment of Sutherland's causal structure. In addition to the implications sketched out above, this study also examines the possibility that individuals may be caught in a state of neutral motivation toward marijuana use—the indeterminate case noted by Sutherland. As with positively motivated individuals, the probability of getting high remains zero when neutral motivation is coupled with a lack of exposure to the necessary techniques for marijuana use. However, *among those who have learned the techniques, the expected probability of getting high on marijuana will only approach 50% for individuals with a neutral balance of motives and attitudes toward marijuana.* In the absence of a determinate state of motivation, use and nonuse remain equiprobable outcomes within the scope of differential association theory.

DATA

Samples

The following assessment of these implications is based on reanalyses of data gathered in two in-class surveys of university undergraduates. As reported in greater detail elsewhere, one survey was conducted at the University of Minnesota (Orcutt, 1975)·

and the other at Florida State University (Orcutt, 1978). Approximately half of the respondents in both surveys received a questionnaire focusing on alcohol use while the other half completed a parallel form dealing with marijuana use. This analysis will be restricted to students at each school who filled out the marijuana questionnaire—444 Minnesota undergraduates and 543 Florida State (FSU) undergraduates.[1]

Measures

The Minnesota and FSU questionnaires included nearly identical measures of three variables that are crucial to an examination of differential association theory: (1) primary group association with patterns of marijuana use, (2) subjective definition of marijuana use, and (3) personal use to get high. In both data sets, the following item serves as a measure of primary group association (Friends): "Of your *four closest friends,* how many would you say use marijuana at least once a month?" The measure of subjective definition is based on the following question: "How would you generally characterize your opinions toward marijuana?" In the Minnesota survey, response options ranged from "highly negative" to "highly positive" on a five-point Likert scale, while at FSU responses were scaled (again, in five Likert categories) from "negative" to "positive." The middle response category in both surveys was "undecided." For most of the analyses reported below, responses to these items were collapsed and recorded as dummy variables—Neutral (1 = undecided) and Positive (1 = either of the two positive responses)—with the two negative responses scored as 0 for both dummy terms.

Finally, the dependent variable for this study—personal use of marijuana to get high—is based on the following item included in both surveys:

Which of the following statements best describes the approximate number of times you have gotten "high" on marijuana during the past year?

1. I did not use marijuana during the past year.
2. I used marijuana during the past year, but did not get "high."
3. I got "high" on marijuana during the past year, but only once or twice.
4. I got "high" on marijuana at least 3 times during the past year, but not more than 12 times.
5. I got "high" on marijuana more than 12 times during the past year.

An important feature of this item is that it measures a respondent's self-reported ability to get high which, for Becker (1953), is a defining characteristic of a marijuana user. That is, this measure distinguishes between those who are minimally competent users—who have acquired the physical and subjective techniques for getting high—and those who are not. Therefore, according to Becker's conception, respondents who

---

[1] The samples at each school were drawn from classes in the major undergraduate colleges and represent broad cross-sections of these respective student bodies. Of the students attending class on the days of administration, 92% returned usable questionnaires at Minnesota and 97% returned usuable questionnaires at FSU.

checked either of the first two statements should be classified as nonusers. Thus, the dependent variable in this analysis is a proportional measure of initiation into marijuana use—Ownuse—based on a binary scoring of nonusers (0 = statements 1 or 2) versus users (1 = statements 3, 4, or 5).

ANALYSIS

Descriptive Statistics

Table 13.1 shows means and standard deviations for the variables employed in this analysis for each university subsample and for the total sample. As indicated by the subsample means for Ownuse, the FSU subsample contains a substantially higher proportion of marijuana users than does the Minnesota subsample (X = .475 versus X = .345). Similarly, the mean number of Friends who use for FSU respondents exceeds the mean for Friends in the Minnesota data (X = 1.803 versus X = 1.230). These subsample differences are consistent with Sutherland's (1956:11–12; Cressey, 1960) macro-level principle of differential social organization; that is, variations in rates of norm-violating behavior reflect variations in the organization of groups (for and against the deviant act) within which differential association occurs. Thus, despite the overall difference in proportions of users in the two subsamples, the zero-order correlations between Ownuse and Friends are virtually identical within these two university samples (Minnesota r = .646 versus FSU r = .663). More importantly, when Ownuse is simultaneously regressed on Friends and on a dummy variable for subsample (Minnesota = 0; FSU = 1) in the combined data set, the subsample effect disappears completely (partial Beta = .008 versus zero-order r = .132). In short, the epidemiological difference in the prevalence of marijuana use across these subsamples can be explained as a direct "expression of. . . differential group organization" (Sutherland, 1956:11). All subsequent analyses of micro-level implications of

TABLE 13.1 Variable means and standard devations (in parentheses) for Minnesota (N = 444), FSU (N = 543), and combined samples (N = 987)

Variable	Minnesota	FSU	Combined
Own use (1 = User)	.345	.475	.416
	(.476)	(.500)	(.493)
Friends (0-4)	1.230	1.803	1.545
	(1.423)	(1.568)	(1.530)
Neutral (1 = Neutral	155	.121	.137
Definition)	(.363)	(.327)	(.344)
Positive (1 = Positive	.372	.497	.441
Definition)	(.484)	(.500)	(.497)

Sutherland's theory are based on data from the combined samples as described in the last column of Table 13.1.

Marijuana Use as a Contingency of Associations and Definitions

Table 13.2 presents a three-way array of data from the combined samples that bears on the theoretical issues raised earlier. Here, Ownuse—the proportion of respondents who got high on marijuana—is cross-classified with number of Friends who use and with the trichotomous measure of Definition of marijuana. An inspection of these data reveals substantial evidence of the contingent patterning predicted by differential association theory.

First, the far left-hand column of Table 13.2 shows respondents whose four closest associates include no marijuana users. Assuming (from Becker, 1953) that the subjective and behavioral techniques necessary for marijuana use are learned primarily through interaction with friends who use, the ability and probability of getting high should be minimal among these particular respondents. Accordingly, the proportion of users in this column approaches zero among those with negative (.026) or neutral (.086) definitions, and only amounts to one-fourth (.260) of those with positive definitions. Thus, as expected, an absence of interpersonal associations with patterns of marijuana use is generally sufficient for nonuse of the drug.

Second, the top row of Table 13.2 shows respondents scored as "negative" on the Definition variable. In line with the motivational argument that a negative balance of definitions will be a sufficient condition for nonuse of marijuana, the vast majority of respondents across this row of the table are nonusers. A notable exception is the peculiar combination of negative respondents whose four closest friends all use marijuana; six of these nine individuals got high on marijuana during the past year. Save for this small group of respondents—who constitute "deviant cases" for differential association theory—individuals with negative definitions generally remain nonusers irrespective of the number of friends who use.

Third, consider those respondents scored as "positive" on Definition in the bottom row of Table 13.1. In contrast to respondents with negative definitions of the drug, the patterning of use among those who are positively motivated is strongly related to number of friends who use. Note, especially, the sharp increment in Ownuse among those positive respondents with just one friend who uses (.613). This is striking evidence for the implication that techniques necessary for getting high on marijuana can be acquired through contact with a single "criminal pattern." Once they are beyond this initial technical threshold, the proportion of willing respondents who engage in marijuana use continues to increase as a direct function of Friends. Among those with positive definitions whose four closest friends all use marijuana—where the differential association ratio is "far above unity"—marijuana use is a virtual certainty (.945).

Finally, an intriguing pattern of results appears in the middle row of Table 13.2: respondents scored as "neutral" on Definition. As noted above, very few neutral respondents were able to get high when none of their closest friends use. When one out of four friends use, one out of four neutral respondents also reported getting high (.237). The proportion of users increases to exactly .500 when two friends use. From that point on, *use and nonuse remain equiprobable even when most or all of the respondents' four closest friends use marijuana*. Clearly, this pattern reflects the "uncertain" outcome of differential association anticipated by Sutherland under the condition of neutral or balanced motivations.

In sum, these observations in Table 13.2 tend to bear out nearly all of the theoretical implications discussed earlier. While one cell of this table stands out as a possible exception, these data are generally consistent with the precise, contingent predictions that follow from the causal structure of differential association theory. The next section presents a more formal statistical analysis of the system of nonadditive/nonlinear relationships implied by the theory.

NONLINEAR/NONADDITIVE ESTIMATIONS

Table 13.3 presents the results of four multiple regression (OLS) estimations of Ownuse as a function of the independent variables (Friends, Neutral and Positive dummies). The regression equations in the two left-hand columns are based on the total combined sample, whereas the two right-hand equations are based on all cases except the nine "deviant cases" constituted by respondents with negative definitions and four close friends who use marijuana. For the total sample and the restricted sample, the first equation includes only the "main effects" of the independent variables—the linear/additive estimates typically employed in previous research on differential association and marijuana use (for example, Akers et al., 1979; Jaquith, 1981). A second equation was calculated including two additional product terms allowing for interaction between Friends and each of the Definition dummies (Interact1 = Friends X Neutral; Interact2 = Friends X Positive) plus an additional quadratic term (Quadfrnds = Friends X Friends) allowing for nonlinear effects on Ownuse of number of friends who use.

TABLE 13.2 Observed proportion of users by friends who use and definition

Definition	Number of four closest friends who use marijuana				
	0	1	2	3	4
Negative	.026	.148	.225	.182	.667
	(265)	(.81)	(40)	(22)	(9)
Neutral	.086	.237	.500	.500	.571
	(58)	(38)	(22)	(10)	(7)
Positive	.260	.613	.770	.893	.945
	(50)	(62)	(74)	(84)	(165)

* Base Ns in parentheses

These nonlinear/nonadditive specifications are based, of course, on the contingent causal structure of differential association theory.[2] The interaction terms reflect the expectation that the strength or slope of the relationship between Ownuse and Friends will be conditioned on and limited by respondents' subjective Definitions of marijuana. Furthermore, at least among Neutral and Positive respondents, the slope of the Ownuse/Friends relationship should be steeper in the initial range of friends from zero to one—where the increment in learning opportunities is greatest—than at higher values of Friends. These nonlinear influences of Friends should be captured in negative coefficients for the quadratic term Quadfrnds.

TABLE 13.3 Main effects (linear/additive) and nonlinear/nonadditive OLS estimations of ownuse as a function of friends and definition for full sample and for sample excluding "deviant cases"

		Total Sample		Excluding "Deviant Cases"	
		Main Effects	NonLinear/ Nonadditive	Main Effects	NonLinear Nonadditive
Friends	b=	.134**	.175**	.131**	.172**
	se=	.009	.027	.009	.027
	Beta=	.415	.544	.404	.529
Neutral	b=	.106**	.059	.110**	.038
	se=	.033	.043	.033	.042
	Beta=	.074	.041	.007	.027
Positive	b=	.427**	.311**	.436**	.266**
	se=	.028	.042	.029	.043
	Beta=	.430	.313	.440	.268
Interact 1	b=		.055		.102**
	se=		.029		.031
	Beta=		.062		.116
Interact 2	b=		.086**		.149**
	se=		.023		.027
	Beta=		.277		.481
Quadfrnds	b=		-.026**		-.039
	se=		.008		.008
	Beta=		-.317		-.477
Constant	a=	.007	.017	.006	.025
	se=	.017	.019	.017	.019
Equation	R=	.740	.745	.742	.753
Adj.	R^2	.546	.552	.550	.564
F for Increment in R^2		5.873**		11.541**	

[2] Respondents with negative definition and 4 friends who use (n = 9)

* $p < .05$ ** $p < .01$

[2] Following Stolzenberg (1979), a quadratic (parabolic) function—as opposed to a logarithmic specification—is estimated due to its relative ease of interpretation and to facilitate comparison of the linear and nonlinear effects of Friends in the full equations.

FIGURE 13.1   Nonlinear/nonadditive estimate of ownuse (solid line) and observed proportion of users (broken line) by friends who use and definition

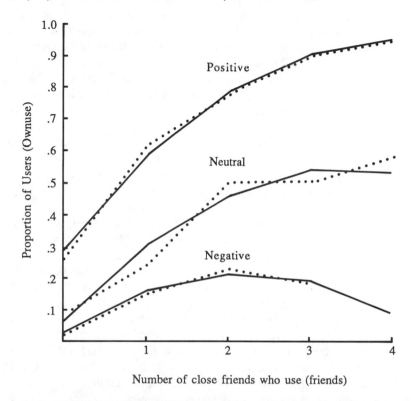

Number of close friends who use (friends)

As shown in the first column in Table 13.3, the linear, additive effects of differential association with Friends who use and subjective Definition of marijuana individually and jointly explain substantial shares of the variance in marijuana use. For the total sample, the main effects of these independent variables are highly significant and together account for over half of the variation in Ownuse ($R^2 = .546$).

However, interpretation of the simple main effects of predictors is highly questionable in the presence of higher-order interactions between them (Finney, Mitchell, Cronkite, and Moos, 1984; Stolzenberg, 1979). This is borne out in the nonlinear/nonadditive estimation of Ownuse for the total sample. The addition of the two interaction terms and the quadratic term yields a significant increment in R^2 over the main effects equation ($R^2 = .552$, $F = .5873$, $p < .01$).[3] The individual effects for Quadfrnds ($b = .026$) and for Interact2 ($b = .086$)—the slope for Positive Definition

---

[3] Neither the set of dummy interaction terms nor the quadratic term made statistically significant contributions to variance explained in Ownuse when entered individually into the regression equations. However, this is not inconsistent with the theoretical structure being examined here, which implies a saturated model including both interaction and nonlinear effects.

adjusted for interaction with Friends—are both highly significant. The main effect for the dummy variable Neutral is no longer significant in the full equation, whereas the interaction of Neutral with Friends (Interact1) is almost significant at p = .063. These results indicate that the slopes of Ownuse on Friends among respondents with Neutral definitions and, especially, Positive definitions are not only steeper than the relatively flat slope among Negative respondents, but that these slopes are nonlinear—that is, steeper at smaller values of Friends. The nonsignificant main effect of Neutral is consistent with the theoretical implication that the origin of this slope (that is, when Friends = 0) should approximate the origin for Negative definition—with both origins approaching zero. However, the significant main effect for the Positive dummy in the full model (b = .311) is inconsistent with this same theoretical argument.

A much closer fit to theoretical expectations is obtained with estimations that exclude as missing data the nine "deviant cases" of Negative respondents who report having four close friends who use marijuana.[4] While the main effects model for this restricted sample is very similar to that for the total sample, several key effects in the nonlinear/nonadditive estimation are markedly clearer. Both product terms for inter-action and the quadratic term are statistically significant, and their net contribution to variance explained in Ownuse is substantial (R^2 = .564, F = 11.541, p < .01). Again, as expected, the main effect of Neutral is trivial and not significantly different from the Negative reference category. Similarly, the main effect of the Positive dummy is reduced substantially in the full model, with its standardized effect being smaller than the standardized effect of its interaction (Interact^2) with Friends (Beta = .268 versus Beta = .481). As shown graphically in Figure 13.1, this nonlinear/nonadditive equation describes a pattern of three divergent, curvilinear slopes: (1) among Negative respon-dents, a relatively flat (parabolic) slope of Ownuse on Friends with an origin near zero and a terminal value approaching zero; (2) among Neutral respondents, a moderate, decelerating slope with an origin near zero and a terminal value approaching .500; and (3) among Positive respondents, a relatively steep, decelerating slope with an origin of .291 and a terminal value approaching 1.0. These estimates closely approximate the observed proportions of users plotted in Figure 13.1 and illustrate the mathematical elegance of the causal structure of differential association theory.

CONCLUSION

One purpose of this analysis has been to offer both a theoretical and empirical rebuttal to Cressey's (1960) influential verdict on the untestable "organizing principle" of differential association. An attempt has been made to show how a number of precise implications for one form of deviant behavior—marijuana use—can be readily derived

---

[4] These "deviant cases" are difficult to explain within the scope of differential association theory or, indeed, any theory of deviant behavior save for a very elementary "peer pressure" explanation. They could result from a variety of factors including measurement error, inadequacies of the cross-sectional design, or, perhaps, instances of very negative experience with marijuana on one or two occasions during the past year.

from the theory and submitted to empirical test. In fact, perhaps no other theory of deviance can generate such exact conditional predictions about the initiation of any deviant act. In addition, this exercise demonstrates that empirical work on differential association and other micro-level explanations of deviant behavior should go beyond the common strategy of focusing on variance "explained" by main effects of independent variables in linear estimations. The explanatory power of Sutherland's theory is manifested less in impressive R^2s than in the subtle patterning of contingent, nonlinear relationships examined here.

In light of the enduring strengths of Sutherland's original formulation, it is important to ask what has been gained—or lost—by subsequent efforts to recast differential association theory "in a more sophisticated and testable form in the language of modern learning theory" (Burgess and Akers, 1966: 131; Adams, 1973; Jeffrey, 1965). Most notably, Burgess and Akers explicitly abandoned Sutherland's deductive system of necessary and sufficient causes in basing their "differential association-reinforcement" theory on the more loosely integrated inductive principles of Skinnerian operant conditioning.[5] They replaced Sutherland's parsimonious system of technical and motivational contingencies with a more complex array of learning mechanisms and variables that enter into the process of differential reinforcement. Yet, as critics have noted (Jaquith and Orcutt, 1982; Strickland, 1982), the causal linkages between the various elements in this elaborate framework are not clearly specified. In his review of nearly two decades of work on the theory—which is now generally known as "social learning theory"—Akers (1985:57) granted that it is still marked by "unresolved ambiguities" and "only goes so far in specifying. . . ahead of time. . . [t]he actual relationships of the variables" in particular empirical applications.

Accordingly, Akers et al. (1979:639) were forced to employ a relatively crude analytical strategy in their initial assessment of the social learning framework using survey data: "We test the general hypothesis from the theory that adolescent marijuana and alcohol use and abuse are related to each of the [five] major sets of variables and to all of them combined." Their test of this "hypothesis" mainly involved a descriptive assessment of the net loss in explained variance when each of five sets of social learning variables was eliminated from main-effects regression equations. It is worth noting that the two sets of variables most closely tied to Sutherland's original formulation— differential association and favorable/unfavorable definitions—appear to account (parsimoniously) for virtually all of the explained variance in their measure of marijuana use (Akers et al., 1979: 647; Jaquith and Orcutt, 1982). More importantly,

---

[5] Burgess and Akers (1966:13) acknowledged the "importance of stating. . . propositions in a formal, deductive fashion" but viewed "this task [as] subsidiary to the more urgent task" of modernizing differential association theory in the image of Skinner's (1953) "behavior theory." A distinctive characteristic of theoretical work in the Skinnerian tradition is the use of inductive rather than deductive strategies for theory construction (Marx, 1963; Reynolds, 1971). That is, the law-like principles of learning in Skinnerian theory were each "discovered" through an inductive process of experimentation on subhuman organisms, replication, and empirical generalization. As summary statements of different empirical regularities, the various principles of operant conditioning do not comprise an integrated theoretical system. Although Akers' (1985) most recent rendition of his theoretical position places less emphasis on its Skinnerian heritage, it is still marked by the peculiar features and limitations of inductive theory (Marx, 1963:14–19).

the markedly low level of specificity and precision in their empirical predictions casts serious doubt on the claim that social learning theory is "more testable" than differential association theory. As Merton points out (1957: 98, emphasis in original), "Precision is an integral element of the criterion of *testability*." At least in the case of marijuana use, the evidence on this crucial measure of *testability* weighs heavily in favor of Sutherland's original formulation.

In sum, reports of the demise of differential association theory—that it has been outdated by developments in social learning theory and "has virtually no importance whatsoever" (Vold and Bernard, 1986:225)—seem greatly exaggerated. Other recent research also testifies to the continuing vitality of Sutherland's approach. For instance, Jackson, Tittle, and Burke (1986; Tittle, Burke, and Jackson, 1986) showed that differential association theory provides a coherent explanation of the likelihood of six criminal offenses (including marijuana use) and two noncriminal offenses in a sample of adults. Their results, coupled with those presented here, suggest that differential association theory may be unrivaled by more recent theories in both the breadth and precision of its empirical implications. Clearly, Sutherland's work is still worth a close look.

REFERENCES

Adams, Reed
1973 Differential association and learning principles revisited. Social Problems 20:458–470.
Akers, Ronald L.
1985 Deviant Behavior: A Social Learning Approach (3rd ed.). Belmont, CA: Wadsworth.
Akers, Ronald L., Martin D. Krohn, Lonn Lanza-Kaduce, and Marcia Radosevich
1979 Social learning and deviant behavior: A specific test of a general theory. American Socio-
        logical Review 44:636–655.
Becker, Howard S.
1953 Becoming a marijuana user. American Journal of Sociology 59:235–243.
1963 Outsiders: Studies in the Sociology of Deviance. New York: Free Press.
Burgess, Robert L. and Ronald L. Akers
1966 A differential association-reinforcement theory of criminal behavior. Social Problems
        14:128–147.
Cressey, Donald R.
1960 Epidemiology and individual conduct: A case from criminology. Pacific Sociological
        Review 3:47–58.
DeFleur, Melvin L. and Richard Quinney
1966 A reformulation of Sutherland's differential association theory and a strategy for
        empirical verification. Journal of Research in Crime and Delinquency 3:1–22.
Finney, John W., Roger E. Mitchell, Ruth C. Cronkite, and Rudolph H. Moos
1984 Methodological issues in estimating main and interactive effects: Examples from coping/
        social support and stress field. Journal of Health and Social Behavior 25:85–98.
Jackson, Elton F., Charles R. Tittle, and Mary Jean Burke
1986 Offense-specific models of the differential association process. Social Problems
        33:335–356.

Jaquith, Susan M.
1981 Adolescent marijuana and alcohol use: An empirical test of differential association theory. Criminology 19:271–280.
Jaquith, Susan M. and James D. Orcutt
1982 Social learning theory and the use of psychoactive substances: A critical and empirical assessment. Presented at the annual meeting of the Midwest Sociological Society.
Jeffrey, C. Ray
1965 Criminal behavior and learning theory. Journal of Criminal Law, Criminology, and Police Science 56:294–300.
Jensen, Gary F.
1972 Parents, peers, and delinquent action: A test of the differential association perspective. American Journal of Sociology 78:562–575.
Johnson, Richard E.
1979 Juvenile Delinquency and Its Origins: An Integrated Theoretical Approach. Cambridge: Cambridge University Press.
Kandel, Denise B., Ronald C. Kessler, and Rebecca Z. Margulies
1978 Antecedents of adolescent initiation into stages of drug use: A developmental analysis. In Denise B. Kandel (ed.), Longitudinal Research on Drug Use: Empirical Findings and Methodological Issues. Washington, D.C.: Hemisphere.
Krohn, Marvin D.
1974 An investigation of the effect of parental and peer association on marijuana use: An empirical test of differential association theory. In Marc Riedel and Terence P. Thornberry (eds.), Crime and Delinquency: Dimensions of Deviance. New York: Praeger.
Marcos, Anastasios C., Stephen J. Bahr, and Richard E. Johnson
1986 Test of a bonding/association theory of adolescent drug use. Social Forces 65:135–161.
Marx, Melvin H.
1963 The general nature of theory construction. In Melvin H. Marx (ed.), Theories in Contemporary Psychology. New York: Macmillan.
Massey, James L. and Marvin D. Krohn
1986 A longitudinal examination of an integrated social process model of deviant behavior. Social Forces 65:106–134.
Matsueda, Ross L.
1982 Testing control theory and differential association: A causal modeling approach. American Sociological Review 47:489–504.
Merton, Robert K.
1957 Social Theory and Social Structure (revised and enlarged ed.). New York: Free Press.
Orcutt, James D.
1975 Deviance as a situated phenomenon: Variations in the social interpretation of marijuana and alcohol use. Social Problems 22:346–356.
1978 Normative definitions of intoxicated states: A test of several sociological theories. Social Problems 25:385–396.
Reynolds, Paul Davidson
1971 A Primer in Theory Construction. Indianapolis: Bobbs-Merrill.
Skinner, B.F.
1953 Science and Human Behavior. New York: Macmillan.
Stolzenberg, Ross M.
1979 The measurement and decomposition of causal effects in nonlinear and nonadditive models. In Karl F. Schuessler (ed.), Sociological Methodology 1980. San Francisco: Jossey-Bass.

Strickland, Donald E.

1982 "Social learning and deviant behavior: A specific test of a general theory"; a comment and critique. American Sociological Review 47:162–167.

Sutherland, Edwin H.

1947 Principles of Criminology (4th ed.). Philadelphia: Lippincott.

1956 The Sutherland Papers. Albert Cohen, Alfred Lindesmith, and Karl Schuessler (eds.). Bloomington: University of Indiana Press.

Tittle, Charles R., Mary Jean Burke, and Elton F. Jackson

1986 Modeling Sutherland's theory of differential association: Toward an empirical clarification. Social Forces 65:405–432.

Vold, George B. and Thomas J. Bernard

1986 Theoretical Criminology (3rd ed.). New York: Oxford.

Voss, Harwin L.

1964 Differential association and reported delinquent behavior: A replication. Social Problems 8:78–85.

James D. Orcutt is a Professor of Sociology at Florida State University. His interests include deviance theory and the sociology of drugs and alcohol.

Point of View
The Dramatization of Evil

FRANK TANNENBAUM

... IN THE CONFLICT between the young delinquent and the community there develop two op posing definitions of the situation. In the beginning the definition of the situation by the young delinquent may be in the form of play, adventure, excitement, interest, mischief, fun. Breaking windows, annoying people, running around porches, climbing over roofs, stealing from pushcarts, playing truant—all are items of play, adventure, excitement. To the community, however, these activities may and often do take on the form of a nuisance, evil, delinquency, with the demand for control, admonition, chastisement, punishment, police court, truant school. This conflict over the situation is one that arises out of a divergence of values. As the problem develops, the situation gradually becomes redefined. The attitude of the community hardens definitely into a demand for suppression. There is a gradual shift from the definition of the specific acts as evil to a definition of the individual as evil, so that all his acts come to be looked upon with suspicion. In the process of identification his companions, hang-outs, play, speech, income, all his conduct, the personality itself, become subject to scrutiny and question. From the community's point of view, the individual who used to do bad and mischievous things has now become a bad and unredeemable human being. From the individual's point of view there has taken place a similar change. He has gone slowly from a sense of grievance and injustice, of being unduly mistreated and punished, to a recognition that the definition of him as a human being is different from that of other boys in his neighborhood, his school, street, community. This recognition on his part becomes a process of self-identification and integration with the group which shares his activities. It becomes, in part, a process of rationalization; in part, a simple response to a specialized type of stimulus. The young delinquent becomes bad because he is defined as bad and because he is not believed if he is good. There is a persistent demand for consistency in character. The community cannot deal with people whom it cannot define. Reputation is this sort of public definition. Once it is established, then unconsciously all agencies combine to maintain this definition even when they apparently and consciously attempt to deny their own implicit judgment.

Early in his career, then, the incipient professional criminal develops an attitude of antagonism to the regulated orderly life that he is required to lead. This attitude is hardened and crystalized by opposition. The conflict becomes a clash of wills. And experience too often has proven that threats, punishments, beatings, commitments to institutions, abuse and defamation of one sort or another, are of no avail. Punishment breaks down against the child's stubbornness. What has happened is that the child has been defined as an "incorrigible" both by his contacts and by himself, and an attempt at a direct breaking down of will generally fails.

The child meets the situation in the only way he can, by defiance and escape—physical escape if possible, or emotional escape by derision, anger, contempt, hatred, disgust, tantrums, destructiveness, and physical violence. The response of the child is just as intelligent and intelligible as that of the schools, of the authorities. They have taken a simple problem, the lack of fitness of an institution to a particular child's needs, and have made a moral issue out of it with values outside the child's ken. It takes on the form of war between two wills, and the longer the war lasts, the more certainly does the child become incorrigible. The child will not yield because he cannot yield—his nature requires other channels for pleasant growth; the school system or society will not yield because it does not see the issues involved as between the incompatibility of an institution and a child's needs, sometimes physical needs, and will instead attempt to twist the child's nature to the institution with that consequent distortion of the child which makes an unsocial career inevitable. The verbalization of the conflict in terms of evil, delinquency, incorrigibility, badness, arrest, force, punishment, stupidity, lack of intelligence, truancy, criminality, gives the innocent divergence of the child from the straight road a meaning that it did not have in the beginning and makes its continuance in these same terms be so much the more inevitable.

The only important fact, when the issue arises of the boy's inability to acquire the specific habits which organized institutions attempt to impose upon him, is that this conflict becomes the occasion for him to acquire another series of habits, interests, and attitudes as a substitute. These habits become as effective in motivating and guiding conduct as would have been those which the orderly routine social institutions attempted to impose had they been acquired.

This conflict gives the gang its hold because the gang provides escape, security, pleasure, and peace. The gang also gives room for the motor activity which plays a large role in a child's life. The attempt to break up the gang by force merely strengthens it. The arrest of the children has consequences undreamed of, for several reasons.

First, only some of the children are caught though all may be equally guilty. There is a great deal more delinquency practiced and committed by the young groups than comes to the attention of the police. The boy arrested, therefore, is singled out in specialized treatment. This boy, no more guilty than the other members of his group, discovers a world of which he knew little. His arrest suddenly precipitates a series of institutions, attitudes, and experiences which the other children do not share. For this boy there suddenly appear the police, the patrol wagon, the police station, the other delinquents and criminals found in the police lock-ups, the court with all its agencies such as bailiffs, clerks, bondsmen, lawyers, probation officers. There are bars, cells, handcuffs, criminals. He is questioned, examined, tested, investigated. His history is gone into, his family is brought into court. Witnesses make their appearance. The boy, no different from the rest of his gang, suddenly becomes the center of a major drama in which all sorts of unexpected characters play important roles. And what is it all about? About the accustomed things his gang has done and has been doing for a long time. In this entirely new world he is made conscious of himself as a different human being than he was before his arrest. He becomes classified as a thief, perhaps, and the entire world about him has suddenly become a different place for him and will remain different for the rest of his life.

THE DRAMATIZATION OF EVIL

The first dramatization of the "evil" which separates the child out of his group for specialized treatment plays a greater role in making the criminal than perhaps any other experience. It cannot be too often emphasized that for the child the whole situation has become different. He now lives in a different world. He has been tagged. A new and hitherto non-existent environment has been precipitated out for him.

The process of making the criminal, therefore, is a process of tagging, defining, identifying, segregating, describing, emphasizing, making conscious and self-conscious; it becomes a way of stimulating, suggesting, emphasizing, and evoking the very traits that are complained of. If the theory of relation of response to stimulus has any meaning, the entire process of dealing with the young delinquent is mischievous in so far as it identifies him to himself or to the environment as a delinquent person.

The person becomes the thing he is described as being. Nor does it seem to matter whether the valuation is made by those who would punish or by those who would reform. In either case the emphasis is upon the conduct that is disapproved of. The parents or the policeman, the older brother or the court, the probation officer or the juvenile institution, in so far as they rest upon the things complained of, rest upon a false ground. Their very enthusiasm defeats their aim. The harder they work to reform the evil, the greater the evil grows under their hands. The persistent suggestion, with whatever good intentions, works mischief, because it leads to bringing out the bad behavior that it would suppress. The way out is through a refusal to dramatize the evil. The less said about it the better. The more said about something else, still better.

The hard-drinker who keeps thinking of not drinking is doing what he can to initiate the acts which lead to drinking. He is starting with the stimulus to his habit. To succeed he must find some positive interest or line of action which will inhibit the drinking series and which by instituting another course of action will bring him to his desired end.[1]

The dramatization of the evil therefore tends to precipitate the conflict situation which was first created through some innocent maladjustment. The child's isolation forces him into companionship with other children similarly defined, and the gang becomes his means of escape, his security. The life of the gang gives it special mores, and the attack by the community upon these mores merely overemphasizes the conflict already in existence, and makes it the source of a new series of experiences that lead directly to a criminal career.

In dealing with the delinquent, the criminal, therefore, the important thing to remember is that we are dealing with a human being who is responding normally to the demands, stimuli, approval, expectancy, of the group with whom he is associated. We are dealing not with an individual but with a group.

> In a study of 6,000 instances of stealing, with reference to the number of boys involved, it was found that in 90.4 per cent of the cases two or more boys were known to have been involved in the act and were consequently brought to court. Only 9.6 per cent of all the cases were acts of single individuals. Since this study was based upon the number of boys brought to court, and since in many cases not all of the boys involved were caught and brought to court, it is certain that the percentage of group stealing is therefore even greater than 90.4 per cent. It cannot be doubted that delinquency, particularly stealing, almost invariably involves two or more persons.[2]

That group may be a small gang, a gang of children just growing up, a gang of young "toughs" of nineteen or twenty, or a gang of older criminals of thirty. If we are not dealing with a gang we may be dealing with a family. And if we are not dealing with either of these especially we may be dealing with a community. In practice all these factors—the family, the gang, and the community—may be important in the development and the maintenance of that attitude towards the world which makes a criminal career a normal, an accepted and approved way of life.   Direct attack upon the individual in these circumstances is a dubious undertaking. By the time the individual has become a criminal his habits have been so shaped that we have a fairly integrated character whose whole career is in tune with the peculiar bit of the environment for which he has developed the behavior and habits that cause him to be apprehended. In theory isolation from that group ought to provide occasion for change in the individual's habit structure. It might, if the individual were transplanted to a group whose values and activities had the approval of the wider community, and in which the newcomer might hope to gain full acceptance eventually. But until now isolation has meant the grouping in close confinement of persons whose strongest common bond has been their socially disapproved delinquent conduct. Thus the attack cannot be made without reference to group life.

[1]John Dewey, *Human Nature and Conduct*, p. 35. New York, 1922.
[2]Clifford R. Shaw and Earl D. Myers, "The Juvenile Delinquent." The Illinois Crime Survey, pp. 662-663, Chicago, 1929.

The attack must be on the whole group; for only by changing its attitudes and ideals, interests and habit,s can the stimuli which it exerts upon the individual be changed. Punishment as retribution has failed to reform, that is, to change character. If the individual can be made aware of a different set of values for which he may receive approval, then we may be on the road to a change in his character. But such a change of values involves a change in stimuli, which means that the criminal's social world must be changed before he can be changed.

THE SCAPEGOAT IS A SNARE AND A DELUSION

The point of view here developed rejects all assumptions that would impute crime to the individual in the sense that a personal shortcoming of the offender is the cause of the unsocial behavior. The assumption that crime is caused by any sort of inferiority, physiological or psychological, is here completely and unequivocally repudiated.

This of course does not mean that morphological or psychological techniques do not have the value in dealing with the individual. It merely means that they have no greater value in the study of criminology than they would have in the study of any profession. If a poor IQ is a bad beginning for a career in medicine, it is also a poor beginning for a career in crime. If the psychiatrist can testify that a psychopath will make an irritable doctor he can prove the same for the criminal. But he can prove no more. The criminal differs from the rest of his fellows only in the sense that he has learned to respond to the stimuli of a very small and specialized group; but that group must exist or the criminal could not exist. In that he is like the mass of men, living a certain kind of life with the kind of companions that make that life possible.

This explanation of criminal behavior is meant to apply to those who more or less consistently pursue the criminal career. It does not necessarily presume to describe the accidental criminal or the man who commits a crime of passion. Here perhaps the theories that would seek the cause of crime in the individual may have greater application than in attempting to deal with those who follow a life of crime. But even in the accidental criminal there is a strong presumption that the accident is the outcome of a habit situation. Any habit tends to have a background of social conditioning.

> A man with the habit of giving way to anger may show his habit by a murderous attack upon some one who has offended. His act is nonetheless due to habit because it occurs only once in his life. The essence of habit is an acquired predisposition to *ways* or modes of response, not to particular acts except as, under special conditions, these express a way of behaving. Habit means special sensitiveness or accessibility to certain classes of stimuli standing predilections and aversions, rather than bare recurrence of specific acts. It means will.[3]

In other words, perhaps the accidental criminal also is to be explained in terms such as we used in discussing the professional criminal.

[3] Dewey, op. cit., p. 42.

BIBLIOGRAPHY

American Academy of Medicine. *Physical Bases of Crime, a symposium contributed to the annual meeting in Minneapolis, 1913*. Mack Printing Co., Easton, Pennsylvania, 1914.

American Eugenics Society. Report of the President, June 20, 1926. New Haven, 1926.

Beccaria, Cesare. *An Essay on Crimes and Punishments*. London, 1767.

Berman, Louis. *The Glands Regulating Personality*. The Macmillan Company, New York, 1928.

Cantor, Nathaniel. *Crime, Criminals and Criminal Justice*. Henry Holt and Company, New York 1932.

DeQuiros, B. *Modern Theories of Criminality*. (Modern Criminal Science Series.) Little, Brown & Company, Boston, 1911.

Dewey, John. *Human Nature and Conduct*. Henry Holt and Company, New York 1922.

Ellis, Havelock. *The Criminal*. Walter Scott Publishing Company, Ltd., London, 1890.

Ferri, E. *Criminal Sociology*. (Modern Criminal Science Series.) Little, Brown & Company, Boston, 1917.

Garofalo, Raffaelle. *Criminology*. (Modern Criminal Science Series.) Little, Brown & Company, Boston, 1914.

Gault, Robert H. *Criminology*, D.C. Heath and Company, Boston, 1932.

Giardini, Giovanni. "A Report on the Italian Convict." *A Psychological and Educational Survey of 1916 Prisoners in the Western Penitentiary of Pennsylvania*. The Board of Trustees of the Western Penitentiary, Pittsburgh, 1927.

Gillin, John L. *Criminology and Penology*. The Century Company, New York, 1926.

Glueck, Sheldon, and Glueck, Eleanor T. *500 Criminal Careers*. Alfred A. Knopf, New York 1930. *500 Delinquent Women*. Alfred A. Knopf, New York, 1934. *1000 Juvenile Delinquents*. Harvard University Press. Cambridge, 1934.

Goddard, Henry H. *Feeble-Mindedness, its Causes and Consequences*. The Macmillan Company, New York. 1914. *Human Efficiency and Levels of Intelligence*. University of Princeton Press, Princeton, 1920.

Goring, Charles. *The English Convict*. His Majesty's Stationery Office, London, 1913.

Grimberg, Leizer E. *Emotion and Delinquency*. Brentano's. New York, 1928.

Halpern, Irving; Stanislaus, J.; and Botein. B. *The Slum and Crime*. New York, 1934.

Kurella, H. *Cesare Lombroso, A Modern Man of Science*. Rebman, Ltd., London, 1911.

Lichtenstein, Perry M. *A Doctor Studies Crime*. D. Van Nostrand Company, New York, 1934.

Lombroso, Cesare. *Crime, its Causes and Remedies*. (Modern Criminal Science Series.) Little, Brown & Company, Boston, 1911.

Moley, Raymond. *Our Criminal Courts*. Minton, Balch & Co., New York, 1920.

Morris, Albert. *Criminology*. Longmans. Green & Co., New York, 1934.

New York State. Reports of the New York Crime Commission. Legislative Documents.

Parsons, Philip Archibald. *Crime and the Criminal*. Alfred A. Knopf, New York, 1926.

Ploscowe, Morris. "Some Causative Factors in Criminality." National Commission on Law Observance and Enforcement, No. 13, *Report on the Causes of Crime*, Vol. I. Government Printing Office, Washington, D.C., 1931.

Pound, Roscoe. *Criminal Justice in America*. Henry Holt and Company, New York, 1930.

Saleilles, Raymond. *The Individualization of Punishment*. (Modern Criminal Science Series.) Little, Brown & Company, Boston, 1913.

Schlapp, Max G., and Smith, Edward H. *The New Criminology*. Boni & Liveright, New York, 1928.

Shaw, Clifford R. *Delinquency Areas*. The University of Chicago Press, Chicago, 1934.

Shaw, Clifford R., and McKay, Henry D. "Social Factors in Juvenile Delinquency." National Commission on Law Observance and Enforcement, No. 13, *Report on the Causes of Crime,* Vol. II. Government Printing Office, Washington, D.C., 1931.

Sutherland, Edwin H. *Principles of Criminology.* J. B. Lippincott Company, Philadelphia, 1934.

Thrasher, Frederic M. *The Gang.* The University of Chicago Press, Chicago, 1927.

White, William A. *Crime and Criminals.* Farrar & Rinehart, New York, 1933. *White-Williams Foundation: Five Years' Review for the Period Ending December* 31, 1921.

A New Theory
of Delinquency and Crime

WALTER C. RECKLESS

CONTAINMENT THEORY is an explanation of conforming behavior as well as deviancy.[1] It has two reinforcing aspects: an inner control system and an outer control system. Are there elements within the self and within the person's immediate world that enable him to hold the line against deviancy or to hue to the line of social expectations? The assumption is that strong inner and reinforcing outer containment constitutes an insulation against normative deviancy (not constitutional or psychological deviancy), that is, violation of the sociolegal conduct norms.

A MIDDLE RANGE THEORY

Containment theory does not explain the entire spectrum of delinquency and crime. It does not explain crime or delinquency which emerges from strong inner pushes, such as compulsions, anxieties, phobias, hallucinations, personality disorders (including inadequate, unstable, antisocial personalities, etc.), from organic impairments such as brain damage and epilepsy, or from neurotic mechanisms (exhibitionists, peepers, fire setters, compulsive shop lifters). All told these cases are minimal. And containment theory does not explain criminal or delinquent activity which is a part of "normal" and "expected" roles and activities in families and communities, such as the criminal tribes of India, Gypsy vocations and trades (very similar to the former), begging families, and

Source: Reckless, Walter C. "A New Theory of Delinquency and Crime." *Federal Probation,* Vol. 25 (December) 1961:42-46. Reprinted by permission of Federal Probation.
[1] For the complete statement on Containment Theory, see Walter C. Reckless, *The Crime Problem* ,3rd Ed. New York: Appleton-Century-Crofts, 1961, pp. 335-359.

certain phases of delinquency subculture and organized crime. Between these two extremes in the spectrum of crime and delinquency is a very large middle range of norm violation, perhaps as big as two-thirds to three-quarters of officially reported cases as well as the unreported cases of delinquency and crime. Containment theory seeks to explain this large middle range of offenders. According to its place on the spectrum of delinquency and crime, one might say that it occupies the middle position.

A QUICK REVIEW OF CRIMINOLOGICAL THEORIES

Before proceeding further, it might be a good idea to see in what directions theory in criminology is pointing at present. Since the early 19th century we have had a long succession of theories, most of which have not stood the test of time. It is possible to assemble these theories into three main camps of schools: (1) biological and constitutional theory—often called the school of criminal biology—in which the mainsprings of deviancy are sought in the inherited physical and mental makeup of man; (2) psychogenic theory, in which the formation of antisocial character is traced to faulty relationships within the family in the first few years of life; and (3) sociological theory, in which the pressures and pulls of the social milieu produce delinquent and criminal behavior.

Mention should be made of some of the specific theories. The dominating theory in Europe today is still the all-inclusive one which falls into the school of criminal biology. It points to the inheritance of weaknesses or pronenesses toward crime and delinquency (plus pressure from a bad environment).[2] Many variants of this theory have shown up in recent years: The attempt to prove inheritance of proneness through the method of studying criminal twins (Lange);[3] the attempt to identify body-mind types (Kretschmer);[4] the general acceptance throughout Europe in the past 25 years of several criminally-oriented types of psychopaths, based on inherited proneness (according to Kurt Schneider);[5] the attempt to identify and explain habitual (serious) offenders as contrasted with occasional offenders or offenders of opportunity, according to early onset which in turn points to inheritance of proneness (Irwin Frey);[6] the specification of the mesomorphic somatotype (muscular) as the type of constitution which is most usually related to delinquency (first according to William Sheldon[7] and later to the Gluecks).[8]

The psychogenic school probably claims August Aichhorn as its fountainhead. According to Aichhorn,[9] faulty development in the first few years of life makes it impossible for the child to control his impulses. The child lingers on as a sort of

---

[2] Franz Exner, *Kriminologie*. Berlin, 1949, pp. 115-120.

[3] Johannes Lange, *Crime and Destiny*, translated by Charlotte Haldane, New York: C. Boni, 1930.

[4] E. Kretschmer, *Physique and Character*, translated by W.I.H. Sprott. New York: Harcourt, Brace & Co., 1925.

[5] Kurt Schneider, *Psychopathische Persönlichkeiten*, 6th Ed. Berlin, 1943.

[6] Irwin Frey, *Die Frühkriminelle Rückfallsverbrecher*. Basel, 1951, pp. 95-98, 103, 253.

[7] William H. Sheldon, *Varieties of Delinquent Youth*. New York: Harper and Brothers, 1949, p. 727.

[9] August Aichhorn, *Wayward Youth*. New York, 1936.

principle in life. Friedlander[10] indicates that this faulty development in the first few years of life adds up to an antisocial character structure, incapable of handling reality properly. Redl,[11] who is also a disciple of Aichhorn, calls attention to the failure of the child to develop a management system over his impulsivity; that is, fails to develop a good ego and super ego.

The sociologists, ever since Ferri[12] (Italy, c. 1885), have been calling attention to bad environmental conditions. This was echoed by Bonger,[13] who placed the blame for disproportional crime and delinquency among the proletariat on the pressures of the capitalistic system. However, the American sociologists in the twenties pointed to conditions of social or community disorganization, rather than factors related to poverty. They became engrossed with identifying the location and characteristics of high delinquency areas of the city, specifying family disruption and conflict instead of broken home, and calling attention to the modal importance of companionship in delinquency.

It was not until around 1940 that a basic American Sociological theory of delinquency and criminal behavior was propounded. This was done by Sutherland and it was called differential association.[14] According to this theory, delinquent or criminal behavior is learned as is most other kinds of behavior—learned in association with others, according to the frequency, intensity, priority, and duration of contacts. Sutherland's theory really is not basically different from the one announced by Tarde[15] 50 years earlier, which regarded criminal behavior as a product of imitation of circulating patterns. Glaser[16] fairly recently proposed differential identification as a substitute for differential association. One takes over the models of behavior from those (reference) groups with which one identifies. But this does not have to be a face-to-face or person-to-person identification. (One can identify with the Beatniks without having actual physical contact with them.)

Still more recently Albert Cohen,[17] picking up the lead from Whyte's *Street-Corner Society*, contended that working class boys who turned their backs on middle-class virtues and values, found the solution for their status problems in the delinquency subculture of the gang. And most recently of all is the theory propounded by Cloward and Ohlin[18] that urban slum boys gravitate to delinquency subculture when they discover they do not have access to legitimate avenues of success.

[10] Kate Friedlander, *The Psycho-Analytic Approach to Delinquency*. New York: International Universities Press, 1947.

[11] Fritz Redl and David Wineman, *Children Who Hate*. Glencoe, Illinois: The Free Press, 1951.

[12] Enrico Ferri, *Criminal Sociology*. New York: Appleton and Co., 1896.

[13] W. G. Bonger, *Criminality and Economic Conditions*, translated by H.P. Horton. Boston: Little, Brown and Co., 1916.

[14] Edwin H. Sutherland, *Principles of Criminology*, 4th Ed. Philadelphia: J.B. Lippincott Co., 1947, pp. 6-7.

[15] Gabriel Tarde, *Penal Philosophy* translated by R. Howell. Boston: Little, Brown and Co., 1912.

[16] Daniel Glaser, "Criminality Theories and Behavioral Images," *American Journal of Sociology*, Vol. 61, 1956, p. 440.

[17] Albert K. Cohen, *Delinquent Boys: The Culture of the Gang*. Glencoe, Illinois: The Free Press, 1955, pp. 128-133.

[18] R. A. Cloward and Lloyd Ohlin, *Delinquency and Opportunity*. Glencoe, Illinois: The Free Press, 1960.

COMMENT ON THE THEORIES

Working backward in commenting on these theories, one might say that Cloward's theory only applies to those forms of delinquency which are part and parcel of the role structure of delinquency subculture. Jackson Toby[19] makes the estimate that this might only be 10 percent of the whole spectrum of delinquency. Assuming that Cloward's focus is very restricted, his theory does not account for the boys who do not gravitate toward the fighting gang, the criminal gang, and the retreatist groups (drugs). It does not specify that the ones who do gravitate to the three types of subculture have internalized an awareness of inaccessibility to legitimate success goals. It does not indicate that there are degrees of participation in gangs and that delinquency involvement of some members might be nil.

Cohen's theory has somewhat more merit. Somewhere and somehow in the growing-up process, slum boys turn their backs on middle-class values and look to street-corner groups to come to their aid. But Cohen is not able to specify the boys who do or do not turn their back on middle-class virtues and opportunities and gravitate to the street corner. He does not indicate whether only some of the boys in the street corner get involved in delinquent acts, as Shaw and Thrasher did a generation ago. So we have two interesting sociological formulations here, but not much realistic applicability.

Sutherland's differential association theory was meant to be a general theory, applying to the entire spectrum of delinquency and crime, from low to high in the class structure and across the board in personality. The trouble with Sutherland's theory (as well as Tarde's and Glaser's) is that it does not explain who *does* and who *does not* take up with carriers of delinquent patterns or who internalizes and who does not internalize delinquent models of behavior.

Coming now to the contributors to theory in the psychogenic school (Aichhorn, Redl, *et al.*), one should observe that at the most they only occupy a small end of the total spectrum of delinquency and crime. It is granted that there are some individuals whose ego and super ego development is too weak or poor to control impulses and to handle ordinary expectancies. But it is not at all clear just which children succumb to or are recipients of faulty socialization in the first few years of life. And it is not clear just which of the children, teenagers, late adolescents, and adults who are supposed to have little control over their impulse system run afoul the laws and regulations of society and those who do not.

One certainly finds it difficult to specify just exactly what the proneness is that is supposed to be the mainspring of serious, habitual, and early-starting offenders (criminal biology). It seems to be a sort of weakness in character. The evidence for the inheritance of proneness is very skimpy and most unimpressive, a sort of unreliable family-tree assessment by clinicians.

William Sheldon was able to specify the different kinds of somatotypes, much more definitely than Kretschmer was able to specify his body-mind types. A group of 200 problem youth in a Boston hostel, according to Sheldon, tended to have mesomorphic (athletic) body types along with several related forms of mental deviancy. The Gluecks discovered that among 500 delinquent and 500 nondelinquent boys the

[19] Private circulated comment on the Cloward and Ohlin book, 1961.

delinquents showed up very much more mesomorphic than the nondelinquents. The mesomorphs were found by the Gluecks to have a higher delinquency potential than other body types. Associated with mesomorphy were strength, social assertiveness, uninhibited motor responses, less submissiveness to authority. While mesomorphy does not explain all of delinquent behavior in the Gluecks' sample, it is certainly associated with a large segment of it and seems to reinforce many of the mental, emotional, and family traits connected with delinquency. Future studies will have to confirm the mesomorphic potential in delinquency.

GLUECKS: 4 TO 1 CAUSAL LAW

Out of their research on 500 delinquent and 500 nondelinquent boys, the Gluecks[20] proposed a five-point causal law. According to this formulation, delinquents are distinguishable from nondelinquents (1) physically, in being essentially mesomorphic; (2) temperamentally, in being restless, impulsive, aggressive, destructive; (3) emotionally, in being hostile, defiant, resentful, assertive, nonsubmissive; (4) psychologically, in being direct, concrete learners; (5) socioculturally, in being reared by unfit parents. This might be looked upon as a 4 to 1 law: four parts individual and one part situational. Items 2, 3, and 5 were chosen from among more than 100 overlapping traits, which distinguished delinquents from nondelinquents. The use of more sophisticated statistical methods would have enabled the Gluecks to find the two or three components within this maze of overlapping items which basically differentiate the delinquents from the nondelinquents. Nevertheless, the 4 to 1 causal law still stands as one of the few formulations which is worth attempting to confirm, qualify, or disprove by more rigorous research methods in the future. The law covers most of the spectrum of juvenile delinquency as we know it in the United States, certainly insofar as the full spectrum is represented by 500 boys from Boston who had been committed by juvenile courts to state schools in Massachusetts for delinquency.

INGREDIENTS OF INNER AND OUTER CONTAINMENT

In contrast to the buck-shot approach of the Gluecks, that is shooting out in all directions to explore and discover, containment theory seeks to feret out more specifically the inner and outer controls over normative behavior. It is attempting to get closer on the target of delinquency and crime by getting at the components which regulate conduct.

Inner containment consists mainly of self-components, such as self-control, good self-concept, ego strength, well-developed superego, high frustration tolerance,

---

[20] Sheldon and Eleanor Glueck, *Unraveling Juvenile Delinquency*, New York: The Commonwealth Fund, 1950, pp. 218-282.

high resistance to diversions, high sense of responsibility, goal orientation, ability to find substitute satisfactions, tension-reducing rationalizations, and so on. These are the inner regulators.

Outer containment represents the structural buffer in the person's immediate social world which is able to hold him within bounds. It consists of such items as a presentation of a consistent moral front to the person, institutional reinforcement of his norms, goals, and expectations, the existence of a reasonable set of social expectations, effective supervision and discipline (social controls), provision for reasonable scope of activity (including limits and responsibilities) as well as for alternatives and safety-valves, opportunity for acceptance, identity, and belongingness. Such structural ingredients help the family and other supportive groups contain the individual.

Research will have to feret out the one or two elements in inner and outer containment which are the basic regulators of normative behavior. Undoubtedly in the lists cited above there are items which, if present, determine the existence of other items and cause most of the regulation of conduct. Likewise, research must indicate the way in which the inner and outer regulatory systems operate conjointly. How much self-strength must be present in a fluid world with very little external buffer? How much weakness in self components is an effective external buffer able to manage?

SUPPORTING RESEARCH

The research and observations so far which give support to containment theory are the following:

1. According to Albert J. Reiss,[21] as a result of a study of Chicago delinquents who failed and succeeded on probation, the relative weakness of personal and social controls accounts for most cases of delinquency. Reiss found, however, that the personal controls had more predictive efficiency than the social controls as far as recidivism was concerned.

2. Nye[22] presented evidence to the effect that trends toward delinquent behavior are related to four control factors: (a) direct control which comes from discipline, restrictions, punishments; (b) internalized control which is the inner control of conscience; (c) indirect control which is exerted by not wanting to hurt or go against the wishes of parents or other individuals with whom the person identifies, and (d) the availability of alternative means to goals. Nye contends that his social control theory should not be applied to compulsive behavior or the behavior influenced by delin-quency subcultures. He feels that the more indirect control is effective, the less need

[21] Albert J. Reiss, Jr., "Delinquency as the Failure of Personal and Social Controls," *American Sociological Review*, Vol. 16, 1951, pp. 196-206.

[22] F. Ivan Nye, *Family Relationships and Delinquent Behavior*. New York: John Wiley and Sons, Inc., 1958, pp. 3-4.

for direct control; the more internalized control is effective, the less need for any other type of control.

   3. Reckless and Dinitz[23] found that a favorable concept of self insulated 12-year-old boys in the slum against delinquency, including perceptions about self, companions, home, and school. A poor concept of self, including perceptions that one is likely to get into trouble, his friends are in trouble, his family and home are unsatisfactory, that he will not finish school, and so on, was associated with delinquency vulnerability in 12-year-old slum boys. Four years later, followup contact revealed that the good self concept group had pretty much held the line and the favorable direction, while the poor self concept group had gravitated in unfavorable directions, 35 percent being involved with the law three times on an average. Reckless and Dinitz look upon a good or poor self-concept as an internalization of favorable or unfavorable socialization.

   4.   As a result of his observations on hyperaggressive, hostile children, Redl[24] identifies 22 functions of the ego in managing life situations. He conceives of the ego as the manager in the behavior control system, while the super ego is looked upon as the system which gives the signals to the ego. Redl, as is true of Aichhorn disciples, recognizes, particularly at the extremes, ego shortage and ego strength as well as a sick conscience and a healthy one.

   Containment theory points to the regulation of normative behavior, through resistance to deviancy as well as through direction toward legitimate social expectations. It may very well be that most of the regulation is in terms of a defense or buffer against deflection. At any rate, it appears as if inner and outer containment occupies a central or core position in between the pressures and pulls of the external environment and the inner drives or pushes. Environmental pressures may be looked upon as a condition associated with poverty or deprivation, conflict and discord, external restraint, minority group status, limited access to success in an opportunity structure. The pulls of the environment represent the distractions, attractions, temptations, patterns of deviancy, advertising, propaganda, carriers of delinquent and criminal patterns (including pushers), delinquency subculture, and so forth. The ordinary pushes are the drives, motives, frustrations, restlessness, disappointments, rebellion, hostility, feelings of inferiority, and so forth. One notices at once that Bonger as well as Cloward fall into pressure theory, while Tarde, Sutherland, and Glaser fall into pull theory.
   In a vertical order, the pressures and pulls of the environment are at the top or the side of containing structure, while the pushes are below the inner containment.

---

[23] Walter C. Reckless, Simon Dinitz, and Ellen Murray, "Self Concept as an Insulator against Delinquency," *American Sociological Review,* Vol. 21, 1956, p. 745; "The Self Component in Potential Delinquency and Potential Non-Delinquency," *Ibid.,* Vol. 22, 1957, p. 569; Dimon Dinitz, Barbara Ann Kay, Reckless, "Group Gradients in Delinquency Potential and Achievement Score of Sixth Graders," *American Journal of Orthopsychiatry,* Vol. 28, 1958, pp. 598-605; Frank Scarpitti, *et al.,* "The 'Good' Boy in a High Delinquency Area: Four Years Later," *American Sociological Review,* Vol. 25, 1960, pp. 555-558.
   [24] Fritz Redl and David Wineman, *Children Who Hate.* Glencoe, Illinois: The Free Press, 1951, pp. 74-140.

If the individual has a weak outer containment, the pressures and pulls will then have to be handled by the inner control system. If the outer buffer of the individual is relatively strong and effective, the individual's inner defense does not have to play such a critical role. Likewise, if the person's inner controls are not equal to the ordinary pushes, an effective outer defense may help hold him within bounds. If the inner defenses are of good working order, the outer structure does not have to come to the rescue of the person. Mention has already been made of the fact that there are some extraordinary pushes, such as compulsions, which cannot be contained. The inner and outer control system is usually not equal to the task of containing the abnormal pushes. They are uncontainable by ordinary controls.

SEVEN TESTS OF VALIDITY

1. Containment theory is proposed as the theory of best fit for the large middle range of cases of delinquency and crime. It fits the middle range cases better than any other theory.

2. It explains crimes against the person as well as the crimes against property, that is the mine run of murder, assault, and rape, as well as theft, robbery, and burglary.

3. It represents a formulation which psychiatrists, psychologists, and sociologists, as well as practitioners, can use equally well. All of these experts look for dimensions of inner and outer strength and can specify these strengths in their terms. Differential association and/or pressure of the environment leave most psychiatrists and psychologists cold and an emphasis on push theory leaves the sociologists for the most part cold. But all of the experts can rally around inner and outer weaknesses and strengths.

4. Inner and outer containment can be discovered in individual case studies. Weaknesses and strengths are observable. Containment theory is one of the few theories in which the microcosm (the individual case history) mirrors the ingredients of the macrocosm (the general formulation).

5. Containment theory is a valid operational theory for treatment of offenders: for restructuring the milieu of a person or beefing up his self. The most knowledgeable probation workers, parole workers, and institutional staff are already focusing to some extent on helping the juvenile or adult offender build up ego strength, develop new goals, internalize new models of behavior. They are also working on social ties, anchors, supportive relationships, limits, and alternative opportunities in helping to refashion a new containing world for the person.

6. Containment theory is also an effective operational theory for prevention. Children with poor containment can be spotted early. Programs to help insulate vulnerable children against delinquency must operate on internalization of stronger self components and the strengthening of containing structure around the child.

7. Internal and external containment can be assessed and approximated. Its strengths and weaknesses can be specified for research. There is good promise that such assessments can be measured in a standard way.

Finally, it is probable that the theory which will best supplement containment theory in the future will be "damage theory," according to which a light to dark spectrum of damage produces maladjustment and deviancy. The problem here is to find measures to isolate the less serious and less obvious damage cases and to estimate how far into the middle range of delinquency and crime the lighter impairments go.

There are many variables in the personality of the delinquent and the delinquency-producing situation itself which the investigators may not readily discern and which themselves may constitute the critical factors involved in the delinquent act. The investigator may inadvertently focus upon conspicuous and seemingly important factors involved in the delinquent act which, in the end, will reveal very little of the essential nature of delinquent behavior. Many ambitious studies have erred in this direction despite enormous expenditures of time and effort.

—Block and Flynn in
Delinquency: The Juvenile
Offender in America Today.

Techniques of Neutralization
A Theory of Delinquency

GRESHAM M. SYKES
DAVID MATZA

IN ATTEMPTING TO UNCOVER the roots of juvenile delinquency, the social scientist has long since ceased to search for devils in the mind or stigma of the body. It is now largely agreed that delinquent behavior, like most social behavior, is learned and that it is learned in the process of social interaction.

The classic statement of this position is found in Sutherland's theory of differential association, which asserts that criminal or delinquent behavior involves the learning of (a) techniques of committing crimes and (b) motives, drives, rationalizations, and attitudes favorable to the violation of law.[1] Unfortunately, the specific content of what is learned—as opposed to the process by which it is learned—has received relatively little attention in either theory or research. Perhaps the single strongest school of thought on the nature of this content has centered on the idea of a delinquent subculture. The basic characteristic of the delinquent sub-culture, it is argued, is a system of values that represents an inversion of the values held by respectable, law-abiding society. The world of the delinquent is the world of the law-abiding turned upside down and its norms constitute a countervailing force directed

---

Source: Sykes, Gresham M. and David Matza. "Techniques of Neutralization: A Theory of Delinquency." *American Sociological Review,* Vol. 22 (December): 664–670.

[1] E.H. Sutherland, *Principles of Criminology,* revised by D.R. Cressey, Chicago: Lippincott, 1955, pp. 77–80.

[2] Albert K. Cohen, *Delinquent Boys,* Glencoe, Ill.: The Free Press, 1955.

against the conforming social order. Cohen[2] sees the process of developing a delinquent sub-culture as a matter of building, maintaining, and reinforcing a code for behavior which exists by opposition, which stands in point by point contradiction to dominant values, particularly those of the middle class. Cohen's portrayal of delinquency is executed with a good deal of sophistication, and he carefully avoids overly simple explanations such as those based on the principle of "follow the leader" or easy generalizations about "emotional disturbances." Furthermore, he does not accept the delinquent sub-culture as something given, but instead systematically examines the function of delinquent values as a viable solution to the lower-class, male child's problems in the area of social status. Yet in spite of its virtues, this image of juvenile delinquency as a form of behavior based on competing or countervailing values and norms appears to suffer from a number of serious defects. It is the nature of these defects and a possible alternative or modified explanation for a large portion of juvenile delinquency with which this paper is concerned.

The difficulties in viewing delinquent behavior as springing from a set of deviant values and norms—as arising, that is to say, from a situation in which the delinquent defines his delinquency as "right"—are both empirical and theoretical. In the first place, if there existed in fact a delinquent sub-culture such that the delinquent viewed his illegal behavior as morally correct, we could reasonably suppose that he would exhibit no feelings of guilt or shame at detection or confinement. Instead, the major reaction would tend in the direction of indignation or a sense of martyrdom.[3] It is true that some delinquents do react in the latter fashion, although the sense of martyrdom often seems to be based on the fact that others "get away with it" and indignation appears to be directed against the chance events or lack of skill that led to apprehension. More important, however, is the fact that there is a good deal of evidence suggesting that many delinquents *do* experience a sense of guilt or shame, and its outward expression is not to be dismissed as a purely manipulative gesture to appease those in authority. Much of this evidence is, to be sure, of a clinical nature or in the form of impressionistic judgments of those who must deal firsthand with the youthful offender. Assigning a weight to such evidence calls for caution but it cannot be ignored if we are to avoid the gross stereotype of the juvenile delinquent as a hardened gangster in miniature.

In the second place, observers have noted that the juvenile delinquent frequently accords admiration and respect to law-abiding persons. The "really honest" person is often revered, and if the delinquent is sometimes overly keen to detect hypocrisy in those who conform, unquestioned probity is likely to win his approval. A fierce attachment to a humble, pious mother or a forgiving, upright priest (the former, according to many observers, is often encountered in both juvenile delinquents and adult criminals) might be dismissed as rank sentimentality, but at least it is clear that the delinquent does not necessarily regard those who abide by the legal rules as immoral. In a similar vein, it can be noted that the juvenile delinquent may exhibit great resentment if illegal behavior is imputed to "significant others" in his immediate social

---

[3] This form of reaction among the adherents of a deviant subculture who fully believe in the "rightfulness" of their behavior and who are captured and punished by the agencies of the dominant social order can be illustrated, perhaps, by groups such as Jehovah's Witnesses, early Christian sects, nationalist movements in colonial areas, and conscientious objectors, during World War I and II.

environment or to heroes in the world of sport and entertainment. In other words, if the delinquent does hold to a set of values and norms that stand in complete opposition to those of respectable society, his norm-holding is of a peculiar sort. While supposedly thoroughly committed to the deviant system of the delinquent sub-culture, he would appear to recognize the moral validity of the dominant normative system in many instances.[4]

In the third place, there is much evidence that juvenile delinquents often draw a sharp line between those who can be victimized and those who cannot. Certain social groups are not to be viewed as "fair game" in the performance of supposedly approved delinquent acts while others warrant a variety of attacks. In general, the potentiality for victimization would seem to be a function of the social distance between the juvenile delinquent and others and thus we find implicit maxims in the world of the delinquent such as "don't steal from friends" or "don't commit vandalism against a church of your own faith."[5] This is all rather obvious, but the implications have not received sufficient attention. The fact that supposedly valued behavior tends to be directed against disvalued social groups hints that the "wrongfulness" of such delinquent behavior is more widely recognized by delinquents than the literature has indicated. When the pool of victims is limited by considerations of kinship, friendship, ethnic group, social class, age, sex, etc., we have reason to suspect that the virtue of delinquency is far from unquestioned.

In the fourth place, it is doubtful if many juvenile delinquents are totally immune from the demands for conformity made by the dominant social order. There is a strong likelihood that the family of the delinquent will agree with respectable society that delinquency is wrong, even though the family may be engaged in a variety of illegal activities. That is, the parental posture conducive to delinquency is not apt to be a positive prodding. Whatever may be the influence of parental example, what might be called the "Fagin" pattern of socialization into delinquency is probably rare. Furthermore, as Redl has indicated, the idea that certain neighborhoods are completely delinquent, offering the child a model for delinquent behavior without reservations, is simply not supported by the data.[6]

The fact that a child is punished by parents, school officials, and agencies of the legal system for his delinquency may, as a number of observers have cynically noted, suggest to the child that he should be more careful not to get caught. There is an equal or greater probability, however, that the child will internalize the demands for conformity. This is not to say that demands for conformity cannot be counteracted. In fact, as we shall see shortly, an understanding of how internal and external demands

[4] As Weber has pointed out, a thief may recognize the legitimacy of legal rules without accepting their moral validity. Cf. Max Weber, T*he Theory of Social and Economic Organization* (translated by A.M. Henderson and Talcott Parsons), New York: Oxford University Press, 1947, p. 125. We are arguing here, however, that the juvenile delinquent frequently recognizes *both* the legitimacy of the dominant social order and its moral "rightness."

[5] Thrasher's account of the "Itschkies"—a juvenile gang composed of Jewish boys—and the immunity from "rolling" enjoyed by Jewish drunkards is a good illustration. Cf. F. Thrasher, *The Gang, Chicago:* The University of Chicago Press, 1947, p. 315.

[6] Cf. Solomon Kobrin, "The Conflict of Values in Delinquency Areas," *American Sociological Review,* 16 (October, 1951), pp. 653–661.

for conformity are neutralized may be crucial for understanding delinquent behavior. But it is to say that a complete denial of the validity of demands for conformity and the substitution of a new normative system is improbable, in light of the child's or adolescent's dependency on adults and encirclement by adults inherent in his status in the social structure. No matter how deeply enmeshed in patterns of delinquency he may be and no matter how much this involvement may outweigh his associations with the lawabiding, he cannot escape the condemnation of his deviance. Somehow the demands for conformity must be met and answered; they cannot be ignored as part of an alien system of values and norms.

In short, the theoretical viewpoint that sees juvenile delinquency as a form of behavior based on the values and norms of a deviant sub-culture in precisely the same way as law-abiding behavior is based on the values and norms of the larger society is open to serious doubt. The fact that the world of the delinquent is embedded in the larger world of those who conform cannot be overlooked nor can the delinquent be equated with an adult thoroughly socialized into an alternative way of life. Instead, the juvenile delinquent would appear to be at least partially committed to the dominant social order in that he frequently exhibits guilt or shame when he violates its proscriptions, accords approval to certain conforming figures, and distinguishes between appropriate and inappropriate targets for his deviance. It is to an explanation for the apparently paradoxical fact of his delinquency that we now turn.

As Morris Cohen once said, one of the most fascinating problems about human behavior is why men violate the laws in which they believe. This is the problem that confronts us when we attempt to explain why delinquency occurs despite a greater or lesser commitment to the usages of conformity. A basic clue is offered by the fact that social rules or norms calling for valued behavior seldom if ever take the form of categorical imperatives. Rather, values or norms appear as *qualified* guides for action, limited in their applicability in terms of time, place, persons, and social circumstances. The moral injunction against killing, for example, does not apply to the enemy during combat in time of war, although a captured enemy comes once again under the prohibition. Similarly, the taking and distributing of scarce goods in a time of acute social need is felt by many to be right, although under other circumstances private property is held inviolable. The normative system of a society, then, is marked by what Williams has termed *flexibility*; it does not consist of a body of rules held to be binding under all conditions.[7]

This flexibility is, in fact, an integral part of the criminal law in that measures for "defenses to crimes" are provided in pleas such as nonage, necessity, insanity, drunkenness, compulsion, self-defense, and so on. The individual can avoid moral culpability for his criminal action—and thus avoid the negative sanctions of society— if he can prove that criminal intent was lacking. *It is our argument that much delinquency is based on what is essentially an unrecognized extension of defenses to crimes, in the form of justifications for deviance that are seen as valid by the delinquent but not by the legal system or society at large.*

These justifications are commonly described as rationalizations. They are viewed as following deviant behavior and as protecting the individual from self-blame

---

[7] Cf. Robin Williams, Jr., *American Society,* New York: Knopf, 1951, p. 28.

and the blame of others after the act. But there is also reason to believe that they precede deviant behavior and make deviant behavior possible. It is this possibility that Sutherland mentioned only in passing and that other writers have failed to exploit from the viewpoint of sociological theory. Disapproval flowing from internalized norms and conforming others in the social environment is neutralized, turned back, or deflected in advance. Social controls that serve to check or inhibit deviant motivational patterns are rendered inoperative, and the individual is freed to engage in delinquency without serious damage to his self image. In this sense, the delinquent both has his cake and eats it too, for he remains committed to the dominant normative system and yet so qualifies its imperatives that violations are "acceptable" if not "right." Thus the delinquent represents not a radical opposition to law-abiding society but something more like an apologetic failure, often more sinned against than sinning in his own eyes. We call these justifications of deviant behavior techniques of neutralization; and we believe these techniques make up a crucial component of Sutherland's "definitions favorable to the violation of law." It is by learning these techniques that the juvenile becomes delinquent, rather than by learning moral imperatives, values or attitudes standing in direct contradiction to those of the dominant society. In analyzing these techniques, we have found it convenient to divide them into five major types.

The Denial of Responsibility. In so far as the delinquent can define himself as lacking responsibility for his deviant actions, the disapproval of self or others is sharply reduced in effectiveness as a restraining influence. As Justice Holmes has said, even a dog distinguishes between being stumbled over and being kicked, and modern society is no less careful to draw a line between injuries that are unintentional, i.e., where responsibility is lacking, and those that are intentional. As a technique of neutralization, however, the denial of responsibility extends much further than the claim that deviant acts are an "accident" or some similar negation of personal accountability. It may also be asserted that delinquent acts are due to forces outside of the individual and beyond his control such as unloving parents, bad companions, or a slum neighborhood. In effect, the delinquent approaches a "billiard ball" conception of himself in which he sees himself as helplessly propelled into new situations. From a psychodynamic viewpoint, this orientation toward one's own actions may represent a profound alienation from self, but it is important to stress the fact that interpretations of responsibility are cultural constructs and not merely idiosyncratic beliefs. The similarity between this mode of justifying illegal behavior assumed by the delinquent and the implications of a "sociological" frame of reference or a "humane" jurisprudence is readily apparent.[8] It is not the validity of this orientation that concerns us here, but its function of deflecting blame attached to violations of social norms and its relative independence of a particular personality structure.[9] By learning to view himself as more acted upon than acting, the delinquent prepares the way for deviance from the dominant normative system without the necessity of a frontal assault on the norms themselves.

[8] A number of observers have wryly noted that many delinquents seem to show a surprising awareness of sociological and psychological explanations for their behavior and are quick to point out the causal role of their poor environment.

[9] It is possible, of course, that certain personality structures can accept some techniques of neutralization more readily than others, but this question remains largely unexplored.

The Denial of Injury. A second major technique of neutralization centers on the injury or harm involved in the delinquent act. The criminal law has long made a distinction between crimes which are *mala in se* and *mala prohibita*—that is between acts that are wrong in themselves and acts that are illegal but not immoral—and the delinquent can make the same kind of distinction in evaluating the wrongfulness of his behavior. For the delinquent, however, wrongfulness may turn on the question of whether or not anyone has clearly been hurt by his deviance, and this matter is open to a variety of interpretations. Vandalism, for example, may be defined by the delinquent simply as "mischief"—after all, it may be claimed, the persons whose property has been destroyed can well afford it. Similarly, auto theft may be viewed as "borrowing," and gang fighting may be seen as a private quarrel, an agreed upon duel between two willing parties, and thus of no concern to the community at large. We are not suggesting that this technique of neutralization, labelled the denial of injury, involves an explicit dialectic. Rather, we are arguing that the delinquent frequently, and in a hazy fashion, feels that his behavior does not really cause any great harm despite the fact that it runs counter to law. Just as the link between the individual and his acts may be broken by the denial of responsibility, so may the link between acts and their consequences be broken by the denial of injury. Since society sometimes agrees with the delinquent, e.g., in matters such as truancy, "pranks," and so on, it merely reaffirms the idea that the delinquent's neutralization of social controls by means of qualifying the norms is an extension of common practice rather than a gesture of complete opposition.

The Denial of the Victim. Even if the delinquent accepts the responsibility for his deviant actions and is willing to admit that his deviant actions involve an injury or hurt, the moral indignation of self and others may be neutralized by an insistence that the injury is not wrong in light of the circumstances. The injury, it may be claimed, is not really an injury; rather, it is a form of rightful retaliation or punishment. By a subtle alchemy the delinquent moves himself into the position of an avenger and the victim is transformed into a wrong-doer. Assaults on homosexuals or suspected homosexuals, attacks on members of minority groups who are said to have gotten "out of place," vandalism as revenge on an unfair teacher or school official, thefts from a "crooked" store owner—all may be hurts inflicted on a transgressor, in the eyes of the delinquent. As Orwell has pointed out, the type of criminal admired by the general public has probably changed over the course of years and Raffles no longer serves as a hero;[10] but Robin Hood, and his latter day derivatives such as the tough detective seeking justice outside the law, still capture the popular imagination, and the delinquent may view his acts as part of a similar role.

To deny the existence of the victim, then, by transforming him into a person deserving injury is an extreme form of a phenomenon we have mentioned before, namely, the delinquent's recognition of appropriate and inappropriate targets for his delinquent acts. In addition, however, the existence of the victim may be denied for the delinquent, in a somewhat different sense, by the circumstances of the delinquent act itself. Insofar as the victim is physically absent, unknown, or a vague abstraction (as is often the case in delinquent acts committed against property), the awareness of the victim's existence is weakened. Internalized norms and anticipations of the reactions

[10] George Orwell, *Dickens, Dali, and Others,* New York: Reynal, 1946.

of others must somehow be activated, if they are to serve as guides for behavior; and it is possible that a diminished awareness of the victim plays an important part in determining whether or not this process is set in motion.

The Condemnation of the Condemners. A fourth technique of neutralization would appear to involve a condemnation of the condemners or, as McCorkle and Korn have phrased it, a rejection of the rejectors.[11] The delinquent shifts the focus of attention from his own deviant acts to the motives and behavior of those who disapprove of his violations. His condemners, he may claim, are hypocrites, deviants in disguise, or impelled by personal spite. This orientation toward the conforming world may be of particular importance when it hardens into a bitter cynicism directed against those assigned the task of enforcing or expressing the norms of the dominant society. Police, it may be said, are corrupt, stupid, and brutal. Teachers always show favoritism and parents always "take it out" on their children. By a slight extension, the rewards of conformity—such as material success—become a matter of pull or luck, thus decreasing still further the stature of those who stand on the side of the law-abiding. The validity of this jaundiced viewpoint is not so important as its function in turning back or deflecting the negative sanctions attached to violations of the norms. The delinquent, in effect, has changed the subject of the conversation in the dialogue between his own deviant impulses and the reactions of others; and by attacking others, the wrongfulness of his own behavior is more easily repressed or lost to view.

The Appeal to Higher Loyalties. Fifth, and last, internal and external social controls may be neutralized by sacrificing the demands of the larger society for the demands of the smaller social groups to which the delinquent belongs such as the sibling pair, the gang, or the friendship clique. It is important to note that the delinquent does not necessarily repudiate the imperatives of the dominant normative system, despite his failure to follow them. Rather, the delinquent may see himself as caught up in a dilemma that must be resolved, unfortunately, at the cost of violating the law. One aspect of this situation has been studied by Stouffer and Toby in their research on the conflict between particularistic and universalistic demands, between the claims of friendship and general social obligations, and their results suggest that "it is possible to classify people according to a predisposition to select one or the other horn of a dilemma in role conflict."[12] For our purposes, however, the most important point is that deviation from certain norms may occur not because the norms are rejected but because other norms, held to be more pressing or involving a higher loyalty, are accorded precedence. Indeed, it is the fact that both sets of norms are believed in that gives meaning to our concepts of dilemma and role conflict.

The conflict between the claims of friendship and the claims of law, or a similar dilemma, has of course long been recognized by the social scientist (and the novelist) as a common human problem. If the juvenile delinquent frequently resolves his dilemma by insisting that he must "always help a buddy" or "never squeal on a friend,"

[11] Lloyd W. McCorkle and Richard Korn, "Resocialization Within Walls," The Annals of the American Academy of Political and Social Science, 293, (May, 1954), pp. 88–98.

[12] See Samuel A. Stouffer and Jackson Toby, "Role Conflict and Personality," in *Toward a General Theory of Action,* edited by Talcott Parsons and Edward A. Shils, Cambridge: Harvard University Press, 1951, p. 494.

even when it throws him into serious difficulties with the dominant social order, his choice remains familiar to the supposedly law-abiding. The delinquent is unusual, perhaps, in the extent to which he is able to see the fact that he acts in behalf of the smaller social groups to which he belongs as a justification for violations of society's norms, but it is a matter of degree rather than of kind.

"I didn't mean it." "I didn't really hurt anybody." "They had it coming to them." "Everybody's picking on me." "I didn't do it for myself." These slogans or their variants, we hypothesize, prepare the juvenile for delinquent acts. These "definitions of the situation" represent tangential or glancing blows at the dominant normative system rather than the creation of an opposing ideology; and they are extensions of patterns of thought prevalent in society rather than something created *de novo*.

Techniques of neutralization may not be powerful enough to fully shield the individual from the force of his own internalized values and the reactions of conforming others, for as we have pointed out, juvenile delinquents often appear to suffer from feelings of guilt and shame when called into account for their deviant behavior. And some delinquents may be so isolated from the world of conformity that techniques of neutralization need not be called into play. Nonetheless, we would argue that techniques of neutralization are critical in lessening the effectiveness of social controls and that they lie behind a large share of delinquent behavior. Empirical research in this area is scattered and fragmentary at the present time, but the work of Redl,[13] Cressy,[14] and others has supplied a body of significant data that has done much to clarify the theoretical issues and enlarge the fund of supporting evidence. Two lines of investigation seem to be critical at this stage. First, there is need for more knowledge concerning the differential distribution of techniques of neutralization, as operative patterns of thought, by age, sex, social class, ethnic group, etc. On *a priori* grounds it might be assumed that these justifications for deviance will be more readily seized by segments of society for whom a discrepancy between common social ideals and social practice is most apparent. It is also possible however, that the habit of "bending" the dominant normative system—if not "breaking" it—cuts across our cruder social categories and is to be traced primarily to patterns of social interaction within the familial circle. Second, there is need for a greater understanding of the internal structure of techniques of neutralization, as a system of beliefs and attitudes, and its relationship to various types of delinquent behavior. Certain techniques of neutralization would appear to be better adapted to particular deviant acts than to others, as we have suggested, for example, in the case of offenses against property and the denial of the victim. But the issue remains far from clear and stands in need of more information.

In any case, techniques of neutralization appear to offer a promising line of research in enlarging and systematizing the theoretical grasp of juvenile delinquency. As more information is uncovered concerning techniques of neutralization, their origins, and their consequences, both juvenile delinquency in particular, and deviation from normative systems in general may be illuminated.

---

[13] See Fritz Redl and David Wineman, *Children Who Hate,* Glencoe: The Free Press, 1956.

[14] See D.R. Cressey, *Other People's Money,* Glencoe: The Free Press, 1953.

ARTICLE 17

Toward an Interactional Theory of Delinquency

TERENCE P. THORNBERRY

Contemporary theories of delinquency are seen as limited in three respects: they tend to rely on unidirectional causal structures that represent delinquency in a static rather than dynamic fashion, they do not examine developmental progressions, and they do not adequately link processual concepts to the person's position in the social structure. The present article develops an interactional theory of delinquency that addresses each of these issues. It views delinquency as resulting from the freedom afforded by the weakening of the person's bonds to conventional society and from an interactional setting in which delinquent behavior is learned and reinforced. Moreover, the control, learning, and delinquency variables are seen as reciprocally interrelated, mutually affecting one another over the person's life. Thus, delinquency is viewed as part of a larger causal network, affected by social factors but also affecting the development of those social factors over time. *

A VARIETY OF SOCIOLOGICAL THEORIES have been developed to explain the onset and maintenance of delinquent behavior. Currently, three are of primary importance: social control theory (Hirschi, 1969), social learning theory (Akers, 1977), and integrated

Source: Thornberry, Terence P. "Toward an Interactional Theory of Delinquency." *Criminology,* Vol. 25(4), 1987:863–891. Reprinted by permission of the American Society of Criminology.

* The present work was supported in part by the Office of Juvenile Justice and Delinquency Prevention, grant number 86-JN-CX-0007; the views expressed are those of the author and not necessarily those of the funding agency. I would like to thank Drs. Robert A. Silverman of the University of Alberta and Margaret Farnworth, Alan Lizotte, and Hans Toch of the University at Albany for providing helpful comments on earlier drafts of this article.

models that combine them into a broader body of explanatory principals (Elliott, Ageton, and Canter, 1979; Elliott, Huizinga, and Ageton, 1985).

Control theory argues that delinquency emerges whenever the social and cultural constraints over human conduct are substantially attenuated. As Hirschi states in his classic presentation (1969), control theory assumes that we would all be deviant if only we dared. Learning theory, on the other hand, posits that there is no natural impulse toward delinquency. Indeed, delinquent behavior must be learned through the same processes and mechanisms as conforming behavior. Because of these different starting points, control and learning models give causal priority to somewhat different concepts, and integrated models capitalize on these complementary approaches. Muting the assumptive differences, integrated theories meld together propositions from these (and sometimes other theories—for example, strain) to explain delinquent behavior.

Although these approaches have substantially informed our understanding of the causes of delinquency, they and other contemporary theories suffer from three fundamental limitations. First, they rely on unidirectional rather than reciprocal causal structures. By and large, current theories ignore reciprocal effects in which delinquent behavior is viewed as part of a more general social nexus, affected by, but also affecting, other social factors. Second, current theories tend to be nondevelopmental, specifying causal models for only a narrow age range, usually midadolescence. As a result, they fail to capitalize on developmental patterns to explain the initiation, maintenance, and desistance of delinquency. Finally, contemporary theories tend to assume uniform causal effects throughout the social structure. By ignoring the person's structural position, they fail to provide an understanding of the sources of initial variation in both delinquency and its presumed causes. In combination, these three limitations have led to theories that are narrowly conceived and which provide incomplete and, at times, misleading models of the causes of delinquency.

The present article develops an interactional theory of delinquency that addresses and attempts to respond to each of these limitations. The model proposed here pays particular attention to the first issue, recursive versus reciprocal causal structures, since the development of dynamic models is seen as essential to represent accurately the interactional settings in which delinquency develops.

Origins and Assumptions

The basic premise of the model proposed here is that human behavior occurs in social interaction and can therefore best be explained by models that focus on interactive processes. Rather than viewing adolescents as propelled along a unidirectional pathway to one or another outcome—that is, delinquency or conformity—it argues that adolescents interact with other people and institutions and that behavioral outcomes are formed by that interactive process. For example, the delinquent behavior of an adolescent is formed in part by how he and his parents *interact* over time, not simply by the child's perceived, and presumably invariant, *level* of attachment to parents.

Moreover, since it is an interactive system, the behaviors of others—for example, parents and school officials—are influenced both by each other and by the adolescent, including his or her delinquent behavior. If this view is correct, then interactional effects have to be modelled explicitly if we are to understand the social and psychological processes involved with initiation into delinquency, the maintenance of such behavior, and its eventual reduction.

Interactional theory develops from the same intellectual tradition as the theories mentioned above, especially the Durkheimian tradition of social control. It asserts that the fundamental cause of delinquency lies in the weakening of social constraints over the conduct of the individual. Unlike classical control theory, however, it does not assume that the attenuation of controls leads directly to delinquency. The weakening of controls simply allows for a much wider array of behavior, including continued conventional action, failure as indicated by school dropout and sporadic employment histories, alcoholism, mental illness, delinquent and criminal careers, or some combination of these outcomes. For the freedom resulting from weakened bonds to be channeled into delinquency, especially serious prolonged delinquency, requires an interactive setting in which delinquency is learned, performed, and reinforced. This view is similar to Cullen's structuring perspective which draws attention to the indeterminancy of deviant behavior. "It can thus be argued that there is an *indeterminate* and not a determinate or etiologically specific relationship between motivational variables on the one hand and any particular form of deviant behavior on the other hand" (Cullen, 1984: 5).

Although heavily influenced by control and learning theories, and to a lesser extent by strain and culture conflict theories, this is not an effort at theoretical integration as that term is usually used (Elliott, 1985). Rather, this paper is guided by what we have elsewhere called theoretical elaboration (Thornberry, 1987). In this instance, a basic control theory is extended, or elaborated upon, using available theoretical perspectives and empirical findings to provide a more accurate model of the causes of delinquency. In the process of elaboration, there is no requirement to resolve disputes among other theories—for example, their different assumptions about the origins of deviance (Thornberry, 1987:15–18); all that is required is that the propositions of the model developed here be consistent with one another and with the assumptions about deviance stated above.

Organization

The presentation of the interactional model begins by identifying the central concepts to be included in the model. Next, the underlying theoretical structure of the proposed model is examined and the rationale for moving from unidirectional to reciprocal causal models is developed. The reciprocal model is then extended to include a developmental perspective, examining the theoretical saliency of different variables at different developmental stages. Finally, the influence of the person's position in the social structure is explored. Although in some senses the last issue is logically prior to the others, since it is concerned with sources of initial variation in the causal variables, it is discussed last so that the reciprocal relationships among the concepts—the heart of an interactional perspective—can be more fully developed.

THEORETICAL CONCEPTS

Given these basic premises, an interactional model must respond to two overriding issues. First, how are traditional social constraints over behavior weakened and, second, once weakened, how is the resulting freedom channelled into delinquent patterns? To address these issues, the present article presents an initial version of an interactional model, focusing on the interrelationships among six concepts: attachment to parents, commitment to school, belief in conventional values, associations with delinquent peers, adopting delinquent values, and engaging in delinquent behavior. These concepts form the core of the theoretical model since they are central to social psychological theories of delinquency and since they have been shown in numerous studies to be strongly related to subsequent delinquent behavior (see Elliott et al., 1985, Chs. 1–3, for an excellent review of this literature).

The first three derive from Hirschi's version of control theory (1969) and represent the primary mechanisms by which adolescents are bonded to conventional middle-class society. When those elements of the bond are weakened, behavioral freedom increases considerably. For that freedom to lead to delinquent behavior, however, interactive settings that reinforce delinquency are required. In the model, those settings are represented by two concepts—associations with delinquent peers and the formation of delinquent values—which derive primarily from social learning theory.

For the purpose of explicating the overall theoretical perspective, each of these concepts is defined quite broadly. Attachment to parents includes the affective relationship between parent and child, communication patterns, parenting skills such as monitoring and discipline, parent-child conflict, and the like. Commitment to school refers to the stake in conformity the adolescent has developed and includes such factors as success in school, perceived importance of education, attachment to teachers, and involvement in school activities. Belief in conventional values represents the granting of legitimacy to such middle-class values as education, personal industry, financial success, deferral of gratification, and the like.

Three delinquency variables are included in the model. Association with delinquent peers includes the level of attachment to peers, the delinquent behavior and values of peers, and their reinforcing reactions to the adolescent's own delinquent or conforming behavior. It is a continuous measure that can vary from groups that are heavily delinquent to those that are almost entirely nondelinquent. Delinquent values refer to the granting of legitimacy to delinquent activities as acceptable modes of behavior as well as a general willingness to violate the law to achieve other ends.

Delinquent behavior, the primary outcome variable, refers to acts that place the youth at risk for adjudication; it ranges from status offenses to serious violent activities.

Since the present model is an interactional one, interested not only in explaining delinquency but in explaining the effects of delinquency on other variables, particular attention is paid to prolonged involvement in serious delinquency.

THEORETICAL STRUCTURE

The present section develops the reciprocal structure of the interactional model by examining the interplay of the concepts just defined. It begins by describing (Figure 17.1) the way in which these variables are typically represented in predominately recursive theories of delinquency (see, for example, Johnson, 1979: Weis and Seder-strom, 1981; Elliott et al., 1985).

In these models, all the variables are temporally ordered; earlier ones affect later ones, but there is no provision for feedback or reciprocal causal paths. The unidirectional specification can be illustrated by examining the relationship between attachment to parents and associations with delinquent peers. According to the model, attachment to parents reduces the extent to which the child associates with delinquent peers, an assertion consistent with common observation and empirical research (for example, Poole and Regoli, 1979). Yet, by implication, the model also states that associations with delinquent peers exerts no causal influence on the extent to which the child is attached to parents. If peer associations were thought to influence attachment to parents, then this effect would have to be specified and estimated. As seen in Figure 17.1, reciprocal effects of this type are excluded by design.

The second feature to note about this model is that it treats delinquency entirely as an outcome of a social process rather than as an integral part of that process. Models

---

FIGURE 17.1   A typical recursive causal model of delinqunecy

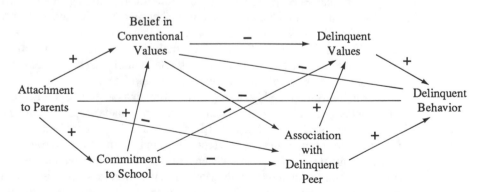

such as this assert that various social factors cause delinquent behavior but ignore the possibility that delinquency and its presumed causes are part of a reciprocal causal structure, mutually influencing one another over the person's life span. For example, these models state that associations with delinquent peers increase the likelihood of delinquent conduct, an obviously reasonable assertion, but ignore the possibility that delinquent conduct affects the likelihood and intensity of associations with delinquent peers. Similar statements can be made for the other relationships in which delinquency is embedded.

It should be noted at the outset that there is nothing inherently incorrect with recursive models; if the causal processes are unidirectional, recursive models offer a correct specification and should be used. It is only when the causal processes are in fact reciprocal that models such as these lead to problems of misspecification and incorrect interpretations of causal effects. The remainder of this section develops the argument that unidirectional models are inadequate and that reciprocal models are required to understand the causes of delinquency, precisely because delinquency is embedded in an interactive social process, affected by and affecting other variables. As a starting point, the findings of three recent panel studies that examine both unidirectional and reciprocal models of delinquent conduct are considered.

Empirical Findings

Thornberry and Christenson (1984) estimated a reciprocal causal structure for unemployment and criminal involvement, both measured at the individual level, for a sample of young adult males. They found that unidirectional models, either from unemployment to crime or from crime to unemployment, were inadequate to model the causal process. Overall, their findings:

> offer strong support for a reciprocal model of crime causation. Consistent with our theoretical specification, unemployment has significant instantaneous effects on crime and crime has significant effects, primarily lagged effects, on unemployment (1984:408).

Liska and Reed (1985) studied the relationship among three control theory variables, attachment to parents, success in school, and delinquency. Although their results differed somewhat for blacks and whites, these variables appear to be embedded in a reciprocal causal loop. Overall, "the analysis suggests that parental attachment affects delinquency, that delinquency affects school attachment, and that school attachment affects parental attachment" (Liska and Reed, 1985:556–557).

Finally, Burkett and Warren (1987) estimate a panel model for four variables: religious commitment, belief in the sinfulness of marijuana use, associations with peers who use marijuana, and self-reported marijuana use. Their basic finding suggests that religious commitment and belief affect marijuana use indirectly, through association with delinquent peers. They also present consistent evidence that these four variables are reciprocally related over time. Marijuana use increases associations with delinquent peers, and associations with delinquent peers reduce religious commitments. In addition, marijuana use at time one significantly affects both religious commitment

FIGURE 17.2   A reciprocal model of delinquent involvement at early adolescence [a]

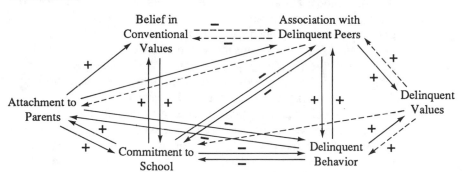

[a]solid lines represent stronger effects; dashed lines represent weaker effects.

and beliefs at later times and "this, in turn, contributes to deeper involvement with marijuana-using peers and subsequent continued use in response to direct peer pressure" (1987:123).

All three of these studies derive primarily from a social control framework, but use different data sets, variables, and analytic techniques. Nevertheless, all provide empirical support for the improved explanatory power of reciprocal models. The pattern of relationships observed in these studies strongly suggests that reciprocal causal models are necessary to model adequately the social settings in which delinquent behavior emerges and develops.

These findings also suggest that previous tests of delinquency theories based on recursive causal structures are both incomplete and misleading. As Thornberry and Christenson (1984:399) point out, such tests:

> are incomplete since estimates for reciprocal paths simply cannot be obtained. More importantly, recursive tests can produce misleading results since estimates of unidirectional effects obtained from them may be in substantial error. Conceivably, recursive tests could indicate a unidirectional effect between two variables, i.e., X→Y, when the actual relationship (as estimated from a nonrecursive model) could indicate either that the variables are reciprocally related, i.e., X↔Y, or that the direction of the causality is actually reversed, i.e., X←Y (see Heise, 1975:191–93; Hanushek and Jackson, 1977:79–86).

If any or all of these errors exist, and results of recent research suggest they do, then current theories of delinquency, which have been strongly influenced by the results of recursive studies, are inadequate to describe the actual processes in which delinquency is embedded. Because of this, it is important to develop and test interactional models that allow for reciprocal effects.

MODEL SPECIFICATION

A causal model allowing for reciprocal relationships among the six concepts of interest—attachment to parents, commitment to school, belief in conventional values, association with delinquent peers, delinquent values, and delinquent behavior—is presented in Figure 17.2. This model refers to the period of early adolescence, from about ages 11 to 13, when delinquent careers are beginning, but prior to the period at which delinquency reaches its apex in terms of seriousness and frequency. In the following sections the model is extended to later ages.

The specification of causal effects begins by examining the three concepts that form the heart of social learning theories of delinquency—delinquent peers, delinquent values, and delinquent behavior. For now we focus on the reciprocal nature of the relationships, ignoring until later variations in the strength of the relationships.

Traditional social learning theory specifies a causal order among these variables in which delinquent associations affect delinquent values and, in turn, both produce delinquent behavior (Akers, Krohn, Lanza-Kaduce, and Radosevich, 1979; Matsueda, 1982). Yet, for each of the dyadic relationships involving these variables, other theoretical perspectives and much empirical evidence suggest the appropriateness of reversing this causal order. For example, social learning theory proposes that associating with delinquents, or more precisely, people who hold and reinforce delinquent values, increases the chances of delinquent behavior (Akers, 1977). Yet, as far back as the work of the Gluecks (1950) this specification has been challenged. Arguing that "birds of a feather flock together," the Gluecks propose that youths who are delinquent seek out and associate with others who share those tendencies. From this perspective, rather than being a cause of delinquency, associations are the result of delinquents seeking out and associating with like-minded peers.

An attempt to resolve the somewhat tedious argument over the temporal priority of associations and behavior is less productive theoretically than capitalizing on the interactive nature of human behavior and treating the relationship as it probably is; a reciprocal one. People often take on the behavioral repertoire of their associates but, at the same time, they often seek out associates who share their behavioral interests. Individuals clearly behave this way in conventional settings, and there is no reason to assume that deviant activities, such as delinquency, are substantially different in this regard.

Similar arguments can be made for the other two relationships among the delinquency variables. Most recent theories of delinquency, following the lead of social learning theory, posit that delinquent associations lead to the formation of delinquent values. Subcultural theories, however, especially those that derive from a cultural deviance perspective (Miller, 1958) suggest that values precede the formation of peer groups. Indeed, it is the socialization of adolescents into the "lower-class culture" and its particular value system that leads them to associate with delinquent peers in the first place. This specification can also be derived from a social control perspective as demonstrated in Weis and Sederstrom's social development model (1981) and Burkett and Warren's social selection model (1987).

Finally, the link between delinquent values and delinquent behavior restates, in many ways, the basic social psychological question of the relationship between attitudes and behavior. Do attitudes form behavior patterns or does behavior lead to attitude formation? Social psychological research, especially in cognitive psychology and balance models (for example, Festinger, 1957; Brehm and Cohen, 1962) points to the reciprocal nature of this relationship. It suggests that people indeed behave in a manner consistent with their attitudes, but also that behavior is one of the most persuasive forces in the formation and maintenance of attitudes.

Such a view of the relationship between delinquent values and behavior is consistent with Hindelang's findings:

> This general pattern of results indicates that one can "predict" a respondent's self approval [of illegal behaviors] from knowledge of that respondent's involvement/non-involvement [in delinquency] with fewer errors than vice-versa (1974:382).

It is also consistent with recent deterrence research which demonstrates that the "experiential effect," in which behavior affects attitudes, is much stronger than the deterrent effect, in which attitudes affect behavior (Paternoster, Saltzman, Waldo, and Chiricos, 1982; Paternoster, Saltzman, Chiricos, and Waldo 1983).

Although each of these relationships appears to be reciprocal, the predicted strengths of the associations are not of equal strength during the early adolescent period (see Figure 2). Beliefs that delinquent conduct is acceptable and positively valued may be emerging, but such beliefs are not fully articulated for 11- to 13-year-olds. Because of their emerging quality, they are viewed as more effect than cause, produced by delinquent behavior and associations with delinquent peers. As these values emerge, however, they have feedback effects, albeit relatively weak ones at these ages, on behavior and associations. That is, as the values become more fully articulated and delinquency becomes positively valued, it increases the likelihood of such behavior and further reinforces associations with like-minded peers.

Summary: When attention is focused on the interrelationships among associations with delinquent peers, delinquent values, and delinquent behavior, it appears that they are, in fact, reciprocally related. The world of human behavior is far more complex than a simple recursive one in which a temporal order can be imposed on interactional variables of this nature. Interactional theory sees these three concepts as embedded in a causal loop, each reinforcing the others over time. Regardless of where the individual enters the loop, the following obtains: delinquency increases associations with delinquent peers and delinquent values; delinquent values increase delinquent behavior and associations with delinquent peers; and associations with delinquent peers increases delinquent behavior and delinquent values. The question now concerns the identification of factors that lead some youth, but not others, into this spiral of increasing delinquency.

Social Control Effects

As indicated at the outset of this essay, the premise of interactional theory is that the fundamental cause of delinquency is the attenuation of social controls over the person's conduct. Whenever bonds to the conventional world are substantially weakened, the individual is freed from moral constraints and is at risk for a wide array of deviant activities, including delinquency. The primary mechanisms that bind adolescents to the conventional world are attachment to parents, commitment to school, and belief in conventional values, and their role in the model can now be examined.

During the early adolescent years, the family is the most salient arena for social interaction and involvement and, because of this, attachment to parents has a stronger influence on other aspects of the youth's life at this stage than it does at later stages of development. With this in mind, attachment to parents[1] is predicted to affect four other variables. Since youths who are attached to their parents are sensitive to their wishes (Hirschi, 1969:16–19), and, since parents are almost universally supportive of the conventional world, these children are likely to be strongly committed to school and to espouse conventional values. In addition, youths who are attached to their parents, again because of their sensitivity to parental wishes, are unlikely to associate with delinquent peers or to engage in delinquent behavior.

In brief, parental influence is seen as central to controlling the behavior of youths at these relatively early ages. Parents who have a strong affective bond with their children, who communicate with them, who exercise appropriate parenting skills, and so forth, are likely to lead their children towards conventional actions and beliefs and away from delinquent friends and actions.

On the other hand, attachment to parents is not seen as an immutable trait, impervious to the effects of other variables. Indeed, associating with delinquent peers, not being committed to school, and engaging in delinquent behavior are so contradictory to parental expectations that they tend to diminish the level of attachment between parent and child. Adolescents who fail at school, who associate with delinquent peers, and who engage in delinquent conduct are, as a consequence, likely to jeopardize their affective bond with their parents, precisely because these behaviors suggest that the "person does not care about the wishes and expectations of other people. .." (Hirschi, 1969:18), in this instance, his or her parents.

Turning next to belief in conventional values, this concept is involved in two different causal loops. First, it strongly affects commitment to school and in turn is affected by commitment to school. In essence, this loop posits a behavioral and attitudinal consistency in the conventional realm. Second, a weaker loop is posited between belief in conventional values and associations with delinquent peers. Youths who do not grant legitimacy to conventional values are more apt to associate with delinquent friends who share those views, and those friendships are likely to attenuate further their beliefs in conventional values. This reciprocal specification is supported by Burkett and Warren's findings concerning religious beliefs and peer associations (1987). Finally, youths who believe in conventional values are seen as somewhat less likely to engage in delinquent behavior.

Although belief in conventional values plays some role in the genesis of delinquency, its impact is not particularly strong. For example, it is not affected by delinquent behavior, nor is it related to delinquent values. This is primarily because belief in conventional values appears to be quite invariant; regardless of class of origin

---

[1] The term "attachment to parents" is used throughout the text, but it is clear that parent surrogates— for example foster parents or guardians—can also perform this function.

or delinquency status, for example, most people strongly assert conventional values (Short and Strodtbeck, 1965:Ch. 3). Nevertheless, these beliefs do exert some influence in the model, especially with respect to reinforcing commitment to school.

Finally, the impact of commitment to school is considered. This variable is involved in reciprocal loops with both of the other bonding variables. Youngsters who are attached to their parents are likely to be committed to and succeed in school, and that success is likely to reinforce the close ties to their parents. Similarly, youths who believe in conventional values are likely to be committed to school, the primary arena in which they can act in accordance with those values, and, in turn, success in that arena is likely to reinforce the beliefs.

In addition to its relationships with the other control variables, commitment to school also has direct effects on two of the delinquency variables. Students who are committed to succeeding in school are unlikely to associate with delinquents or to engage in substantial amounts of serious, repetitive delinquent behavior. These youths have built up a stake in conformity and should be unwilling to jeopardize that investment by either engaging in delinquent behavior or by associating with those who do.

Low commitment to school is not seen, however, as leading directly to the formation of delinquent values. Its primary effect on delinquent values is indirect, via associations with delinquent peers and delinquent behavior (Conger, 1980:137). While school failure may lead to a reduced commitment to conventional values, it does not follow that it directly increases the acceptance of values that support delinquency.

Commitment to school, on the other hand, is affected by each of the delinquency variables in the model. Youths who accept values that are consistent with delinquent behavior, who associate with other delinquents, and who engage in delinquent behavior are simply unlikely candidates to maintain an active commitment to school and the conventional world that school symbolizes.

Summary: Attachment to parents, commitment to school, and belief in conventional values reduce delinquency by cementing the person to conventional institutions and people. When these elements of the bond to conventional society are strong, delinquency is unlikely, but when they are weak the individual is placed at much greater risk for delinquency. When viewed from an interactional perspective, two additional qualities of these concepts become increasingly evident.

First, attachment to parents, commitment to school, and belief in conventional values are not static attributes of the person, invariant over time. These concepts interact with one another during the developmental process. For some youths the levels of attachment, commitment, and belief increase as these elements reinforce one another, while for other youths the interlocking nature of these relationships suggests a greater and greater attenuation of the bond will develop over time.

Second, the bonding variables appear to be reciprocally linked to delinquency, exerting a causal impact on associations with delinquent peers and delinquent behavior; they also are causally effected by these variables. As the youth engages in more and more delinquent conduct and increasingly associates with delinquent peers, the level of his bond to the conventional world is further weakened. Thus, while the weakening of the bond to conventional society may be an initial cause of delinquency, delinquency eventually becomes its own indirect cause precisely because of its ability to weaken further the person's bonds to family, school, and conventional beliefs. The implications of this amplifying causal structure is examined below. First, however, the available support for reciprocal models is reviewed and the basic model is extended to later developmental stages.

Support for Reciprocal Structures

The previous section developed a theoretical rationale for moving from recursive to reciprocal causal structures of delinquency. Using an interactional perspective, delinquent behavior, especially sustained involvement with serious delinquent behavior, was viewed as part of an ongoing social process rather than simply a product of other social variables. The present section reviews sources of theoretical and empirical support for this perspective.

First, this model is logically consistent with the approaches of many other theoretical models; see, for example, those proposed by Hirschi (1969), Akers (1977), Elliott et al. (1979, 1985), Weis and Sederstrom (1981), and Snyder and Patterson (in press). Indeed, the present model can be viewed as a logical extension of those theories since it explicitly specifies reciprocal effects that have, until recently, remained largely implicit in criminological theory and research.

Second, as indicated above, recent panel studies that estimate reciprocal effects produce consistent support for this perspective. Whether concerned with unemployment and crime (Thornberry and Christenson, 1984), attachment to parents, commitment to school and delinquency (Liska and Reed, 1985), or religion, peers, and marijuana use (Burkett and Warren, 1987), each of these analyses suggest that there are substantial feedback effects involving delinquency and its presumed causes.

Third, using data from the National Youth Survey, Huizinga and Elliott (1986) report a number of significant reciprocal effects. Although they did not observe feedback effects from delinquent behavior to the conventional bonding variables posited by interactional theory, they do report reciprocal effects among the elements of the bond. They also report that delinquent behavior and associations with delinquent peers are mutually reinforcing (Huizinga and Elliott, 1986:12). Finally, they report that exposure to delinquent friends has significant feedback effects on a wide range of variables, including "internal deviant bonds, perceived sanctions, normlessness, prosocial aspirations, and involvement in prosocial roles" (Huizinga and Elliott, 1986:14).

Fourth, a large number of studies have found that delinquent behavior (including drug use) measured at one time has significant effects on the presumed "causes" of delinquency measured at a later time. Among the variables found to be affected by prior delinquency are educational and occupational attainment (Bachman, O'Malley, and Johnston, 1978: Kandel and Logan, 1984); dropping out of high school (Elliott and Voss, 1974; Bachman et al., 1978; Polk et al., 1981; Thornberry, Moore, and Christenson, 1985); unemployment (Bachman et al., 1978; Thornberry and Christenson, 1984); attachment to parents (Paternoster et al., 1983); commitment to school

(Paternoster et al., 1983; Liska and Reed, 1985; Agnew, 1985); and belief in conventional values (Hindelang, 1974; Paternoster et al., 1983; Agnew, 1985). These empirical findings are quite consistent with theory that posits that delinquent behavior is not only produced by other social variables, but also exerts a significant causal influence on those variables.

DEVELOPMENTAL EXTENSIONS

The previous section developed a strategy for addressing one of the three major limitations of delinquency theories mentioned in the introduction—namely, their unidirectional causal structure. A second limitation is the nondevelopmental posture of most theories which tend to provide a cross-sectional picture of the factors associated with delinquency at one age, but which do not provide a rationale for understanding how delinquent behavior develops over time. The present section offers a developmental extension of the basic model.

Middle Adolescence

First, a model for middle adolescence, when the youths are approximately 15 or 16 years of age is presented (Figure 17.3). This period represents the highest rates of involvement in delinquency and is the reference period, either implicitly or explicitly, for most theories of delinquent involvement. Since the models for the early and middle

FIGURE 17.3   A reciprocal model of delinquent involvement at middle adolescence[a]

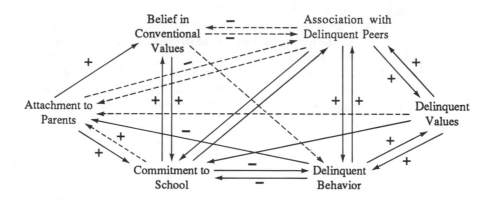

[a]Solid lines represent stronger effects; dashed lines represent weaker effects

adolescent periods have essentially the same structure and causal relationships (Figure 17.2 and 17.3), discussion focuses on the differences between them and does not repeat the rationale for individual causal effects.

Perhaps the most important difference concerns attachment to parents which is involved in relatively few strong relationships. By this point in the life cycle, the most salient variables involved in the production of delinquency are likely to be external to the home, associated with the youth's activities in school and peer networks. This specification is consistent with empirical results for subjects in this age range (Johnson, 1979:105; and Schoenberg, 1975, quoted in Johnson). Indeed, Johnson concludes that "an adolescent's public life has as much or more to do with his or her deviance or conformity than do 'under-the-roof' experiences" (1979:116).

This is not to say that attachment to parents is irrelevant; such attachments are involved in enhancing commitment to school and belief in conventional values, and in preventing associations with delinquent peers. It is just that the overall strength of parental effects are weaker than at earlier ages when the salience of the family as a locus of interaction and control was greater.

The second major change concerns the increased importance of delinquent values as a causal factor. It is still embedded in the causal loop with the other two delinquency variables, but now it is as much cause as effect. Recall that at the younger ages delinquent values were seen as emerging, produced by associations with delinquent peers and delinquent behavior. Given their emergent nature, they were not seen as primary causes of other variables. At midadolescence, however, when delinquency is at its apex, these values are more fully articulated and have stronger effects on other variables. First, delinquent values are seen as major reinforcers of both delinquent associations and delinquent behavior. In general, espousing values supportive of delinquency tends to increase the potency of this causal loop. Second, since delinquent values are antithetical to the conventional settings of school and family, youths who espouse them are less likely to be committed to school and attached to parents. Consistent with the reduced saliency of family at these ages, the feedback effect to school is seen as stronger than the feedback effect to parents.

By and large, the other concepts in the model play the same role at these ages as they do at the earlier ones. Thus, the major change from early to middle adolescence concerns the changing saliency of some of the theoretical concepts. The family declines in relative importance while the adolescent's own world of school and peers takes on increasing significance. While these changes occur, the overall structure of the theory remains constant. These interactive variables are still seen as mutually reinforcing over time.

Later Adolescence

Finally, the causes of delinquency during the transition from adolescence to adulthood, about ages 18 to 20, can be examined (Figure 17.4). At these ages one should more properly speak of crime than delinquency, but for consistency we will continue to use the term delinquency in the causal diagrams and employ the terms delinquency and crime interchangeably in the text.

FIGURE 17.4   A reciprocal model of delinquent involvement at later
adolescence[a]

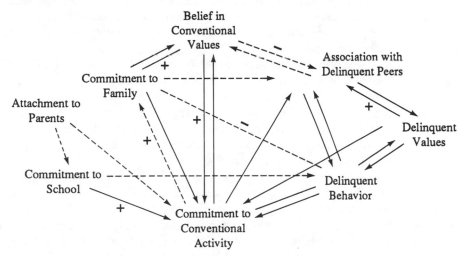

[a]Solid lines represent stronger effects; dashed lines represent weaker effects.

Two new variables are added to the model to reflect the changing life circumstances at this stage of development. The more important of these is commitment to
conventional activities which includes employment, attending college, and military
service. Along with the transition to the world of work, there is a parallel transition from
the family of origin to one's own family. Although this transition does not peak until
the early 20s, for many people its influence is beginning at this stage. Included in this
concept are marriage, plans for marriage, and plans for childrearing. These new
variables largely replace attachment to parents and commitment to school in the
theoretical scheme; they represent the major sources of bonds to conventional society
for young adults.

Both attachment to parents and commitment to school remain in the model but
take on the cast of exogenous variables. Attachment to parents has only a minor effect
on commitment to school, and commitment to school is proposed to affect only
commitment to conventional activities and, more weakly, delinquent behavior.

The other three variables considered in the previous models—association with
delinquent peers, delinquent values, and delinquent behavior—are still hypothesized
to be embedded in an amplifying causal loop. As indicated above, this loop is most
likely to occur among adolescents who, at earlier ages, were freed from the controlling
influence of parents and school. Moreover, via the feedback paths delinquent peers,
delinquent values, and delinquent behavior further alienate the youth from parents and
diminish commitment to school. Once this spiral begins, the probability of sustained
delinquency increases.

This situation, if it continued uninterrupted, would yield higher and higher rates
of crime as the subjects matured. Such an outcome is inconsistent with the desistance

that has been observed during this age period (Wolfgang, Thornberry, and Figlio, 1987). Rates of delinquency and crime begin to subside by the late teenage years, a phenomenon often attributed to "maturational reform." Such an explanation, however, is tautological since it claims that crime stops when adolescents get older, because they get older. It is also uninformative since the concept of maturational reform is theoretically undefined.

A developmental approach, however, offers an explanation for desistance. As the developmental process unfolds, life circumstances change, developmental milestones are met (or, for some, missed), new social roles are created, and new networks of attachments and commitments emerge. The effects of these changes enter the processual model to explain new and often dramatically different behavioral patterns. In the present model, these changes are represented by commitment to conventional activity and commitment to family.

Commitment to conventional activity is influenced by a number of variables, including earlier attachment to parents, commitment to school, and belief in conventional values. And once the transition to the world of work is made, tremendous opportunities are afforded for new and different effects in the delinquency model. Becoming committed to conventional activities—work, college, military service, and so on—reduces the likelihood of delinquent behavior and associations with delinquent peers because it builds up a stake in conformity that is antithetical to delinquency.

Moreover, since the delinquency variables are still embedded in a causal loop, the effect of commitment to conventional activities tends to resonate throughout the system. But, because of the increased saliency of a new variable, commitment to conventional activities, the reinforcing loop is now set in motion to *reduce* rather than increase delinquent and criminal involvement.

The variable of commitment to family has similar, albeit weaker, effects since the transition to the family is only beginning at these ages. Nevertheless, commitment to family is proposed to reduce both delinquent associations and delinquent values and to increase commitment to conventional activity. In general, as the individual takes on the responsibilities of family, the bond to conventional society increases, placing additional constraints on behavior and precluding further delinquency.

These changes do not occur in all cases, however, nor should they be expected to since many delinquents continue on to careers in adult crime. In the Philadelphia cohort of 1945, 51% of the juvenile delinquents were also adult offenders, and the more serious and prolonged the delinquent careers were, the greater the odds of an adult career (Wolfgang et al., 1987; Ch. 4).

The continuation of criminal careers can also be explained by the nature of the reciprocal effects included in this model. In general, extensive involvement in delinquency at earlier ages feeds back upon and weakens attachment to parents and commitment to school (see Figures 17.2 and 17.3). These variables, as well as involvement in delinquency itself, weaken later commitment to family and to conventional activities (Figure 17.4). Thus, these new variables, commitment to conventional activities and to family, are affected by the person's situation at earlier stages and do not "automatically" alter the probability of continued criminal involvement. If the initial bonds are extremely weak, the chances of new bonding variables being established to break the cycle towards criminal careers are low and it is likely that criminal behavior will continue.

Behavioral Trajectories

The manner in which reciprocal effects and developmental changes are interwoven in the interactional model can be explicated by the concept of behavioral trajectories. At early adolescence, some youths are very weakly attached to their parents, very weakly committed to school, and do not grant legitimacy to conventional values. As indicated above, they are the most likely youngsters for high delinquency involvement. (The term delinquency involvement summarizes the causal loop containing delinquent behavior, delinquent values, and association with delinquent peers.) In turn, the high delinquency involvement further attenuates the bonding to parents and to school. This early adolescent situation continues during middle adolescence and substantially reduces the chances of the person reestablishing (or perhaps establishing) bonds to conventional society during late adolescence.

In brief, a behavioral trajectory is established that predicts increasing involvement in delinquency and crime. The initially weak bonds lead to high delinquency involvement, the high delinquency involvement further weakens the conventional bonds, and in combination both of these effects make it extremely difficult to reestablish bonds to conventional society at later ages. As a result, all of the factors tend to reinforce one another over time to produce an extremely high probability of continued deviance.

On the other hand, one can imagine many young adolescents who, at the outset, are strongly attached to their parents, highly committed to school, and believe in conventional values. The theoretical model predicts that this high level of bonding buffers them from the world of delinquency. Moreover, the reciprocal character of this loop establishes a behavioral trajectory for these youths that tends towards increasing conformity. Their initial strong conventional bonds reduce the chances of involvement in delinquency and thereby increase the chances of commitment to conventional activities and the like at later ages.

Thus, we can conceive of at least two types of adolescents with differing and diverging behavioral trajectories. In one trajectory, social bonds become progressively weaker and delinquent behavior progressively more likely, while in the other commitment to conformity becomes progressively stronger and delinquent behavior progressively less likely.

Of course, if there are these extremes, there are also intermediate cases. In many ways they are the most interesting since their eventual outcome is much more in doubt. For example, there are some youths who have a relatively high level of attachment to parents but low commitment to school (or vice versa). These adolescents are more likely candidates for delinquency involvement than are youths with both high attachment and commitment. But, should the delinquent involvement occur, its feedback effect on the bonding variables is less certain. While the delinquency may further reduce the already weak commitment to school, the strong attachment to parents may serve as a buffer to offset some of the negative feedback. Such a situation, in which the initial bonding variables are neither extremely high nor extremely low, allows for rather varied patterns of interactive effects as the developmental process unfolds. Moreover, the prediction of the eventual outcome for such youths awaits more direct empirical evidence establishing the relative strength of these competing effects.

The concept of behavioral trajectories raises an important theoretical issue. It suggests that the initial values of the process variables play a central role in the entire process since they set the basic path of the behavioral trajectories. Because of this, it is theoretically important to account for variation in those initial values. In the present paper the role of one general class of variables, position in the social structure, is used to illustrate this issue.

STRUCTURAL EFFECTS

Structural variables, including race, class, sex, and community of residence, refer to the person's location in the structure of social roles and statuses. The manner in which they are incorporated in the interactional model is illustrated here by examining only one of them, social class of origin.

Although social class is often measured continuously, a categorical approach is more consistent with the present model and with most theories of delinquency that incorporate class as a major explanatory variable—for example, strain and social disorganization theories. For our purposes, the most important categories are the lower class, the working lower class, and the middle class.

The lower class is composed of those who are chronically or sporadically unemployed, receive welfare, and subsist at or below the poverty level. They are similar to Johnson's "underclass" (1979). The working lower class is composed of those with more stable work patterns, training for semiskilled jobs, and incomes that allow for some economic stability. For these families, however, the hold on even a marginal level of occupational and economic security is always tenuous. Finally, the middle class refers to all families above these lower levels. Middle-class families have achieved some degree of economic success and stability and can reasonably expect to remain at that level or improve their standing over time.

The manner in which the social class of origin affects the interactional variables and the behavioral trajectories can be demonstrated by comparing the life expectancies of children from lower- and middle-class families. As compared to children from a middle-class background, children from a lower-class background are more apt to have (1) disrupted family processes and environments (Conger, McCarty, Wang, Lahey, and Kroop, 1984; Wahler, 1980); (2) poorer preparation for school (Cloward and Ohlin, 1960); (3) belief structures influenced by the traditions of the American lower class (Miller, 1958; Anderson, 1976); and (4) greater exposure to neighborhoods with high rates of crime (Shaw and McKay, 1942; Braithwaite, 1981). The direction of all these effects is such that we would expect children from lower-class families to be *initially* less bonded to conventional society and more exposed to delinquent values, friends, and behaviors.

As one moves towards the working lower class, both the likelihood and the potency of the factors just listed decrease. As a result, the initial values of the interactional variables improve but, because of the tenuous nature of economic and social stability for these families, both the bonding variables and the delinquency variables are still apt to lead to considerable amounts of delinquent conduct. Finally, youths from middle-class families, given their greater stability and economic security, are likely to start with a stronger family structure, greater stakes in conformity, and higher chances of success, and all of these factors are likely to reduce the likelihood of initial delinquent involvement.

In brief, the initial values of the interactional variables are systematically related to the social class of origin. Moreover, since these variables are reciprocally related, it follows logically that social class is systematically related to the behavioral trajectories described above. Youngsters from the lowest classes have the highest probability of moving forward on a trajectory of increasing delinquency. Starting from a position of low bonding to conventional institutions and a high delinquency environment, the reciprocal nature of the interrelationships leads inexorably towards extremely high rates of delinquent and criminal involvement. Such a view is consistent with prevalence data which show that by age 18, 50%, and by age 30, 70% of low SES minority males have an official police record (Wolfgang et al., 1987).

On the other hand, the expected trajectory of middle-class youths suggests that they will move toward an essentially conforming life-style, in which their stakes in conformity increase and more and more preclude serious and prolonged involvement in delinquency. Finally, because the initial values of the interactional variables are mixed and indecisive for children from lower-working-class homes, their behavioral trajectories are much more volatile and the outcome much less certain.

Summary: Interactional theory asserts that both the initial values of the process variables and their development over time are systematically related to the social class of origin. Moreover, parallel arguments can be made for other structural variables, especially those associated with class, such as race, ethnicity, and the social disorganization of the neighborhood. Like class of origin, these variables are systematically related to variables such as commitment to school and involvement in delinquent behavior, and therefore, as a group, these structural variables set the stage on which the reciprocal effects develop across the life cycle.

CONCLUSION

The present article has developed an interactional theory of delinquent behavior. Unlike traditional theories of delinquency, interactional theory does not view delinquency merely as an outcome or consequence of a social process. On the contrary, it views delinquent behavior as an active part of the developmental process, interacting with other social factors over time to determine the person's ultimate behavioral repertoire.

The initial impetus towards delinquency comes from a weakening of the person's bond to conventional society, represented, during adolescence, by attachment to parents, commitment to school, and belief in conventional values. Whenever these three links to conformity are attenuated, there is a substantially increased potential for delinquent behavior.

For that potential to be converted to delinquency, especially prolonged serious delinquency, however, a social setting in which delinquency is learned and reinforced is required. This setting is represented by associations with delinquent peers and delinquent values. These two variables, along with delinquent behavior itself, form a mutually reinforcing causal loop that leads towards increasing delinquency involvement over time.

Moreover, this interactive process develops over the person's life cycle, and the saliency of the theoretical concepts vary as the person ages. During early adolescence, the family is the most influential factor in bonding the youth to conventional society and reducing delinquency. As the youth matures and moves through middle adolescence, the world of friends, school, and youth culture becomes the dominant influence over behavior. Finally, as the person enters adulthood, new variables, especially commitment to conventional activities and to family, offer a number of new avenues to reshape the person's bond to society and involvement with delinquency.

Finally, interactional theory posits that these process variables are systematically related to the person's position in the social structure. Class, minority-group status, and the social disorganization of the neighborhood of residence all affect the initial values of the interactive variables as well as the behavioral trajectories. Youths from the most socially disadvantaged backgrounds begin the process least bonded to conventional society and most exposed to the world of delinquency. Furthermore, the reciprocal nature of the process increases the chances that they will continue on to a career of serious criminal involvement. On the other hand, youths from middle-class families enter a trajectory which is strongly oriented toward conformity and away from delinquency.

But, regardless of the initial starting points or the eventual outcome, the essential point of an interactional theory is that the causal process is a dynamic one that develops over the person's life. And delinquent behavior is a vital part of that process; it is clearly affected by, but it also affects, the bonding and learning variables that have always played a prominent role in sociological explanations of delinquency.

EPILOGUE

The version of interactional theory presented here is an initial statement of this perspective and does not represent a complete model of all the factors that are associated with delinquency. For example, the role of other structural variables, especially race and sex, which are so strongly correlated with delinquency, has to be fully explicated to better understand the sources of both the delinquency and bonding variables. Similarly, greater attention needs to be paid to the influence of early childhood behaviors and family processes since it is increasingly clear that delinquency is part of a progressive sequence that begins at much earlier ages (Patterson and Dishion, 1985; Loeber and Stouthamer-Loeber, 1986).

In addition, other process variables similar to those incorporated in Figure 17. 2 through 4 need to be considered. For example, the general issue of gang membership and co-offending should be examined in an interactional setting as should concepts such as self-concept and self-efficacy. Finally, developmental stages have been represented here by rough age categories, and they require more careful and precise definition in terms of physical maturation and psychological growth.

Despite these, and no doubt other, limitations, this article accurately represents the basic structure of an interactional theory of delinquency. It has identified the theory's core concepts and described the manner in which they are reciprocally related to account for the initiation of delinquency and its development over time. In the coming years, the theory described here will be developed theoretically and tested empirically.[2]

REFERENCES

Agnew, Robert (1985) Social control theory and delinquency: A longitudinal test. Criminology 23:47–62.

Akers, Ronald (1977) Deviant Behavior: A Social Learning Perspective. Belmont: Wadsworth.

Akers, Ronald L., Marvin D. Krohn, Lonn Lanza-Kaduce, and Marcia Radosevich (1979) Social learning theory and deviant behavior. American Sociological Review 44:635–655.

Anderson, Elijah (1976) A Place on the Corner. Chicago: University of Chicago Press.

Bachman, Jerald G., Patrick M. O'Malley, and John Johnston (1978) Youth in Transition: Adolescence to Adulthood—Change and Stability in the Lives of Young Men. Ann Arbor: Institute for Social Research.

Braithwaite, John (1981) The myth of social class and criminality reconsidered. American Sociological Review 46:36–58.

Brehm, J.W. and Arthur R. Cohen (1962) Explorations in Cognitive Dissonance. New York: Wiley.

Burkett, Steven R. and Bruce O. Warren (1987) Religiosity, peer influence, and adolescent marijuana use: A panel study of underlying causal structures. Criminology 25:109–131.

Cloward, Richard A. and Lloyd E. Ohlin (1960) Delinquency and Opportunity: A Theory of Delinquent Gangs. Glencoe: Free Press.

Conger, Rand D. (1980) Juvenile delinquency: Behavior restraint or behavior facilitation? In Travis Hirschi and Michael Gottfredson (eds.), Understanding Crime. Beverly Hills: Sage.

Conger, Rand D., John A. McCarty, Raymond K. Wang, Benjamin B. Lahey, and Joseph P. Kroop (1984) Perception of child, child-rearing values, and emotional distress as mediating links between environmental stressors and observed maternal behavior. Child Development 55:2,234–2,247.

Cullen, Francis T. (1984) Rethinking Crime and Deviance Theory: The Emergence of a Structuring Tradition. Totowa, NJ: Rowman and Allanheld.

Elliott, Delbert S. (1985) The assumption that theories can be combined with increased explanatory power: Theoretical integrations. In Robert F. Meier (ed.). Theoretical Methods in Criminology. Beverly Hills: Sage.

[2] The Rochester Youth Development Study, supported by the Office of Juvenile Justice and Delinquency Prevention and directed with my colleagues Alan Lizotte. Margaret Farnworth, and Susan Stern, is designed to examine the basic causes and correlates of delinquency from this perspective.

Elliott, Delbert S., Suzanne S. Ageton, and Rachelle J. Canter (1979) An integrated theoretical perspective on delinquent behavior. Journal of Research on Crime and Delinquency 16:3–27.

Elliott, Delbert S., David Huizinga, and Suzanne S. Ageton (1985) Explaining Delinquency and Drug Use. Beverly Hills: Sage.

Elliott, Delbert S. and Harwin L. Voss (1974) Delinquency and Dropout. Lexington: Lexington Books.

Festinger, Leon (1957) A Theory of Cognitive Dissonance. Stanford: Stanford University Press.

Glueck, Sheldon and Eleanor Glueck (1950) Unraveling Juvenile Delinquency. Cambridge: Harvard University Press.

Hanushek, Eric A. and John E. Jackson (1977) Statistical Methods for Social Scientists. New York: Academic Press.

Heise, David R. (1975) Causal Analysis. New York: Wiley.

Hindelang, Michael J. (1974) Moral evaluations of illegal behaviors. Social Problems 21:370–384.

Hindelang, Michael J., Travis Hirschi, and Joseph G. Weis (1981) Measuring Delinquency. Beverly Hills: Sage.

Hirschi, Travis (1969) Causes of Delinquency. Berkeley: University of California Press.

Huizinga, David and Delbert S. Elliott (1986) The Denver High-Risk Delinquency Project. Proposal Submitted to the Office of Juvenile Justice and Delinquency Prevention.

Johnson, Richard E. (1979) Juvenile Delinquency and Its Origins. Cambridge: Cambridge University Press.

Kandel, Denise B. and John A. Logan (1984) Patterns of drug use from adolescence to young adulthood I. Periods of risk for initiation, continued risk and discontinuation. American Journal of Public Health 74:660–667.

Krohn, Marvin D. and James Massey (1980) Social and delinquent behavior: An examination of the elements of the social bond. Sociological Quarterly 21, 529–543.

LaGrange, Randy L. and Helene Raskin White (1985) Age differences in delinquency: A test of theory. Criminology 23:19–46.

Loeber, Rolf and Magda Stouthamer-Loeber (1986) Family factors as correlates and predictors of juvenile conduct problems and delinquency. In Norval Morris and Michael Tonry (eds.). Crime and Justice: An Annual Review of Research Chicago: University of Chicago Press.

Liska, Allen and Mark Reed (1985) Ties to conventional institutions and delinquency. American Sociological Review 50:547–560.

Matsueda, Ross (1982) Testing social control theory and differential association. American Sociological Review 47:489–504.

Miller, Walter B. (1958) Lower class culture as a generating milieu of gang delinquency. Journal of Social Issues 14:5–19.

Paternoster, Raymond, Linda E. Saltzman, Gordon P. Waldo, and Theodore G. Chiricos (1982) Perceived risk and deterrence: Methodological artifacts in perceptual deterrence research. Journal of Criminal Law and Criminology 73:1,238–1,258.

Paternoster, Raymond, Linda E. Saltzman, Theodore G. Chiricos, and Gordon P. Waldo (1983) Perceived risk and social control: Do sanctions really deter? Law and Society Review 17:457–479.

Patterson, Gerald R. and Thomas S. Dishion (1985) Contributions of families and peers to delinquency. Criminology 23:63–80.

Polk, Kenneth, Christine Adler, Gordon Bazemore, Gerald Blake, Sheila Cordray, Garry Coventry, James Galvin, and Mark Temple (1981) Becoming Adult: An Analysis of Maturational Development from Age 16 to 30 of a Cohort of Young Men. Final Report of the Marion County Youth Study. Eugene: University of Oregon.

Polk, Kenneth, Christine Adler, Gordon Bazemore, Gerald Blake, Sheila Cordray, Garry Coventry, James Galvin, and Mark Temple (1981) Becoming Adult: An Analysis of Maturational Development from Age 16 to 30 of a Cohort of Young Men. Final Report of the Marion County Youth Study. Eugene: University of Oregon.

Poole, Eric D. and Robert M. Regoli (1979) Parental Support, delinquent friends and delinquency: A test of interactional effects. Journal of Criminal Law and Criminology 70:188–193.

Schoenberg, Ronald J. (1975) A Structural Model of Delinquency. Unpublished doctoral dissertation. Seattle: University of Washington.

Shaw, Clifford R. and Henry D. McKay (1942) Juvenile Delinquency and Urban Areas. Chicago: University of Chicago Press.

Short, James F. Jr., and Fred L. Strodtbeck (1965) Group Processes and Gang Delinquency. Chicago: University of Chicago Press.

Snyder, J. and Gerald Patterson (In Press) Family interactions and delinquent behavior. Child Development.

Thornberry, Terence P. (1987) Reflections on the advantages and disadvantages of theoretical integration. Presented at the Albany Conference on Theoretical Integration in the Study of Crime and Deviance.

Thornberry, Terence P. and R.L. Christenson (1984) Unemployment and criminal involvement: An investigation of reciprocal causal structures. American Sociological Review 49:398–411.

Thornberry, Terence P., Margaret Farnworth, and Alan Lizotte (1986) A Panel Study of Reciprocal Causal Model of Delinquency. Proposal submitted to the Office of Juvenile Justice and Delinquency Prevention.

Thornberry, Terence P., Melanie Moore, and R.L. Christenson (1985) The effect of dropping out of high school on subsequent delinquent behavior. Criminology 23:3–18.

Wahler, R. (1980) The insular mother: Her problems in parent-child treatment. Journal of Applied Behavior Analysis 13:207–219.

Weis, Joseph G. and John Sederstrom (1981) The Prevention of Serious Delinquency: What to Do? Washington, D.C., U.S. Department of Justice.

Wolfgang, Marvin E., Terence P. Thornberry, and Robert M. Figlio (1987) From Boy to Man—From Delinquency to Crime: Followup to the Philadelphia Birth Cohort of 1945. Chicago: University of Chicago Press.

Exploring Integration of Theoretical Levels of Explanation
Notes on Gang Delinquency

JAMES F. SHORT, JR.

THE GOALS OF THIS PAPER are modest and straightforward: 1) to suggest a rationale for integrating levels of explanation; 2) to suggest alternatives to simplifying assumptions which ignore well established knowledge; 3) to identify relationships between levels of explanation which might foster their integration.[1]

Levels of explanation refer to what is to be explained as well as to how it is to be explained. As I will use these terms, the *individual* level seeks to explain *behaviors of individuals*, while the *macrosocial* level focuses on *rates* and *types* of behavior. Explanation at the individual level is in terms of characteristics of individuals, while at the macro-level it is on social and cultural system differences. The *microsocial* level directs attention to behavioral outcomes of *ongoing behavioral events* and seeks explanation in terms of interaction processes characteristic of such events (see Short, 1985; Cohen and Short, 1976). The relevance of each level of explanation to the other levels is what theoretical integration is about.

Source: Short, James F., Jr. "Exploring Integration of Theoretical Levels of Explanation: Notes on Gang Delinquency." In Messner, Steven, Marvin Krohn and Alan Liska (Eds.). *Theoretical Integration in the Study of Deviance and Crime: Problems and Prospects*. Albany: SUNY Press, 1989. Reprinted by permission of SUNY Press and James F. Short, Jr.

[1] I use as an exemplar, my own research and that of others on gang delinquency. See Short and Strodtbeck, 1965 (the 1974 edition included a new introduction and a list of papers published subsequent to the earlier edition); also Short, 1974, 1985, and forthcoming.

The rationale is simple. Theoretical and empirical advance, as well as effective social policy, require knowledge that transcends the limitations of levels of explanation standing alone. Yet scholarly disciplines and practitioners in juvenile justice remain by and large locked in departments, research units, and programs which, if not mutually exclusive, tend to be compartmentalized and insular. Nevertheless, it is clear that there is much overlap among disciplines, and between disciplines and practitioners, in the nature of their interests in delinquency and delinquents.

SIMPLIFYING ASSUMPTIONS AND "GRAY AREAS" OF KNOWLEDGE

The fact that "one cannot say everything at once" forces decisions as to how to organize theory and research. We do so clumsily, often by the use of simplifying assumptions. Simplifying assumptions are useful, indeed necessary, but they often become little more than "easy ways out" of the difficult task of critical examination and use of knowledge from other disciplines or research traditions[2] Thus, for example, the assumption that there is *a* human nature or that human nature is *either* fixed and anti-social *or* malleable and developing is untenable and unnecessary. As knowledge of genetic limitations and potentialities has grown, it has become clear that biology and experience interact, and that physiological conditions *in combination* with social processes and conditions shape human development

Similarly, the manner in which individual compositional features of social and cultural systems affect those systems, and the outcomes of events within them, is critical to macro- and microsocial levels of explanation. Recent research on crime and communities, for example, suggests that communities, as well as individuals, have "careers in crime" (see Reiss and Tonry, 1986). The manner in which these careers relate to the sorts of individuals who comprise communities must be neither assumed nor ignored.

The discovery that involvement in minor delinquencies is virtually universal has led some to assume that it is unnecessary to inquire as to why young people commit delinquent acts. It is important only to know "why don't" they do so. Increasingly, that question is being posed as, "why don't they commit *serious* crimes," for that is the more popular (and troubling) question (see Blumstein, et al., 1986; cf., Gottfredson and Hirschi, 1986). Most criminal involvement also is varied and widespread, rather than esoteric, specialized, or confined to a small minority. In view of these facts it makes little sense to ask what distinguishes delinquents from nondelinquents. Nor is it sufficient to limit inquiry to "why do" and "why don't" young people commit delinquent behaviors. Etiologically-relevant questions must concern the processes and mechanisms of motivation *and* control, in different social systems and subcultures, which account for variations in behavior.

A very large number of adolescent (and preadolescent) behaviors are of sufficient concern to adults that they have been legally proscribed. Many of these change

---

[2] See, also, Swigert, this volume. The subject matter of simplifying assumptions of one discipline are, of course, often of primary interest to other disciplines.

over time and circumstance. Motivations of "reactors" to such behaviors, as well as offenders, also vary.[3] Finally, those who engage in acts defined as delinquent do so only occasionally. Even the most seriously delinquent boy or girl does not spend much of his or her time committing delinquent acts; and most youngsters in even the highest "delinquency areas" do not become seriously delinquent. It is in "gray areas," such as that between "normal" adolescent behaviors and those that stretch the bonds and the boundaries of control beyond toleration levels in families and communities, that different levels of explanation become critical. Subcultures and related group processes help to explain both why some *individuals* "do" and others "do not" commit proscribed behaviors, and/or the circumstances in which some individuals will or will not do so. The strength of "mainstream" cultural norms varies, as do local community toleration levels. When either of these is weak or ambiguous, the "push" needed to encourage participation in law breaking is lessened. The ambiguity of general American norms concerning "cheating" on income tax, "sharp" business dealings, "macho" images and the use of violence to settle disputes, lends support to those who would commit both property and person offenses (see Matza and Sykes, 1961). In some communities "hustling" is "hard work" and a way of life (Valentine, 1978). When opportunities for illegal gain exist and when community or group norms support illegal behavior, or group processes lead in that direction, legal proscriptions may lack force. Research at the microsocial level is necessary for more precise understanding of the situations or circumstances under which group processes supercede conventional norms, and the mechanisms by which individual decision-making leads to delinquent versus nondelinquent behavior choices.

Such broadly-sketched parameters leave many questions unanswered, e.g., which boys and girls make which choices, or have such choices made for them by others; why delinquency episodes occur when and where they do; what sorts of "occasions" give rise to delinquency on the part of what sorts of youngsters. Still another "gray area" thus concerns the processes, mechanisms, and types of life events which "trigger" delinquent episodes and/or lead to greater individual commitment to deviant identities.

DELINQUENCY AS COLLECTIVE BEHAVIOR

The remainder of this paper focuses on relationships between levels of explanation of individual and group behaviors among members of delinquent gangs. Observations are drawn chiefly, but not exclusively, from studies conducted in Chicago during the period, 1959 through the early 1970s (see Short and Strodtbeck, 1965, 1974; Short and Molland, 1976).

The research is embedded in the following widely accepted theoretical principles

---

[3] Gibbs (1985) notes that the absence of "reactive" variables in major theories of etiology of crime and delinquency "may have led criminologists to shift their attention from these. . . to labelling theory" (p. 48).

regarding subcultural formation: 1) "social separation produces cultural differentia-tion" (Glaser, 1971); 2) available alternative choices for action are socially structured, (see Merton, 1938; also Stinchcombe, 1975); and 3) "the crucial condition for the emergence of new cultural forms is the existence, *in effective interaction with one another, of a number of actors with similar problems of adjustment*" (Cohen, 1955, p. 59).[4]

The gangs we studied fit the following defining criteria: 1) recurrent congrega-tion outside the home; 2) self-defined inclusion/exclusion criteria and continuity of affiliation; 3) a territorial basis consisting of customary hanging and ranging areas, including self-defined use-and-occupancy rights; 4) a versatile activity repertoire; and 5) organizational differentiation, e.g., by authority, roles, prestige, friendship or special interest cliques. [5]

Macrosocial observations

All of the "gang communities" (where the lower-class gang and non-gang groups were located) were characterized by lower socioeconomic status indicators. There were, however, marked differences between the black and white gang areas, e.g., income levels and overcrowded living conditions; no white gang community studied was as disadvantaged as the least disadvantaged black gang community. The latter were also more disadvantaged with respect to family stability and other institutional measures. In sum, members of the black gangs lived in communities consisting of the "unstable poor," while the white gangs resided in working-class communities among the "stable poor" (Miller, 1964).[6]

[4] The impact on young people of policies and practices of local institutions, and of events in local communities, is critical (see Schwartz, 1987). Even the most thorough studies of the historical macro-level forces that have shaped contemporary youth cultures (e.g., Schwendinger and Schwendinger, 1985) are weakened by the absence of information concerning the socialization experiences of young people in families and community institutions, and the mechanisms by which they influence individual and group behavior (see Short, 1985b).

[5] These are adapted from Miller (1981). I omit Miller's specification of the centrality of four types of activity (hanging out, relations with the opposite sex, illegal activities, and recreational-athletic activities) on the grounds that it is behavior that we wish to explain. Miller's types and subtypes of law-violating youth groups may also be viewed as dependent variables. The specific nature of the subcultures and related behavior of the gangs we studied is discussed in Short and Strodbeck, 1965 and Short, 1985.

Consistent with the importance accorded group-definition of gang status, the basic design of the research compared gangs with adult-sponsored groups comprised of the same or similar age, race, and gender peers from the gang neighborhoods. Youth groups from middle-class neighborhoods also were studied, but we did not systematically interview youth workers with nongang groups, nor did we place field observers with these groups. Timing and the shifting nature of the field situation made it impossible always to use the several methods of data collection utilized in the study with precisely the same boys. Group membership changed over time, while our police record checks, interviews, and assessments, occurred periodically or at a single point in time. Field observations of the gangs extended over an initial period of approximately five years, but gangs were added to the study over that period. The follow-up study, conducted a dozen years after

[6] Use of the term, "unstable poor," to describe the families and communities of black gang members is not intended to be evaluative; the term is simply indicative of the instability of circumstances in their lives. (See Liebow, 1967; Hannerz, 1969; Valentine, 1978; Anderson, 1978).

Youth groups from the black and white middle-class communities were "better off" than any of the gang communities, but the white middle-class community, and the white middle-class boys studied, were more affluent than the black middle-class boys and their local community (see Short and Strodtbeck, 1965; also Cartwright, et al., 1975).

Life in the white gang areas revolved around conventional institutions such as the Catholic church, local political organizations, and "improvement associations" (a euphemism in some instances for keeping blacks from moving into their neighborhoods). Ethnic organizations and extended kinship groups, unions and other job relationships and formally organized recreational patterns (e.g., bowling leagues) were important sources of community stability for both adults and young people. Neighborhood taverns, often with a distinct ethnic clientele, were the exclusive domain of neighborhood adults.

Life in the black gang communities was characterized by informal neighboring from the vantage of front-door steps or stair landings, and by socializing in local taverns and pool halls and other quasi-public settings such as "quarter parties." There was a great deal of mingling of young people and adults which sometimes resulted in delinquent episodes such as the following observation of a "quarter party":

> This woman who is called "Ma" was giving the party. There was a lot of drinking—inside, outside in the cars, in the alleys, everywhere. There were Rattlers (the gang to which the worker was assigned) and a bunch of boys from the (housing) projects. They had two rooms, neither of them very large. There was some friction going on when I got there—boys bumping each other, and stuff like this. There were a lot of girls there. Must have been about 50 to 75 people in these two rooms, plus another 20 or 25 outside. There were some older fellows there, too—mainly to try and grab one of these younger girls. The girls were doing a lot of drinking—young girls, 12- and 13-year olds. The age group in this party must have been from about 11 to 30's. There were girls there as young as 11, but no boys younger than about 15. The girls are there as a sex attraction, and with the older boys and men around, you know the younger boys aren't going to do any good.
>
> We had one real fight. One of David's sisters was talking to one of these boys from the projects. I guess she promised to go out to the car with him. To get outside you had to go out this door and down this hall, and then out on the porch and down the stairs. She went as far as the porch. As she got out there, I guess she changed her mind. By this time the guy wasn't standing for any "changing the mind" business, and he started to pull on her. She yelled for David, and he came running out. All he could see was his sister and a guy he didn't know pulling on her. David plowed right into the guy. I guess he hit him about 15 times and knocked him down and across the street, and by the time I got there the guy was lying in the gutter. I took David off to the side and told Gary to get the guy out of there.
>
> Duke, Red, and Mac were standing eight or ten feet away, sort of watching these project boys. This one boy goes up the street on the other side and comes up behind David and me. We don't see him. All of the sudden Duke runs right past me and he plows into this guy. Duke said, "Well look, man, the guy was sneaking up behind you and I wasn't gonna have him hit you from behind! I did it to protect you."
>
> I got the guy up and he said, "I wasn't going to hit you. I just wanted to see what was going on." But Duke says, "Let's run all these project guys out." I talked them out of it.

I said, "Look, don't you think you've done enough? The police aren't here yet, but if you start anything else somebody is bound to call them. The party is still going on so why don't we all just go back inside. No sense in breaking up a good thing. You paid your quarter." (Adapted from Short and Strodtbeck, pp. 110-111.)

In contrast to the relationships between black gang members and local adults, white gang boys more often found themselves openly at odds with proprietors of local hangouts and other adults and adult institutions, particularly concerning drinking (which was virtually universal), drug use (which was rare among most of these boys), sexual delinquency, and general rowdyism. Stealing was tacitly condoned by adult "fences" and other purchasers of stolen goods, but deeply resented by local residents who had been victimized, and feared by others. In communities undergoing racial transition (during the period of study this included most lower-class white communities in Chicago) the rowdyism complained of was at times turned to advantage and encouraged by local adults. An apposite case is the following:

At approximately 12:30 at night, I was hanging with a group of 15 to 20 members of the Amboys, Bengals, Sharks, and a few Mafia, at the corner of the park. The group was a mixed one of boys and girls ranging in age from 16 to 20. For the most part, they were sitting or reclining in the park, talking, drinking beer, or wrestling with the girls. They were not unusually loud or boisterous because a policeman on a three-wheeler had been by a half-hour earlier and had warned them of the lateness of the hour.

I noticed a solitary teen-age figure ambling along on the sidewalk heading toward the Avenue, but paid no particular heed. As the figure neared the group, he made no effort to swerve over and join the group but continued by. This was an oddity, so I watched the youth as he neared the curb where I was sitting. I suddenly realized that the boy was black, and in danger if detected. I did not dare do or say anything for fear of alerting the kids, and for a few minutes I thought he could pass by without detection. However, a Bengal who had been drinking beer spotted him and immediately asked, "Am I drunk or is that a Nigger?" The attention of the entire group was then focused on the black youth, who by this time had stepped off the curb and was walking in the center of the street.

Behind him, however, consternation and anger arose spontaneously like a mushroom cloud. I heard muttered threats, "Let's kill the bastard," "Get the mother-fucker," "Come on, let's get going." Even the girls agreed.

Within seconds, about a dozen of the kids began running after the black youth. Realizing that I was unable to stem the tide, I yelled out "Hey man, look alive." The boy heard me in mid-stride, but did not turn around. Again I found it necessary to shout a warning as the white teenagers were rapidly overtaking him. At my second outcry, the black youth turned around and saw the white kids closing in on him. Without hesitation, he took off at full speed with the white mob at his heels yelling shouts of "Kill the bastard—don't let him get away."

I remained standing by my car, joined by three Amboys who did not participate in the chase. The president of the Amboys shook his head, stating that his guys reacted like a bunch of kids whenever they saw a colored guy, and openly expressed his wish that the boy would get away. Another Amboy in an alibi tone, excused his non-participation by explaining that he couldn't run fast enough to catch anybody. Harry merely stated that the black kid didn't bother him, so why should he be tossed in jail for assaulting a stranger.

> We could hear the progress of the chase from the next block. There were shouts and outcries as the pursued ran down the street and his whereabouts were echoed by the bedlam created by his pursuers. Finally, there was silence and we waited for approximately fifteen minutes before the guys began to straggle back. As they returned, each recited his share of the chase. Barney laughingly related that Guy had hurdled a parked car in an effort to tackle the kid, who had swerved out into the street. He said he had entered a coal yard, looking around to find where the boy had hidden, when an adult from a second floor back porch warned that he had better get out of there as the coal yard was protected by a large and vicious Great Dane.
>
> The black youth apparently had decided that he couldn't outrun his tormentors and had gone in and out of back yards until he was able to find a hiding place. His pursuers began to make a systematic search of the alleys, garages, back yards, corridors, etc. *The boys were spurred on to greater efforts by the adults of the area who offered advice and encouragement.* One youth laughingly related that a woman, from her bedroom window, kept pointing out probable hiding places in her back yard so that he would not overlook any sanctuary. Other youths related similar experiences. Glen related that as the youths turned onto X street, he began to shout to the people ahead in the block that "a Nigger was coming" so that someone ahead might catch or head off the boy. (Adapted from Short and Strodtbeck, pp. 112-114.)

This scene was typical of late evening gatherings of boys and girls at "their" park in a neighborhood that was unsuccessfully resisting invasion by black families. In both of these field reports, macro-level phenomena (the ecological setting, normative properties of the community, and the general structure of relationships between young people and adults) set the stage for events which resulted in delinquent behavior. In both, the "action" is a function of the ongoing interaction of parties involved in the events. There is, of course, much we do not and cannot know about these events—their outcomes (and other possible outcomes)—but it is clear that the behavior observed cannot be understood without reference to both macro- and micro-level phenomena.

Because of the racial ecology of Chicago, black and white gangs did not fight with one another. Black gangs were deeply embedded in lower-class cultural and community settings. In contrast, many black families in the vanguard of invasion of white residential areas were able to do so as a result of relative economic affluence (see Bursick, 1986).

The individual level of explanation

Direct evidence of "common crime" role models in the black gang areas is found in field observations:

> That poolroom down there is nothing but hustlers—the worst type of people in the area—prostitutes dressed kind of flashy, and their pimps. There was one guy, a dope addict, wears his shades, one of the regulars. He was shooting pool, and he recognized me and spoke to me and to the fellows.
>
> The three of us started shooting a game on the back table. There was a conversation that the older fellows were having on one of the front tables about some kind of robbery

that they had just pulled. They had been busted. They were all teasing one of the guys that was shooting, about the fact that he was caught. The police had him chained around the lamp post. He got his hand out of one of the cuffs, but he still had one of the cuffs on. He couldn't get it off, and they were teasing him. Everyone in the poolroom was aware of what was going on. (Adapted from Short and Strodtbeck, p. 108.)

The "business as usual" nature of criminal behavior in the black gang communities is further illustrated by another detached worker's report that a street dealer in marijuana was enclosing a note with her new address in each bag she sold. Customers were thanked for their business and asked to continue their patronage in her new location.

Such crime as existed in the white gang communities was more covert. The white gangs also were less visible in their communities, to younger children as well as adults, than was the case in the black communities. Field observations confirmed these differences. While attending an evening of boxing matches between members of two black gangs, I was seated at ringside with the leader of one of the gangs. Several preteen boys were seated immediately back of us. One of these boys, aged 9 or 10, whispered loudly (and admiringly) to another, "That's Buck, president of the Cobras." Pre-teens also were much in evidence at other social occasions, involving gang members, far more so than in comparable gatherings in the white gang areas.

These observations were confirmed by interview responses of boys in each of the six research design strata (black and white lower-class gang and non-gang, and black and white middle-class) concerning their perceptions of legitimate and criminal opportunities (see Cloward and Ohlin, 1960; Short, Rivera, and Tennyson, 1965). Legitimate educational and occupational opportunities tended strongly to be perceived as more open by whites than by blacks, by middle-class than be lower-class boys, and by nongang than by gang boys. Perceptions of adult "clout" and helpfulness to young people followed this same pattern. Responses indicative of integration of the carriers of criminal and noncriminal values, criminal learning structures, and visibility of criminal careers were precisely the opposite.

A consistent picture emerged also from interviews with boys and adults they had "nominated" as those with whom they had the *most contact* (see Rivera and Short, 1967a). Gang members were more isolated from the conventional adult world, more embedded in the lower-class milieu, and less likely to receive assistance from adults than were nongang boys from the same communities. Middle-class boys were more favored in each respect. The contrast was especially notable among the black youngsters studied, and among their "significant adults." Gang members, compared to their non-gang counterparts, had little reason to believe that adults were willing or able to help them in substantial ways. Analysis of the boys' evaluations of adult roles suggested that detached workers played a *compensating*, albeit quite limited, role for gang boys *vis a vis* the adult world (see Short, Rivera, and Marshall, 1964). Study of the occupational choices of the boys found *social relationships with adults* to be more influential than were the boys' perceptions of mobility chances of neighborhood peers, again highlighting the importance of adult relationships, again to the detriment of the gang boys (see Rivera and Short, 1967b).

All of these observations suggest that adult-world macro-level influences are "translated" by means of conventional socialization processes, such as those specified in social learning theory (Akers, 1977) and social cognitive theory (Bandura, 1986).

The "social disability" hypothesis

Very early in the research, field observations indicated that lower-class boys and girls lacked social assurance and possessed few social skills. Detached workers frequently reported that members of their gangs did not feel comfortable when outside "the area" and that they were ill at ease in many social situations. The following excerpt from a detached worker's report is apposite, and suggests as well that members of the gang under observation had a low degree of mutual obligation to one another outside of the gang context. The worker is describing events prior to and during the annual banquet of the YMCA of Metropolitan Chicago, a very large, "dressy" affair attended by many of the city's political, business and philanthropy leaders.

> I talked it over with Duke. Duke wanted me to get him a date with one of the YMCA girls from the downtown office. I told him I thought maybe he'd be better to take Elaine because she's never been to a downtown affair. Elaine has a baby girl who is a year old and one that's three. Duke's never taken her to a real nice place. I had an extra ticket and I said, "Well, Duke, seeing that you and Butch get along real well, maybe Butch would go."
>
> Duke said, "No, no, we don't want to take Butch because he doesn't know how to eat out in company."
>
> I smiled and said "Crisake, he knows just as much as you do."
>
> "No, he just don't know how to eat out in company." Then he went back to the time I took them to the Prudential Building. I suggested that we go in and get a cup of coffee, but Butch said, "No, we'd better go back to the area and get a hot dog or Polish [sausage]." And Duke was all for it, too, because he didn't want to go there either. They're real shy about going into a strange place that's real nice. Earlier in the summer I took Duke, Butch, and Harry out to Lake Meadows, and they were real shy. They didn't want to go in because they felt they weren't dressed good enough. Anyway, Duke didn't feel Butch was qualified. So I said "Okay, how about Harry?"
>
> "Hell no. Harry hasn't got enough clothes to go."
>
> On the way to the banquet I told them approximately what was going to go on, about the main speaker being President Eisenhower's doctor. When we got to the amphitheater, I dropped Elaine, Alice [Duke's aunt and the worker's date for the evening], and Duke and I went to park the car. I told him to go in and check the coats. He looked around and finally came back because he didn't know where they were supposed to go. Then I found the tables and I put Duke and Elaine together.
>
> Over-all, he had a real good time. Elaine complained because Duke insulted her. Duke was trying to show her how to cut the meat. He said Elaine didn't know which hand to hold the knife in. She was real hungry and she ate everything but the meat, because Duke was rapping on her so much. She felt real bad for not having eaten the meat. She didn't know whether it would have been appropriate to have Duke cut her meat or not. (Adapted from Short and Strodtbeck, pp. 219-220.)

The boys' lack of social skills was advanced as a possible explanation for aggressive behavior both within the gang and in relations between gangs (see Short and Strodtbeck, 1965; Gordon, 1967). In the absence of social skills, verbal aggression, body punching, wrestling, and aggressive posturing serve as a sort of least common denominator for interpersonal relationships. Boys who possess more advanced social skills often are rewarded with leadership positions. The gang provides no encouragement for (and often discourages) the development or the exercise of skills necessary to function in such conventional settings as school, work, or marriage, however. Again, a field report is illustrative:

> Fuzzhead, a member of the Chiefs, approached the detached worker in a pool hall hangout and began to talk very seriously about his plans to get and keep a job so that he could provide for the girl he wanted to marry. The worker probed Fuzzhead and, finding him deadly in earnest, encouraged the boy in these ambitions and indicated his willingness to help him secure a steady job. In the midst of the conversation other Chiefs entered the pool hall and came over to where the worker and Fuzzhead were conversing. Upon discovering the topic of conversation they began ridiculing Fuzzhead's ambitions. Fuzzhead abruptly discontinued this discussion and withdrew from the conversation. (Adapted from Short and Strodtbeck, p. 222.)

Participation in the gang does little to prepare young people for conventional adult roles. Being "street wise" is not an asset in most available low-level jobs. Toughness, physical and verbal aggression often are counter productive on the job, as is the casual attitude toward *time* which is displayed in hanging activities. Demands for punctuality, perseverance, and quality performance likewise are alien to gang culture. As a socializing context, the gang runs counter to many requirements of modern civilization (see Inkeles, 1966).

Systematic testing of individual gang boys

Several more systematic and rigorous individual-level measures also differentiated among our samples. Gang boys made the lowest scores on six measures of intelligence, designed specifically so as not to be biased against lower-class and gang subjects (see Cartwright, et al., 1980). Gang members were followed in these measures, by lower-class nongang and middle-class nongang boys, in that order. In each class-by-gang-status category, black youngsters scored lower than did their white counterparts.

From the same set of testing routines, Desmond Cartwright and his colleagues also found that the gang boys differed from the nongang boys on several personality factors. The data suggest that gang boys tended to be more uncertain of themselves, more self-critical and self-questioning, and to have a poor regard for self. The tests also provided evidence that the gang boys were less decisive and more suggestible, and they had more difficulty in task concentration. They had poor immediate memory, were slower in making judgements, and they were less effective on performance tests. The gang boys appeared to be more cautious, more easily distracted, and more concerned with how they were doing relative to their peers than were the other boys.

Early socialization, normative ambiguity, and delinquent behavior

Trutz Trotha (1974) has explored the linkage between macrosocial, microsocial, and individual levels of explanation, based largely on the research literature from the United States. Trotha's analysis is based on a proposition drawn from role theory, viz., that socialization is a process of learning the *predictability of the behavior of others*. Conversely, one's own responses to the behavior of others are expected to be predictable in order that social interaction and "normal community life" may be facilitated. In this way much human behavior acquires a "taken for granted" quality.

Trotha notes that many inner-city communities are characterized by normative ambiguity and by inconsistency in the observation of conventional norms and sanctioning behavior. There is ample evidence of normative ambiguity in other segments of society, but it is among the ghetto underclass that ambiguity with respect to crime and delinquency is most evident (see Valentine, 1978; Liebow, 1967; Anderson, 1980; Wilson, 1987). Petty crime, police activity, welfare workers and government bureaucracies are a constant presence in many slum communities, yet law enforcement and the bureaucracies of government and business often seem more a part of the problems than of the solutions to individual and community ills. One result of this combination of circumstances is a "hustling" orientation to life. These factors combine to reduce the predictability of behavior and of life in general.

An inability to *tolerate ambiguity* has been found to be associated with a large number of personal characteristics, including the need for social approval, anxiety, and a negative self-concept . . . .. Ambiguity and unpredictability on the scale found in many urban ghetto communities may strain even those who have a high tolerance for ambiguity. A causal mechanism, which regrettably cannot be documented from this research, thus may exist between life conditions among the urban underclass, intolerance of ambiguity, and the social disabilities of gang boys.[7]

Trotha attributes the polarities found in Walter Miller's "focal concerns of the lower class" to a combination of reduced behavioral predictability, normative ambiguity and inconsistency in sanctioning (see Miller, 1958). This, for example, belief that luck or "fate" largely determines one's life chances is enhanced by conditions of disadvantage that are beyond one's control, and by the necessity to hustle as a means of economic survival. Universal dependency needs heighten the need for "automony" under such circumstances.

Trotha's focus on the predictability of behavior is relevant, as well, to the role of the unsocialized aggressive adolescent in the gang (Hewitt and Jenkins, 1946). Given the highly aggressive nature of much interpersonal interaction within the gang, one might expect such behavior to be approved, perhaps even rewarded. While systematic evidence is lacking, this appears not to be the case. The phenomenon was so rare in the gangs we studied that the one such case which clearly fit the category was noteworthy. The young man in question was a member of perhaps the most feared conflict gang in

---

[7] The ghetto urban underclass had not yet been "discovered" when our studies were being conducted. Its rapid consolidation since that time has been documented by Julius Wilson (1987) and others. The black gangs we studied were, in any case, "truly disadvantaged" in the same ways as the present-day ghetto

the city. His frequent outbursts of temper and assaults on others, within and outside the gang, led the boys to regard him as "crazy" and undependable, and he was actively shunned by many. He often behaved aggressively in situations in which aggression was inappropriate, even by gang standards. His presence made the group more vulnerable to police intervention, and his low status in the gang was related to this fact, as well.

The microsocial level of explanation

As is suggested from the field observations, microsocial processes may be helpful in explaining the "proximate" causes of behavior, and in linking macro- and individual-level theories. In this respect, our research focused particularly on group process mechanisms involved in precipitating delinquent behavior or in decisions to "join the action" once started. These included (a) the reactions of gang leaders to status threats; (b) the reactions of gangs (or segments of gangs) to status threats; and (c) a utility-risk paradigm of individual decision-making in situations involving the group (see Short and Strodtbeck, chapters 2, 8, 9, and 11).

Our attention was first drawn to the reactions of gang leaders to status threats by an apparently dramatic reversal of behavior on the part of Duke, a strong gang leader, following his return from a brief period of jail detention. Duke was a very cool leader of a tough, conflict-oriented gang of black teenagers. More socially skilled than the others, he maintained his position by cultivating nurturant relationships with other members of the gang and by negotiating with other leaders in intergang councils.

Upon his return from detention, Duke began "acting very unusual," provoking conflict with rival gangs. The boys responded enthusiastically to Duke's aggressive behavior, but he soon returned to being cool. It appeared that, for a brief period, Duke simply catered to the most broadly held normative characteristics of the group. Following reestablishment of his leadership role, and with the support of the detached worker, he was able to resume his customary mode of relating to the group.

As similar cases came to our attention, we were able to formulate what we believe to be the general mechanism at work. Abstracting the basic theoretical elements of this mechanism facilitates empirical and theoretical exploration of its generality, and possible integration of levels of explanation. A fundamental individual-level principle, common to the behavioral sciences, holds that behavior is adaptive, or problem-solving, i.e., reactive. The nature of any particular adaptation depends heavily on the nature of the problem of which the behavior is a response. The definition of any condition or situation is problematic, in turn, is in large part determined by social and cultural factors, e.g., culturally or socially defined desiderata (or, conversely, things to be avoided).[8]

In the adolescent gang world we studied in Chicago, and apparently in other adolescent social worlds, *status vis a vis one's peers* was a major problem. The saliency

---

[8] Some problems may, of course, be rooted in biological imperatives or limitations (see Pollack, et al., 1983) Even so, such problems are likely to be mediated by macro- and perhaps microsocial definitions, perceptions, and interactive effects.

of status, and the intensity with which related problems were experienced (e.g., the perception of status *threat*) varied a great deal in different situations and for boys occupying different roles in the group. Solutions to status problems were deeply embedded in normative properties and processes of the group.

The extent to which this principle applies to *group* behavior is not clear, though our research suggests that it does. We found evidence of the operation of the status threat mechanism, for example, in *group* behavior, as when rival gangs confronted one another "accidentally" on the street, or in public settings such as attendance at a professional basketball game.

Incidents such as these provided grist for the mill of individual and group status among fighting gangs, and they served to perpetuate the investment of these boys in their gang "rep." They also served the image of these boys as street warriors whose group norms required their participation in conflict with rival gangs. Without the detailed accounting of the incidents available through the field research, such an interpretation would seem reasonable. The normative explanation is inadequate on several grounds, however. In nearly all cases, fights were quickly and easily stopped. In none of the cases observed did all of the boys participate in the fighting or related delinquent behaviors.

Careful review of many incidents suggests that those most centrally involved were gang leaders and boys striving for leadership, and other core members. Membership roles and personal investment in the gang are variable among both groups and individuals, and such variation influences the likelihood of involvement in the give and take of such incidents.

The influence of normative properties of the group in most gang members thus appears to be tenuous and largely situational. The Chicago gangs were characterized by loose criteria of membership, frequently changing membership, and relatively low cohesion except under special circumstances that drew members together. Members of the gangs came and went for days or weeks at a time, and unless they occupied particularly strong leadership or other roles central to the group, most were hardly missed.

Situational factors, group solidarity, and behavior

The reaction of groups to situations in which group status is threatened, or in which status may be enhanced, supports observations made by others concerning the importance of the *group qua group* to the behavior of group members. Miller, et al.'s (1967) documentation of the occurrence of physically and verbally aggressive behaviors among members of a Boston gang found that the great majority of these acts were directed toward other members of the gang. Most served group purposes, e.g. demonstrating personal characteristics related to group acceptance and prestige.

The gang thus may be seen as an arena for status achievement, maintenance, and defense among young men who lack both skills and opportunities for status outside of this context. Violent exchanges within the gang and delinquent responses to status threats often are the result of reliance upon the lowest common denominator of skills and understandings with broad appeal within the group. The greater social skills possessed by gang leaders, and their generally supportive and nurturant style of leadership, confirms the value of group membership to gang members. Ironically, the leaders often were exposed as a result to situations in which there was a high risk of delinquency involvement.

Together with observations by Klein and Crawford (1967) concerning gang solidarity, these findings suggest that gang delinquency is a function of a combination of individual characteristics of members, internal group dynamics, and external pressures. Other field observers also have documented the importance of internal group processes and relationships with external environment in gang formation and behavior (see Yablonsky, 1962; Jansyn, 1966; and Brymmer, 1967).

The importance of cultural differences

Group processes are circumscribed by cultural differences. Differences between group and individual fighting reported by the Cambridge (England) Study in Delinquent Development are instructive in this respect. David Farrington and his colleagues (1981) report that the nature of aggressive incidents depended heavily on whether they were group fights or simply altercations between individuals. Individual fights more often involved "hostile aggression" and feelings of anger, while group fights were more *instrumental* in character (e.g., coming to the aid of a friend or to gain status). Group fights occurred most frequently in pubs and streets, often in both. Compared to individual fights they more frequently involved weapons and resulted in serous injuries. The young men who took part in group fighting were more likely than individual combatants to belong to "anti-social groups." Case studies suggest that group fighting was a matter largely of lifestyle, rather than of participating in conflict gangs.[9]

CONCLUSION

This chapter does little more than lay the groundwork for more formal integration of levels of explanation for collective (in this case, gang) delinquency. The microsocial level of explanation appears to be useful in linking the macrosocial and individual levels, as well as in its own right. The microsocial level is the least understood of the levels of explanation. Yet it bears on important and neglected issues. It may, for example, offer a way out of sociology's chronic difficulties with the concept of norm, and our failure to explain the circumstances in which normative properties of groups become manifest in behavior, are modified, and ignored.

---

[9] Ironically, medical concerns (e.g., with AIDS) may lead to additional field work with gangs whereas concerns with violence and other criminal behavior by gangs since the 1960s has not.

Perhaps, as Gibbs (1981) suggests, the explanatory power of "group norms" has been over-emphasized. The manner in which "normative properties" of groups are manifest in attitudes and in behavior varies a great deal between and among individuals, and in different types of situations. This chapter suggests some of the microsocial processes and mechanisms that "translate" normative properties of groups into individual and group behavior.

Bridging concepts are needed between social psychological and social structural explanations. The *gang* appears to be such a concept for understanding juvenile delinquency (see Firestone, 1976). Concepts alone are insufficient, however. The microsocial level of explanation, implying methods, data, and theory, is likely to be a necessary part of the bridging and integrating task.

REFERENCES

Akers, Ronald L. (1977) Deviant Behavior: A Social Learning Approach. 2nd ed. Belmont: Wadsworth.

Anderson, Elija. (1978) A Place on the Corner. Chicago: University of Chicago Press.

Bandura, Albert. (1986) Social Foundations of Thought and Action: A Social Cognitive Theory. Englewood Cliffs: Prentice-Hall.

Blumstein, Alfred, Jacqueline Cohen, Jeffery A. Roth, and Christy A. Visher. (1986) Criminal Careers and "Career Criminals'" vol. 1. Panel on Research on Criminal Careers, National Research Council. Washington, D.C.: National Academy Press.

Brymmer, Richard A. (1967) "Toward a Definition and Theory of Conflict Gangs." paper presented at the annual meeting of the Society for the Study of Social Problems.

Bursick, Robert J. (1986) "Ecological Stability and the Dynamics of Delinquency." Pp. 35-66 in Communities and Crime, Crime and Justice, vol. 8, edited by Albert J. Reiss, Jr. and Michael Tonry. Chicago: University of Chicago Press.

Cartwright, Desmond S., Barbara Tomson, and Hershey Schwartz. (1975) Gang Delinquency. Monterey, CA: Brooks/Cole.

Cloward, Richard A. and Lloyd E. Ohlin. (1960) Delinquency and Opportunity: A Theory of Delinquent Gangs. Glencoe, Il: Free Press.

Cohen, Albert K. (1955) Delinquent Boys: The Culture of the Gang. Glencoe, Il: Free Press.

Cohen, Albert K. and James F. Short, Jr. (1976) "Crime and Juvenile Delinquency." Pp. 47-100 in Contemporary Social Problems, edited by Robert K. Merton and Robert Nisbet. Contemporary Social Problems. 4th edition.   N.Y.: Harcourt, Brace, and Jovanovich.

Firestone, Harold. (1976) "The Delinquent and Society: The Shaw McKay Tradition. Pp. 23-49 in Delinquency, Crime, and Society, edited by James F. Short, Jr. Chicago: University of Chicago Press.

Gibbs, Jack P. (1986) Norms, Deviance, and Social Control: Conceptual Matters. N.Y.: Elsevier-North Holland.

Gibbs, Jack P. (1985) "The Methodology of Theory Construction in Criminology." Pp. 23-50 in Theoretical Methods in Criminology, edited by Robert F. Meier, Beverly Hills: Sage.

Glaser, Daniel (1971) Social Deviance. Chicago: Markham.

Gordon, Robert A. (1967) "Social Class, Social Disability, and Gang Interaction." American Journal of Sociology 73:42-62.

Gottfredson, Michael and Travis Hirschi. (1986) "The True Value of Lambda Would appear to be Zero: An Essay of Career Criminals, Criminal Careers, Selective Incapacitation, Cohort Studies, and Related Topics." Criminology 24:213-234.

Hannerz, Ulf. (1969) Soulside: Inquiries Into Ghetto Culture and Community. N.Y.: Columbia University Press.

Inkeles, Alex. (1966) "Social Structure and the Socialization of Competence." Harvard Educational Review 36:265-283.

Jansyn, Leon R. (1966) "Solidarity and Delinquency in a Street Corner Group." American Sociological Review 31:265-283.

Klein, Malcolm W. and Lois Y. Crawford. (1967) "Groups, Gangs, and Cohesiveness." Journal of Research in Crime and Delinquency 4:63-75.

Liebow, Elliott. 1967. Tally's Corner. Boston: Little, Brown.

Matza, David and Gresham Sykes. (1961) "Juvenile Delinquency and Subterranean Values." American Sociological Review 26:712-719.

Merton, Robert K. (1957) "Social Structure and Anomie." Pp. 131-194 in Social Theory and Social Structure. edited by Robert Merton. Glencoe, Il.: Free Press.

Miller, S.M. (1964) "The American Lower Class: A Typological Approach." Social Research.

Miller, Walter B. (1981) "Gangs, Groups, and Serious Youth Crime." Pp. 115-138 in Critical Issues in Juvenile Delinquency, edited by David Shichor and Delos H. Kelly. Lexington, Mass: D.C. Heath.

Miller, Walter B., Mildred S. Geertz, and Henry S. G. Cutter. (1961) "Aggression in a Boys' Street-Corner Group." Psychiatry 24:283-98.

Pollack, Vicki. Sarnot Mednick, and William F. Gabrielli, Jr. (1983) "Crime Causation: Biological Theories." Pp. 308-316 in Encyclopedia of Crime and Justice. vol. 1. New York: Macmillan.

Reiss, Albert J., Jr. and Michael Tonry. (1986) Communities and Crime. Chicago: University of Chicago Press.

Rivera, Ramon and James F. Short, Jr. (1967a) "Significant Adults, Caretakers, and Structures of Opportunity: An Exploratory Study." Journal of Research in Crime and Delinquency 4:76-97.

Rivera, Ramon and James F. Short, Jr. (1967b) "Occupational Goals: A Comparative Analysis." Pp. 70-90 in Juvenile Gangs in Context: Theary, Research, and Action, edited by Malcolm W. Klein and Barbara C. Meyerhoff. Englewood Cliffs: Prentice-Hall.

Schwartz, Gary. (1987) Beyond Rebellion or Conformity: Youth and Authority in America. Chicago: University of Chicago Press.

Schwendinger, Herman and Julia Siegel Schwendinger. (1985) Adolescent Subcultures and Delinquency. New York: Praeger.

Short, James F., Jr. (1974) "Youth, Gangs, and Society: Macro- and Micro- Sociological Process." Sociological Quarterly 15:20-31.

_____. (1985a) "The Level of Explanation Problem in Criminology." Pp. 51-72 in Theoretical Methods in Criminology, edited by Robert F. Meier. Beverly Hills: Sage.

_____. (1985b) "Review Essay: Adolescent Subcultures and Delinquency." Criminology 23:181-191.

_____. Forthcoming. Delinquency and Society. Englewood Cliffs: Prentice-Hall.

Short, James F., Jr. and John Moland, Jr. (1976) "Politics and Youth Gangs." Sociological Quarterly 17:162-179.

Short, James F., Jr., Ramon Rivera, and Harvey Marshall. (1964) Pacific Sociological Review 7:59-65.

Short, James F., Jr. Ramon Rivera, and Ray A. Tennyson. (1965) "Perceived Opportunities, Gang Membership, and Delinquency." American Sociological Review 30:56-67.

Short, James F., Jr. and Fred L. Strodtbeck. (1965) Group Process and Gang Delinquency. Chicago: University of Chicago Press.

Stinchcombe, Arthur L. (1975) "Merton's Theory of Social Structure." Pp. 11-13 in The Idea of Social Structure: Papers in Honor of Robert K. Merton, edited by Lewis A. Coser. New York: Harcourt, Brace and Jovanovich.

Trotha, Trutz. (1974) Jugendliche Bandendelinquenz. Stuttgart: Verlag.

Valentine, Bettylou. (1978) Hustling and Other Hard Work: Life Styles in the Ghetto. New York: Free Press.

Wilson, William Julius. (1987) The Truly Disadvantaged: The Inner City, the Underclass, and Public Policy. Chicago: University of Chicago Press.

Yablonsky, Lewis. (1962) The Violent Gang. N.Y.: MacMillan.

Summary and Discussion

WE INTRODUCED this section on the causes of juvenile delinquency by defining *theory* as "a carefully structured statement explaining the causal relationship between systemically established facts or variables." Thus, an etiological theory is the end result of empirical testing of hypotheses, concepts, and generalizations. The purpose of theory is to offer logical, valid, and reliable accounts of observed events or phenomena.

Beyond their common commitment to the objectivity and empiricism of the scientific method of inquiry, the various scholarly disciplines develop and build their theories from diverse and unique perspectives. For example, biological theories have emphasized physical attributes, genetics, and the physiological and biological changes that accompany puberty, in accounting for delinquent behavior. On the other hand, psychologists and psychiatrists generally trace illegal youthful conduct to individual pathologies involving some combination of mental, emotional, and personality maladjustments.

The sociological perspective that dominates the theories presented in this book insists that we must understand and interpret human behavior in its social context. While the sociological explanations of juvenile delinquency presented in this section focus on a wide variety of social variables in the life situations and backgrounds of juvenile delinquents, all the sociological theories share the same basic thesis and perspective. They do not view delinquency as the result of some biological or psychological factor in the individual. Rather, they look to social structure, cultural values, group associations, and societal response to norm violating behavior, for a better understanding of juvenile delinquency.

In order to enhance study and comparison, the huge volume and variety of sociological theories explaining juvenile delinquency often have been organized and summarized into convenient typologies. For instance, the articles in Part Two can be divided into five typological groups of causal theories: Social Strain Theories, Cultural Transmission Theories, Social Learning Theories, Social Control Theories, and Labeling Theories. At least one example of each of these explanatory types has been included:

1. *Social Strain Theories* concentrate on the frustrated success goals of lower class youths as etiologically related to juvenile misconduct. This kind of explanation is represented by Robert Merton's Anomie Theory.

2. *Cultural Transmission Theories* are exemplified in the article by Walter B. Miller who pointed to lower-class values in the form of six focal concerns which he identified as promoting and reinforcing gang delinquency among lower class boys.

3. *Social Learning Theories* include Edwin Sutherland and Donald Cressey's Theory of Differential Association which credits the delinquent's conduct to effective socialization from delinquent peers and role models who favor law-violating behavior over law-abiding behavior. The article by James Orcutt operationalized the variables of differential association and found support for the precept that juvenile delinquency is socially learned. The article by Thompson and his associates also found support for the social learning approach.

4. *Social Control Theories* help explain both conforming and nonconforming behavior by focusing on internalized social control (self-control) and societal restraints external to the individual that ordinarily constrain most individuals to abide by the major norms of their social group. The articles by Walter Reckless and by Gresham Sykes and David Matza in this section explain delinquency as resulting from a weakening or neutralizing of these control mechanisms.

5. *Social Labeling Theories* offer an explanation of delinquency that originates in the societal perception and judgment of behavior as deviant and the subsequent delinquent label and "locked-in role assignment." Frank Tannenbaum's theoretical construct of "tagging" is an appropriate description of this theoretical model.

After reviewing these diverse sociological theories, it is reasonable to inquire about their singular or collective ability to explain and predict delinquent behavior. Researchers in the field generally agree that while each theoretical contribution presented in this section sheds considerable light on selected dimensions of the delinquency problem, no single sociological theory offers a definitive, all encompassing, explication of cause. On the contrary, continued scrutiny and testing of these theories have revealed several serious limitations. Common and conspicuous short-comings of many sociological theories of juvenile delinquency are the absence of adequate explanations of female participation in illegal activity and the erroneous idea that delinquency was primarily a phenomenon involving lower-class youths.

Renewed interest in the generation of more refined and complete sociological theories of juvenile delinquency is likely to develop in these future directions:

1. A stronger research thrust toward understanding conformity as a key to comprehending deviant behavior. This reverse approach is based on the premise that it may be more helpful to expand our knowledge of why most youths do *not* become

delinquent than to continue pursuing insights about the very small minority who do become officially defined as juvenile delinquents.

2. The implementation of interdiscilplinary theory-building endeavors by bold and innovative scholars is long overdue and is a promising frontier of new knowledge regarding the etiology of juvenile delinquency. James Short, in his article in this section, "Exploring Integration of Theoretical Levels of Explanation: Notes on Gang Delinquency," adroitly underscores the mutual concerns and overlap among academic disciplines as potentially fruitful areas of investigation.

3. New efforts toward the integration of existing sociological theories of delinquency should substantially enhance explanatory and predictive power. Despite their obvious utility, typologies of theories of delinquency and other forms of human behavior—as cited in this summary and throughout the literature—are seldom comprised of discrete categories of behavior or explanation. There is almost always considerable overlap of the various types comprising a typology. In addition, many of the theorists were contemporaries or colleagues and their theoretical insights often have common conceptual roots and contribute to one another—a practice totally in harmony with the principle of "the accumulative nature of knowledge" endorsed by all disciplines. Therefore, it is reasonable to expect scholars active in the study of juvenile delinquency to move toward the natural synthesis of some existing theories.

The synthesis of existing theories of delinquency is exemplified by Terence Thornberry's article in this section, "Toward an Interactional Theory of Delinquency." Thornberry brings together elements of Social Control Theory, Social Learning Theory, and other delinquency variables into his own interactional and developmental model of delinquency.

While the theories represented by the articles in Part Two offer a variety of explanations for juvenile delinquency, there are more points of similarity than departure among them. As we continue to study the problem of juvenile delinquency, it appears that a more thorough understanding will result from focusing on and integrating these similarities than from debating their differences.

Questions for Review and Discussion

1. Define Travis Hirschi's theoretical concept of "the social bond." How does it account for juvenile delinquency?

2. How did William Thompson and his associates empirically test Hirschi's Control Theory of Delinquency? What were their findings?

3. Define Robert Merton's theoretical concept of anomie. How may it be applied to explain various forms of juvenile delinquency?

4. What were the six focal concerns of the lower-class identified by Walter Miller? How did he relate these values to juvenile delinquency?

5. In your own words, use Edwin Sutherland and Donald Cressey's Theory of Differential Association in linking criminal and delinquent behavior to the socialization or learning process.

6. How did James Orcutt empirically test Sutherland's Theory of Differential Association? What were his findings?

7. What did Frank Tannenbaum mean, in his article "The Dramatization of Evil," when he described "the process of making the criminal as a process of tagging"?

8. How does Walter Reckless' Containment Theory explain both conforming and nonconforming behavior? Identify and describe the functioning of inner and outer containment.

9. Outline and explain the five "techniques of neutralization" in the theory of delinquency formulated by Gresham Sykes and David Matza. According to the theory how do juveniles rationalize and justify delinquent behavior?

10. Why did Terrance Thornberry seek to synthesize several existing theorectical constructs into his Interactional Theory of Delinquency?

11. According to James Short's article, what is meant by "theoretical levels of explanation"? What kinds of theoretical integration does Short suggest?

PART THREE

The Social Context of Juvenile Delinquency

INTRODUCTION

HUMAN BEINGS, like other organisms, respond to an intrinsic and powerful social imperative. We are attracted and drawn together into the company of others like ourselves where, through mutual aid, we enhance personal and species survival. Thus, we form alliances, associations, groups, and societies—both large and small. Collectively, the members of our species overcome much of their vulnerability and establish communities, build cities, and develop cultures and subcultures that generally out-live specific generations of associated humans.

Sociologists have specialized in the study of human behavior in groups and collectivities. They have determined that there is great variability in the origin, size, composition, duration, and intensity of interaction of such human aggregates. In addition to being a product of human needs and interaction, the group also serves as a catalyst and backdrop for all sorts of subsequent human behavior. For example, the study of the group context of juvenile delinquency has been a rich field of research for sociologists and criminologists. In this section, we focus on three common social groupings as they relate to delinquent behavior: the neighborhood gang, the family, and the youth subculture.

We begin with a synopsis of Frederick Thrasher's classic, 1927 book *The Gang*. Thrasher identified 1,313 gangs in Chicago and presented a grim picture of lower class, predatory youths in his day. He systematically described the attitudes and activities of the gangs and traced their origin back to the spontaneous and innocuous play groups of neighborhood boys growing up in an environment of conflict and social disorganization.

Maynard Erickson and Gary Jensen follow with their 1977 reaffirmation of the group premise and the legitimacy of the sociological inquiry in juvenile deviance. However, in their "Delinquency is Still Group Behavior," Erikson and Jensen utilized self-report data to broaden the group basis of delinquency from urban gangs of lower-class males to the small peer group that may be found wherever there are young people who socially support deviant behavior.

Lewis Yablonsky's "The Delinquent Gang as a Near-Group" offers helpful theoretical insights into the organization and functions of gangs. He concluded that the delinquent gang is organizationally midway between the stability of the established group and the spontaneous, unruly mob. Thus, according to Yablonsky, the gang is a kind of social collective in its own right, with characteristics suited to meet the specific needs of its members.

Howard and Barbara Myerhoff, in their "Field Observations of Middle Class Gangs," broadened the lower-class stereotype of gangs to include groups of middle-class youngsters engaged in illegal conduct. The Myerhoffs' description of the values, attitudes, social skills, affluence, and access to automobiles of middle-class gangs—and the attitude of adults in their environment—is in striking contrast to those of lower-class gangs.

The role of the family in preventing or contributing to delinquency falls under the scrutiny of Gary Jensen. In his "Parents, Peers, and Delinquent Action: A Test of the Differential Association Perspective," Jensen concluded that paternal supervision and support, and the child's positive attachment to parents, consistently tend to neutralize the negative influence of delinquent patterns and peers external to the home environment.

"Family Relationships and Delinquency" is also the subject of the article by Stephan Cernkovich and Peggy Giordano. However, rather than the traditional focus on the premises that an intact relationship between parent(s) and child supports conforming behavior in the youth and a broken relationship between parent(s) and the child is conducive to delinquency, the authors' researched a multidimensional set of family interactions. Cernkovich and Giordano probed the following set of family interactions as they may relate to offspring delinquency: control and supervision, identity support, caring and trust, intimate communication, instrumental communication, parental disapproval of peers, and conflict. Their analysis also sought relationships between the set of family interaction variables and the race and sex composition of the family, as well as the presence of either or both parents.

The third collectivity discussed in this section that has been identified as a source of deviant behavior for many young people and delinquency for some is the youth subculture. Participation is a matter of degree with many millions of young Americans attracted to the generally innocuous music, language, fads, and fashions that distinguish their generation. At the same time, some youth of every generation manifest extreme alienation from their parents and the larger society and dominant culture and promote a counterculture with conflicting and troublesome values, attitudes, and behaviors. While Jack Bynum's article explores the hippie phenomena of the late 1960's, he identifies and analyzes youthful frustration and the search for social identity that characterize the alienated youth of every generation, including the punk rockers of the 1980's.

In "The appearance of Youthful Subculture: A Theoretical Perspective on Deviance," Lynne Richards captures our attention with her theoretically grounded analysis of the origin, appearance, and behavior of deviant youth subcultures. Richards brings together anomie, socialization, deviant labeling, and other constructs in her argument that the uniform subcultural dress of alienated youths serves as flaunted, symbolic displays of their deviant values that are followed by reactive responses throughout the larger society.

Frederick M. Thrasher *The Gang*.
Chicago: University of Chicago Press. 1927.

THE AUTHOR

Frederick Milton Thrasher was born in Shelbyville, Indiana on February 2, 1892. He received his undergraduate education at DePaul University and accomplished his graduate work in sociology at the University of Chicago, graduating with his master's degree in 1917 and the doctorate (Ph.D.) in 1926. While at Chicago, Thrasher had the enviable opportunity to interact as student or colleague with Robert Park, Ernest Burgess, Clifford Shaw, Henry McKay, and many other excellent scholars on the sociology faculty. Without doubt, Thrasher's lifelong interest in gang dynamics and delinquency in an urban milieu was initially generated through these Chicago contacts.

In 1927, Professor Thrasher began his long and illustrious career as a sociology faculty member at New York University. In addition to his research, teaching, and professional publications in the area of juvenile delinquency, he served as a member of President Hoover's White House Conference on Child Health and Protection, member of the Criminal Justice Advisory Committee for the American Law Institute, member of the Attorney General's Conference on Delinquency Prevention, Chairman of the Action Committee for Delinquency Prevention, and as Secretary of the National Crime Prevention Institute.

Thrasher died in March 1962 at 70 years of age.

The Book

The Gang by Frederick M. Thrasher was first published in 1927 and intended as a text for undergraduate instruction. Robert E. Park wrote a preface. At that time, there was general consensus that Thrasher's well-written and detailed account was the definitive work on urban youth gangs in the United States. This conviction and popularity was underscored by a second edition in 1936 and a third edition—prefaced by James F. Short, Jr.—in 1963.

In one major sense, the title of the book is a misnomer. Rather than "the gang," Thrasher identified and studied 1,313 gangs in Chicago—a prodigious, seven-year task. In addition, as Park notes in his preface, the focus of Thrasher's work is actually on "gangland"; that is, "a study of the gang and its habitat, and in this case, the habitat is a city slum" (p. ix).

The author's intrinsic and consistant sociological perspective is apparent throughout the book. Thrasher perceived and explained gangs as social groups whose emergence and behavior is best understood in the larger context of social change and disorganization, cultural expectations and conflicts, and impacting social institutions, nccds, and circumstances. His close analysis resulted in a wide range of useful sociological insights regarding the ecology, etiology, composition, organization, activities, and types of gangs that came under his scrutiny.

METHODOLOGICAL APPROACH

Thrasher's impressive 580 page treatise on Chicago's youth gangs is qualitative and descriptive. His accounts of gang phenomena are distilled into reasonable, objective conclusions—much like good investigative reporting—perhaps reflecting the author's early experience and writing style as a newspaper reporter.

The substantive content of *The Gang* rests heavily on reports, case studies, conversations and interviews with gang members, and similar data made available to Thrasher by the Juvenile Court of Cook County, Chicago Police Department, Chicago/Cook County School for Boys, Public Schools, Chicago Department of Public Welfare, and over a score of other public and private agencies. To procure the cooperation of these many diverse agencies—as well as the collection and preparation of the data—is evidence of Thrasher's interpersonal skills and devotion to his research endeavor.

There is a major ecological dimension to Thrasher's methodology. One of his first tasks was to spatially identify the geographic locales of the distinctive gangs in Chicago. He prepared a map of the city showing were various gangs and ethnic enclaves were located at that time. This map was included with early editions of the book (in a pocket inside the back cover) and readers were urged to read Chapter I with the map in hand.

FINDINGS AND CONTRIBUTIONS

Frederick Thrasher's study receives special stature and significance from scholars and students of youth gang phenomena who realize that many of his findings fill an important niche in the evolving and accumulating body of sociological knowledge about gangs. Not only did Thrasher validate and expand earlier, often fragmentary, information—but his insights forshadowed and laid the vital conceptual foundations for many sociological investigations and theories by others that were to follow in this area. A few examples will illustrate Thrasher's seminal contributions and their transitional role:

Ecology

The Gang was initially published in 1927. Building on Burgess's (1925) "Zone of Transition" idea in which an inner city neighborhood of poverty, physical decay, and ethnic minorities is seen as an environment especially conducive to social problems. Thrasher found that gangs of predatory youth flourished in urban slums. Thrasher called these "interstitial areas"— situated between better organized and socially controlled areas, and often adjacent to railroad tracks, rivers, and business or industrial districts. Fifteen years later, Clifford Shaw and Henry McKay (1942) empirically verified and expanded this concept in their studies of inner city "high delinquency areas."

Typology

Thrasher found that a gang is the product of a kind of natural evolution progressing over time from a loosely organized, innocent, neighborhood play group of youngsters to a more alienated, cohesive, organized, predacious group of young men. He further discovered that there is great diversity in gangs. Depending upon where a particular gang might be in its developmental process and the kinds of opportunities and role models available in its environment, a gang would tend to specialize in certain forms of delinquency. Based on these findings, Thrasher developed a typology of delinquent gangs. Each type of gang was distinguished by certain organizational and behavioral characteristics. Thrasher's typology included the diffuse or rudimentary gang, the solidified or conflict oriented gang, the conventional gang or athletic club, the criminal gang, and the secret society which places inordinate value on mysterious symbols and rituals. It takes little imagination to perceive the usefulness of Thrasher's preliminary work and early typology of gangs to the later typological formulations of Albert Cohen (1955), Richard Cloward and Lloyd Ohlin (1960), and others.

Etiology

Frederick Thrasher's contributions to the theoretical explanations of collective or gang delinquency are impressive. He successfully gathered the relevant and helpful theoretical fragments from other past and contemporary scholars, refocused and applied them to the gangs he was studying, blended in his own etiological insights, and left valuable building blocks for the future use of sociological theorists in developing and refining viable explanations of juvenile delinquency.

In brief, Thrasher concluded that the slum habitat, the city wilderness, as it has been called, produces gangs. More specifically, he "stressed as causes of delinquency the disorganized features of slum life and the grinding impact of urban industrialism on migrant and immigrant cultures" (Platt, 1969:4). To Thrasher, the poor, lower-class youth of such neighborhoods are not only spatially interstitial—separated away from the larger society and between more desirable areas—but socially interstitial as well.

That is, they are caught between conflicting and confusing sets of norms or behavioral expectations at home, school, and at work. They realize, personally and collectively, that they have "fallen through the cracks" around mainstream society and have an overwhelming sense of their own marginal social status and unfulfilled needs.

> Gangs represent the spontaneous effort of boys to create a society for themselves where none adequate to their needs exists . . . The gang . . . offers a substitute for what society fails to give; and it provides a relief from suppression and distasteful behavior. It fills a gap and affords an escape . . . Thus the gang . . . arising through conflict, is a symptom of disorganization in the larger social framework (Thrasher, 1936:37-38).

Thrasher's definition of the gang—based upon his exhaustive study of 1,313 gangs, and reflecting his theoretical explanations of their origin and behavior—is still one of the best definitions available to us:

> The gang is an interstitial group originally formed spontaneously, and then integrated through conflict. It is characterized by the following types of behavior: meeting face to face, milling, movement through space as a unit, conflict, and planning. The result of this collective behavior is the development of tradition, unreflective internal structure, *espirit de corps,* solidarity, morale, group awareness, and attachment to a local territory (1936:57).

Limitations

When compared to some current sociological research, Thrasher's work may appear to be unsophisticated. Strenuous efforts are made to enhance validity and reliability of findings and conclusions through advanced methodological and statistical operations that were not developed or applied to sociological investigations in Thrasher's day. Therefore, such a comparison is irrelevant. In *The Gang,* Thrasher's skillful combination of qualitative and quantitative data was quite advanced for that time (1927) and still stands as a superb model for such efforts today.

A more critical problem is Thrasher's omission of exactly how he reached certain generalizations. While his data and reasoning are apparently regarding the ecological placement of gangs and his tabular data clearly support his conclusions regarding the numerical, age, and ethnic composition of the gangs he studied, Thrasher gives little indication of how he moved from case studies and interviews to generalizations about gang development, organization, and ideology. However, looking back from the vantage point of today, Thrasher becomes less vulnerable on this point. Many of his well-reasoned conclusions and generalizations were largely substantiated by subsequent researchers.

In more recent research, the emphasis has changed from social disorganization as the seedbed for juvenile gangs to incorporate the realization that lower-class neighborhoods *are* organized, albeit different from theorganization in middle-and upper-class districts. Several theorists (Cohen, 1955; Cloward and Ohlin, 1960) contended that the emergence and delinquent activities of gangs represented an anomic reaction of lower-class youths to dominant middle-class standards. Walter Miller (1958) argued that much of the delinquent behavior of lower-class gangs is actually a genuine reflection of lower-class values that deviate from middle-class culture. "This view of gang life as an integral part of lower-class subculture" led James Short, in his preface to the 1963 edition of *The Gang,* "to assert that gangs do not cause delinquency, although it is through gangs that much delinquency occurs" (Cavan and Ferdinand, 1981:213).

REFERENCES

Burgess, E.W. (1925) The growth of the city. In *The City.* R.E. Park, E.W. Burgess, and R.D. Mckinie (Eds). Chicago: University of Chicago Press, pp. 47-61.

Cavan, R.S. and Ferdinand, T.N. (1981) *Juvenile Delinquency* (4th ed.). New York: Harper & Row.

Cloward, R.A. and Ohlin, L.E. (1960) *Delinquency and Opportunity.* New York. Free Press.

Cohen, A.K. (1955) *Delinquent Boys: The Culture of the Gang.* New York: Free Press.

Miller, W.B. (1958) Lower class culture as a generating milieu of gang delinquency. *Journal of Social Issues 14* (Summer): 5-19.

Platt, A.M. (1969) *The Child Savers: The Invention of Delinquency.* Chicago: University of Chicago Press.

Shaw, C.R. and McKay, H.D (1942) *Juvenile Delinquency in Urban Areas.* Chicago: University of Chicago Press.

Thrasher, F.M. (1946) *The Gang.* Chicago: University of Chicago Press.

ARTICLE 19

Delinquency is Still Group Behavior!
Toward Revitalizing the Group Premise in the Sociology of Deviance*

MAYNARD L. ERICKSON
GARY F. JENSEN

ONE OF THE FUNDAMENTAL NOTIONS in the original development of the sociological study of delinquency was the notion that "delinquency is a group phenomenon," meaning that the context and major referrents for delinquent behavior involve adolescent groups. This "group premise" was in fact one of the major justifications for sociological claims to the field. Moreover, the most popular theoretical works on delinquency through the mid-1960's took "gangs" and "delinquency subcultures." or "contracultures," as their main unit of analysis.[1] In short, the very subject matter of the sociology of delinquency was its group characteristics.

However, since the mid-1960's there has been a movement away from "the study

* This paper is based on data gathered as part of a larger study of "Community Tolerance and Measures of Delinquency" supported by a grant from the National Institute of Mental Health (MH22350). The authors wish to express their gratitude to the entire research staff (especially James Creechan, Karen Wilkinson, Grant Stitt and James Galliher) for their work in gathering and analyzing the data.

Source: Erickson, Maynard L. and Gary F. Jensen. "Delinquency is still Group Behavior!: Toward Revitalizing the Group Premise in the Sociology of Deviance." *Journal of Criminal Law and Criminology.* Vol. 68 (2), 1977:262-273. Reprinted by special permission of Northwestern University School of Law.

[1] R. Cloward & L. Ohlin, Delinquency and Opportunity (1960); A. Cohen, Delinquent Boys (1955); Cloward, *Illegitimate Means, Anomie, and Deviant Behavior,* 24 AM, Soc. Rev. 164 (1959); Miller, *Lower Class Culture as a Generating Milieu of Gang Delinquency,* 14 J. Soc. Issues 5 (1958).

of gangs" to a focus on delinquent "behavior" or acts.[2] Such a shift has been supported by the observation that the emphasis on gangs, subcultures, roles and careers "prematurely and unnecessarily restrict(s) the study of delinquency to small segments of the population . . . "[3]

Delinquent behavior is distributed more pervasively in the social structure than in lower-class male delinquent gangs and is more readily measured through survey techniques. Thus, most current empirical studies focus on delinquent behavior regardless of its group or individual nature. With the demise of the subcultural perspectives, the group premise (which does not require exclusive focus on gangs) has been forgotten or ignored.

Not only has empirical work come to concentrate on individualistic action, but the delinquency theories which inherited the field from subcultural theory, primarily labeling and deterrence theories, have yet to explicitly encompass the group premise in their perspectives or to fully explore its implications for their arguments.[4] Any theorist is free to stipulate those phenomena which are relevant, and each may simply deny the relevance of the group nature of delinquency or leave it to the reader to guess its role. Yet thus far, labelling and deterrence theorists have not declared the group premise to be outside the domain of relevant phenomena. Instead, they appear simply to have forgotten that premise in order to emphasize other variables, such as "deviant identity," "secondary deviance" and "self-conceptions" (in the case of labelling theorists), or "perceived risks" and "costs" of deviance to individuals (in the case of deterrence theory). Each tends to focus on the actor's response to potential and actual sanctions and labels.

[2] T. Hirschi. Causes of Delinquency (1969); Hindelang, *The Commitment of Delinquents to Their Misdeeds: Do Delinquents Drift?*, 17 Soc. Prob. 502 (1970); Hindelang, Age, Sex and the Versatility of Delinquency *Involvements*, 18 Soc. Prob. 522 (1971); Hirschi & Stark, *Hellfire and Delinquency*, 17 Soc. Prob. 202 (1969); Jensen, *"Crime Doesn't Pay"; Correlates of a Shared Misunderstanding*, 17 Soc. Prob. 189 (1969); Jensen, *Delinquency and Adolescent Self-Conceptions: A Study of the Personal Relevance of Infraction*, 20 Soc. Prob. 84 (1972); Jensen, Parents, Peers and Delinquent. Action: A Test of the Differential Association Hypothesis, 78 AM. J. Soc. 562 (1972); Waldo & Chiricos, *Perceived Penal Sanction and Self-reported Criminality: A Neglected Approach to Deterrence Research*, 19 Soc. Prob. 522 (1972); Williams & Gold, From *Delinquent Behavior to Official Delinquency*, 20 Soc. Prob. 209 (1972).

[3] T. Hirschi, *supra* note 2. at 52-53.

[4] Three theoretical perspectives seem to hold center stage: labelling, deterrence and radical criminology. See Gibbs & Erickson, Major *Developments in the Sociological Study of Deviance*. 1 Ann. Rev. Soc. 21 (1975), for a review of recent developments.

Several theorists have begun to "hint" at ways in which group notions could be incorporated into labelling and deterrence theories. For example, Thorselland Klemke point out that labeling analyses stress "the importance of the impact of societal reaction on the deviant person rather than focusing upon his psychological or sociological characteristics." They then go on to suggest factors which can shape the impact of labelling, such as, deviant career stage, confidentiality, attitude towards labellers, permanency of the label, societal reaction to labels and prevalence of labels. While there are hints suggesting the importance of group context the issue is never directly addressed. Thorsell & Klemke, *The Labelling Process: Reinforcement and Deterrent?* 6 L. Soc'y Rev. 393 (1972).

Even more recently Tittle suggests specifications of labelling and deterrence theory in terms of types of norms, characteristics of offenders, characteristics of sanctions, the kind of behavior involved, diffusion of sanction effects, career stage, community context and perceptual dimensions of sanctions. Again, the group nature of delinquency may be implicit in such theoretical specifications of current theory but it is rarely, if ever, dealt with directly. Tittle, Deterrents or Labeling?, 53 Soc. Forces 399 (1975).

The major purpose of this article, however, is not to criticize those theories which currently hold center stage in delinquency and deviance research; its purpose is merely to suggest that an important observation is being neglected both theoretically and empirically. While the claim that delinquency is a group phenomenon has been propounded since at least 1927, very little is known about the complete scope of the premise.[5] Moreover, unless the issue is revitalized in the sociology of deviance, little more will be known. The current investigation attempts to explore one aspect of the group premise—the group properties of delinquent acts—and to illustrate how current perspectives could be given new vitality and direction if peer group phenomena were more explicitly integrated into such theories.

PAST RESEARCH

Even though a vast amount of official data has been cited to support the view that delinquency is group behavior,[6] only a few basic questions concerning the issue can presently be answered. The cumulative data on the group nature of delinquent acts suggests that (1) although group violation rates vary among acts, there are very few acts (primarily offenses related to "incorrigible" behavior, such as running away and defiance of parents) where offenses occur as often alone as in group context;[7] (2) official sources of data overestimate by approximately 20% the amount of group violations,[8] and (3) there is little or no significant variation between socio-economic status categories, in terms of the *pattern of group violations* among acts, and the absolute levels of group violation rates.[9]

At present, one cannot answer with confidence the most basic questions concerning the group premise: Is there a relatively constant underlying social property ("groupness") of various types of delinquent action? Are the group properties of delinquent acts constant by gender? Are they constant from community to community? Can the patterns noted in data collected in the early 1960's be found in data collected in the mid-1970's? More generally, is the group premise applicable over time and space?

[5] The complete scope of the phrase "delinquency is a group phenomenon" has never been explicated. However, no matter how narrow the scope is taken to be, it includes within its meaning the claims that (1) most delinquent acts are social events involving several individuals—the so-called group context of the behavior, and (2) one of the most important sources of motivation and support for engaging in delinquent conduct is peer groups. In the present study, "group delinquency", "group violation rates" *will be used to refer to delinquent behavior* (i.e., violation of legal rules by juveniles) *that occurs in the company of others*. For

[6] Id. at 114-15.

[7] Id. at 114-29; M. Gold, Delinquent Behavior in an American City 82 (1970).

[8] Erickson, *supra* note 5; Erickson, *Group Violations and Official Delinquency: The Group Hazard Hypothesis,* 11 Criminology 127 (1973).

[9] Erickson, *Group Violations, Socio-economic Status and Official Delinquency,* 52 Soc. Forces 41 (1973).

STUDY DESIGN

In an attempt to answer these questions unofficial data is used: namely, self-reports of high school students in four southern Arizona communities which vary considerably in terms of size, dominant industry and industrial diversity. The urban community is a "standard metropolitan statistical area" with a population of about 400,000 and and economy oriented around mining, manufacturing, tourism, a military base, and a university. The three smaller communities, whose populations range from 1200 to 8000, encompass a "mining" town, a "tourist" town and a town commonly depicted as a "ranching" community.

As part of a larger project involving adults, police and adolescents, questionnaires were administered to a total of 1700 high school students (53% male, 47% female). This number included 427 students (51% male, 49% female) from three small-town high schools and 1273 students (54% male, 46% female) from three high schools in the urban community. Questionnaires were administered in either a classroom or cafeteria setting by project staff subject to variable restrictions set by each school administration. The three small-town high schools, which required signed parental consent for a student to take part in the study, yielded samples of between 25% an 35% of the student population.[10] The urban schools allowed the questionnaire to be administered in social studies and English classes, resulting in samples of approximately 50% of each school's population. Two of the urban schools allowed parents to "excuse" students from participating, although very few did so, while the third urban school encouraged all students to complete the questionnaire. In all cases, steps were taken to assure students that participation was strictly voluntary and the questionnaires anonymous.[11]

The group violation rates (GVR) were measured similarly to earlier research by asking subjects how many times during the last twelve months they had committed each of a variety of delinquent acts and then how many of these times they were with others.[12] The acts encompass eighteen offenses which could result in adjudication as

[10] A number of observations should be made concerning the possible effects of these procedural differences. If significant urban-rural differences are in fact found, then *one* explanation might be that group delinquencies were underestimated in the *written* parental consent samples as compared to the less restricted urban samples. If stability and agreement are found, it would be difficult to argue that the procedural difference eliminated differences that would have been there otherwise. Moreover, since there are three rural samples with identical restrictions and three urban samples with their own constant set of restrictions, stability and variation can be assessed within these sets as well as between. Finally, it should also be noted that where comparisons were possible, there was close correspondence between data on parental occupation and education and on the occupational structure and educational attainment of the populace according to the 1970 census. Even measures of delinquency based on juvenile court reports for the two counties involved parallel findings.

[11] No code numbers were used and teachers were asked to either leave the room or to leave the administration of the questionnaire entirely to the staff. Students were allowed to exchange questionnaires before answering in order to alleviate suspicions of secret codes and were told to place their own

[12] Group violation rates refer to the proportion (%) of violations that are known to or reported to have been violated in the company of others. For convenience the formula is simply: $GVR = GV/TV \times 100$, where GVR = group violation rates; VG = acts committed in the company of others; TV = total violations; and 100 simply removes the decimal point.

TABLE 19.1 Group violation rates (GVR)[a] by school subsamples

| | Urban | | | | | | | | Small Town | | | | Totals | |
| | Western | | Parochial | | Central | | Mining | | Tourist | | Ranch | | | |
Setting	GVR	Freq.	GVR	Freq.	GVR	Freq.	GVR	Freq.	GVR	Freq.	GVR	Freq.	GVR	Freq.
Drunk	91	8573	92	6026	94	5008	94	6135	84	1304	98	1113	93	28159
Drinking	90	14065	90	11154	91	7119	90	9499	81	2034	88	1744	90	45615
Marijuana	86	9495	92	6031	87	7778	87	9257	90	2510	90	1801	88	36872
Drugs	81	1515	76	497	83	1700	84	1842	71	409	72	150	80	6113
Vandalism	79	455	80	370	91	362	75	257	68	54	90	34	80	1532
Burglary	78	722	74	128	76	88	85	118	78	11	7	127	78	1094
Auto Theft	70	104	58	52	77	52	59	82	50	9	43	5	64	304
Truancy	69	6887	64	765	66	4318	75	1483	59	236	69	169	68	13858
Grand Theft	68	158	48	10	78	54	60	14	—	—	81	10	66	246
Smoking	64	10032	76	6286	64	5450	64	6531	61	3007	63	2496	67	33802
Armed robbery	64	123	33	2	100	1	54	9	50	1	100	1	57	137
Robbery	62	124	40	60	33	3	54	37	75	7	25	1	52	232
Petty Theft	60	610	54	211	64	236	49	135	53	25	28	14	55	1231
Shoplifting	46	953	55	582	46	399	51	778	42	113	43	44	50	2869
Runaway	36	31	30	15	44	370	33	9	14	2	38	6	34	433
Assault	28	552	32	31	18	16	19	26	31	4	12	3	25	632
Defy parents	26	1652	26	2318	25	1301	24	3213	29	75	38	215	26	8774
Fights	22	154	26	121	18	66	13	49	25	16	23	7	20	413

[a]Proportion of acts reported to have been committed in the company of peers.

a delinquent or an incorrigible in the state of Arizona. Ten of the eighteen acts are comparable to those utilized in earlier studies, thus allowing comparisons between studies as well as among the different schools, communities and sub-groups in the present study.

FINDINGS

The frequency of self-reported group violations (Freq.) and group violation rates (GVR) for the eighteen delinquent acts are summarized in Table 19.1 for the six high school samples. As in prior research, considerable variation was found in the proportion of acts committed in the company of peers. In general, drunkenness, drinking and use of marijuana are most likely to be group activities. Between 84% and 98% of self-reported drunkenness incidents were reported to have been committed in the company of others, as were between 81% and 91% of drinking incidents and between 86% and 92% of incidents of marijuana use. Such a pattern is quite consistent with what is commonly known about the social and recreational nature of these activities. Group violation rates were also high for the use of other illicit drugs, ranging between 71% and 84%. Other acts which ranked relatively high in terms of group violation rates were burglary and vandalism.

Some acts by the very nature of the setting and circumstances in which they occur are likely to be individual acts and rank low in terms of group violation rates. For example, defying parents (incorrigibility), is likely to involve the individual adolescent acting alone in a stance contrary to parents. Similarly, running away from home is likely to be an individual action. These low group violation rates do not indicate that peer relationships are irrelevant to such actions. An adolescent's peer group may be an ultimate source of conflict with parents and a retreat from the home situation even though the act is committed alone.

TABLE 19.2 Rank order correlations (RHO's) between group violation rates (GVR) for pairs of school subsamples[a]

	Western	Central	Mining	Tourist	Ranch
Parochial	.92	.71	.93	.88	.69
Western		.86	.97	.88	.80
Central			.79	.65	.95
Mining				.91	.79
Tourist					.63

[a]Coefficient of concordance = .86.

Two other offenses were uniformly low in group violation rates: assault and fights. Obviously, these offenses by nature involve more than one person; however, the questionnaire asked whether anyone was "helping" the adolescent. At least in terms of self-reports, beating up or hurting someone intentionally and getting into fights are likely to be individual conflicts.

The most striking finding for the six subsamples is the similarity in group violation rates for each act relative to other acts. As summarized in Table 19.2, the rank order correlations of all acts in terms of group violation rates for all pairs of schools range between .63 and .97. The coefficient of concordance (a summary measure of overall concordance in rank orderings) is .85 and statistically significant beyond the .001 level. Therefore, it is safe to conclude that there is a stable order to these acts in terms of the particular underlying group property being examined.

Not only is there a good deal of stability in the rank ordering of the acts but the *levels* of actual group violation rates are also quite similar. For example, in Table 19.2 there are 265 sample-by-sample differences in group violation rates for the eighteen acts, and of these, only thirty-six (13.6%) were greater than 20%. In fact, 64% of the differences were less than or equal to 10%. Of course, there was greater variation for some acts than others. Whether one considers differences greater than 10% or greater than 20%, it appears that one-third of the acts account for most such differences. Armed robbery, robbery, auto theft, vandalism, petty theft and grand theft accounted for 92% of the differences greater than 20% and 62% of the differences greater than 10%. There were *no* differences greater than 20% for eleven of the eighteen acts. Several of the most variable acts are very rarely committed; hence the group violation rates should be very unstable from sample to sample, as the most disparate group violation rates tend to occur when comparing samples with very low frequencies of involvement. Thus, for 265 tests of significance involving group violation rates for pairs of schools, only thirty-four were statistically significant at the .05 level. The average difference for all 265 comparisons was only 14%. Removing armed robbery from the computation above reduces the average difference to only 9%. In sum, there is considerable stability in the rank order of offenses in terms of group violation rates and there are rarely any significant differences from sample to sample in the magnitude of such rates.

GROUP VIOLATION RATES BY GENDER

While delinquent behavior has been typically viewed as a male phenomenon, this image is even more prominent in depictions of gangs and group delinquency. Traditionally, gangs of adolescent males have most concerned the public and, until recently, have received the most attention in sociological criminology. However, together with an apparent rise in female criminality and a growing concern with sex roles and their influence on behavior, female "gangs" have been receiving increasing notoriety.[13] Since earlier research on group violations, and virtually all on delinquency

[13] *See, e.g.*, F. Adler, Sisters In Crime (1975).

TABLE 19.3 Group violation rates (GVR) by community and gender[a]

| | Urban | | | | Small Town | | | |
| | Male | | Female | | Male | | Female | |
	GVR	Freq.	GVR	Freq.	GVR	Freq.	GVR	Freq.
Drunk	91	13535	94	6072	93	5561	94	2991
Drinking	86	22036	95	10302	86	8684	92	4593
Marijuana	85	15075	93	8229	87	7222	89	6346
Drugs	82	2452	76	497	83	1700	84	1842
Vandalism	81	1068	84	119	72	294	90	51
Burglary	74	659	87	279	81	122	86	34
Grand Theft	67	152	69	56	52	54	66	42
Smoking	63	8151	73	3819	65	851	80	1037
Auto Theft	69	220	33	2	68	23	50	1
Truancy	67	11713	71	10055	61	5846	66	6188
Petty Theft	48	179	67	8	53	44	50	1
Armed robbery	60	593	54	464	45	105	54	69
Robbery	52	124	100	2	58	11	-	-
Shoplifting	45	1446	59	488	42	438	61	497
Runaway	38	32	33	384	44	13	11	4
Assault	25	213	36	386	23	31	6	2
Fights	23	2898	30	2373	16	648	42	2855
Defy parents	23	309	21	32	14	58	21	14

[a]Coefficient of concordance (w) = .94 (p .000): Mean rank order correlation coefficient (R) = .88.

has been limited to males, very little is known about the "groupness" of female delinquency.[14]

On the basis of the findings thus far, one would expect that any claim about the group nature of female delinquency based on official statistics would be grossly misleading. Just (as Erickson found) as official statistics overestimate the extent of group delinquency because of the nature of the offenses for which males are arrested, official figures underestimate the "groupness" of female delinquency.[15] Numerous studies using official statistics have shown an inordinate concentration of sexual offenses, runaway offenses and incorrigibility among female as compared to male offenders.[16] These offenses rank low in group violation rates. In contrast, self-report studies of delinquency suggest striking similarity in pattern of delinquency for the two

[14] In his 1960 data, Gold does report that sex, age and race made little difference for acting alone. M. Gold, *supra* note 7, at 91.

[15] Erickson, *supra* note 5, at 120.

[16] Gibbons & Griswald, *Sex Differences Among Juvenile Court Referrals*, 42 Soc. & Soc. Research 106 (1957); Morris *Female Delinquency and Relational Problems*, 43 Soc. Forces 82 (1964).

TABLE 19.4   Rank order correlations (Rho's) between group violation rates (GVR) for subgroups

	Urban Female	Small Town Male	Small Town Female
Urban Male	.76	.96	.91
Urban Female		.81	.94
Small Town Male			.88

sexes, the major differences appearing in rates rather than types of self-reported offenses.[17] To the degree that boys tend to be arrested for offenses ranking high in group violation rates and girls tend to be arrested for offenses low in terms of group violations, official statistics will give a baised "individualistic" image of female delinquency.

The group violation rates for males and females in urban and small-town settings are summarized in Table 19.3 and the rank order correlations for all pairs of subgroups are presented in Table 19.4. Again, one finds a great deal of concordance in the rank ordering of delinquent acts in terms of group violation rates. The rank order correlation coefficients range between .76 and .96 and the overall measure of concordance is .90 (statistically significant beyond the .001 level). There is a tendency, however, for the lowest rank order correlations to involve cross-sex comparisons. For example, all of the coefficients below .90 involved male-female comparisons. The largest rank order coefficients were obtained when comparing females in the two settings or males in the two settings.

As in sample comparisons, there appears to be considerable stability in actual levels of group violation rates between sexes as well as between settings. The average difference between males and females is only 12% and only four of thirty-five differences exceed 20%. However, there are consistent, statistically significant differences between males and females in *both* samples for shoplifting, grand theft, truancy, defiance and drinking. The only other significant difference occurs between urban males and urban females for marijuana use. As revealed in Table 19.3, these differences are quite small.

A surprising findings is that females in both urban and rural settings tend to have group violation rates that are higher than their male counterparts. For urban settings, the female group violation rate exceeded the male rate for thirteen of eighteen offenses. For ten offenses (burglary, shoplifting, vandalism, smoking, truancy, auto theft, defiance, drinking, drunkenness, marijuana and drugs) the female group violation rates exceeded that for males in both settings. Moreover, of the statistically significant male-female differences, grand theft is the only offense where males exceeded females.

[17] M. Gold, supra note 7, at 64: Hindelang. *Age, Sex and the Versatility of Delinquency Involvements*. 18 Soc. Prob. 522, 533 (1971); Jensen & Eve. *Sex Differences in Delinquency*, in Criminology (forthcoming, 1976).

Females had significantly higher group violation rates for shoplifting, truancy, defiance and drinking in both settings and significantly higher group violation rates for marijuana use in the urban setting. Thus, while females tend to commit fewer delinquent acts,[18] *when such acts do occur* females are just as likely as males to commit most offenses in the company of peers. Some offenses are significantly more likely to be group acts for females, while only one offense is less likely to be a group act for females as for males. One can thus conclude that the image of female delinquency as individualistic activities of loners is not supported by the data.

COMPARISON WITH OTHER GROUP PROPERTIES STUDIES

As noted earlier, considerably more official than unofficial (self-reported) data has been brought to bear on the group context of delinquent acts. In fact, from the vast self-reported literature there are still only two studies that are directly relevant to the group properties issue and a few that bear indirectly on the issue.[19] One of these studies utilized self-reported data gathered in Utah approximately ten years ago from a composite sample limited to white males, fifteen to seventeen years old, and was used in modeling the present investigation. An early analysis was based on fifty incarcerated youths, fifty probationers and fifty high school students.[20] Subsequent analyses were bases on a larger composite sample (N = 336) representing these same three categories.[21] It was impossible to compare group violation rates found in the present research with rates for twelve acts from the early analysis and with rates for ten acts drawing on subsequent analyses. Moreover, while not as directly comparable, comparisons can be made with a 1960 study by Gold bases on male and female high school students in Flint, Michigan.[22]

[18] Significant differences were found in the frequency of delinquent acts of most sorts in these data. Males significantly exceeded females for the most serious offenses with little difference for the less serious offenses, See M. Erickson & G. Jensen, Sex and Self-reported Delinquency (unpublished manuscript available from Maynard L. Erickson or Gary F. Jensen, Department of Sociology, U. of Ariz., Tuscon, Ariz.).

[19] Other research has dealt with this issue but using very different techniques. For example, Klein sets forth the proportion of incidents with companions reported, but draws his data from anecdotal information and probation records for "gang clusters" in Los Angeles. Such sources depend on what happened to be recorded and may underestimate group incidents for some acts and overestimate for others. Klein, *supra* note 7.

Exploring the social versus solitary nature of delinquent involvements of 337 male Catholic students in Berkeley, California. Hindelang utilizes self-reports but focuses on the type of *delinquents* (solitary, mixed and social) rather than the characteristics of acts. Hindelang, *The Social Versus Solitary Nature of Delinquent Involvements*, 2 Brit. J. Soc. 167 (1971).

The interest here is in the group quality of *events, incidents* or *acts* which occur in a community rather than the characteristics of the "delinquents" involved. A small proportion of the offenders in the community may be "social" offenders and yet account for most of the incidents in the community. Group "delinquency" may be the major problem in a community irrespective of the proportion of delinquent youth who might fall in one or another category.

[20] Erickson, *supra* note 5.

[21] Erickson, *Group Violations and Official Delinquency: The Group Hazard Hypothesis,* 11 Criminology 127 (1973); Erickson, *supra* note 9.

[22] M. Gold, *supra* note 7.

TABLE 19.5   Group violation rates (GVR) of urban and small town males for previous studies and the present study

	Utah Males (N = 150)		Utah Males (N = 336)		Arizona Small Town Males		Arizona Urban Males	
	GVR	Frequency	GVR	Frequency	GVR	Frequency	GVR	Frequency
Vandalism	91	4538	75	4881	72	294	81	1068
Burglary	84	690	67	1950	81	199	74	659
Drinking	78	11033	82	10105	86	8684	86	22032
Grand theft	78	184	64	457	68	23	69	220
Narcotics	77	22	-	-	78	779	82	2451
Petty theft[a]	72	14106	60	17560	45	105	60	593
Auto Theft	72	638	61	1215	52	54	67	152
Armed robbery	69	16	-	-	58	11	52	124
Truancy	60	6754	55	11277	65	851	63	8151
Fights	55	7138	58	6145	14	58	23	309
Runaway	50	766	45	1036	44	13	38	32
Defy parents	17	7111	27	7069	16	649	23	2883

[a]For the Utah data two items were combined (theft less than $2.00 and theft $2.00 to $50.00) to make petty theft comparable for the two studies.

Not only does there appear to be a good deal of stability among samples, settings and sex categories within the present study, but, as summarized in Table 19.5, there is a great deal of concordance between the findings in the Utah research and the group violation rates found for small-town males and urban males. The rank order correlations (Rho's) for small-town and urban males in comparison to the Utah sample of 150 are .84 and .87, respectively. For the ten comparable acts using the larger Utah sample the rank order correlations were .93 for small-town males and .98 for urban males. The sample used in the earliest analysis included a greater proportion of "official delinquents" than the sample used in subsequent analyses. Thus, one would expect greater correspondence between the findings of the present study and the larger of the two earlier samples, since the present investigation did not purposely stratify by official delinquency.

Examining group violation rates act by act reveals considerable agreement between the two bodies of data. For example, the average difference between group violation rates using the larger Utah sample is only 10% and would have been much lower if the extreme differences for "fighting" were excluded. This difference in group violation rates for fighting in the two studies probably resulted from differences in wording of questions used in collecting those data. In the Utah research, adolescents were asked to indicate how many times others were *watching or helping* during the fight, while the present study merely asked how many times someone was *helping*.

Finally, while the group violation rates are not presented, Gold does present the rank orders for the acts he studied.[23] Eleven acts were comparable enough to make some rank order comparisons possible. Comparing Gold's results with those for the four subsamples in the current investigation yields rank order correlations similar to those for Utah and Arizona. For urban males, the coefficient was -.87 and for urban females it was -.86. It was -.81 for the small-town males and -.78 for small-town females. It is interesting to note that the rank order correlations are stronger for the urban comparisons, since Gold's study was based on an urban sample. At any rate, the order of acts in terms of group violation rates is persistent in quite disparate samples and settings for different bodies of research covering a fifteen-year period.

SOURCES OF ORDER IN PATTERNS OF AND LEVELS OF GROUP VIOLATION RATES

While the data thus far have suggested considerable stability both in rank orders and absolute levels of group violation rates, more analysis is needed to address fully the possible sources of order in group violation rates across time and space. One consideration—the institutional context of the act—was noted earlier when it was suggested that defiance of parents and running away from home are generated from conflict situations within the family and that other adolescents are not likely to be present at the moment of conflict. Another consideration might be the nature of the social learning process involved. Drug use of all kinds, but particularly marijuana use and drinking, have been depicted as primarily recreational activities unusually dependent on social reinforcement.[24] Acts such as theft and robbery result in acquisition of money or goods, while drug use results in highly subjective states, and whether commonly used illicit drugs are intrinsically rewarding independent of social reinforcement is problematic. Learning to recognize and define the effects of drugs may be far more contingent on peer-based learning than is the case for more instrumental offenses. Moreover, illegal drugs, and to a lesser extent, alcohol are not as pervasively distributed among the population as are property and goods. Access to property and goods is not as dependent on association with others as is access to illegal substances. Finally, it should be noted that some of the more serious property crimes, such as burglary, require more sophisticated knowledge and possibly more emotional support than do others.

[23] *Id.* at 85.
[24] H. Becker, *Outsiders: Studies in the Sociology of Deviance* (1963); E. Goode, *Drugs in American Society* (1972).

GROUP VIOLATION RATES AND OFFENSE SERIOUSNESS

Delinquent offenses differ considerably in seriousness, and the earlier research reported a rank order correlation of .58 between judge and probation officers' evaluations of seriousness and group violation rates. Using data reported in Erickson's 1971 paper, the rank order correlations between evaluations of seriousness and group violation rates in the present investigation were +.45 and +.44 for small-town and urban males respectively. For the ten comparable offenses in the 1973 paper, the rank order correlations between the Provo evaluations and group violation rates were +.33 and +.35.

Another aspect of this research dealt with community evaluation of the seriousness[25] of offenses, allowing a further examination of the relation between seriousness and group violation rates. While there was a a great deal of concordance between adults, juveniles, small-town and urban residents in the rank order of delinquent acts in terms of seriousness (rank order correlations for evaluations ranging from .91 and .97), there was virtually no correlation between seriousness and group violation rates. The rank order correlation was only +.12 for the sample as a whole.

There were certain offenses which were widely discrepant in ranking by group violation rates and seriousness. The most consistently out-of-order offenses were drinking, assault, smoking, truancy, marijuana use and armed robbery. Three of these offenses—drinking, armed Robbery and truancy—were also badly out of order in comparison with the Utah studies.

Moreover, even within sets of similar acts, seriousness does not consistently order offenses in terms of group violation rates. For example, while smoking is characterized by lower group violation rates than drinking or marijuana use (see Table 19.3), the latter two offenses are nearly identical in group violation rates even though marijuana use is consistently evaluated as more serious. For males, grand theft exceeds petty theft and shoplifting in group violation rate, but for females, grand theft has the lowest group violation rate.

If broad categories of offenses are considered, sizable discrepancies can be noted between evaluations of seriousness and group violation rates. Drug offenses tend to be evaluated low in seriousness but high in "groupness." Offenses such as auto theft and robbery rank high in terms of seriousness but fall towards the middle in terms of group violation rates. Status offenses such as running away from home and parental defiance rank low in both seriousness and groupness. In sum, seriousness as measured by public evaluation does not appear to be a major source of order in group properties in this investigation. There may, however, be other ways of defining seriousness (for example, actual legal responses) which would be in greater concordance with patterns of group violation rates.

[25] Offense seriousness was measured using magnitude estimate methods. Questions of the following form were administered to all juvenile subjects and random samples of adults and policemen in each community studied. Respondents were asked "If the number 100 was used to indicate how serious stealing something worth less than $100 is, what number would you give (description of the act)?" The median values of responses to the question for each type of act represents the seriousness of the act. The use of medians is now conventional in using magnitude estimation methods. Hamblin, *Social Attitudes: Magnitude Measure-*

CONCLUSION AND BROADER IMPLICATIONS

A number of conclusions concerning delinquency as a group phenomenon appear justifiable by the data. One can conclude that delinquent acts generally occur in "the company of peers" and that such tendencies vary from offense to offense. Drug offenses tend to have the highest group violation rates while status offenses, other than drinking and smoking, have the lowest. Second, there is considerable concordance in the group properties of delinquent acts across time and space with high rank order correlations and there are few significant sample differences within this study or, for that matter, between the results of the present investigation and data gathered over a decade ago in Utah and Michigan. Earlier findings were replicated over time and space. Third, one can seriously question the individualistic image of female delinquency, since what significant differences there are suggest that females may be proportionately more likely to commit offenses in a group context than males. Official data have tended to give an image of female delinquency biased towards status offenses and this bias may translate into an erroneous image of female delinquency. Finally, the variations in group violation traits are *not* attributable to seriousness as measured by adult and juvenile evaluations.

Relevance for Present Theories

Earlier in this article, it was suggested that labelling and deterrence theories, two of the three major theoretical perspectives on deviance which hold center stage today, would both benefit greatly by an emphasis on the group nature of delinquent behavior. As a review of the literature and the data presently demonstrate, *delinquency is still group behavior!* Labeling theory would perhaps be given new vitality by a much stronger emphasis on peer group variables, including the premise that the majority of delinquent acts are committed in concert. Recognition of the latter might well be interpreted to suggest that full-blown "deviant identities" could and probably do develop in peer group settings *before* individuals are ever reacted to—a possibility seemingly denied by labeling theorists.[26] Furthermore, if, as a study by Erickson has suggested, violations in groups increase the probability of arrest and labelling, the relevance of group violation rates to labeling notions is clear.[27] In addition, an emphasis on "peer group" variables would perhaps save labelling from the purely individualistic perspective which many argue it now holds. Even if it is conceded that important processes begin with reaction, it seems crucial to recognize and emphasize that one's attachment to a delinquent (deviant) peer group may have profound impact on the potential effects of labelling for self-identity and career patterns. Even those labelling theorists who recognize peer phenomena as relevant give insufficient emphasis to peer variables.

---

[26] In fact, the tendency to ignore or dismiss primary deviance or prelabelled behavior is a major source of the criticism in most recent, radical critiques of labelling theory. *See* Taylor, Walton & Young, The New Criminology 139 (1973); Young, *Working-class Criminology*, in Critical Criminology 63 (I. Taylor, P. Walton and J. Young eds. 1975).

[27] Erickson, *Group Violations and Official Delinquency: The Group Hazard Hypothesis*, 11 Criminology 127 (1973).

Deterrence theory also suffers from inadequate attention to social context variables and is inordinately individualistic in orientation. The deterrence process is seemingly psychological. The inclusion of peer group variables would not only make the theory more sociological but might very well clear up some of the present confusion about the relative and highly unpredictable effects of variables like perceived certainty and severity.

Even the premise that most delinquent acts arc group events is theoretically relevant to deterrence theory. It suggests that in a group context, a host of important variables are probably operating to dilute the effects of individualistic variables, such as perceived certainty. Specifically, peer pressure in a given situation may make perceived certainty impotent as an explanatory variable. On the other hand, one might well find that in situations where an individual is alone, perceived certainty is the most important variable for explaining rates of behavior. The general point, of course, is that a whole new set of issues is raised for both labelling and deterrence theory when group violations and peer group phenomena are made central to those theories.

Broader Implications

The findings presented here have implications for issues even broader than the accurate depiction of delinquency as a group phenomenon and for labelling and deterrence theory. For example, in a recent work on "subcultural" theories of "urbanism," Claude Fisher reiterates the widely-accepted view that not only is urbanism correlated with high rates of "unconventionality," but also that this difference is particularly prominent for group or subcultural unconventionality.[28] He argues that "a small town may have a few delinquent youths, but only in a large city will there be sufficient numbers (*i.e.*, a critical mass) sufficiently distinctive to establish a viable delinquent subculture." He does note, however, that "little has been done to estimate systematically the effects of 'grouping' across various realms of action."[29]

Of course, even the assumption that urbanism is correlated with delinquent behavior, while widely accepted, has yet to be demonstrated. In fact, a recent study of rural Oregon youth as compared to a similar study in Philadelphia[30] leads Polk to conclude that "non-metropolitan youths have just about as many run-ins with the law as metropolitan youths, and the causes of these confrontations are often of roughly equal seriousness in both towns and cities."[31] While the present study concentrates on group violation rates of delinquent acts rather than volume, it can also be reported that there were few statistically significant differences between urban and small-town males in rates of self-reported delinquency. When there were differences, the mining town tended to be characterized by the greatest involvement. The urban community and the tourist town fell in the middle, with the farm town having the lowest rates.

[28] Fischer, *Toward a Subcultural Theory of Urbanism*, 80 Am. J. Soc. 1319, 1328-30 (1975).

[29] Id. at 1328.

[30] M. Wolfgang, B. Figlio & T. Sellin, *Delinquency in a Birth Cohort* (1972).

[31] K. Polk, Teenage Delinquency in Small Town America (1974) (Research Report 5, Center for Studies of Crime and Delinquency, National Institute of Mental Health).

The county encompassing the three small-town communities actually had a juvenile court referral rate greater than the two standard metropolitan statistical areas in the state. If rural Oregon and Philadelphia youth are comparably delinquent, and Arizona youth from small towns of between 1200 and 8000 population do not differ significantly from those in a city of 350,000, then it is time seriously to question common images of rural-urban differences in delinquency.

The present analysis suggests that at least as a peer group phenomenon, there is little difference between small-town delinquency and urban delinquency. However, the notion of a "delinquent subculture" is sufficiently vague that these findings might be dismissed as peripheral to the argument. On the other hand, other researchers attempting to assess delinquent values report that the attitudes towards law-breaking of the rural adolescents they studied were similar to attitudes found among adolescents in "hard-core" delinquency areas of large cities and, in fact, were not significantly different from those of older, institutionalized delinquents.[32] Even research on adults has suggested an homogenization of attitudes between rural and urban populations.[33] Such findings tend to be ignored or dismissed by those dedicated to the preservation of rurality as a major variable in explaining deviance.

At the present time, there is no adequate justification for arguing that the group properties of delinquent acts (or the distribution of delinquent acts or values) vary between small towns and large metropolitan areas. If "delinquent subcultures" are ultimately defined in such a way that evidence gathered thus far can be dismissed, or if the relevant comparisons end up being between "megalopolis" and "farmers," then the theory would explain very little. If, however, such variables are to retain their status as general explanatory variables in the study of deviance, there must be some effort to explain the lack of theoretically predicted differences. This analysis leads one to question traditional images of male-female delinquency and suggests that it is time to move beyond academic *a priori* dedication to a thorough empirical analysis of urban-rural differences in delinquency as individual and group behavior.

[32] Ball & Lilly, *Juvenile Delinquency in a Rurban County*, 9 J. Research Crime & Delinquency 69 [33] van Es & Brown, *The Rural-Urban Variable Once More: Some Individual Level Observations*, 39 Rural Soc. 373 (1974).

[33] van Es & Brown, *The Rural-Urban Variable Once More: Some Individual Level Observations*, 39 Rural Soc. 373 (1974).

The Delinquent Gang as a Near Group*

LEWIS YABLONSKY

THIS PAPER IS based on four years of research and direct work with some thirty delinquent gangs in New York City. During this period I directed a crime prevention program on the upper West Side of Manhattan for Morningside Heights, Inc., a community social agency sponsored by fourteen major institutions including Columbia University, Barnard, Teacher's College, Union Theological Seminary, and Riverside Church.

Approaches used in data gathering included field study methods, participant observation, role-playing, group interaction analysis, and sociometry. The data were obtained through close daily interaction with gang boys over the four-year period during which I was the director of the project.

Although data were obtained on 30 gangs, the study focused on two, the Balkans and the Egyptian Kings. It was the latter which committed the brutal killing of a polio victim, Michael Farmer, in an upper west side park of New York City. The trial lasted over three months and received nation-wide attention. These two groups were intensively interviewed and contributed heavily to the formulation of a theory of near-groups. In addition to the analysis of the gang's structure, a number of delinquent gang war events produced vital case material.

There is a paucity of available theory based on empirical evidence about the structure of delinquent gangs. Two landmarks in the field are Thrasher's *The Gang* and Whyte's *Street Corner Society*. Some recent publications and controversy focus on the emergence of gangs and their function for gang members. Professor Cohen deals with

* This is a revised version of a paper delivered at the Eastern Sociological Meetings in New York City, April 11, 1959. The theory of near-groups and gang data presented in this paper is part of a forth-coming volume on gangs by the author.

Source: Yablonsky, Lewis "The Delinquent Gang as a Near Group." *Social Problems,* Vol. 7 (Fall), 1959:108-117. Reprinted by permission of the Society for the Study of Social Problems ©1959.

emergence of gangs and their function for gang members. Professor Cohen deals with gangs as sub-cultures organized by working-class boys as a reaction to middle-class values (1). In a recent publication Block and Nederhoffer discuss gangs as organizations designed to satisfy the adolescent's striving for the attainment of adult status (2).

Although partial group structuring has been extensively discussed in sociological literature on "groups," "crowds," and "mobs," my gang research revealed that these collectivity constructs did not seem to adequately describe and properly abstract the underlying structural characteristics of the delinquent gang. Consequently, I have attempted here to construct a formulation which would draw together various described social dimensions of the gang under one conceptual scheme. I call this formulation Near-Group Theory.

NEAR-GROUP THEORY

One way of viewing human collectivities is on a continuum of organization characteristics. At one extreme, we have a highly organized, cohesive, functioning collection of individuals as members of a sociological group. At the other extreme, we have a mob of individuals characterized by anonymity, disturbed leadership, motivated by emotion, and in some cases representing a destructive collectivity within the inclusive social system. When these structures are observed in extreme, their form is apparent to the observer. However, in viewing these social structures on a continuum, those formations which tend to be neither quite a cohesive integrated group nor a disturbed mal-functioning mob or crowd are often distorted by observers in one or the other direction.

A central thesis of this paper is that mid-way on the group-mob continuum are collectivities which are neither groups nor mobs. These are structures prevalent enough in a social system to command attention in their own right as constructs for sociological analysis. Near-groups are characterized by some of the following factors:

1. diffuse role definition,
2. limited cohesion,
3. impermanence,
4. minimal consensus of norms,
5. shifting membership,
6. disturbed leadership, and
7. limited definition of membership expectations. These factors characterize the near-group's "normal" structure.

True groups may manifest near-group structure under stress, in transition, or when temporarily disorganized; however, at these times they are moving toward or away from their normative, permanent structure. The near-group manifests its homeostasis in accord with the factors indicated. It never fully becomes a *group* or a *mob*.

THE GANG AS A NEAR-GROUP PATTERN

Some recent sociological theory and discourse on gangs suffers from distortions of gang structure to fit a group rather than a near-group conception. Most gang theorizing begins with an automatic assumption that gangs are defined sociological groups. Many of these misconceived theories about gangs in sociological treatises are derived from the popular and traditional image of gangs held by the general public as reported in the press, rather than as based upon empirical scientific investigation. The following case material reveals the disparities between popular reports of gang war behavior and their organization as revealed by more systematic study.

The official report of a gang fight, which made headlines in New York papers as the biggest in the city's history, detailed a gang war between six gangs over a territorial dispute.* The police, social workers, the press, and the public accepted a defined version of groups meeting in a battle over territory. Research into this gang war incident, utilizing a near-group concept of gangs, indicates another picture of the situation.

N.Y. Daily News
NIP 200—PUNK FIGHT NEAR COLUMBIA CAMPUS
By Grover Ryder and Jack Smee
A flying squad of 25 cops, alerted by a civilian's tip, broke up the makings of one of the biggest gang rumbles in the city's turbulent teen history last night at the edge of Columbia University campus on Morningside Heights.

N.Y. Herald Tribune
POLICE SEIZE 38, AVERT GANG BATTLE—RIVERSIDE PARK RULE WAS GOAL
Police broke up what they said might have been "a very serious" battle between two juvenile factions last night as they intercepted thirty-eight youths.

N.Y. Times
GANG WAR OVER PARK BROKEN BY POLICE
The West Side police broke up an impending gang fight near Columbia University last night as 200 teenagers were massing for battle over exclusive rights to the use of Riverside Park.

N.Y. Journal-American
6-GANG BATTLE FOR PARK AVERTED NEAR GRANT'S TOMB
COPS PATROL TROUBLE SPOT
Police reinforcements today patrolled Morningside Heights to prevent a teenaged gang war for "control" of Riverside Park.

World-Telegram and Sun
HOODLUM WAR AVERTED AS COPS ACT FAST
38 to 200 Seized near Columbia
by Richard Graf

* New York Newspaper Headlines—June 11, 1955.

Fast police action averted what threatened to be one of the biggest street gang fights in the city's history as some 200 hoodlums massed last night on the upper West Side to battle over "exclusive rights" to Riverside Park.

Depth interviews with 40 gang boys, most of whom had been arrested at the scene of the gang fight, revealed a variety of reasons for attendance at the battle. There were also varied perceptions of the event and the gangs involved reported simply in the press as "gangs battling over territory." Some of the following recurring themes were revealed in the gang boys' responses.

Estimates of number of gang boys present varied from 80 to 5,000.

Gang boys interviewed explained their presence at the "battle" as follows:

I didn't have anything to do that night and wanted to see what was going to happen.

Those guys called me a Spic and I was going to get even. (He made this comment even though the "rival" gangs were mostly Puerto Ricans.)

They always picked on us. (The "they" is usually a vague reference.)

I always like a fight; it keeps up my rep.

My father threw me out of the house; I wanted to get somebody and heard about the fight.

The youth who was responsible for "calling on" the gang war—the reputed Balkan Gang leader—presented this version of the event:

That night I was out walkin' my dog about 7:30. Then I saw all these guys coming form different directions. I couldn't figure out what was happening. Then I saw some of the guys I know and I remembered we had called it on for that night.

I never really figured the Politicians (a supposed "brother Gang" he had called) would show.

Another boy added another dimension to "gang war organization":

How did we get our name? Well, when we were in the police station, the cops kept askin' us who we were. Jay was studying history in school—so he said how about The Balkans. Let's call ourselves Balkans. So we told the cops—we're the Balkans—and that was it.

Extensive data revealed this was not a case of two organized groups meeting in battle. The press, public, police, social workers, and others projected group conceptions onto a near-group activity. Most of the youths at the scene of the gang war were, in fact, participating in a kind of mob action. Most had no real concept of belonging to any gang or group; however, they were interested in a situation which might be exciting and possibly a channel for expressing some of their aggressions and hostilities. Although it was not necessarily a defined war, the possibilities of a stabbing or even a killing were high—with a few hundred disturbed and fearful youths milling around in the undefined situation. The gang war was not a social situation of two structured teen-aged armies meeting on a battlefield to act out a defined situation; it was a case of two near-groups in action.

Another boy's participation in this gang war further reveals its structure. The evening of the fight he had nothing to do, heard about this event and decided that he would wander up to see what was going to happen. On his way to the scene of the rumored gang fight he thought it might be a good idea to invite a few friends "just to be on the safe side." This swelled the final number of youths arriving at the scene of the gang fight, since other boys did the same. He denied (and I had no reason to disbelieve him) belonging to either of the gangs and the same applied to his friends. He was arrested at the scene of the "battle" for disorderly conduct and weapon-carrying.

I asked him why he had carried a knife and a zip gun on his person when he went to the gang fight if he did not belong to either of the reputed gangs and intended to be merely a "peaceful observer." His response: "Man, I'm not going to a rumble without packin'." The boy took along weapons for self-defense in the event he was attacked. The possibilities of his being attacked in an hysterical situation involving hundreds of youths who had no clear idea of what they were doing at the scene of a gang fight was, of course, great. Therefore, he was correct (within his social framework) in taking along a weapon for self-protection.

These characteristic responses to the situation when multiplied by the numbers of others present characterizes the problem. What may be a confused situation involving many aggressive youths (belonging to near-groups) is often defined as a case of two highly mechanized and organized gang groups battling each other with definition to their activities.

In another "gang war case" which made headlines, a psychotic youth acted out his syndrome by stabbing another youth. When arrested and questioned about committing the offense, the youth stated that he was a member of a gang carrying out retaliation against another gang, which was out to get him. He attributed his assault to gang affiliation.

The psychotic youth used the malleable near-group, the gang, as his psychotic syndrome. Naploeon, God, Christ, and other psychotic syndromes, so popular over the years, may have been replaced on city streets by gang membership. Not only is it a convenient syndrome, but some disturbed youths find their behavior as rational, accepted, and even aggrandized by many representatives of society. Officials such as police officers and social workers, in their interpretation of the incident often amplify this individual behavior by a youth into a group gang war condition because it is a seemingly more logical explanation of a senseless act.

In the case of the Balkans, the societal response of viewing them as a group rather than a near-group solidified their structure. After the incident, as one leader stated it, "lots more kids wanted to join."

Another gang war event further reveals the near-group structure of the gang. On the night of July 30, 1957, a polio victim named Michael Farmer was beaten and stabbed to death by a gang varyingly known as the Egyptian Kings and the Dragons. The boys who participated in this homicide came from the upper West Side of Manhattan. I had contact with many of these boys prior to the event and was known to others through the community program I directed. Because of this prior relationship the boys cooperated and responded openly when I interviewed them in the institutions where they were being held in custody.*

---

* The research and interviewing at this time was combined with my role as consultant to the Columbia Broadcasting System. I assisted in the production of a gang war documentary narrated by Edward R. Murow, entitled "Who Killed Michael Farmer?" The documentary tells the story of the killing through the actual voices of the boys who committed the act.

Responses to my interviews indicated the near-group nature of the gang. Some of the pertinent responses which reveal this characteristic of the Egyption King gang structure are somewhat demonstrated by the following comments made by five of the participants in the killing. (These are representative comments selected from over ten hours of recorded interviews.)

I was walking uptown with a couple of friends and we ran into Magician (one of the Egyptian King gang leaders) and them there. They asked us if we wanted to go to a fight, and we said yes. When he asked me if I wanted to go to a fight, I couldn't say no. I mean I could say no, but for old time's sake, I said yes.

Everyone was pushin' and I pulled out my knife. I saw this face—I never seen before, so I stabbed it.

He was laying on the ground lookin' up at us. Everyone was kicking, punching, stabbing. I kicked him in the jaw or someplace; then I kicked him in the stomach. That was the least I could do was kick 'im.

They have guys watching you and if you don't stab or hit somebody, they get you later. I hit him over the head with a bat. [Gang youths are unable to articulate specific individuals of the vague "they" who watch over them.]

I don't know how many guys are in the gang. They tell me maybe a hundred or a thousand. I don't know them all. [Each boy interviewed had a different image of the gang.]

These comments and others revealed the gang youths' somewhat different perceptions and rationale of gang war activity. There is a limited consensus of participants as to the nature of gang war situations because the gang structure—the collectivity which defines gang war behavior—in amorphous, diffuse, and malleable.

Despite the fact of gang phenomena taking a diffuse form, theoreticians, social workers, the police, the press, and the public autistically distort gangs and gang behavior toward a gestalt of clarity. The rigid frame of perceiving gangs as groups should shift to the fact of gangs as near-groups. This basic redefinition is necessary if progress is to be made in sociological diagnosis as a foundation for delinquent gang prevention and correction.

THE DETACHED GANG WORKER

The detached-worker approach to dealing with gangs on the action level is increasingly employed in large cities and urban areas throughout the country. Simply stated, a professional, usually a social worker, contacts a gang in their milieu on the street corner and attempts to redirect their delinquent patterns into constructive behavior.

Because of the absence of an adequate perceptual framework, such as the near-group concept, detached gang workers deal with gang collectivities as if they were organized like other groups and social organizations. The following principle stated in a New York City Youth Board manual on the detached gang worker approach reveals this point of view:

Participation in a street gang or club, like participation in any natural group, is a part of the growing-up process of adolescence. Such primary group associations possess potentialities for positive growth and development. Through such a group, the individual can gain security and develop positive ways of living with other individuals. Within the structure of his group the individual can develop such characteristics as loyalty, leadership, and community responsibility (3, p.107).

This basic misconception not only produces inaccurate reports and theories about gang structure but causes ineffectual work with gangs on the action level. This problem of projecting group structure onto gangs may be further illuminated by a cursory examination of detached gang worker projects.

Approaching the gang as a group, when it is not, tends to project onto it a structure which formerly did not exist. The gang worker's usual set of notions about gangs as groups includes some of the following distortions:

1. the gang has a measurable number of members,
2. membership is defined,
3. the role of members is specified,
4. there is a consensus of understood gang norms among gang members, and
5. gang leadership is clear and entails a flow of authority and direction of action.

These expectations often result in a group-fulfilling prophecy. A group may form as a consequence of the gang worker's view. In one case a gang worker approached two reputed gang leaders and told them he would have a bus to take their gang on a trip to the country. This gang had limited organization; however, by travel-time there were 32 gang members ready to go on the trip. The near-group became more organized as a result of the gang worker's misconception.

This gang from a near-group point of view was in reality comprised of a few disturbed youths with rich delusional systems who had need to view themselves as leaders controlling hordes of other gang boys in their fantasy. Other youths reinforce this ill-defined collectivity for a variety of personal reasons and needs. The gang, in fact, had a shifting membership, no clarity as to what membership entailed, and individualized member images of gang size and function.

The detached worker, as an agent of the formal social system, may thus move in on a gang and give a formerly amorphous collectivity structure and purpose through the projection of group structure onto a near-group.

NEAR-GROUP STRUCTURE

Research into the structure of 30 groups revealed three characteristic levels of membership organization. In the center of the gang, on the first level, are the most psychologically disturbed members—the leaders. It is these youths who require and need the gang most of all. This core of disturbed youths provides the gang's most cohesive force. In a gang of some 30 boys there may be five or six who are central or core members because they desperately need the gang in order to deal with their personal problems of inadequacy. These are youths always working to keep the gang together and in action, always drafting, plotting, and talking gang warfare. They are the center of the near-group activity.

At a second level of near-group organization in the gang, we have youths who claim affiliation to the gang but only participate in it according to their emotional needs at given times. For example, one of the Egyptian Kings reported that if his father had not given him a "bad time" and kicked him out of the house the night of the homicide, he would not have gone to the corner and become involved in the Michael Farmer killing. This second-level gang member's participation in the gang killing was a function of his disturbance on that particular evening. This temporal gang need is a usual occurrence.

At a third level of gang participation, we have peripheral members who will join in with gang activity on occasion, although they seldom identify themselves as members of the gang at times. This type of gang member is illustrated by the youth who went along with the Egyptian Kings on the night of the Farmer killing, as he put it, "for old time's sake." he just happened to be around on that particular evening and went along due to a situational condition. He never really "belonged" to the gang nor was he defined by himself or others as a gang member.

The size of gangs is determined in great measure by the emotional needs of its members at any given point. It is not a measure of actual and live membership. Many of the members exist only on the thought level. In the gang, if the boys feel particularly hemmed in (for paranoid reasons), they will expand the number of their near-group. On the other hand, at other times when they feel secure, the gang's size is reduced to include only those youths known on a face-to-face basis. The research revealed that, unlike an actual group, no member of a near-group can accurately determine the number of its membership at a particular point in time.

For example, most any university department member will tell you the number of other individuals who comprise the faculty of their department. It is apparent that if there are eight members in a department of psychology, each member will know each other member, his role, and the total number of members of the department. In contrast, in examining the size of gangs or near-group participation, the size increases in almost direct relationship to the lack of membership clarity. That is, the second-and third level members are modified numerically with greater ease than the central member. Third level members are distorted at times to an almost infinite number.

In one interview, a gang leader distorted the size and affiliations of the gang as his emotional state shifted. In an hour interview, the size of his gang varied from 100 members to 4,000, from five brother gangs or alliances to 60, from about ten square blocks of territorial control to include jurisdiction over the five boroughs of New York City, New Jersey, and part of Philadelphia.

Another characteristic of the gang is its lack of role definition. Gang boys exhibit considerable difficulty and contradiction in their roles in the gang. They may say that the gang is organized for protection and that one role of a gang is to fight. How, when, whom, and for what reason he is to fight are seldom clear. The right duties and obligations associated with the gang member's role in the gang varies from gang boy to gang boy.

One gang boy may define himself as a protector of the younger boys in the neighborhood. Another defines his role in the gang as "We are going to get all those guys who call us Spics." Still other gang boys define their participation in the gang as involuntarily forced upon them, through their being "drafted." Moreover, few gang members maintain a consistent function or role within the gang organization.

Definition of membership is vague and indefinite. A youth will say he belongs one day and will quit the next without necessarily telling any other gang member. I would ask one gang boy who came into my office daily whether he was a Balkan. This was comparable to asking him, "How do you feel today?"

Because of limited social ability to assume rights, duties, and obligations in constructive solidified groups, the gang boy attaches himself to a structure which requires limited social ability and can itself be modified to fit his mometary needs. This malleability factor is characteristic of the near-group membership. As roles are building blocks of a group, diffuse role definitions fit in adequately to the near-group which itself has diverse and diffuse objectives and goals. The near-group, unlike a true group, has norms, roles, functions, cohesion, size, and goals which are shaped by the emotional needs of its members.

GANG LEADERSHIP CHARACTERISTICS

Another aspect of near-groups is the factor of self-appointed leadership, usually of a dictatoral, authoritarian type. In interviewing hundreds of gang members one finds that many of them give themselves some role of leadership. For example, in the Egyptian Kings, approximately five boys defined themselves as "war counsellors." It is equally apparent that, except on specific occasions, no one will argue with this self-defined role. Consequently, leadership in the gang may be assumed by practically any member of the gang if he so determines and emotionally needs the power of being a leader at the time. It is not necessary to have his leadership role ratified by his constituents.

Another aspect of leadership in the gang is the procedure of "drafting" or enlisting new members. In many instances, this pattern of coercion to get another youth to join or belong to the gang becomes an end in itself, rather than a means to an end. In short, the process of inducing, coercing, and threatening violence upon another youth, under the guise of getting him to join, is an important gang leader activity. The gang boy is not truly concerned with acquiring another gang member, since the meaning of membership is vague at best; however, acting the power role of a leader forcing another youth to do something against his will becomes meaningful to the "drafter."

GANG FUNCTIONS

In most groups some function is performed or believed to be performed. The function which it performs may be a constructive one, as in an industrial organization, a P.T.A. group, or a political party. On the other hand, it may be a socially destructive group, such as a drug syndicate, a group of bookies, or a subversive political party. There is usually a consensus of objectives and goals shared by the membership, and their behavior tends to be essentially organized group action.

The structure of a near-group is such that its functions not only vary greatly and shift considerably from time to time, but its primary function is unclear. The gang may on one occasion be organized to protect the neighborhood; on another occasion, to take over a particular territory; and on still another, it may be organized in response to or for the purpose of racial discrimination.

The function of near-groups, moreover, is not one which is clearly understood, known, and communicated among all of its members. There is no consensus in this near-group of goals, objectives, or functions of the collectivity—much near-group behavior is individualistic and flows from emotional disturbance.

A prime function of the gang is to provide a channel to act out hostility and aggression to satisfy the continuing and momentary emotional needs of its members. The gang is a convenient and malleable structure quickly adaptable to the needs of emotionally disturbed youths, who are unable to fulfill the responsibility and demands required for participation in constructive groups. He belongs to the gang because he lacks the social ability to relate to others and to assume responsibility for the relationship, not because the gang gives him a "feeling of belonging."

Because of the gang youth's limited "social ability," he constructs a social organization which enables him to relate and to function at his limited level of performance. In this structure norms are adjusted so that the gang youth can function and achieve despite his limited ability to relate to others.

An example of this is the function of violence in the near-group of the gang. Violence in the gang is highly valued as a means for the achievement of reputation or "rep." This inversion of societal norms is a means for quick upward social mobility in the gang. He can acquire and maintain a position in the gang through establishing a violent reputation.

The following comments by members of the Egyptian Kings illustrate this point:

> If I would of got the knife, I would have stabbed him. That would have gave me more of a build-up. People would have respected me for what I've done and things like that. They would say, "There goes a cold killer."
>
> It makes you feel like a big shot. You know some guys think they're big shots and all that. They think, you know, they got the power to do everything they feel like doing.
>
> They say, like, "I wanna stab a guy," and the other guy says, "Oh, I wouldn't dare to do that." You know, he thinks I'm acting like a big shot. That's the way he feels. He probably thinks in his mind, "Oh, he probably won't do that." Then, when we go to a fight, you know, he finds out what I do.
>
> Momentarily, I started to thinking about it inside: den I have my mind made up I'm not going to be in no gang. Then I go on inside. Something comes up den here come all

my friends coming to me. Like I said before, I'm intelligent and so forth. They be coming to me—then they talk to me about what they gonna do Like, "Man, we'll go out here and kill this guy." I say, "Yeah." They kept on talkin' and talkin'. I said, "Man, I just gotta go with you." Myself, I don't want to go, but when they start talkin' about what they gonna do, I say,"So, he isn't gonna take over my rep. I ain't gonna let him be known more than me." And I go ahead just for selfishness.

The near-group of the gang, with its diffuse and malleable structure, can function as a convenient vehicle for the acting out of varied individual needs and problems. For the gang leader it can be a super-powered organization through which (in his fantasy) he dominates and controls "divisions" of thousands of members. For gang members, unable to achieve in more demanding social organizations, swift and sudden violence, is a means for quick upward social mobility and the achievement of a reputation. For less disturbed youths, the gang may function as a convenient temporary escape from the dull and rigid requirements of a difficult and demanding society. These are only some of the functions the near-group of the gang performs for its membership.

NEAR-GROUP THEORY AND SOCIAL PROBLEMS

The concept of the near-group may be of importance in the analysis of other collectivities which reflect and produce social problems. The analysis of other social structures may reveal similar distortions of their organization. To operate on an assumption that individuals in interaction with each other, around some function, with some shared mutual expectation, in a particular normative system as always being a group formation is to project a degree of distortion onto certain types of collectivities. Groups are social structures at one end of a continuum; mobs are social structures at another end; and at the center are near-groups which have some of the characteristics of both, and yet are characterized by factors not found fully in either.

In summary, these factors may include the following:

1. Individualized role definition to fit momentary needs.
2. Diffuse and differential definitions of membership.
3. Emotion-motivated behavior.
4. A decrease of cohesiveness as one moves from the center of the collectivity to the periphery.
5. Limited responsibility and sociability required for membership and belonging.
6. Self-appointed and disturbed leadership.
7. A limited consensus among participants of the collectivities' functions or goals.
8. A shifting and personalized stratification system.
9. Shifting membership.
10. The inclusion in size of phantasy membership.

11. Limited consensus of normative expectations.
12. Norms in conflict with the inclusive social system's prescriptions.

Although the gang was the primary type of near-group appraised in this analysis, there are perhaps other collectivities whose structure is distorted by autistic observers. Their organization might very well include adult gangs varyingly called the "Mafia," the "National Crime Syndicate," and so-called International Crime Cartels. There are indications that these social organizations are comparable in organization to the delinquent gang. They might fit the near-group category if closely analyzed in this context, rather than aggrandized and distorted by mass media and even Senate Committees.

Other more institutionalized collectivities might fit the near-group pattern. As a possible example, "the family in transition" may not be in transition at all. The family, as a social institution, may be suffering from near-groupism. Moreover, such standardized escape hatches of alcoholism, psychoses, and addictions may be too prosaic for the sophisticated intellectual to ultilize in escape from himself.

For him, the creation and perpetuation of near-groups requiring limited responsibility and personal commitment may be a more attractive contemporary form for expressing social and personal commitment may be a more attractive contemporary form for expressing social and personal pathology. The measure of organization or disorganization of an inclusive social system may possibly be assessed by the prevalence of near-group collectivities in its midst. The delinquent gang may be only one type of near-group in American society.

REFERENCES

1. Cohen, Albert K., Delin*quent Boys* (Glencoe: The Free Press, 1955)
2. Block, Herbert, and Arthur Nederhoffer, *The Gang* (New York: The Philosophical Library, 1958).
3. Furman, Slyvan S., *Reaching the Unreached* (New York: Youth Board, 1952).

ARTICLE 21

Field Observations of Middle Class "Gangs"*

HOWARD L. MYERHOFF
BARBARA G. MYERHOFF

THE SOCIOLOGICAL LITERATURE about gangs contains at least two sharply conflicting descriptions of the extent of gang structure and the nature of their values. In the most prevalent view, the gang is seen as a kind of primary group, highly structured, relatively permanent and autonomous, possessing a well-developed delinquent subculture which is transmitted to new members. The gang is interpreted as meeting strongly felt needs of its members and as providing a collectively derived solution to common problems of adjustment. Different writers who hold this view have stressed different problems, but nearly all have agreed that one of the most important functions of the gang is to establish bonds of loyalty and solidarity between members of a tightly knit peer group.

Cohen[1] has identified the primary needs met by the gang as those of resolving status frustration for lower class boys, and providing an expression of masculine identification for middle class boys. Parsons[2] has also emphasized the achievement of

* The observations reported in this paper were carried out as part of a Youth Studies Center developmental project, which ultimately led to an action-research program concerned with the treatment of delinquent gangs. Both the developmental project and the action-research program, now in process, received support from the Ford Foundation. The authors would like to thank A. W. McEachern of the Youth Studies Center, University of Southern California, for his generous and valuable assistance, criticism, and encouragement. A shorter version of this paper was read at the annual meeting of the Pacific Sociological Association in Sacramento, April 1962.

Source: Reprinted from *Social Forces,* Vol. 42 (March) 1964: 328-336. "Field Observations of Middle Class 'Gangs'" by Howard L. Myerhoff and Barbara G. Myerhoff. Copyright © The University of North Carolina Press.

[1]Albert K. Cohen, *Delinquent Boys: The Culture of the Gang* (Glencoe: Free Press, 1955).
[2]Talcott Parsons, "Certain Primary Sources and Patterns of Aggression in the Social Structure of the Western World," reprinted in Mullahy (Ed.), *A Study of Interpersonal Relations* (New York: Grove Press, Evergreen Edition, 1949).

sexual identity as a problem dealt with by delinquent behavior. Cloward and Ohlin,[3] following Merton's conception, have specified the discrepancy between aspirations toward success goals and opportunities for achieving them as the problem giving rise to gang behavior. Kvaraceus and Miller[4] have stressed the inherent conflict between lower and middle class values and the delinquent's predisposition to the former in explaining gang behavior. Eisenstadt[5] and Block and Neiderhoffer[6] have pointed to the gang as a collective response to the adolescent's striving toward the attainment of adulthood and the frustrations attendant on the transition from one age status to another. These authors identify different components of the gang subculture according to their interpretation of its function, but implicit or explicit in all these position is the view of the gang as an integrated and relatively cohesive group.

A strikingly different interpretation of the structure of gangs describes them as informal, short lived, secondary groups without a clear-cut, stable delinquent structure. Lewis Yablonsky[7] has suggested a conceptualization of the gang as a "near-group," specifying the following definitive characteristics: diffuse role definitions, limited cohesion, impermanence, minimal consensus on norms, shifting membership, emotionally disturbed leaders, and limited definition of membership expectations. On a continuum of the extent of social organization, Yablonsky locates the gang midway between the mob at one end and the group at the other. The gang is seen as in a state of equilibrium, moving sometimes closer to one end of the continuum and sometimes the other, but never actually becoming completely disorganized like a mob or completely organized like a group. He contends that detached worker programs, by treating the gang as a true group, may actually make it one. When a detached worker acknowledges a gang's leaders, recognizes its territory, membership, name, and purpose, he crystallizes its organization, lending it a structure which it did not previously have. This Yablonsky calls the "group-fulfilling prophecy."

The gangs he has observed are, in actuality, quite different from groups. They are "near-groups" which have a diffuse and malleable structure that enables them to meet the varied and individual needs of the members. For many gang members who are unable to meet the demands and responsibilities of more structured social organizations, it is the gang's very lack of organization and absence of expectations which constitute its primary sources of satisfaction. Youths affiliate with a gang not for a feeling of belonging and solidarity but because it is an organization within which they can relate to others in spite of their limited social abilities. The flexibility of gang organization means that it can meet diverse, momentary needs of the members who,

[3] Richard A. Cloward and Lloyd E. Ohlin, *Delinquency and Opportunity: A Theory of Delinquent Gangs* (Glencoe: Free Press, 1961).

[4] William C. Kvaraceus and Walter B. Miller, *Delinquent Behavior: Culture and the Individual* (Washington, D.C.: National Education Association, 1959).

[5] S. N. Eisenstadt, From Generation to Generation: Age Groups and Social Structure (Glencoe: Free Press, 1956).

[6] Herbert A. Bloch and Arthur Niederhoffer, *The Gang: A Study of Adolescent Behavior* (New York: Philosophical Library, 1958).

[7] Lewis Yablonsky, "The Delinquent Gang as a Near-Group," *Social Problems,* Vol. 7 (Fall 1959), pp. 108-117.

accordingly, participate in it with varying intensity. Yablonsky suggests that in a gang there are a few core members surrounded by a large number of peripheral members to whom the gang is much less important and who are more loosely attached to it.

James F. Short, Jr. objects to Yablonsky's description of the gang as a near-group on the grounds that he has overstated the case.[8] but agrees nevertheless, that gangs do not have "the stability of membership, the tight knit organization and rigid hierarchical structure which is sometimes attributed to them.[9] Most of the groups he had observed have the kind of shifting membership which Yablonsky described.

The supervisor of a large, long-lived detached worker program in Los Angeles with many years of gang experience there and in Harlem has given a description much like that of Yablonsky.[10] He observed that delinquent gangs seldom act as a corporate group and that most of their anti-social activities are committed in groups of two's or three's, or by a single person. He found communication between members to be meager and sporadic, reflecting the same limitations in social abilities that Yablonsky identified. In fact, one of the goals of his detached worker program is the structuring of gangs into social groups, encouraging cooperation and communication between members and a gradual assumption of social responsibilities. When successful, a detached worker is able to form a gang into a club which elects officers, collects dues, arranges activities, and eventually establishes nondelinquent norms and role expectations. Thus by substituting the status factions of membership in an organized social group for delinquent activities, the program provides an aspect of socialization which gang members have not previously experienced. The program is able, in this way, to prepare gang members to meet the requirements and responsibilities of conventional, adult social life. The technique is apparently the self-conscious application of what Yablonsky has called "the group-fulfilling prophecy," and seems to be quite a successful one.

The field observations presented here are based on the experiences of a participant-observer who spent two weeks among several groups of deviant and non-deviant middle class youths in a suburb of Los Angeles. These observations are particularly pertinent to the prevailing conflicting interpretations of the extent of gang structure. The middle class youngsters described here were located through lists of "hangouts" provided by local police, school authorities, and probation officers. The observer "hung around" these places and when asked who he was, which was seldom,

---

[8] In a recent article Pfautz raised the question of whether Yablonsky's "near-group" concept is necessary. He suggests that Yablonsky's findings could be more productively recast into the the theoretical traditions of collective behavior in general and social movements in particular. Certainly, Pfautz's point that this would widen the theoretical relevance of Yablonsky's findings is well-taken. There are two reasons for the author's preference for the near-group concept rather than a collective behavior orientation: first an immediate concern with indicating the point similarity between these observations and those reported by Yablonsky, regardless of the conceptual framework he uses in describing them, and second, the authors' feeling that in view of the fragmented and discontinuous state of the literature on the subject, it is at present more important to compare and relate studies of adolescent collective deviant activities to one another than to more general sociological issues and concepts. Harold W. Pfautz. "Near-Group Theory and Collective Behavior "A Critical Reformulation," *Social Problems,* Vol. 9 (Fall 1961), pp. 167-174.

[9] James F. Short, Jr., "Street Corner Groups and Patterns of Delinquency," A Progress Report from National Institute of Mental Health Research Grant, M-3301 (Chicago, March 1961), p. 20.

[10] Alva Collier, personal communication (Los Angeles, 1961).

explained that he was a writer doing a series of articles on teenagers. The youngsters talked freely in front of and to the observer, and after a short time included him in many of their activities, such as house and beach parties, drag races, car club meetings, bull sessions, and bowling. Altogether, about eighty youngsters ranging in age between fifteen and eighteen were observed. All were Caucasian, most in high school, Protestant, and in appearance and manner readily distinguishable from the lower class boys and girls who occasionally mixed with them.

Impressions, activities, and conversations were recorded by the observer in a daily journal and roughly classified into the following categories: values and peer interactions, deviant activities, and group organization.[11] It should be kept in mind that these comments are observations, not findings. Many authors have lamented the dearth of speculation about as well as empirical observations of gangs, in both the middle and lower classes. Cohen and Short recently said about middle class delinquent subcultures: "The saddest commentary, however, is that we are faced with a poverty of speculation, without which there can be no meaningful research, without which, in turn, there can be no conclusions that are more than speculation."[12] These observations and comments lead to some of the speculation which must precede meaningful empirical research, and their greatest value may prove to be heuristic.

VALUES AND PEER INTERACTIONS

The youngsters observed, like most groups of teenagers, were rather uniform in dress and demeanor. Their self- possession and poise, along with elaborate grooming and expensive, well-tended clothes combined to give an impression of urbanity and sophistication beyond what would normally be expected of this age group. For most events, the girls wore tight capris, blouses or cashmere sweaters, silver fingernail and toenail polish, towering intricate coiffeurs, brush-applied iridescent lipstick, and heavy eye makeup. The boys, like the girls, were uniformly clean, and like them preferred their pants as tight as possible; levis were rarely seen. Usually an Ivy League shirt was worn outside the pants and over this a nylon windbreaker. At beaches both boys and girls wore bikinis, and apparently no one without a deep and even tan ever dared appear. The overall impression fostered was one of careful, elegant casualness sustained in manner as well as appearance. The complete absence of the social and physical awkwardness usually associated with adolescence was indeed striking.

The content of conversation among these groups did not differ appreciably from what one would expect to find among most teenagers; it concerned clothes, dates, sex, school classes and activities, bridge, sports, and so forth. But no subject dominated the conversation as much as the car, which seemed an object of undying, one might say

---

[11] These field observations precisely conform to what Zelditch has called Type I information. This consists of incidents and histories, and treats as data the meanings assigned to and explanations given for activities as well as the behavior itself. Morris Zelditch, Jr., "Some Methodological Problems of Field Studies," *American Journal of Sociology.* Vol. 67 (March 1962), pp. 566-576.

[12] Albert K. Cohen and James F. Short, Jr., "Research in Delinquent Subcultures," *Journal of Social Issues,* Vol. 14, No. 3 (1958), p. 34.

morbid, fascination. The majority of girls and boys owned their own cars and virtually all had access to a car, usually a late model American or foreign sports car. "Custom jobs" were not rare and cars were often "shaved," "chopped," "channeled," and "pinstriped." All were scrupulously clean and highly polished. The argot concerning the car was as elaborate and subtle as one might expect in view of its importance; such matters as "dual quads," "turning seven grand," "slicks," "3:7 trans ratio" were frequently discussed with great intensity. Driving skill and mechanical expertise were prized far above mere ownership of a desirable car.

The car, in fact, permeated every aspect of these youngsters' social life. The size of groups which gathered was usually limited by the number a single car could hold, and when several cars congregated, at drive-ins for example, youngsters demonstrated a distinct unwillingness to leave the car. Radios in cars were never off and all activities took place against a background of popular music. The car also affected the places frequented, with drive-in movies and restaurants preferred. After school and on weekends, many of these youngsters could be seen slowly cruising in their cars, up and down the neighborhood streets, greeting acquaintances, chatting, taking friends for short rides, all with an air of easy sociability. These cruises in manner and purpose were reminiscent of the Spanish late afternoon *Paseo*, in which young people stroll casually up and down streets closed off for that purpose. The cars were the location for nearly all social events engaged in by these youngsters. They were the site of bull sessions, drinking bouts, and necking parties. In all the car provided a mobile parlor, clubhouse, dining room, and bedroom; it was at once the setting and symbol of much of adolescent deviant and nondeviant sociability and sexuality.

Several writers have emphasized the dominant role of the car in patterns of middle class deviance. Warrenberg and Balistrieri[13] found auto theft to be characteristic of "favored groups," older white boys who had better relations with peers and came from more desirable neighborhoods than did boys charged with other types of offenses. T.C.N. Gibbens[14] studied adolescent car thieves in London and also found them to be a "favored group," not because they lived in better neighborhoods but because they came from homes which were intact and affectionate. All these findings and impressions may be interpreted as supporting the contention of Parsons[15] and Cohen[16] that the primary middle class problem to which delinquency is a response is the establishment of masculine identity. Indeed, the sexual significance of the car has been widely recognized. Gibbens comments that: "In the simplest cases joy-riding is of the common 'proving' type, in which an overprotected lad from a 'good' home commits an offense to prove his masculinity . . . . The daring act represents a bid for independence, and the car provides a feeling of power in which he feels so lacking. . . ."[17] Certainly, this view is corroborated by the observations of middle class youths offered here, among whom the car, if not a sufficient cause of masculinity, is at least a necessary condition for it.

[13] William W. Wattenberg and James Balistrieri, "Automobile Theft: A 'Favored Group' Delinquency," *American Journal of Sociology,* Vol. 57 (May 1952), pp. 575-579.

[14] T.C.N. Gibbens, "Car Thieves," *British Journal of Delinquency,* 7-9 (1957-1959), pp. 257-265.

[15] Parsons, *op. cit.*

[16] Cohen, *op. cit.*

[17] Gibbens, *op. cit.,* p. 262.

In view of the importance of the car, it was not surprising to find that the only formal social organizations to which many of these youngsters belonged were car clubs, whose membership often transcended the class and age affiliations typical of the more informal gatherings. These clubs usually consist of about fifteen members and are devoted to the building and legal and illegal racing of cars. In order to be admitted, youngsters' cars must undergo rigorous police safety inspections and members may be expelled or excluded for too many traffic tickets. In marked contrast to the informal groups, these clubs are highly structured. Meetings are regular and frequent, membership is stable, leaders are elected for specified terms, and the clubs have names, plaques, and jackets. The meetings are conducted strictly according to Roberts' Rules of Order, fines are levied for infractions of rules, dues are collected, and events are planned in detail and in advance. A well-developed pattern of mutual aid and extensive coopera- tion has been established, and it is not unusual for members to pool money, skills, and time to build a car which is entered in races and rallies by the entire group. It is obviously no accident that the only object around which spontaneous, unsupervised yet structured groups form is the car.

DEVIANT ACTIVITIES

The deviant behavior of the groups observed varied greatly in seriousness. Some of their activities may be considered deviant only because technically illegal, such as curfew violation and beer drinking, while more serious infractions such as theft and narcotics are less common. The more serious deviant activities seemed to involve the least number of people at one time; youngsters were alone or with a friend or two on these occasions. The less serious infractions were not usually the purpose of a gathering but were rather incidental to another activity. These included spontaneous drag racing, drinking, and much sexual activity.

Of the more serious violations, theft was certainly the most common. Many boys spoke of frequent and regular stealing, often from employers. Ready access rather than need or desire seemed to determine the choice of stolen objects. These items were seldom traded or converted into cash. Great pride was evidenced in the cleverness with which the thefts were executed and a good performance seemed more important than the acquisition of goods. Several boys boasted about never having been caught although they had been engaging in this activity for years. The stolen goods were by no means small, inexpensive, or easily portable, but included such items as tires, car radios, phonographs, tape recorders, and television sets. Great care was taken in order to ensure that stolen goods were not missed. Thefts were timed so as to coincide with events such as inventories, and the filling of orders.

It is not possible on the basis of these observations to estimate the frequency of these thefts, but one can say with certainty that they were by no means uncommon. This phenomenon appears to be very similar to 'white collar crime" and as such raises questions as to the generalizability of theories of delinquency causation based solely on socio-economic variables. As Wattenberg and Balistrieri have pointed out: "The point of impact of the concept of [white collar crime] lies in its assumption that the form of anti-social or illegal conduct rather than its frequency varies from . . . class to class in our society."[18] It may well be that the "white collar delinquent" engages in as many anti-social activities as do lower class youngsters, but a combination of factors, particularly the form of delinquency, interact to prevent these activities from coming to the attention of the authorities, or if apprehended, prevent the middle class youngsters from being officially handled and recorded. Indeed, there is already much evidence to suggest this is the case.[19]

The same discretion, judgment, and self-possession which characterized thefts was observed in the homosexual, and to a lesser degree, the heterosexual gatherings. These events were held in private homes and occasionally included slightly older boys from nearby colleges. They were not events which were likely to attract the attention of police or even parents. The homosexual youngsters often met one another at small cabarets, coffee houses, and bars in which few lower class teenagers or adults were to be seen. They also met in several private clubs whose members were primarily upper and middle class teenage homosexuals. These youngsters were typically inconspicuous and did not indulge in egregious displays of homosexuality either in dress or manner. While in the clubs, many were openly solicitous and flirtatious, but upon leaving, their more conventional manners were resumed. The same caution was apparent among those who purchased and used narcotics, usually marijuana. It was smoked at small, quiet parties, rarely while driving or in public places. It was not unusual to hear these poised, well-dressed youngsters speak of stealing, using narcotics, and the advantages and disadvantages of their respective college choices in the same tone of voice and conversation.

The middle class group anti-social activities which *do* come to the attention of the authorities are of a rather different nature than those just described. Several examples of these were provided by a local probation officer assigned to the neighborhood. On one occasion, he recalled, a group of about ten boys went back and forth across a busy intersection between 5:30 and 6:30 in the evening, effectively bring traffic to a complete standstill until dispersed by the police. Another time, a car full of boys drove slowly down a main shopping street spraying the well dressed shoppers with the contents of a fire extinguisher. One incident involved a group of boys who stole an old car and took it to a vacant lot and while one boy drove the car around in circles, the others threw stones at it, until it was nothing but a battered corpse.

There is a mischievous, often amusing overtone to all these incidents; they are not the kind likely to be though malicious or violent. Rather, they are spontaneous and gratuitous, proving nothing but providing "kicks." This behavior is not the kind which is likely to seriously alarm parents or police. It has none of the grim overtones usually associated, correctly or not, with activities of lower class gangs. In general, the nonviolent nature of the deviant activities of these youngsters is salient, and personal

[18] Wattenberg and Balistrieri, *op. cit.*, p. 575.
[19] A. L. Porterfield, "Delinquency and Its Outcome in Court and College," *American Journal of Sociology,* Vol. 48 (1943), pp. 199-208; Ivan F. Nye and James F. Short, Jr., "Scaling Delinquent Behavior," *American Sociological Review,* Vol. 22 (1957), pp. 326-331.

aggression rare. The anti-social activities observed among these groups rarely took the form of open defiance of authority; manipulation rather than rebellion appeared to be the preferred technique for handling trouble with authorities. Cohen and Short have postulated just such a difference between lower and middle class delinquency:

> . . . we are persuaded that further research will reveal subtle but important differences between working class and middle class patterns of delinquency. It seems probable that the qualities of malice, bellicosity, and violence will be underplayed in the middle class subcultures and that these subcultures will emphasize more the deliberate courting of danger . . . and a sophisticated, irresponsible, "playboy" approach to activities symbolic in our culture, of adult roles and centering largely around sex, liquor, and automobiles.[20]

How closely that description fits the middle class groups observed is readily apparent.

Interestingly enough, even while engaging in flagrant, frequent infractions of the law, these youngsters sustained the opinion that their activities would in no way interfere with their future plans. They did not define themselves as delinquents or even troublemakers and did not expect others to do so. More likely than not, upon graduating from high school and entering college, as most planned to do, these youngsters will leave their deviant activities behind without a trace in the form of official records, self-definition, or residues of unpleasant experiences with authorities. The police seemed to share this expectation. An incident was observed in which a boy was picked up for drinking and curfew violation. In the patrol car he expressed his concern lest the occasion jeopardize his chances for entering college. The officer, who had until that point been rather surly, hastened to reassure the boy that such a possibility was quite unlikely, and implied that nothing would come of the visit to the station.

The same expectations were shared by the people who worked at the places where these youngsters congregated—waitresses, life guards, theater managers—who did not feel that even as a group they constituted a serious nuisance. Their tolerance is no doubt increased by middle class youngsters' liberal spending habits which make it worth their while to put up with an occasional annoyance. But in addition their attitudes are affected by the usually pleasant relations they have with these boys and girls, whose interpersonal experiences with adults and peers are more harmonious and extensive than those observed among the more socially inadequate lower class gangs observed by Yablonsky and the supervisor of the detached worker program in Los Angeles. This difference in social ability is hardly surprising in view of the middle classes' traditional specialization in entrepreneurial activities. The techniques of smooth social relations are the bread and butter of the middle classes, and middle class teenagers, deviant and nondeviant alike, demonstrate remarkable agility in the manipulation of social situations. Their interpersonal skills enable them to control their social environment to a much greater degree than possible for lower class teenagers who have not had the opportunity to acquire and perfect these techniques.

---

[20] Cohen and Short, *op. cit.*, p. 26.

GROUP ORGANIZATION

It can be seen that the groups observed, with the exception of disturbed leadership, precisely conform to Yablonsky's description of a near-group. Certainly, they do not qualify for the term "gang" as it is usually used, nor do they have well-developed delinquent values. On the contrary, the similarity between these youngsters' values and those of the adult, dominant society is conspicuous. Such a continuity has been suggested by Matza and Sykes[21] in a recent article in which they contend that the values underlying much juvenile delinquency are far less deviant than commonly portrayed, due to a prevailing oversimplification of middle class values. The authors argue that existing alongside the official, dominant values in society is another conflicting set which they call subterranean. These are values which are frequently relegated by adults to leisure time pursuits and are not ordinarily allowed to interfere with the regular course of a conventional life. Matza and Sykes pointed out that the content of these subterranean values has been described by Veblen in his portrayal of the "gentleman of leisure"—disdain for work, identification of masculinity with tough, aggressive behavior, and the search for thrills and adventures. The authors feel that the delinquent emphasizes a society's subterranean values but instead of relegating them to after-hours activities, he makes them a way of life, a code of behavior. The delinquent, then, has not evolved an original set of values but has only taken over one aspect of those held by most people along with their publicly proclaimed, respectable middle class values.

J. A. Pitt-Rivers[22] has suggested the concept "infra-structure" to describe what Matza and Sykes have referred to as subterranean values. The infra-structure is a set of values which exists alongside and in opposition to the official beliefs and behavior required by the formal systems of authority. It is not merely a set of separate beliefs held by one segment of the community but is that part of the social structure consisting of the personal, internalized version of officially endorsed values. The two systems are seen by Pitt-Rivers as interdependent, representing the private and public morals held simultaneously by everyone in the social system. The opposition of the value systems creates a structural tension or ambivalence which, though never really sharp enough to seriously endanger the social order, nevertheless provides a predisposition to deviance from officially prescribed behavior. The relation between the two systems is continuous, and while certain people or groups are more influenced by one system than the other, both affect all behavior to some degree.

In the light of the observations presented here, one may postulate that just as certain individuals and social groups are closer to one set of these values than the other, so are different age groups. Adolescence may be understood as a period in the life span of the individual when he is closer to deviant or subterranean values than he will be as an adult or has been as a child. Several authors have conceptualized adolescence as a

---

[21] David Matza and Gresham M. Sykes, "Juvenile Delinquency and Subterranean Values," *American Sociological Review*, Vol. 26 (October 1961), pp. 712-719.

[22] J. A. Pitt-Rivers, *The People of the Sierra* (Chicago: University of Chicago Press, Phoenix Edition, 1961).

period of license, a time for social and sexual exploration. Benedict[23] has pointed out the expectation that the adolescent will be irresponsible, though as an adult a few years later he can no longer be, and Erikson[24] has described adolescence as a psychosocial moratorium, set aside for experimentation in establishing an identity prior to the assumption of adult roles. One implication which can be drawn from these interpretations is that a teenager's "deviant behavior" may be in actuality a phase in his history when he is allowed and even expected to behave in accord with a set of subterranean values which do not disappear when he becomes an adult but instead are acted upon only on more appropriate occasions.

The adolescent in our culture, it is suggested, may be viewed as an aristocrat, a gentleman of leisure who, for a time, is not required to work but is allowed to play, explore, test limits, indulge his pleasures, and little else besides. This description of the delinquent as a kind of aristocrat closely resembles Finestone's characterization of the black teenage narcotic addict.[25] The "cat" is an individual who has developed an elaborate repertoire of manipulative techniques for dealing with the world, eschewing violence in favor of persuasion and charm. "He seeks through a harmonious combination of charm, ingratiating speech, dress, music, the proper dedication to his 'kick' and unrestrained generosity to make of his day to day life itself a gracious work of art."[26] The similarity between this depiction of the "cat" and the youngsters described here is indeed remarkable, especially in light of the differences between them in race, class, and circumstance.

There is, then, much reason to think that Matza and Sykes are justified in urging that delinquency might be better understood as an extension of the adult conforming world rather than as discontinuous with it. One advantage of this interpretation is that it allows for a single explanation of lower and middle class delinquency and thus avoids the inconsistency inherent in theories which specify the influence of socio-economic factors in the etiology of lower class delinquency and psychological factors in the etiology of middle class delinquency. It is likely that much may be gained by exploring the similarity between the delinquent and the rest of society rather than his deviance from it. Certainly these observations suggest that middle class deviants may differ from lower class delinquents not in the frequency of their anti-social activities, but only in the form which they take and the sophistication, social intelligence, judgment, and skill with which they are executed.

SUMMARY

These observations have raised several important issues concerning the structure and values of delinquent groups. It may be that the extent of gang structure is frequently exaggerated and that such groups may not be as cohesive, structured, and stable as they

[23] Ruth Benedict, "Continuities and Discontinuities in Cultural Conditioning," reprinted in Mullahy (Ed.), *A Study of Interpersonal Relations* (New York: Grove Press, Evergreen Edition, 1949).

[24] Erik H. Erikson, *Childhood and Society* (New York: W. W. Norton, 1950).

[25] Harold Finestone, "Cats, Kicks and Color," *Social Problems*, Vol 5 (July 1957), pp. 3-13.

[26] *Ibid.*, p. 5.

are commonly depicted. The groups described here manifested all but one of the characteristics (disturbed leadership) described by Yablonsky as those of a near-group. There is a coincidence of opinion based on three sets of observations (Yablonsky's, the supervisor of a detached worker program in Los Angeles, and those reported in this paper) suggesting that the common conception of the gang as a highly organized primary group is not always accurate and may be the result of the gross exaggerations made possible by the dearth of empirical observations of gangs. Exaggeration may also have taken place in the extent of the differences between delinquent values and those of the dominant society. The observations reported in this paper are in accord with the suggestions of Matza and Sykes that the delinquent subculture is an extension of values held by most members of the society but indulged in less openly and less often. Certainly the behavior and beliefs of the middle class youngsters observed are not dramatically different from those of most conventional teenagers or adults.

In view of these three sets of observations, the following questions may be asked:

1. How often and to what extent are gangs primary groups with elaborate delinquent subcultures, and how prevalent are such groups when compared with the loosely structure, secondary, impermanent collectivities with little or no delinquent subculture such as those described here?

2. In view of the conflicting characterizations of the extent of gang structure and the nature of gang values, would not there be more scientific value in describing gangs in terms of at least these two variables rather than primarily on the basis of the content of their deviant activities?

3. To what extent, if any, does adult recognition, particularly in the form of the assignment of detached workers to gangs, legitimize and formalize these groups, lending them a cohesion and solidarity which they previously might not have had?

4. Has the emphasis on the deviant activities of these groups obscured their similarity to conventional teenagers and adults, thereby exaggerating the differences between delinquents and non-delinquents? And

5. Would it not be more fruitful to examine the extent and nature of the similarities rather than differences between deviant and non-deviant teenagers and adults?

The action implications of these questions are far-reaching. If, as Yablonsky suggests, the gang meets different needs for different members, a uniform approach on a gang basis is inappropriate. More suitable would be an attempt to help individual members develop the interpersonal skills which would enable them to participate in structured, socially accepted groups. Or, by deliberately applying techniques such a Yablonsky's "group-fulfilling prophecy," gangs might be made into non-deviant clubs. And, if delinquent values are but a continuation of one aspect of the accepted value system subscribed to by most law-abiding people, a program designed to integrate these values into a more appropriate place in deviant youngsters' lives (for example, by providing socially acceptable means of expressing aggression and seeking adventure) would be more honest and effective than attempts to eliminate them altogether.

At this stage, only one firm conclusion is justified. The variables in terms of which gangs can best be understood have not yet been identified and are not likely to be until widespread and systematic empirical observation is conducted. The impressions reported here suggest just how valuable and unsettling such observation may prove.

Parents, Peers, and Delinquent Action
A Test of the Differential Association Perspective[1]

GARY F. JENSEN

This study attempts to go beyond the well-documented relationship between delinquent associations and involvement in delinquency to a consideration of the independent consequences of delinquent peers, parents, and "delinquent" definitions for delinquent action. The data fail to support Sutherland and Cressey's argument that family life is relevant to delinquency only when "delinquent patterns" are available to copy. Using a variety of measures of availability of deviant patterns, paternal supervision and support were found to be negatively related to delinquency to approximately the same degree under almost all conditions. Moreover, delinquent peers and paternal supervision and support were both found to influence delinquency involvement regardless of definitions favorable and unfavorable to the violation of the law. The family, peers, and definitions relevant to law breaking appear to exert independent effects on delinquency which are not adequately encompassed by etiological perspectives that introduce such definitions as intervening between other important variables and delinquency.

Source: Jensen, Gary F. "Parents, Peers, and Delinquent Action: A Test of the Differential Association Perspective." *American Journal of Sociology*, Vol. 78 (November) 1972: 562-575. Reprinted by permission of The University of Chicago Press.

[1] The data utilized in this paper were collected as part of the Richmond Youth Study under the direction of Alan B. Wilson (Survey Research Center, University of California, Berkeley). I gratefully acknowledge my debt to Travis Hirschi. This paper elaborates, in part, on some aspects of his earlier analysis of the Richmond data as reported in *Causes of Delinquency* (Berkeley: University of California Press, 1969).

INTRODUCTION

Most empiricle tests of the differential association perspective on delinquency (Sutherland and Cressey 1966, pp. 77-100) have focused on the most basic relationship implied by the theory: association with delinquent peers is assumed to lead to differential exposure to "definitions favorable to the violation of the law" and is subsequently examined in relation to delinquent behavior.[2] A strong positive relationship has been well documented (Glueck and Glueck 1950, pp. 163-64; Short 1957, pp. 233-39; Voss 1964, pp. 74-85; Erickson and Empey 1965, pp. 268-82). The present study represents an attempt to go beyond the usual concern with the direct relationship between differential association and delinquency to an assessment of the consequences of peers, parents, and definitions for delinquency involvement and an empirical examination of the ability of the theory to encompass a certain set of "known" relationships between patterns of family life and delinquency.

DIFFERENTIAL ASSOCIATION AND THE FAMILY

An adequate theory of delinquency must be able to encompass the persistent finding that the nature of parent-child relationships is a fairly important determinant of involvement in delinquency (Healy and Bronner 1936; Glueck and Glueck 1950; Nye 1958; Gold 1963; Hirschi 1969), and the differential association perspective has been posited as just such a theory.[3] Recognizing such persistent relationships, Sutherland and Cressey (1966, pp. 226-27) argue that most family variables are related to delinquency through the following two processes:

> A child may be driven from the home by unpleasant experiences and situations or withdraw from it because of the absence of pleasant experiences, and thus cease to be a functioning member of an integrated group... The important element is that isolation from the family is likely to increase the child's associations with delinquency behavior patterns and decrease his associations with antidelinquency behavior patterns.
>
> The home may fail to train the child to deal with community situations in a law-abiding manner. That is, delinquency patterns may not be present in the home, but the home may be neutral with respect to delinquency of the child . . . Again, whether such a "neutral" child becomes delinquent or not will depend upon his associations with delinquent and antidelinquent patterns outside the home.

[2] Two notable exceptions are Hirschi's *Causes of Delinquency* (1969) and Hackler's study of "norms vs. others" as predictors of delinquency (1968, pp. 92-106).

[3] Since the hypotheses to be tested in this analysis treat conditions of family life as independent variables and delinquency as the dependent variable, our analysis and interpretations are in terms of that assumed caysal ordering. However, it should be recognized that delinquency may be causally implicated in generating certain conditions of family life as well. Similarly, when we test certain notions derived from the differential association perspective, the interpretation is in terms of the ordering suggested by such theorists. Again, it should be recognized that, even where the associations suggest that certain relationships do exist, the causal direction may be quite different from that assumed by a particular theorist.

The first of these two processes encompasses situations of isolation or alienation from the home as distinct from the failure of the home to present antidelinquent patterns. In the latter situation, the child is not necessarily driven or withdrawn from the family, but the family situation is such that he fails to develop attitudes, inhibitions or definitions which work against the violation of the law.

> In either case, whether the "unattached" child becomes delinquent depends on his associations *outside the home* (Sutherland and Cressey 1966, pp. 227-28).
>
> These two processes are important because they increase the probability that a child will come into intimate contact with delinquents and will be attracted by delinquent behavior.
>
> A child does not necessarily become delinquent because he is unhappy. Children in unhappy homes may take on delinquency patterns if there are any around for them to acquire.

While the stress is placed on contacts outside the home, Sutherland and Cressey do note that a child may learn to be delinquent in the home as well. They feel, however, that peers of the same sex are more important than parents in shaping the behavior of adolescents, whether in delinquent or antidelinquent directions. Hence, their emphasis is on contact with children of the same age and sex.[4]

In sum, while numerous theorists and researchers have supported a theoretical model locating the development of delinquent behavior in the nature of direct and indirect control by the family over the teenager, Sutherland and Cressey's arguments add a qualifying condition to the model. The lack of control by the parents is argued to be associated with delinquent behavior only in situations where there are delinquent patterns around to copy. In short, the known relationships between qualities of family life and delinquency are thought to hold up only within certain contexts.

Robert Stanfield (1966, pp. 411-17) has found several patterns of "interaction" consistent with such an hypothesis. For example, using appearances in a court for one or more juvenile offenses as his measure of delinquency, he found parental discipline to be more strongly related to delinquency among low-status families than high-status families, and he interprets that finding as suggested the "unpleasant family experiences are more likely to produce delinquency in circumstances where there is an alternative cultural pattern that is favorable to the violation of the law." However, recent research (Hirschi 1969, pp. 212-23) suggests little, if any, correlation between family status and acceptance of alternative cultural patterns favorable to the violation of the law. While such findings cast doubt on the notion that it is such "cultural" patterns which account for the conditioning effect of social status, it may be that status is related to association with delinquents and that such associations increase the probability of delinquency through group pressure rather than through socialization into competing cultural

---

[4] Other authors have argued that a "Fagin" pattern of socialization is rare (Sykes and Matza 1957. p. 665); and, in support of such contentions, Hirschi (1969, pp. 94-97) has found that irrespective of social class standing, attachments to one's parents are negatively related to delinquency. He notes that "the lower-class parent even if he is himself committing criminal acts, does not publicize this fact to his children. . . . He operates to foster obedience to a system of norms to which he himself may not conform."

standards alone. At any rate, Stanfield's study is a suggestive indirect test of the "interaction hypothesis," based on a small, homogeneous, and nonrandom sample.

This study attempts a more direct and encompassing test through an examination of the relationship between direct and indirect parental control and delinquency under conditions varying in the availability of delinquent patterns, utilizing data from a large heterogeneous random sample of adolescents.[5] Moreover, since differential association theory had put so much emphasis on "definitions," we test some rather basic but as yet unexamined claims of the theory involving such normative phenomena. Do delinquent peers influence acceptance of unconventional cultural standards, and, if so, do delinquent peers affect delinquency only through such alternative cultural patterns? One of the major implications of Short ans Strodtbeck's (1965) group-process perspective on delinquency is that delinquent peers can influence involvement in delinquency independently of definitions favorable and unfavorable to the violation of the law. While such definitions are likely to be related to delinquent behavior and to be in part, a product of interaction with delinquent friends, it can by hypothesized that the delinquent peer group may be a source of "situationally induced motives" (Briar and Piliavan 1965, pp. 35-45) and that delinquent peers can thus provide the impetus to deviate before one has come to accept unconventional definitions and quite often in spite of commitments to conventional normative standards.

STUDY DESIGN

These relationships will be examined utilizing questionnaire data gathered as part of the Richmond Youth Study by the Survey Research Center (University of California at Berkeley) in 1965. The population consisted of the 17,500 students entering the 11 junior and senior high schools of Western Contra Costa County in the fall of 1964. While the original sample consisted of both black and nonblack, male and female adolescents in grades 7 through 12, the present analysis was carried out on the 1,588 nonblack males in the sample.[6]

---

[5] One of the many findings in Hirschi's (1969, pp. 154-55) earlier multivariate analysis of this body of data was that attachment to parents is negatively related to delinquency, regardless of number of delinquent friends an adolescent has. In the present analysis, we elaborate on that finding through more extensive controls for exposure to criminogenic influences as well as "definitions" favorable to law breaking. Moreover, while Hirschi focused on the independent role of such attachments in the etiology of delinquency, the present analysis focuses more extensively on the differential association theorists' prediction of interaction effects.

[6] The sample was drawn from the student population of Western Contra Costa County, California, which is located in the San Francisco-Oakland metropolitan area, bordered by Berkley and San Francisco and San Pablo Bays. The largest city in the area is Richmond, which is primarily an industrial community, with more than 60% of the employed males holding manual jobs. For more extensive details on the area, see Wilson (1966). The nonblack segment of the sample consisted primarily of Caucasians (90%), with a small portion of Orientals and "others." For a more detailed discussion of sampling and data-gathering procedures, see Wilson, Hirschi, and Elder (1965) and Hirschi (1969).

The dependent variable, delinquent behavior, was measured by the respondent's answers to a series of six questions concerning offenses of varying degrees of seriousness.[7] Only acts committed within a year previous to the administration of the questionnaire are included in the score. The respondents are categorized as admitting to no delinquent acts, one delinquent act, and two or more delinquent acts.

Supervision and emotional support by the father were measured by means of questionnaire items. Paternal supervision was assessed by asking respondents to answer "usually," "sometimes," or "never" to the following questions:(1) Does your father know where you are when you are away from home? and (2) Does your father know who you are with when you are away from home? Parental support was measured by answers to three questions: (1) Does your father seem to understand you? (2) Have you ever felt unwanted by your father? (3) Would your father stick by you if you really got into bad trouble?

Number of close delinquent friends, perceptions of "trouble" in the neighborhood, and official delinquency rates of the schools attended are each used as indicators of variation in the presence of delinquent patterns. Respondents were asked, "Have any of your close friends ever been picked up by the police?" and were categorized for purposes of analysis into those with zero, one or two, and three or more delinquent friends. The adolescents in the sample were also presented the statement "Young people are always getting into trouble" and were asked whether or not it applied to their neighborhood. These two items are similar to measures of differential association used in other studies (Short 1957, pp. 335-36). Utilizing police data gathered from the Richmond and San Pablo police departments and the Contra Costa County Sheriff's Office, the schools sampled were ranked in terms of the percentage of nonblack "official delinquents" and classified as "high, "medium," and "low." There was not sufficient variation in self-reported delinquency from school to school to rank them in terms of self-reported delinquency.

As DeFleur and Quinney (1966, p. 7) specify in their formalization of the differential association theory, it is criminal motives, attitudes, and techniques which are assumed to effectively result in the overt commission of crimes. Associating with delinquents is thought to be conducive to learning definitions favorable to the violation of the law, and an excess of such definitions over antidelinquent definitions is assumed to lead to delinquency. Sykes and Matza (1957, pp. 664-70) suggest that "techniques of neutralization" are a crucial component of these definitions, in that a definition favorable to the violation of legal codes can be viewed in one sense as a justification of deviant behavior. Two of the items making up the "definitions" score are implicated in a discussion of these techniques: (1) most things that people call "delinquency" don't really hurt anyone, and (2) policemen try to give all kids as even break. The first item is concerned with the "denial of injury." while the second is assumed to be involved

---

[7] Self-reported delinquency was measured by responses to the following questions: (1) have you ever taken little things (worth less than $2.00) that did not belong to you? (2) have you ever taken things of some value (between $2.00 and $50.00) that did not belong to you? (3) have you ever taken things of large value (worth over $50.00) that did not belong to you? (4) have you ever taken a car for a ride without the owner's permission? (5) have you ever banged up on purpose something that did not belong to you? (6) not counting fights you may have had with a brother or sister, have you ever beaten up on anyone on purpose?

in the "condemnation of the condemners." Two other items went into the score: (1) it's alright to get around the law if you can get away with it, and (2) to get ahead, you have to do some things which are not right. On all but the police item, "strongly agree" or "agree" was coded zero; "undecided, 1", and "disagree" or "strongly disagree," 2. The codes were reversed for the police item. These four items were combined to form a score that measures criminal attitudes or definitions favorable to the violation of the law. No measure of the respondent's knowledge of techniques was available, limiting this study to a score measuring only the attitudinal content of the learning that leads to delinquency.

Gamma, a symmetrical measure of association with a "proportional reduction in error" interpretation appropriate to an ordinal level of measurement (Goodman and Kruskal 1954, pp. 732-64; Costner 1965, pp. 341-53) and percentage distributions are used to assess the association between variables. The differential association variables are controlled by subdivision, and the relationships of paternal supervision and support to delinquent behavior are examined within these subcategories.

FINDINGS

The zero-order relationships among paternal supervision and support, number of delinquent friends, perception of neighborhood trouble, and delinquent behavior are summarized in table 22.1. All of the gamma coefficients are statistically significant at the .01 level. As expected, both paternal supervision and support are negatively related to delinquency. Moreover, the data are consistent with Sutherland and Cressey's argument that the nature of a child's home life can affect the probability that he will come into intimate contact with delinquency peers, in that paternal supervision and support are negatively related to intimate associations with others who have been picked up by the police. They are similarly related to "delinquent" attitudes and beliefs and to perceptions of trouble in the neighborhood. However, as the strength of the relationship suggests, many well-supervised and emotionally supported adolescents have delinquent friends, engage in delinquent action, and exhibit tenuous commitments to conventional moral standards.

TABLE 22.1   Zero-order gamma Coefficients

Variables	Delinquent Friends	Delinquent Definitions	Neighborhood Trouble	Delinquent Behavior
Paternal supervision	-.37	-.25	-.18	-.28
Paternal support	-.28	-.29	-.23	-.30
Delinquent friends	. . .	.43	.26	.60
Delinquent definitions	. . .	. . .	.18	.38
Neighborhood trouble	. . .	. . .	. . .	.25

TABLE 22.2 Self-reported delinquency within "definitions" subgroups, by delinquent friends

| | Definitions Favorable and Unfavorable to the Violation of the Law | | | | | | | | |
| | Unfavorable (%) | | | Neutral (%) | | | Favorable (%) | | |
Self-reported Delinquent Act	0	1-2	3-4	0	1-2	3-4	0	1-2	3-4
0	78	64	38	69	49	34	60	37	20
1	18	26	24	19	33	33	24	33	29
2+	4	10	38	11	18	34	15	30	51
N	251	81	34	202	105	98	91	86	138
Gamma	-.17	-.26	-.17						

The three differential association variables are, in turn, related to involvement in delinquent behavior. The more delinquent associates one has, the more likely he is to be delinquent. Similarly, the less the attachment to the conventional normative system and the greater the perception of trouble in the neighborhood, the greater the tendency toward delinquent action. Not only are all three related to the overall measure of delinquency, but each was found to be associated with every act that went into the overall measure as well with all the gamma coefficients in the expected direction and significant at the .01 level. Moreover, number of delinquent friends, neighborhood trouble, and the definitions score are interrelated as well with an especially strong relationship exhibited between intimate associations with delinquents and "delinquent" attitudes and beliefs. Associating with persons assumed to embrace attitudes and beliefs favorable to the violation of the law is, as expected, positively associated with embrace of such attitudes and beliefs.

However, as predicted on the basis of group-process and situational-inducement perspectives on delinquency, association with delinquents and the definitions score are independently related to delinquency involvement (table 22.2). Together, these two variables differentiate adolescents in terms of delinquency fairly well. While only 22% of the adolescents with no delinquent friends and a preponderance of definitions unfavorable to the violation of the law have committed one or more delinquent acts, fully 80% of the adolescents at the other end of the continuum fall in that category. However it is clear that the effect of the number of delinquent friends on delinquency is not solely a product of socialization into competing normative standards. The partials are somewhat smaller than the zero-order coefficient of .60 but are still quite strong relative to other relationships in the data. As suggested by Briar and Piliavan (1965), it may be that adolescents with delinquent friends are more likely to experience short-run, situationally induced pressures to deviate.

TABLE 22.3 Self-reported delinquency within "delinquent friends" subgroups, by paternal supervision

Self-reported Delinquent Acts	Number of delinquent friends								
	3+ (%)			1-2 (%)			0 (%)		
	Low	Medium	High	Low	Medium	High	Low	Medium	High
0	26	28	30	39	50	59	60	78	74
1	21	37	35	36	28	29	28	17	18
2+	53	35	36	26	22	13	13	5	8
N	119	57	98	90	60	111	120	96	346
Gamma		.17			.26			.17	

To assess Sutherland and Cressey's (1966) hypothesis, it is necessary to go beyond the zero-order relationships to an examination of more complex three-variable relationships. For example, tables 22.3 and 22.4 summarize the relationships between paternal supervision and support and delinquency involvement, controlling for number of delinquent friends. It turns out that, while parental supervision is negatively related to the number of close delinquent friends and number of delinquent friends is positively associated with delinquency, the relationship between supervision and delinquent behavior persists within all three categories of delinquent friends. The data fail to support Sutherland and Cressey's (1966) argument, in that the association

TABLE 22.4 Self-reported delinquency within "delinquent friends" subgroups, by paternal emotional support

Self-reported Delinquent Acts	Number of delinquent friends											
	3+ (%)				1-2 (%)				0 (%)			
	Low	2	3	High	Low	2	3	High	Low	2	3	High
0	21	20	33	43	44	52	49	56	61	68	71	80
1	24	39	33	26	30	30	36	32	21	22	21	17
2+	55	41	33	31	26	18	15	12	18	10	8	3
N	104	59	51	49	86	54	47	72	104	100	140	190
Gamma		—.27				—.15				—.28		

TABLE 22.5 Self-reported delinquency within neighborhood contexts, by paternal supervision

| | Young Always Getting in Trouble | | | | | | | | |
| | Agree (%) | | | Undecided (%) | | | Disagree (%) | | |
Self-reported Delinquent Acts	Low	Medium	High	Low	Medium	High	Low	Medium	High
0	27	70	39	46	52	63	52	57	69
1	29	9	28	25	27	23	24	30	22
2+	44	21	32	29	21	14	24	13	9
N	90	43	71	72	62	124	243	169	468
Gamma		—.20			—.25			—.28	

is equally strong among those with three or more delinquent friends and among those with no delinquent friends at all. Thus, paternal supervision appears to be related to delinquency, irrespective of the availability of delinquent patterns as measured by the number of close delinquent friends. Similarly, supportive or affectionate father-son relationships are negatively related to delinquent behavior within each of the delinquent-friends subdivisions, with each variable contributing independently to delinquent behavior.

By subdividing on the basis of perceptions of trouble in the neighborhood, it was possible to test the hypothesis that "if the family is in a community in which there is

TABLE 22.6 Self-reported delinquency within neighborhood contexts, by paternal emotional support

| | Young in Neighborhood Always in Trouble | | | | | | | | | | | |
| | Agree (%) | | | | Undecided (%) | | | | Disagree (%) | | | |
Self-reported Delinquent Acts	Low	2	3	High	Low	2	3	High	Low	2	3	High
0	34	40	40	67	47	47	60	72	49	57	68	69
1	20	20	34	23	22	34	27	21	27	28	21	22
2+	46	40	26	10	31	22	12	7	24	15	11	9
N	83	45	35	31	81	65	48	57	212	157	204	278
Gamma		—.32				—.30				—.25		

no pattern of theft, the children do not steal, no matter how much neglected or how unhappy they may be at home" (Sutherland and Cressey 1966, P. 227). The data indicate that paternal supervision is negatively related to delinquency even when respondents disagree that the young are always getting into trouble in their neighborhood (see table 22.5). In fact, supervision is actually slightly less strongly related to delinquency in neighborhoods where the young are perceived as always in trouble than among those where they are perceived as little trouble.

Neither does paternal support appear to interact significantly with perceived trouble (table 22.6). Emotional support does lead to slightly greater percentage differences among respondents in neighborhoods high in trouble. However, the relations persist within all subdivisions, and the gamma coefficients are only slightly different. As was the case with number of delinquent friends, when perception of trouble in the neighborhood is used to measure the availability of delinquent behavior patterns, the data fail to reveal the predicted pattern of interaction.

Table 22.7 summarizes the relationships between paternal supervision and support and self-reported delinquency in schools with variable delinquency rates; and, again, there appears to be no tendency for direct and indirect paternal control to make any greater difference in high-rate schools than in low-rate schools. For example, the gamma coefficients combining all low-rate schools (7.6%-10.8% with an official record) were -.26 for the paternal support measure and -.30 for paternal supervision as compared with -.32 and -.27 for all high-rate schools combined (26.2%–32.7% officially delinquent). Again, we fail to find support for the interaction hypothesis. Whether in a school with a high rate or a low rate of official delinquency, paternal

TABLE 22.7 Gamma coefficients relating self-reported delinquency to paternal supervision and support within schools

Schools and Percentage Officially Delinquent		Self-Report by Supervision	Self-Report by Support
High rate:			
	33%	-.30 (N = 92)	-.27 (N =93)
	29%	.03 (N = 31)	-.19 (N = 29)
	26%	-.29 (N = 215)	-.30 (N = 212)
	26%	-.17 (N=151)	-.29 (N=144)
Middle rate:			
	21%	-.44 (N = 102)	-.43 (N = 100)
	21%	-.41 (N=112)	-.44 (N=100)
	19%	-.10 (N = 29)	-.11 (N = 26)
Low rate:			
	11%	-.32 (N = 285)	-.15 (N = 267)
	11%	-.28 (N = 143)	-.39 (N = 140)
	8%	-.27 (N = 184)	-.38 (N = 177)

TABLE 22.8 Self-reported delinquency with "definitions" subgroups, by paternal supervision

Self-reported Delinquent Acts	Definitions Favorable to Violation								
	Favorable (%)			Neutral (%)			Unfavorable (%)		
	Low	Medium	High	Low	Medium	High	Low	Medium	High
0	26	44	45	50	54	64	68	75	78
1	29	36	28	29	30	24	21	16	17
2+	46	20	27	21	17	12	12	8	5
N	145	59	115	127	115	229	96	73	245
Gamma		-.29			-.20			-.18	

supervision and support differentiate adolescents in terms of admitted delinquent acts equally well.

We have already seen that the probability of embracing "definitions favorable to the violation of the law" increases with increases in the number of close friends who have been picked up by the police. These definitions are, in turn, associated with delinquency involvement. Moreover, each of these variables, independent of the other, is related to delinquency. When the "definitions" score is held constant by subdivision, we find that paternal supervision and support are related to delinquent behavior in all

TABLE 22.9 Self-reported delinquency within "definitions" subgroups, by paternal emotional support

Self-reported Delinquent Acts	Definitions Favorable to Violation											
	Favorable (%)				Neutral (%)				Unfavorable (%)			
	Low	2	3	High	Low	2	3	High	Low	2	3	High
0	26	39	46	50	52	46	63	70	70	69	74	79
1	30	29	31	30	27	32	26	23	16	22	17	18
2+	44	32	23	20	21	21	11	7	14	9	9	4
N	131	75	52	54	132	99	101	121	70	68	104	159
Gamma		-.29				-.25				-.16		

subgroups as well (see tables 22.8 and 22.9). The relationships are slightly stronger among those with attitudes and beliefs conductive to lawbreaking than among those committed to more conventional standards, in that father's supervision and support are slightly more likely to have an effect among those who express attitudes and beliefs conducive to the violation of the law. In short, parental surveillance and support may make for a somewhat greater difference in delinquency involvement among adolescents who are not committed to conventional normative standards and who hold attitudes favorable to the violation of the law. Among adolescents committed to conventional standards, such external parental control may have lesser impact because of the marked strength of internal controls resulting from a firm acceptance of conventional definitions.[8] This interaction should not mask the fact that, contrary to Sutherland and Cressey's (1966) arguments, parental supervision and support are related to delinquency even in categories exhibiting definitions unfavorable to the violation of the law.

SUMMARY AND CONCLUSIONS

This study attempts to go beyond the usual concern with the relationships between delinquent companions and delinquent behavior to an assessment of arguments using differential association theory to encompass certain "known" relationships. Consistent with previous research and as predicted on the basis of the theory, the number of delinquent friends, the perception of "trouble" in the neighborhood and the variable acceptance of attitudes and beliefs favorable to the violation of legal codes were significantly related to involvement in delinquent action. Moreover, those associating with delinquents are more likely to be delinquent, regardless of the effect of these associations on their attitudes and beliefs. This finding tends to support theories of delinquency which stress the importance of group pressure, group processes, and short-term situational motivations in the explanation of delinquency.

Using several alternative measures of the availability of delinquent patterns, the findings consistently tended to cast doubt on Sutherland and Cressey's (1966) arguments concerning the home and family in relation to delinquent behavior. Number of delinquent friends had little effect on the relationship between paternal supervision and delinquency. Nor did it have much of an effect on the association between affectionate father-son relationships and delinquent behavior. The case was similar when neighborhood patterns and school-delinquency rates were held constant. Some interaction was noted when definitions or verbalizations favorable to the violation of the law were controlled: the two family variables were more highly related to delinquent behavior among those whose definitions were most favorable to the violation of the law. However, the relationships persisted within all subdivisions.

---

[8] This finding is consistent with the claims of "containment theorists" (e.g., Reckless 1966, pp. 223-30; 1967) that elements of "inner containment" may play a greater role as deterrents to delinquency in situations of weak "outer containment" than in situations where external controls are more likely to be operative. For a critical analysis and reformulation of the containment perspective, see Jensen (1970, pp. 1-14; 1972).

In sum, what goes on in the family situation appears to have a significance of its own which is not encompassed by the differential association perspective as presented by Sutherland and Cressey (1966). The neutral or isolated child is more likely to be delinquent than the child who is loved by and attached to his parents even when delinquent patterns "outside the home" are scarce or absent. Moreover, contrary to some studies (Watt and Maher 1958, pp. 321-30), these data suggest that attitudes toward one's parents do affect attitudes toward public law and morality but that direct and indirect parental control have effects on delinquent behavior independent of such beliefs and attitudes. In short, the family has effects on delinquency involvement which cannot be attributed to the "internalization" of values, beliefs, or attitudes towards the law. Such findings are inconsistent with theories that view attitudes and beliefs concerning legal prescriptions as "the" variables accounting for the consequences of family life for delinquency.

As Marvin Olsen (1968, pp. 117-29) points out, actors are led to perpetuate patterns of social organization, not merely because they come to accept certain social norms as their own, but also through processes of social sanctioning, social manipulation, identification, and compliance. Just as actual and potential reactions of delinquent peers can influence behavior without necessarily shaping normative commitments at the same time, so the sensitivity of children to the actual and potential reactions of their parents may shape their behavior even if they do not form commitments to such standards. The theory of differential association stresses "definitions" and "cultural" variables (values, norms, and beliefs) to such an extent that processes shaping human behavior other than internalization of normative standards tend to be slighted.

REFERENCES

Briar, Scott, and Irving Piliavin. (1965) "Delinquency, Situational Inducements and Commitments to Conformity." *Social Problems* 13 (1): 35-45.

Costner, Herbert L, (1965) "Criteria for Measures of Association." *American Sociological Review* 30 (June): 341-52.

DeFleur, Melvin, and Richard Quinney, (1966) "A Reformulation of Sutherland's Differential Association Verification. "*Journal of Research in Crime and Delinquency* 3 (January): 1-11.

Erickson, Maynard L., and Lamar T. Empey, (1965) "Class Position, Peers, and Delinquency." *Sociology and Social Research* 49 (April): 268-82.

Glueck, Sheldon, and Eleanor Glueck, (1950) *Unraveling Juvenile Delinquency.* Cambridge, Mass.: Harvard University Press.

Gold, Martin, (1963) *Status Forces in Delinquent Boys.* Ann Arbor: University of Michigan, Institute for Social Research.

Goodman, Leo A., and William H. Kruskal. (1954) "Measures of Association for Cross Classification."*Journal of the American Statistical Association* 49 (December): 732-64.

Hackler, James C. (1968) "Predictors of Deviant Behavior: Norms vs. the Perceived Anticipations of Others." *Canadian Review of Sociology and Anthropology* 5 (2): 92-106.

Healy, William, and Augusta Bronner. (1936) *New Light on Delinquency and Its Treatment.* New Haven, Conn.: Yale University Press.

Hirschi, Travis, (1969) *Causes of Delinquency.* Berkley: University of California Press.

Jensen, Gary F. (1970) "Containment and Delinquency: Analysis of a Theory." *University of Washington Journal of Sociology* 2 (November): 1-14.

———. (1972) "Delinquency and Adolescent Self-Conceptions: A Study of the Personal Relevance of Infraction." Ph. D. dissertation, University of Washington.

Nye, F. Ivan, (1958) *Family Relationships and Delinquent Behavior.* New York: Wiley

Olsen, Marvin E. (1968) *The Process of Social Organization.* New York: Holt, Rinehart & Winston.

Reckless, Walter C. (1966) "A New Theory of Delinquency and Crime." In *Juvenile Delinquency*, edited by Rose Giallombardo. New York: Wiley.

———. (1967) *The Crime Problem*, 4th ed. New York: Appleton-Century-Crofts.

Short, James F. (1957) "Differential Association and Delinquency." *Social Problems* 4 (January): 233-39.

Short, James F. Jr., and Fred L. Strodtbeck. (1965) *Group Process and Gang Delinquency.* Chicago: University of Chicago Press.

Stanfield, Robert Everett. (1966) "The Interaction of Family Variables and Gang Variables in the Aetiology of Delinquency." *Social Problems* 13 (Spring): 411-17.

Sutherland, Edwin H., and Donald R. Cressey. (1966) *Principles of Criminology.* 7th ed. Philadelphia: Lippincott.

Sykes, Gresham M., and David Matza. (1957) "Techniques of Neutralization: A Theory of Delinquency." *American Sociological Review* 22 (December): 644-70.

Voss, Harwin L. (1964) "Differential Association and Reported Delinquency Behavior: A Replication." *Social Problems* 12 (Summer): 78-85.

Watt, Norman, and Brendan A. Maher. (1958) "Prisoner's Attitudes toward Home and the Judicial System." *Journal of Criminal Law and Criminology* 49 (November-December): 321-30.

Wilson, Alan B. (1966) "Western Contra Costa County Population, 1965: Demographic Characteristics." Mimeographed. Berkeley, Calif.: Survey Research Center.

Wilson, Alan B., Travis Hirschi, and Glen Elder. (1965) "Secondary School Survey." Techni-

ARTICLE 23

Family Relationships and Delinquency*

STEPHEN A. CERNKOVICH
PEGGY C. GIORDANO

Family interaction and attachment assume prominent roles in social control theories of delinquency. However, the degree of conceptualization and the measurement strategies generally employed arguably are inadequate to capture the real dynamic quality of such relationships and to specify their effects on delinquency involvement. The purpose of this research is to distinguish more precisely those family interaction mechanisms which are associated with delinquency. The analysis, based on a sample of 824 adolescents, leads to the specification of seven distinct family interaction dimensions: control and supervision, identity support, caring and trust, intimate communication, instrumental communication, parental disapproval of peers and conflict. Compared with research based on a single attached-unattached dimension, this multidimensional model gives a much more complete and precise sense of the kind of relationships which exist between parents and their more or less delinquent children. In addition, the analysis shows that the family interaction variables have similar effects on delinquency in both-parent, mother-only, and mother/stepfather homes. The analysis by race, sex, and race-sex subgroups suggests, however, that while there is a core of family attachment dimensions that is important for all adolescents, there are several important subgroup differences.

The study of the relationship between the family and juvenile delinquency has had a curious history, ebbing and flowing with the times and with the dominance of alternative theoretical perspectives. This area is best characterized, however, by a

* This research was supported by PHS Research Grant No. MH 29095, National Institute of Mental Health, Center for Studies of Antisocial and Violent Behavior. We would like to thank two anonymous *Criminology* reviewers for their helpful comments.

Source: Cernkovich, Stephen A. and Peggy C. Giordano, "Family Relationships and Delinquency." *Criminology,* Vol. 25 (2), 1987:295-321. Reprinted by permission of the American Society of Criminology.

relative lack of interest on the part of criminologists—by the belief that family variables are not nearly as important as peer, school, and various structural factors in understanding delinquent behavior patterns (compare Rodman and Grams, 1967; Wilkinson, 1974). While there are numerous examples of research on the link between the family and delinquency scattered throughout the literature, it is telling that the major, and perhaps the best work to date—Nye's 1958 study—is now almost 30 years old.

Further, many researchers appear to agree with Nye's assessment (1958: 49) that "the family is functionally and normatively more important to girls than to boys." Insofar as criminologists have not been very interested in female delinquency, and because much of the research in this area is seriously flawed, it is not surprising that the study of the relationship between the family and delinquency lags far behind other areas of research and theory development. Although the emergence of social control theory in recent years has reintroduced the importance of family variables for understanding delinquency, the status of the family in delinquency theory and research remains a lowly one. Gove and Crutchfield (1982: 301) have summarized the status of this body of research:

> Although there exists a substantial body of empirical literature regarding the effects of family variables on delinquency, much of it is either atheoretical or is linked to perspectives so dated that they are no longer considered fruitful.

Gove and Crutchfield (1982: 302) go on to note that there is considerable evidence that the family is (or should be) related to delinquency involvement. In fact, this is one of the most replicated findings in the literature.

> The literature consistently indicates that (1) one-parent homes, (2) poor marriages, (3) lack of parental control, (4) ineffectual parental behavior. . ., (5) association with delinquents as opposed to nondelinquents, and (6) very poor parent-child relationships are associated with delinquency (however it is defined). All of these factors influencing delinquency have in common that they are likely to be a consequence of parental behavior, with parental behavior being casually linked to a lack of effective role models, a lack of a natural home environment, and a lack of parental supervision (which could explain their childrens' propensity to associate with delinquent friends) (Gove and Crutchfield, 1982: 304).

Yet much of this evidence has been ignored or downplayed by criminologists. Bordua (1962) has attributed this to a desire to avoid "psychologizing." That is, while criminologists include in their analyses such structural or social variables as social class, blocked opportunities, and peer relations, such variables as personality characteristics and parent-child relationships are avoided because they are "too psychological." This is yet another example of the misguided loyalty to artificial disciplinary boundaries which is far too characteristic of the social sciences.

As significant as this relative neglect of family variables is the quality of the data itself, as well as the general theoretical approach taken in examining these data. Nye suggested some time ago (1958: 34) that it is not the structure of the family per se which is causally related to delinquency, but rather the actual relationships and interaction patterns which are the key variables. Still, it is rather obvious that the primary sociological focus, with the important exception of some recent research from a control theory perspective, either has been on structural variables (for example, broken homes, family size, birth order). or interactional variables treated in an almost structural, either-or way (for example, poor marital relations, parental supervision and control, maternal employment). While theoretical lip service usually is paid to the notion that the important variables are probably social-psychological and interactional in nature, the analysis have tended to be primarily structural and macrosociological, only touching the interactional surface.

Studies of the relationship between broken homes and delinquency offer a good illustration. Many of the articles examining this relationship begin by asserting that far more important than the effects of the actual parental separation and/or living in a broken home on the child are the familial problems and conflicts that led to the separation in the first place. It appears to be generally accepted that harmonious yet physically broken homes are far less detrimental to the development and mental health of the child than are physically intact but psychologically broken homes (compare Wells and Rankin, 1986; Patterson and Dishion, 1985; Rosen, 1985; Shoemaker, 1984; Arnold and Brungardt, 1983; Rutter and Giller, 1984). Once this is asserted, however, much of the research in this area turns to a dichotomous, structural variable—broken/unbroken home—as the major antecedent to delinquency. Post hoc interpretations are then offered as to why broken homes apparently are related to delinquency. These explanations usually center on patterns of family interaction, but little or no data has been collected on the nature and quality of these relationships. Most studies of the broken home and delinquency, for example, have divided families into two discrete categories—broken and unbroken—and (Empey, 1982: 164) give "absolutely no clue as to the quality of life within either of them."

Research on the effects of maternal employment on child development offers another example of the approach usually taken. Researchers appear to agree that maternal employment affects behavior indirectly, through such factors as lack of supervision, loss of direct control, and attenuation of close relationships. Similarly, most agree that its effects depend on a number of conditions, such as social class background, race, the attitudes of family members regarding maternal employment, whether the employment is full-or part-time, and so forth (see Etaugh, 1980, and Hoffman, 1974, for thorough reviews of this literature). Once this is noted, however, the analysis tend to focus on the structural level. As Hirschi (1969: 237-238) has noted, for example, Nye considered the loss of direct control due to maternal employment (as the reason for the relationship between maternal employment and delinquency) as so obvious that he did not even bother to analyze the relationship in any detail. Yet, as Hoffman (1974) has suggested, working mothers might very well be stricter and impose even more rules than non-working mothers—the demands of their dual rule may require a higher degree of structure in order for the household to run smoothly. She expresses surprise (Hoffman, 1974; 205) that few studies have obtained data on such basic child-rearing behaviors as these.

The typical study deals only with two levels—the mother's employment status and a child characteristic. The many steps in between—family roles and interaction patterns, the child-rearing practices—are rarely measured. . . . The distance between an antecedent condition like maternal employment and a child characteristic is too great to be covered in a single leap. Several levels should be examined in a single study to obtain adequate insight into the processes involved.

While a few researchers stand out because of their attempts to measure the nature and quality of family relationships (see, for example, Johnson, 1986; Agnew, 1985; LaGrange and White, 1985; Canter. 1982; Wiatrowski, Griswold, and Roberts, 1981; Krohn and Massey, 1980; Norland, Shover, Thorton, and James, 1979; and Hirschi, 1969), the degree of conceptualization and/or the measurement strategies generally employed are arguably inadequate to capture the full range or the real dynamic quality of the relationships. For example, although Norland et al. (1979) were interested in intrafamily conflict and delinquency, apparently only one question was included to measure family conflict: "There is a lot of tension and conflict in my home." Similarly, Canter (1982), in one of the more theoretically and methodologically sophisticated studies, conceptualized and measured family involvement as the amount of time the adolescent spends with his/her family, and parental influence by the single item, "How much have your parents influenced what you've thought or done?" While these kinds of questions are clearly on the right track, they are not comprehensive measures of the nature, quality, and dynamics of the interactions which characterize relationships among family members. Research in the area has rarely gone beyond the very basic, surface level measures of family attachment and involvement.

With such a background in mind, Gove and Crutchfield, (1982: 317) have thrown down the gauntlet:

> It is time that we start taking the relationship between family characteristics and delinquency very seriously and systematically determine the precise mechanisms of how family characteristics are related to delinquency.

CONCEPTUAL ORIENTATION

The purpose of this article is to specify more precisely those family interaction mechanisms which are associated with delinquency involvement. Along with the peer group, the family is a major arena for social interaction, personal growth, and social and emotional maturation. But while the dynamics of peer group interaction have been the object of considerable criminological research (see Giordano, Cernkovich, and Pugh, 1985, for a review of this literature), family structure has attracted most of the attention of criminologists interested in the effects of family variables on delinquency. More and better research on the role of internal family dynamics clearly is needed. This article will report on the relationship of several dimensions of internal family dynamics to delinquent behavior. Since previous delinquency theory and research has stressed the role of broken homes, race and sex, this article also will examine the impact of family factors within categories of these sociodemographic variables.

The authors' theoretical orientation builds directly upon the work of Hirschi (1969). In his discussion of the family and delinquency, Hirschi maintains that attachment to parents forms the basis of conformity. Eschewing the concept of internalization, he believes (1969: 94) that it is the attachment itself that is important:

> The more strongly a child is attached to his parents, the more strongly he is bound to their expectations, and therefore the more strongly he is bound to conformity with the legal norms of the larger system.

But exactly what constitutes attachment? Hirschi suggests that it is the parents' "psychological presence" in the child's mind during tempting situations that is the key. In this sense, direct control, per se, is relatively unimportant (1969: 89-90):

> The child is less likely to commit delinquent acts not because his parents actually restrict his activities but because he shares his activities with them; not because his parents actually know where he is, but because he perceives them as aware of his location. Following this line of reasoning we can say that the more the child is accustomed to sharing his mental life with his parents, the more he is accustomed to seeking or getting their opinion about his activities, the more likely he is to perceive them as part of his social and psychological field, and the less likely he would be to neglect their opinion when considering an act contrary to law—which is, after all, a potential source of embarrassment and/or inconvenience to them.

Accepting this, how does one know if a child is attached or not, or more accurately, how can one determine the degree of attachment? One strong indicator is communication between the child and his/her parents. Hirschi maintains (1969: 93-94) that the extent and nature of communication are as important as feelings of affection in this regard—that the degree of psychological presence of the parent is dependent in part upon the extent to which the child communicates with the parent.

Hirschi's data and reasoning about the importance of family attachment are convincing. However, it is desirable to be more specific with regard to exactly what constitutes this important dimension of attachment. Hirschi is somewhat ambiguous in this regard. On the other hand, he often gives the impression that attachment is a unidimensional construct; indeed, this is usually the way in which the theory is interpreted by others—attachment is one of four ways in which individuals are bound to the social order. At other times, however, as when he concentrates on the communication origins of attachment or on the feelings of affection which characterize attachment, Hirschi gives the impression that attachment is more multidimensional in nature.

The authors of this article believe the multidimensional interpretation to be the more accurate of the two. However, neither Hirschi nor other social control theorists and researchers have systematically identified what these dimensions might be. The purpose of this research is to examine the impact on delinquency of several dimensions of family attachment and interaction. As will be discussed in detail below, the analysis leads to the specification of seven conceptually distinct dimensions of family interaction.

In addition to this elaboration of the Hirschi model, the authors are also interested in whether the effects of these variables are consistent across different types of family structure, or whether there are important in interactional dynamics by family type. For example, is parental attachment more important in inhibiting delinquency in single-parent homes than in those where two parents are present? Hirschi argues that attachment to *a* parent is the important variable; that is, attachment to two parents does not mean the child is doubly insulated. If he is correct (and his data do support this position), this would explain "the fact that one-parent family is virtually as efficient a delinquency controlling institution as the two-parent family, contrary to expectations deriving from 'direct control' hypotheses" (1969: 103). This general issue of the effect of family structure on delinquency will be explored using a multidimensional model of family interaction. It is quite conceivable that some dimensions of family interaction will operate similarly in different family structures while others may be unique to a particular kind of structure.

Finally, the article will examine whether there are sex or race differences in the influence of family interaction variables. Previous research leads one to believe that there are (compare Krohn and Massey, 1980), but as noted previously, this research has typically been based on a unidimensional conceptualization of family attachment. The multidimensional model used here will shed some important light on these demographic differences.

RESEARCH DESIGN

The data for this study are based on a 1982 sample of adolescents living in private households in a large North Central Standard Metropolitan Statistical Area. In order to obtain a cross section of youth between 12 and 19 years of age geographically dispersed throughout the metropolitan area, a multistage modified probability sample design was used in which geographically defined area segments were selected with known probability. The segments were stratified, using the most up-to-date census data available (1980), on the basis of racial composition and average housing value. Within the segments, households and eligible respondents were selected for interviews to fill specified sex and race quotas; no specific age quotas were allocated, although the ages of respondents were tracked as the interviews were conducted to ensure adequate representation of teens of all ages.

A total of 942 interviews was successfully completed. Of these, 51% were with adolescent females, 49% with males; 45% of the respondents were white, the remaining nonwhites being predominately black (50% of the total sample). The respondents ranged in age from 12 through 19: 21% were either 12 or 13, 32% 14 or 15, 32% 16 or 17, and 15% 18 or 19 years of age.[1]

Delinquency involvement was measured by a modified version of Elliott and Ageton's (1980) self-report delinquency scale. Twenty-seven individual delinquent

[1] The survey was managed by National Analysts, Inc. Interviews were conducted from late April through late June of 1981. Informed consent and written permission were obtained from each respondent and parent/guardian prior to the interview. The National Analysts staff validated 54% of the interviews to ensure that proper protocol was followed.

behaviors were represented in the scale; subjects indicated how many times during the past year they had committed each act. The coding scheme was as follows: never = 0, once or twice a year = 2, once every 2-3 months = 5, once a month = 12, once every 2-3 weeks = 22, once a week = 52, and 2-3 times a week or more = 130. These numerical codes were derived by extrapolating the implied frequency over the period of one year.

In order to avoid some fairly serious limitations inherent in more typical measures of delinquency (compare Cernkovich et al., 1985; Hindelang, Hirschi, and Weis, 1981), a frequency/seriousness-based offender typology will be used as the dependent variable in the following analysis. This typology defines five levels of increasingly serious and frequent delinquent involvement; nonoffenders are those youth who reported no major offenses and no minor offenses; low-frequency minor offenders are those who reported no major offenses and a low rate of minor offenses; high-frequency minor offenders reported no major offenses but a high rate of minor offenses; high -frequency minor offenders reported no major offenses but a high rate of minor offenses; low-frequency major offenders reported a low rate of major offense involvement, while high frequency major offenders reported a high rate of major offenses. The offender index is coded from 1 through 5, with high-frequency major offenders receiving the highest score.[2]

A number of family variables are included in this study. Home Status defines the youth's structural family living arrangement. Rather than follow the convention of defining as broken any home which is characterized by the absence of at least one biological parent, the authors discriminated among several types of family structures (Wells and Rankin, 1986: 81-82). This is made possible by the representation of several family types in the sample: 49% of the subjects lived with both parents, 28% with mother only, 3% with father only, 11% with mother and stepfather, 3% with father and stepmother, and 6% with other relatives. However, because an analysis of variance revealed few significant differences in family factor characteristics by home status, and because of small sample sizes for three of the categories (that is, only 23 cases in father-stepmother homes, 26 in father-only homes, and 53 in other-relative homes), the analysis will be restricted to both-parent (n = 462), mother-only (n = 265), and mother-stepfather (n = 103) living arrangements. This decision combined with some minor missing data problems reduces the sample size to 824. While it would be preferable for

---

[2] The typology is based on the distinction between major and minor offenses. Twenty one of the 27 self-report items were used to construct major and minor offense subscales. The composition of the two scales is as follows:

Major: motor vehicle theft, grand theft, aggravated assault, selling hard drugs, rape, robbery, and breaking and entering.

Minor: throwing objects at cars or people, running away, lying about age, petty theft, prostitution, sexual intercourse, cheating on tests, simple assault, disorderly conduct, public drunkenness, theft $5-$50, truancy, drug use, and alcohol use.

For the minor offense subscale, 1-47 reported acts was defined as low frequency, 48 or more as high frequency. This is the median cutoff for those reporting any minor offense involvement. For the major offense subscale, 1-4 reported acts was defined as low frequency, 5 or more as high frequency. This is the median cut off for those reporting any minor offense involvement. For a more detailed description of the construction of the offender index, the reader is referred to the author's earlier work (Cernkovich et al., 1985).

the full range of living arrangements to be represented in the analysis, the use of these three has several advantages: they are clearly among the most typical in American society—the Bureau of Census (1985:4) reports that 75% of all children under 18 live in two-parent homes (the Census Bureau does not, unfortunately, further break this category into natural parent and stepparent homes), 20% in mother-only homes, 2% each in father-only and other-relative homes, and the remainder in nonrelative homes; the categories used represent family living arrangements which long have been of interest to criminologists; and such a breakdown represents a significant improvement over the more crude broken-intact distinction usually made in criminological research.

The interview schedule included 28 family-related items, each coded in a 1-to-5 Likert format. A principle components factor analysis of the pooled items using oblique rotation resulted is seven distinct scales. A loading criterion of .500 was used for scale inclusion. The factor loadings of the individual items and the scale reliabilities are presented in the appendix. The seven scales are as follows:

Control and Supervision refers to the extent to which parents monitor the behavior of their children. This scale is represented by three items: "My parents want to know who I am going out with when I go out with other boys (girls)"; In my free time away from home, my parents know who I'm with and where I am" (from Minor, no date); My parents want me to tell them where I am if I don't come home right after school." High scores on this scale reflect high levels of control and supervision.

Identity Support during adolescence is particularly important because of the uncertainties and self-doubts which characterize this period of the life cycle. Positive identity support is characterized by the belief that parents respect, accept, and support the youth for what he is. This dimension is measured by the following negatively worded items: "My parents sometimes put me down in front of other people"; "Sometimes my parents won't listen to me or my opinions"; "My parents sometimes give me the feeling that I'm not living up to their expectations"; "My parents seem to wish I were a different type of person" (from Minor, no date). High scores on this scale indicate high levels of identity support.

Caring and Trust is an index of the degree of intimacy of a relationship. Probably the most critical area of support a family can provide to offspring is a basic sense of caring, trust, and affection. This dimension is measured by the following items: "My parents often ask about what I am doing in school" (from Hirschi, 1969); "My parents give me the right amount of affection" (from Gold and Reimer, 1972); "One of the worst things that could happen to me would be finding out that I let my parents down"; "My parents are usually proud of me when I've finished something I've worked hard at"; My parents trust me" (from Minor, no date); "I'm closer to my parents than a lot of kids my age" (from Minor, no date); High scale scores reflect high levels of caring and trust.

Intimate Communication refers to the sharing of private thoughts and feelings. Hirschi (1969:90) recognized intimacy of communication between parent and child as an important dimension of attachment. The factor analysis isolated three items (all from West and Zingle, 1969) as indicative of this dimension: "How often do you talk to your parents about the boy/girl whom you like very much?"; How often do you talk to your parents about questions or problems about sex?"; "How often do you talk to your parents about things you have done about which you feel guilty?" High scores on this scale are indicative of high levels of intimate communication.

Hirschi"s (1969:90) findings suggest that it is not just communication with parents per se that is important, but rather the *content* of that communication. Specifically, he found that the discussion of future plans was an important index of attachment. In the present research, Instrumental Communication is defined as a variable separate from intimate communication. It is measured by the following items (all from West and Zingle, 1969): "How often do you talk to your parents about problems you have at school?"; "How often do you talk to your parents about your job plans for the future?"; "How often do you talk to your parents about problems with your friends."; "How often do you talk to your parents about how well you get along with your teachers?"; High levels of instrumental communication are indicated by high scale scores.

Parental Disapproval of Peers is, of course, all too descriptive of many parent-child relationships during adolescence. This variable is indexed by the following two items: "In general, what do your parents think of your friends?" (from Hirschi, 1969); "In general, what do your parents think of your boyfriend/girlfriend?" High scale scores reflect high levels of parental disapproval. Conflict is the extent to which parents and adolescents have arguments or disagreements with one another. Two items were flagged by the factor analysis as measuring this dimension: "How often do you have disagreements or arguments with your parents?"; How often do you purposely not talk to your parents because you are mad at them?" High levels of parent-child conflict are indicated by high scale scores.

ANALYSIS AND FINDINGS

Before examining the findings, it should be noted that the cross-sectional research design does not permit one to resolve completely the issue of causal order. It is quite conceivable, for example, that high degrees of control and supervision, conflict, and parental disapproval of peers *follow* delinquency rather than precede it. While control theory does provide a theoretical rationale for assuming that family dynamics precede delinquency, there is also good reason to suspect that delinquency involvement affects family interaction as well. No doubt there is some truth to this reciprocal relationship. However, family attachments are formed long before youths begin to engage in delinquent behavior. Adolescents who are strongly attached to their families in the first place are unlikely to become involved in delinquency; as a result, there is no serious delinquency among these youths to threaten family attachment. Youths at the other end of the continuum, however, are more likely to become involved in delinquency (through association with delinquent peers or other intermediary processes) precisely because of their lack of family attachment. Their involvement in delinquency thus only reinforces already weak attachments. While there is considerable support for this position (compare Hirschi, 1969; Elliott, Ageton, and Huizinga, 1985), the reader is cautioned that the cross-sectional design used here cannot firmly establish the causal order of the variables.

TABLE 23.1 Mean family relationship scores by sex, race, home status, and level of delinquency (age controlled)

	Caring and Trust		Control and Supervision[a]		Intimate Communication		Identity Support[b]		Parental Disapproval of Peers[c]		Conflict		Instrumental Communication	
	Mean	F	Mean	F	Mean	F	Mean	F	Mean	F	Mean	F	Mean	F
Sex														
Male (n = 401)	4.02	7.57**	3.78	80.33***	2.49	12.09***	3.29	.010	2.16	.069	2.23	11.07***	3.34	9.00**
Female (n = 423)	3.94		4.27		2.74		3.37		2.02		2.43		3.57	
Race														
White (n = 363)	3.88	17.01***	3.98	7.18***	2.68	2.36	3.32	.155	2.07	.638	2.51	12.40***	3.45	.263
Nonwhite (n = 461)	4.06		4.08		2.58		3.34		2.10		2.19		3.47	
Home Status														
Both Parents (n = 458)	4.00	1.60	4.04	2.65	2.60	.563	3.37	.882	2.05	.351	2.27	2.17	3.46	.206
Mother Only (n = 264)	3.96		3.98		2.62		3.31		2.13		2.34		3.45	
Mother/Stepfather (n = 102)	3.95		4.14		2.73		3.24		2.14		2.57		3.49	
Delinquent Involvement														
Nonoffender (n = 71)	4.25	10.02***	4.36	5.13***	2.63	.822	3.80	11.30***	1.88	6.52***	1.56	12.58***	3.81	8.46***
Low-frequency Minor (n = 305)	4.07		4.12		2.66		3.43		1.98		2.24		3.57	
High-frequency Minor (n = 196)	3.95		4.03		2.65		3.30		2.11		2.40		3.48	
Low-frequency Major (n = 153)	3.89		3.89		2.62		3.20		2.17		2.50		3.26	
High-frequency Major (n = 99)	3.73		3.73		2.43		2.96		2.40		2.78		3.16	

[a] Sex-by-race interaction ($F = 4.11$*); Sex-by-home status-by-delinquency interaction ($F = 2.02$*)

[b] Delinquency-by-sex interaction ($F = 2.90$**); Sex-by-race interaction ($F = 3.76$*)

[c] Sex-by-home status interaction ($F = 3.22$*)

*$p < .05$ **$p < .01$ ***$p < .001$

Table 23.1 presents the results of a four-way analysis of variance for each of the family dimensions by sex, race, home status, and level of delinquency. Age is controlled as a covariate. As expected, there are significant sex differences on most of the family dimensions: caring and trust, control and supervision, intimate communication, conflict, and instrumental communication. Surprisingly, males report a higher mean level of caring and trust, while females report more conflict with parents. As would be predicted from past research, however, females are subjected to greater control and supervision than are males, and they are more likely to engage in both intimate and instrumental communication with their parents.. The only significant race differences in family characteristics occur for caring and trust and control and supervision, for which nonwhites report the highest rates, and conflict, for which whites report the highest levels. To the extent that the selected factors represent different dimensions of family attachment, it is clear from the outset that a simplistic attached-unattached dichotomy would have masked some important variation by sex and race.

Importantly, however, none of the seven family factors differ significantly by home status. This clearly weakens the traditional argument that broken homes, female-headed homes, or those with stepfathers are *necessarily* negative and/or disadvantageous socialization environments. At least for the family dimensions specified, all three family structures are characterized by similar levels of attachment and interaction. To the extent that such family dimensions are related to delinquency (and they are, as shall be seen shortly), one would expect to find essentially the same patterning of relationships within the three home status categories. This issue will be taken up in greater detail in the regression analysis.

With the exception of intimate communication, each of the family relationship dimensions is significantly related to delinquency involvement. The differences are most apparent for identity support and conflict. Mean levels of identity support decrease in a linear fashion across the five offender categories, with nonoffenders reporting the highest and high-frequency major offenders the lowest levels. On the other hand, conflict means increase from the nonoffender to the high-frequency major offender category. These and the remaining patterns shown in Table 23.1 are consistent with preliminary expectations—delinquents have lower levels of caring and trust, control and supervision, identity support, and instrumental communication; on the other hand, the most delinquent youths are more likely to have conflicts with their parents, and the parents of delinquents are more likely than other parents to disapprove of their children's friends. When compared with the results of studies based on a single attached-unattached dimension, this analysis of seven distinct family interaction dimensions begins to give a more complete and precise sense of the kind of relationships which exist between parents and their relatively more or less delinquent children.

Before turning to this issue in more detail, the analysis of variance revealed several interaction terms which should be noted. First is that between sex and race for the control and supervision dimension. Nonwhite females report the greatest level of supervision (4.29), white males the least (3.68). The pattern of means (3.86 for nonwhite males, 4.25 for white females) clearly reveals that the sex difference is more important of the two; that is, while there are large control and supervision differences by sex within race subgroups, the race differences within sex categories are unimpressive. Second, although there are no main race or sex effects for identity support, there is a significant sex-race interaction: among the four race-sex groupings, nonwhite females (3.43) report the greatest levels of identity support; the remaining three groups report significantly lower levels (white females = 3.29, white males = 3.35, and nonwhite males = 3.26).

Third, there is a significant sex-home status interaction for the parental disapproval of peers variable. Among males, respondents in mother-only (2.19) and both-parent (2.17) homes report higher levels of parental disapproval than those in mother/stepfather homes (2.00). Among females, however, those in mother/stepfather homes report the highest levels (2.25 versus 1.94 in both-parent and 2.07 in mother-only homes). Thus, it is only in mother/stepfather homes that females report greater disapproval rates than males. In fact, it is this category (females in mother/stepfather homes) which has the highest mean level of disapproval. This is contrary to what was expected, given the widespread assumption that stepfathers cause more difficulty for male than for female children. On the other hand, it is not altogether inconsistent with the female delinquency literature which assumes that broken homes have a more negative effect on females than upon males (compare Datesman and Scarpitti, 1975).

Finally, there are also two interesting interaction terms involving family dimensions and delinquency. First is the delinquency-sex interaction for identity support. Female nonoffenders report the highest identity support levels by far. In fact, it is only among nonoffenders that male-female differences in identity support are significantly different (3.31 versus 3.99). For the other four offender categories, the male-female means are virtually identical. As would be expected high-frequency major offenders, both male (2.96) and female (2.97), report the lowest levels of identity support. The other interaction term involves delinquency, sex, and home status in the case of control and supervision. What is most apparent in the pattern of means is that females are subjected to more control than males in all three home status categories; and this is true for all levels of delinquency involvement as well. This is powerful evidence of the extent to which adolescent females are supervised as compared to their male counterparts. Overall, female nonoffenders in mother/stepfather homes report the greatest levels of control and supervision (although all females in the mother/stepfather category, regardless of level of delinquency, report almost equally high levels). On the other hand, male high-frequency major offenders from mother-only homes report the least amount of control and supervision.[3]

The analysis of variance results presented in Table 23.1 suggest some interesting patterns. However, these data are primarily descriptive in nature. The discussion turns now to the regression analysis in order to be more definitive about the relative effects of these variables on delinquency involvement. Table 23.2 presents the correlation matrix of delinquency, age, and the seven family interaction factors. With the exception of intimate communication, which is not significantly associated with delinquency at thezero-order, all of the family dimensions are moderately associated with delinquency involvement in the expected direction. The matrix also indicates that while most of the family factors are associated with one another, the coefficients are

---

[3] The reader is cautioned against interpreting this as a firm conclusion, as small cell sizes in a three-way interaction may produce unstable means.

Table 23.2 Correlation matrix

	Delinquency	Control and Supervision	Identity Support	Caring and Trust	Intimate Communication	Instrumental Communication	Disapproval of Peers	Conflict	Age
Delinquency	1.000	-.221	-.218	-.191	-.051	-.194	.188	.192	.105
Control and Supervision		1.000	.052	.393	.279	.317	-.150	-.062	-.147
Identity Support			1.000	.339	.172	.177	-.226	-.338	.004
Caring and Trust				1.000	.343	.400	-.261	-.321	-.063
Intimate Communication					1.000	.486	-.114	-.058	.055
Instrumental Communication						1.000	-.200	-.117	-.077
Disapproval of Peers							1.000	.176	.010
Conflict								1.000	.012
Age									1.000

TABLE 23.3 Regression analysis by home status

	Total Sample			Both Natural Parents			Mother Only			Mother/Stepfather		
	Unstandardized			Unstandardized			Unstandardized			Unstandardized		
	b	s.c.	Beta	b	s.c.	Beta	b	s.c.	Beta	b	s.c.	Beta
Caring and Trust	-.054	.070	-.031	-.116	.103	-.062	-.066	.129	-.038	.128	.251	.085
Control and Supervision	-.181	.055	-.122	-.167	.083	-.102	-.229	.100	-.167	.021	.188	.042
Intimate Communication	.124	.045	.099	.113	.064	.089	.110	.085	.094	.128	.149	.110
Identity Support	-.181	.046	-.135	-.213	.068	-.153	-.126	.081	-.102	.003	.134	.002
Parental Disapproval of Peers	.138	.049	.090	.093	.072	.060	.131	.090	.089	.251	.151	.181
Conflict	.105	.031	.114	.102	.045	.107	.146	.057	.163	.089	.092	.109
Instrumental Communication	-.169	.055	-.115	-.187	.082	-.121	-.196	.093	-.150	-.404	.158	-.291
Age	.045	.019	.072	.052	.028	.083	.011	.038	.018	.044	.060	.075
Race Dummy	.011	.075	.005	.035	.105	.015	-.192	.153	-.076	.024	.236	.011
Sex Dummy	.302	.080	.127	.390	.114	.163	.092	.147	.041	.240	.259	.106

F = 15,874 (p < .001)
Multiple R = .384
R² = .147

F = 8,909 (p < .001)
Multiple R = .408
R² = .166

F = 4.78 (p < .001)
Multiple R = .400
R² = .160

F = 1.71 (p < NS)
Multiple R = .400
R² = .160

not of sufficient magnitude to create problems of multicollinearity in the regression analysis.

The data in Table 23.3 summarize the results of a series of regression equations for the total sample and the three home status categories. The results of these analyses are presented separately for the various home status categories because the authors wanted to test the hypothesis that family interaction dynamics affect delinquency similarly for various types of family living arrangements. Sex and race are entered into the equations as dummy variables (coded 1 for males, 0 for females, and 1 for whites, 0 for nonwhites). Finally, age is included in each of the equations because of its association with both delinquency and control and supervision.

A general review of the data in Table 23.3 reveals that the family interaction variables explain relatively small portions of the variance in delinquency. This is disappointing, though not totally unexpected. The explained variance could have been boosted considerably had peer and school variables, for example, been included in the model. However, the goal of this inquiry is not to test a model of how, for example, family and peer associations combine to induce/inhibit delinquency. Rather, the concern is more specifically with the impact of several dimensions of family interaction on delinquency across different types of family structure. The aim is to investigate whether the multidimensional conceptualization of family interaction clarifies the relationship between the family and delinquency beyond that conveyed by more simplistic broken/intact and attached/unattached models.

Before proceeding, it should be noted that the equation for the mother/stepfather home is not statistically significant, and that only one of the slope coefficients (instrumental communication) is significant. This is in part a function of the small size of this category (n = 102), and the consequent larger standard errors of the estimates, which makes statistical significance more difficult to attain. Thus, while it would be misleading to make too much of these data, there are several noteworthy features about this subgroup. First, the single largest unstandardized slope coefficient (-.404 for instrumental communication) in the table is found in the mother/stepfather family. Similarly, parental disapproval of peers is more strongly related to delinquency among youths in mother/stepfather homes than in any home status category. Last are several reversals in the sign of the coefficient (caring and trust, control and supervision, and identity support). Whether these coefficients are indicative of real and important differences in the dynamics of family interaction patterns in mother/stepfather homes as opposed to alternative living arrangements, or whether they are unstable products of insufficient sample size and large standard errors, is not known. A guess is that they reflect real differences. It is tempting to argue, for example, that control and supervision is not as effective in inhibiting delinquency in such homes and that disapproval of peers takes on greater importance because of the resentment that the youth has for the stepfather as an "outsider." The fact that the unstandardized coefficient for intimate communication is largest in this family structure seems to support this logic as well. There is certainly support for this general interpretation in the delinquency literature (compare Johnson, 1986). Because of uncertainty about the statistical significance of the data, however, this group will be excluded from the discussion which follows. To echo Johnson's (1986) sentiment, there does seem to be something unique about mother/stepfather families, and future researchers are urged to include larger samples of mother/stepfather homes in order to examine these possibilities with greater certainty in the conclusions.

Turning to the other subgroups in Table 23.3, it is clear that the family interaction variables have similar effects on delinquency in varying family structures. All of the variables are associated with delinquency in the expected direction, with the exception of intimate communication. Intimate communication is actually *positively* associated with delinquency in the total sample and in both-parent and mother-only homes. This is difficult to explain, especially since intimate communication is associated with all of the other variables in the expected direction (see Table 23.3).

Adolescents who are willing to discuss with their parents such sensitive matters as boyfriends, girlfriends, and sex apparently are not so attached to their parents that delinquency is attenuated. This is ironic since communication between parent and child on such sensitive and private matters is presumably an index of a strong, intimate relationship which, in turn, is an important deterrent to delinquency (at least according to social control theory). It may be, however, that family discussions about girlfriends, boyfriends, and sex are not good indices of intimate communication. Perhaps these are topics of discussion between all adolescents and their parents; hence they do not discriminate between intimate and nonintimate relationships. There is, however, another possible interpretation.

Although detailed data on the nature and context of these conversations were not collected, it is conceivable that many of them are parent-initiated, often against the wishes of the child. One can envision the youth, cornered by the parents, being forced to discuss what are very personal and often embarrassing matters. Under these conditions, it is not difficult to see why this is not a valid index of the intimacy of a relationship and why it is not negatively associated with delinquency (as shown in Table 23.4 this relationship is strongest among males, especially white males; to the extent that males find it more difficult than females to discuss private and intimate matters with their parents, the post hoc explanation presented here makes some sense). The reader is cautioned, however, that this is pure speculation since the authors do not have any data which speak directly to the issue.

Comparison of the unstandardized regression coefficients across groups indicates that all of the family interaction variables are similarly related to delinquency involvement in the total sample, mother-only, and both-parent homes. While this does not necessarily mean that home status is an unimportant variable in delinquency involvement, it does suggest that similar family dynamics are operating within various types of family structure. If there are indeed family structure differences in delinquency involvement, then one must look elsewhere; such differences are not evident in the family dimensions the authors have examined. (They do appear in the mother/stepfather category but, as indicated above, the authors do not have confidence that the sample size is sufficient to pursue these differences.) This position is supported by separate analyses of the relationship between family structure and delinquency (not shown here) which found no significant relationship, either in the total sample or in any of the sex, race, or race-sex subgroups.

Within mother only and both parent homes, however, the *relative importance* of the family interaction variables does vary. In both-parent homes identity support, instrumental communication, conflict, and control and supervision are most important

TABLE 23.4 Understandardization regression coefficients (standard error) and varience in delinquency explained by family factors and age

Sample Group	Caring and Trust	Control and Supervision	Intimate Communication	Identity Support	Parental Disapproval of Peers	Conflict	Instrumental Communication	Age	RSQ	F of Equation
Males (n = 405)	-.083 (.110)	-.257 (.079)	.201 (.070)	-.164 (.068)	.151 (.072)	.053 (.046)	-.197 (.080)	.064 (.028)	.122	7.67*
Females (n = 425)	-.016 (.091)	-.102 (.077)	.065 (.059)	-.177 (.063)	.148 (.068)	.160 (.042)	-.154 (.074)	.029 (.027)	.142	9.76*
Whites (n = 364)	.034 (.105)	-.211 (.076)	.207 (.072)	-.231 (.071)	.206 (.077)	.113 (.045)	-.279 (.081)	.056 (.028)	.178	10.76*
Nonwhites (n = 461)	—	-.289 (.071)	.059 (.061)	-.175 (.062)	.120 (.066)	.091 (.044)	-.114 (.076)	.026 (.027)	.112	8.03*
White Males (n = 174)	-.139 (.177)	-.219 (.120)	.375 (.115)	-.261 (.110)	.206 (.118)	.038 (.065)	-.396 (.118)	.064 (.043)	.225	6.61*
Nonwhite Males (n = 228)	-.034 (.148)	-.269 (.107)	.087 (.092)	-.104 (.090)	.123 (.093)	.058 (.067)	-.060 (.112)	.060 (.039)	.075	2.52**
White Females (n = 190)	-.050 (.137)	.070 (.110)	.097 (.090)	-.147 (.090)	.165 (.099)	.184 (.060)	-.138 (.107)	.075 (.036)	.175	5.50*
Nonwhite Females (n = 233)	-.034 (.128)	-.226 (.109)	.052 (.082)	-.195 (.089)	.130 (.095)	.135 (.060)	-.149 (.104)	-.004 (.039)	.145	5.36*

*p < .001   **p < .01

(as determined by the relative magnitude of their standardized Beta coefficients). In mother-only homes, however, control and supervision is most important, followed by conflict and instrumental communication. These differences in relative importance, however, are not large, and the authors are reluctant to conclude that differential family interaction patterns are operating. Rather, the data continue to suggest that similar processes are involved in various family structures. Instrumental communication, identity support, control and supervision, and conflict appear to be significantly related to delinquency in all family contexts. The multidimensional conceptualization of family interaction thus permits one to be much more specific about the nature of these processes than do more unidimensional attached/unattached models.

In addition to the analyses represented by the data in Table 23.3, several potential interactions among the variables (for example, race-sex, sex-intimate communication, conflict-intimate communication) were also tested. With one exception, these did not add significantly to the variance accounted for by main effects. This exception is the interaction between intimate communication and instrumental communication in both-parent homes (b = −.331). The most delinquent youths have the lowest score on the product of these two variables. This suggests that a combination of high instrumental communication and high intimate communication is indicative of strong attachment and has a delinquency inhibiting effect. An analysis of variance using a dichotomized version of this interaction term (the product of the two variables, each split at the median) shows that high-frequency major offenders have the lowest scores and low-frequency minor offenders the highest. The pattern of means is perfectly linear across the five offender categories, with the exception of nonoffenders, who have a mean value below that of low-frequency minor and high-frequency minor offenders. The authors have speculated on the uniqueness of this nonoffender group elsewhere (Giordano et al., 1986).

Because the race and sex dummies included in the analysis presented in Table 23.3 suggest tha these variables affect delinquency involvement even after family interaction patterns have been controlled (that is, males are significantly more delinquent than females in all family contexts, while blacks are considerably more delinquent than whites in mother-only homes), and because the literature suggests important sex and race differences in the impact of family variables on delinquency (compare Rankin, 1983; Gove and Crutchfield, 1982), one last analysis was performed. The data in Table 23.4 present unstandardized regression coefficients for the family interaction dimensions by sex, race, and race-sex subgroups. While the authors would have liked to present breakdowns for race and sex groups by homes status (for example, intact white homes, mother-only black homes) the small samples which result when the data are combined in this way prohibited doing so.

As the data in Table 23.4 show, the amount of variance in delinquency explained by the model ranges from a high of 22.5% among white males to a low of 7.5% for nonwhite males[4] . While the explained variance is again disappointing, the data do

---

[4] While R^2 differences are compared across groups, the reader is reminded that R^2 is in part a function of a particular subgroup's variance. Because this can lead to potentially misleading conclusions, unstandardized regression coefficients will also be compared across groups, and the standard errors of these estimates will be presented.

reveal several interesting patterns. First, the model accounts for slightly more variance among females than among males (14.2% versus 12.2%). To the extent that the model specified here is a social control model, this is consistent with previous arguments that control theory does a better job of explaining female than male delinquency (compare Krohn and Massey, 1980). Still, the variance explained for the two groups is quite similar, due in part to a more complete measurement of family interaction patterns in the model presented here. Previous research based on a unidimensional attachment variable may have masked differences in the particular *dimensions* of attachment which inhibit delinquency among males and females. For example, the data show that although the total explained variance is similar among males and females, the relative importance of the variables is not. Among males, control and supervision, intimate communication, and instrumental communication are most important (as determined by the relative magnitude of the coefficients). For females, however, identity support, conflict, instrumental communication, and parental disapproval of peers are the strongest predictors. This seems to suggest that while family attachment is important in inhibiting delinquency among all adolescents, the various dimensions of this bond operate somewhat differentially among males and females.

Second, the family variables also do considerably better in accounting for the delinquency of whites than for nonwhites (17.8% versus 11.1%). For both groups, control and supervision, identity support, disapproval of peers, and instrumental communication are important predictors. With the exception of the supervision variable, however, the coefficients are considerably larger among whites than among nonwhites. For whites, instrumental communication is clearly the best predictor, while among nonwhites, control and supervision heads the list.

Third, among the four race-sex subgroups, the model explains more variance in delinquency among whites, male (22.5%) and female (17.5%), than among nonwhites, male (7.5%), or female (14.5%). While identity support seems to be important in all four subgroups, there are important differences by group in relative salience of the variables. Instrumental communication and intimate communication are the strongest predictors by far among white males, while control and supervision is most important among nonwhite males, conflict among white females, and control and supervision among nonwhite females. These differences offer further support for the contention that it is important to distinguish among various dimensions of family interaction and attachment so that one can specify which ones operate similarly and which operate differentially across particular subgroups.

Finally, a comparison of the unstandardized coefficients reveals, with few exceptions, that control and supervision, identity support, parental disapproval of peers, and instrumental communication are significantly related to delinquency involvement across all of the subgroups. On the other hand, intimate communication is more salient for whites, males, and especially white males than for any of the other subgroups (an examination of the instrumental communication-intimate communication interaction discussed earlier produced unstandardized coefficients of -.363 for whites, -.379 for males and -.460 for white males), while conflict is most predictive of delinquency among females generally, and white females in particular. In conjunction with the above data, these findings suggest that while there is a core of family attachment dimensions that appears important for all adolescents, there are several important subgroup differences which demand attention in subsequent research.

DISCUSSION

Much of the literature dealing with the family and delinquency is characterized by a dichotomous attached/unattached conception of family relationships and a broken-intact model of family structure. The purpose of this article has been to show that a more detailed elaboration of the elements constituting family attachment provides a more rigorous test of exactly how family processes affect delinquency. Examining the effect of these relationships within different types of families also allows one to be more unambiguous about the relationship between family processes and family structure.

Although the explained variance in delinquency accounted for by the model is small, this does not mean that family variables are unimportant in understanding and predicting delinquency involvement. While there is no doubt that peer and school variables, for example, are more powerful predictors, the data (as well as considerable theory and previous research) indicate that family processes are too important to be excluded from criminological explanations. Family relationships assume a major role in one of the most powerful models of delinquency—social control theory. To the extent that more and more research is being conducted to test the propositions of this model, it is incumbent upon criminologists to attend to basic problems of conceptualization and measurement. Only when family interaction processes are properly conceptionalized and operationalized can one begin to sort out the relative importance of family, peer, school, and other variables, and to specify how such factors might interact in their effect on delinquency. This research represents a modest step in this direction.

The findings indicate that while there is no significant variation by family structure. Significant relationships between all but one of the family interaction dimensions and delinquency, coupled with the lack of any significant relationship between family structure and delinquency in the data, suggest that internal family dynamics are considerably more important than family structure in affecting delinquency. The family variables specified seem to have similar affects on delinquency in all types of family structures. The findings do not suggest that the effects of broken homes are mediated by family interaction dynamics, as is commonly assumed. Indeed, the findings indicate that there is no broken home effect (whether there might be a differential official reaction to delinquency on the basis of family structure [compare Johnson, 1986) is an important, though separate issue; since the data are confined to self-reported delinquency, the authors cannot address this issue). However, the small number of cases in father-only, father/stepmother, and mother/stepfather homes forced a restriction of the analyses to both-parent and mother-only homes. As a result, research based on larger samples of these types of family structures, especially mother/stepfather homes, is required before any definitive conclusions can be drawn.

On the other hand, the regression analysis for the various sex, race, and race-sex subgroups suggest both important similarities and differences in the impact of family dynamics on delinquency. Subsequent research should pursue these in greater detail.

All of these findings complicate the presumed relationship between the family and delinquency. The data make it clear that the traditional attached/unattached and broken/intact dichotomies mask many of the specific internal dynamics of family relationships. At the same time, these data point to the multidimensional nature of family attachment. While the family factors identified are associated with one another, they are clearly separate dimensions which have differential impacts on delinquency. It is equally obvious that there is considerable variation among sociodemographic subgroups in both the utility of the family variables, as measured by the explained variance, and in the specific combination of variables that are predictive of delinquency. It will be the task of future research to analyze these subtleties and to specify the causal ordering of their effects.

REFERENCES

Agnew, Robert (1985) Social control theory and delinquency: A longitudinal test, Criminology 23: 47-61.

Arnold, William R. and Terrance M. Brungardt (1983) *Juvenile Misconduct and Delinquency*. Boston: Houghton Mifflin.

Bordua, David (1962) Some comments on theories of group delinquency. *Sociological Inquiry* 32:245-260.

Canter, Rachelle J. (1982) Family correlates of male and female delinquency. *Criminology* 20: 149-167.

Cernkovich, Stephen A., Peggy C. Giordano, and M.D. Pugh (1985) Chronic offenders: The missing cases in self-report delinquency research. *Journal of Criminal Law and Criminology* 76: 301-326.

Datesman, Susan K. and Frank R. Scarpitti (1975) Female delinquency and broken homes: A reassessment. *Criminology* 13: 33-55.

Elliott, Delbert and Suzanne Ageton (1980) Reconciling race and class differences in self-reported and official estimates of delinquency. *American Sociological Review* 45: 95-110.

Elliott, Delbert, David Huizinga, and Suzanne Ageton (1985) Explaining Delinquency and Drug Use. *The National Youth Survey,* Project Report No. 21, Boulder, CO: Behavioral Research Institute.

Empey, LeMar T. (1982) *American Delinquency*: Its Meaning and Construction (rev. ed.). Homewood, IL: Dorsey.

Etaugh Claire (1980) Effects of nonmaternal care on children: Research evidence and popular views. *American Psychologist* 35: 309-317.

Giordano, Peggy C. Stephen A. Cernovich, and M.D. Pugh (1986) Friendships and delinquency. *American Journal of Sociology* 91: 1,170-1202.

Gold ,Martin and David J. Reimer (1974) Changing Patterns of Delinquent Behavior Among Americans 13 to 16 Years Old, 1967-1972. *Report No. 1 of the National Survey of Youth.* Ann Arbor: Institute of Social Research, University of Michigan (NIMH Grant No. MH 20575).

Gove, Walter R. and Robert D. Crutchfield (1982) The family and juvenile delinquency. *The Sociological Quarterly* 23: 301-319.

Hindelang, Michael J., Travis Hirschi, and Joseph G. Weis (1981) *Measuring Delinquency.*
Beverly Hills: Sage.

Hirschi, Travis (1969) Causes of Delinquency. Berkley: *University of California Press.*

Hoffman, Lois Wladis (1974) Effects of maternal employment on the child: A review of the research. *Developmental Psychology* 10: 204-228.

Johnson, Richard E. (1986) Family structure and delinquency: General patterns and gender differences *Criminology* 24: 65-84.

Krohn, Marvin D. and James L. Massey (1980) Social control and delinquent behavior: An examination of the elements of the social bond. *The Sociological Quarterly:* 529-543.

LaGrange, Randy L. and Helene Raskin White (1985) Age difference in delinquency: A test of theory. *Criminology* 23: 19-45.

Minor, William No Date *Maryland Youth Survey.* Institute of Criminal Justice and Criminology. College Park, University of Maryland.

Norland, Stephen, Neal Shover, William E. Thorton, and Jennifer James (1979) Intrafamily conflict and delinquency. *Pacific Sociological Review* 2: 223-240.

Nye, F. Ivan (1958) *Family Relationships and Delinquent Behavior.* New York: Wiley.

Patterson, Gerald R. and Thomas J. Dishion (1985) Contributions of families and peers to delinquency. *Criminology* 23: 63-79.

Rankin, Joseph H. (1983) The family context of delinquency. *Social Problems* 30: 466-479.

Rodman, Hyman and Paul Grams (1967) Juvenile delinquency and the family: A review and discussion. *Task Force Report:* Juvenile Delinquency and Youth Crime. The President's Commission on Law Enforcement and the Administration of Justice. Washington, D.C.: U.S. Government Printing Office.

Rosen, Lawrence (1985) Family and delinquency. Structure or function? *Criminology* 23: 553-573.

Rutter, Michael and Henri Giller (1984) *Delinquency*: Trends and Perspectives. New York: Guilford.

Shoemaker, Donald J. (1984) *Theories of Delinquency: An Examination of Explanations of Delinquent Behavior.* New York: Oxford University Press.

United States Bureau of the Census (1985) Marital Status and Living Arrangements: March 1984. *Current Population Reports,* Series P-20, No. 399. Washington, D.C.: U.S. Government Printing Office.

Wells, L. Edward and Joseph H. Rankin (1986) The broken homes model of delinquency: Analytic issues. *Journal of Research in Crime Delinquency* 23: 68-93.

West, Lloyd and Harvey W. Zingle (1969) A self-disclosure inventory for adolescents. *Psychological Reports* 23: 439-445.

Wiatrowski, Michael D., David B. Griswold, and Mary K. Roberts (1981) Social control theory and delinquency. *American Sociological Review* 46: 525-541.

Wilkinson, Karen (1974) The broken family and juvenile delinquency: Scientific explanation of ideology? *Social Problems* 21: 726-739.

Stephen A. Cernkovich is Professor of Sociology at Bowling Green State University. His research interests include conceptualization and measurement in criminology and chronic juvenile offenders.

Peggy C. Giordano is Professor of Sociology at Bowling Green State University. Her research focuses on the role of peer relationships in the etiology of adolescent problems, including pregnancy, psychological distress, and involvement in delinquency.

APPENDIX 23.1   Family Scale Reliabilities and Factor Loadings

---

Caring and Trust (response form at ranges along a five-point scale from "strongly agree" to "strongly-disagree"). Alpha = .757

1. My parents often ask about what I am doing in school. .586
2. My parents give me the right amount of affection. .731
3. One of the worst things that could happen to me would be finding out that I let my parents down. .636
4. My parents are usually proud of me when I've finished something I've worked hard at. .698
5. My parents trust me. .616
6. I'm closer to my parents than a lot of kids my age are. .636

Identity Support (response format ranges along a five-point scale from "strongly agree" to "strongly disagree"). Alpha = .690

1. My parents sometimes put me down in front of other people. -.699
2. Sometimes my parents won't listen to me or my opinions. -.708
3. My parents sometimes give me the feeling that I'm not living up to their expectations. -.761
4. My parents seem to wish I were a different type of person. -.643

Intimate Communication (response format ranges along a five-point scale from "very often" to "never"). Alpha = .673

1. How often do you talk to your parents about the boy/girl whom you like very much? .824
2. How often do you talk to your parents about questions, or problems about sex? .798
3. How often do you talk to your parents about things you have done about which you feel guilty? .589

Control and Supervision (response format ranges along a five-point scale from "strongly agree" to "strongly disagree"). Alpha = .691

1. My parents want to know who I am going out with when I go out with boys/girls. .774
2. In my free time away from home, my parents know who I'm with and where I am. .742
3. My parents want me to tell them where I am if I don't come home right after school. .815

Conflict (response format ranges along a five-point scale from "two or more per week" to "hardly ever or never"). Alpha = .615

1. How often do you have disagreements or arguments with your parents? .822
2. How often do you purposely not talk to your parents because you are mad at them? .817

Instrumental Communication (response format ranges along a five-point scale from "very often" to "never"). Alpha = .654

1. How often do you talk with your parents about problems you have at school? -.680
2. How often do you talk with your parents about your job plans for the future? -.545
3. How often do you talk with your parents about problems with your friends? -.645
4. How often do you talk with your parents about how well you get along with your teachers? -.794

Parental Disapproval of Peers (response format ranges along a five-point scale from "strongly approve" to "strongly disapprove"). Alpha = .475

1. In general, what do your parents think of your friends? .756
2. In general, what do your parents think of your boyfriend/girlfriend? .730

The Youth Subculture
*The Hippies of Haight-Ashbury**

JACK E. BYNUM

IN THE 1960's, San Francisco was a West Coast center for the hippies, the unnumbered thousands of young Americans, who in their rejection of the social order established by their parents, sought to establish a new morality and a new lifestyle based on the "hang-loose ethic" of "doing your own thing." And for a few years the ordinary drab Haight-Ashbury district was transformed into a colorful, carnival-like land of bohemians where everything goes.

During the mid-sixties, to drive through the area at any time of day or night was to become entangled in the biggest traffic jam in San Francisco. Streams of automobiles and bus loads of tourists constantly converged on the scene to get a first-hand story to tell relatives back in more conservative parts of the country. I remember my first drive through "Hippie-land." My reactions were typical of the outsider. Everything looked so strange to my uninitiated eyes that I did what many visitors did the first time: I rolled up the car windows and locked all the doors! A bit later I began to realize that the tourist or occasional visitor, staring goggle-eyed from the sanctity of his automobile isn't really seeing much of the local culture. It was then that I decided to get onto the streets and interact with the hippies.

I also realized that my traditional business suit and grooming would evoke little rapport. "Should I let my beard grow, wear beads, sandals, and a dirty sweat shirt?" I asked myself. I invited my wife to throw on an old blanket and come along, but she saw neither duty nor challenge in such an adventure. So, finally, dressed in casual attire, I arrived alone on the corner of Haight and Ashbury Streets. But not alone for long; for a person was immediately engulfed in the sights, sounds, smells, and people of the Haight-Ashbury district.

---

* Research was conducted in the mid-1960s; revised and edited in 1988 specifically for this volume.

359

The great majority of the "sidewalk society" with which I mingled was young, white, and between 15 and 25 years of age. The vast majority of the males wore their hair long. Sideburns. mustaches, and beards were also common among those who were old enough to grow them (this was several years before an abundance of facial hair became more acceptable for males in the larger society). In addition, unless one knew differently, a few minutes close to large groups of hippies could cause one to wonder if soap and deodorant were unavailable in that part of the world. It became apparent that part of the behavior I was observing was a scornful rejection of the typically attired, deodorized facade of middle-class society and culture. Casual grooming, or no grooming at all, seemed to be part of the lifestyle for both sexes.

I estimated that the four blocks of the immediate Haight-Ashbury intersection contained at least 700 hippies. They were extremely social—strolling in two's and three's, or lounging in groups of five to twenty on the sidewalks, curbs, and porches. Generally, there was a great deal of talk and movement. Most of them were dressed in garments unlike the customary clothing of Americans, but their dress conformed very much among themselves. Serapes and sandals, together with the long hair and assorted beads and bracelets seemed to be a kind of identifying hippie trademark. Beyond these standardized, uniform dress characteristics, there was room for a wide variety of costume and appearance; the more colorful and uninhibited, the more acceptable to the subculture. Many hippies were barefooted. Some young men were stripped to the waist. A number of girls wore micro-skirts; one was wearing a loin cloth. Another young woman with a huge tattoo on her shoulder wore no blouse.

At the other extreme, many individuals were fantastically overdressed. Some were wearing long, flowing robes, supplemented by small metal bells on their ankles and around their necks. One youth was dressed in a colonial garb, complete with lace-trimmed shirt with glass buttons and high collar, over knicker-type pantaloons. Another wore an ancient naval officer's jacket over faded ragged jeans. He had bare feet.

As I walked down the sidewalk, something fluttered in front of my face. It was a small pink cardboard box, suspended by a paper streamer from a third floor window. On the box was a sign which read "extra change for Marijuana." I followed with my eyes up the streamer, and there in the window was a young girl of no more than 13 who was smiling down at me and literally fishing with the box in the street for contributions. Besides extensive begging, other hippie economic activities included very aggressive peddling of home-crafted baskets, hand-woven cloth, drawings, and underground magazines (the *Oracle, Maverick* and *Berkeley Barb*) which articulated and promoted the hippie ideology. A number of small shops operated by more enterprising hippies and catering to the subculture life style were scattered along Haight Street. The houses, sidewalks, and hippie automobiles in the area were decorated and covered with the so-called psychedelic colors, grafitti, and slogans, such as "Turn on; Tune in; and Drop out!" Translated, this suggested: "Turn on with drugs; Tune in to life; and Drop out of school and the middle-class society!" Another slogan in abundance was: "Haight is love!"

The hippies talked a great deal about love. While I am not too prudish or inclined to stand in the way of love, it was a bit awkward climbing over a pile of six amorous male and female hippies stretched out on the sidewalk next to my automobile. I wandered into two hippie shops where their posters and poems were displayed for viewing and for sale. Contrary to expectations, everything they drew, painted, or wrote was not sex-oriented, though this is not to say there wasn't a great deal of sex on display in various forms. I found the hippies outgoing and gregarious, although their boldness sometimes intimidated me. (Before my sojourn was over, several of them pointed out to me that I was probably unredeemable from the "straight-society" because of my advanced age. I was over 30!) Occasionally, hippies would come down the street like strolling minstrels playing on guitars, flutes, and other instruments. In nearby Golden Gate Park, The Grateful Dead performed a frenzied public concert.

Those hippies crowded together on the sidewalks gladly talked with me and welcomed interviews. However, they badly outnumbered me and when I attempted to establish communication, they quickly determined that I was an outsider and gave me a bad time with rude and obscene words and gestures. When one girl solicited me for money, a big, bearded, wild-looking fellow came up close to me and yelled in a loud voice: "Let's hear what the man says! Let's hear what the man says!" This was intended, I believe, to intimidate and embarrass members of the outgroup into "contributing," and it succeeded very well.

I finally formulated a technique whereby I could talk with just one or two hippies at a time. I noticed that many of them were hitch-hiking towards the ocean beaches to the west. I got back into my automobile and began picking them up. By isolating them in a car it became possible to separate one or two at a time from the large crowds and to establish a more natural dialogue and communication. It was during those forty or more trips between Haight-Ashbury district and the beach that I made my first significant discovery: When one or two hippies were isolated in an automobile with me, there was an abrupt and startling change of personality from that displayed on the sidewalks when I had faced overwhelming groups of them. In the vehicle they immediately abandoned their breezy bravado and became much more discreet and personally responsible. I realize that their dominance over strangers and the Haight-Ashbury neighborhood only existed when they were in large supportive groups that continually reinforced the subcultural value for alienation. In addition, the insulting behavior they exhibited on the sidewalk was only possible when they could hide in the unstructured anonymity of the crowd.

I used an unstructured, conversation-type interview with just two basic questions: (1) "What is a hippie?" and (2) "What does the 'scene' mean?" (referring to the hippie phenomena in the Haight-Ashbury district). While I received many sincere and spontaneous answers, there was little consensus of responses to these questions.

Definitions of "hippie" ranged from "Child of God" to "flower power" to "revolutionary." Similarly, my passengers to the beach were often uncertain whether they were hippies or not, and often expressed a need for such middle-class values as education, employment, and money.

To my inquiry about the meaning of the "scene" in which I tried to get close to the values or ideology that lay behind hippie behavior, I ran into a confusing array of interpretations and little agreement among my subjects. Amazingly, I discovered that many of those bizarre looking people who talked so openly about "free love" and "popping pills" were from well-to-do families in middle-class or upper-class suburbs of San Francisco. Of course, many run-away youngsters swelled the hippie ranks, but the middle-class element had escaped many researchers. It became apparent that many of these teenage youths were pseudo-hippies, the week-end or vacation variety "playing hippie" for a little while before returning to the homes and schools of the larger society. I also encountered those who were retreating from society because of some failure and those who were helplessly hooked on drugs and operated in a semi-daze. Later, I met a few "guru-philosopher types" who usually loitered in the coffee houses and sought to set down the theory and rationale that formed the ideological base for the Haight-Ashbury "scene." It was these individuals, who were usually older and had a measure of leadership or charisma, who sought to explain the hippie life style and behavior as more than short-term hedonism and an alternative to boredom as suggested by most of the hippies I encountered.

In general, I was told that they were not rebelling as much as rejecting the "phony, middle-class values and culture that dominate the world and restrict true freedom and creativity." The hippies were scornful and amused at those of us who spend our lives "following an overstructured, artificial plan laid down by society, such as scheduled eating, sleeping, studying, working and 'leading respectable lives' according to old-fashioned and meaningless rules."

They felt that most adults were hypocrites. For example, we sanctify marriage yet so many are "secretly cheating." The hippies argued that the marriage institution is ridiculous and that love, sex and companionship are "natural and free." They believed that all of us are seeking "mind-expanding experiences" and that drugs are the avenue to this emotional and mental experience rather than education as suggested by conservative and restrictive society.

Some hippies claimed that they had found and were practicing a kind of religion—a type of primitive, long-lost Christianity that the contemporary church does not possess. They claimed to be truly pacifistic and to truly love one another. One of their most popular posters depicted Jesus with this caption:

> WANTED: Jesus of Nazareth—a professional agitator; full beard, condemned to death by respectable society and the pigs [the police].

The hippies identified with this image of Jesus as a downtrodden, misunderstood hippie promoting a new lifestyle.

Those were some of their public proclamations as they shouted together at the "straight outsider" on the sidewalks of Haight-Ashbury, or chanted in unison at the feet of a hippie guru. In short, they claimed to be the social movement leading to the future and challenged existing social institutions (education, religion, government, economy, and family) as illegitimate and irrelevant to the needs of contemporary young people. However, privately, seated in my car, they often added something more: disillusionment, loneliness, and fear. Several asked me to help negotiate their return to home and families, which I was able to accomplish for some with a few telephone calls. Many young hippies confided that they had been unable to compete effectively for grades in school and simply dropped out; others that they were estranged from their parents; still others that it was drugs rather than ideology that had brought them to the Haight-Ashbury. One youth solemnly put into words what many others had articulated less eloquently: "We are just a lot of lost people. We don't know what to do, so we identify with the people of Haight-Ashbury."

Perhaps the most glaring deficiency I found in the hippie movement was the failure of many individual hippies to maintain, or even explain, their convictions when separated from the group. This seems to indicate a lack of genuine solidarity that is necessary if any movement is to survive for very long. Because of this and the absence of a clearcut and widely accepted ideology, I concluded that the hippie phenomenon was not a viable social movement. However, it has been remembered as an extreme manifestation of the youth subculture during the 1960s.

My second set of conclusions had to do with their strange clothing and was reached purely by accident. After completing the trips to the beach and conversation-interviews with the hippies, I returned to the Haight Street sidewalk. As I grew tired of walking, I took a stationary position and watched the busy scene as the hippies walked by. And then it dawned on me that I was actually seeing a parade-like ritual! I was astonished to see the same characters repeatedly passing in front of me. A great many of those young people had no place to go. They would reach the end of the short neighborhood, turn around, walk back, and then repeat the trip. The barefooted fellow in the old naval officer's uniform walked by me four times in 30 minutes. The girl with the tattoo passed before my wondering eyes six times. The poor exhibitionist in the colonial garb paraded by me a record nine times in 45 minutes! Then I got part of the point and meaning: It was the same costumes on the same people parading by to get some kind of fulfillment out of the shocked stares of tourists and visitors like me. But that was only part of it. I am convinced that I was seeing some desperate efforts on the part of the young people to resolve personal and social identity crises.

More support for this notion began to accumulate as I observed several members of the Hell's Angels Motorcycle Club mingling in the crowd. It was very warm that Sunday afternoon and perspiration was pouring from the faces of the Hell's Angels. Yet they did not remove their heavy, leather jackets. Why? Could it be so spectators would see the frightening skull and crossed bones insignia on their backs and recognize them as "Hell's Angels"? It appeared to me that many, perhaps most, of the people on Haight Street in San Francisco were literally begging for identity, recognition, and some kind of status, even if it was deviant identity and status! And they got it by "doing their own thing." Many failed in school, failed at work, failed at finding love, and failed at achieving all those middle-class values and objectives that they claimed to repudiate. Perhaps this is why they declare that society is wrong to impose such unreasonable values on everyone. And with the attention-grabbing clothing and behavior they may be crying out: "Hey, I'm alive! I'm here! I'm somebodyListen to me!"

The last insight derived from this field experience with the San Francisco hippie community may be the most useful since it was about myself. When I first arrived on Haight Street, I hesitated to stop long in one spot, or look long at individuals. The unabashed frankness and lack of inhibitions of the hippies, as well as their overwhelming numbers, inhibited me. Finally, this feeling wore off, and I began to analyze my own feelings of fear.

We conforming members of the larger society may fear the hippies for one or both of the following reasons. First of all, we fear the hippies are subhuman in some way; that these deviant, strange-looking people (according to our socialized standards) might hurt us physically. This is the instant reaction when first-time visitors to Haight Street roll up the windows and lock the doors of their automobiles.

Second, we may be afraid that the hippies are superhumans; that they might hurt us intellectually; that they may be right, and we may be wrong; that they have found something good or true, and it is a threat to our established and traditional ways of thinking and doing things.

I believe that the hippie subculture and lifestyle told us some important things about our changing society. Moreover, they openly and candidly confronted society with the reality of its own hypocrisy in a great many areas, ranging from war and peace to personal morality. An ancient Hebrew proverb sums up the point succinctly: "The fathers have eaten sour grapes and the children's teeth are set on edge."

Serious students of human behavior generally agree that the hippie of the 1960s was the offspring of larger society, a social mutation that pitifully and publically condemned the failures of preceding generations and institutions.

If we have been frightened by a Frankenstein monster, perhaps we should reflect that it is our own creation, the consequence of denying our younger generation meaningful responsibility and participation in the social process. This is the point of Nicholas Von Hoffman's insightful book, *We Are The People Our Parents Warned Us Against* (1968). Perhaps this is the message behind all of the symbolic interaction on Haight Street: "We ar just a lot of lost people and don't know what to do."

SUGGESTED READINGS

Earisman, Delbert L. (1968). *Hippies in our Midst*. Philadelphia: Fortress Press.

Keniston, Kenneth. (1965). *The Uncommitted: Alienated Youth in American Society*. New York: Harcourt, Brace and World.

Patridge, William L. (1973). *The Hippie Ghetto: The Natural History of a Subculture*. New York: Holt, Rinehart and Winston.

Simons, J.I. and Barry Winograd. (1967). *It's Happening*. Santa Barbara: Marc Laird.

Von Hoffman, Nicholas. (1968). *We Are The People Our Parents Warned Us Against*. Chicago: Quadrangle Books.

Yablonsky, Lewis. (1968). *The Hippie Trip*. New York: Pegasus.

The Appearance
of Youthful Subculture
A Theoretical Perspective on Deviance

LYNNE RICHARDS

A number of theoretical perspectives can be united to form a comprehensive explanation of the formation and dissolution of deviant subcultures. Using this theoretical framework, the role of appearance is herein promulgated as being a primary and contributing factor to this subcultural process. Examinining the Teddy Boy subculture of the 1050s and the Hippie subculture of the 1960s, it is shown that appearance factors 1) add credibility to the deviant role; 2) provide a descriptive embodiment of the deviance, to which society reacts; 3) serve as flaunted symbols of deviance in retaliatory counterpride displays; and 4) contribute cues for imitation by mass society, thereby initiating social repair.

SELF-ENHANCEMENT THEORY suggests that all human behavior is directed toward constructing and supporting a perception of self that is positive and conducive to esteem (Sirgy, 1982). Thus, deviant behavior can be perceived as merely unconventional or socially unacceptable means for acquiring positive perceptions of the self. Within the investigation delineated herein, this self-enhancement perception of deviance was united with concepts generated by a number of other theoretical perspectives to form a comprehensive interpretation of the formation of deviant subculture (see Table 25.1). Ideas concerning the social and psychological functions of appearance were then applied to that theoretical framework, resulting in an explanation in which appearance represented a key ingredient in the subcultural process.

Source: Richards, Lynne. "The Appearance of Youthful Subculture: A Theoretical Perspective on Deviance." *Clothing and Textiles Research Journal,* Vol. 6 (Spring) 1988:56-64. Reprinted by permission.

The subsequent theoretical explanation was tested against two real world youthful deviant subcultures: the British Teddy Boys and the American Hippies. These social groups were selected for analysis due to the fact that they were sufficiently remote in time to insure the total completion of the formation and dissolution process while being recent enough for primary data to be adequately available. In addition, the Teddy Boys of Great Britain and the Hippies of America represented two different social class backgrounds, nationalities and decades, thereby providing breadth to the testing of the theoretical explanation.

THE FORMATION OF DEVIANT SUBCULTURE

As noted, self-enhancement theory suggests that all human behavior is aimed at the generation of positive perceptions of the self and self-esteem. Thus, collective social behavior would be that which reinforces self-perceptions for the majority of the members of a social group or, alternately, the self-perceptions of a powerful and controlling minority. Thus, social rules (folkways and moves) represent behavioral programmers which direct the members of society into those actions which have, in the past, proved successful for maintaining esteem for the majority or controlling minority.

Social rules are learned through socialization, usually beginning in early childhood. The degree to which an individual becomes committed to and internalizes social rules is determined by the amount of self-enhancement that accrues from conformity during socialization. Reinforcement of self-esteem received from significant others in response to behavior which conforms to social rules, increases both an individual's desire to repeat the behavior and his/her perceptions of the rightness of that behavior and the corresponding social rule. When the family or society fails to reward compliance with social rules, however, commitment to those rules is subsequently weak (Hewitt, 1970).

Shame is an emotional experience antithetical to self-enhancement. Thus, fear of shame acts as a socio-psychological tool by which individuals are restrained from breaking social rules. For those rules which have been thoroughly internalized during socialization, fear of self-shaming may be sufficient to induce continued conformity. However, for those rules evidencing less stringent personal commitment, fear of being caught and experiencing social shame may act as a social deterrent. To decrease the likelihood that social rules will be broken, a society can install intensive socialization mechanisms and thereby create protective barriers (fear of shaming) against nonconformity (Sagarin, 1977).

Deviant rule-breaking occurs when life situations arise for which existing rules are inadequate and when mechanisms are available for circumventing self or social shame. Controlled anonymity or secrecy, lying and self-deception all represent common means for avoiding shame. Those social rules which have been most strongly internalized have the greatest potential for evoking shame when transgressed. Therefore, those same rules require the most substantial amounts of deceit, in the event of rule-breaking, to protect the perception of self from denigration (Sagarin, 1977).

TABLE 25.1 Theoretical propositions employed in the development of a comprehensive explanation of deviant subculture formation

Theoretical Perspective	*Proposition*
Self-enhancement	All human behavior, including deviant behavior, is directed toward enhancement of self-esteem.
Anomie	Societies promulgate goals and means of goal attainment; such goals and means may not be equally enhancing for all individuals, thereby motivating a search for alternative behavior patterns.
Functional Deviance	Deviance is a necessary component in all societies, serving clearly to distinguish acceptable behavior (which is self-enhancing for the majority) from unacceptable (deviant) behavior.
Cognitive Consistency/ Dissonance	To alleviate mental discomfort caused by conflicting perceptions of others, mental processes are simplified through categorization of individuals as totally conforming or nonconforming, thereby increasing the strength with which the deviant label is applied to nonconformists.
Self-fulfilling Prophesy	The degree to which a nonconformist identifies with a socially promulgated deviant label depends upon the strength with which that label is applied or proclaimed.
Deviant Labeling	If the nonconformist accepts the deviant label, he/she attempts to alleviate social isolation by seeking the companionship of others with a similar label, thereby forming a deviant subcultural group.
Subcultural Leadership	Mass society imitates subcultural behavior, thereby reducing the differences between the subculture and larger society and initiating social repair.

Anomie theory suggests that all societies promulgate specific goals, as well as means by which those goals can be realized. These institutionalized means vary in the degree to which they are effective in the pursuit of socially approved goals. In those societies with ineffective means, social rules may be broken in order to create new avenues for goal realization. For example, lower class individuals may find their pathway to success blocked by discrimination or lack of financial and educational resources. Thus, deviating methods may be adopted in order to obtain the materialistic acquisitions associated with the goal of upward mobility. Deceit mechanisms would be initiated to forestall self or social shaming as a result of the deviance (or rule breaking) (Merton, 1979).

Douglas (1970) maintained that deviance and respectability are two opposing concepts linked together in the same manner as night versus day, goodness versus evil, life versus death. In other words, deviance (rule-breaking) is unacceptable behavior only to the degree to which acceptable behavior has been defined. Similarly, the functionalist theory of deviance contends that deviant behavior is an integral and necessary component of all societies, serving to delineate clearly the boundaries of acceptable behavior (Dentler & Erickson, 1979; Durkheim, 1979).

By adhering to acceptable behavior (rules) a person can perceive the self as being right and thereby enhance self-esteem. However, rightness is only meaningful if there is concurrently a clear definition of wrongness. Individuals are therefore motivated to promulgate actively their own behavior modes as being right and to do so by pointing out opposite behavior modes as being wrong. Thus, labeling others as being deviant serves to upgrade the self-esteem of rule-conformists. The more effectively that opposing individuals can be tagged as deviant and wrong, the more effectively can the positive label of "rule-abiding" be applied to the self.

It can be seen, then, that acts are not deviant in and of themselves. Acts must first be observed by persons who subscribe to an opposing form of rule-governed behavior, after which the acts (and actors) must then be labeled as deviant by members of that audience. Thus, it is the social audience that inadvertently creates deviance by delineating what is considered acceptable versus unacceptable behavior.

Cognitive consistency (or cognitive dissonance) theory suggests that individuals seek ways to alleviate the mental discomfort caused by conflicting information (Mischel, 1968). For example, if an individual is observed committing some form of deviant, rule-breaking behavior, that behavior is perceived as conflicting with the conformity required for group membership. Cognitive dissonance, or discomfort, results from the perception of a group member whose behavior is apparently predictable (rule-conforming) sometimes and unpredictable (rule-breaking) at other times. To reduce this dissonance and foster consistency of expectations, the sometimes nonconformist is perceived as being deviant in general, thereby strengthening the application of the deviant label to the social transgressor. According to Balch and Kelly (1979), deviance becomes a "master status" which overshadows all information to the contrary.

The degree to which a rule-breaking individual identifies with the deviant label (i.e., self-fulfilling prophesy) depends, in part, upon the degree of social conflagration which his/her nonconformity has caused. The greater the number of individuals who voice agreement with the deviant label, as well as the vociferousness with which that label is proclaimed, the more convinced will be the nonconformist that he/she is in fact, deviant. The mass media, by reporting instances of observed deviance to society at large, serves to foster a social outcry against the rule-breaking and subsequent mass labeling of the deviant. In the words of Tannenbaum. (1979),

> The person becomes the thing he is described as being the parents . . .the police . . . the court . . . .their very enthusiasm defeats their aim. The harder they work to reform the evil the greater the evil grows under their hands. The way out is through a refusal to dramatize the evil. The less said about it the better (pp. 162-163).

Mass labeling serves to isolate the deviant from the more conforming members of society. The interactionist, or labeling, theory of deviance suggests that after an individual acquiesces to a perception of the difference from others, he/she then attempts to alleviate social isolation by seeking the company of persons who are similarly different (Tannenbaum, 1979). The subsequent formation of a deviant subgroup fosters the promulgation of new subcultural rules of conduct supportive of that rule-breaking behavior labeled as deviant by the larger society. Conformity to the social rules of the subculture, defined as right by members of that subgroup, serves to enhance wounded self-perceptions. As with the social rules of the larger society, those of the subculture are likewise enshrouded with a fear of shaming which acts as a deterrent to nonconformity by members of the subculture (Sagarin, 1977).

The presence of subcultures within a society signifies a struggle for supremacy among a number of lifestyles and value systems. Although deviance can be viewed as a creative response to irrelevant, ineffectual social rules, members of society are more likely to perceive nonconformity as a potentially destructive force undermining the security of that which is familiar. Enthusiastic mass media delineations of the activities, lifestyle and appearances associated with the offending subcultures fuel a "moral panic" and lead to an eventual perception of the deviants as "folk devils" Brake, 1985). Clarke, Hall, Jefferson and Roberts (1976) described a moral panic as,

> . . . a spiral in which the social groups who perceive their world and position threatened, identify a responsible enemy and emerge as the vociferous guardian of traditional values (p. 72).

As the publicized conflict between society and subculture escalates, the deviant group often retaliates against the derisive labeling and ridicule with expressions of aggressive countermoralism. After all, to members of the subculture, those members of the larger society are deviating in regards to subcultural social rules and are thus deserving of social shaming. Corresponding with countershaming are counterpride displays, in which symbols of the deviance are arrogantly flaunted (Sagarin, 1977). Eventually, seemingly innocuous symbols may, of themselves, become objects of derision which augment a moral panic, due to association with and use by the deviants (Clarke, 1976).

To summarize the aforementioned process of deviant subculture formation, a situation arises within society for which existing social rules of conduct are inadequate, thus creating motivation for not conforming to or breaking those rules. The social rules, however, are protected by a fear of self and/or social shaming, necessitating the generation of defensive deceptions against shame. If the rules are transgressed and if the nonconforming behavior is observed by members of the social audience, society is alerted to the attack against the established social rule structure. Subsequent delineation of the so-called wrong behavior serves to define more clearly the social rules, or right behavior, as adhered to by the majority. The initial perceptions of a deviant act evolve into perceptions of the individual as being deviant. Deviant labeling isolates the individual and encourages the seeking out of others similarly labeled. The subsequent formation of a deviant subgroup results in the generation of new social rules protected by a fear of shaming. As the deviants cohere, the subculture is perceived (by members of the larger society) as being a threat to social stability. Symbols which visually distinguish members of the subculture from members of the larger society serve to accentuate the ensuing social conflict.

As previously discussed, the presence of disparity between socially promulgated goals and means for achieving goals motivates deviant rule-breaking and subsequent formation of subcultures. Brake (1974) has suggested that the specific *nature* of the frustration experienced, due to conflict between goals and means, depends upon the social class background of the actor. For example, a lower class child, having been socialized into the value system of the working class (emphasizing toughness, excitement, autonomy and fate), is confronted in the public schools with the middle class means to success (control of aggression, deferred gratification, respect for property, ambition and responsibility). Being uncommitted to these new prescriptions, the lower class child fails to succeed and the lower class rules which are adopted in early childhood prove ineffectual. On the other hand, a middle class child may be subjected to goal expectations (often the academic or athletic hopes of parents and teachers) which are beyond his/her natural abilities. In other words, no effectual means for success are available, given the excessive goals. Wealthy youth may be promised materialistic goal realization in the form of allowances or inheritances, regardless of individual achievement, thereby negating the value of the means whereby goals are usually obtained (Hewitt, 1970).

Because the frustrations which motivate deviance spring from differing social orientations, the subsequent subcultures tend to reflect specific class identifications. As Rubington and Weinberg (1973) observed, "The crucial condition for the emergence of new cultural forms is the existence . . . of a number of actors with similar patterns of adjustment" (p.233). Likewise, most nonconforming individuals do not deviate from all of the social rules learned during socialization but only from those which somehow pertain to the frustrated need for self-esteem. Thus, some social class rule orientations are carried over into subculture formation, strengthening the identification of the subculture with a particular social class value system.

Individuals who are attracted to subcultural membership select a group which 1) is congruent with their social class and educational background, 2) offers an apparent solution to the conflict between social goals and means of goal attainment, and 3) presents an enhancing identity in regards to self-image. Adolescence is both a time when subcultures seem to have a special attraction and a time for serious searching for identity (Roach, 1969). Especially for lower class youth, a subculture can provide opportunities for acquiring self-enhancement through achieved (rather than ascribed) status.

Brake (1985) and Clarke (1976) have discussed subcultural solutions to social contradictions (between goals and means) as being magical rather than real. In other words, subcultural solutions more frequently reflect pathways to temporary escapism than bona fide alternatives. (In this light, subcultural solutions are congruent with those forms of self-deception used to reduce sensations of nonconformist shame.) The construction of a subcultural identity detached from and in a plane beyond the frustrating reality of class membership, occupation and/or school represents one such magical solution to social inequities. By lifting the subcultural identity out of the social milieu from which it spawned, new and more attainable criteria can be devised for evaluating and enhancing self-perceptions.

Youthful subcultures tend to be masculine oriented and controlled with females acting as peripheral appendages. Brake (1985) suggested that, while males search for alternative identities through subcultural membership, conformity to the social rule of marriage remains of primary importance to many females, especially lower class girls. Therefore, these females tend to maintain a traditional feminine role even within the subculture and to acquiesce to male supremacy. McRobbie and Garber (1976) contended that females have marginal roles in youthful subcultures because they have more central roles within a different range of activities (i.e., home-related). As role alternatives become increasingly available to females, female youth may also participate more fully in the subcultural identity search.

SUBCULTURAL APPEARANCE

Subcultural dress can be perceived to be a form of conspicuous consumption in that clothing is consciously and conspicuously used by members to communicate group identity as well as the values, beliefs and focal concerns of the subculture. In addition, a unique subcultural appearance suggests disassociation from the larger culture while simultaneously acting to unify group members.

As previously discussed, subcultures can provide magical solutions to the inequities of life by lifting the individual out of an identity defined by traditional social class criteria. The new identity revolves around subcultural rules and expectations which are within attainable reach of the members. Subcultural dress serves to add credibility to the new identity while enhancing the unreal or escapist characteristics of the subcultural role. By looking like, as well as acting like, someone from outside the boundaries of the larger culture, the individual proclaims his ineligibility for evaluation under the existing social rule system—a system which, in some way, is perceived to be a threat to self-esteem. Disassociation from the larger social group, then, is communicated through adherence to subcultural dress.

Similarity in dress among members of a subculture serves to designate the boundaries of the group (Clarke, 1976; Clarke et al., 1976). Joseph and Alex (1972) have suggested that through group identification a particular mode of appearance becomes a totemic emblem of that group. A totem, by broad definition, is an object believed to be related to a group and to embody the characteristics of that group. Thus the dress of a subculture is totemic to the degree to which 1) it is perceived to be intrinsic to the subculture and 2) it symbolically reflects the values, beliefs and focal concerns of the group. Brake (1985) used the term "homology" to discuss the close fit between the material objects of a subculture (including items of clothing and adornment) and the characteristic behavior of group members. Behavior, of course, is the outward manifestation of values, beliefs and focal concerns.

As an embodiment of group values, beliefs and focal concerns, the components of subcultural dress reflect symbolic meanings which make statements about the subculture. The specific meanings of subcultural dress may be unintelligible to persons outside the group, however, in that the symbolism may represent a form of "argot" (i.e., the secret jargon of a subgroup) (Brake, 1985). While a subcultural style of appearance may suggest chaos to members of the larger society, to those who are cognizant of the visual jargon, subcultural appearance reveals a meaningful order. The symbolic meanings of subcultural appearance are always most apparent to the initial innovators of a subculture (Hebdige, 1979). For persons who later join, the subcultural appearance symbolizes group identity in general. However, the specific meanings originally associated with individual components of the subcultural style are less apparent to these late arrivers.

As previously discussed, the frustrations which motivate deviance spring from differing social class situations, and therefore subsequent subcultures tend to reflect specific class identifications. Since most nonconforming individuals do not deviate from all social class rules, some social class orientations are carried over into the subculture. Thus, by reflecting the values, beliefs and focal concerns of the subculture, subcultural dress also contains symbolic components associated with aspects of the larger parent social class. Hebdige (1979) has maintained that "subcultural styles are mutations and extensions of existing codes rather than the pure expression of creative drives . . . they are meaningful mutations" (pp. 130-131).

It is the *difference* between subcultural dress and that of the larger parent culture that is the most significant visual factor in subcultural style. It is the difference which portrays the separation of the subculture from its parent social class. Greater visual difference between the styles characteristic of the subculture and the larger society suggests greater rapture between the two groups in terms of values, beliefs and focal concerns. It is the *nature* of these appearance differences, however, that symbolizes the reason for the separation or, in other words, which values, beliefs and focal concerns represent the point of contention.

As noted, subcultural dress contains many symbolic components congruent with aspects (including appearance) of the larger parent culture. A "bricoleur" is someone who deliberately rearranges selected symbolic components of language (here, nonverbal language) to create a new and different message (Clarke, 1976). Hebdige (1979) related this concept of bricolage to radical Surrealism, in which the juxtaposition of "two apparently incompatible realities" creates an "explosive junction" (p. 106). Thus, the manipulation of components of dress to juxtapose seemingly incompatible cues (as defined by appearance norms of the larger society) creates a visual explosive junction symbolic of the seeming incompatibility of the two groups and their potentially explosive differences.

Klapp (1972) labeled this subcultural emphasis on visual difference as "style rebellion," defined as the "use of fashion more or less deliberately as symbolic protest, an effort to shock . . ." (p. 330). Thus, style rebellion is merely a form of "counterpride display." The deviant group retaliates against derisive labeling from the larger culture by pridefully flaunting visual symbols of their deviance. Such flaunting of symbols can eventually extend social contempt from the deviant individual to the symbol of deviance. Thus, not unlike the behavior of Pavlov's dog, society begins to exhibit intolerance and persecution at the sight of a visual cue of deviance rather than waiting for observation of the deviant act.

Subculture leadership theory, as it pertains to fashion change, suggests that clothing designers find inspiration in the dress styles of cultural subgroups (Sproles, 1985). This inspiration is then transferred into clothing products for mass consumption. Once subcultural styles are mass consumed, they no longer communicate difference between the subculture and larger society, thereby negating the most important communicative aspect of subcultural dress. In the words of Klapp (1972) "style invasion" threatens the identity of a subculture when "the number of new adopters threatens to swamp the original group and wipe out its boundaries" (p. 332). Style invasion thereby acts to repair the divided social order by reducing the difference factor.

More complete social recuperation, or repair of the divided social order, depends upon 1) the use of subcultural symbols by mass consumers as well as 2) the relabeling of subcultural deviant behavior as being acceptable (Hebdige, 1979). Sagarin (1977) identified this repair process as the pathway by which social rules are changed. A subculture promulgates an exaggerated form of nonconformity into social awareness, eliciting an initial defensive action followed by gradual social acquiescence. Thus, subcultural dress can be perceived as a motivating force behind the change of fashion and appearance norms, introducing seemingly incompatible styles which mass society may initially reject but eventually imitate to some degree.

Working Class Example: The Teddy Boys

"Through the dank mews of Shoreditch and over the littered bomb sites of Stepney slouch some of the nattiest young men in Britain. They are Edwardians—the dead end kids of London." Thus were the Teddy Boys (or Edwardians) introduced by *Newsweek* (Britain: . . . , p. 47) in 1954.

The dreary postwar British environment fostered improved economic opportunities for working class youth. Realizing a little spending money, these youth idled away leisure hours in streetcorner crap games or local dance halls (Britain: . . ., 1954). These activities alone, however, introduced little excitement, status or acclaim into lives overshadowed by the pursuit of dead-end unskilled or semi-skilled jobs.

The Teddy Boys represented an example of working class youth who, socialized into the value and belief systems of lower social strata, found their pursuit of self-enhancement stymied in a world governed by middle class norms. Deviance (rule breaking) and subsequent social labeling fostered the formation of a subculture in which new rules sanctioned nonconformist (and occasionally violent) activities, deemed to be self-enhancing (Great Britain . . ., 1956).

To glamorize their leisure hours, to enhance self-esteems, and in keeping with the trickle-down theory of fashion diffusion (Sproles, 1985),these working class youth adopted a postwar dress style prevalent among young English men of higher social status: the Edwardian suit. This Edwardian costume of the early 1950s represented a reinterpretation of a turn-of-the-century male dress style. The most recognizable feature of the Teddy Boy version included a coat with velvet collar, a narrow tie and slim drainpipe trousers. Lower class affiliation with this Edwardian dress, however, soon motivated the middle and upper classes to abandon the style (Jefferson, 1976) Thus, the Edwardian suit became a symbol of subcultural separation from the larger society by default.

British newspapers faithfully reported Teddy Boy deviance as well as their association with the foppish Edwardian dress (Damage. . ., 1954). The *Tailor and Cutter*, a tailoring trade journal, lamented that

> by a series of vicious coincidences all the old ladies who have been beaten up lately, all the modest young men who have had their faces slashed, and all the poor little pussy cats who have had tin cans tied to their tails have been beset by wicked young dandies in Edwardian clothes (Edwardian? . . . , 1953, p. 2).

These accounts served to confirm the rightness of the larger conforming society by pointing out the wrongness of the youthful deviants. In addition, the descriptions aided in the visual categorization of the deviant. By describing the outer container of the inner deviant nature, the Teddy Boy became a publicly recognizable entity. Contempt for the Teddy Boy's violent acts therefore expanded to encompass the symbol of his deviant group: the Edwardian suit. An editorial writer commented that "no doubt dozens of young men who like to wear drainpipe trousers and bootlace ties are law-abiding but their uniform has been disgraced. They should either discard it or share the disgrace" (Rock & Cohen, 1970, p. 298).

For the Teddy Boys, the Edwardian costume represented a magical solution to their low status position in British society. Donning this male symbol of upper class attire visually separated the Ted from the traditional working class environment. Thus, congruent with the concepts of totemism and homology (i.e., the embodiment of cultural values, beliefs and focal concerns), the Edwardian suit symbolized subcultural frustrations concerning lower class status and subsequent desires for social mobility and self-enhancement opportunities. The coat with velvet collar and narrow tie suggested a lifestyle of leisure, rather than physical labor. The surrealistic explosive junction of incompatible objects could then be perceived as being the placement of a seemingly elegant costume against the backdrop of a working class neighborhood.

A typical Edwardian suit cost about $90, paid in installments from an unskilled or semi-skilled laborer's salary. Although the Ted was not above attacking an enemy was brass studded belts and bicycle chains, care was always taken not to damage the magical (and expensive) Edwardian suit (Lights Out . . , 1954). If apprehended by the police, Teddy Boys reportedly surrendered without a struggle to avoid spoiling their elegant dress. Why did the Teddy Boys so highly value their costume? According to a British boys' club leader, "It makes him feel smart—important" (Britain: . . ., 1954, p. 48).

Media coverage not only introduced the Teddy Boys to the public but served to introduce the Ted to himself as well (Rock & Cohen, 1970). Social stereotyping clearly delineated just how to dress and behave in order to conform to subcultural Teddy Boy rules. The Edwardian dresser was also informed by newspapers and magazine articles that, due to his clothing choice, he automatically possessed a socially predetermined nature. For example, according to the chairman of the Dartford Juvenile Court, Edwardian suits were ". . . flashy, cheap and nasty, and stamp the wearer as a particularly undesirable type" (Ridiculous. . ., 1954, p. 4). Such deviant labeling and emphasis upon a supposedly uniform style of dress acted to increase solidarity among the Teddy Boys by widening social and visual differences from the larger culture.

The moral panic which ensued isolated Teddy Boys from the activities of conforming, respectable youth. Exclusion was as much upon the basis of Edwardian appearance, however, as upon evidence of deviant behavior (Town Warns . . . , 1954). For example, the manager of a dance hall in New Cross informed a group of youth: "You cannot come in. You're not properly dressed—and you know it. You will not be allowed in if you wear velvet lapels, drainpipe trousers, slim jim ties or other Teddy Boy outfits" (Rock & Cohen, 1970, p. 298). Similarly, a committee of the Osford City Council recommended that Teddy Boys be banned from dances in the town hall, with decisions for exclusion being made on the basis of "exaggerated Edwardian styles of dress" (Proposed . . . , 1955, p. 4). Thus the mere wearing of *symbols* had become the basis for labeling, isolation and contempt.

British Teddy Boys were most dominant from 1953 through 1955. Thereafter, working class youth began migrating into a diversity of other deviant subcultural groups, donning new esoteric styles. Thus, contrary to the proposed theoretical perspective, visual difference between the Teds and the larger society did not disappear due to subcultural leadership in fashion. The Edwardian suit had been mass produced *before* the Teddy Boys adopted the style, not as a result of their identification with it. This finding has suggested that social repair due to subcultural leadership may not be initiated in cases of lower class deviant groups.

Middle Class Example: The Hippies

The Hippies composed a middle and upper class youthful subculture whose members began "dropping out" of conventional society during the early 1960s. By 1967, there were an estimated 300,000 Hippies in the United States alone (Brown, 1967; Feigelson, 1970). The Hippie movement, paralleling the previously discussed pattern of deviance and subculture formation, emerged from a perceived incompatibility between socially established goals (as reflected in the materialistic American Dream) and means of goal attainment (hard work, deferred gratification and submergence of individualistic identity). However, unlike the Teddy Boy situation (in which the means were ineffectual for realization of socially approved success), Hippies perceived the goals to be incompatible with the perceived high cost of the means. Was "success" worth working always for tomorrow and becoming a cardboard replica of other success-seekers? Rejecting the means for goal attainment and devaluing the goals themselves, the Hippie subculture devised new social rules for experiencing life and evaluating human worth.

Paramount within Hippie philosophy was an insistence upon personal authenticity. Individuals were encouraged to express their true selves, rather than merely to act as mobilizing forces behind a collection of role masks (Berger, 1967). Since social roles help define identity, the Hippie rejection of roles as a component of self led to a shadowy internal perception of personal identity. This lack of well defined identity boundaries, rather than being a source of concern, symbolized for the Hippie a potential for identity growth and expanded, transcendental awareness of self. (According to Willis [1976], this search for true self, through transcendence, also motivated the

Hippie use of drugs.) Adherence to prescribed social roles, then, was believed artificially to compartmentalize and to limit self-realization (Willis, 1978).

Congruent with the search for true self was the Hippie emphasis upon unrestrained self-expression or freedom from all inhibition. According to Abbie Hoffman, a Hippie spokesman, the power to forbid was the only thing to be forbidden within the new society (Feigelson, 1970). Similarly, the Hippie movement advocated active participation rather than passive spectating, as applied to all forms of self-expression. A person did not have to be an accomplished artist, musician or dancer before painting, singing or dancing. The personal pleasure derived from self-expression, no matter how crude, far exceeded the value of the resulting product. As stated by Davis (1967), "All men are artists, and who cares that some are better at it than others; we can all have fun!" (p.13).

The emphasis upon the right of all individuals to express and be accepted as their true selves promulgated the underlying theme of love within the Hippie subculture. A true Hippie, one who had successfully realized and internalized the all-accepting doctrine of Hippie philosophy, indiscriminately exuded love for all human beings. In innocence, the Hippies believed that unconditional love would eventually bring societies to realize the errors of their ways; love would cure all social ills (Dropouts. . ., 1967).

> And thus in love we have declared the purpose of our hearts plainly, without flattery, expecting love, and the same sincerity from you, without grumbling, or quarrelling, being Creatures of Your own Image and mould, intending no other matter herein, but to observe the Law of righteous action, endeavoring to shut out of the Creation, the cursed thing, called particular Propriety, which is the cause of all wars, blood-shed, theft, and enslaving Laws, that hold people under misery (Sabine, 1941, p.276).

Thus wrote Gerald Winstanley, a member of the seventeenth century British Diggers. Adopting the Digger name and philosophy of love, the Hippie Diggers (of San Francisco, Los Angeles, Boston and New York) distributed free food to persons in need. They also maintained a Free Store, where anyone (Hippie or non-Hippie) could obtain clothing, furniture, books and other items free of charge (Free Store. . ., 1967). Thus, some Hippies attempted to push their concept of love beyond the realm of mere philosophical rhetoric (The Hippies are . . . , 1967).

The Hippie lifestyle also reflected elected poverty in rebellion against the materialism of the larger culture. Paralleling this with the exploration for identity, Davis (1967) wrote " . . . they proclaim that happiness and a meaningful life are not to be found in things, but in the cultivation of the self and by an intensive exploration of inner sensibilities with like-minded others" (p.13).

Hippie poverty was augmented by the perception of employment as being a sporadic activity for the purpose of occasionally earning "bread," rather than as a means to self-enhancement (Buff, 1970; Dropouts. . ., 1967). Eight-to-five employment was seen as artificially compartmentalizing time in the same way that roles dissected self-identity. Also undermining commitment to any form of work ethic among the Hippies was the preponderant subcultural enchantment with the here and now (Berger, 1967). At the same time that Hippie youth were questioning the value of sought after goals, they were also facing the fact that future plans could easily be obliterated in a nuclear holocaust. Thus, they were propelled by their environment into stressing the importance of experiencing the immediate moment.

The clothing associated with the Hippie subculture did, at first glance, appear to be a meaningless, unpredictable assortment of diverse items and styles. Males, sporting beards and long hair, dressed in tie-dyed shirts, T-shirts with subcultural logos, leather vests, faded and tattered jeans, army jackets, vintage hats, beads, embroidered headbands, white sheets, diverse theatrical costumes, sandals and/or bare feet. Females, often having waist-length hair, wore long "granny" dresses, jeans, peasant blouses, miniskirts, blanket capes, ragged furs, beads, sandals and/or bare feet. Handmade belts, pendants, wire-rimmed glasses, uniquely colored sunglasses and body paints were adopted by both sexes (Buff, 1970; Dropouts..., 1967; Wolf, 1968). Further analysis of such conglomerated appearances, however, reveals the esoteric nature of Hippie dress.

Congruent with the concepts of totemism and homology (i.e., embodiment of cultural values, beliefs and focal concerns), the Hippie appearance symbolically communicated major aspects of the subcultural philosophy. The wide assortment of clothing styles associated with Hippie appearance was, in itself, indicative of the emphasis upon freedom of expression and search for identity. Under the new subcultural rules it was acceptable to appear in any manner of dress as long as that appearance was an authentic expression of the self or search for the self (as opposed to the rule-conforming uniforms behind which the "squares" were believed to hide). Since it was the pleasure of self-expression that was of uppermost importance rather than the end product of that expression, the success of an outfit was defined in terms of its fun rather than by aesthetic or functional criteria.

The conscious election of poverty as a lifestyle (thereby "dropping out" of middle class materialism) often included a conscious selection of appearance cues symbolic of the Hippie identification with the oppressed. Tattered and faded clothing, bare feet, tangled and uncombed hair, and an unwashed body sufficiently separated the Hippie from any suggestion of affluence. Elected poverty, as well as lack of concern for the future, reduced wardrobe planning and maintenance to a minimum. The unpredictable assortment of costume items which made up a particular outfit, rather than being a conscious expression of self, may at times have been a reflection of only those things which were readily available for wear. Wolf (1968) observed that as the Hippie movement progressed and indigence became more fact than choice, the clothing of Hippies began to appear authentically shabby. Increasing numbers of the subculture availed themselves of the Diggers' charity, acquiring nondescript clothing from the bins in the Free Store.

It was the idiosyncratic nature of Hippie dress which most clearly differentiated members of that subculture from the larger society. Although the nature of the difference symbolized the philosophical concerns of the subculture (as discussed above), the mere fact of visual difference represented a conscious effort on the part of subculture to show disassociation from the larger society.

Several aspects of Hippie deviance were of particular interest to the mass media, namely their use of drugs and their liberal sexual attitudes. While publicizing these apparently newsworthy characteristics, the media also served to delineate for society the appearance for deviance. Thus, deviance was provided with an identifiable embodiment (Dropouts . . . , 1967; Inside . . ., 1967).

As occurred with the Teddy Boy and his suit, social contempt for Hippie deviance expanded to encompass the visual appearance of the deviant group. During the ensuing moral panic, the components of Hippie appearance were perceived as symbols of the nonconformist threat against social stability: tattered clothing was indicted as a threat to the traditional work ethic; dirtiness was seen to undermine the traditional definition of respectability; while masculine long hair and beaded jewelry reportedly served to destroy traditional sex roles.

Long hair on men represented an especially pronounced catalyst for social contempt, and the presence of this one visual cue alone became the basis for labeling and isolation. The "Establishment" even initiated a counter-attack—a publicity campaign designed to stamp out long hair. Billboards began to appear along American highway, reading "Beautify America: Cut Your Hair." In a retaliatory move against this social derision, the Hippies flaunted their long hair and other symbols of differentness. In such a showing of counterpride display, one Hippie male stated: "If you ask me why I have my hair long, I'd say, principally because I like it . . . and to kick society in the bollocks . . . wave my fingers at them . . . " (Willis, 1978, p.96).

Bricolage, the rearrangement of known symbols to create a new message or meaning, was a common factor in Hippie appearance. No single component of Hippie dress was new, or never before known, but the innovative combination of those components successfully created new messages concerning social and economic philosophy. In many cases, the rearrangement of cues incorporated the Surrealistic combination of seemingly incompatible components (as defined by the appearance norms of the larger society), resulting in an explosive junction. It was the junction of incompatibility which begged for the attention of society and, once obtained, served to flaunt a suggested indifference to social rules. For example, by the standards of society, long hair (a feminine appearance cue) on a male body represented the combination of incongruent factors. As Hippie deviance became more clearly defined and publicly proclaimed, the incompatibility of long hair on a male body became a symbol of explosive incompatibility and polarization between Hippies and non-Hippies. To a similar but often lesser degree, the combination of other incongruent appearance cues served to flaunt the Hippie disregard for social rules: a brocade jacket worn with faded and patched jeans, a heavy wool cape worn in the summer, bare feet in sandals during the winter, a shirt cut from an American flag, or a Roman toga on a twentieth century metropolitan street corner.

Mass media coverage of the Hippie subculture not only served to inflame public indignation but also assisted in the eventual creation of "plastic" (imitation) Hippies (The flowering. . . , 1967; Hippies. . .,1967; Inside. . . 1967). Youngsters and oldsters alike were provided with a visual formula whereby to flirt with the appearance of liberalism. Weekend Hippies emerged, only to disappear again on Monday mornings. Suggestions of Hippiedom began to peek from the pages of slick, high fashion publications. In keeping with the subcultural leadership theory of fashion change, invasion of the Hippie style had begun (Party. . . , 1967). With a mass consumption of

Hippie style, the line of demarcation between that subculture and the larger society was blurred. The labeling of "deviant" became less applicable on the basis of appearance cues alone. Flaunting deviant symbols before the face of society became less effective toward initiation, society acted to mend the rift and recuperate.

In 1968, The American Hippie movement evolved into the Youth International Party (Yippies) in response to a Presidential election. Social love was abandoned for social politics. Apolitical Hippies left the movement and the cities, searching for peace and expressive freedom in the agrarian countryside (Here come..., 1968). In 1969, a few remaining militant Yippies were dubbed the "Crazies," a term that in Underground vernacular ironically came to mean anarchists who refused to accept discipline (Feigelson, 1970).

DISCUSSION AND SUMMARY

Style rebellion (as applied to clothing and adornment) represents an indigenous component within the social formation and dissolution of deviant subcultures. Appearance factors initially serve and add credibility to the magical or escapist identity sought by members of a deviant subculture by symbolizing the new group's values, beliefs and focal concerns. Those same appearance cues later provide a descriptive embodiment of the deviance to facilitate the social labeling and isolation of the nonconformist. Those same cues are then employed by the subculture in counterpride displays, during which the symbols of deviance are publicly flaunted. And finally, in situations of middle and upper class deviant subcultures, those same cues are eventually initiated by members of mass society, thereby undermining the component of difference between the two groups and initiating social repair.

The results of this investigation suggested that the social class origin of a subculture may determine the process whereby an appearance different to that of the larger society is acquired and/or lost. The Teddy Boys actually sought visual *similarity* with the rest of British male society by imitating a dress style worn by individuals of higher status. The Hippies, on the other hand, intentionally pursued visual difference as a symbol of disassociation. The Teddy Boy appearance disappeared due to a change of clothing style by members of the subculture. The Hippie appearance of difference disappeared due to an imitative change by the larger society.

Applying self-enhancement concepts to the above mentioned class differentiations, it can be suggested that the collective behavior of both the subculture and the larger society were directed toward reinforcing self-esteem. In the instance of the lower class Teddy Boys, the subculture sought self-enhancement through visual identification with the upper classes (i.e., the adoption of the upper class Edwardian suit) after which members of the larger society sought self-enhancement through visual disassociation with the lower class (i.e., abandonment of the Edwardian suit). Once the potential of the suit had been thereby diminished, lower class youth changed to more enhancing appearance alternatives.

In the Hippie example, the upper and middle class subculture sought self-enhancement through disassociation from a society perceived to advocate demeaning values (i.e., materialism, aggression, etc.) through adoption of an esoteric appearance of differentness. Subsequently, as liberalism became respectable the members of the larger society enhanced self-esteem by emulating the subculture, thereby reducing visual difference between the two groups. Thus, it might be concluded that the trickle down theory of fashion is operative in cases of lower class subculture appearance, whereas the subcultural leadership theory of fashion is most applicable to upper and middle class subcultures. Further studies are needed to test these ideas.

The close ties between appearance cues and the formation of deviant subcultures suggest a relationship between the variability permitted in dress within a given society and the prevalence of subcultures within the same society. One might expect that within those societies which strictly limit variability in dress (i.e., enforce uniform clothing) the formation of deviant subcultures would be correspondingly limited. However, further investigation of subcultural appearance is needed also to ascertain the degree to which subculture formation and dissolution is actually dependent upon these factors.

REFERENCES

Balch, R. & Kelly, D. (1979). Reactions to deviance in a junior high school. In D. Kelly (Ed.). *Deviant behavior* (pp.24-41). New York: St. Martin's Press.

Berger, B. (1967, December). Hippie morality: More old than new. *Trans-Action, 5*, 19-23.

Brake, M. (1974, December). The skinheads. *Youth and Society, 6*, 179-200.

Brake, M. (1985). *Comparative youth culture.* London: Routledge & Kegan Paul.

Britain: Foppish dead-enders. (1954, May 17). *Newsweek, 43*, 47-48.

Brown, J. (1967). *The Hippies.* New York: Time.

Buff, S. (1970). Greasers, Dupers and Hippies: Three responses to the adult world. In L. Howe (Ed.). *The white majority* (pp. 60-77). New York: Random House.

Clarke, J. (1976). Style. In S, Hall & Y. Jefferson (Eds.), *Resistance through rituals* (pp. 175-191). London: Hutchinson.

Clarke, J. Hall, S., Jefferson, T. & Roberts, B. (1976). Subcultures, cultures and class. In S. Hall & T. Jefferson (Eds.), *Resistance through rituals* (pp. 9-74). London: Hutchinson.

Damage in southend train. (1954, July 5). *The Times,* p. 3.

Davis, F. (1967, December). Why all of us may be Hippies someday. *Trans-Action, 5*, 10-18.

Dentler, R., & Erikson, K. (1979). The functions of deviance in groups. In D. Kelly (Ed.), *Deviant Behavior* (pp. 56-69). New York: St. Martin's Press.

Douglas, J. (1970). *Deviance and respectability.* New York: Basic Books.

Dropouts with a mission. (1967, February 6). *Newsweek, 69*, 92-95.

Durkheim, E. (1979). The normal and the pathological. In D. Kelly (Ed.), *Deviant behavior* (pp. 51-55). New York: St. Martin's Press.

Edwardian? Cut it out. (1953, November 14). *Daily Herald,* p. 2.

Feigelson, N. (1970). *The underground revolution: Hippies, Yippies and others.* New York: Funk & Wagnalls.

The flowering of the Hippies. (1967, September). *Atlantic Monthly, 220*, 63-72.

Free Store. (1967, October 14). *New Yorker, 43*, 49-51.

Great Britain: The Teds (1956, September 24). *Time, 68* 27-28.

Hebdige, D. (1979). *Subculture: The meaning of style.* London: Methuen and Co.

Here come the Yippies. (1968, March 11). *Newsweek*, 71, 68.

Hewitt, J. (1970). *Social stratification and deviant behavior*. New York: Random House.

Hippies —a passing fad? (1967, October 23). *U.S. News and World Report*, 63, 42-44.

The Hippies are coming (1967, June 12). *Newsweek*, 69 28-29.

Inside the Hippie revolution (1967, August 22). *Look, 31*, 58-61, 63-64.

Jefferson T. (1976). Cultural responses to the Teds. In S. Hall & T. Jefferson (Eds.), *Resistance through rituals* (pp. 81-86). London: Hutchison.

Joseph, N., & Alex, N. (1972, January). The uniform: A sociological perspective. *American Journal of Sociology, 77*, 719-730.

Klapp, O. (1972). *Currents and unrest*. New York: Holt, Rinehart & Winston.

Lights out, petting aboard Teddy train. (1954, May 24). *Daily Herald*, p. 5.

McRobbie, A., & Garber, J. (1976). Girls and subcultures. In S. Hall & T. Jefferson (Eds.), *Resistance through rituals* (pp. 209-222). London: Hutchinson.

Merton, R. (1979). Social structure and anomie. In D. Kelly (Ed.), *Deviant behavior* (pp. 110-121). New York: St. Martin's Press.

Mischel, W. (1968). *Personality and assessment*, New York: John Wiley & Sons.

Party face put-on. (1967, November 28). *Look,* 31, 52-55. Proposed dance ban on Teddy boys. (1955, September 30). *The Times*, p. 4.

Ridiculous Edwardian suit. (1954, March 25). *The Times*, p. 4.

Roach, M. (1969, November). Adolescent dress. *Journal of Home Economics, 61*, 693-697.

Rock P., & Cohen S. (1970). The Teddy boy. In V. Bogdanor & R. Skidelsky (Eds.), *The age of affluence, 1951-1964*. London: Macmillan.

Rubington, E., & Weinberg, M. (1973). *Deviance: The interactionist perspective*. New York: Macmillan.

Sabine, G. (1941). *The works of Gerrard Winstanley*. Ithaca, NY: Cornell University Press.

Sagarin, E. (1977). *Deviance and social change*. London: Sage.

Sirgy, M. (1982, December). Self concept in consumer behavior: A critical review. *Journal of Consumer Research, 9*, 287-300.

Sproles, G. (1985). Behavioral science theories of fashion. In M. Solomon (Ed.), *The psychology of fashion* (pp. 55-70). Lexington, MA: D.C. Heath.

Tannenbaum, F. (1979). Definition and dramatization of evil. In D. Kelly (Ed.), *Deviant behavior* (pp. 160-165). New York: St. Martin's Press.

Town warns Teddy Hooligans. (1954, May 25). *Daily Herald*, p. 5.

Willis, P. (1976). The cultural meaning of drug use. In S. Hall & T. Jefferson (Eds.), *Resistance through rituals* (pp. 106-118). London: Hutchinson.

Willis P. (1978), *Profane culture*, London: Routledge & Keagan Paul.

Wolf, L. (1968). *Voices from the love generation*. Boston: Little, Brown and Co.

Summary and Discussion

In this section we have viewed the juvenile delinquent in three common collectivities which can supply the companions, catalyst, and context for his or her illegal conduct. The gang, the family, and the youth subculture not only represent influential reference groups that help shape motives, attitudes, values, personality, and character of youths, but are often etiologically relevant to deviant behavior.

Frederick Thrasher's landmark book, *The Gang,* led the way for an extensive series of studies focusing on the inner city, lower-class aggregate of youths who, in their poverty and alienation, develop a reactive and delinquent subculture. According to Thrasher and numerous others, youths join gangs because of economic and status frustration, to attain friendship networks, to demonstrate defiance of parents, schools, and other traditional authorities, and out of fear and vulnerability in a tough neighborhood. While much gang interaction may be relatively innocuous and recreational, the solidarity of the membership and the unique and defiant values of the gang subculture tend to reinforce and reward delinquent behavior. During the 1980s, the size and illegal activities of adolescent street gangs in Los Angeles, Chicago, Miami, and other cities have rapidly expanded, eliciting widespread community alarm. These contemporary, central city gangs are characterized by sophisticated and lucrative drug franchising and homicidal violence.

The second reading in Part Three, "Delinquency is Still Group Behavior . . ." is by Maynard Erickson and Gary Jensen, who empirically broadened the scope of inquiry beyond the organized gang subculture. Erickson and Jensen present evidence to support their contention that most delinquency is committed in small social groups. While there is some variation in group dynamics according to type of offense, they found that females are generally more social than males in their delinquent escapades.

While collective behavior is more generally applied by sociologists to fads, fashions, panics, riots, and social movements, Lewis Yablonsky's article "The Delinquent Gang as a Near-Group" theoretically argues that inner city gang activity also, is often another form of collective behavior. Yablonsky concluded that the gang is organizationally and functionally midway between the formally organized social group and the unruly mob. If Yablonsky's thesis is correct, it would follow that some of the usual explanations of collective behavior might be applicable to gang behavior.

For example, mass hysteria, mob lynchings, and other spontaneous and ordinarily unreasonable public outbursts are often explained by collective behaviorists with the contagion theory. According to contagion theory, human emotions are "contagious" under some circumstances and can quickly sweep through a crowd and elicit extraordinary levels of fear, anger, or even criminal behavior. Thus, some of the especially wanton, vicious, and confounding conduct of street gangs may be partially traced to an overwhelming emotional contagion motivating gang members.

A whole new dimension was added to the study of gang delinquency by Howard and Barbara Myerhoff and other scholars who proved that gang delinquency is not solely a lower-class phenomenon. Although the social class stratification system has long been a fruitful area of sociological inquiry, with similarities and differences in social class subcultures and lifestyles well established, the comparative analysis of social class gang delinquency is rather recent. In the Myerhoffs' article, "Field Observation of Middle Class Gangs," it becomes clear that both lower and middle-class youngsters engage in collective delinquency. However, the deviance of middle-class youths was more likely to center on activities involving automobiles and was carried out with an attitude of casual mischief. Perhaps the most intriguing class difference in delinquency lies in the societal perception and reaction to middle-class misbehavior. The favored middle-class youths and the adults in their milieu rationalized and accepted much illegal conduct as temporary, harmless and nonthreatening to the promising educational and occupational futures projected for these youths.

Investigators seeking to track down the original causes of juvenile delinquency have been repeatedly drawn back to the delinquent's family as a social context and as etiologically relevant. The biological family is the primary social group for nearly every child and must bear a major responsibility for the youth's successful or unsuccessful internalization of societal standards of behavior. It has often been suggested that the effectiveness of this socialization process for youths can be altered and distorted by certain unhappy events and circumstances that can occur within the family (e.g., parental battles, divorce, spouse and child abuse, and educational and economic deprivation).

Two articles in Part Three address inner-family relationships as they might retard or encourage offspring delinquency: "Parents, Peers, and Delinquent Action..."by Gary Jensen, and "Family Relationships and Delinquency" by Stephen Cernkovich and Peggy Giordano. The independent variables examined include parental supervision and support, the child's positive attachment to parents, intimate communication, and caring and trust. These authors point to how parental failure in these important child-rearing skills can indirectly generate subsequent delinquent behavior.

The last two articles in Part Three deal with the youth subculture in the United States which manifests itself with distinctive fads, fashions, musical taste, language, and even values and ideology that often contrast sharply with those generally espoused by older generations. In "The Youth Subculture: The Hippies of Haight-Ashbury," Jack Bynum's foray into the hippie counterculture of the 1960s leaves us with one of many colorful descriptions of an extreme element of American youths at that time. Bynum found a set of fascinating and paradoxical set of behaviorisms. For example, the hippies alternated between paralyzing apathy and frenetic hyperactivity; between brazen deviance from societal norms and rigid overconformity with one another; between public defiance and a private cry for help. While the hippies of the 1960s were a highly visible form of youthful alienation and rejection of traditional values and norms, it was actually a microcosm of bohemian behavior that characterizes a small minority of youths in every generation. To most former hippies, (and the rest of us whose rebellion was less sensational), it was an altruistic and transitional search for identity and purpose or the last "sowing of wild oats" before rejoining the larger society. Most students of adolescence and youthful behavior agree that such phenomena are at least partially reflective of the marginal position occupied by youths in our society in which they are denied full participation, and meaningful responsibility and social status. For a few, the denial and deviance of the youth subculture is the seedbed for more serious delinquent behavior.

Lynne Richards, in her article, "The Appearance of Youthful Sub culture: A Theoretical Perspective on Deviance," makes an unusual and productive approach to explaining extreme forms of the youth subculture whose nonconforming behavior often crosses the line into delinquency. She also sheds considerable light on the societal reaction to such youthful deviance. Richards combines acute sociological insights with her professional expertise in dress and appearance in identifying and analyzing the conflicts between youth subcultures and their parent culture. In the end, she sees a series of subsequent societal reactions, ranging sequentially from retaliation, to imitation, to social repair.

In conclusion of Part Three, the common thread linking these articles is that membership in rather naturally occurring social collectives and groupings can produce behavior that is nonconforming and deviant from the standards of the larger society.

Questions for Review and Discussion

1. According to Frederick Thrasher in his book, *The Gang,* what is the link between the slum habitat or "interstitial area" and the emergence and delinquent activities of urban youth gangs?

2. What implications are suggested by Maynard Erickson and Gary Jensen in their article, "Delinquency is Still Group Behavior" regarding the group context and differences in male/female delinquency, urban/rural delinquency, and types of offense?

3. Based on Lewis Yablonsky's "The Delinquent Gang as a Near-Group", differentiate between the organization and functions of the typical social group, the unstable mob, and the delinquent gang.

4. Based on the article, "Field Observations of Middle Class 'Gangs' " by Howard and Barbara Myerhoff, what are the similarities and differences between middle- and lower-class delinquent groups? Apparently, middle-class youths (as well as the adults in their environment) generally perceive their illegal activities as transitory and nonserious. Why?

5. What factors in the home and family were cited by Gary Jensen in his article "Parents, Peers, and Delinquent Action . . ." as associated with increased and decreased probabilities of delinquency by the children?

6. List and describe the factors in the home and family identified by Stephan Cernkovich and Peggy Giordano in their article, "Family Relationships and Delinquency" that relate to offspring delinquency? Also, how do race and sex composition of the family affect delinquency potential?

7. The hippies of the 1960s were an extreme manifestation of the youth subculture in the United States. Gleaned from the article by Jack Bynum, can you explain the hippie values and attitudes that conflict with the culture of middle class society? Why would these values and attitudes of the hippie ideology lead some young people to engage indelinquent behavior?

8. According to Lynne Richards in her article, "The Appearance of Youthful Subculture: A Theoretical Perspective on Deviance," what are the symbolic meanings of the uniform dress and appearance of members of the youth subculture? Describe the various reactions of the larger society.

PART FOUR

Society Versus
the Juvenile Delinquent

INTRODUCTION

PART FOUR EXAMINES the confrontations experienced by juvenile law violators as they interact with adults in the larger society. The focus is upon the social arenas of the schools, streets, and the juvenile court. We use the term *social arena* to describe the settings in which juveniles confront the adult normative system. It appropriately connotes the highly competitive struggle for dominance, and in a sense, social survival experienced by many adolescents as they move from the more private domain of home and family to the more public social milieu of the schools and streets. If their behavior in these public settings are construed as significantly disruptive, harmful, threatening, or antisocial, then there is a strong possibility that they will come into contact with the police and the juvenile court. These contacts are almost invariably confrontational in nature and, in many instances, begin the process of officially identifying a youth as a juvenile delinquent.

An appropriate beginning for the study of the confrontation between juvenile delinquents and the larger American society is a synopsis of the classic book *The Child Savers* written in 1969 by Anthony Platt. Platt traced the development of a group of social reformers in America during the late 19th and early 20th centuries and their influence on the handling of juvenile law violators. The "Child Savers" as they became known, viewed delinquency as a direct result of the poverty and generally deplorable living conditions of the inner city slums. They believed that delinquency, like a "disease," if diagnosed and treated early enough, could be "cured." Their influence on society, and especially the newly developed juvenile court system had significant and lasting impact on the handling of delinquents by the police, courts, and correctional officers in this country.

Kenneth Polk takes a comprehensive look at the relationship between juvenile delinquency and the school experience. His research which used data from a longitudinal cohort analysis of adolescent males confirmed that there is a significant linkage between school success and adult success. His article explains a complex relationship among family, school, and adult status. Polk's final analysis proposes that a variety of familial variables such as ethnicity, social class, place of residence, and early socialization, largely set the stage for success or failure in school. The school experience becomes a large determinant of whether troublesome behavior is likely to develop. If problematic behavior is developed, and supported by a peer culture, the youth is likely to become identified and officially labeled as a juvenile delinquent. Whether the delinquency label is applied appears to have significant impact upon the later behavior of youths in their adult years.

The third contribution to this section is from William Pink who also examines the link between the school experience and delinquency. He argues that the schools create and promote a two-trajectory system which takes one group of youths along an educational path toward academic success and preparation for success as an adult, while the other group is directed toward academic failure and lack of preparation for success in the adult world. Pink develops a detailed strategy for creating effective changes in the schools which would help prevent juvenile delinquency and provide better avenues for occupational success among those youths currently flooding the juvenile justice system.

When youths are not in school, they tend to spend a great deal of their time on the streets. Cruising the streets in automobiles—seemingly a national past time for many youths—frequenting pool halls, video arcades, and bowling alleys, or simply "hanging out" on the streets and sidewalks of major cities and small towns alike are frequent activities for youths during their teenage years. Many of these activities are likely to bring youths into contact with the police. Irving Piliavin and Scott Briar in their article "Police Encounters with Juveniles," analyze these police-juvenile contacts. Their observational study indicates that police have wide discretion in how they handle juveniles on the streets. This discretion, especially as it relates to the decision to detain, arrest, and officially process juveniles as delinquent appears strongly affected by variables such as the youth's record of prior offenses, race, appearance, and overall demeanor.

Douglas Smith and Christy Visher further examine the variation in the handling of juveniles by the police. Their research indicates that police discretion in the processing of juveniles is influenced by both legal and extralegal factors. The decision to take a suspect into custody is significantly influenced by the race and demeanor of the suspect as well as the presence or absence of bystanders. Another important variable seems to be the influence exerted on the police by the victim. Interestingly, their data indicated that the sex of the offender had very little impact on the decision to arrest.

Alan Neigher's article shifts our attention from the streets to the social arena of the juvenile court. He analyzes the impact of one of the most important landmark decisions of the U.S. Supreme Court regarding the juvenile court process. The Gault Decision of 1967, provided for the extension of many of the procedural rights outlined in the Bill of Rights and the 14th Amendment to the U.S. Constitution known as "due process" to youths appearing in juvenile courts. Neigher outlines the rights granted youths by the Gault decision and discusses the long-term ramifications of the ruling for juvenile justice.

Anne Rankin Mahoney's article also addresses the issue of due process in the juvenile courts. One right not extended to juveniles by the landmark Gault decision was that of trial by jury. This basic right afforded adult offenders in criminal court traditionally has been denied to youths appearing in juvenile court. Nevertheless, in some cases, juvenile courts have allowed a youth's case to be heard before a jury. Mahoney first gives a brief historical overview of juveniles' right to trial by jury and discusses the difficulty in measuring the impact of jury trials. Although difficult to assess, Mahoney contends that it is quite possible that youths who ask for jury trials may in fact receive a more negative disposition as the courts might penalize them for making such a request. At the very least, data indicate that the setting of a jury trial significantly delays processing the case.

In the next article, McNally teams with colleague Diane Dwyer to explore what they view as the potential demise of the juvenile court. Dwyer and McNally insist that the underlying philosophy of the juvenile court, especially that of *parens patriae* which viewed the court as a "superparent" acting on behalf of youths who appear there were well-conceived and important. The authors argue that the unique orientation of the juvenile court must be reaffirmed and retained.

The final article in Part Four, Tom Seligson's "Are They Too Young to Die?" addresses one of the most controversial issues in American society today. In a thought provoking article, Seligson points out that the United States may be the only country in the world which executes its children. Profiling some of the youths on death row awaiting execution for crimes committed while juveniles, Seligson explores the ultimate confrontation between juvenile delinquents and adult authority—capital punishment.

Anthony M. Platt, *The Child Savers: The Invention of Delinquency.* Chicago: University of Chicago Press. 1969.

THE AUTHOR

ANTHONY M. PLATT was born in Manchester, England on April 27, 1942. He received his bachelor's degree in law and his master's degree from the University of Oxford. Platt's graduate work at the University of California, Berkeley led to a master's degree (1965) and a doctorate in criminology (1966). *The Child Savers: The Invention of Delinquency* was originally Platt's doctoral dissertation at Berkeley where the young scholar was instructed and influenced, and his research encouraged, by some of the most distinguished sociologists and criminologists of that time, including Aaron Cicourel, Richard Korn, Joseph Lohman, David Matza, and Philip Selznick.

From 1966 to 1968, Platt was a research fellow at the Center for Studies in Criminal Justice at the University of Chicago where his research focus on the child savers continued. At that institution, Professors Howard Becker and Sheldon Messinger contributed their critical discussions and editorial expertise to the further polishing of the manuscript.

In 1968, Platt returned to his alma mater at Berkeley as a member of the faculty of the School of Criminology. Since 1977, he has been in the Division of Social Work, California State University, Sacramento. In addition to his ongoing research, teaching, and professional publications in the areas of law, criminology and delinquency, Professor Platt has served as Associate Director, Task Force on Group Violence, the President's Commission on the Causes and Prevention of Violence, and as Editor of the journal, *Crime and Social Justice.* In 1980, he received the Paul Tappan Award for "Outstanding Contributions to the Field of Criminology" from the Western Society of Criminology.

THE BOOK

The Child Savers: The Invention of Delinquency was initially published in 1969 and a second edition followed in 1977. However, the importance and authoritative quality of the study was recognized very early. Even prior to publication, Platt's thesis was being cited by other scholars in the field, including several references by authors participating in the prestigious *Task Force Report: Juvenile Delinquency and Youth Crime,* published in 1967.

One of Platt's major objectives in the book was to trace the late 19th century and early 20th century emphasis and legal enforcement of a set of basic values and behavioral expectations for American youth. Actually, such values as hard work, education, religion, and attitudes of deference and dependence toward adults have much older roots. However, near the end of the 19th century—as industrialization, urbanization, and secularism intensified and as crime and other social problems increased in the emerging mass society—it seemed to many prominent and concerned citizens that the Protestant Work Ethic, moral reliability, and other traditional values should be restated and reapplied. These social reformers directed their special attention at Chicago and other cities where large numbers of lower-class youths were perceived as indolent, aimless, and predestined by brutal living conditions to ultimate criminality.

The popular opinion of that day held that a causal link existed between the inner city slum neighborhoods in which these youngsters lived and their seemingly automatic involvement with corrupting habits and crime. Moreover, this view was supported by the explanatory theories of delinquency from several sociologists who stressed environmental decay and social disorganization. The penologist, Enoch Wines succinctly summarized this perspective when he wrote of these children:

> Their destitution, their vagrant life, their depraved habits, their ragged and filthy condition forbid their reception into the ordinary schools of the people. It is from this class that the ranks of crime are continually recruited, and will be so long as it is permitted to exist. They are born to crime, brought up for it. They must be saved (Platt, 1969:132).

Thus, the stage was set for the entrance of the "Child Savers"—a group of affluent and politically influential social reformers—who, near the turn of the century, were able to institute a powerful new program of social control over many American children and youths.

The Child Savers diagnosed nonconforming behavior in harmony with the *medical model,* utilizing such analogous terms as "disease" and "contagion." In other words, crime was viewed as a kind of social pathology, and young people manifested the antisocial behavioral symptoms of criminality as a result of being exposed to it in their environment. The older the criminal, the more chronic the "sickness," and chances of recovery were considered to be less than those for a young person (Platt, 1969:45).

Motivated by idealism, the Child Savers perceived the rehabilitation of lower class children destined for lives of crime as a matter of life and death. They mobilized their resources and not only took direct action to intervene in the lives of so-called wayward youths, but to shape public opinion and affect the passage of legislation designed to support their ideology. They castigated and sought to eliminate saloons and brothels as temptations to youthful depravity. They profoundly influenced the newly emerging juvenile court system in Illinois and large numbers of children and youth were denied due process and institutionalized because a dominant segment of society labeled them as having criminal propensities and in need of a more wholesome environment. According to Platt, the Child Savers literally "invented" juvenile delinquency by calling attention to new categories of youthful deviance and demanding societal response. Although they sincerely believed that their actions were humanitarian and benevolent strategies to protect the nation's young people, they were often intrusive, punitive, and unconstitutional (Arnold and Brungardt, 1983:6–7).

METHODOLOGICAL APPROACH AND STYLE

The *Child Savers* is a skillful and highly readable blend of historical and sociological content. Platt's thorough historical research successfully chronicles the development, dogma, and activities of an important dimension of the progressive movement in an era of rapid and often traumatic social change. He demonstrates considerable sociological knowledge and sophistication as he challenges popular theories of juvenile misbehavior and analyzes the social impacts of the Child Savers' program. Finally, the author's well-reasoned discussions of the juvenile court and the immediate and long-range effects of the Child Savers on criminal and juvenile law reflect his earlier legal training.

SOME MAJOR FINDINGS AND CONTRIBUTIONS

Under the auspices of the Child Savers, the existing reformatory system of the 19th century and the new juvenile court system which originated in Illinois in 1899, were rigorously modified. These institutions formalized and implemented a strict mode of adjudication and institutional regimen for "troublesome" youth. The Child Savers' treatment program included the following principles:

> (1) Young offenders must be segregated from the corrupting influences of adult criminals. (2) 'Delinquents' need to be removed from their environment and imprisoned for their own good and protection. Reformatories should be guarded sanctuaries, combining love and guidance with firmness and restraint. (3) 'Delinquents' should be assigned to reformatories without trial and with minimal legal requirements. Due process is not required because reformatories are intended to reform and not to punish. (4) Sentences should be indeterminate, so that inmates are encouraged to cooperate in their own reform and recalcitrant 'delinquents' are not allowed to resume their criminal careers....(Platt, 1969:54).

In addition to his lucid explanation of the Child Savers' ideology and treatment program, and the concomitant stigma and injustices inflicted upon lower-class youth, Platt also repudiated the oversimplified, causal relationship between slum neighborhoods and juvenile delinquency popularized by some social theorists and reformers of that day. By interjecting other independent variables, such as social labeling and the organization of juvenile justice, Platt and other writers have underscored the truly complex etiology of juvenile delinquency (Cicourel, 1968:24–25).

LIMITATIONS

Platt's documentation of the excesses of the Child Savers is so devastating that it is possible to overlook some of their ideas that were constructive and useful. For example, they suggested that "young offenders be segregated from the corrupting influences of adult criminals" (Platt, 1969:54). To have applauded this position would not have weakened the validity of Platt's indictment.

In a similar vein, the author's pessimistic evaluation of the effectiveness of the 1967 U.S. Supreme Court Gault Decision is obvious (Platt, 1969:161–169). With just two years between the Gault Decision and the publication of the *Child Savers,* Platt appears premature and hopeless in his evaluation. Certainly, Gault *was* a landmark decision aimed at reversing some of the negative residuals of the *Child Savers* in the adjudication process for juveniles. Reformation must begin somewhere, and a United States Supreme Court Decision advocating due process for juveniles was a worthy step in the right direction. Again, such an appreciation would not have weakened Platt's powerful thesis.

Comments and suggestions such as these are of such a mild and minor nature that they hardly qualify as a critique. The excellence of Platt's work is undiminished and the Child Savers remains a major contribution to the literature on juvenile delinquency and corrections.

REFERENCES

Arnold, W.R. and Brungardt, T.M. (1983). *Juvenile Misconduct and Delinquency.* Boston: Houghton Mifflin Company.

Cicourel, A.V. (1968). *The Social Organization of Juvenile Justice.* New York: John Wiley & Sons.

Platt, A.M. (1969). *The Child Savers: The Invention of Delinquency.* Chicago: University of Chicago Press.

Taskforce report: Juvenile Delinquency and Youth Crime. (1967). The President's Commission on Law Enforcement and Administration of Justice. Washington, D.C.: U.S. Government Printing Office.

ARTICLE 26

Schools and the Delinquency Experience

KENNETH POLK

*The basic proposition examined here is that school experience is an
important factor in understanding delinquency but that before this
statement can be examined, it is necessary to elaborate an institutional
theory which weaves together family-school-adult work role linkages.
Secondary data and findings drawn from an ongoing cohort study of
284 adolescent males in the Pacific Northwest are used to show that
adult success is related to school success, school success is related to
family status characteristics, school status and social class exert
independent effects on delinquency, and that adult careers, both
successful and deviant, are functions of adolescent school and delinquency labels.*

ANY COMPREHENSIVE DISCUSSION of juvenile delinquency must, sooner or later, center on
the school. In present-day industrial society, the school has come to occupy a
fundamental role in the lives of young people generally—and of delinquents in a
particular way. This importance rests on a number of considerations. More is involved
here than the fact that schools have become virtual age-based social ghettos, shielding
the young from contact with persons at a short distance either older or younger in age
(although this segregation is an important feature of the distinctive forms of youthful
behavior that are likely to bear such titles as "adolescent subculture" or "teenage

Source: Polk, Kenneth. "Schools and the Delinquency Experience."*Criminal Justice and Behavior,*
Vol. 2 (December) 1975: 315-338. Reprinted by permission of Sage Publications, Inc.

Author's Note: The research on which this paper is based is supported by funds granted by the
National Institute of Mental Health (Grant No. MH14806 "Maturational Reform and Rural Delinquency").

society"). Operating within the context of a "credentialed" society, to use the term suggested by Pearl (1972), how well a young person competes in school has enormous consequences for *future* status. The ultimate credential earned in the future is, in fact, the accumulation of countless little credentials in the present and past that take the form of grades, units, and credits. As assumptions about status futures lead to the development of such bureaucratic procedures as curriculum organization, tracking, ability grouping, and grading, these act backward into the status *present* of the child. Who the person is in the present, in the social world of the school, is significantly related to assumptions about who she or he might become. How well the student performs in school, or is seen to perform, comes to provide an important identity "fix" for the establishment of youthful status in school and community. Additionally, a significant part of the social activities provided for the young are organized within and around the school, both formally and informally. Providing a framework for a wide range of social activities (including unconventional and deviant activities), the school extends into the lives of adolescents well beyond the regular school hours.

It would seem only reasonable that the centrality of the school for the adolescent experience generally would extend in the specific form of adolescent behavior we call delinquency. In the sections which follow there will be an examination of a variety of ways that school behavior and delinquency can be seen to intertwine. Describing such interconnections, in other words, will require that a number of features of school behavior be elaborated, rather than one simple feature such as academic performance.

THE DEFINITION OF DELINQUENCY

The starting point, however, is delinquency, and the first task is to explicate the meaning, or in this case the meanings, to be given to this term. A starting point is law and legal process. Juvenile delinquency is based in law. Technically, it consists of those persons who have been legally processed and identified as "delinquent youth." As we review literature and data here, then, the search will focus on one definition of delinquency which is grounded in official processing of youth by police and courts.

There are enormous difficulties with such a definition. For one, as Elliott and Voss (1974:12) observe, it can unwittingly introduce the assumption that there are only two kinds of children—delinquent and nondelinquent. For another, definition based on official processing will contain biases that can be shown to be connected with such processing (for example, see Goldman, 1963). Furthermore, a legal definition based on official processing will combine in unknown and unknowable ways (without considerable additional information) two very different things: some form of *action* on the part of a young person (at least in most instances), combined with some *reaction* on the part of official agents. Hidden in single records are variations in both action and reaction, the result being a label "delinquency" that will suffer from lack of uniformity of meaning. Finally, most theories of youth deviance have a conception of troublesome behavior that do not mesh neatly with simple official records. Virtually all pose processes of alienation, reaction, and rebellion that imply much richer behavior than will ever be available from organizational processing data.

Despite all these difficulties, in these pages one focus of the measure of deviance will be official processing. Juvenile delinquency is a legal term, which, aside from whatever other logical problems are posed, does combine the assumption that some act has occurred with the official response to that act. The logical precision of this definition is clear, whatever the theoretical problems that might follow.

One way to utilize such a definition, and yet come to grips with the resultant problems, is to elaborate an additional conception which permits the inclusion of an additional definition or definitions. That is what is proposed here. At this point some hard decisions must be made. One well-accepted alternative is the utilization of measures of self-report of delinquent activity (for examples, see Elliott and Voss, 1974; Clark and Wenninger, 1962; Short and Nye, 1957–1958; and Short, 1958). These have the virtue of focusing the definition on legal process while avoiding the problem of unknown variations in the reaction process. As Elliott and Voss (1974:14) observe:

> The point of reference for an operational definition of delinquency must be the legal code, not the conduct norms of particular social groups. The significance of the proscriptions in the legal code is that there is some probability of official response to behavior that violates the statutes. Although official action does not necessarily occur when a delinquent act is detected, it is largely restricted to these acts.

There are yet some difficulties in describing youthful misconduct that are not resolved by definitions, either self-report or official, that remain close to the legal code. Much of the time the theoretical interest in delinquency does not result simply with law-violating behavior, but with a life style that is assumed to be attached to such behavior. One of the clearest illustrations can be found in Cohen's (1955) description of the "delinquency subculture," where the definition evolved around behavior among adolescent groupings characterized by malice, short-run hedonism, nonutilitarian actions, an emphasis on group autonomy, and versatility, all of which evolved among working-class boys through a complex process of reaction formation against their failure in school (and the consequent failure in status aspirations). Another is found in the work of Stinchcombe (1964), who focuses theoretically on issues of rebellion and alienation (among high school youth) as virtually independent phenomena, relegating actual delinquency to a relatively minor role. A characteristic of these theoretical discussions is that what they describe is a general orientation to the world, an orientation imbedded in a set of values and behavior that extends well beyond simple acts of delinquency.

The second definition of delinquency that will be used here will also enter into these murky waters. In general, the intent is to define an orientation, on the part of the young person, which leads to a willingness to engage in forms of behavior, especially peer behavior, which render the individual vulnerable to punishment and sanction by adults. Drawing the boundaries around this set poses problems that cannot be dealt with in the limited space of these pages. What can be done is to assert what are thought to be the major aspects of such an orientation, reserving the elaboration and theoretical justification for another work.

At the core of this troublesome orientation is a set of values and behaviors that evolve around a peer subculture that is in some respects oppositional to standards of behavior established for adolescents by adults. Thus, there is an emphasis on certain forms of behavior either disapproved of or discouraged by adults (drinking, smoking, fighting, and "cruising," to give illustrations), along with the necessary value orientations calling for a rejection of the claims of adults on adolescent behavior, substituting instead peers as the proper persons to establish standards for behavior. Adolescents caught up in this view of the world, in other words, are likely to support peer claims on their behavior and to reject to some degree the attempts of adults (such as parents or teachers) to lay claims on adolescent behavior.

There are two or three aspects of this definition of a "troublesome orientation" that should be clarified. One, it is viewed as being inherently probabilistic. It is not a fixed "thing" which a young person "gets," and, once "got," has forever. It is instead an orientation, a loose way of life, which a youngster may drift into and out of, episodically. Second, it is important to stress the notion of vulnerability. What such an orientation does is, probabilistically, to render the young person vulnerable to adult sanctions. This permits the connection of this perspective to the "labeling" perspective, i.e., a function of the troublesome orientation is to increase the probability that the young person will be vulnerable to a variety of negative labels controlled by adults, especially those organizationally based in the school (slow, emotionally disturbed, noncollege, and the like) or in the juvenile justice system (arrest, probation, adjudication, and the like). Third, this view sees acts of delinquency as episodically imbedded within the troublesome orientation. The young person who drifts into the troublesome orientation may in turn be pressured or drift into specific acts of delinquency, such acts being consistent with this orientation (not a necessary result).

THE MEANING OF THE SCHOOL EXPERIENCE

In discussing the relationship between school experience and delinquency, the second definitional problem encountered centers around the meaning of the school experience. At this point, the analysis must become a little complicated. An easy way out would be to focus on a given bit of school behavior—grades or truancy, for example—and show the connection between these and delinquency. Such a procedure has some appeal because it is both easy to do and the results are rather dramatic. The problem is, however, that we must decide what such findings mean, and to do that requires the exposition of some theory, first about school and then about delinquency as it relates to school.

The description of the school experience to be given here starts from the assumption that much of the meaning of what goes on in school is to be found at its termination point: the introduction of the young person into the world of work. It is relatively easy in this society to obtain a ranking of occupations from high to low in terms of a variety of indicators of social and economic status. It is a common sociological observation that in a relatively few decades, this nation (along with many other rapidly industrializing nations) has moved from a system where one inherited her or his occupation from the parent to a condition where one moves into an occupation as a result of a complex negotiation of barriers, notably established in the educational system. Education, in other words, has come to serve a "gatekeeper" function, consigning elite positions to some by means of a complex system of progressive, cumulative credentials, conferring lower status on others through a graded series of progressively lowered credentials.

To take the experience in what is seen here as the *logical* order (which is backward from the *experienced* order), to achieve those positions which consistently score high in the occupational ranking scales—such as judge, physician, lawyer, or college professor—one must negotiate some system of professional and graduate education which leads to a graduate degree (M.D., J.D., or Ph.D.), which in turn requires, in most instances, not only the completion of an undergraduate degree, but the completion of the undergraduate degree with some clear evidence of exemplary merit (indicated both by high levels of academic performance and through letters of recommendation).

Preceding college is the high school experience where the aspiring candidate must have the credentials and the diploma, and further must display evidence of high academic achievement as indicated by the grade point average, but even more; the high achievement must be in the "right" courses, namely those identified as college preparatory. Prior to this is the elementary experience, where the students with high promise are streamed together in the high-ability groups, wherein they receive the requisite educational content to prepare them for the later steps.

The argument here is that this process of sorting out the elites is a basic and fundamental dynamic of the educational system. Much of what happens in school must be understood in terms of this process, including often what appears to be content. Vast numbers of students understand very well—when confronted by paramecia, *Mill on the Floss, Beowulf,* or the Articles of Confederation—that what is important is certainly not their interest in these, nor even their understanding, but instead what grade they will receive on the test that covers such topics. Students learn early in the game, in other words, that academic experiences are to be treated *instrumentally* as means to further ends, rather than *intrinsically* in terms of interest or enthusiasm with the substance (this is not to deny that some students, and some teachers, do, in fact, become "involved" in their work).

Further, major features of this system are that there is a tight interlocking between the institutional levels and that much of what happens early is justified and rational-ized—by students, teachers, and the organizations—in terms of the destination. Some college courses are designed deliberately to fail large proportions of students, espe-cially in preprofessional programs, in order to sort the wheat from the chaff; tracking of college preparatory students is viewed as necessary both to provide the college bound the requisite academic training and to avoid exposing noncollege students to material which would have no meaning and would, in the view of educators, be beyond them anyway; the ability grouping of elementary students is necessary in order to provide the bright students, again in the view of educators, with the necessary basic academic skills that assure that they will be qualified to take advantage of the college preparatory classes at the secondary level. This grouping/tracking/grading system is relatively tightly linked, and the meaning of the "status flows" that are generated lies in the terminal links with the adult work world.

While this perspective emphasizes the importance of status destination as a fundamental feature of the institutional logic of educational institutions, it does not deny the relevance of status origins. An important aspect of the form of education that has been described is that it is fundamentally competitive: it is designed so that there are both winners and losers. Wins and losses are not randomly distributed, however, and this is where the family background enters the analysis. The first few years of the young person are spent in the family context. One way that the family experience can be viewed is that of making some children more vulnerable to being cast in the role of "loser." Again, this notion of vulnerability emphasizes that the basic reason that children are vulnerable at all is the set of institutional decisions which require that some must fail. The institution creates the categories (in the early years consisting of low-ability groups) that produce the vulnerability. Family background factors then interact to expose some children to such failure, these factors consisting of such things as belonging to a lower social class, being a member of a minority group, speaking a different language, or living in the wrong part of town, to give some of the more traditional sociological variables. The conception of family vulnerability used here goes beyond these basically institutional or structural variables, however, since it is clear that some children in the categories that would appear to be the most vulnerable do in fact succeed, and some that would seem least vulnerable fail. There are operating family and personal "competence" variables whereby young persons even in vulnerable settings have conveyed to them a range of behavioral and attitudinal competences (such as competence in the linguistic style of the school) that permit them to compete effectively, whereas other young persons, even from what would appear to be less vulnerable settings, do not possess such competences and thus are cast in the role of loser.

This conception of the school experience sees the school years as caught between status origins and status destinations, serving as a competitive battleground in the present for the young.

THE SCHOOL EXPERIENCE AND DEVIANCE

Among the many results of this competition, a significant element is that of the potential for the evolution of deviance and deviant careers. The educational system can be viewed as having an explicit concern for the potential for deviance as it relates specifically to the issue of status futures. At a psychological level, for the individual youthful actor, a message is communicated, for example, to the person who is doing well that indicates that engaging or being caught engaging in acts of problematic deviance poses significant threats to the future career. The student planning, say, a career that winds through law school and into the legal profession is confronted with a purely rational constraint either to avoid certain patterns of deviance or at least to be very careful not to get caught. At an institutional level, the school manifests a great concern for idleness and tends to fill up the free time of the promising student with a great variety of activities. The argument is, again, probabilistic. It is not that the high-status potential student will always avoid trouble; rather, there are a variety of personal and institutional constraints operating to restrain entry into deviance and then into deviant careers.

For the student doing poorly, quite a different situation exists. Such students can be explicitly excluded from the social activities of the school by virtue of their low academic output. Once cut away from the school, they encounter a real bind because a majority of the community recreational and social activities provided for the young are monitored through the school system. The poor performer is thusly doubly done in: excluded both from the formal activities of the school and from the legitimate adult community. For such an adolescent, the economic and occupational constraints are not powerful. Whatever the costs of deviance (anxiety, threat to dignity, physical and psychological abuse), the future occupational costs are not operating to the same degree as for the "good" student. Further, the organization is not constraining his time—nor are there clear, legitimate alternatives.

Such a student has one major alternative: involvement in the world of adolescent peers and peer culture. To the extent that this culture provides supports for a range of behavior that runs counter to adult expectations (cruising, drinking, and so on), it can be viewed as increasing the probability that a young person will engage in public acts of deviance and be labeled as deviant by the official control agencies.

EARLY ADULT LIFE: ACHIEVEMENT AND DEVIANCE

The argument here is that these promissory experiences are in fact connected with experiences in early adulthood. Functioning as institutional systems, there evolve over time patterns of institutional career "flows," the consequences of which are clearly observable (or at least these should be) in what happens as young persons move into early adulthood. The "straight" students, who have maintained institutional careers as exemplary students and who have avoided the definition of deviant, should show high levels of access to adult success and low levels of adult criminality. On the other hand, the unsuccessful students, especially those who accumulate over time public definitions as deviants, can be expected to show both high levels of official adult deviance and low levels of access to adult success.

THE PROMISSORY AND INSTITUTIONAL
CHARACTER OF THE ARGUMENT

What should be clear by now about this formulation is, first, that it is based on notions of probabilistic promise. The two sets of institutions, socialization and social control, are both seen as being fundamentally based on notions of youthful promise. This is perhaps clearest in the case of the educational/work linkage since the process is so clearly based on notions of recruitment, selection, and preparation. But this logic of the status future operates in the social control institutions as well. The contemporary concern about the negative effects of labeling and stigma, and the consequent emphasis on diversion, provides an obvious demonstration of this point. The argument to eliminate these negative processes contains the premise that the alternative need is to protect the interests of the child, especially with respect to the future. In fact, the whole range of status offenses (ungovernable behavior, endangering one's welfare, out of control, being in manifest danger of engaging in lewd or immoral conduct) can be viewed explicitly within this future-oriented, promissory framework. The reason why these statutes are provided is to protect the future interests of the child, to redirect her or him during these youthful years so that "worse problems don't develop later." The concern for the protection of the future of children is so strong, in fact, that the legal system is willing to promulgate unconstitutionally vague conditions for the imposition of the coercive power of the state in order to accomplish the task. Not only is the *intent* of the juvenile justice system to protect (however one may question the effectiveness of such procedures) the futures of children, it also in its *processes* uses as a basic criterion for decision-making the perceived future potential of the child. The child most likely to be either ignored or diverted is the individual who exhibits a multitude of symptoms of success, i.e., if the individual who is doing well in school, who is involved in a lot of legitimate school activities, who is part of the inner circle, and so on happens to be arrested, it is highly likely that the justice system will extend to the limit its capacity to nonintervene. The cases where intervention is likely to be viewed as necessary are instances where there are, instead of indicators of success, symptoms of failure and illegitimacy. It is in such cases that there is likely to be a perceived need for the social control institutions to enter into the scene, quite likely *with the intent of protecting the interests of the child,* i.e., to engage in action to try to improve the status future prospects of the child, at least in terms of the control aspects of status.

A further feature of this status future argument is that the system operates *bureaucratically,* such that *organizational careers* evolve out of the institutional organization of status. In the contemporary world, terms such as "college prep" or "delinquent" derive their basic meaning in bureaucratic process. Interlocking sets of *institutional labels* are generated which derive their logic and meaning in organizational process, and one must sort out issues at the institutional level before discourse about individual issues around labeling can make much sense. Thus, it is important to know how the label exists in the first place, and the role it plays within the institutional context, before it is possible to make sense of the question of how one kind of actor, e.g., the teacher, is able to impose upon another kind of actor, e.g., the student, one or another type of label, e.g., bright or dumb.

Finally, this perspective argues that critical intersections exist between institutional labels in the "socializing" and in the "social control" bureaucracies. The process of building a career definition of a deviant, to give a specific example, is likely to be a slow and cumulative process, involving the building up over time of failure labels in the socializing institutions and "need for control" labels in the social control institutions. The importance of this assumption is that, first, it avoids the mistake of viewing a single negative label event as a catastrophic and transforming experience without reference to the context of other labels. Certainly some experiences which produce labels can lead to basic transformation of identity, e.g., murderer, narc, or spy. It seems likely, however, that a single experience with delinquency, when that experience is contradicted by powerful institutional definitions of success may have limited impact. The exact same offense, at the exact same time, for another young person with a history of unsuccessful and problematic behavior labels, may have quite different institutional and personal consequences. Second, as illustrated in this last instance, it calls attention to the hypothesis that much of the basis for the imposition of control labels may lie well outside the social control system. If success and nonsuccess have their definition in the institutional intersections of work, school, and family experiences, and if the definition of nonsuccess is a fundamental feature of individuals who ultimately occupy the most persistent and problematic categories of career delinquents, then attempts to alter basic behavior patterns within the context of the social control institutions may be of little consequence. This includes attempts to "radically nonintervene," since the basic features of social vulnerability remain. Putting it another way, for those persons caught most firmly in the intersection of institutional processes that lead to social vulnerability, the presence of the justice system is merely one of a gamut of problematic roles that must be negotiated, however unsuccessfully. However important it may be for social policy to urge and support the limitation of the power of the juvenile justice system, for those young persons who are most vulnerable the critical features of the vulnerability remain: they will possess few educational credentials and have virtually no chance to enter the job market in a satisfying and legitimate role, to give but two features of such vulnerability.

SOME SUPPORTIVE EVIDENCE

The nature of this exercise creates a unique set of demands for a discussion of data. What will be done here will be to examine the key set of institutional intersections and to generate either data drawn from previously published research or new data, depending on the nature of the question and what data are available. The new data will be drawn from an ongoing longitudinal investigation of adolescents in a medium-sized county (1960 population: 120,888) in the Pacific Northwest. A 25% random sample was drawn from a sample frame consisting of all male sophomores enrolled in the schools of the county in 1964. From a total of 309 subjects selected, 284 usable interviews were obtained, giving a response rate of 92%. The one-hour interviews conducted by the project staff members covered a range of demographic, school, family, work, and peer variables. To these data were added grade point average from school transcripts and delinquency reports from juvenile court records. Further description of this study can be found in Polk and Schafer (1972).

The discussion of evidence will be organized by asking a series of questions:

1. Is there evidence of a connection between school performance and adult success? The question is seen as one of the most critical to the argument, since most of the premises are based on the notion of the institutional connection between school and work. Here a variety of supporting evidence can be cited. Census results persistently report that the highest paying occupations are professional and technical positions, i.e., those requiring the most education (Bureau of the Census, 1973a: 1 and 1973b: 213), and, furthermore, these are the occupations with the highest prestige ranking (Miller, 1971: 201). Using as a criterion the amount of lifetime earnings, males with four or more years of college will earn over the courses of their lifetime approximately twice the income of persons who do not finish high school, and recent research suggests that this gap is widening over time (U.S. National Center for Educational Statistics, 1975: 22). A strong connection does seem to exist, then, between the educational and work institutions.

2. Is there evidence of a connection between indicators of family power/vulnerability and school performance? Here again, there seems to be wide and general support for the proposition from the literature. Certainly, countless studies have been conducted which show the relationship between class and performance, i.e., to use the language of this argument, that a working-class background, one measure of family vulnerability, renders it more likely that the child will come to be defined as academically unsuccessful (a review, summary, and annotation of a great number of such studies can be found in Squibb, 1973). Using less abstract and less neutral language, Pearl (1965: 92) argues: "'special ability classes,' 'basic track,' or 'slow learner classes' are various names for another means of systematically denying the poor adequate access to education."

3. Is there evidence of a connection between school performance and deviance? As before, so much evidence exists for this basic premise from earlier research that there is little need for extensive discussion. Considerable data have been gathered showing the relationship between such academic performance variables as grades, tracking or streaming, dropping out, and deviance/delinquency (for examples, see Polk and Schafer, 1972; Stinchcombe, 1964; Hargreaves, 1967; and Elliott and Voss, 1974).

4. Is there evidence of significant independent connections between family background, school performance, and deviance? Now the argument begins to grow more complex. Perhaps it is time to draw upon some actual data, especially to make sense of the earlier distinction between delinquency and the troublesome life style. Extracting part of a table from a previously published study, it can be seen that when the simultaneous effects of class background and academic performance on deviant behavior are examined, both contribute some independent effect, but the strongest effects are a result of academic performance (see Table 26.1). Persistently, the percentage differences are greater in the contrasts between academic performance categories than is true for the social class categories. Note here that the pattern is the same for the measure of official delinquency as it is for the wider measures of troublesome behavior. We will use this consistency to argue in the tables which follow that there is at least some reason to presume that it may be legitimate to link the specific behavior of official delinquency to a wider troublesome life style. (Making this assumption is necessary both because in some studies to be cited the only measure of deviance available is delinquency and because in other cases the tables would be too complex if a great number of deviance outcome measures were included. Nonetheless,

TABLE 26.1 Percentage of troublesome and delinquent responses by social class background and grade point average

| | Grade Point Average | | | |
| | High | | Low | |
Troublesome Item	(1) White Collar (N = 111)	(2) Blue Collar (n = 77)	(3) White Collar (n = 28)	(4) Blue Collar (n = 44)
"Friends in Trouble"	30	43	75	64
"Drink with Friends"	46	52	75	61
"Enjoy Cruising"	57	61	82	84
"Peers vs. Principal"	52	48	83	70
"Peers vs. Parents"	28	31	65	46
"Peers vs. Police"	59	57	82	79
"Drink Beer"	35	44	64	72
"Like to Fight"	18	20	43	48
"Official Delinquency"	14	21	36	41

Mean Percentage Difference by:
  a. Social Class, indicated by comparing columns
      1) 1 vs. 2 = 4.2%
      2) 3 vs 4 = 4.4%
  b. G.P.A. indicated by comparing columns
      1) 1 vs. 3 = 29.6%
      2) 2 vs. 4 = 20.9%
Source: Polk, 1969

while the empirical measure is based on delinquency, the theoretical conception of delinquency that is being suggested nests such behavior in the context of a wider troublesome life style.)

5. Is there evidence that when academic failure occurs the nature of the involvement with adolescent peers mediates between the deviant and nondeviant experiences? At this point we can draw on some original data. Among those young persons in the Pacific Northwest study who were academically unsuccessful, the level of delinquency involvement varies considerably by involvement in the teenage culture. Using a composite measure of teenage culture suggested by Galvin (1975), students with low grades who had little involvement with teenage culture had low levels of delinquency (14%), while among failing students with high involvement with teenage culture, close to half (46%) became labeled as juvenile delinquents.

6. Is there evidence that the connection between educational performance and deviance extends into early adult life? At this point we begin to explore virtually virgin territory, since few previous research findings exist on the link between adolescent or adult school careers and adult criminality. Data from the Pacific Northwest cohort indicate that such a link can be traced. Looking first at high school performance, slightly over half (54%) of individuals with low grade point averages (low meaning in this case below 2.00) had been charged with an adult offense, in contrast with 23% so charged among individuals with higher grade point averages. A similar pattern exists in the case of adult educational attainment. Drawing the line at three years or more of college completed (since some of the successful elements of the cohort are at the time this research is being done still in college), we find low levels of adult criminality (15%) among those with high adult educational attainment, and high levels of criminality (39%) among those with less educational attainment.

7. Is there evidence of a connection between the labels attached by the socializing (school) and the social control (juvenile court) institutions to *adolescent* and *adult* criminality? To get at this question, it is helpful to generate a table (see Table 26.2); the resultant data indicate strong links between these institutional experiences. Among the small group of individuals who had both delinquent and academically unsuccessful labels, the level of adult criminality was quite high (83%). At the opposite extreme, relatively low levels of adult criminality (18%) were observed among individuals who were both academically successful and nondelinquent as adolescents. Interestingly, if the young person had earned a label of delinquent, in half the cases (50%) even the experience of academic success was not powerful enough to protect against the eventual experience with adult criminal behavior, while 40% of the nondelinquent youth who were academically unsuccessful were pulled toward adult criminality.

8. Is there evidence of a link between the labels attached by the socializing (school) and the social control (juvenile court) institutions to adolescents and adult success? We unfortunately cannot obtain a good test of this question from the Pacific Northwest data, since as of this writing some of the potentially successful elements of the cohort are still in college. Nonetheless, if we use as a temporary measure of potential adult success significant levels of higher education involvement, we can draw upon some previous research to look tentatively at the issue (Noblit, 1974). The findings of that study (see Table 26.3) indicate that, as might be expected from the earlier discussion, the highest levels of adult success (75% with high educational attainment)

TABLE 26.2 Percentage of individuals with Adult Criminal Records by Delinquency status as adolescent and by high school grade point average

| | *Percentage Criminal* | |
	Delinquent	*Non-Delinquent*
High G.P.A.	50 (N = 32)	18 (N = 164)
Low G.P.A.	83 (N = 18)	40 (N = 38)

TABLE 26.3 Percentage of young persons with high access to adult success (defined by college attendance) by academic performance and delinquency

| | Percentage with High Access to Adult Success | |
	Delinquent	Non-Delinquent
High G.P.A.	60	75
Low G.P.A.	26	20

Source: Noblit, 1973

are found among young persons with high levels of academic success as adolescents who were not involved with the juvenile justice system. An interesting facet of these findings is that these data are somewhat interactive. What is observed is that the basic factor operating among the most vulnerable is simply academic failure, i.e., among those with low grade point averages the level of success attainment is low, regardless of delinquency involvement (26% of the low g.p.a. delinquents, and 20% of the low g.p.a. nondelinquents being considered as successful adults, the difference between these two categories appearing to be nonsignificant). The barrier to adult success is, apparently, first and foremost academic. Once you have failed, you have little chance to succeed, and the experience of delinquency does not make your chances any worse. Among the academically successful, on the other hand, the experience of delinquency does appear to suppress the level of success (60% achieving high levels of educational attainment, contrasted with the earlier mentioned 75% among the high g.p.a. nondelinquents).

DISCUSSION

By now the case should be taking shape. What is being suggested is that a number of issues must be considered to make sense of the link between the school experience and delinquency. Implied in these terms is an exceptionally complex network of institutional interconnections. Perhaps it would be useful at this point to restate the suggested viewpoint in diagrammatic form (see Figure 26.1). Starting in the correct temporal sequence, the family can be viewed as establishing the basic support conditions that create either more powerful or more vulnerable young persons (with vulnerability being a result of such considerations as social class, ethnicity, place of residence, family competence variables, and so on). Using a variety of evidence regarding one feature of vulnerability, it does appear that an argument can be made that a likely path of the vulnerable youth is low academic success in elementary and secondary school. Once the school has operated in the lives of children for a few years, the evidence suggests that school status may be an important ingredient in setting up the paths to troublesome behavior, with a likely path from high academic achievement being drawn to less troublesome behavior. Among low academic performers, it is suggested that an

FIGURE 26.1 Suggested status flows among socializing (family, school, work) and social control (police, courts, training schools) institutions

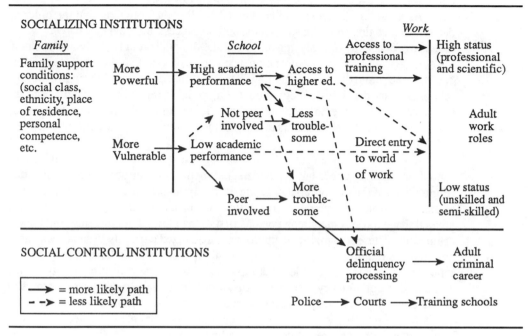

important condition affecting the flow into deviance may be the quality of the peer experience. If the low performers are not caught up in the supportive teenage culture, the likely path may be to less troublesome behavior. On the other hand, if the unsuccessful youth is surrounded by a supportive peer culture, a likely path may be into a troublesome life style pattern, a feature of which is official delinquency.

At this point, the patterns become complex enough to cause difficulty for simple summarization. On the one hand, the path to adult success seems to be open primarily to those who continue to perform well academically, especially those who avoid the delinquency label, while on the other hand, adult success appears to be closed to the academically unsuccessful, with the probability of success being not much better for the nondelinquents among the school failures. The paths to adult deviancy appear to lead through both the educational and the delinquency labeling processes, with the highest levels of adult criminality occurring where the individual as an adolescent was labeled as both delinquent and failure, while a much less likely path traces through academic success and nondelinquency.

Again, it should be emphasized that these labels are seen, first, as arising out of the bureaucratic and organizational processes. School grades and tracks have their origins and meaning in the process of sorting that leads to the adult work world. Further, the suggested view emphasizes strongly that the labeling experiences are institutionally interconnected and are best understood in terms of specific patterns of interconnections. It simply does not mean much to say that academic achievement is correlated with delinquency. One must have a conception, according to the suggested perspective, regarding what education is about, and then how under particular conditions the level of delinquency may be higher or lower.

As a further note, it should be pointed out that the argument that the ordering derives its meaning from the end points, both in success and deviance careers, refers to the suggested way of analyzing and understanding the order from the viewpoint of the outside analyst. There is some evidence which suggest that the adolescent actors "in the scene" build their understanding from their immediate experiences. For the high school student, the terms college prep or failure have immediate meaning, and the social statuses, however much these are based in institutional futures, are likely to be evaluated by the adolescent actors in terms of their status present (see Elliott and Voss, 1974: 204).

A view has been developed here that suggests that there is a link between the school and delinquency, but that understanding the connection requires explication (Figure26.1) of the institutional ordering of family-to-school-to-adult work role system. It is in these structural orderings that the basic patterns of vulnerability are created that expose some young persons first to the label of delinquency and then to criminality. These socializing institutions are organized currently in such a way as to assure, even require, that some young persons will come to be labeled in ways that render them socially vulnerable. Seeking the sources of the social vulnerability that are evidenced in delinquency, in other words, necessitates an exploration of features of bureaucratic organization and function, rather than a focus on individual pathology. Furthermore, positive action to address these patterns of vulnerability requires social policies that go well beyond diversion or radical nonintervention, since, as frequently expressed, these make little or no reference to the institutional ordering of the socializing institutions.

REFERENCES

Clark, J.P. and E.P. Wenniger (1962). "Socio-economic class and area correlates of illegal behavior among juveniles." *Amer. Soc. Rev.* 27 (December): 826–834.

Cohen, A.K. (1955). Delinquent Boys. New York: *Free Press*.

Elliott, D.S. and H.L. Voss (1974). *Delinquency and Dropout*. Lexington, Mass.; D.C. Heath.

Galvin, J.L. (1975). "Youth culture and adult success." Ph.D. dissertation. University of Oregon, Department of Curriculum and Instruction. September. (unpublished)

Goldman, N. (1963). *The Differential Selection of Juvenile Offenders for Court Appearances*. New York: National Council on Crime and Delinquency.

Hargreaves, D.H. (1967). *Social Relations in a Secondary School*. London: Routledge & Kegan Paul.

Miller, H.P. (1967). *Rich Man, Poor Man*. New York: Thomas Y. Crowell.

Noblit, G. (1973). "Delinquency and access to success: a study of the consequences of the delinquency label." Ph.D. dissertation. University of Oregon, Department of Sociology. (unpublished)

Pearl A. (1972). Atrocity of Education. New York: E.P. Dutton.

——(1965). "Youth in lower class settings," in Muzafer Sherif and Carolyn W. Sherif (eds.) Problems of Youth. Chicago: *Aldine.*

Polk, K. (1969). "Class, strain, and rebellion among adolescents." *Social Problems* 17 (Fall): 214–224.

——and W.E. Schafer (1972). Schools and Delinquency. Englewood Cliffs, N.J.: *Prentice-Hall.*

Short, J.F., Jr. (1958). "Differential association with delinquent friends and delinquent behavior." *Pacific Soc. Rev.* 1: 20–25.

——and F.I. Nye (1957–1958). "Reported behavior as a criterion of deviant behavior." *Social Problems* 5: 207–213.

Squibb, P.G. (1973). "Education and class." *Educational Research* 15 (June): 194–209.

Stinchcombe, A. (1964). *Rebellion in a High School.* Chicago: Quadrangle. U.S. Bureau of the Census (1973a) Census of the Population: 1970. Subject Reports, Final Report PC (2)-8B, Earnings by Occupation and Education, Washington, D.C.: Government Printing Office.

——(1973b) Census of the Population: (1970). Subject Reports, Final Report PC (2)-5B Educational Attainment. Washington, D.C.: Government Printing Office.

U.S. National Center for Educational Statistics (1975). *Digest of Educational Statistics—* (1974). Washington, D.C.: Government Printing Office.

ARTICLE 27

Schools, Youth, and Justice

This article posits that using the literature on school effectiveness as a basis for creating effective schools, holds the most promise for developing an efficient and cost-effective delinquency prevention strategy. It is argued that typical organizational and instructional practices of schools, maintain a two-trajectory system of education that ill-prepares low trajectory youth for success in school and the out-of-school world, and thus creates the conditions that generate troublesome and delinquent behavior. A detailed strategy for creating effective schools is presented that is grounded in the notion of using collaborative group decision making to develop specific plans for local school improvement. It is argued that effective schools, orchestrated with changes in the occupational arena, will reduce the flow of juveniles into the justice system.

Those who cannot remember the past are condemned to repeat it.
—Santayana

MUCH HAS BEEN WRITTEN about the phenomenon called juvenile delinquency. It is a problem that is persistent in the face of a variety of strategies designed to realize its eradication. It is not a problem unique to American society. While the type and number of offenses may vary, no society has found a "cure." Thus, developing state and federal policy in the field of juvenile justice is fraught with problems (such as, how should the

Source: Pink, William T. "Schools, Youth, and Justice." Crime and Delinquency Vol. 30 (July) 1984: 439-461. Reprinted by permission of Sage Publications, Inc.

police respond to first time status offenders, what "treatment" options should be used by the juvenile court when processing youths who have committed serious property offenses, or what prevention strategy deserves funding for experimentation). About the only thing agreed on by those working in the field is that there appear to be no easy quick-fix solutions.

While much data exists about the types of offenses committed, the distribution of offenses by race, class, sex, and geography, and the relative effectiveness of different "treatments," decisions, and policy, and most especially changes to existing policy, these are more often based on political expediency and cost factors than on sound evidence and reasoning. Further confounding this decision-making process is the fact that policy is frequently made without any serious exploration of the contextual realities facing juveniles in both the school and occupational arenas, and without the benefit of valid data about the comparative effectiveness of different "treatments" on randomly assigned youths (see Pink, 1982a).

There have been a number of theories proposed to explain the etiology of delinquency. Some have been empirically tested, at least in part. As yet, however, no single theory has been entirely successful in describing the reason young people engage in delinquent acts and/or in describing a "treatment" that would eliminate or significantly reduce recidivism. These theories of delinquency fall into one of three categories: First, theories that attempt to describe the conditions, personal and/or situational, that cause young people to become involved in delinquent acts. The outcome is prevention strategies; Second, theories that attempt to describe the conditions, either personal and/or situational, that cause young people to continue committing delinquent acts. The outcome is remediation strategies; Third, theories that attempt to describe the conditions, either personal and/or situational, that cause young people to commit and continue committing delinquent acts. The outcome is a set of related strategies that focus on both prevention and remediation.

In the majority of cases, interventions have been based on these competing theories of delinquency. It is self-evident that these interventions bring with them varying limitations. Intervention aimed at prevention may well reduce the numbers of youths reaching the juvenile court, but it does nothing to help those that do reach the court. Intervention aimed at remediation may well help those reaching the court, but does nothing to stem the tide arriving at the court steps. Thus it would seem that a strategy that focuses on both prevention and remediation is the only defensible course of action.

Given the magnitude of the task to develop a theory of delinquency and a set of prevention and remediation interventions, to say nothing of the space limitations of a journal article, the present focus will be narrowed to the issue of prevention. The article does, however, talk to the issue of remediation when developing the framework for thinking about the critical factors driving youths into delinquent involvements.

In developing a position that calls for us to rethink prevention strategies, five points need to be advanced at the outset. First, the schooling experience is the critical factor in the development of adolescent identity and careers. Second, intervention in schools offers the best opportunity to develop effective prevention. Third, recent research on school improvement and effectiveness suggests both a content and process for such intervention. Fourth, the articulation between schooling and early occupational careers must be made more explicit. Fifth, the juvenile justice system must work in concert with school districts and other community service agencies to orchestrate change in school, social, and occupational arenas to maximize the success experiences for all youths. In short, it is argued that manageable and cost-effective reforms in the schooling and occupational arenas can be effective in directing youths away from delinquent involvements and into pro-social and productive activities.

TOWARD A THEORY OF DELINQUENCY

Historically, theories of delinquency have been class based. They have emphasized the personal limitations of individuals, or classes of individuals, and the relationship between these individuals and the social structure of society. Researchers such as Cloward and Ohlin (1960), Cohen (1955), and Miller (1958) have argued that working-class boys have difficulty accessing the opportunity structure of society. The school is seen as an important arena for gaining conventional status and success. Boys failing to gain such conventional status and success seek other ways to enjoy status and success. The result is delinquent behavior. Both Cohen (1955) and Merton (1968) argue that all people aspire to the attainment of commonly defined (success) goals. Merton argues that people strive to achieve these goals by using institutionally prescribed means, but that these means are inversely related to social class position. For Merton, such barriers lead some to the use of illegitimate channels to achieve these stated goals. Cohen extends this line of reasoning to state that the focus of this blocked goal attainment for lower-class youths is the school. In short, these class-based theories suggest that either personal or class-related limitations, together with differential access to the opportunity structure of society, both cause and maintain a subculture of delinquency.

Recent evidence about the scope of delinquency has indicated that it can no longer be accurately characterized as a working-class activity. Consequently, more contemporary theories have attempted to reconceptualize why youths engage in delinquent acts. Theories and perspectives variously named Strain, Control, Interactional, and Labeling have appeared in the literature. Central to most of these explanations is the notion that some youths are less bound to, or committed to, the traditional values and institutions of society than are their peers; this may be caused by a lack of success, or too few binding structures, or a combination of stigmatizing labels and the negative impact of associating with delinquent peers. Regardless of the theory, this group of youths is seen as vulnerable and therefore more likely to engage in delinquent activity. Such youths tend to be identified both by the school and justice system and targeted for "treatment." As a result of this process of identification, these youths are frequently separated from their less deviant peers. It is argued that they become typed or labeled as deviant, and that the "treatment" that was designed to help them frequently becomes part of the problem, in that it serves to maintain a deviant identity. Lemert (1967) called this process Secondary Deviance. Again, the school is seen as an important arena for the development of this differential attachment or commitment to conventional values and behavior.

In attempting to reconceptualize the causes of delinquency, Hirschi (1969:132) has argued that "the causal chain runs from academic incompetence to poor school performance to disliking of school to rejection of the school authority to the commission of delinquent acts." While others would want to add that this supports a class position, since lower-class youths generally do poorer in school than do middle-class youths, we cannot assume that academic incompetence (however measured) is a direct outcome of social class origin. Moreover, Hirschi's data do not support such an interpretation. A more refined position regarding the movement of youths from class origins to class destination posits that early in a student's school career, decisions are made about ability and educability that mesh with commonplace organizational practices of schools, that is, ability grouping, tracking, and special education remediation, that in turn serve, over time, to solidify both in-school and out-of-school identities for students that finally govern options in both career and life choices (Kelly, 1978; Pink, 1978 and 1982; Pink and Noblit, 1977; Polk and Schafer, 1972). What this position suggests is that students, regardless of ascriptive characteristics such as I.Q., class, race, and sex, are more likely to become involved in delinquent activity if they have a school career that involves placement in low status or low academic groups, together with treatment by the school that indicates restricted rather than unrestricted career and life choices. While it is evident that disproportionate numbers of working-class, low measured I.Q., minority, and male students have this experience in schools, •
this should not be seen as support for the position that it is *these* characteristics that "cause" delinquent involvements. Sufficient evidence exists to demonstrate that when controlling these variables, the relationship between the school experience and delinquency remains strong (Hargreaves, 1967; Ogbu, 1974; Rist, 1970; Schafer and Olexa, 1971).

SCHOOLS AND DELINQUENCY REVISITED: THE DEVELOPMENT OF STUDENT IDENTITY

Students attending school are routinely compared with each other using a common yardstick, usually scores in a standardized achievement test. Frequently, schools also make placement and personal decisions about students based on factors such as personal appearance, language facility, and previous teacher comments (Cicourel and Kitsuse, 1963; Goodlad, 1984; Pink and Sweeney, 1978; Rist, 1970 and 1978). The net result is that students are placed into one of two pathways or educational strands that have not only immediate significance on what students will do and be expected to do in school but also, of more long range importance, for what students will be able to do when they leave school. Simplistically, the two pathways can be characterized as academic/success/high status/college preparatory/professional occupation in orientation and nonacademic/failure/low status/non-college/low skill occupation in orientation. This distinction can possibly best be understood by viewing schools as a means for providing each student cultural capital that allows him or her to thrive and prosper in the postschool world. The greater the capital, the greater the likelihood of enjoying prosperity. Students in the low trajectory, however, enjoy limited opportunity to gain sufficient capital for such prosperity. That is to say, the school is organized in such a way that prevents low trajectory students from getting the same educational opportunities as their high trajectory peers, which in turn translate into limited options in the occupational arena (see Apple, 1982; Berg, 1971; Bourdieu and Passerson, 1977; Bowles and Gintis, 1976; Young and Whitty, 1977).

This categorization of students into these two trajectories may begin very informally in the elementary school, via such practices as ability grouping within the heterogeneous classroom and singling out students for Chapter I remediation. It becomes more formalized through the junior high school and high school years, via practices such as tracking students into differentially paced class sections, and/or differentiated curricular strands (such as, college prep, commercial, basic, remedial). While these practices may not be seen by students, teachers, and parents as a formal district-wide mechanism for classifying students, nevertheless they function in a very systematic way to separate students into these two distinct pathways or trajectories. This pattern may be even less visible and understood in urban districts where entire schools may be organized in such a way as to provide students *only* the nonacademic/ failure/low status/noncollege/low skill occupational pathway. This may explain, in part, why delinquent involvement is highest in urban districts with a high concentration of minority students.

What is revealed by such a systematic analysis of the link between students' status origins, schooling experiences, and occupational/life options is that the school is the major arena in which students forge their identities. More precisely, it is the school that is the major force in manipulating or shaping student identity. The kind of person a student becomes, including the range of skills he or she acquires, is in great part a direct function of the type of learning environment created by the school. Consequently, it can be reasoned that students enjoying success in school, that is, the high trajectory students, are likely to be committed to the goals of the institution and unlikely to be engaging in delinquent activity. By contrast, students enjoying little success in school, that is, the low trajectory students, are unlikely to be committed to the goals of the institution, but likely to be engaged in delinquent activity. These students have little to lose by engaging in delinquent activity. Interestingly, a range of data support such an interpretation of student behavior (Kelly and Pink, 1973; Ogbu, 1974; Polk, 1969; Toby and Toby, 1962).

What is it about schooling that is so influential in shaping student identity? How do decision about educability made early in a student's school career relate to options in the postschool career? What is the relationship between placement in an academic track, the kind of schooling experience enjoyed, and occupational choice? While there appear to be a number of interrelated factors that shape the answers to these questions, they can be organized under three headings: (a) Developing Skills, (b) Developing Competence, and (c) Developing Status.

Developing Skills

The school is the central institution for dispensing the skills prized in contemporary society. Mastering these valued skills, such as reading, writing, and conceptual thinking, serves as a ticket for subsequent entry into a wide number of educational, occupational, and social arenas. Placement in the high trajectory or pathway signals to teachers, student, and parents that it is an expectation that the student can achieve high quality work and thus can legitimately aspire to success in postschool arenas. Conversely, placement in the low trajectory signals to all low expectations for both school and postschool success.

Evidence would indicate that students assigned to low ability groups or tracks and expected to be inferior in performance and behavior to their peers assigned to high ability groups or tracks, infrequently develop the level of skill of their better situated peers. To the extent that this pattern is set in place in the early elementary years determines that it is here where intervention in the form of educational reform should begin. Targeting intervention in later years may be too late. Is this differential school performance a function of social class, race, or I.Q. differences? Research evidence suggests it is not. Studies controlling these and other sociopsychological factors show that students in the low trajectory consistently perform poorly, academically and behaviorally, compared to their high trajectory peers (Hargreaves, 1967; Jones et al., 1972; Rosenbaum, 1976; Rutter et al., 1979; Willis, 1977). Evidence would suggest that the learning environment experienced by low trajectory students in school is qualitatively different from that experienced by high trajectory students. Factors such as teacher expectations for work load and behavior, the amount of academic learning time accumulated per day, frequent diagnosis of individual learning difficulties, and the number and intensity of teacher interactions involving both school related and personal matters, all significantly differentiate the schooling experience of high and low trajectory students. The fact is that students placed in the high trajectory setting have greater opportunities to learn skills and be successful within the school setting than students placed in a low trajectory setting. Where skills are important marketable attributes, it is clear that the way schools are commonly organized and managed systematically prevents a sizeable proportion of the student body from acquiring these skills. Mastering a skill such as reading early in the school career is important for both learning *all* other subjects in the school setting and being able to learn independently in the out-of-school setting. Moreover, a failure to read gains in importance the longer it remains unremediated. Graduating from school with less than a ninth-grade reading level becomes a serious handicap within the occupational arena. It is through this manipulation of the skills acquired by students that schools play such a central role in defining student identity. Moreover, by withholding essential skills from students, the school becomes a primary instrument in creating vulnerability to delinquent involvement.

Developing Competence

The school provides the major arena in which students can demonstrate competence. Inasmuch as the school defines the criteria for both competence and incompetence, explicitly by teaching and enforcing rules of learning, inquiry, and conduct, implicitly by the expectations of staff for differential achievement and behavior, and placing students into the high or low trajectories (such placement carrying with it both formal and informal messages about the educability of students located in different trajectories), then adolescent competence is defined largely by the academic label carried by the student. In short, schools define a competent youth as one who does well academically, conforms to the rules of the building, and shows the proper deference to adults. By contrast, an incompetent youth is one who demonstrates academic and behavior problems. Even nonacademic extracurricular activities such as sports, debate, or drama, activities that provide a second avenue for demonstrating competence, usually carry the prerequisite of maintaining passing grades. Thus students having academic difficulties, this is, students in the low trajectory, are not only constantly reminded of their inferiority to their more successful peers, but also denied opportunities to develop such competence.

From this analysis of the way the organization of schooling functions to manipulate the students' sense of competence, it is easy to see why low trajectory students may develop low commitment to the school and its value system, have a low sense of competence or self-worth within the school arena, and thus become disproportionately involved in troublesome and/or delinquent behavior. For them, school has little meaning or relevance for either their immediate or more long range lives. While many students do not come to understand the significance of their school career until after they have entered high school, nevertheless, the evidence suggests that beginning in the early elementary grades, the troublesome students come disproportionately from the low trajectory group.

The full meaning of this manipulation of the students' sense of competence is made explicit when we look at the institutionalization of these two trajectories from elementary through junior high to high school. As emphasized above, students showing initial academic difficulty and placed in low trajectory ability groups or tracks, are unlikely *ever* to catch up to their peers who are placed in the high trajectory. This is in part a function of the learning environment of the remediation program offered to low achievers. It is also a function of the perceived difference between the two trajectories. Simply stated, the problem is that assignment to a low trajectory is not part of a competent student's biography, and assignment there frequently brings the student into contact with a different and more restrictive set of rules and expectations that function to increase the probability of being further labeled as incompetent and a troublemaker. This, over time, so fills out the biography with information about negative labels and stigmatizing behaviors that students find it difficult to escape even when moving from school to school. The result is that students having difficulty in school infrequently develop a sense of competence within the school arena.

Developing Status

By controlling access to the skills acquired by students, together with the sense of competence students develop as an outgrowth of this skills acquisition, the school functions as the major arena in which students gain status. Who you are in the school setting, and to a large degree who you are in the out-of-school setting, is defined by the value structure of the school. The school values and rewards academic competence by conferring high status on students demonstrating such competence. It also rewards, via status, acceptable social and physical competence—again, a minimum level of academic competence must be maintained to remain eligible for such status. It is no accident, therefore, that subcultures found in schools are based in large part on the distinctions inherent in the two trajectory system: high status and rewards being differentially enjoyed by high trajectory students when contrasted with their low trajectory peers (see Coleman, 1961; Gordon, 1957; Hargreaves, 1967; Polk and Pink, 1971). Again, it seems reasonable to argue that students without status in an institution that is the major dispenser of both formal and informal adolescent status may, without encouragement to do otherwise, develop a low commitment to the rules and goals of that institution. Moreover, it seems reasonable to argue that low trajectory students, devoid of status *and* a way to improve their status, will demonstrate their low stake in schooling by continuing to do poorly academically and by engaging in troublesome and delinquent behavior (Ogbu, 1974; Pearl, 1972; Pink, 1982b; Schafer and Olexa, 1971; Willis, 1977).

DELINQUENCY PREVENTION THROUGH SCHOOL IMPROVEMENT

Historically, schools have not enjoyed much support as an avenue for delinquency prevention. This may have been a mistake. Popular theories of delinquency have placed the motivation for delinquent involvement with psychogenic and/or social distinctions: factors clearly outside the control of schools (Aichhord, 1955; Burt, 1938; Cohen, 1955; Grossbard, 1962; Hathaway and Monaches, 1953; Merton, 1968; Reiss, 1952; Toby, 1957). Moreover, much large-scale educational research about the impact of schools on the cognitive and social development of students has reported that the school has little importance when compared with family characteristics (see Coleman et al., 1966; Jencks et al., 1972; Rehberg and Rosenthall, 1978). While the school may have been seen as unimportant, schooling has enjoyed a more central role.

The recently developed concepts of normalization and deinstitutionalization, that is, removing status offenses from the statutes, and seeking community-based diversion options rather than committing "low-risk" youths to correctional institutions, have recognized the importance of delinquent youths continuing their education *with* nondelinquent youth. Unfortunately, youth participating in such diversion options have frequently found themselves placed back in the same low trajectory educational settings that originally contributed to their delinquent involvement. Returning students to an unchanged school setting with the expectation that things might go better the second time around, is not a defensible remediation strategy.[1] Thus, while education has been seen as important, the process and structure of education has yet to be seen as equally important. Predictably, as the results of past diversion efforts focused on the school have been less than commendable, policymakers have tended to look elsewhere for prevention/remediation strategies.

---

[1] Other strategies such as in-school suspension rooms, or special classes for the severe underachiever are frequently used. They are usually ineffective as both a remediation for low achievers and antisocial behavior. This lack of success can be attributed in great part to the fact that little attempt is made to change the learning environment and teach these students using different instructional strategies (See Chobot and Garibaldi, 1982; Deal and Nolan, 1978; Newman, 1981).

Alternative Schools as Prevention

The alternative school is one strategy that recognizes the importance of changing the process of delivering education to low trajectory students.[1] However, in the majority of school districts attempting such a strategy, alternative schools usually become "dumping grounds" for troublesome youths in the district. To date, the major concern has been how to remove troublesome students from their regular school. Less effort has been expended in thinking through the content of an alternative education for the student.[2] Thus, the educational setting of alternative schools differs little from that experienced in the schools from which the students were transferred: as a consequence, such students infrequently overcome the learning deficits that initially caused them to be placed in the low trajectory group. Not only is such an alternative school perceived as inferior to regular schools, but by association, are those students who attend. In short, a most promising institutional response to low achievement and troublesome behavior is frequently so conceptually flawed that it becomes part of the problem, not the solution, to low achievement and antisocial behavior. We should also note that alternative schools are found almost exclusively at the high school level. Problems for elementary or junior high students are thus completely unaddressed by this intervention.[3]

All is not lost, as there are some beacons of hope on the educational terrain. Gold and Mann (1983:306), for example, have reported on a study of experimental alternative schools that comes close to testing the notion that changing the educational setting in fundamental ways will reduce delinquent involvements. The authors were interested in locating a certain type of alternative school to test the notion that failure in school leads to low self-esteem that leads, in turn, to efforts to counteract it—such responses could range all the way from alienation and withdrawal to rebelliousness and delinquent acts:

> The alternative school programs made special efforts (1) to provide their students, who had had histories of scholastic failure, with experiences of success, largely through individualized instruction and evaluation: and (2) to provide social support from warm, accepting teachers. According to the theory, scholastic success and social support were hypothesized to raise the students' self-esteem and strengthen the social bonds that integrate students' self-esteem and strengthen the social bonds that integrate students with their schools. Thus, the provocation to be delinquent would be reduced, the social constraints against delinquency would be strengthened, and consequently disruptive and delinquent behavior would decline.

---

[2] Newman (1981), for example, argues that alternatives should be evaluated on criteria such as: voluntary choice, clear and consistent goals, small size, participation, extended and cooperative roles, and integrated work. His analysis reveals that few schools respond to low achieving and/or troublesome youths by implementing these principles for reducing student alienation.

[3] There is a lesson here to be learned from public health, where approximately 90% of monies are targeted at prevention, and the remaining 10% at remediation. Preventing the learning and development problems that contribute to driving students into delinquent involvements should be the main focus of delinquency prevention. Focusing on the junior and senior high school student may be too late if we want to impact learning and development difficulties that often originate with the type of schooling experiences existing in kindergarten classrooms. It is the elementary school that should be the *prime* focus in delinquency

While this study lacked random assignment to treatments and a mixing of "problem" with "normal" students, the findings nevertheless are supportive of the notion that a restructured learning setting can improve academic achievement and reduce delinquent involvement. The study is important because it demonstrates that relatively minor modifications in the schooling experience, independent of factors such as family, I.Q. and social class, can impact student achievement, self-esteem, and delinquent involvement.

The schools in the Gold and Mann study attempted to change both how the curriculum was taught as well as the setting in which it was taught. The authors report significant changes in delinquent involvements. What these three schools failed to do was successfully reintegrate the students with their high trajectory peers and work to reduce the barriers to successful movement from school to occupations. That is, the prevention intervention did not result in making its graduates competitive with the average graduate of the high trajectory who was enrolled in the conventional school. The danger here is that a separatist program for troublesome youths can become a spoiled image program. If only "bad" students are enrolled, then stigma attaches to both the program *and* all those who attend. A second danger is that a credential earned from such a program can be viewed as inferior to a credential earned at a "conventional" school. This is important because the credential becomes a part of the permanent record of the student and thus becomes a factor in *every* transaction in the occupational arena (such as, a GED versus a conventional diploma). A better intervention strategy is one that keeps all types of students enrolled in the program, thus opening occupational options rather than closing them off. While the outcome of this separatist strategy can be seen as a limitation of the intervention, it should not be a surprise. Until very recently, the literature on schooling effects offered few suggestions about alternative strategies for low trajectory youths. However, some recent research about both the content and the process of school improvement is beginning to provide an outline of how this might be accomplished. The significance of this new research is that it suggests that the typical low trajectory student *can* learn and be successful if schools are structured and teach in certain ways.

Creating Effective Schools

The pioneer work of researchers such as Brookover and his associates (1978 and 1979) and Edmonds (1979), has led to a body of research and writing known as The Effective Schools literature. Contrary to the widely disseminated findings of the large-scale surveys previously reported by Coleman (1966) and Jencks et al. (1972), the effective schools literature suggests that there are specific characteristics of schools that, if present, make schooling effective. Edmonds (1979: 16) defines effective schools as those that "bring children of the poor to those minimal masteries of basic school skills that now describe minimally successful pupil performance for the children of the middle class." This initial work has served to popularize five components of effective schools: strong administrative leadership, high expectations for student achievement, an orderly atmosphere conducive to learning, an emphasis on basic skill acquisition, and frequent monitoring of pupil progress. The result has been that many districts have begun effective school projects and/or targeted district-wide staff development at the five specific characteristics. The premise has been, if some schools why not all schools? Sadly, as with some other promising interventions, most school districts have acted without understanding the substance of the five characteristics, the relationship between the characteristics, or the most effective ways to implement the characteristics at the individual school level. Moreover, districts have tended to use *only* this literature to shape their intervention. Thus, in the majority of cases, school effectiveness is defined narrowly as student achievement in reading and mathematics, and the major avenue to achieve this is utilizing the five components enumerated by Edmonds. Consequently, the results of effective school interventions in cities such as St. Louis, Milwaukee, and New York have been less than spectacular.

These mixed results should not be surprising since the effective schools literature on which interventions are based is at best incomplete. Several researchers (MacKenzie, 1983; Pink, 1983 and 1984; Purkey and Smith, 1983; and Rowan et al., 1983) have detailed a series of limitations with the literature that indicates why it *cannot* be seen as a blueprint for school improvement. In particular, they note (a) that the data are predominantly correlational rather than longitudinal, (b) that there is little agreement concerning the definition of an effective school, or of the five components, (c) that it is not clear if and how the components are nested together, (d) that it is not clear if the components are in any priority order, or enjoy any strengths relative to each other, (e) that the literature does not specify how the effective school characteristics were originally created in the school studied, *or* how they are currently maintained, and (f) that it is not clear how best to transport the five characteristics from school to school. Pink (1983) also emphasizes that this literature does not discuss the best classroom instructional arrangements to facilitate learning for the low trajectory students. What is needed, as Pink (1983) and Purkey and Smith (1983) argue, is a synthesis of research on school improvement. Such a synthesis would draw from diverse literature (such as, school effects, school change, school organization, classroom instruction, participation, and staff development) and would begin to *detail* the characteristics of effective schools (such as, what does a principal do in asserting strong leadership? What organizational arrangements contribute to an orderly school atmosphere? What instructional strategies are most effective for high and low trajectory students?). Such a synthesis is in its infancy. As it develops, it will reveal gaps in our knowledge where additional research is needed.

Despite these limitations that seriously hamper schools using *only* the effective schools literature to inform efforts at school improvement, there are some extremely promising outcomes from this broad interest in creating effective schools that speak directly to delinquency prevention. First, it has helped to restore faith in the schools as a means to improve student achievement and behavior. Second, it has focused attention on the need to change school practices to improve the learning of low trajectory youth. Third, it has provided a framework within which to conceptualize both the assessment of current practices and their subsequent refinement. Fourth, it has provided a language and a set of ideas that parents can use to gain access to the debate about the goals, objectives, and outcomes of schooling. Fifth, it has provided a focus to draw together relatively diverse research about schools and school effectiveness (such as, literature on classroom effectiveness, expectations, school organization, staff development, and school change).

The promise of the school effectiveness movement is that it might well produce some systematic knowledge about how best to teach and organize for students who arrive at school with very different interests, experiences, and levels of skills. This has a great deal to do with delinquency prevention.

Effective Schools as Prevention

The position developed so far is that the creation of effective schools is a potentially effective delinquency prevention strategy. Moreover, the fact that previous attempts to improve the education of delinquent or predelinquent youths have proved to be poor preventive strategies, does not diminish the potential of *this* strategy. The previous school-based intervention strategies were ineffective because they did not take into account the relationship among the students' location in the two trajectory system, differential opportunities for learning, and available career options. The difficulties with using only the effective schools literature to create effective schools notwithstanding, it is argued that by dismantling the two trajectory system, and providing varied and equitable opportunities for *all* youths to develop skills, competence, and status, then *all* students will enjoy more positive and successful experiences than negative and unsuccessful experiences during these critical formative years. As a consequence of making schooling more meaningful and rewarding students would have more to gain by engaging in prosocial rather than delinquent behavior. Obviously, the next level of concern is aligning the occupational arena with the product of the newly created effective school: it is essential that the promise of success offered to low trajectory youths through the creation of an effective school be realized through wide, rather than restricted, career options. The ability to translate the skills, competence, and status gained in school into mobility and success within the occupational arena is a key factor in the conceptualization of schooling as an effective delinquency prevention strategy. Without such a correspondence, school will continue to be unimportant in the lives of youths. The result will be a continuing flow of youths into the justice system.

While it is important to recognize the urgent need to reshape the occupational arena, it is clearly beyond the scope of this article to detail a plan for such a reorganization. It is possible, however, to detail a six-point, low cost strategy for creating effective schools. It must be emphasized that this strategy draws on findings from several sets of literature in addition to the effective schools research, that is, school change, classroom and school organization, classroom instruction, participation, and staff development.

1. Each school district should create a climate that encourages and supports innovation and change based on research evidence about effective instructional and organizational practices. The recent series of reports focusing on the current status of public education can provide the platform for such reforms. Public interest is currently high with respect to school improvement.

   With this climate of support for change, emphasis should be placed on the development of school specific programs based on student needs, and a method of delivering that program that is grounded in the research on effective instructional and organizational practice. This plan should detail school activities for an academic year and should be evaluated annually. The key to success here is that this planning process involve both the staff and community (including students and parents) in collaborative planning and decision making. As collegial relationships are built, and common goals and expectations developed, then a greater sense of partnership can be forged between the school and the community it serves.

2. Each school should develop a specific plan that details both the content and the process of the following six components identified as key in the school improvement literature:

a. Instruction: How will teachers teach in this school? What shared assumptions, beliefs, or norms are held about the act of teaching? Will homework be assigned? How much homework, and how is it coordinated between subjects? How do we handle discipline? How is grouping to be managed? How will students not mastering the required material be retaught? What teaching styles are appropriate for the range of students in the school? How can we decrease classroom interruptions and increase academic learning time for all students? How can student achievement be monitored? How will teacher fidelity to agreed upon instructional strategies be monitored? What organizational changes must be made to ensure that *all* students learn the basic curriculum?

b. Expectations: How will high expectations for student learning be projected by staff and administration? What teacher behaviors contribute to maximizing student achievement? How can teachers monitor and provide feedback to each other about their teaching? How can parents be involved in projecting expectations for success to students?

c. Curriculum Alignment: How can objectives and assessment be matched with instruction? What skills should be taught in what sequence to students? How are resources used to focus on skills indentified as essential? What assessment methods should be used to check for mastery? How can skills be broken down into smaller units for testing for mastery? What organizational arrangements, such as grade level meetings, will facilitate coordination of curriculum alignment activities?

d. Climate: How can the learning environment of schools be improved? How can student excellence be acknowledged? How can orderly and attractive schools be created and maintained over time? What practices foster high student and faculty morale?

e. Leadership: What is the appropriate role of the school administration in creating and maintaining an effective school? What are faculty perceptions of the administration style? How can school administrators best facilitate instructional improvement? What leadership roles can faculty play in school improvement? How can school administrators develop and use collaborative planning and shared decision making to improve schools? How can administrators best utilize the strengths of faculty in facilitating school improvement?

f. Parent/Community Involvement: What roles can parents and community play to aid with school improvement efforts? What organizational changes can be made to involve parents and community in collaborative decision making?

These components are important elements in schools found to be effective in improving student achievement and reducing troublesome and delinquent behavior: they should be the focus of local school improvement efforts. In answering specific questions such as these, the plan will make the goals and objectives of schooling clear. It is also important to focus the improvement on all six components. The plan should detail how the various activities proposed will be evaluated, as well as what staff development activities will be required to assist faculty, administration, and community to implement these activities. The emphasis here is on the benefit derived from involving *all* those involved in the educative process, *including* students at the junior and senior high levels, in working through not only the goal setting but also the form and substance of the school improvement plan.[4] The result of this planning process will be more than public knowledge of what schools are trying to do. The process also sensitizes schools to the needs and aspirations of the community. Throughout this planning process, it is essential that the participants have access to current knowledge about the best practices in each component as they develop school improvement plans.

3. Local school districts must provide the support needed to actualize school improvement plans: one important support is guaranteeing the stability of faculty and administration for a three- to five-year period. This involves commitment from school superintendents to a considerable measure of autonomy for schools in their district, as well as the availability of technical and content knowledgeable staff. Discretionary funds should be made available to schools to customize programs to the objectives developed in their improvement plan. Without this level of endorsement and support, as contrasted with a district-wide mandate that certain things "will be done" (such as, the designation by the central office that certain schools will be part of an effective schools project), the potential for such school based planning is minimized.

4. School districts must develop ways of rewarding faculty for giving time and energy to school improvement activities. This might take the form of providing time during the school day and/or additional salary to engage in planning. Without a system to recognize and reward teachers for important contributions to school improvement, the process is likely to be given a low priority and result in inconsequential school improvement plans.

5. Each school district must develop an ongoing staff development plan for teachers and administrators that emphasizes improving knowledge and understanding

---

[4] It cannot be overemphasized that successful implementation of an effective school plan depends on the faculty, administration, and community seeing the value of the changes and "buying into" the change strategies. It is not a question of "can the effective practices be implemented in the average school," but rather, "is the school and its community willing to invest in bringing these practices into their school?" Cost is not a critical factor. Most of the practices require a change in thinking and organizing for instruction, rather than large injections of additional monies. Mandating change is clearly a questionable tactic. Ownership of the improvement plan appears to be the key to successful implementation of the change strategy. The major focus is on improving instruction and organization of schools by using the research on effective practice, and *not* on the significantly more costly factors such as lengthening the school day and year, merit pay for teachers, reducing class size, and reducing the number of classes taught each day, that are being promoted in many recent national commissions and reports.

about effective instruction and organization. It is essential, for example, that school improvement plans contain ways to restructure the learning experience for low trajectory youths by incorporating the most effective instructional techniques (such as, mastery learning, direct teaching, student team games). Thus, the staff development effort *must* be able to deliver assistance and training in areas slated for improvement in the plans. The staff development should enable teachers and administrators to gain new knowledge and skills, practice these new skills, and receive continuous feedback and coaching concerning this practice. It should also create opportunities for both to work cooperatively in making instructional decisions that are based on sound research evidence. It is imperative that staff development be continuous throughout the school year, and that time be provided for these activities during the school day. Evidence suggests that the typical one-shot in service format is ineffective with respect to bringing about a change in behavior. Without time to plan for change, little change occurs.

6. In order to bring practice at the local school level into line with what is known from research to be effective, staff development activities must be tied to teacher and administrator evaluation. Ongoing monitoring of the school improvement plan is essential. In short, teachers and administrators should be hired and fired on their ability, *after* intensive staff development involving knowledge dissemination, practice, coaching, and feedback to model effective instructional and organizational practices has taken place.

In summary, it has been argued that effective schools, schools that improve the achievement of all students and reduce the incidence of delinquent involvements, *can* be created by (a) synthesizing knowledge about successful instructional and organizational practices, (b) incorporating such practices into specific educational improvement action plans, (c) providing staff development for faculty and administrators concerning the implementation of these practices, (d) monitoring the implementation and outcomes of these practices, and (e) annually modifying school improvement plans to reflect what has been learned during the previous year. In this way, all students attending schools will have the opportunity to succeed and maintain a range of options for postschool careers.[5] The result should be significantly fewer youths entering the juvenile justice system.[6] The next test becomes whether the occupational arena can be restructured to accommodate in an equitable way, well-prepared students from

---

[5] Two important ideas are implicit in this conception of an effective school. First, that schools can teach with equal facility students at either end of the learning continuum. Here, students achieving below grade level will learn at rates equal to or greater than students achieving at or above grade level. Second, that all students can learn in the *same* school. This latter idea is important because it brings into question the commonplace practice of isolating academically deficient and/or troublesome students into separate classrooms or buildings.

[6] The justice system can contribute to this process by engaging in activities such as (a) funding research on effective instructional and organizational practices, (b) sitting on school improvement planning teams, (c) collaborating on the articulation of schooling with work experience, (d) providing information to students on issues such as drug and alcohol dependence, and (e) facilitating the integration of youths with community agencies.

different class, race, and ethnic backgrounds in significantly greater numbers than ever
before.

REFERENCES

A Nation at Risk: The Imperative for Educational Reform. (1983). Washington, D.C.: Govern-
ment Printing Office.
Aichord, A. (1955). *Wayward Youth*. New York: Meridian Books.
Apple, M.W. (1982). "Reproduction and contradiction in education," in M.W. Apple (ed.)
Cultural and Economic Reproduction in Education. London: Routledge and Kegan Paul.
Berg, I. (1971). *Education and Jobs*. Boston: Beacon Press.
Bourdieu, P. and J.C. Passeron (1977) Reproduction in Education, Society and Culture. London:
Sage.
Bowles, S. and H. Gintis (1976). Schooling in Capitalist America. New York: *Basic Books*.
Brookover, W.B., et al. (1978). "Elementary school social climate and school achievement."
Amer. Educational Research J. 15: 552–565. (1979). School Social Systems and Student
Achievement: Schools Can Make a Difference. New York: *Praeger*.
Burt, C. (1938). The Young Delinquent. England: *Univ. of London Press*.
Chobot, R.B. and A. Garibaldi (1982). "In school alternatives to suspension: a description of ten
school districts' progress." Urban Rev. 14: 317–336.
Cicourel, A. and J. Kitsuse (1963). The Educational Decision Makers. New York: *Free Press*.
Cloward, R.A. and L.E. Ohlin (1960). Delinquency and Opportunity: A Theory of Delinquent
Gangs. New York: *Free Press*.
Cohen, A. (1955). Delinquent Boys. Glencoe, IL: *Free Press*.
Coleman, J.S. (1961). The Adolescent Society. New York: *Free Press*.
Coleman, J.S., et al. (1966). Equality of Educational Opportunity. Washington, DC: Govern-
ment Printing Office.
Deal, T. and R. Nolan (1978). Alternative Schools. Chicago: Nelson Hall.
Edmonds, R. (1979). "Effective schools for the urban poor." *Educational Leadership* 37:15–29.
Gold, M. and D. Mann (1983). "Alternative schools for troublesome youth." *Urban Rev*. 14:
305–316.
Goodlad, J. (1984). A Place Called School. New York: McGraw-Hill.
Gordon, C.W. (1957). The Social System of the High School. Glencoe, IL: *Free Press*.
Grossbard, A. (1962). "Ego deficiency in delinquents." *Social Casework* (April): 71–78.
Hathaway, S. and E.D. Monaches (eds.) (1953). Analyzing and Predicting Juvenile Delinquency
with the Minnesota Multiphasic Personality Inventory. Minneapolis: *Univ. of Minnesota
Press*.
Hargreaves, D.H. (1967). Social Relations in a Secondary School. New York: *Humanities Press*.
Herschi, T. (1969). Causes of Delinquency. Berkeley: *Univ. of California Press*.
Jencks, C., et al. (1972). Inequality: A Reassessment of the Effects of Family and Schooling in
America. New York: *Basic Books*.
Jones, J., et al. (1972). "Increasing the gap." *Education and Urban Society* 4: 339–349.
Kelly, D.H. (1978). How the School Manufactures Misfits. South Pasadena: *Newcal Publica-
tions*.
Kelly, D.H. and W.T. Pink (1973). "School commitment, youth rebellion and delinquency."
Criminology (February): 473–485.
Lemert, E.M. (1967). Human Deviance, Social Problems and Social Control. Englewood Cliffs,
NJ: Prentice Hall.

MacKenzie, D.E. (1983). "Research for school improvement: an appraisal of some recent trends." *Educational Researcher* 12: 5–17.

Merton, R.K. (1968). Social Theory and Social Structure. New York: *Free Press*.

Miller, W.B. (1958). "Lower class culture as a generating milieu of gang delinquency." J. of Social Issues XIV: 5–19.

Newman, F.M. (1981) "Reducing alienation in high schools: implications of theory." Harvard Educational Rev. 51: 546–564.

Ogbu, J. (1974). The Next Generation. New York: Academic Press. (1978). Minority Education and Caste: The American System in Cross-Cultural Perspective. New York: *Academic Press*.

Pearl, A. (1972). The Atrocity of Education. St. Louis: New Critics Press.

Pink, W.T. (1978). "Rebellion and success in the high school." *Contemporary Education* 49: 78–84. (1982a). "Academic failure, student social conflict and delinquent behavior." *Urban Rev.* 14: 141–180. (1982b). "The school principal and school climate: effects on disruption and academic performance," in G. Noblit and B. Johnson (eds.) The Principal and School Desegregation: An Anthology of Interpretive Studies. Springfield, IL: Charles C. Thomas. (1983). "Translating the literature on effective schools into practice: some words of caution." Presented at the AESA meetings, November, Milwaukee, Wisconsin. (1984). "Creating effective schools: problems in translating the literature into practice." *Educational Forum*.

Pink, W.T. and G.W. Noblit (1977). "The consequences of labeling in early adult careers." *Education* 98: 32–40.

Pink, W.T. and M. Sweeney (1978). "Teacher nomination, deviant career lines and the management of stigma in the junior high school." *Urban Education XIII*: 361–380.

Polk, K. (1969). "Class, strain and rebellion among adolescents." *Social Problems* 17:214–223.

Polk, K. and W.T. Pink (1971). "Youth culture and the school: a replication." *British J. of Sociology* (June): 160–171.

Polk, K. and W. Schafer (eds.) (1972). Schools and Delinquency. Englewood Cliffs: Prentice Hall.

Purkey, S.C. and M.S. Smith (1983). "Effective schools: a review. " *Elementary School J.* 83:427–452.

Rehberg, R. and E. Rosenthall (1978). Class and Merit in the American High School. New York: *Longman*.

Reiss, A.J., Jr. (1952).   "Social correlates of psychological types of delinquency." *Amer. Soc. Rev.* (December): 710–718.

Rist, R. (1970). "Social class and teacher expectation." *Harvard Educational Rev.* 49: 411–451. (1978). The Invisible Children: Social Integration in American Society. Cambridge: *Harvard Univ. Press*.

Rosenbaum, J.E. (1976). Making Inequality. New York: John Wiley.

Rowan, B., et al. (1983). "Research on effective schools: a cautionary note." *Educational Researcher* 12: 24–31.

Rutter, M., et al. (1979). Fifteen Thousand Hours. Cambridge: *Harvard Univ. Press*.

Schafer, W. and C. Olexa (1971). Tracking and Opportunity, Scranton, PA: Chandler.

Toby, J. (1957). "The differential impact of family disorganization." *Amer. Soc. Rev.* (October): 505–512.

Toby, J. and M. Toby (1962). "Low school status as a predisposing factor in sub-cultured delinquency." New Brunswick: *Rutgers University (mimeo)*.

Willis, P.E. (1977). Learning to Labour. Farnsborough, England: *Saxon House*.

Young, J. and G. Whitty (eds.) (1977). Society, State and Schooling. Guildford, England: *Falmer Press*.

Police Encounters
with Juveniles[1]

IRVING PILIAVIN
SCOTT BRIAR

*In an observational study of police officers' contacts with juveniles the
authors reached these conclusions: (1) Wide discretion was exercised by
policemen in dealing with youthful offenders. (2) The exercise of this
discretion was affected by a few readily observable criteria, including
boys' prior offense records, race, grooming, and demeanor. Among first
offenders particularly, but to some degree among all offenders, a youth's
demeanor was a major criterion for determining what police disposition
he would be given. Officers estimated that 50–60 per cent of first offense
dispositions were based on this criterion. (3) The differential in arrest
and apprehension rates between Negroes and whites was not simply a
consequence of a greater offense rate among the former or police bias.
To some extent this differential was due to the fact that Negroes more
often than Caucasians exhibited those aspects of demeanor associated
by officers with "true" delinquent boys.*

As THE FIRST of a series of decisions made in the channeling of youthful offenders
through the agencies concerned with juvenile justice and corrections, the disposition
decisions made by police officers have potentially profound consequences for apprehended juveniles. Thus arrest, the most severe of the dispositions available to police,

Source: Piliavin, Irving and Scott Briar. "Police Encounters with Juveniles." *American Journal of
Sociology* Vol. 70 (September) 1964: 206–214. Reprinted by permission of the University of Chicago Press
and the authors.

[1] This study was supported by Grant MH-06328-02, National Institute of Mental Health, United
States Public Health Service.

may not only lead to confinement of the suspected offender but also bring him loss of social status, restriction of educational and employment opportunities, and future harassment by law-enforcement personnel.[2] According to some criminologists, the stigmatization resulting from police apprehension, arrest, and detention actually reinforces deviant behavior.[3] Other authorities have suggested, in fact, that this stigmatization serves as the catalytic agent initiating delinquent careers.[4] Despite their presumed significance, however, little empirical analysis has been reported regarding the factors influencing, or consequences resulting from, police actions with juvenile offenders. Furthermore, while some studies of police encounters with adult offenders have been reported, the extent to which the findings of these investigations pertain to law-enforcement practices with youthful offenders is not known.[5]

The above considerations have led the writers to undertake a longitudinal study of the conditions influencing, and consequences flowing from, police actions with juveniles. In the present paper findings will be presented indicating the influence of certain factors on police actions. Research data consist primarily of notes and records based on nine months' observation of all juvenile officers in one police department.[6] The officers were observed in the course of their regular tours of duty.[7] While these data do not lend themselves to quantitative assessments of reliability and validity, the candor shown by the officers in their interviews with the investigators and their use of officially frowned-upon practices while under observation provide some assurance that the materials presented below accurately reflect the typical operations and attitudes of the law-enforcement personnel studied.

The setting for the research, a metropolitan police department serving an industrial city with approximately 450,000 inhabitants, was noted within the community it served and among law-enforcement officials elsewhere for the honesty and superior quality of its personnel. Incidents involving criminal activity or brutality by

[2] Richard D. Schwartz and Jerome H. Skolnick, "Two Studies of Legal Stigma," *Social Problems,* X (April, 1962), 133–42; Sol Rubin, *Crime and Juvenile Delinquency* (New York: Oceana Publications, 1958); B.F. McSally, "Finding Jobs for Released Offenders," *Federal Probation,* XXIV (June, 1960), 12–17; Harold D. Lasswell and Richard C. Donnelly, "The Continuing Debate over Responsibility: An Introduction to Isolating the Condemnation Sanction," *Yale Law Journal,* LXVIII (April, 1959), 869–99.

[3] Richard A. Cloward and Lloyd E. Ohlin, *Delinquency and Opportunity* (Glencoe, Ill.: Free Press, 1960), pp. 124–30.

[4] Frank Tannenbaum, *Crime and the Community* (New York: Columbia University Press, 1936), pp. 17–20; Howard S. Becker, *Outsiders: Studies in the Sociology of Deviance* (New York: Free Press of Glencoe, 1963), chaps. i and ii.

[5] For a detailed accounting of police discretionary practices, see Joseph Goldstein, "Police Discretion Not To Invoke the Criminal Process: Low Visibility Decisions in the Administration of Justice," *Yale Law Journal,* LXIX (1960), 543–94; Wayne R. LaFave, "The Police and Non-enforcement of the Law—Part I," *Wisconsin Law Review,* January, 1962, pp. 104–37; S.H. Kadish, "Legal Norms and Discretion in the Police and Sentencing Processes," *Harvard Law Review,* LXXV (March, 1962), 904–31.

[6] Approximately thirty officers were assigned to the Juvenile Bureau in the department studied. While we had an opportunity to observe all officers in the Bureau during the study, our observations were concentrated on those who had been working in the Bureau for one or two years at least. Although two of the officers in the Juvenile Bureau were Negro, we observed these officers on only a few occasions.

[7] Although observations were not confined to specific days or work shifts, more observations were made during evenings and weekends because police activity was greatest during these periods.

members of the department had been extremely rare during the ten years preceding this study; personnel standards were comparatively high; and an extensive training program was provided to both new and experienced personnel. Juvenile Bureau members, the primary subjects of this investigation, differed somewhat from other members of the department in that they were responsible for delinquency prevention as well as law enforcement, that is, juvenile officers were expected to be knowledgeable about conditions leading to crime and delinquency and to be able to work with community agencies serving known or potential juvenile offenders. Accordingly, in the assignment of personnel to the Juvenile Bureau, consideration was given not only to an officer's devotion to and reliability in law enforcement but also to his commitment to delinquency prevention. Assignment to the Bureau was of advantage to policemen seeking promotions. Consequently, many officers requested transfer to this unit, and its personnel comprised a highly select group of officers.

In the field, juvenile officers operated essentially as patrol officers. They cruised assigned beats and, although concerned primarily with juvenile offenders, frequently had occasion to apprehend and arrest adults. Confrontations between the officers and juveniles occurred in one of the following three ways, in order of increasing frequency: (1) encounters resulting from officers' spotting officially "wanted" youths; (2) encounters taking place at or near the scene of offenses reported to police headquarters; and (3) encounters occurring as the result of officers' directly observing youths either committing offenses or in "suspicious circumstances." However, the probability that a confrontation would take place between officer and juvenile, or that a particular disposition of an identified offender would be made, was only in part determined by the knowledge that an offense had occurred or that a particular juvenile had committed an offense. The bases for and utilization of non-offenses related criteria by police in accosting and disposing of juveniles are the focuses of the following discussion.

SANCTIONS FOR DISCRETION

In each encounter with juveniles, with the minor exception of officially "wanted" youths,[8] a central task confronting the officer was to decide what official action to take against the boys involved. In making these disposition decisions, officers could select any one of five discrete alternatives:

1. outright release
2. release and submission of a "field interrogation report" briefly describing the circumstances initiating the police-juvenile confrontation.
3. "official reprimand" and release to parents or guardian
4. citation to juvenile court
5. arrest and confinement in juvenile hall.

[8] "Wanted" juveniles usually were placed under arrest or in protective custody, a practice which in effect relieved officers of the responsibility for deciding what to do with these youths.

Dispositions 3, 4, and 5 differed from the others in two basic respects. First, with rare exceptions, when an officer chose to reprimand, cite, or arrest a boy, he took the youth to the police station. Second, the reprimanded, cited, or arrested boy acquired an official police "record," that is, his name was officially recorded in Bureau files as a juvenile violator.

Analysis of the distribution of police disposition decisions about juveniles revealed that in virtually every category of offense the full range of official disposition alternatives available to officers was employed. This wide range of discretion resulted primarily from two conditions. First, it reflected the reluctance of officers to expose certain youths to the stigmatization presumed to be associated with official police action. Few juvenile officers believed that correctional agencies serving the community could effectively help delinquents. For some officers this attitude reflected a lack of confidence in rehabilitation techniques; for others, a belief that high case loads and lack of professional training among correctional workers vitiated their efforts at treatment. All officers were agreed, however, that juvenile justice and correctional processes were essentially concerned with apprehension and punishment rather than treatment. Furthermore, all officers believed that some aspects of these processes (e.g., judicial definition of youths as delinquents and removal of delinquents from the community), as well as some of the possible consequences of these processes (e.g., intimate institutional contact with "hard-core" delinquents, as well as parental, school, and conventional peer disapproval or rejection), could reinforce what previously might have been only a tentative proclivity toward delinquent values and behavior. Consequently, when officers found reason to doubt that a youth being confronted was highly committed toward deviance, they were inclined to treat him with leniency.

Second, and more important, the practice of discretion was sanctioned by police-department policy. Training manuals and departmental bulletins stressed that the disposition of each juvenile offender was not to be based solely on the type of infraction he committed. Thus, while it was departmental policy to "arrest and confine all juveniles who have committed a felony or misdemeanor involving theft, sex offense, battery, possession of dangerous weapons, prowling, peeping, intoxication, incorrigibility, and disturbance of the peace," it was acknowledged that "such considerations as age, attitude and prior criminal record might indicate that a different disposition would be more appropriate."[9] The official justification for discretion in processing juvenile offenders, based on the preventive aims of the Juvenile Bureau, was that each juvenile violator should be dealt with solely on the basis of what was best for him.[10] Unofficially, administrative legitimation of discretion was further justified on the grounds that strict enforcement practices would overcrowd court calendars and detention facilities, as well as dramatically increase juvenile crime rates—consequences to be avoided because they would expose the police department to community criticism.[11]

---

[9] Quoted from a training manual issued by the police department studied in this research.

[10] Presumably this also implied that police action with juveniles was to be determined partly by the offenders' need for correctional services.

[11] This was reported by beat officers as well as supervisory and administrative personnel of the juvenile bureau.

In practice, the official policy justifying use of discretion served as a demand that discretion be exercised. As such, it posed three problems fur juvenile officers. First, it represented a departure from the traditional police practice with which the juvenile officers themselves were identified, in the sense that they were expected to justify their juvenile disposition decisions not simply by evidence proving a youth had committed a crime—grounds on which police were officially expected to base their dispositions of non-juvenile offenders[12]—but in the *character* of the youth. Second, in disposing of juvenile offenders, officers were expected, in effect, to make judicial rather than ministerial decisions.[13] Third, the shift from the offense to the offender as the basis for determining the appropriate disposition substantially increased the uncertainty and ambiguity for officers in the situation of apprehension because no explicit rules existed for determining which disposition different types of youths should receive. Despite these problems, officers were constrained to base disposition decisions on the character of the apprehended youth, not only because they wanted to be fair, but because persistent failure to do so could result in judicial criticism, departmental censure, and, they believed, loss of authority with juveniles.[14]

DISPOSITION CRITERIA

Assessing the character of apprehended offenders posed relatively few difficulties for officers in the case of youths who had committed serious crimes such as robbery, homicide, aggravated assault, grand theft, auto theft, rape, and arson. Officials generally regarded these juveniles as confirmed delinquents simply by virtue of their involvement in offenses of this magnitude.[15] However, the infraction committed did not always suffice to determine the appropriate disposition for some serious offenders;[16] and, in the case of minor offenders, who comprised over 90 per cent of the youths against whom police took action, the violation per se generally played an insignificant role in the choice of disposition. While a number of minor offenders were seen as serious delinquents deserving arrest, many others were perceived either as "good" boys whose offenses were atypical of their customary behavior, as pawns of undesirable associates or, in any case, as boys for whom arrest was regarded as an unwarranted and possibly harmful punishment. Thus, for nearly all minor violators and for some serious

[12] In actual practice, of course, disposition decisions regarding adult offenders also were influenced by many factors extraneous to the offense per se.

[13] For example, in dealing with adult violators, officers had no disposition alternative comparable to the reprimand-and-release category, a disposition which contained elements of punishment but did not involve mediation by the court.

[14] The concern of officers over possible loss of authority stemmed from their belief that court failure to support arrests by appropriate action would cause policemen to "lose face" in the eyes of juveniles.

[15] It is also likely that the possibility of negative publicity resulting from the failure to arrest such violators—particularly if they became involved in further serious crime—brought about strong administrative pressure for their arrest.

[16] For example, in the year preceding this research, over 30 per cent of the juveniles involved in burglaries and 12 per cent of the juveniles committing auto theft received dispositions other than arrest.

delinquents, the assessment of character—the distinction between serious delinquents, "good" boys, misguided youths, and so on—and the dispositions which followed from these assessments were based on youths' personal characteristics and not their offenses.

Despite this dependence of disposition decisions on the personal characteristics of these youths, however, police officers actually had access only to very limited information about boys at the time they had to decide what to do with them. In the field, officers typically had no data concerning the past offense records, school performance, family situation, or personal adjustment of apprehended youths.[17] Furthermore, files at police headquarters provided data only about each boy's prior offense record. Thus both the decision made in the field—whether or not to bring the boy in—and the decision made at the station—which disposition to invoke—were based largely on cues which emerged from the interaction between the officer and the youth, cues from which the officer inferred the youth's character. These cues included the youth's group affiliations, age, race, grooming, dress, and demeanor. Older juveniles, members of known delinquent gangs, Negroes, youths with well-oiled hair, black jackets, and soiled denims or jeans (the presumed uniform of "tough" boys), and boys who in their interactions with officers did not manifest what were considered to be appropriate signs of respect tended to receive the more severe dispositions.

Other than prior record, the most important of the above clues was a youth's *demeanor*. In the opinion of juvenile patrolmen themselves the demeanor of apprehended juveniles was a major determinant of their decisions for 50–60 per cent of the juvenile cases they processed.[18] A less subjective indication of the association between a youth's demeanor and police disposition is provided by Table 28.1, which presents the police dispositions for sixty-six youths whose encounters with police were observed in the course of this study.[19] For purposes of this analysis, each youth's demeanor in the encounter was classified as either co-operative or un-cooperative.[20] The results clearly reveal a marked association between youth demeanor and the severity of police dispositions.

[17] On occasion, officers apprehended youths whom they personally knew to be prior offenders. This did not occur frequently, however, for several reasons. First, approximately 75 per cent of apprehended youths had no prior official records; second, officers periodically exchanged patrol areas, thus limiting their exposure to, and knowledge about, these areas; and third, patrolmen seldom spent more than three or four years in the juvenile division.

[18] While reliable subgroup estimates were impossible to obtain through observation because of the relatively small number of incidents observed, the importance of demeanor in disposition decisions appeared to be much less significant with known prior offenders.

[19] Systematic data were collected on police encounters with seventy-six juveniles. In ten of these encounters the police concluded that their suspicions were groundless, and consequently the juveniles involved were exonerated; these ten cases were eliminated from this analysis of demeanor. (The total number of encounters observed was considerably more than seventy-six, but systematic data-collection procedures were not instituted until several months after observations began.)

[20] The data used for the classification of demeanor were the written records of observations made by the authors. The classifications were made by an independent judge not associated with this study. In classifying a youth's demeanor as co-operative or un-cooperative, particular attention was paid to: (1) the youth's responses to police officers' questions and requests; (2) the respect and deference—or lack of these qualities—shown by the youth toward police officers; and (3) police officers' assessments of the youth's

TABLE 28.1   Severity of police disposition by youth's demeanor

Severity of police disposition	Youth's Demeanor		
	Co-operative	Un-cooperative	Total
Arrest (more severe)	2	14	16
Citation or official reprimand	4	5	9
Informal reprimand	15	1	16
Admonish and release (least severe)	24	1	25
Total	45	21	66

The cues used by police to assess demeanor were fairly simple. Juveniles who were contrite about their infractions, respectful to officers, and fearful of the sanctions that might be employed against them tended to be viewed by patrolmen as basically law-abiding or at least "salvageable." For these youths it was usually assumed that informal or formal reprimand would suffice to guarantee their future conformity. In contrast, youthful offenders who were fractious, obdurate, or who appeared nonchalant in their encounters with patrolmen were likely to be viewed as "would-be tough guys" or "punks" who fully deserved the most severe sanction: arrest. The following excerpts from observation notes illustrate the importance attached to demeanor by police in making disposition decisions.

1. The interrogation of "A" (an 18-year-old upper-lower-class white male accused of statutory rape) was assigned to a police sergeant with long experience on the force. As I sat in his office while we waited for the youth to arrive for questioning, the sergeant expressed his uncertainty as to what he should do with this young man. On the one hand, he could not ignore the fact that an offense had been committed; he had been informed, in fact, that the youth was prepared to confess to the offense. Nor could he overlook the continued pressure from the girl's father (an important political figure) for the police to take severe action against the youth. On the other hand, the sergeant had formed a low opinion of the girl's moral character, and he considered it unfair to charge "A" with statutory rape when the girl was a willing partner to the offense and might even have been the instigator of it. However, his sense of injustice concerning "A" was tempered by his image of the youth as a "punk," based, he explained, on information he had received that the youth belonged to a certain gang, the members of which were well known to, and disliked by, the police. Nevertheless, as we prepared to leave his office to interview "A," the sergeant was still in doubt as to what he should do with him.

As we walked down the corridor to the interrogation room, the sergeant was stopped by a reporter from the local newspaper. In an excited tone of voice, the reporter explained that his editor was pressing him to get further information about this case. The newspaper had printed some of the facts about the girl's disappearance, and as a consequence the girl's father was threatening suit against the paper for defamation of the girl's character. It would strengthen the newspaper's position, the reporter explained, if the police had information indicating that the girl's associates, particularly the youth the sergeant was about to interrogate, were persons of disreputable character. This stimulus seemed to resolve the sergeant's uncertainty. He told the reporter, "unofficially," that the youth was known to be an undesirable person, citing as evidence his membership in the delinquent gang. Furthermore, the sergeant added that he had evidence that this youth had been intimate with the girl over a period of many months. When the reporter asked if the police were planning to do anything to the youth, the sergeant answered that he intended to charge the youth with statutory rape.

In the interrogation, however, three points quickly emerged which profoundly affected the sergeant's judgment of the youth. First, the youth was polite and co-operative; he consistently addressed the officer as "sir," answered all questions quietly, and signed a statement implicating himself in numerous counts of statutory rape. Second, the youth's intentions toward the girl appeared to have been honorable; for example, he said that he wanted to marry her eventually. Third, the youth was not in fact a member of the gang in question. The sergeant's attitude became increasingly sympathetic, and after we left the interrogation room he announced his intention to "get 'A' off the hook," meaning that he wanted to have the charges against "A" reduced or, if possible, dropped.

2. Officers "X" and "Y" brought into the police station a seventeen-year-old white boy who, along with two older companions, had been found in a home having sex relations with a fifteen-year-old girl. The boy responded to police officers' queries slowly and with obvious disregard. It was apparent that his lack of deference toward the officers and his failure to evidence concern about his situation were irritating his questioners. Finally, one of the officers turned to me and, obviously angry, commented that in his view the boy was simply a "stud" interested only in sex, eating, and sleeping. The policemen conjectured that the boy "probably already had knocked up half a dozen girls." The boy ignored these remarks, except for an occasional impassive stare at the patrolmen. Turning to the boy, the officer remarked, "What the hell am I going to do with you?" And again the boy simply returned the officer's gaze. The latter then said, "Well, I guess we'll just have to put you away for a while." An arrest report was then made out and the boy was taken to Juvenile Hall.

Although anger and disgust frequently characterized officers' attitudes toward recalcitrant and impassive juvenile offenders, their manner while processing these youths was typically routine, restrained, and without rancor. While the officers' restraint may have been due in part to their desire to avoid accusation and censure, it also seemed to reflect their inurement to a frequent experience. By and large, only their occasional "needling" or insulting of a boy gave any hint of the underlying resentment and dislike they felt toward many of these youths.[21]

[21] Officers' animosity toward recalcitrant or aloof offenders appeared to stem from two sources: moral indignation that these juveniles were self-righteous and indifferent about their transgressions, and resentment that these youths failed to accord police the respect they believed they deserved. Since the patrolmen perceived themselves as honestly and impartially performing a vital community function

PREJUDICE IN APPREHENSION AND DISPOSITION DECISIONS

Compared to other youths, Negroes and boys whose appearance matched the delinquent stereotype were more frequently stopped and interrogated by patrolmen—often even in the absence of evidence that an offense had been committed[22] —and usually were given more severe dispositions for the same violations. Our data suggest, however, that these selective apprehension and disposition practices resulted not only from the intrusion of long-held prejudices of individual police officers but also from certain job-related experiences of law-enforcement personnel. First, the tendency for police to give more severe dispositions to Negroes and to youths whose appearance corresponded to that which police associated with delinquents partly reflected the fact, observed in this study, that these youths also were much more likely than were other types of boys to exhibit the sort of recalcitrant demeanor which police construed as a sign of the confirmed delinquent. Further, officers assumed, partly on the basis of departmental statistics, that Negroes and juveniles who "look tough" (e.g., who wear chinos, leather jackets, boots, etc.) commit crimes more frequently than do other types of youths.[23] In this sense, the police justified their selective treatment of these youths along epidemiological lines: that is, they were concentrating their attention on those youths whom they believed were most likely to commit delinquent acts. In the words of one highly placed official in the department:

> If you know that the bulk of your delinquent problem comes from kids who, say, are from 12 to 14 years of age, when you're out on patrol you are much more likely to be sensitive to the activities of juveniles in this age bracket than older or younger groups. This would be good law enforcement practice. The logic in our case is the same except that our delinquency problem is largely found in the Negro community and it is these youths toward whom we are sensitized.

As regards prejudice per se, eighteen of twenty-seven officers interviewed openly admitted a dislike for Negroes. However, they attributed their dislike to experiences they had, as policemen, with youths from this minority group. The officers reported that Negro boys were much more likely than non-Negroes to "give us a hard

---

warranting respect and deference from the community at large, they attributed the lack of respect shown them by these juveniles to the latters' immorality.

[22] The clearest evidence for this assertion is provided by the overrepresentation of Negroes among "innocent" juveniles accosted by the police. As noted, of the seventy-six juveniles on whom systematic data were collected, ten were exonerated and released without suspicion. Seven, or two-thirds of these ten "innocent" juveniles were Negro, in contrast to the allegedly "guilty" youths, less than one-third of whom were Negro. The following incident illustrates the operation of this bias: One officer, observing a youth walking along the street, commented that the youth "looks suspicious" and promptly stopped and questioned him. Asked later to explain what aroused his suspicion, the officer explained, "He was a Negro wearing dark glasses at midnight."

[23] While police statistics did not permit an analysis of crime rates by appearance, they strongly supported officers' contentions concerning the delinquency rate among Negroes. Of all male juveniles processed by the police department in 1961, for example, 40.2 per cent were Negro and 33.9 per cent were

time," be unco-operative, and show no remorse for their transgressions. Recurrent exposure to such attitudes among Negro youth, the officers claimed, generated their antipathy toward Negroes. The following excerpt is typical of the views expressed by these officers:

> They (Negroes) have no regard for the law or for the police. They just don't seem to give a damn. Few of them are interested in school or getting ahead. The girls start having illegitimate kids before they are 16 years old and the boys are always "out for kicks." Furthermore, many of these kids try to run you down. They say the damnedest things to you and they seem to have absolutely no respect for you as an adult. I admit I am prejudiced now, but frankly I don't think I was when I began police work.

IMPLICATIONS

It is apparent from the findings presented above that the police officers studied in this research were permitted and even encouraged to exercise immense latitude in disposing of the juveniles they encountered. That is, it was within the officers' discretionary authority, except in extreme limiting cases, to decide which juveniles were to come to the attention of the courts and correctional agencies and thereby be identified officially as delinquents. In exercising this discretion policemen were strongly guided by the demeanor of those who were apprehended, a practice which ultimately led, as seen above, to certain youths, (particularly Negroes[24] and boys dressed in the style of "toughs") being treated more severely than other juveniles for comparable offenses.

But the relevance of demeanor was not limited only to police disposition practices. Thus, for example, in conjunction with police crime statistics the criterion of demeanor led police to concentrate their surveillance activities in areas frequented or inhabited by Negroes. Furthermore, these youths were accosted more often than others by officers on patrol simply because their skin color identified them as potential troublemakers. These discriminatory practices—and it is important to note that they are discriminatory, even if based on accurate statistical information—may well have self-fulfilling consequences. Thus it is not unlikely that frequent encounters with police, particularly those involving youths innocent of wrongdoing, will increase the hostility of these juveniles toward law-enforcement personnel. It is also not unlikely that the frequency of such encounters will in time reduce their significance in the eyes of apprehended juveniles, thereby leading these youths to regard them as "routine." Such responses to police encounters, however, are those which law-enforcement personnel perceive as indicators of the serious delinquent. They thus serve to vindicate and reinforce officers' prejudices, leading to closer surveillance of Negro districts, more frequent encounters with Negro youths, and so on in a vicious circle. Moreover, the consequences of this chain of events are reflected in police statistics showing a

---

[24] An unco-operative demeanor was presented by more than one-third of the Negro youths but by only one-sixth of the white youths encountered by the police in the course of our observations.

disproportionately high percentage of Negroes among juvenile offenders, thereby providing "objective" justification for concentrating police attention on Negro youths.

To a substantial extent, as we have implied earlier, the discretion practiced by juvenile officers is simply an extension of the juvenile-court philosophy, which holds that in making legal decisions regarding juveniles, more weight should be given to the juvenile's character and life-situation than to his actual offending behavior. The juvenile officer's disposition decisions—and the information he uses as a basis for them—are more akin to the discriminations made by probation officers and other correctional workers than they are to decisions of police officers dealing with non-juvenile offenders. The problem is that such clinical-type decisions are not restrained by mechanisms comparable to the principles of due process and the rules of procedure governing police decisions regarding adult offenders. Consequently, prejudicial practices by police officers can escape notice more easily in their dealings with juveniles than with adults.

The observations made in this study serve to underscore the fact that the official delinquent, as distinguished from the juvenile who simply commits a delinquent act, is the product of a social judgment, in this case a judgment made by the police. He is a delinquent because someone in authority has defined him as one, often on the basis of the public face he has presented to officials rather than of the kind of offense he has committed.

Survey Research Center and Center for the Study of Law and Society
University of California, Berkeley

ARTICLE 29

Street-Level Justice

Situational Determinants of Police Arrest Decisions*

DOUGLAS A. SMITH
CHRISTY A. VISHER

In this paper we examine variations in police arrest practices. Data collected in 1977 from police encounters with suspects indicate that arrest practices reflect legal and extra-legal factors. The decision to take a suspect into custody is influenced by such features of the situation as the dispositional preferences of victims, the race and demeanor of the suspect, and the presence of bystanders. Furthermore, the seriousness of the offense increases the chances of arrest. Contrary to much existing literature, males and females are equally likely to be arrested. The relevance of these findings to theoretical models of police behavior is discussed and the implications of our analysis for studies of criminal processing in general are considered.

POLICE OCCUPY A UNIQUE and powerful position in our system of justice. Unlike other decision-makers in the criminal justice system (e.g., prosecutors, judges), police officers make legal decisions in a context of low visibility. Consequently, they have wide discretionary power over who will be subject to legal intervention and control. In

Source: Smith, Douglas A. and Christy A. Visher. "Street-Level Justice: Situational Determinants of Police Arrest Decisions." *Social Problems* Vol. 29 (December) 1981: 167–177. Reprinted by permission of the Society for the Study of Social Problems c 1981.

* This research was made possible, in part, by a grant from the National Science Foundation (No. G143949) to the Workshop in Political Theory and Policy Analysis at Indiana University. Neither the workshop nor the National Science Foundation bear any responsibility for the analysis or interpretation presented here. The authors thank Roger Parks, Alan Lizotte, Charles Tittle and the anonymous reviewers of *Social Problems* for their insights and criticisms of previous drafts. Correspondence to Douglas Smith, Department of Sociology.

part, the power of the police rests on their ability to regulate the flow of persons to other social control agencies (Clark and Sykes, 1974). This institutional location of the police has broad consequences for those against whom the law is applied (Bottomley, 1973; Piliavin and Briar, 1964). Arrest not only threatens individual liberty but involves many other social and economic liabilities as well. Hence, whether police invoke the law consistently or not is a central issue in the study of police behavior.

Police have a legal mandate to enforce the law uniformly. Early models of police behavior portrayed the police as ministerial officers operating under the strict rule of law (e.g., Kadish, 1962). But a policy of full enforcement, which uniform enforcement implies, is neither possible nor desirable because of conflicting organizational goals, diverse situational demands and the dependence of police on the communities they serve (Goldstein, 1963; Manning, 1977; Quinney, 1970; Wilson, 1968). Moreover, several studies have demonstrated the myth of complete enforcement (Black, 1970; Lundman, 1974; Lundman *et al.*, 1978; Piliavin and Briar, 1964; Reiss, 1971; Skolnick, 1966). Most scholars concur that selective enforcement is a routine aspect of contemporary police work.

When the potentially profound consequences of arrest are combined with the norm of selective enforcement, several critical issues emerge. The most central one is: upon what criteria is the law being invoked? One answer to this question is that enforcement reflects the underlying dimensions of stratification in society (Black, 1976; Cook, 1967; Galliher, 1971; Silver, 1967). Specifically, members of socially disadvantaged groups such as blacks and youth are more likely to be taken into custody independent of the seriousness of their behavior. Opposing this view is a conception of the police as equally responsive to the interests of all social groups (Blau and Scott, 1962). Within this framework, police arrest decisions reflect the seriousness of particular violations rather than the situation or characteristics of the violator.

These two models of police behavior may, however, possess only limited promise for advancing our understanding of arrest decisions. In encounters with suspects police often make arrests quickly. This precludes a careful weighing of information on the part of the police and forces them to act on the basis of salient situational characteristics. Indeed, several writers suggest that these external cues are powerful determinants of arrest decisions (Bittner, 1967; Cumming *et al.*, 1965; Pepinsky, 1975). Moreover, many of these situational factors do not fit neatly into either the consensus or conflict model of policing. For example, if police decisions to arrest are influenced by the presence of bystanders neither theoretical camp could claim to have expected this relationship.

But the absence of an integrated theoretical model is not the only impediment to a more complete understanding of police decision making. Equally troublesome is that the empirical literature on police behavior only paints an impressionistic image of arrest decisions. Previous research has looked primarily at the relationship between arrest and limited combinations of extra-legal variables. Indeed, a recent review of the empirical literature on the determinants of police behavior characterized this research as "a series of bivariate assertions about the impact of certain variables on police behavior" (Sherman, 1980:70). Consequently, the relative contribution of various predictors of the arrest decision remains problematic.

Our analysis has several objectives. Since much of the previous empirical work on arrest decisions has been based on only two data sets pertaining to police-citizen contacts (the Black-Reiss data collected in 1966 and the Sykes-Clark data from 1970), new data of this type are introduced. The data for this study represent police-citizen contacts observed in 1977 in 24 police departments. First, we determine the strength of association between arrest and variables included in previous research on police arrest practices. Second, we estimate the relative importance of various factors in the arrest decision. Third, we estimate a causal model reflecting the interrelations among these variables and the decision to arrest.

PREVIOUS RESEARCH

One situational variable that is frequently discussed in the literature on police-citizen encounters is the way police enter the scene. The majority of police-citizen encounters are reactive, rather than proactive (Black, 1971; Reiss, 1971). Police-initiated encounters generally involve minor offenses and appear to differ substantially from reactive encounters. Police may be granted less legitimacy in proactive encounters and react more aggressively to establish a position of authority (Friedrich, 1977). Some studies report a higher proportion of arrests in proactive encounters (Black, 1971; Lundman, 1974). However, police may have a greater range of options in handling encounters they initiate themselves since these encounters are less visible to the police organization and, unlike mobilizations initiated by a dispatcher, are not necessarily a matter of departmental record. Thus, the influence of type of mobilization on arrest decisions is unclear.

Location of the encounter is an additional factor that may relate to an officer's decision to arrest a suspect. Lundman (1974) found that police made more arrests for drunkenness in enclosed public places, such as bars, than in open public places or private places. Conversely, others suggest that when police are asked to maintain order they are less likely to use formal authority in private places than in public ones (Black, 1976; Wilson, 1968).

The salient feature of the spatial location may be the presence or absence of bystanders (Bittner, 1970; Westley, 1953). The presence of an audience may threaten police control of the situation and prompt formal action to re-establish authority. Police may find it necessary to quickly control a situation and arrest a suspect when an audience is present. On the other hand, police might informally warn or reprimand a suspect if the encounter is not conspicuous to others. For example, Friedrich (1977) found that arrest decisions are more likely when at least 10 citizens are present.

The primary legal explanation of arrest decisions is the seriousness of the offense. Police are more likely to arrest both adult and juvenile suspects when the offense is a felony rather than a misdemeanor (Black, 1971; Black and Reiss, 1970; Friedrich, 1977; LaFave, 1965; Lundman et al., 1978; Piliavin and Briar, 1964).

The influence of suspect characteristics (race, age, gender, demeanor) on arrest decisions has generated some debate. While most researchers agree that blacks are more likely to be stopped, interrogated, and subsequently arrested (Black, 1971; Black and Reiss, 1970; Bogomolny, 1976; Lundman *et al.*, 1978; Friedrich, 1977; Piliavin and Briar, 1964), interpretations of this pattern are diverse. Some argue that the higher arrest rate for blacks reflects a greater incidence of disrespectful and hostile behavior by black suspects toward police (Black, 1971). Others maintain that the effect of race on arrest decisions disappears when the seriousness of the offense is held constant (Black and Reiss, 1970; Terry, 1967). Thus, whether blacks occupy a disadvantaged status in arrest situations independent of other aspects of their behavior is problematic.

Most studies of police behavior analyze either juvenile or adult samples. As a result, little is known about the influence of the suspect's age on arrest decisions. Some early studies (LaFave, 1965; Piliavin and Briar, 1964) suggest that officers exercise considerably more discretion towards juveniles, but we lack systematic evidence on this issue.

Gender differences in arrest have been examined directly. Several studies of police-citizen encounters indicate that women are much less likely to be stopped, interrogated, or arrested than men (Friedrich, 1977; McEachern and Bauzer, 1967; Pastor, 1978; Rubinstein, 1973). This may suggest that police view female suspects as less threatening and less dangerous than male suspects. Alternatively, police encounters with female suspects might involve more minor offenses which end in an arrest less often. But, when victim reports are compared with official arrest records, female offenders appear over-represented in arrest statistics for serious offenses (Hindelang, 1979). Thus, the influence of gender on arrest decisions is unclear.

The demeanor of the suspect also influences police decisions to invoke the law. Indeed, much research indicates that antagonistic or hostile suspects run a greater risk of being arrested (Bittner, 1967; Black, 1971; Black and Reiss, 1970; Lundman *et al.*, 1978; Piliavin and Briar, 1964; Reiss, 1971; Sykes and Clark, 1975).

Another situational factor in arrest decisions is the presence and actions of complainants. Police rely on information from victims for evidence about the offense. Similarly, officers may consider the complainant's request for arrest or leniency when making arrest decisions. Several studies report that police encounters with isolated suspects ended in arrest less often than encounters where a complainant was present (Black and Reiss, 1970; Lundman et al., 1978). However, Lundman (1974) found that the presence of a complainant was not related to arrests for public intoxication. Also, when citizens explicitly request an arrest, police tend to comply (Black, 1970; Black, 1971; Black and Reiss, 1970; Friedrich, 1977; Lundman *et al.*, 1978). Conversely, police rarely arrest a suspect if a complainant asks them not to (Black, 1971; LaFave, 1965). As a result, complainant presence and complainant preference for arrest seem to be important determinants of police decisions to invoke the law.

Our final predictor of arrest is the victim-suspect relationship. Previous research suggests that police make arrests more often when the suspect is a stranger to the victim (Black, 1971; LaFave, 1965; Friedrich, 1977), but less often when the victim and suspect are friends, acquaintances or relatives. These findings suggest that law varies directly with relational distance (Black, 1976).

DATA

The data used in the current analysis were collected as part of a larger evaluation of police services conducted in 1977. Trained civilians riding on 900 patrol shifts recorded information on 5,688 police-citizen encounters. These data represent 24 police departments in the metropolitan areas of St. Louis, Missouri, Rochester, New York, and Tampa-St. Petersburg, Florida. Those cases which did not contain a suspect were eliminated from the analysis. Traffic stops were also excluded since arrest, while possible, occurs rarely in these encounters. Finally, since coding characteristics of the suspect was a major concern, all cases were excluded where there were multiple suspects heterogenous in race, age or gender. The final sample contains data on 742 encounters.

FINDINGS

Table 29.1 presents descriptive statistics and the percent arrested within categories of each independent variable. The majority of these encounters were responses to citizen requests for police service. A slight tendency exists for the encounters to occur in public places, and in about half of the encounters, bystanders, who were not directly involved, observed the police-suspect interaction. As to the characteristics of the suspects encountered by the police, 51.6 percent were white and 81.7 percent were male. The predominant age was 19 to 35 years. A minority of the suspects exhibited antagonistic or hostile behavior toward the police. About half of the encounters occurred without a victim present. In the remaining cases, 21.3 percent of the victims requested that the suspect be arrested, 35.4 percent requested that the matter be disposed of informally, and 43.3 percent expressed no preference for a type of disposition. Finally, the majority of police contacts with suspects involved misdemeanor offenses.

The bivariate relationship between arrest and the independent variables in the data are also shown in Table 29.1. But our focus in this analysis is to estimate the *relative* contribution of these variables to arrest decisions. A multivariate method is necessary to assess which factors have an effect on arrest probabilities independent of other determinants of arrest. Since the dependent variable (arrest) is dichotomous, our model violates several assumptions of the ordinary least-squares method (Hanushek and Jackson, 1977). Consequently, a probit model is estimated (Finney, 1971; Gunderson, 1974).[1]

The results of the probit analysis are shown in Table 29.3. The independent variables follow the coding presented in Table 29.2. To determine which variables have a net effect on arrest probabilities, we estimated a model including all possible

[1] Probit estimates have some desirable properties. Since they are maximum likelihood estimates they are Best Asymtotically Normal (BAN). Moreover, z tests can be computed to test if specific estimates are significantly different from zero. For two-tailed tests, z of 1.96 reflects significance at the .05 level and a value of 2.57 is significant at the .01 level. For one-tailed tests, z of 1.65 and 2.33 indicate significance at the .05 and .01 levels respectively.

TABLE 29.1 Data on the encounters in the sample and the proportion of arrests for various subsamples

Characteristic	N	Percent of Total	Percent Arrested	X^2	p
Police Entry					
Proactive	238	32.1	12.6	4.56	.03
Reactive	504	67.9	19.2		
Location					
Public	437	56.9	15.3	2.08	.15
Private	305	41.1	19.7		
Bystanders Present					
Yes	397	53.5	22.9	19.42	<.01
No	345	46.5	10.4		
Victim Preference					
No Victim	398	52.6	14.3	56.76	<.01
No Preference	149	20.1	18.8		
Informal Disposition	122	16.4	6.6		
Formal Disposition	73	9.8	46.6		
Suspect Characteristics					
Non-white	359	49.4	21.4	8.62	<.01
White	383	51.6	13.1		
Male	606	81.7	17.7	.49	.48
Female	136	18.3	14.7		
Under 19 Years	225	30.3	15.6	.91	.64
19-35 Years	345	48.5	17.1		
Over 35 Years	172	23.2	19.2		
Demeanor or Suspect					
Civil	611	82.3	12.8	44.44	<.01
Antagonistic	131	17.7	37.4		
Victim-Suspect Relationship					
No Victim	398	53.64	14.3	17.28	<.01
Known	269	36.26	16.7		
Strangers	75	10.11	34.2		
Offense					
Felony	87	11.7	42.5	42.86	<.01
Misdemeanor	655	88.3	13.7		
All Encounters	742		17.1		

predictors of arrest. These estimates appear as the *full model* in Table 29.3. Then we re-estimated this model using only the significant predictors of arrest. These estimates appear as the *reduced model*. Our discussion turns to the results in Table 29.3.

Failure to display deference toward an officer significantly increases the probability of arrest net of other factors. The police mission is to maintain social order (Banton, 1964), but the law is only one resource available to the officer to control a situation. The ability of police to regulate encounters rests, in part, on the extent to

TABLE 29.2 Description of variables in probit estimation

Variable Name	Description of Variables
Police Entry	0 = Reactive (citizen initiated) 1 = Proactive (police initiated); x = .321
Location	0 = Public places (on street parking lot) 1 = Private places (inside bar, store, private residence); x = .411
Bystanders	0 = No bystanders present 1 = Bystanders present; x = .535
Informal Disposition	1 = Victim requests informal disposition (warn offending party, release suspect) 0 = All other cases; x = .164
Formal Disposition	1 = Victim requests arrest 0 = All other cases; x = ,098
Suspect Race	1 = White 0 = Non-white; x = .528
Suspect Sex	1 = Male 0 = Female; x = .817
Suspect Age	1 = Under 19 years 2 = 19 to 35 years 3 = Over 35 years; x = 1,936
Suspect Antagonistic	1 = Antagonistic (hostle attitude, cursed officer, refused to cooperate) 0 = Civil (all other cases); x = .377
Victim Knows Suspect	1 = Victim and suspect are known to each other 0 = All other cases; x = .362
Victim Stranger to Suspect	1 = Victim and suspect are strangers 0 = All other cases; x = .101
Felony	1 = Felony offense (auto theft, burglary, assault, breaking and entering, rape) 0 = Misdemeanor (shoplifting, drunkenness, vandalism, trespassing, disturbing the peace); x = .117
Arrest	1 = Arrest 0 = No arrest; x = .171

which citizens defer to police authority. Where possible, police often prefer to establish order without arrest (Muir, 1977). Antagonistic behavior toward the police is a symbolic rejection of their authority which may necessitate more formal means of control.

Previous literature suggests that the bivariate association between race and arrest is spurious. That is, controlling for levels of antagonism or seriousness of the offense eliminates the race/arrest relationship. Current data, however, indicate that race does matter. After controlling for the effects of all other variables in the model (which includes demeanor and offense seriousness), black suspects are more likely to be arrested. Several scholars discuss the influence of danger on police activity and the tendency of police to identify "symbolic assailants" on the basis of salient cues

exclusively. Both have some bearing on decisions to invoke the law.

Arrest decisions also reflect other motivations. Police work involves controlling people, and this task is facilitated by the inequality of power and authority between police and the public. Some of our findings suggest that police act in ways to maintain this disparity. Antagonistic suspects, for example, offer a direct challenge to police authority and police respond with a higher incidence of arrests in these encounters. Moreover, the presence of bystanders may amplify the need of police to appear in control of the encounter. And as these data indicate, the presence of bystanders increases the probability of arrest. Additionally, arrest decisions reflect a dimension of police pragmatism. Arrest is less likely to occur when the victim and suspect know each other. This probably reflects police perceptions that the victim will not cooperate fully in the subsequent adjudication.

These data also have implications for the study of criminal processing in general. Consider two populations: a pool of offenders whom the police encounter and a subsample of those taken into custody. Our analysis indicates that the latter population is not a random sample of the former. Attrition from the criminal justice system at the stage of arrest is systematically biased. Consequently, studies which test the relationship between individual characteristics and later criminal justice outcomes such as bail decisions or sentencing often discuss bias at a particular stage of the criminal justice system without considering the non-random nature of the sample at that particular point. As a result, studies of disadvantage in the criminal justice system subsequent to arrest decisions are, at best, conservative statements of the extent to which bias exists in the overall sanctioning process.

Our findings are also relevant to the continuing debate over various measures of criminality. For many years, Uniform Crime Reports (UCR) were a widely accepted source of data on the extent of criminal behavior in a population. Researchers developed self-report indicators because they thought that official indicators of crime were biased. Recently, victimization data have been used to resolve the discrepancy between official and self-report sources. Hindelang (1978), for example, argues that the high rates of crime by blacks in the UCR arrest data reflect their higher level of involvement in criminal activity rather than a selection bias. We suggest a qualification to that conclusion. In this analysis we find repeated evidence that arrests are not applied randomly to individuals. Selection bias does exist at the arrest stage. But the current data are more heterogenous with respect to the types of offenses considered. Thus, Hindelang's argument may apply for more serious personal offenses but might not hold as well for less serious criminal activity.

Finally, a few caveats. While this study documents the relevance of situational factors in the application of law, much research still should be done. Several potentially important sources of influence in the arrest process are not addressed in this paper. Specifically, characteristics of the officer and victim may be important determinants of the decision to arrest and most studies, including the present, simply do not address these possibilities directly. Moreover, organizational properties of police departments may influence officer behavior on the street. Finally, patterns of enforcement may depend upon characteristics of the specific neighborhoods in which the encounters occur. These issues raise opportunities for future research.

REFERENCES

Banton, Michael (1964). The Policeman in the Community. New York: Basic Books.

Bayley, David and H. Mendelsohn (1969). Minorities and The Police: Confrontation in America. New York: Free Press.

Bittner, Egon (1967). "The police on skid row: A study of peace keeping." *American Sociological Review* 32:699–716. (1970). The Functions of Police in Modern Society, National Institute of Mental Health. Washington D.C.: Government Printing Office.

Black, Donald (1970). "The production of crime rates." *American Sociological Review* 35:733–748. (1971) "The social organization of arrest." Stanford Law Review 23:63–77. (1976). The Behavior of Law. New York: Academic Press.

Black, Donald and Albert J. Reiss (1970). "Police control of juveniles." *American Sociological Review* 35:63–77.

Blau, Peter and M.R. Scott (1962). Formal Organizations. San Francisco: Chandler.

Bogomolny, Robert (1976). "Street patrol: The decision to stop a citizen." *Criminal Law Bulletin* 12:544–582.

Bottomley, A.K. (1973). "Police discretion in law enforcement." Pp. 35–83 in A.K. Bottomley (ed.), *Decisions in the Penal Process*. South Hackensack, N.J.: F.B. Rothman and Co.

Clark, John P. and Richard Sykes (1974). "Some determinants of police organization and practice in a modern industrial democracy." Pp. 455–494 in Daniel Glaser (ed.), *Handbook of Criminology. Beverley Hills*: Sage Publications.

Cook, W. (1967). "Policemen in society: Which side are they on?" *Berkeley Journal of Sociology* 12:117–129.

Cumming, E., I. Cumming and L. Edell (1965). "Policemen as philosopher, guide and friend." *Social Problems* 12:276–286.

DeFleur, Lois (1975). "Biasing influences on drug arrest records: Implications for deviance research." *American Sociological Review* 40:88–103.

Finney, D.J. (1971). Probit Analysis. Cambridge: Cambridge *University Press*.

Friedrich, Robert J. (1977). "The impact of organization, individual and situational factors on police behavior." Unpublished Ph.D. dissertation, University of Michigan.

Galliher, John (1971). "Explanations of police behavior." *Sociological Quarterly* 12:308–318.

Goldstein, Herman (1963). "Police discretion: The ideal versus the real." *Public Administration Review* 23:140–148.

Gunderson, Morley (1974). "Retention of trainees: A study with dichotomous dependent variables." *Journal of Econometrics* 2:79–93.

Hanushek, Eric A. and John E. Jackson (1977). Statistical Methods for Social Scientists. New York: *Academic Press*.

Hindelang, Michael (1978). "Race and involvement in common law personal crime." American Sociological Review 43:93–109. (1979). "Sex differences in criminal activity." *Social Problems* 27:143–156.

Kadish, S.H. (1962). "Legal norms and discretion in the police and sentencing processes." *Harvard Law Review* 75:904–931.

LaFave, Wayne R. (1965). Arrest: The Decision to Take a Suspect into Custody. Boston: Little, Brown and Co.

Lundman, Richard (1974). "Routine arrest practices: A commonwealth perspective." *Social Problems* 22:127–141.

Lundman, Richard, Richard E. Sykes and John P. Clark (1978). "Police control of juveniles." *Journal of Research in Crime and Delinquency* 15:74–91.

McEachern, A.W. and Riva Bauzer (1967). "Factors related to disposition in juvenile police contacts." Pp. 148–60 in Malcolm Klein (ed.), Juvenile Gangs in Context. Englewood Cliffs: *Prentice Hall.*

McKelvey, Richard and William Zavonia (1975). "A statistical model for the analysis of ordinal level dependent variables." *Journal of Mathematical Sociology* 4:103–120.

Manning, Peter K. (1977). Police Work: The Social Organization of Policing. Cambridge: *MIT Press.*

Muir, William K. Jr. (1977). Police: Street Corner Politicians. Chicago: *University of Chicago Press.*

Pastor, Paul (1978). "Mobilization in public drunkenness control: A comparison of legal and medical approaches." *Social Problems* 25:373–384.

Pepinsky, Harold (1975). "Police decision making." Pp. 21–52 in D. Gottfredson (ed.), Decision Making in the Criminal Justice System. National Institute of Mental Health. Washington, D.C.: U.S. Government Printing Office.

Piliavin, Ivan and Scott Briar (1964). "Police encounters with juveniles." *American Journal of Sociology* 70:206–214.

Quinney, Richard (1970). The Social Reality of Crime. Boston: Little, Brown and Co.

Reiss, Albert J. (1971). The Police and the Public. New Haven, Conn.: Yale University Press.

Rubinstein, Jonathan (1973). City Police. New York: Farrar, *Straus and Giroux.*

Sherman, Lawrence (1980). "Causes of police behavior: The current state of quantitative research." *Journal of Research in Crime and Delinquency* 17:69–100.

Silver, Allan (1967). "The demand for order in civil society," Pp. 1–24 in David Bordua (ed.). *The Police*: Six Sociological Essays. New York: John Wiley and Sons.

Skolnick, Jerome (1966). Justice Without Trial. New York: John Wiley and Sons.

Stinchcombe, Arthur L.(1963). "Institutions of privacy in the determination of police administrative practice." *American Journal of Sociology* 63:150–160.

Sykes, Richard and John P. Clark (1975). "A theory of deference exchange in police-civilian encounters." *American Journal of Sociology* 81:584–600.

Terry, Robert (1967). "The screening of juvenile offenders." *Journal of Criminal Law, Criminology and Police Science* (June): 173–181.

Westley, William A. (1953). "Violence and the police." American *Journal of Sociology* 59:34–41.

Wilson, James Q. (1968). Varieties of Police Behavior. Cambridge: Harvard University Press.

ARTICLE 30

The Gault Decision
Due Process and the Juvenile Courts

ALAN NEIGHER

ON MAY 15, 1967, the Supreme Court of the United States ruled that juvenile courts must grant to children many of the procedural protections required in adult criminal trials by the Bill of Rights. In this, the *Gault*[1] decision, the Supreme Court for the first time considered the constitutional rights of children in juvenile courts.

It is not questioned that *Gault* will have a major impact on the future of juvenile courts in this country, many of which having for years operated under a philosophy that made ordinary procedural safeguards seem evil. It is submitted, however, that the *Gault* decision is neither a panacea for children in trouble nor an onerous burden for juvenile law enforcement officers. The decision will hopefully protect young people from being given indeterminate "correctional" sentences for making allegedly obscene phone calls that no one thinks necessary to verify. The decision may make life a bit more difficult for judges and probation officers. It is clear that at the very least, *Gault* will grant some semblance of consistent legal protection to the child.

But there are some popular misconceptions concerning the scope of *Gault*. As an example, the front page of the May 16, 1967, *New York Times* headlined an otherwise excellent summary of the decision as follows: "High Court Rules Adult Code Holds in Juvenile Trials. . . Finds Children Are Entitled to the Basic Protections Given in Bill of Rights."[2] But the decision does not accord to juveniles all of the protections of the Bill of Rights. All juvenile courts—with the exception of the District of Columbia—are, in fact, state courts. The Bill of Rights has not yet been made

---

Source: Neigher, Alan. "The Gault Decision: Due Process and the Juvenile Courts." *Federal Probation*, Vol. 31 (December) 1967:8–18. Reprinted by permission of Federal Probation.
[1] *In Re Gault*, 387 U.S. 1 (1967).
[2] *New York Times*, May 16, 1967, p. 1, col. 1 (city ed.).

applicable in its entirety to state criminal proceedings. Further, the *Gault* decision was limited to but a few Bill of Rights issues. This must be kept in mind, although, as will be later noted, the decision was as significant for what it *suggested* as it was for what it actually held as binding legal precedent.

Thus, before the decision may be discussed in terms of its implications for the juvenile courts, a brief examination is in order as to what the "basic protections" of the Bill of Rights are, and whether these protections have been extended to state (and thereby juvenile) proceedings.

BILL OF RIGHTS AND THE FOURTEENTH AMENDMENT

The Bill of Rights[3] means the first Ten Amendments to the newly written Federal Constitution, proposed to the state legislatures by the First Congress in 1789. The Bill of Rights was intended to be a series of limitations on the three *federal* branches: The Congress, the Executive, and the Judiciary. These proposed limitations were a practical political necessity, to mollify local concern over the sanctity of state autonomy in many areas of the law, and thereby speed ratification by the necessary nine state legislatures.

Of these Ten Amendments, six are not directly related to the criminal process. These are the First, Second, Third, Seventh, Ninth, and Tenth. Left for consideration, therefore, are the Fourth, Fifth, Sixth, and Eighth Amendments. And of these four, the Fourth and Eighth were not at issue in *Gault* and will be treated briefly.

Before these Amendments are discussed, the Fourteenth Amendment must be considered because it is closely related to the concept of federalism and because it affects not only those Amendments related to the criminal process, but also the entire Ten Amendments and their applicability to the states.

The Bill of Rights was expressly intended to be a check on federal power. There was nothing in the original Constitution to prevent the states from formulating their own systems of criminal administration, and indeed, the Tenth Amendment provides that "The powers not delegated to the United States by the Constitution; nor prohibited by it to the States, are reserved to the States respectively, or to the people."

After the Civil War, almost a century after the ratification of the Constitution (which included the Bill of Rights), Amendments Thirteen, Fourteen, and Fifteen were enacted, largely for the benefit of the newly emancipated slaves. Amendment Thirteen abolished slavery; Amendment Fifteen provided that race, color, or previous condition of servitude shall not be a disability for voting.

Amendment Fourteen was written partly to assure fair and equitable treatment on the part of state authorities to the newly emancipated. For our purposes, its most pertinent part is Section 1, which provides: ". . . No State shall make or enforce any law which shall abridge the privileges or immunities of citizens of the United States; nor

---

[3] For excellent summaries of the entire Constitution from which much of the following material on the Bill of Rights is drawn, see Antieau, *Commentaries on the Constitution of the United States* (1960), and The Younger Lawyers Committee of the Federal Bar Association, *These Unalienable Rights* (1965).

shall any State deprive any person of life, liberty, or property, *without due process of law*; nor deny to any person within its jurisdiction the equal protection of the laws."

Thus, the "due process" clause of the Fifth Amendment was made applicable to the states. However, the vague and sweeping concept of due process was slow in making its impact felt on the states which had been left virtually autonomous in formulating criminal procedures. But in recent years, on a case-by-case basis, the Supreme Court has made *some* of the Bill of Rights protection binding on the states through the due process clause of the Fourteenth Amendment. Of those protections now applicable to the states included are several under those Amendments not relevant to the criminal process (especially freedom of speech under the First Amendment), and these need not be considered here.

The Fourth Amendment was largely a reaction to the Writs of Assistance issued in the colonies prior to the Revolution, which gave British revenue officers nearly unlimited authority to search private dwellings and to seize goods. Consequently, the Fourth Amendment reflects the Founders' jealous regard of the right to privacy—to be secure against unreasonable invasion of one's person, property, and home. The Fourth Amendment now applies in full to both federal and state authorities.

The Fourth Amendment provides for the security of people "in their persons, houses, papers, and effects against unreasonable searches and seizures." The laws pertaining to warrants—for both search and arrest—are too technical to be set out here. Suffice it to say that, as to searches and seizures of property, unless there is consent, individuals and their possessions or dwellings cannot be searched or seized without a warrant, except when this is justified by the surrounding circumstances and is done in a reasonable manner.

The Fourth Amendment prohibits unwarranted and unreasonable arrests, but it does not require that the police obtain a warrant for every arrest. The police may arrest without a warrant where the arresting officer actually sees the commission of a misdemeanor or a felony; also, the arresting officer may arrest without a warrant when he has "probable cause" to believe a felony has been committed. Probable cause is difficult to define precisely, but it may generally be stated that it is the existence of such facts and circumstances as would lead a reasonable person to believe that the suspect to be arrested is guilty of the offense.

Where a warrant must be obtained, it must specifically describe the person to be arrested. A general warrant—one that is to be filled in at the arresting officer's convenience—is not valid. An arrest made pursuant to an invalid warrant is unlawful. A warrant for either arrest or search and seizure may be issued only by a magistrate or judge; police officers have no authority to issue warrants.

THE FIFTH AMENDMENT

The First Congress included a specific provision regarding grand jury indictments as the first clause of the Fifth Amendment. The purpose of the provision is to insure that persons will not be brought to trial arbitrarily when there is no reasonable basis for believing they are guilty of a crime, and that those who are brought to trial will be adequately informed of the charges against them. The Supreme Court has held that the due process clause of the Fourteenth Amendment does not require a state to provide grand jury indictment, so long as the state provides other means of insuring justice to the accused.

The next clause provides that no person "shall . . . be subject for the same offense to be twice put in jeopardy of life or limb." The Founders' sense of fair play led them to include in the Fifth Amendment the concept that the Government should not be able to harass and persecute a man by trying him repeatedly for the same offense. The double jeopardy prohibition has not yet been binding on the states. However, the states are bound by the due process clause of the Fourteenth Amendment; thus, successive trials which flaunt the principles of justice and fair play are not permitted.

The Fifth Amendment next provides that no person "shall be compelled in any criminal case to be a witness against himself...." The history of inquisition and torture in the Old World gave the Founders ample reason to provide against the idea that a man should be forced to incriminate himself by his own words. The privilege has two aspects: (1) the right to be free from coercion designed to extract a confession; and (2) the right to remain silent without having an inference of guilt drawn from that silence.

Freedom from coerced confessions has long been recognized as basic to due process and neither federal nor state governments may extract a confession by force. Force need not be physical; mental coercion such as threats or interrogation to the point of exhaustion would make a confession coerced, and thereby invalid.

The second aspect of the privilege against self-incrimination is the right to remain silent. This is the right invoked by those who "take the Fifth." This right, too, has recently been extended to apply to the states under the Fourteenth Amendment. A criminal defendant has the right to refuse to testify entirely; his failure to take the stand may not even be commented upon by the prosecution in either the federal or state courts. A witness, on the other hand, must take the stand if called, and must claim the privilege one question at a time. The privilege applies not only to criminal trials, but extends also to those before congressional committees, grand juries, and administrative agencies.[4]

The privilege against self-incrimination was highly relevant to the *Gault* decision.

Following the self-incrimination provision appears the most sweeping concept of American jurisprudence: that no person shall "be deprived of life, liberty or property without due process of law." We have seen that the "due process" concept was later duplicated in the Fourteenth Amendment.

If there exists a legal concept not susceptible of precise definition it is due process. It means justice; it means judicial fair play. It is perhaps the very essence of our constitutional tradition. It is both "substantive" and "procedural"—it prohibits the making of laws that are unfair in themselves, and it prohibits unfair application of the law.

---

[4] The privilege has one notable exception: A person has no right to remain silent if a statute (federal or state) gives him immunity from prosecution—that is, if the government is prevented from prosecuting him on the basis of his testimony.

Due process applies to Congress in its law-making authority, and forbids laws that are arbitrary or unreasonable. And when the Executive Branch exercises a law-making or rule-making function, it, too, must exercise substantive due process.

Procedural due process requires that the laws, once made, be applied fairly. It means that an individual has the right to be fairly heard before he stands to lose life, liberty, or property. It requires a fair trial in a criminal case and a hearing by an impartial tribunal in a property case.

Procedural due process considerations were at the heart of the Gault decision.

THE SIXTH AMENDMENT

The Sixth Amendment is of particular importance to the *Gault* decision. Of the entire Bill of Rights, it is the one most particularly concerned with the rights of an accused in a Federal criminal trial. The text of the Sixth Amendment follows:

> In all criminal prosecutions, the accused shall enjoy the right to a speedy and public trial, by an impartial jury of the State and District wherein the crime shall have been committed, which District shall have been previously ascertained by law, *and to be informed of the nature and cause of the accusation; to be confronted with the witnesses against him;* to have compulsory process for obtaining witnesses in his favor, *and to have the assistance of Counsel for his defense.* [Emphasis added.]

The right to a jury trial in criminal prosecutions was considered so important to the Founders that they included the right in the main body of the Constitution as well as in the Bill of Rights: Article III, Section 2, commands that the "Trials of all Crimes, except in Cases of Impeachment, shall be by Jury . . . ."

The Sixth Amendment establishes the basic requirement that the accused be tried by the traditional jury of 12. On the other hand, the states are *not* required to provide trial by jury, although many do by virtue of their own constitutions. Some states provide for juries of 8 or 10, rather than 12. However, the Fourteenth Amendment mandate that the states provide due process requires that whatever form of trial the states do provide must be fair.

Not "all criminal prosecutions" by the Federal Government require jury trials. Military trials, criminal contempt proceedings, or petty offenses punishable by small fines or short periods of imprisonment may be conducted without juries. When the right to jury trial applies, this right may be waived, and the defendant may be tried by a judge alone, where both the defendant and the Government so agree, with the consent of the trial judge.

The Sixth Amendment further provides that "the accused enjoy . . . a speedy and public trial." The history of the Inquisition and the Court of the Star Chamber was not lost on the Founding Fathers. These Courts were notorious for their practices of detaining accused persons for long periods, and interrogating witnesses in secret. The Sixth Amendment provided against these abuses by insuring that the accused has the right to defend himself while witnesses and evidence are still available. The wisdom of this protection is readily apparent if one considers the anxiety involved in a prolonged criminal prosecution. Thus, if an accused is not afforded a speedy trial, he may not be tried at all. As to what constitutes a "speedy trial" suffice it to say that standards of reasonableness must govern. The right to a speedy trial has not yet been held binding upon the states under the Fourteenth Amendment, although an obvious prolongment would probably violate due process.

The right to a *public* trial is a basic right under due process, and this right does extend to defendants in trials conducted by the states. The presence of the public and representatives of the press acts as a guarantee that the court will proceed appropriately. The Supreme Court has not yet determined whether all trials must be freely open to the public or whether circumstances will permit a limitation on the type of spectators allowed.

The next protection afforded under the Sixth Amendment is the right to an impartial jury. The definition of "impartial" as used here has two aspects. First, there must be an opportunity for a cross section of the community to serve as jurors. Exclusion because of race, religion, national origin, or economic status violates the defendant's Sixth Amendment rights, whether the trial be federal or state. The cross-section concept does *not* require that every jury be composed of all the various racial, religious, ethnic, or economic groups of the community. It does prohibit court officials from *systematically* excluding any of these groups.

Second, the right to an impartial jury also involves the problem of publicity surrounding the trial. The First Amendment guarantees of free speech and freedom of the press must be balanced against the accused's right to be accorded a jury that will consider his case with an open mind. Modern communications techniques have added great complexity to this problem. The Supreme Court held in the case of Dr. Sam Sheppard that due process is violated where widespread newspaper publicity saturates the community so as to make it virtually impossible to find a panel of impartial jurors.

The Sixth Amendment next requires that a person be tried by "an impartial jury of the State and District wherein the crime shall have been committed, which District shall have been previously ascertained by law." This provision insures that a person will be tried only in that area where the crime was committed—where evidence and witnesses should be readily available, unless circumstances dictate that an impartial trial can only be had elsewhere. It is also required that Congress define in advance the boundaries of the Districts in which crimes shall be tried. The Supreme Court has not yet dealt with the issue of whether the due process clause of the Fourteenth Amendment limits the states in determining where trials for state offenses may be held.

Of great relevance to the *Gault* decision is the next phrase of the Sixth Amendment, which provides that the accused shall enjoy the right "to be informed of the nature and cause of the accusation." Thus, the accused must be informed of the charges against him sufficiently in advance of the court proceedings to allow him a reasonable opportunity to prepare a defense. Also, such notice must specify the alleged misconduct with reasonable particularity. Again this guarantee obtains, whether the trial be federal or state.

The second clause of the Sixth Amendment also was critical to the *Gault* decision. It provides that the accused shall enjoy the right "to be confronted with the witnesses against him." The philosophy underlying this clause is that the accused should be met by his accusers face-to-face, and be able to subject the testimony of the witnesses against him to cross-examination. The right to confrontation is a basic due process protection and applies to state, as well as to federal courts.

The Sixth Amendment next provides that an accused be entitled to have the court compel witnesses to appear and testify if they are unwilling to come voluntarily. A refusal to so compel witnesses to testify on behalf of the accused violates the right to a fair trial, and consequently offends the due process clause. Although the Supreme Court has not dealt directly with the issue, it does not seem likely that such a basic fair trial protection would fail to be held binding on the states under the Fourteenth Amendment.

Finally, the Sixth Amendment provides that the accused shall "have the assistance of counsel for his defense." There was no right to counsel prior to the enactment of the Bill of Rights, and the accused had to rely on the graces of the trial judge to act as his counsel. The inclusion of this right in the Sixth Amendment reflected the belief of the Founders that most defendants are vastly unprepared to protect themselves against the resources of the state's prosecution machinery. The accused today in both federal and state proceedings has the right to counsel in felony cases, and in misdemeanor cases where the accused is in jeopardy of incarceration. In such cases, the recent *Escobedo* and *Miranda* decisions have extended the right to counsel beyond the trial state; the accused is now entitled to counsel when the investigation focuses upon him so as to attempt to elicit incriminating statements. The reader should note that it is at this point, also, that the Fifth Amendment's privilege against self-incrimination attaches.

THE EIGHTH AMENDMENT

Statutes prohibiting excessive bail and cruel and unusual punishment had been enacted in precolonial England and in the constitutions of a number of colonies. These prohibitions were reflected in the Eighth Amendment which reads: "Excessive bail shall not be required, nor excessive fines imposed, nor cruel and unusual punishment inflicted."

It has not been definitely settled whether the provisions of the Eighth Amendment are applicable to the states under the Fourteenth Amendment.

Bail is a mechanism designed to insure the appearance of a defendant in court; by posting bail, the defendant undertakes to guarantee his appearance in court or else forfeit a sum of money. The amount of bail required is generally set by the magistrate who commits an arrested person to custody. Not every accused person is entitled to bail—military personnel and those accused of capital crimes are generally denied such release. But where the accused is entitled to bail, the Eighth Amendment requires that it not be "excessive." Such factors as the defendant's criminal history, the seriousness of the crime and ability to pay are relevant to the issue of excessiveness. There is generally no right to bail after conviction pending appeal; requests for such bail are left largely to the discretion of the trial judge.

As to the excessive fine provision, it is generally left to Congress to prescribe the limits of fines and to the trial courts to decide what fine should be imposed in a particular case. The Supreme Court has refused to review fines levied by the lower federal courts.

There are no precise standards as to what constitutes cruel and unusual punishment. The death penalty is not of itself cruel and unusual; what is forbidden by very early tradition of Anglo-American law is the infliction of unnecessary pain in the execution of the death sentence.

It is apparent that the Eighth Amendment, like its companions, leaves many problems unanswered, especially because the Eighth Amendment's prohibitions are not yet binding on the states. The law of bail—especially as it applies to the indigent accused—is in a state of re-evaluation. There are those who have argued, in the wake of the Chessman case, that long delay in execution is cruel and unusual punishment; indeed, there are many who argue that by modern standards, the death penalty is itself cruel and unusual punishment.

It is not pretended that the above summary of certain of the Bill of Rights criminal protections is an authoritative treatise. Indeed, entire volumes have been written on some individual Amendments. It is only hoped that the reader be informed of these protections so that the *Gault* decision might be placed in its proper constitutional perspective.

THE CASE OF THE "LEWD AND INDECENT" PHONE CALL

Gerald and another boy were taken into custody in the morning of June 8, 1964, by the Sheriff of Gila County, Arizona. The police were acting upon a verbal complaint from a Mrs. Cook, a neighbor of the boys, that she received a lewd and indecent phone call. Both of Gerald's parents were at work that morning and no notice of the police action was left at their home. Gerald's mother learned of his being taken to the Children's Detention House only after Gerald's older brother went to look for him at the home of the other boy. At the Detention Home, the mother and brother were told "why Jerry was there" and that a hearing would be held the next day at 3 o'clock.

A petition praying for a hearing was filed on June 9 by an Officer Flagg which recited that "said minor is under the age of 18 years and in need of protection of this Honorable Court [and that] said minor is a delinquent minor." The petition was not served on the Gaults and they first saw it 2 months later.

On June 9, a hearing was held in the chambers of Juvenile Judge McGhee with Gerald, his mother, his brother and the probation officers being present. No formal or informal record of this hearing was made. Judge McGhee questioned Gerald about the telephone calls without advising him of a right to counsel or a privilege against self-incrimination. There is conflicting testimony as to Gerald's answers. Both Officer Flagg and Judge McGhee stated that Gerald admitted making at least one of the indecent remarks while Mrs. Gault recalled that her son only admitted dialing Mrs. Cook's number.

Gerald was released from the detention home without explanation on either the 11th or the 12th (again the memories of Mrs. Gault and Officer Flagg conflict) pending further hearings; a hearing was held before Judge McGhee on June 15th. Mrs. Gault asked that Mrs. Cook be present but was told by the Judge that "she didn't have to be present." Neither the Gaults nor Officer Flagg remembered any admission by Gerald at this proceeding of making the indecent remarks, though the judge did remember Gerald's admitting some of the less serious statements. At the conclusion of the hearing, Gerald was committed as a juvenile delinquent to the State Industrial School "for the period of his minority [6 years] unless sooner discharged by due process of law."

No appeal is permitted under Arizona law in juvenile cases. Gerald filed a writ of habeas corpus with the Supreme Court of Arizona which was referred to the Superior Court for hearing. Among other matters, Judge McGhee testified that he acted under a section of the Arizona Code which defines a "delinquent child" as one who (in the judge's words) is "habitually involved in immoral matters." The basis for the judge's conclusion seemed to be a referral made 2 years earlier concerning Gerald when the boy allegedly had "stolen" a baseball glove "and lied to the Police Department about it." No petition or hearing apparently resulted from this "referral." The judge testified that Gerald had violated the section of the Arizona Criminal Code which provides that a person who "in the presence of or hearing of any woman or child . . . uses vulgar, abusive or obscene language, is guilty of a misdemeanor . . . ." The penalty for an adult convicted under this section is a fine of $5 to $50, or imprisonment for not more than 2 months.

The Superior Court dismissed the habeas corpus petition, and Gerald sought review in the Arizona Supreme Court on many due process grounds. The Arizona Supreme Court affirmed the dismissal of the petition.

The appellants, in their appeal to the United States Supreme Court, did not raise all of the issues brought before the Supreme Court of Arizona. The appeal was based on the argument that the Juvenile Code of Arizona is invalid because, contrary to the due process clause of the Fourteenth Amendment, the juvenile is taken from the custody of his parents and committed to a state institution pursuant to proceedings where the Juvenile Court has virtually unlimited discretion, and in which the following basic rights are denied: Notice of the charges; right to counsel; right to confrontation and cross-examination; privilege against self-incrimination; right to a transcript of the proceedings; and right to appellate review.

These were the questions before the Supreme Court in the *Gault* decision. The Court explicitly noted that other issues passed upon by the Supreme Court of Arizona, but not presented by the appellants to the Supreme Court of the United States, would not be considered. This is consistent with the Court's strict practice of reviewing—if it chooses to review at all—only those issues actually presented to it.

THE DECISION

The *Gault* decision was handed down May 15, 1967, a little over 5 months after its oral argument was heard by the Supreme Court. Mr. Justice Fortas wrote the opinion for the majority which was, in effect, 8 to 1. Justice Fortas was joined by Chief Justice Warren and Justices Brennan, Clark, and Douglas. Mr. Justice Black concurred with the result but argued that juveniles in jeopardy of confinement be tried in accordance with all of the Bill of Rights protections made applicable to the states by the Fourteenth Amendment.[5] Mr. Justice White concurred with the majority except for Part V concerning self-incrimination, confrontation, and cross-examination which he felt need not be reached, since the decision would be reversed on other grounds.[6] Mr. Justice Harlan concurred in part and dissented in part: he concurred with the majority insofar as it held that Gerald was deprived of due process of law by being denied adequate notice, record of the proceedings, and right to counsel; he dissented on the grounds that the other procedural safeguards imposed by the Court might discourage "efforts to find more satisfactory solutions for the problems of juvenile crime, and may thus now hamper enlightened development of juvenile courts."[7]

Only Mr. Justice Stewart dissented in full. Although acknowledging the short-comings of many of the juvenile and family courts, he maintained that the procedural safeguards imposed by the decision would abolish the flexibility and informality of juvenile courts and would cause children again to be treated as adults.[8]

In summary form, the decision held as follows:

Notice of Charges.[9]—A petition alleging in general terms that the child is "neglected, dependent or delinquent" is sufficient notice under Arizona law.[10] It is not required that the petition be served upon the parents. No facts need be alleged in the initial petition; the Arizona Supreme Court held that such facts need not be alleged until the close of the initial hearing. No petition at all was served upon Gerald or his parents prior to the initial hearing.

The Arizona Supreme Court rejected Gerald's claim that due process had been denied because of failure to provide adequate notice on the following grounds: that "Mrs. Gault knew the exact nature of the charge against Gerald from the day he was taken to the detention home"; that the Gaults had appeared at the two hearings "without objection"; that advance notice of the specific charges or basis for taking the juvenile into custody and for the hearing is not necessary because "the policy of the juvenile law is to hide youthful errors from the full gaze of the public and bury them in the graveyard of the forgotten past."

The Supreme Court rejected these arguments, noting that the "initial hearing" in this case was in fact a hearing on the merits of the case. The Court stated that even if there was validity to the practice of deferring specific notice on the grounds of protecting the child from the public eye, it must yield to the due process requirement of adequate notice. Therefore, a hearing where a youth's freedom and the parent's right to custody are in jeopardy may not be held unless the child and his parents or guardian be first notified in writing of the specific issues that must be met at that hearing. Such notice must be given at the earliest practicable time and sufficiently in advance of the hearing to permit preparation. Mere "knowledge" of the kind Mrs. Gault allegedly had

---

[5] *In Re Gault,* supra note 1, at 59–64.

[6] *Id.* at 64–65.

[8] *Id.* at 78–81.

[9] *Id.* at 31–34.

[10] Ariz. Rev. Stat. ANN. tit. 8, 222 (1955).

of the charges against Gerald does not constitute a waiver of the right to adequate notice because of its lack of particularity.

Right to Counsel.[11]—The Arizona Supreme Court had held that representation of counsel for a minor is discretionary with the trial judge. The Supreme Court disagreed, noting that neither probation officer nor judge can adequately represent the child. Since a proceeding where a child stands to be found "delinquent" and subject to loss of liberty is comparable in gravity to an adult felony prosecution, the juvenile needs the assistance of counsel for the same reasons underlying the inclusion of the right in the Sixth Amendment: The juvenile—even less than the average adult criminal defendant—is not prepared to cope with the complexities of the law or of building an adequate defense. Thus, the due process clause of the Fourteenth Amendment requires that in state proceedings which may result in commitment the child and his parent must be notified of the child's right to be represented by counsel. If they are unable to afford a lawyer, one must be appointed for them.[12]

The Court discounted the holding of the Arizona Supreme Court that since Mrs. Gault knew that she could have appeared with counsel, her failure to do so was a waiver of the right. Notification of the right to counsel plus "specific consideration" of whether to waive the right must precede a valid waiver. Without being expressly advised of the right (and Mrs. Gault was not so advised) there can be no "specific consideration" and thus, no waiver.

Self-Incrimination, Confrontation, and Cross-Examination.[13]—It will be recalled that at the June 9 hearing, Judge McGhee questioned Gerald about the telephone calls without advising him of his right to counsel or his right to remain silent. The judge and Officer Flagg stated that Gerald admitted making at least one of the indecent remarks; Mrs. Gault recalled only that her son admitted dialing Mrs. Cook's number. The Arizona Supreme Court rejected Gerald's contention that he had a right to be advised that he need not incriminate himself, saying that the "necessary felxibility for individualized treatment will be enhanced by a rule which does not require the judge to advise the infant of a privilege against self-incrimination."

The Supreme Court rejected this view and held that any admissions that Gerald allegedly made were improperly obtained in violation of the Fifth Amendments' privilege against self-incrimination. The Court traced the history underlying the privilege, and observed: "one of its purposes is to prevent the State, whether by force or by psychological domination, from overcoming the mind and will of the person under investigation and depriving him of the freedom to decide whether to assist the

---

[11] *In Re Gault, supra* note 1, at 34–42.

[12] The Court emphasized as "forceful" the Report of the President's Commission on Law Enforcement and Administration of Justice, *The Challenge of Crime in a Free Society*, pp. 86–7 (hereinafter cited as NAT'L CRIMECOMM'N REPORT) (1967), which recommended: "Counsel should be appointed as a matter of course wherever coercive action is a possibility without requiring any affirmative choice by child or parent." In *Re Gault, supra* note 1, at 38–40n. 65. Also cited was HEW, *Standards for Juvenile and Family Courts*, Children's Bureau Pub. No. 437–1966, p. 57 (1966) (hereinafter cited as *Standards)* which states: "As a component part of a fair hearing required by due process guaranteed under the 14th Amendment, notice of the right to counsel should be required at all hearings and counsel provided upon request when the family is financially unable to employ counsel." In *Re Gault, supra* note 1, at 39.

[13] Id. at 42–57.

State in securing his conviction." The Court implied that no less than the freedom from coerced confessions is the importance of the reliability, especially as to alleged admissions or confessions from those of Gerald's age, must undergo careful scrutiny for in the Court's words: "It would indeed be surprising if the privilege against self-incrimination were available to hardened criminals but not to children. The language of the Fifth Amendment, applicable to the States by peration of the Fourteenth Amendment, is unequivocal and without exception. And the scope of the privilege is comprehensive."[14]

The State of Arizona argued that the Fifth Amendment provides only that no person "shall be compelled in any *criminal case* to be a witness against himself" and should therefore not apply through the Fourteenth Amendment to state juvenile proceedings. The Supreme Court held that the privilege is not based upon the *type* of proceeding in which it is involved, "but upon the nature of the statement or admission made, the exposure which it invites." Since the privilege may be invoked in a civil or administrative proceeding, the court noted that it would make no difference whether juvenile proceedings are deemed "civil" or "criminal." The Court took the opportunity to express its disapproval with these labels, and noted that in over half of the states juveniles may be placed in adult penal institutions after findings of delinquency.[15] The Court stated: "For this purpose, at least, commitment is a depriviation of liberty. It is incarceration against one's will, whether it is called 'criminal' or 'civil.' And our Constitution guaranteeds that no person shall be 'compelled' to be a witness against himself when he is threatened with deprivation of his liberty. . . ."

The Court noted that "special problems may arise with respect to waiver of the privilege by or on behalf of childre, and that there may well be some differences in technique—but not in principle—depending upon the age of the child and the presence and competence of parents." And as special care must be taken before the privilege is validly waived, so also must admissions obtained without the presence of counsel be subject to the greatest scrutiny. Here we see the Fifth Amendment's self-incrimination provision to be vitally interwoven with the Sixth Amendment's right to counsel.

The "confession" of Gerald, made without counsel, outside of the presence of his parents, and without advising him of his right to remain silent served as a basis for Judge McGhee's finding of delinquency. Since this "admission" or "confession" was obtained in violation of those rights noted above, the Supreme Court searched for another basis on which the judgment might rest. There was none to be found. There was no sworn testimony. The complainant, Mrs. Cook, did not appear. The Arizona Supreme Court held that "sworn testimony must be required of all witnesses" including those related to the juvenile court system. The Supreme Court held that this is not sufficient: In the absence of a valid confession adequate to support the determination of the Court, confrontation and sworn testimony by witnesses available for cross-

---

[14] The Court cited to this point *Standards, supra* note 12, at 49, for authority that prior to a police interview, the child and his parents should be informed of his right to have legal counsel present and to refuse to answer questions. This provision of the *Standards* also suggests that the parents and child be informed

[15] HEW, *Delinquent Children in Penal Institutions,* Children's Bureau Pub. No. 415–1964, p. 1 (1964).

examination were essential for a finding of "delinquency" and a subsequent order depriving Gerald of his liberty.[16] The court made it clear, therefore, that an adjudication of "delinquency" or a commitment to an institution is invalid unless the juvenile is afforded the same protections respecting sworn testimony that an adult would receive in a criminal trial.

Appellate Review and Transcript of Proceedings.[17]—The Supreme court did not specifically decide whether there is a right to appellate review in a juvenile case[18] or whether juvenile courts are required to provide a transcript of the hearings for review, because the decision of the Arizona Supreme Court could be reversed on other grounds. Notwithstanding its failure to rule directly on this issue, the Court pointed out the undesirable consequences of the present case, where: no record of the proceedings was kept; no findings or grounds for basing the juvenile court's conclusions were stated; and the reviewing courts were forced to reconstruct a record while Judge McGhee had the "unseemly duty of testifying under cross-examination as to the events that transpired in the hearings before him."[19]

EPILOGUE

It should be evident to the reader that the legal precedents handed down by the *Gault* decision are neither numerous nor complex. At any proceeding where a child may be committed to a state institution, that child and his parent or guardian must be given notice in writing of the specific charges against the child sufficiently in advance of the proceedings to permit adequate preparation. The child and his parent must be notified of the child's right to be represented by counsel, and if financial considerations so require, counsel must be appointed for them. The child and his parents or guardian must be advised of the child's right to remain silent. Admission or confessions obtained from the child without the presence of counsel must undergo the greatest scrutiny in order to insure reliability. In the absence of a valid confession, no finding of "delinquency" and no order of commitment of the child for any length of time may be upheld unless

[16] For this point, the Court again cited *Standards, supra* note 12, at 72–73, which states that all testimony should be under oath and that only competent material and relevant evidence under rules applicable to civil cases should be admitted into evidence. Also cited was, *e.g.*, Note, "Rights and Rehabilitation in Juvenile Courts," 67 Colum. L. Rev. 281, 336 (1967): "Particularly in delinquency cases, where the issue of fact is the commission of a crime, the introduction of heresay—such as the report of a policeman who did not witness the events—contravenes the purpose underlying the Sixth Amendment right of confrontation." (Footnote omitted.) In *Re Gault, supra* note 1, at 56–57 n. 98.

[17] *Id.* at 57–59.

[18] The Supreme Court has yet to hold that a state is required to provide any right to appellate review, *Griffin v. Illinois,* 351 U.S. 12, 18 (1956).

[19] The Court cited, *e.g.*, *Standards,* supra note 12, at 8, which recommends "written findings of fact, some form or record of the hearing" "and the right to appeal." It recommends verbatim recording of the hearing by stereotypist or mechanical recording. *Id.* at 76. Finally, it urges that the judge make clear to the child and family their right to appeal. *Id.* at 78. Also cited was, *e.g.*, NAT'L CRIME COMM'N REPORT, supra note 12, at 86, which states that "records make possible appeals which, even if they do not occur, import by their possibility a healthy atmosphere of accountability." In *Re Gault, supra* note 1, at 58–69, n. 102.

such finding is supported by confrontation and sworn testimony of witnesses available for cross-examination.

If indeed the *Gault* decision were significant only for the black-letter law, summarized above, the demands made upon our juvenile judges and probation officers would be rather easy to comply with. The few mandates of Gault would eventually become implemented (with, of course, varying degrees of enthusiasm). However, the decision cannot be read solely in the light of its few binding precedents.

Some may recall that it was the same Justice Fortas who wrote for the majority in the *Kent*[20] decision, which a year prior to *Gault* considered the requirement for a valid waiver of "exclusive" jurisdiction of the juvenile court of the District of Columbia so that a youth could be tried in the District's adult criminal court. The essence of *Kent* was that the basic requirements of due process and fairness be met in such a proceeding. But although confined to the narrow issue of waiver proceedings, *Kent* was a prologue to *Gault* insofar as it expressed disenchantment with the course of juvenile justice in this country, which was expressed in an often-quoted sentence: "There is evidence...that there may be grounds for concern that the child receives the worst of both worlds: that he gets neither the protections accorded to adults nor the solicitous care and regenerative treatment postulated for children."[21]

With this warning, an alert was sounded in *Kent* for what would become in *Gault* an indictment of the juvenile courts. Despite the limitation of issues actually adjudicated in the decision, *Gault*, taken as a while, is a comprehensive note of concern over the administration of juvenile justice in this country. Part II of the decision[22] dealing largely with background and history contains 41 footnotes citing materials covering the entire ambit of juvenile justice, from custody to treatment, from probation to psychiatric care, and including numerous books, studies, and articles critical of virtually every aspect of the juvenile process. In Part II the parens patriae doctrine—the concept of the state assuming the role of substitute parent—was challenged on both historical grounds ("its meaning is murky and its historic credentials are of dubious relevance") and on legal grounds ("[T]he constitutional and theoretical basis for this peculiar system is—to say the lease—debatable."). The nomenclature attached to "receiving homes" or "industrial schools" did not, in the Court's view, alter the practical reality that these are institutions of confinement where juveniles may for years be deprived of their liberty. The Court was careful to note that the "substitute parents" of the early reformers' ideology have, in fact, become guards, state employees, and fellow juveniles incarcerated for offenses ranging in scope from "waywardness" to rape and murder.

It is therefore apparent to the reader of Part II of the *Gault* decision that the case was not, as the narrow scope of its holding might wrongly suggest, decided in the abstract. Part II was a harsh and critical prelude to the decision. It was tempered with concern for a system of justice that the Court suggests has fallen short of its early hopes and aspirations, and it was laced with documentation of these failings. It is submitted that the marked distaste for the course of juvenile justice in this country, which permeated the decision, was of itself a prologue (as *Kent* was for *Gault*) for further

[20] *Kent v. United States*, 383 U.S. 541 (1966).
[21] *Id.* at 556, citing Handler. "The Juvenile Courts and the Adversary Systems: Problems of Function and Form," 1965 WIS. L. REV. 7 (other citations omitted).
[22] *In Re Gault, supra* note 1, at 12–31.

decisions by the Supreme Court extending the due process clause into other aspects of juvenile proceedings. To speculate on the direction of such hypothetical extensions would be indeed foolish. As noted earlier, the Supreme Court selects only a small fraction of those cases submitted to it for review, and of these, only those issues necessary to dispose of a case are actually adjudicated (the appellate review and transcript issue in *Gault* is an example).

For those who are understandably concerned with the present, the *Gault* decision leaves many questions unanswered. Mr. Justice Fortas wrote in *Gault* that "neither the Fourteenth Amendment nor the Bill of Rights is for adults alone." But if indeed they are not for adults only, the Fourteenth Amendment and the Bill of Rights are not yet for children completely. The *Gault* decision did not cover the procedures or constitutional rights applicable to the pre-judicial of post-adjudicative stages of the juvenile process.[23] Thus, the body of law now pertaining to the rights of the adult criminal suspect when he is first brought into custody does not yet apply to the juvenile suspect. It is yet to be decided whether the Fourth Amendment's prohibitions against unreasonable searches and seizures, protections made fully binding upon the states, will affect the kind of evidentiary matter admissible against the child in an adjudicatory proceeding. The Fifth Amendment's right to a grand jury indictment and the double jeopardy prohibition have not yet been made fully binding upon the states by the Supreme Court, and their relevance to juvenile proceedings are uncertain.

One may ponder whether prolonged confinement in a "receiving home" pending a hearing on the merits would violate the Sixth Amendment's guarantee of a *speedy* trial, if this right is held to be firmly binding upon the states. The Sixth Amendment's guarantee to a *public* trial, which is binding upon the states, may have significant implications for juvenile hearings, which have by statute in a large proportion of the states been closed to the public. The Sixth Amendment's guarantee that the accused be entitled to have the court compel witnesses to appear and testify, a right closely related to the right of confrontation, has potential relevance to juvenile hearings, and cannot be ignored (although this right is not yet firmly binding upon the states under the Fourteenth Amendment).

One might further consider the Eighth Amendment and its prohibitions against cruel and unusual punishment, excessive fines, and excessive bail. If any or all of the Eighth Amendment is eventually made binding upon the states, how will the course of juvenile justice be affected? Is it cruel and unusual punishment to deny to a child those safeguards not considered by *Gault* and then subject that child to confinement in an institution of limited treatment facilities? Does unconditional relegation to a "receiving home" pending a hearing infringe on the prohibition against excessive bail?

That these issues may legitimately be framed, in the light of the Supreme Court's refusal in *Gault* to accept the traditional noncriminal label attached to juvenile proceedings is, in the writer's opinion, the greatest significance of the decision. It is not possible to even speculate as to the extent to which the Supreme Court is prepared to go in according to juveniles the procedural safeguards available to adults in criminal proceedings. All that is clear is that the sweeping, intangible concept of due process has at last been officially introduced to our juvenile courts.

[23] *Id.* at 13.

ARTICLE 31

Jury Trial for Juveniles
Right or Ritual?[*]

ANNE RANKIN MAHONEY

This study is an exploration of the effects of setting cases for trial in a court that permits jury trials for juveniles. Although few cases actually go to trial, cases set for trial have an impact on juveniles and the court. The study reported here is based on data from a study of 710 youths upon whom delinquency petitions were filed in a suburban court in 1980. Of these youths, 94 had cases set for trial and 7 actually went to trial.

The first part of the article gives a brief historical perspective on the juvenile right to jury trial, discusses why defense attorneys set cases to trial, and describes some of the difficulties in measuring the impact of jury trials. The second part reports on the impact of trial setting in "Suburban Court" on case outcomes and case processing time. A partial correlation analysis shows that here is no significant association between setting a case for trial and either adjudication or final disposition, even when other factors are held constant. Setting a case for trial has a significant association with long case processing times, however. Cases set for trial take almost twice as long as other cases to move from filing to adjudication.

Source: Mahoney, Anne Rankin. "Jury Trials for Juveniles: Right or Ritual?" *Justice Quarterly,* Vol. 2 (December) 1985:553-565. Reprinted by permission of the Academy of Criminal Justice Sciences.

[*] This article is based on research conducted under Grant Number 79-NJ-AX-0034 from the National Institute of Juvenile Justice and Delinquency Prevention, Law Enforcement Assistance Administration, U.S. Department of Justice. Points of view or opinions stated in this document are those of the author and do not necessarily represent the official position or policies of the U.S. Department of Justice.

ALTHOUGH JURY TRIAL is perceived as a fundamental legal right of Americans and is recommended in the juvenile justice standards approved by the Institute of Judicial Administration and the American Bar Association (1980: 51),[1] three quarters of the States have followed the lead of the U.S. Supreme Court, which held in 1971, in McKeiver v. Pennsylvania, that there is no constitutional right to a trial by jury in a juvenile court adjudication.

How important is the right to jury trial for juveniles and what impact does it have on juveniles and courts? Although there is a fair amount of rhetoric and legal analysis of the juvenile right to jury trial in the legal literature, there is very little empirical work on juvenile trials or cases set for trial, either to a jury or to a judge. This article is an attempt to begin to fill that gap, and to stimulate further research on the topic. It is the report of an empirical study of trial setting in one jurisdiction where the right has been available to juveniles for many years. The emphasis here, however, is less on trials held than on trials *set* because much of the force of the right to jury trial rests in its potential. The defendant's right to require the prosecution to bring forth its case and witnesses before a jury is a powerful bargaining tool in and of itself, whether or not the trial ever occurs.

HISTORICAL PERSPECTIVE

Access by juveniles to jury trial has varied over the years as the general legal approach to juveniles has shifted. Juveniles had the right to trial by jury early in American history, when serious juvenile offenders were prosecuted in adult criminal systems and given the same rights as adults (Fox 1970: 1187, 1191). In the late nineteenth century a specialized court for children was established; consequently, the rules of adult criminal procedure were considered inapplicable (McLaughlin and Whisenand 1979; 5).

This orientation dominated the juvenile court until the 1960s, when child advocates became concerned about protecting the rights of juveniles who, as a result of juvenile proceedings, could be deprived of liberty for several years. During this period, three U.S. Supreme Court decisions—*Kent v. United States* (1966), *In re Gault* (1967), and *In re Winship* (1970)—awarded specific due process rights to juveniles. In 1971, the Court deviated from its general pattern of extending due process rights to juveniles by holding in *McKeiver v. Pennsylvania* (1971) that there was no constitutional right to a trial by jury in a juvenile court adjudication. The *McKeiver* decision has prompted numerous law review articles arguing the merits of jury trial for juveniles (see, e.g., Dodd 1971; Keegan 1977; McLaughlin and Whisenand 1979; Rosenberg 1980).

[1] 4.1 Trial by Jury.

A. Each jurisdiction should provide by law that the respondent may demand trial by jury in adjudication proceedings when respondent has denied the allegations of the petition.

B. Each jurisdiction should provide by law that the jury may consist of as few as six persons and that the policy arguments in favor of authorizing jury trials in juveniles cases begin with the same reasons that underlie constitutional provisions authorizing jury trials in criminal cases. The jury trial is seen as important in neutralizing the biased juvenile court judges and because it gives enhanced visibility to the adjudicative process (IJA/ABA, 1980a: 51).

SETTING CASES FOR TRIAL

The right to jury trial is essentially the right to *set* cases for jury trial because most cases set for trial never actually go to trial. Nevertheless, they take up space on overcrowded court dockets, remain potentially time-consuming blocks on attorneys' calendars, and require expanded jury calls.

Although the right to a speedy trial has always been defined as a defendant's right, in fact it is usually the defense attorney who is most eager to delay the defendant's case as long as possible. Defense attorneys set cases for trial for many reasons besides their concern that their client may be innocent, e.g., to gain time in a specific case, as part of plea negotiation, or as part of a strategy to gain stronger position in the courtroom vis-á-vis the prosecutor.

The attorney sometimes seeks time in cases, hoping that the witnesses against the defendant will get tired of coming to court and therefore never testify. Time can calm an irate witness or blur his memory. It can also give an attorney a chance to become familiar with the case or give a youth the chance to improve behavior or get a job.

The logic behind trial setting as part of plea negotiation is simple. The prosecutor does not have the resources to go to trial on all the cases set for trial and therefore should be more willing to reach settlements favorable to youths whose cases have been set for trial in return for not having to try the case (Church 1979: 522). Each party to a plea bargain offers something: the prosecutor offers a lower sentence or a less serious record, while the major lever for the accused is "efficiency." By pleading guilty and avoiding jury trial, the accused saves the prosecutor and the court an expenditure of time and resources (Ewing 1978: 170-71). As Church (1979: 514) notes regarding the criminal court, it is the defendant's right to a jury trial, "with the uncertainty for both sides that its exercise entails," which allows bargaining to occur.

A problem in plea negotiation for juveniles is that in many juvenile courts there is essentially a small range of disposition alternatives. In contrast to lower criminal courts described by Feeley (1979: 464), whose codes delineate criminal offenses in minute detail and provide a fine calibration of penalties, many juvenile codes adhere to the IJA-ABA Juvenile Justice Standards, which limit the penalty for any child to a maximum of two years (IJA-ABA, 1980b). This leaves little distance in what Feeley (1979: 465) calls the "gap between theoretical maximum exposure and the standard rate."

Plea bargaining primarily comes into play for juveniles who have several cases simultaneously pending in court and who thus may be potentially subject to a mandatory sentencing statute. All the unresolved cases of one juvenile comprise a negotiation package. Plea bargaining revolves around efforts to combine the several petitions to drop some of them in order to avoid repeat offender status. Plea bargaining may also result in agreements to omit some of the counts in a single petition. Though this may look impressive to a child and his family, it, like the "standard rate" described by Feeley (1979: 464), often has little practical meaning.

Apart from the individual merits of a particular case, defense attorneys may set cases for trial as part of a larger attempt to establish a position of power in the courtroom. Setting for trial has considerable harassment value. An individual case is not only a case in its own right, but often is part of a public defender's workload, part of a negotiation universe. Setting a particular case for trial may have little connection with a specific case or a client's characteristics. Rather, it is a way to keep the prosecutor off balance, or to maintain a stock of trial cases that can be settled at essentially no cost.

PROBLEMS IN MEASURING THE EFFECT OF RIGHT TO JURY TRIAL

As we attempt to study the right of juveniles to jury trial we are faced with problems. What, for example, is an appropriate measure of the effect of the right to jury trial on juveniles? There are several possibilities: (1) case outcome at both the adjudication and disposition level, (2) time that it takes a case to reach adjudication, (3) a youth's satisfaction with the court process, and (4) an enhanced possibility that "truth" will emerge and the error of convicting an innocent person will be minimized.

Measurement of the effect of trial setting on any of these factors is difficult. The range of options for case outcome is narrow in juvenile court and dispositions are often recommended by decision makers other than the judge. And what effect is one to anticipate? If trial setting is an effective tactic for the defense, we would expect a less severe adjudication or disposition for the defendant whose case is set for trial. However, if youths with more serious cases, and thus a higher likelihood of negative outcomes, are more likely to set for trial, then it may be difficult to separate the potentially positive effect of setting for trial from the potentially negative effect of more serious cases. Trial setting could also lead to more negative outcomes because courts penalize youths who ask for jury trials.

The effect of trial setting on case processing time is probably the easiest factor to measure. We can compare the time it takes to move through court for cases set for trial and those not set for trial, and measure them against time goals specified by several judicial and administrative groups. One problem with measurement of time, however, is that it may be more likely that serious cases are set for trial and also that they take longer to go through the court because of their complexity. We would expect that cases set for trial would take somewhat longer.

It is difficult to measure the third and fourth factors, youth's satisfaction with the court process and the emergence of "truth." Little research has been done on either; and neither is amenable to empirical investigation.

The remainder of this article will explore the impact of setting cases for trial on case outcomes, taking into consideration the influence of other factors, and the impact of trial setting on case processing time. First, it is useful to get some description of the court which provided the context of the research.

DESCRIPTION OF THE COURT AND ITS PROCESS

The Court

The court in which this research was conducted, referred to as "Suburban Court," is part of the general jurisdiction trial court that serves a large, rapidly growing suburban county. In 1980, when the research was conducted, the court consisted of one judge who worked full time handling all juvenile matters, one referee who worked one day a week, one juvenile prosecutor who was joined by an assistant midway through the year, and one Public Defender. The court has a due-process orientation and a strong legalistic tradition that goes back to its earliest days. It adheres to the model of the criminal courts in many ways, and all cases go first to the prosecutor, who makes a decision about whether to file them in court or not. Probation officers are not involved until they are asked to prepare predisposition reports after adjudication, or to help the judge decide whether to grant a "reserved adjudication." The reserved adjudication involves a guilty plea and six months of court supervision, which, if successfully completed, result in dismissal of all charges. Court volume is increasing rapidly and there is throughout the system an expressed concern about rising costs, heavy dockets, and inadequate services.

Court Process

After a petition on a youth is filed in court by the prosecutor, a date is set for an advisement hearing, during which the judge explains the nature of the allegations and the youth's constitutional and legal rights. In 1980, nearly half of the cases took more than three months to move from filing to the Advisement Hearing (Mahoney 1985).

This hearing is the first point in the adjudication process when a youth may enter a plea or request a trial and, in 1980 in the state where Suburban Court is located, all juveniles had the right to a trial before either a judge or a jury of not more than six persons. If a youth appears at advisement without an attorney, yet wants the opportunity to seek legal counsel, he or she is given a date for a later hearing. If the youth denies the allegations at these hearings, the matter is set for a pretrial conference in order to give the youth an opportunity for discovery or to negotiate or plea bargain with the District Attorney to reach a mutually agreeable conclusion of the case.

THE FREQUENCY OF JURY TRIALS

Ninety-four (14 percent) of the 650 youths for whom trial information was available at the completion of the study's data collection phase[2] requested a trial. Over 70 percent of these youths asked for a jury trial rather than a trial to the judge.[3] However, setting for trial was much more common than *going* to trial. Only seven youths (1 percent) were actually adjudicated at trial. Our particular interest here is an analysis of the 94 cases set for trial.

---

[2] Trial information is available on 650 cases of the total 710 cases in the study. Sixty cases having missing values on this variable because they were still pending at the conclusion of the data collection phase

[3] This may be an underestimation of the percentage of cases set for jury trial. There were a few records which did not indicate whether the case was set to a bench or jury trial and all of these were coded as bench trials.

TABLE 31.1 Youths who had their cases set for trial by kind of attorney

| | Kind of Attorney | | | |
	None	Private	Public	No Info.
Percent	5%	17%	33%	
Set for Trial	(16)	(42)	(34)	(2)

PUBLIC DEFENDERS MORE LIKELY TO SET FOR TRIAL

Public Defenders were significantly more likely than other attorneys or youths without attorneys to set cases for trial, as Table 31.1 shows. Slightly over half of the 664 youths for whom information was available on attorney had attorneys (38 percent private attorneys, 15 percent Public Defenders, and 2 percent court appointed counsel). Public Defenders and court appointed counsel were similar in the percentage of cases they set for trial and they were therefore combined in this analysis.

One-third of all youths represented by public attorneys had their cases set for trial compared to 17 percent of the youths with private attorneys and 5 percent of the youths with no attorneys. This high percentage of trial sets among public attorneys lends some support to the hypothesis that Public Defenders use trial sets to establish a position of power vis a vis the prosecutor, especially in light of the finding that public attorneys were no more likely than the others to *go* to trial.

IMPACT OF TRIAL SETTING ON YOUTHS AND COURT

In this article we look at the impact of the right to jury trial on (1) juveniles and their cases, and on (2) the court system. Our discussion of the impact upon juveniles focuses on the effect of jury trial settings on (a) case processing time and on (b) adjudication and disposition. It uses quantitative data from the 1980 study of records of all juveniles who entered the court. The study of the impact of trial setting on the court focuses on the calendar and time problems which trial setting creates for the court, using observation an interview data from the study.

Impact of Trial Setting on Case Processing Time

Case processing time can be measured for categories of cases by computing the mean number of days it takes cases in the category to move from filing in court to either adjudication or final disposition. The means of categories can be compared to see which kinds of cases have the longest processing time. A comparison of the mean case processing time of cases set for trial and those not set for trial shows that cases set for trial take much longer to move from filing to adjudication than do cases not set for trial

TABLE 31.2 Mean number of days from case filing to adjudication for cases set for trial and cases not set for trial

	Set	Not Set
Mean Number Days	232.38	118.11
Number Cases	94	552
Pooled Variance Estimate T value = 12.57		
DF = 664 2-tail probability = 0.000		

(a mean of 232 days compared to 118 days, a difference significant at the .01 level). This difference is due primarily to the long time span between advisement and adjudication for cases set for trial (a mean of 159 days compared to a mean of 52 days). Both of these are longer than the 30 days between filing and adjudication recommended by most standards for juveniles (e.g., IJA-ABA 1980a), but the cases set to trial take five times longer than the recommended time.

The long case processing times were particularly acute for cases set for jury trial. When we compared times of the small number of cases set for bench trial (trial before a judge) with those set for jury trial, we found that jury cases took longer.

One useful indicator of case processing time is the number of days that it takes the lengthiest case in the third quartile to complete a stage in the process. The third quartile case represents the disposition time fo the case that takes longer than 75 percent and less than 25 percent of the cases in the population. This measure indicates the length of time for disposition of the slower cases in court (Church 1978). The third quartile for the advisement to the adjudication state, where no trial was set, was 82 days. However it was 158 days, nearly twice as long, for the cases sent to bench trial, and 209 days for cases set to jury trial. These numbers far exceed any of the time standards for juveniles.

One reason for the long processing times for the cases set for trial is that at least 70 percent of these cases were not adjudicated until the day scheduled for trial. A few more were resolved at continuances after the trial date. In general, once a case was set for trial—for whatever reason—it usually was not resolved before the trial date. The court process allowed for a special pretrial conference, a hearing in which the defense attorney and the prosecutor could arrange for plea negotiation, but only 11 percent of the cases set for trial were resolved in those hearings.

Impact of Trial Setting Upon Adjudication and Disposition

Did juveniles who set for trial reap more positive case outcomes to compensate for their longer case processing times? This section reports on the impact of setting cases for trial upon case outcome. Bench and jury trials are combined because preliminary work did not show any relevant differences between them regarding case outcome.

If defense attorneys indeed win better settlements for their clients by setting cases to trial, then youths set for trial should, as a group, receive more favorable adjudications and dispositions than do youths who are not set for trial. But simple comparisons may not be appropriate, because youths who set for trial may be more likely to have more serious cases and consequently may expect more severe outcomes. In order to sort out the effects of these opposing factors, a partial correlation analysis was carried out, taking into consideration other factors that might be expected to influence case outcome besides trial setting. These other factors include: number of petitions, number of counts, classification of the most serious offense charged, and type of attorney, as well as age and the party who has custody of the juvenile.

Prior record could not be included in this analysis because only 180 of the 710 cases had relevant information, and of these, only 80 showed any records. Presumably the court and the prosecutor also lack this information, since we had full access to all police, prosecutor, and court records used by the court in decision-making. Although we view previous record as an important variable, we feel justified in its exclusion, given the fact that in the large majority of cases the court made judgments about youths knowing that it had no information about prior record.

Table 31.3 shows the association between each of the seven variables and adjudication and disposition, without any other variables taken into account, and the partial correlations holding each variable constant and then holding all the control variables constant at once.

The partial correlation analysis does not show any positive impact of trial setting on case outcomes, either when its effect is considered alone or when the effects of other variables are taken into consideration. The hypothesis that cases set for trial receive less severe outcomes is not supported by the results of the analysis.

A refined outcome variable was created which included both adjudication and disposition outcomes and the differentiation between the different kinds of dismissals—the thought was that there might be some relevant quantitative differences between cases dismissed, for example, for lack of evidence, and those dismissed because of a case pending in another court. Analysis using this more refined measure of case outcome did not change the results reported here.

In conclusion, this study of court records from one suburban juvenile court shows no significant impact of trial setting on case outcomes as defined either by adjudication or final disposition. A partial correlation analysis gives support neither for more positive case outcomes as one might expect if it were used by attorneys to facilitate plea negotiation, nor for more negative outcomes, which might hold true if youths were penalized with more severe outcomes for taking up court time.

Impact of Trial Setting on the Court

Trials or the threat thereof affect courts as well as juveniles and their lawyers. Jury trials can take a substantial amount of time and in a court with only one judge, an unexpectedly lengthy trial can quickly bring the entire juvenile court to a standstill. A minimum amount of time has to be reserved for each scheduled trial and an adequate number of jurors need to be called.

Although only 7 of the 94 cases set for trial went to trial, the trial setting itself affected the court. About three quarters of the cases were not resolved until, on, or after the day of trial, thus keeping dockets full and the possibility of trial open. Although everyone in the court knows that most cases will be settled without trial, no one knows

TABLE 31.3 Zero order partials for adjudication and disposition and seven other variables partial correlations: Trial set and adjudication, trial set and disposition controlling for each variable separately and all six together

Variables	Zero Order Correlations		Partial Correlations	
			Adjudication and Trial Set	Disposition and Trial Set
	Adjudication	Disposition		
Trial Set	-0.0435	-0.0946	—	—
	P=0.163	*P=0.009		
Age	-0.0046	-0.0213	-0.0440	-0.0965
	P=0.459	P=0.296	P=0.160	*P=0.008
Custody of	-0.0783	-0.0022	-0.0470	-0.0947
	P=0.038	P=0.478	P=0.1440	*P=0.009
Number Petitions	0.2595	0.3407	0.0295	-0.0766
	*P=0.0000	*P=0.0000	P=0.253	P=0.027
Number Counts	0.3454	0.4135	+0.0011	-0.0493
	•P=0.0000	*P=0.0000	P=0.490	P=0.108
Class of Offense	0.2714	0.2653	-0.0260	0.0871
	*P=0.000	*P=0.000	P=0.278	P=0.014
Type of Attorney	0.1385	0.1297	-0.0190	-0.0710
	*P=0.001	*P=0.001	P=0.334	P=0.037
None	—	—	-0.0435	-0.0946
		P=0.163	P=0.009	
All Six Control Variables	—	—	+0.0095	-0.0463
			P=0.415	P=0.123

Coefficient Significance
*P = 01

with certainty which cases will be the exception. The more cases the court sets for trial, the more uncertainty with which it has to contend. The jury commissioner sends out jury calls several weeks before the trial date and must base her estimate of juror needs in part on the number of trials scheduled.

In Suburban Court, Monday was set aside for jury trials. One Tuesday when our research observer arrived in court, she found the entire court docket delayed because the jury trial from the previous day had carried over. It was 11:30 a.m. before the regular business of the court could be started, and then it had to be interrupted and the courtroom cleared so that the jury could give its verdict. The morning's docket was finally completed at 1:00, while families and others had been waiting since 8:30 a.m. (SYP 611).

A few weeks later, when the observer inquired why the Tuesday docket was so light, the court clerk explained that she was starting to set fewer matters on Tuesdays in order to leave the day clear for trials that might carry over from Monday (SYP 747). This carried implications for the full range of delinquency matters, pushing all scheduling further into the future. In spite of the expressed concern about keeping time clear for jury trials, few occurred. Observers for the research project were certain they would see a jury trial one Monday, after having been assured late Friday afternoon that *three* jury trials were definitely "on" for Monday. But the observer waited in vain. One youth never appeared, a second case was plea bargained at the last minute, and a third was resolved after a suppression hearing (SYP 305).

DISCUSSION AND POLICY IMPLICATIONS

This study shows that, in Suburban Court, cases set for trial do not have more positive outcomes for youths than do nontrial cases. Furthermore, they take substantially longer to go through the court system. What are the implications of these results? Lawyers set cases for trial for a variety of reasons, but usually one reason is the hope that it will improve the case outcome for their client—yet this study suggests that, at least in this court, it does not. The practices of lawyers in regard to trial setting, like their practices concerning jury selection (Mahoney 1982), may be as much the product of unexamined myths as the result of an empirically based understanding of how courts work.

The finding that trial setting is not associated with differences in case outcome may also provide support for Feeley's argument that in plea bargaining the prosecutor's "offers," although phrased so that they appear to be exceptional "deals," are in fact essentially the "going rate" (1979). Even setting a case for trial may not change this currency of exchange. The right to jury trial for juveniles may be less a right to an impartial jury of peers as conceived in the Constitution, than a *ritual* with little substantive meaning. In a handful of serious cases in which a child denies charges, it may be essential to the cause of justice, but is is unclear how much a jury trial benefits a youth or the community in the great majority of cases.

The difference between jury and nonjury cases in regard to case processing time was striking and bears further exploration. Time is a particularly salient issue in juvenile courts because juveniles are in a period of rapid development and change, while the court itself operates within a jurisdiction that is by definition time-bound (Mahoney 1985). Some time standards (e.g., Florida Rule of Juvenile Procedure 1981) actually establish shorter time frames for juveniles than for adults because legislators believe children have an even greater need for speedy trials than adults. Administrators of courts in which jury trials are an option may want to focus particular attention on ways to reduced this discrepancy, so that children who exercise their right to set for a trial are not penalized by inordinately long case processing times.

Discussions about the issue of jury trial for juveniles usually focus on the incidence and meaning of actual trials, without consideration of the impact of trial sets on the child, the process, and the court. Jury trials may be rare, but trial *sets* may be fairly common and potentially disruptive to a court system. If we want to understand the impact of the right to jury trial on courts, we need to examine the impact of both and how each is used. What is the cost in terms of time, personnel, paper work, and impact on the child of both trials and sets? And what are the outcomes?

In general, we need a better understanding of how the jury alternative changes the dynamics of case processing and case outcomes as well as the negotiating postures of defense and prosecution. Are there ways in which unnecessary trial setting and negative effects of trial setting can be minimized, thus maintaining the right to jury trial without imposing prolonged processing and crowded court dockets? These and other related questions merit consideration and research, which would provide information regarding the right to jury trials for juveniles.

REFERENCES

Church, T. (1978) *Justice Delayed*. Williamsburg, Virginia: National Center for State Courts.
―――― (1979) "In Defense of Bargain Justice." *Law and Society Review* 13:509-525.
Dodd, L. (1971) "The Juvenile Jury Trial Case—A Regrettable Policy Decision." *Louisiana Law Review* 32:133.
Ewing, D. (1978) "Juvenile Plea Bargaining: A Case Study." *American Journal of Criminal Law* 6:167-189.
Feeley, M. (1979) "Pleading Guilty in Lower Courts." *Law and Society Review* 13:461-466.
Florida Rule of Juvenile Procedure (1981) 8.180(a).
Fox, S. (1970) "Juvenile Justice Reform: An Historical Perspective." *Stanford Law Review* (22) 118: 6.
Institute of Judicial Administration & American Bar Association (1980a) *Juvenile Justice Standard Relating to Adjudication*. Cambridge, Massachusetts: Ballinger Publishing Company.
―――― (1980b) *Juvenile Justice Standards: Standards Relating to Dispositions*. Cambridge, Massachusetts: Ballinger Publishing Company.
Keegan, W.J. (1977) "Jury Trials for Juveniles: Rhetoric and Reality." *Pacific Law Journal* 8:811-40.
Mahoney, A.R. (1982) "American Jury Selection Practices and the Ideal of Equal Justice." *The Journal of Applied Behavioral Science* 18.
―――― (1985) "Time and Process in Juvenile Court." *The Justice System Journal* 10:37-55.
McLaughlin, E.J. and L.B. Whisenand (1979) "Jury Trial, Public Trial and Free Press in Juvenile Proceedings: An Analysis of comparison of the IJA/ABA, Task Force and NAC Standards." *Brooklyn Law Review* 46:1-38.
Rosenberg, I.M. (1980) "The Constitutional Rights of Children Charged with Crime: Proposal for a Return to the Not So Distant Past." *University of California—Los Angeles Law Review* 27:656.
Suburban Youth Project (SYP) (1980-81) Unpublished Field Materials.

CASES

1. *In re Gault*, 387 U.S. 2, 87 S. Ct. 1428 (1967).
2. *Kent v. United States*, 383 U.S. 541, 86 S. Ct. 1045 (1966).
3. *McKeiver v. Pennsylvania*, 403 U.S. 528, 91 S. Ct. 1976 (1971).
4. *In re Winship*, 397 U.S. 358, 90 S. Ct. 1068 (1970).

ARTICLE 32

Juvenile Justice

Reform, Retain, and Reaffirm*

DIANE C. DWYER
ROGER B. MCNALLY

INTRODUCTION

THE JUVENILE justice system, and particularly the juvenile court, continues its demise. Parens patriae, its philosophical cornerstone, has slowly been eroded and replaced with the adversarial model of justice. This demise has escalated to the point where many delinquents are now considered adults and held fully culpable for their aberrant behavior. In fact, the Federal posture as promulgated by the Office of Juvenile Justice and Delinquency Prevention (hereafter OJJDP) clearly states that ". . .there is no reason that society should be more lenient with the 16 year old first time offender than a 30 year old first offender" (Regnery, 1985:4). Furthermore, many states have supported this notion by enacting codes (legislatively) to process (certification, waiver, etc.) juvenile offenders in the adult criminal court.

---

*This article is based on a paper prepared for the 1986 Annual Meeting of the American Society of Criminology, Atlanta, Georgia, October 1986. Part of this article previously appeared in the November 17, 1986 issue of *Juvenile Justice Digest* (vol. 14, no. 22), under the title, "A Compromise Is needed in Juvenile Justice Reform."

Source: Dwyer, Diane C. and Roger B. McNally. "Juvenile Justice: Reform, Retain, and Reaffirm." *Federal Probation,* Vol. 51 (September) 1987:47-51. Reprinted by permission of Federal Probation.

This trend, although not surprising, is reshaping the juvenile justice system to the extent that many believe it to be on the verge of extinction. To some, this is a most desirable outcome; however, to others, it signifies a major failure for social justice, especially for adolescents.

This paper is the fourth in a series of research papers ("The Child Savers—Child Advocates and the Juvenile Justice System," "Juvenile Court: An Endangered Species," and "The Juvenile Justice System: A Legacy of Failure?") which have chronicled the birth and transformation of the juvenile justice system. Consequently, this effort is the result of an evolutionary process detailing the present course of events and the consequences should these trends go unabated. The focus of the article will be to critique the OJJDP position on juvenile reform and recommend a more moderate compromise. The authors will call attention to significant new research and the policy reform recommendations of other influential interest groups, namely the National Council of Juvenile an Family Court Judges and the United Nations General Assembly on Criminal Justice.

The authors espouse the position that it is encumbent upon researchers and reformers to identify those elements of the system that are rational and those which need to be replaced. Close attention must be paid to the direction in which the juvenile justice system is heading in order not "to throw out the baby with the bath water."

Historical Perspective

In order to appreciate the present dilemmas, controversies, and conflicts in juvenile justice, it is important to view it from an historical perspective. The longstanding tradition involving state intrusion into the parent-child relationship is rooted in English common law. Implicit in this is the power of the state to intervene in families and to remove children in order to protect the interests of the larger community. Simply stated, this is the court operating on a parens patriae basis, the philosophical spirit of juvenile justice since its inception. This rationale is clearly expressed by the Illinois Supreme Court in 1882:

> It is the unquestioned right and imperative duty of every enlightened government, in its character of parens patriae, to protect and provide for the comfort and well-being of such of its citizens as, by reason of infancy, defective understanding, or other misfortune or infirmity, are unable to take care of themselves. The performance of this duty is justly regarded as one of the most important of governmental functions, and all constitutional limitations must be so understood and construed so as not to interfere with its proper and legitimate exercise.

Hence, with the guiding philosophy of parens patriae, juvenile justice was formally born in 1899. For the next 60 years, this system of justice went relatively unchallenged and unchanged until a flurry of litigation (*Kent, Gault, Winship*) attacked the very spirit of juvenile justice.

From this new perspective the failure of parens partiae to serve the best interest of youth while foregoing the protection of society has evolved to the inevitable; that is neither the restoration of youth nor the protection of the community from his criminal behavior transition.

Transition

With the foundation of the system in serious jeopardy, a series of trends continued to emasculate its integrity. These include the cynicism about rehabilitation; the perceived escalation of violent juvenile behavior; the application of proceduralism to court proceedings; the creation of chronic (violent) offender codes; the general belief in the courts' inability to effectively punish or to treat youth; and a changing public and political atmosphere concerned with a punitive approach to crime and criminals.

Research findings and public policy have supported the notion that the juvenile justice system is too tolerant of juvenile offenders. Two of the most incriminating reports resulting in the reshaping of policy, have been Wolfgang, et al. *Delinquency In a Birth Cohort*, and Martinson's "Nothing Works" studies. The data and implications of these studies have resulted in policy formulation indicating that the juvenile justice system is antiquated, serving *neither* the youth, the victim, nor society.

The response has been a reduction in treatment/therapeutic efforts and a shift to control and incarceration of juveniles. Implicit here is punishment at the exclusion of any other effort since the underlying tone has been that "nothing works" in an appreciable manner to affect recidivism rates.

Juvenile Justice: The Federal Perspective

The Federal government's direction toward juvenile justice for the past 10 years, vis-a-vis OJJDP, has been classically "reactionary." Consistent with public and political trends toward conservatism—and the portrayal, by the media, of juvenile crime escalating out of control and becoming increasingly violent—the response has been that the traditional system of juvenile justice at best is outdated and at worst is a total failure.

With this perception and the public's general attitude toward crime and criminals, the Federal posture has been to alter the juvenile system with "get tough" reform measures. These measures were expressed in policy, the policy of grants, and legislative mandates (i.e., selective incapacitation, preventive detention, certification, etc.) aimed at controlling and punishing those who profile this perception. Assumed here is that the perception is accurate. Some, including the authors, challenge the assumption that juvenile crime has been spiraling out of control. Rather, it is our belief that it is largely media-hyped and grossly overstated [Gilber, 1981].

Nonetheless, a policy review statement (Fall 1985) by Alfred Regnery, chief administrator of OJJDP ("Getting Away With Murder: Why the Juvenile Justice Systems Needs an "Overhaul"), clearly reflects the classical school response to criminal behavior and the corresponding Federal initiatives; namely, punishment is a first priority.

Enlightenment or Futility

Consequently, in an effort to deal with juveniles, pragmatism has slowly been shaping policy predicated on the notion that criminal behavior is largely a matter of choice([Regnery, 85:3). This rationale has resulted in certifying more delinquents to adult courts; tracking chronic offenders in an effort to get them off the streets quicker; maximizing their incarceration; and fostering the position that deterrence and punishment should be the model of justice for juveniles who commit crimes.

Ironically, this response assumes that the traditional efforts to deal with juvenile crime have in fact been a failure and that the "new" findings are clearly valid and therefore rational for the development of contemporary policy. These authors suggest a note of caution.

Wolfgang's Philadelphia studies indicate, among other things, that a small number of chronic delinquents are responsible for a disproportionate amount of serious crime, i.e., "seven percent (7%) of the youths studied were chronically delinquent but accounted for 75% of all serious crimes" [*Juvenile Justice Digest*, 85:1]. One can readily see why, proportionally, selective incapacitation and preventive detention have become the logical conclusion.

This type of reaction reinforces conclusions that criminal behavior is largely an outcome or rationality. This classical school reasoning totally negates factors that should be considered. The concept of maturation is ignored when OJJDP suggests that there is no reason that society should be more lenient with a 16-year-old first-time offender than a 30-year-old and that to maintain a distinction between youth and adults is counterproductive.

Moreover, policies that foster predictive efforts to forecast criminal behavior are not only questionable in terms of validity, but they continue to reinforce stereotyping. Selective incapacitation efforts tend to fall disproportionately on minorities and are entirely retrospective. The implications of this cannot be taken lightly. Targeted individuals are known high-rate offenders based on past criminal behavior. Consequently, tracking efforts result in the identification of the offender only *after* he has committed a crime rather than being prospective.

Folly of Rehabilitation

The hallmark of the juvenile justice system has been the restoration of youth through interventions whose premise are oriented toward rehabilitation. Since Martinson's work of the late sixties suggesting that "with few and isolated exceptions, the rehabilatative efforts that had no appreciable effect on recidivism," (Martinson, 1974:36) subsequent policies embrace deterrence through punishment, e.g., certifying more delinquents to adult court. Aside from exacerbating an already overloaded court docket and overcrowded prison population, this implies the futility of rehabilitation and the desirability of punishment.

Furthermore, the distinct absence of Federal initiatives (grants) to fund programs that are aimed at the restoration of youth through proactive models is a further sign that the Federal government's (OJJDP) priorities are primarily focused on the narrow group of chronic offenders. The freezing of OJJDP's funds for fiscal 1986 and the proposed dismantling of this agency is another clear sign as to the future of juvenile justice in America!

Implications and Current Research

Present attitudes, policy, legislation, etc. toward crime and criminals strongly suggest that crime, regardless of who commits it, is the product of choice and rational decisionmaking. Correspondingly, the response to this line of reasoning is a just deserts model; let the punishment be commensurate with the crime. This classical school thinking, although over two centuries old, has come full cycle, thereby religating the spirit and intent of juvenile justice to the annals of history.

The tide has turned, and one can see the expression of this earlier thinking when scrutinizing the Federal posture. What concerns these authors is the belief that crime is a matter of choice, irrespective of maturational levels or other factors (i.e., psychological problems, etc.) and that the *best* response is the certainty of punishment. This trend totally neglects any of the controversy surrounding deterrence theory.

Research to Consider

The image of rampant, spiraling youth crime has resulted in an intolerance toward selected adolescents. To those few that become labeled the "serious habitual offender," "chronic violent offender," "multiple delinquent offender," etc., the system has widened the net to ensure that deterrence will be a product of swift and certain justice. By waiving those violent delinquents to the adult system, implicit is the belief that this is the most rational response. Moreover, the serious habitual offender label begins to take on multiple meanings. Some states (Minnesota) are waiving to adult court youth who commit two felonies that may be property crimes. Consequently, as more delinquents become labeled serious offenders, the traditional delinquency category diminishes.

Recent research on very violent youth, those who commit murder, produce some intriguing findings that should caution us to this deterrence response and suggest other alternatives to be examined for the violent few.

Dorothy Otnow Lewis (M.D.) et al. have been conducting research on children who commit murder ("Biosychosocial Characteristics of Children Who Later Murder: A Prospective Study") and on youth who are considered very violent ("Violent Juvenile Delinquents"). Their findings are rather timely and suggest an alternative response as compared to conclusions drawn from the Wolfgang studies.

In their study on children who later murder, the researchers document the childhood neuropsychiatric and family characteristics *prior* to the commission of the act. The profile of these children included psychotic symptoms, major neurological impairment, a psychotic first-degree relative, violent acts during childhood, and severe physical abuse (Lewis, et al. 1985:1161). Significant findings included documentation of a history of extreme violence *before* committing murder, the spontaneity, impulsiveness, and the unpredictability of the behavior. When they compared the data of the murderers with that of ordinary delinquents, it was the presence of all five variables (psychotic symptoms, neurological impairment, etc.) that distinguished the murderers from the control group.

Many conclusions were drawn that ". . .suggest violence alone is not as good a predictor of future aggression. . ." (Lewis, et al., 1985:1166). Hence, studies that are focused on tracking chronic antisocial behavior (*after* the commission of criminal acts), such as the Wolfgang studies, may be neglecting some very useful data that may not only assist in explaining violent behavior but point us in an alternative direction to incarceration. More specifically, the researchers suggest that ". . .violent juveniles are likely to be dismissed merely as incorrigible sociopaths and simply incarcerated. . .and that enlightened psychological, educational and medical programs can and should be derived to meet the needs of these multiply damaged children" (Lewis, et al., 1981:318).

Summary and Implications

What does the data suggest? Should we continue on the present course or do these findings necessitate a re-examination of the present trends? Have we been simply overreacting to juvenile cries, or is it time to get tough and accept the erosion of the juvenile justice system as inevitable? Perhaps there is room for change based on sound analysis of past and present trends to embrace a spirit of progressive reform.

These authors believe that the roots, i.e., parens patriae, of juvenile justice were in response to good and needed reforms. The rationale for a separate system of justice is no different today than in the late 1800's; if anything, advocacy is imperative in view of concepts and programs predicated on forecasting future behavior. Furthermore, to ignore the need for a benevolent institutional structure for treating juveniles does and will continue to ignore the fact that adolescents are *not* simply short adults. The punitive response appears to symbolize frustrations with crime and criminals and the need to provide a "quick fix" to a most complex problem.

Transferring youth to criminal court does not appear to be solving any problems other than implying a lack of confidence in the concept of juvenile justice. The consequence has been to broaden the definition of behaviors that qualify one for certification. Additionally, the desired outcome of more arrests, convictions, and lengthier sentences has not been fruitful. A study funded by OJJDP in the early '80s concluded that the apparent reason for transferring/waiving juveniles to adult courts, that they will receive stiffer sentences, does not appear to be substantial. (Hamporian, et al., 1982). Nonetheless, states continue to redefine traditional delinquent behavior for the expressed purpose of "getting tough" even when it has been demonstrated that the disposition will be no, or minor, imprisonment.

In view of recent research studies, Federal efforts have been aimed at early identification, tracking, and, ultimately, incarcerating the chronic violent offender. In order to identify and react to the few who commit a very large, disproportionate amount of crime, these Federal initiatives end up reinforcing the perception that minorities (blacks and Hispanics) are largely responsible for all the violent crimes. This retrospective approach also neglects ethical considerations, as well as ignores empirical problems in prediction efforts (Cohen, 1983). Again, it is difficult not to conclude that many programs, policy decisions, legislative mandates, etc. are born out of frustration rather than logic.

Recommendations

This article is predicated upon the belief of these authors, supported by current research, that Juvenile crime is neither rampant nor becoming increasingly violent. Furthermore, the authors believe that the policy trends of the past 10 years have been primarily reactionary and frequently promulgated from frustration, an intolerance to the violent few, the need to develop "quick fix" responses, i.e., swift and certain punishment, and the belief that youth have been coddled too long in the name of parens patriae.

What follows are recommendations that these authors believe are essential to reforming and restoring the juvenile justice system to a viable, credible social institution, one predicated on *presumptive innocence of those is serves. The authors strongly argue for the retention* of a separate system of justice with its primary goal to safeguard the well-being of the young to assure that they have the right to mature and become responsible adults.

Consequently, the authors *endorse* both the United Nations model code on juvenile justice promulgated August 1985 and the 38 recommendations approved by the National Council of Juvenile and Family Court Judges (NCJFCJ) in July 1984. Embodied in these organizations' policy statements are critical recommendations for the retention of and process for juvenile justice. In general, both organizations struggled with controversial issues relating to philosophy, confidentiality, transfer, research, treatment, disposition, accountability, discretion, etc.

Although these authors support the general policy statements of these organizations, we will highlight some of their recommendations given the data presented in this article. Therefore, the authors recommend:

1. the continued *individualized treatment* approach as the primary goal of juvenile justice. To include the development of medical, psychiatric, and education programs that range from least to most restrictive, according to individual need.

2. that the *chronic, serious juvenile offender*, while being held accountable, be retained within the jurisdiction of the juvenile court. As a resource, specialized programs and facilities to be developed focused on restorations rather than punishment.

3. that the *disposition* of juvenile court have a flexible range for restricting freedom with the primary goal focused on the restoration to full liberty rather than let the punishment fit the crime.

> **a.** that in no case dispositions be of a mandatory nature but left to the "discretion of the judge" based on dispositional guidelines.
>
> **b.** that in no case should a juvenile (under 18 years) be subject to capital punishment.

4. that in situations where the juvenile court judge believes that the juvenile under consideration is non-amenable to the services of the court and based on the youth's present charges, past record in court, his or her age and mental status, may waive jurisdiction.

> **a.** that in all juvenile cases the court of original jurisdiction be that of the juvenile court, and
>
> **b.** the discretion to waive or not be left to the juvenile court judge
>
> **c.** hence, proportionality would be appropriate with these cases. However, these high risk offenders should be treated in small but secure facilities.

5. that policy-makers, reformers, and researchers continue to strive for a greater understanding as to the cause and most desired response to juvenile crime. *Research* should be broad-based rather than limited to management, control, and punishment strategies.

Lastly, these authors call for the appropriation of public money for the support of programs with the expressed *purpose* of serving as a clearinghouse, funding mechanism for traditional and experimental programs, training juvenile justice personnel, and serving the interest of juvenile justice as a significant priority by continuing and stimulating debate.

BIBLIOGRAPHY

Bender, Lauretta. M.D. "Children and Adolescents Who Have Killed." *American Journal of Psychiatry*. Vol. 116, 1959.

Castellano, Thomas C., and Theresa Delorto. "The Justice Model in the Juvenile Justice System: Washington State's Experience." Paper presented at 1986 Academy of Criminal Justice Sciences Annual Meeting. Orlando, FL, March 1986 (unpublished).

Chaiken, Marcia R. and Jan M. Chaiken. "Offender Types and Public Policy." *Crime and Delinquency*. Vol. 30, No. 2, April 1984.

Fischer, Craig. ed. "Judges Urge Guidelines For Disposition of Serious Cases." *Criminal Justice Newsletter*. Vol. 15, No. 2, Nov. 15, 1984.

——. "New Evidence Found of Chronic Delinquency." *Criminal Justice Newsletter*, Vol. 16, No. 24, Dec. 16, 1985.

——. "OJJDP Works with Police to Get Tough with Repeat Offenders." *Criminal Justice Newsletter*, Vol. 15, No. 24, Dec. 24, 1984.

———. "United Nations Congress Adopts Liberal Juvenile Justice Code." *Criminal Justice Newsletter.* Vol. 16, No. 18, Sept. 17, 1985.

Gilber, Seymour. "Treating Juvenile Crime." *New York Times,* Dec. 12, 1981.

Laughlin, Jerry, N. (ed.). *The Juvenile Court and Serious Offenders: 38 Recommendations.* Reno: National Council of Juvenile and Family Court Judges, 1986.

Lewis, Dorothy, et al. "Biopsychosocial Characteristics of Children Who Later Murder: A Prospective Study." *American Journal of Psychiatry,* Vol. 142, No. 10, Oct. 1985.

———. "Violent Juvenile Delinquents: Psychiatric, Neurological, Psychological and Abuse Factors." *Vulnerabilities to Delinquency.* New Haven: Spectrum, 1981.

Martinson, Robert. "What Works? Questions and Answers About Prison Reform." *The Public Interest.* Vol. 35, Spring 1974.

McNally, Roger. "The Juvenile Justice System: A Legacy of Failure?" *Federal Probation.* Vol. 48, No. 4, Dec. 1984.

Metropolitan Court Judges Committee. *Deprived Children: A Judicial Response.* Reno: National Council of Juvenile and Family Court Judges, 1986.

Regnery, Alfred S. "Getting Away With Murder: Why The Juvenile Justice System Needs An Overhaul." *Policy Review.* Vol. 34, Fall 1985.

Von Hirsch, Andrew. "The Ethics of Selective Incapacitation: Observations on the Contemporary Debate." *Crime and Delinquency.* Vol. 30, No. 2, April 1984.

ARTICLE 33

Are They Too Young to Die?

TOM SELIGSON

THE DEATH PENALTY came as a real surprise to me," says Wayne Thompson. "I thought it was a thing of the past. When I was on the streets. I ran around a lot. The only time I watched TV was on Saturday mornings for the cartoons. I never watched the news. I didn't learn about the death penalty until I was in the jail."

Wayne Thompson was 15 when he was arrested along with his half-brother, then 27, and two other men, also in their 20s for the shooting and stabbing death of Charles Keene, Thompson's former brother-in-law, who lived in rural Amber, Okla.

After Keene's body was found in the Washita River, Thompson and the others were convicted of first-degree murder. They were all given the death penalty and sent to McAlester, Oklahoma's turn-of-the-century maximum-security prison. There are 64 convicts currently awaiting execution on McAlester's death row. According to Warden Gary Maynard, Wayne Thompson is the first juvenile locked within its all-brick cells.

Thompson, now 19, is one of 33 inmates on America's death row who are there for crimes committed under the age of 18. Fifteen are white. Eighteen are black. Two are female. All are convicted of murder, usually in combination with another crime. In the continuing and often acrimonious debate about capital punishment, perhaps the most volatile question is whether we should execute juveniles. If Wayne Thompson lived in the Soviet Union, Libya or even South Africa, critics argue, he would not be on death row. America may be alone in the world in executing its young.

According to Victor Streib, a professor of law at Cleveland State University and an authority on the death penalty for juveniles, the United States has executed 281 juvenile offenders throughout its history. The first such execution was in Plymouth Colony in 1642 for the crime of bestiality. The most recent execution was of Jay Kelly Pinkerton (at age 24) in Texas last May. Pinkerton was 17 when charged with

Source: Seligson, Tom. "Are They Too Young to Die?" *Parade,* October 19, 1986: 4-7. Reprinted with permission from *Parade,* copyright © 1976.

TABLE 33.1 States with minimum ages

Among the 36 states that currently have capital punishment, these 27 set a specific minimum age at time the crime was committed:

State	Age
Alabama	14
Arkansas	14
California	18
Colorado	18
Connecticut	18
Georgia	17
Idaho	14
Illinois	18
Indiana	10
Kentucky	14
Louisiana	15
Mississippi	13
Missouri	14
Montana	12
Nebraska	18
Nevada	16
New Hampshire	17
New Jersey	18
New Mexico	18
North Carolina	14
Ohio	18
Oregon	18
Pennsylvania	14
Tennessee	18
Texas	17
Utah	14
Virginia	15

Nine states set no minimum age. Of these, Arizona, Florida, Maryland, South Carolina, Washington and Wyoming provide for age as a mitigating factor. Delaware, Oklahoma and South Dakota have neither a minimum age nor age as a mitigating factor.

---

murdering an Amarillo housewife who lived down the street. Along with Charles Rumbaugh, also in Texas, and Terry Roach in South Carolina. Pinkerton was the third juvenile offender put to death within the last year. Of the 36 states that permit capital punishment, 26 allow it for those who were *under* 18 at the time the crime was committed. In Indiana, where Paula Cooper, 16, was recently condemned to die, executions are permitted for crimes committed from age 10. In Oklahoma, where Thompson was convicted, there is no minimum age at all.

A 1986 Gallup poll found that 70 percent of Americans are in favor of the death penalty. Though there has yet to be a nationwide poll on the execution of juveniles, Streib reports that recent polls of lawyers and law students showed that fewer than 50 percent support the practice. In 1983, the American Bar Association officially opposed it.

Streib himself proposes long-term prison confinement instead. "All of the socio-logical surveys done over the last 50 years show that there is no additional deterrent effect from the death penalty over life in prison." he says. "But even if there were, when you look at the kind of murders teenagers commit, you see they are invariably impulse killers. They also don't have any realistic perception of death. Grandparents die, not kids. If anything, kids are attracted to death-defying behavior. They drive recklessly, they ingest dangerous drugs, they attempt suicide—not really believing they are going to die but because it sounds exciting. So threatening them with death hardly deters them. However, if you threaten a teenager with being grounded for life, take away his car and his girlfriend, and send him away to a dirty hole for life, he knows what that means."

What kind of kid commits murder? Dr. Dorothy Otnow Lewis, a professor of psychiatry at New York University School of Medicine, has studied both adult and juvenile violent offenders. She says most violent youngsters have suffered a head or nervous-system injury or have shown a history of severe psychiatric illness, "Neither of which necessarily causes violence," she notes. "But when these conditions are coupled with growing up in a family in which the youth is horribly abused or witnesses extreme violence, it seems to create a very violent individual. I'm not even sure that his being the victim is as important as seeing extraordinary family violence."

Like many of the other juveniles on death row, Wayne Thompson had certainly witnessed his share of violence. The son of a truck driver, one of eight children, he grew up in Chickasha, Okla. Much of the violence that he witnessed was committed by the brother-in-law he was convicted of killing. "I'd seen him pull a gun on my sister and beat her up," he recalls. "I'd seen him beat my other sisters up. I'd seem take my nephew to the roof of his trailer, hold him upside down and threaten to drop him off, and he used to kick me."

Thompson, whose previous encounters with the law included arrests for shoplifting and assault, had dropped out of the 10th grade just prior to the shooting.

His lawyer, Al Schay, is using the issue of Thompson's age in an attempt to save his life. "My central point," says Schay, "is that with a juvenile, there's simply not as much brain there as with an adult." Says Thompson: "They thought I was too young to drive. Even now, at 19, if I went to buy a beer, they wouldn't sell it to me, because I'm too young. Yet if I shot someone, I'm not too young anymore. Hey, make up your mind."

Paul Magill, on Florida's death row for nine years, points to the same inconsis-tency about age. Magill was 17 and in the 12th grade, a volunteer fireman and a band member, when he was arrested for raping and murdering a store clerk. He says that because of his age, the fire department limited his authority. But there was no limit to the punishment for his crime.

"I couldn't get responsibility for the good in my life, but I could for the bad," he explains. "It seemed to me a double standard." Magill's lawyer, Mike Mello, finds it

TABLE 33.2 Juvenile criminals on death row

Name	State	Age When Crime Was Committed	Time On Death Row
Joseph Auliso	Pennsylvania	15	2 1/2 years
Paula Cooper	Indiana	15	2 months
Wayne Thompson	Oklahoma	15	2 3/4 years
Ronald Ward	Arkansas	15	1 year
Leon Brown	North Carolina	15	2 years
Kevin Hughes	Pennsylvania	16	3 years
Carnel Jackson	Alabama	16	5 years
James Morgan	Florida	16	8 3/4 years
Frederick Lynn	Alabama	16	3 years
Heath Wilkins	Missouri	16	3 months
Jose High	Georgia	16	7 3/4 years
Joseph John Cannon	Texas	17	4 1/2 years
Robert A. Carter	Texas	17	4 1/2 years
Timothy Davis	Alabama	17	6 years
Johnny Frank Garrett	Texas	17	4 years
Gary Graham	Texas	17	5 years
Curtis Paul Harris	Texas	17	7 years
Lawrence Johnson	Maryland	17	4 years
Larry Jones	Mississippi	17	11 1/2 years
Frederick Lashley	Missouri	17	4 years
Andrew Legare	Georgia	17	8 1/4 years
Jesse James Livingston	Florida	17	1 year
Dalton Prejean	Louisiana	17	8 years
David Rushing	Louisiana	17	3 years
Kevin Stanford	Kentucky	17	4 years
Freddie Lee Stokes	North Carolina	17	4 years
Jay Thompson	Indianna	17	4 1/2 years
George Tokmaan	Mississippi	17	5 years
Christopher Berger	Georgia	17	8 years
Janice Buttrum	Georgia	17	5 years
James Trimble	Maryland	17	4 1/2 years
Paul Magill	Florida	17	9 years
Marko Bey	New Jersey	17	3 years

ironic that before Magill's jury was selected, the judge asked all the prospective women jurors whether they had children at home under 18 whom they had to take care of. "That would have been a reason for them to be excused from jury duty," he says.

Though lawyers for condemned juveniles have taken their appeals as far as the U.S. Supreme Court, it has yet to rule directly on the constitutionality of putting juveniles to death. In 1982, in the case of Monty Lee Eddings, a 16-year-old from Oklahoma who killed a police officer, the court ruled that "great weight" must be given to an offender's youth. In a 5-4 decision, it sent the case back for resentencing, ducking the constitutional issue itself. Since *Eddings,* it has refused to consider the matter and turned down a request as recently as January of this year in the case of Terry Roach.

Roach was 17 when he participated in the murder of two teens. Though 25 when he was strapped into South Carolina's electric chair. Roach was retarded, with an IQ of about 70. One of his lawyers, David Bruck, rallied the support of Jimmy Carter, the Secretary General of the UN and Mother Teresa in an attempt to win clemency. Unsuccessful, Bruck was with Roach at the end.

"I read to him in his cell, and it was like reading to a child at bedtime," Bruck recalls. "When his family minister came, Terry asked which prayers would work best at getting him into heaven. That was the mental level on which he was operating. Justice and retribution were concepts beyond his grasp. There was no moral component to his thinking, and that's what immaturity is. It made very real to me that putting an immature person, a kid, into that inexorable process of death is very different from doing it to an adult. It's very dehumanizing to do it anybody, but it's something else again to do it to a kid.

"No one's saying that kids like Terry shouldn't be punished. We're talking about life without parole, or with no parole for decades if they don't get death. The only question we're raising is if we should execute them."

"I see no reason why juveniles should not be executed," says Ernest van den Haag, a professor of jurisprudence at Fordham University. "Either the convict is competent [legally responsible] and knew what he was doing, or he is not. If he is competent, I do not believe his age should make a difference."

Tony Burns, who prosecuted Wayne Thompson, agrees: "Thompson was not your normal 15-year-old kid," he insists. "Chronologically, he may have been 15. But from a maturity and experience level, he was 25 or 30." Asked whether there should be a minimum age at which someone can be put to death, Burns says, "I don't think a 10-year-old should be executed. But I don't think a 10-year-old could have matured to be that violent."

Probably the most common argument made against the execution of juveniles is that, unlike 40-year-old career criminals, the young still offer the chance for rehabilitation. From her work with violent juveniles, NYU's Professor Lewis is convinced that rehabilitation is possible. "Children are more malleable." she says, "They are not yet set in their ways. As psychiatrists, we're not even allowed to make the diagnosis of antisocial personality prior to age 18. The reason is that children are still changing."

"In my experience." she continues, "a lot of kids who have already committed violent acts, even murder, are eminently treatable. I know one who received treatment in a private setting. He had committed murder as a juvenile. He is now an adult. He has a job, a family, and is doing well. He's never gotten into trouble again. But kids who receive such treatment are very rare. And, as far as I know, there aren't any programs for the kids in prison."

There are no programs in McAlester for Wayne Thompson. With the exception of the one hour a day he spends lifting weights in one of the 10-by-30-foot wire enclosures the inmates call "dog kennels." Wayne spends the rest of his time in the cramped cell he shares with his older brother, Tony.

Nevertheless, he is attempting to rehabilitate himself. In the nearly three years he has been on death row, Wayne has grown up. Five-foot-2 and under 100 pounds when arrested, he's now almost 6 feet. He has taught himself to read, and he feels that he has matured while in prison. "When I think back on it, I gave my mom a lot of trouble when I was growing up," he admits. "I didn't want to mind, didn't want to listen or do anything she told me to do. I thought I had all the answers. I also did a lot of things on impulse. Now I think I'm probably more disciplined than most people on the streets."

Paul Magill, the Florida volunteer fireman convicted of rape and murder, believes he has gained a better perspective of himself during his nine years on death row. "I think I needed time in prison." he says. "I needed time to deal with my confused emotions and to be able to understand myself better. On my own, I probably wouldn't have done that."

Magill spends his time writing and reading. He has learned to read Greek. "I used to hate school, and now I love learning," he says. "I couldn't deal with frustration. Now, I can admit when I'm wrong."

Rehabilitated or not, Magill already has had two death warrants signed against him. He could conceivably be executed as early as January. Asked what he would say to those who now determine his fate. Magill replies: "Dead, I can't *do* anything. Alive, I can help people. I can explain what happened to me, and maybe that will help them. I'm not the same person they arrested. And now that I'm able to deal with things better, they want to kill me."

Wayne Thompson tries not to think about being executed. "You think about that, and you're gonna be moping around like an old maid," he says. "You have to develop a positive attitude if you want to change. Besides, if I let myself go, I'll pull my whole family down."

His mother, Dorothy, moved her family from Chickasha to McAlester so she could be near Wayne and his brother. She visits every weekend, talking through a plexiglass window. She says that what hurts her the most are the rules that prevent her from touching Wayne.

Thompson's conviction was recently affirmed in the Oklahoma Court of Criminal Appeals. Tomilou Gentry Liddell, deputy chief of the criminal division of the Oklahoma Attorney General's Office, says that the full process of appeals could take as long as five more years. However, she hopes to speed it up. "We have a policy in our office," she says, "that anytime a defendant is denied one of his appeals, we immediately apply for an execution date on that day."

Oklahoma, which has not had an execution since 1966, prescribes death through intravenous injection. The system is modeled after the one in Texas, where 18 executions have been carried out within the last four years, including that of Jay Kelly Pinkerton in May.

A week before Pinkerton was executed, Virginia Royer, mother of the Amarillo housewife he killed, was not looking forward to it. "I don't mean to be a pansy about it," she said then, "but I can't see how it serves a purpose. What good is it going to do to take another young life?" Acknowledging that the seemingly endless appeal process kept bringing up the pain of her daughter's death, she said that she would have suffered less if they had just locked Pinkerton up indefinitely. "I realize we have to abide by the laws of the land, but I wish we could change the laws," she said.

"The real reform is coming from the states themselves," says Victor Streib. "In the last few years, four or five states have changed their statutes, establishing a minimum age of 18 for execution. New Jersey passed its amendment in January. It appears there is a trend."

Such a development would be in our own best interest, argues David Bruck, who defended Terry Roach: "All I'm saying is that there's a limit to how we should punish people like this. And that limit is somewhere this side of the electric chair. Even if we don't agree that it's a terrible thing to execute kids, simply the fact that the world community has rejected it so uniformly is a reason not to do it. If America really wants to be a beacon of support for human rights around the world, we have to make sure that we respect them ourselves. The spectacle of a country that is unwilling to forswear executing high school-age children is a dismal sight. It's a real symbol of despair and beneath our dignity as a society."

PART FOUR

Summary and Discussion

THE ARTICLES in Part IV have explored and described the confrontations experienced by juvenile delinquents as they interact with adults in the schools, streets, and juvenile courts. While the various authors offered different descriptions and analyses of the social experiences of youths in the schools, streets, and courts, some common elements are discernable throughout all of the readings in Part IV. Notably, in these social arenas adults make the rules, policies, and decisions which govern the behavior or juveniles while they are there. Consequently, confrontations between youths and adults in positions of authority are quite common.

Anthony Platt's book, *The Child Savers: The Invention of Delinquency* traced the development of a large social movement of reformers who emphasized a causal link between the living conditions experienced by youths in inner city slums and law violating behavior. These reformers, through the medical model analogy, insisted that delinquency, like disease, must be identified and diagnosed early so that treatment can prevent its further development, perhaps beyond the point of recovery. The urgency of the perceived dilemma of inner city youths prompted the child savers to intrusive action into the lives of many juveniles. This social movement continues to have residual impact upon the treatment of juveniles in school, on the streets, and within the structure of the juvenile court.

While Kenneth Polk did not advocate the medical model approach to delinquency, his article "Schools and the Delinquency Experience" identifies an important link as existing between living conditions (such as place of residency and social class) and later problems in school. He then points out how the educational process of "sorting out the elites" can lead to subsequent norm violating and delinquent behavior on the part of many youths.

Strong similarities emerge when Polk's article is compared to William Pink's "Schools, Youth, and Justice." Both Polk and Pink argue that the academic success or failure experienced by students in school is one of the most important variables in determining whether a youth is likely to participate in serious law violating behavior and become identified as a juvenile delinquent. The phenomenon of "tracking," or placing students in special curricular programs based upon their past performance, perceived abilities, and often, their social behavior, is viewed by both Polk and Pink as contributing to the problem of juvenile delinquency. They contend that a youth's status can become "fixed" during the educational process, which then shapes possibilities for future social status. Youths labeled as slow, dumb, or problematic, are likely to be directed down an educational path leading to limited occupational possibilities after they leave school. Meanwhile, students viewed as capable of academic success in school are encouraged, challenged, and helped along an educational course which almost assures success in later life. From this perspective, both Polk and Pink see the confrontations between troublesome youths and school officials as directly linked to later confrontations between youths and police in the social arena of the streets.

The article "Police Encounters with Juveniles" by Irving Piliavin and Scott Briar analyzes the social processes involved in police encounters with juveniles in the arena of the streets. Often confrontational in nature, these encounters are largely shaped by the wide latitude in discretion exercised by the police. Piliavin and Briar studied police encounters with juveniles in a metropolitan community with almost half a million residents. Except in extreme cases, virtually every police/juvenile encounter was characterized by the police officer arbitrarily deciding among a variety of dispositional alternatives at his or her disposal. Essentially, the officer could either release the juvenile outright, release the juvenile and file a brief report of the encounter, officially reprimand the juvenile and contact the juvenile's parents, petition the youth to juvenile court, or arrest and temporarily confine the youth in juvenile hall.

Police discretion in choosing among the various alternatives at their disposal tended to focus on a few selected criteria. Important in the decision was the seriousness of the offense committed by the youth. When youths committed serious offenses such as homicide, rape, aggravated assault, arson, grand larceny, and auto theft, police almost always used the option to arrest. However, since most juvenile law violations encountered by the police were not of a serious nature, police relied heavily on other criteria for deciding how to handle most juvenile cases. The youth's race, age, group affiliations, grooming, dress, and demeanor all served as important variables considered by police in exercising their discretion in the handling of juveniles. One of the most significant determinants of how the officers decided to handle a youth's case was the overall demeanor of the youth—especially the amount of deference the juvenile showed the police officer.

In "Street-Level Justice: Situational Determinants of Police Arrest Decision," Douglas Smith and Christy Visher compiled data from 24 police departments examining criteria used by police in the decision-making process regarding making an arrest. Unlike the research by Piliavin and Briar, Smith and Visher's study does not look solely at police encounters with juveniles, but examines police discretion in decision to arrest in encounters across all age groups. While not specifically looking at juvenile encounters with police, their study has important implications for understanding police discretion in the handling of juveniles.

Like Piliavin and Briar, Smith and Visher found that the seriousness of offense was a determining factor, if the offense fell into the serious category, e.g., murder, rape, robbery, and other violent and serious offenses. However, extralegal factors such as race, age and demeanor also were important variables affecting police discretion.

Interestingly, the sex of the offender seemed to have little impact upon police discretion. Smith and Visher found that the presence and the wishes of the victim were of primary importance in determining how police handled offenders. This finding has important implications for understanding encounters between police and juveniles. If adults are the victim of the youthful offender's law violating behavior, or, if adults witness the police-juvenile encounter, their influence on police discretion appears to be significant. If the adults urge the police to arrest, they are much more likely to do so than if the adult victims and/or witnesses prefer that the incident be handled informally. A youth's overall demeanor during the entire incident is likely to exert strong influence over how adults believe the youth should be handled.

The articles by Alan Neigher and Anne Rankin Mahoney address one of the most controversial aspects of the juvenile court—due process. Neigher reviews the impact of the Gault Decision—one of the most influential Supreme Court cases regarding juvenile justice. Prior to 1967, the U.S. Supreme Court consistently hadupheld the basic philosophy of the original 1899 juvenile court that juvenile courts were acting on behalf of the juveniles who appeared before them. This insistence upon the "parental role" of the juvenile court idealized that there was no adversarial relationship between the state and the juvenile, and consequently, there was no need for the Constitutional rights of due process to be extended to youths appearing in juvenile court.

While not extending all of the rights of due process accorded adults charged with crimes, the Gault decision contended that certain constitutional rights should be granted to juveniles appearing before a juvenile court. These rights included: notice of charges against the youth, the right to confront and cross-examine witnesses (as well as the fifth amendment right against self-incrimination), the right to a transcript of all proceedings, and the right to review before an appellate court. In the article "The Gault Decision: Due Process and the Juvenile Court," Neigher points out that while the impact of the Gault decision on juvenile hearings has been significant, it has not meant that all the constitutional rights of due process afforded adults in criminal court are not applied to juveniles. For example, the rights against illegal search and seizure have not been widely applied to juvenile cases, nor has the right to a public jury trial.

It is the issue of the right to trial by jury that is examined by Anne Rankin Mahoney in "Jury Trial for Juveniles: Right or Ritual?" Mahoney asserts that it is not so much the issue of whether juveniles appear before a jury in the juvenile court, but whether merely asking to do so influences the outcome of their cases. Her study of 710 youths petitioned to a suburban juvenile court indicates that even though 94 had their cases set for jury trial, only 7 actually went to trial. Nevertheless, those cases set for trial took almost twice as long to be totally processed as those cases where no trial by jury was requested. Interestingly, there were no significant differences noted in adjudication or disposition in those cases where trials were actually held. Hence, there is no evidence that a trial by jury either hurts or helps a juvenile's case. Rather, her study simply reveals that asking for the trial is very likely to carry the "penalty" of delaying the resolution of the youth's case. Emphasis on the adversarial nature of juvenile justice tends to lower the age for waiver of jurisdiction to adult criminal courts, and in some cases actually provides for automatic waiver of jurisdiction in certain criminal cases. In those cases if a youth commits a serious felony (such as murder), and is over a certain age (often 16), the juvenile is automatically charged with a crime and sent to the adult court. The only way the case would be heard in juvenile court instead, is if a reverse certification hearing occurs in which the criminal court decides to waiver jurisdiction and certify the youth as a juvenile. This essentially reverses what used to be the procedure in most states, where youths were automatically handled by the juvenile court unless a waiver hearing determined that they should stand trial as adults.

The article "Juvenile Justice: Reform, Retain, and Reaffirm" by Diane Dwyer and Roger McNally is one of a four-part series of research papers prepared by McNally and others to chronicle the beginnings and major changes of the juvenile justice system. Dwyer and McNally lament that litigation and the resulting changes in juvenile court proceedings have changed the philosophy and procedures of the juvenile court from paternalism, caring, helping, and treating, to a more adversarial and punitive approach typical of adult criminal court.

Dwyer and McNally contend that the paternalistic and rehabilitative roots of the juvenile court were in themselves important social and legal developments based on sound reasoning and needed social reform. They contend that the current path of changing the juvenile court to one which is modeled on the adversarial adult criminal court system is a serious mistake. They view these changes as a response to the frustration experienced by many people who view the juvenile court as inept and to the general misconception that serious juvenile crime is out of control and increasing at dangerous rates.

The authors strongly argue for the retention of a separate justice system for juveniles. They further believe that the juvenile court must emphasize individualized treatment, wide discretion in the handling and disposition of juvenile cases, and that the court reaffirm its attempts to not only respond to juvenile law violation, but to attempt to address its causes. They argue that the juvenile court must continue to handle the cases of serious violent juvenile offenders unless the court decides in a few cases that jurisdiction should be waived to the adult criminal court. One of the conclusions drawn by Dwyer and McNally is that under no circumstances should a juvenile under 18 years of age be subjected to capital punishment.

The final article, Tom Seligson's "Are They Too Young to Die?" documents the fact that youths under the age of 18 may in fact be subjected to the death penalty. Seligson profiles some of the 33 inmates who were on death row in 1986 awaiting execution for crimes they committed while under the age of 18. He points out that the United States may be the only nation in the world which executes its youths. In a table which lists the minimum age for execution in states which have capital punishment laws, Seligson indicates that nine states specify no minimum age, while those with minimum age limits range from the age of 10 in Indiana to 18 in 10 states. Seligson ends his article by taking the position that the United States cannot hold itself up as an exemplary nation in the worldwide crusade for human rights, while it continues to execute its children.

This section with its emphasis on the confrontation between wayward youths and the law enforcing agencies of larger society reminds all of us of an important principle regarding conforming and deviant behavior. That is, society generally does not come to terms with the individual—rather, each individual must come to terms with society.

Questions for Review
and Discussion

1. What was the basis for Platt's major criticisms of the Child Saver's movement? Did he overlook some of the contributions to juvenile justice made by the child savers?

2. What does Kenneth Polk see as the major problem in the school experience that is likely to be related to juvenile delinquency? What does he mean when he says that school success, family status, and social class exert independent effects on delinquency? Do you agree with his assessment?

3. William Pink contends that the two-trajectory system utilized in the schools "creates the conditions that generate troublesome and delinquent behavior." Do you agree with his assessment? In your opinion, why do schools use a two-trajectory system? How might the problems associated with such a system be reduced or eliminated?

4. What does the article by Irving Piliavin and Scott Briar indicate are the most important variables influencing police discretion in encounters with juveniles? How do their findings differ from those of Douglas Smith and Christy Visher? How are they similar?

5. Should the extralegal factors that influence police discretion in encounters with juveniles be a part of the police officer's decision-making process? Are there ways to reduce the influence of these extralegal factors? Could they ever be totally eliminated? Are there any positive aspects to allowing police such broad discretion in the handling of juvenile cases?

6. What was the impact of the U.S. Supreme Court's Gault Decision on juvenile court proceedings? Do you believe that due process should be a fundamen-

tal part of juvenile justice? What are some of the positive ramifications of the Gault decision? What are some of the negative ramifications?

7. According to Anne Rankin Mahoney, what is likely to be the impact of a youth asking for a jury trial? In your view, should youths be allowed to have jury trials? Should jury trials be a basic part of the juvenile court proceedings? Why? Why not?

8. Diane Dwyer and Roger McNally argue that juvenile courts are in need of reform, but they must be retained and their original mission and philosophy reaffirmed? Do you agree? Why? Why not?

9. What is the major issue raised by Tom Seligson's article, "Are They To Young to Die?" Should juveniles who have committed particularly heinous crimes be subjected to capital punishment? If so, what should be the minimum age for executions? If not, how should these offenders be handled?

10. What common elements do you see running throughout all of the articles in Part IV? What changes do you view as necessary in the schools, handling of juveniles by police, and in the juvenile court, if the problem of juvenile delinquency is to be adequately addressed?

Prevention and Control of Juvenile Delinquency

INTRODUCTION

IN THE FINAL PART of this anthology we look at the issue of social control and efforts to reduce and prevent juvenile delinquency. When sociologists examine social problems such as juvenile delinquency, they realize that it is highly unlikely that any undesirable social condition is likely to be totally eliminated. Rather, it is more realistic to focus on ways in which the negative social impact of these problems may be reduced and perhaps prevented.

Social control refers to the processes used by society to exert influence over its members by negatively sanctioning their deviant behavior. Control methods may be informal, such as gossip, ridicule, and ostracism, or they may be formal, such as fines and imprisonment. Both informal and formal methods of social control are used in efforts to reduce, control, and prevent juvenile delinquency.

We begin Part Five with a synopsis of Edwin Shur's classic book *Radical Non-Intervention*. Operating within the labeling perspective, Schur contends that a large amount of what is defined as juvenile delinquency would be better controlled if it were simply ignored by society. He contends that much of what passes for delinquency treatment, prevention, and formal delinquency control measures today, do not reduce and prevent delinquency, but may in fact, promote it. His final analysis is that the delinquency problem in America must be dramatically "rethought" if effective approaches to the problem are to be developed.

The first article in Part Five, "Negotiating Justice in the Juvenile System ..." by Joyce Dougherty explores one aspect of formal control of juvenile delinquency—the intake procedures of the juvenile court. In her article, Dougherty compares plea bargaining in adult criminal courts with the intake process of the juvenile court. She points out many similarities in the two procedures, yet emphasizes some important differences, especially regarding the lack of safeguards for protecting juveniles' basic institutional rights during the negotiation phase of the intake process.

Whereas Dougherty's article emphasizes the disparities in judicial treatment based on age, Meda Chesney-Lind looks at differential treatment based on sex. In "Girls in Jail," she points out that female delinquents are much more likely than their male counterparts to be jailed for status offenses and other minor crimes—and often spend a longer time in jail than males who may have committed more serious offenses.

Former juvenile court judge H. Ted Rubin looks at two alternatives to jailing or otherwise institutionalizing juveniles in his article "Fulfilling Juvenile Restitution Requirements in Community Correctional Programs." *Restitution* is the requirement that juveniles reimburse their victims for losses or damages suffered from the offense. Community correctional programs typically involve some type of residential program where juveniles go to school part of the day and are recipients of counseling and other rehabilitative efforts to prevent future delinquency. Rubin explores the possibilities for combining these two delinquency control efforts.

The next article, "Delinquency Prevention" is written by William Kvaraceus and reflects some of the frustration associated with delinquency prevention programs and law enforcement practices toward delinquents. Kvaraceus points out that despite society's efforts to rewrite legislation and implement a variety of treatment and prevention programs for juvenile delinquents, delinquency rates have not been reduced. Kvaraceus, much like Schur, points out that society must redefine delinquency and develop a more positive and helpful attitude toward youths if the problems associated with delinquency are to be adequately addressed.

Virginia Burns and Leonard Stern served as consultants on the President's Task Force on Juvenile Delinquency. This excerpt written by them for that *Task Force Report* addresses the issue of delinquency prevention. In "The Prevention of Juvenile Delinquency," Burns and Stern insist that the long-standing tradition of sociologists to study a problem such as juvenile delinquency, yet refrain from making recommendations regarding policies and programs to address the problem, should be discontinued. They indicate that the knowledge and expertise of sociologists who specialize in the study of delinquency must be translated into viable social policies and practices aimed at delinquency prevention. They particularly see the family, schools, and other basic social institutions as the logical focus for delinquency prevention programs and policies.

Don Gibbons asks an intriguing sociological question in his article "Juvenile Delinquency: Can Social Science Find a Cure?" This article is a revised version of Gibbons' keynote address to the Pacific Conference on Juvenile Delinquency held in Tokyo in 1985. In the article, Gibbons presents an overview of the current state of affairs regarding criminological theories regarding the causes of juvenile delinquency and the resulting delinquency prevention strategies spawned by criminological research. Gibbons indicates that societal attitudes toward delinquency prevention clearly have shifted form optimistic to pessimistic as program after program failed to significantly reduce the problem of juvenile delinquency. He concludes by summarizing recommendations regarding the handling of juvenile delinquents, insisting that traditional prevention efforts must be abandoned in favor of an emphasis on diverting as many youths as possible from the juvenile justice system and using institutionalization only as a last resort.

The final article "Rethinking Juvenile Justice." is written by Barry Krisberg and Ira Schwartz. They insist that the problem of juvenile delinquency is greatly misunderstood in American society. They suggest that the widespread notion that there is a steady and alarming increase in serious crimes committed by juveniles is inaccurate. Krisberg and Schwartz contend that data on juvenile arrests, court processing, and detention vary across states in complex and interesting ways. They summarize that it is important for the federal government to play an active role by providing aid to state and local governments in their delinquency reduction and prevention efforts. They conclude that delinquency research must be encouraged and supported. In their view the reforms instituted in the 1970s which focused upon the decriminationlization of status offenses, and diversion of youths from juvenile institutions must be reemphasized. This article concludes Part V and the book with the important conclusion that Americans must seriously reassess the problem of juvenile delinquency.

Edwin M. Schur, *Radical Non-Intervention: Rethinking the Delinquency Problem.* Englewood Cliffs, NJ: Prentice-Hall, 1973.

THE AUTHOR

EDWIN M. SCHUR was born in New York City in 1930. He received an A.B. degree from Williams College in 1952, and an LL.B. from Yale University in 1955. While at Yale Law School he worked closely with Richard C. Donnelly who ignited his interest in "victimless crimes" and related issues. After being admitted to the Bar in Connecticut, he served in the U.S. Army for two years. While stationed in New York, he earned an M.A. in sociology from the New School for Social Research where his teachers included Alfred Schutz and Otto Kirchheimer. He went on to receive his Ph.D. degree in Sociology from the London School of Economics in 1959. His doctoral dissertation was on British policies toward opiate addiction and served as the basis for his first book *Narcotic Addiction in Britain and America* published in 1962.

Schur taught at Wellesley College from 1959 to 1961, and then at Tufts University from 1961 to 1971, serving as chair of the department from 1966 to 1971. Since 1971, he has been on the faculty of New York University where he served as department chair 1971-75. During 1963-64 Schur held a Russell Sage Foundation Residency at the Center for the Study of Law and Society at the University of California, Berkeley; and he was a Visiting Scholar and Social Science Research Fellow at Harvard Law School during 1968-69. From 1971 to 1973 he was a consultant to the Juvenile Justice Standards Project—work which led to the publication of *Radical Non-Intervention.*

A solid sociologist and prolific writer, Schur has authored several other books relevant to the study of delinquency including *Crimes Without Victims* (1965); *Law and Society* (1968); *Our Criminal Society* (1969); *Labeling Deviant Behavior* (1971); *Victimless Crimes* coauthored with Hugo Adam Bedau (1974); *Interpreting Deviance* (1979); and *The Politics of Deviance* (1980).

THE BOOK

Schur begins his book with a chapter entitled "Rethinking the Delinquency Problem." He points out that theories about delinquency causation are contradictory and the data are inconsistent. Consequently, programs of intervention, treatment, and prevention, while well-intended, have been largely unsuccessful and in many cases seem to aggravate the problem.

One of the first problems in dealing with the problem of delinquency, is deciding what it is. Delinquency statutes are often vague, contradictory, and vary widely from one state to another. Schur contends that the label of "delinquent" is grossly over used and widely misunderstood. While delinquency has been heavily researched, Schur points out that public attitudes and beliefs regarding delinquency have been largely ignored by social science research. He believes that many of the public attitudes which have influenced policies toward delinquency are based upon misconceptions about crime and delinquency. Some of these common misconceptions include seeing crime and delinquency as "alien phenomena, as somehow existing *outside of* society, involving attacks *on* society" (p. 10) [italics in the original].

There is also the misconception that crime and delinquency are unique actions that require some type of "special" solutions outside the context of the basic social system. Despite all the evidence to the contrary, delinquency is widely perceived as "abnormal" and the public tends to dichotemize youths into "good" and "bad," "conformists" and "delinquents." Media sensationalism and public fear tend to cause citizens to believe that gang violence, murder, rape, robbery, and other violent offenses comprise the bulk of juvenile delinquency. Actually, as data clearly indicate, the most common forms of juvenile delinquency are *status offenses*—relatively minor law violations such as smoking, drinking, truancy, running away from home, and sexual activities—all of which are legal for adults.

Schur points out the limitations of delinquency typologies used throughout much of the sociological literature. He contends that essentially, delinquency has tended to be approached either from an individual treatment approach or a liberal reform approach. The individual treatment approach tends to focus upon the "differentness" of juvenile offenders and sees delinquency as a symptom of some deeper psychosocial problem. Prevention from this perspective focuses on identifying "predelinquents" and treatment is likely to involve some type of individual therapy. The rehabilitative ideal is pursued through a course of individualized justice and treatment.

The liberal reform approach tends to see delinquency as concentrated in the lower class where individuals are constrained by the social structure. The strain theories of Merton (1938), Cohen (1955), and Cloward and Ohlin (1960) are representative of this approach. Prevention from this perspective is likely to involve work with gangs and other groups in lower class communities in an attempt to open legitimate avenues of success for socially deprived youths. This approach is also cognizant of undesirable conditions in delinquency prevention centers and state training schools and insists that more attention must be paid to the social factors contributing to delinquency.

In contrast to these two dominant approaches, Schur offers a third alternative which he calls "radical non-intervention." This approach assumes that delinquency is widespread throughout society and approaches the problem primarily from the labeling perspective. From this approach, juveniles cannot be neatly divided into categories of delinquent and non-delinquent. Rather, delinquency is seen as being situational in nature primarily defined by societal reaction to specific acts in certain situations. It also gives credence to the "drift" theories (Matza, 1964) which see delinquency as resulting from a series of spontaneous reactions to given social circumstances, rather than from individual pathologies or undesirable social conditions. According to Schur:

> In radical non-intervention delinquents are seen not as having special personal characteristics, nor even as being subject to socioeconomic constraints, but rather as *suffering from contingencies*. Youthful 'misconduct' it is argued, is extremely common; delinquents are those youths who, for a variety of reasons, drift into disapproved forms of behavior and are caught and 'processed' [italics in the original] (p.23).

The radical non-intervention approach emphasizes that the vast majority of all delinquency is comprised of status offenses. From this perspective the intervention of police, courts, and other juvenile authorities in many cases produces more negative results (e.g., labeling, stigma, and further deviance) than the so-called delinquent act. Consequently, this approach calls for radical social change and severe limitations on the jurisdiction of the juvenile court.

Schur provides a detailed analysis of the individual treatment and liberal reform approaches toward delinquency prevention and treatment showing how neither has been effective in reducing delinquency. He points out many of their theoretical and methodological inadequacies and contradictions.

Then, he offers a new way of viewing the delinquency problem which calls for dramatic social change in the way society thinks about the problem of juvenile delinquency. Drawing upon the theories of Frank Tannenbaum (1938), Kai Erikson (1962), Howard Becker (1963), David Matza (1964), and others from the labeling and drift perspectives, Schur outlines a strategy for changing the way society reacts to juvenile misconduct. The main thrust of his argument rests on the idea that much of what is considered juvenile delinquency can in fact be tolerated by society, and fewer negative consequences would result if the behavior were simply ignored. From the radical non-intervention approach, the criminal justice system should be invoked only as a last resort, and then only for behaviors which would be illegal if committed by adults. In short, radical non-intervention calls for social and political "policies that accommodate the widest possible diversity of behaviors . . ." (p. 154), and urges ". . . *leave kids alone wherever possible*" (p. 155) [italics in the original].

Schur argues that delinquency research must focus upon the large amounts of delinquency which goes unreported in official statistics. He also indicates that the labeling theories, drift theories, and control theories (especially as outlined by Hirschi, 1969), offer the most valuable insights for rethinking the delinquency problem. Consistent with Hirschi's control theory, Schur indicates that families and schools must make every effort to develop in juveniles a meaningful social bond to society. He contends that labeling early minor misbehavior of youths as delinquent acts only serves to alienate youngsters from society, and in fact, decreases their sense of attachment to society and conventional norms.

Lest the radical non-intervention approach be seen as an ultra-liberal approach in which any behavior from juveniles would be tolerated, Schur calls for strict enforcement of the legal codes. In other words, legal codes should very explicitly spell out what types of acts will not be tolerated, and then, every effort should be made to enforce those laws. Juveniles would be held accountable for their law violating behavior with specific penalties spelled out the by the statutes. Consequently, from the radical non-intervention approach, while status offenses such as smoking, truancy, and running away from home would be decriminalized, laws against crimes such as burglary, larceny, assault, and other serious crimes would be more strictly enforced.

Schur is also quick to point out that this should not be interpreted as a "get tough" policy either. He indicates that the policy rather than being one of "get tough," simply emphasizes "deal evenly" (p. 169).

LIMITATIONS

Like any major work in juvenile delinquency, *Radical Non-intervention* has not been without its critics. One of the limitations in this work is the problem inherent in the labeling approach to deviance. That is, that while it provides an excellent basis for understanding deviant careers, it sheds little light on the social processes leading to initial norm violation. It has been charged that this perspective provides no etiological explanation for delinquency as it provides no systematic answer as to what caused the deviant behavior in the first place. To some extent Schur overcomes this limitation, however, by incorporating the ideas from drift an control theories which do explain social factors leading to initial norm violation.

Sharper criticism has been leveled at Radical Non-intervention in terms of its policy implications. While some applaud the call for the decriminalization of status offenses and the limiting of juvenile court jurisdiction, others believe that ignoring minor misconduct in children leads to more serious law violation as these youths reach adolescence and young adulthood.

Despite some limitations, *Radical Non-Intervention* stands as a classic work in sociology on the problem of juvenile delinquency. It is based upon sound sociological theory and in the tradition of C. Wright Mills challenges the sociological imagination.

REFERENCES

Becker, Howard S. (1963). *Outsiders*. New York: Free Press

Cloward, Richard A. and Lloyd E. Ohlin (1960). *Delinquency and Opportunity: A Theory of Delinquent Gangs*. New York: Free Press.

Cohen, Albert K. (1955). Delinquent Boys: The Culture of the Gang. New York: Free Press.

Erikson, Kai T. (1962). "Notes on the Sociology of Deviance." *Social Problems* 9 (Spring): 307-314.

Hirschi, Travis (1969). *Causes of Delinquency*. Berkeley: University of California Press.

Matza, David (1964), *Delinquency and Drift*. New York: John Wiley & Sons.

Merton, Robert K. (1938). "Social Structure and Anomie." *American Sociological Review* 3 (October): 672-682.

Tannenbaum, Frank (1938). *Crime and the Community*. Boston: Ginn & Co.

Negotiating Justice in the Juvenile System

A Comparison of Adult Plea Bargaining and Juvenile Intake

JOYCE DOUGHERTY

PROBLEMS WITH A SYSTEM OF DISCRETIONARY JUSTICE

IN THE ADULT CRIMINAL JUSTICE SYSTEM, plea bargaining is a widely accepted, if not controversial, practice. As Meeker and Pontell point out, these "quasi-official" negotiations of justice have "long been the 'normal state of affairs' in [adult] criminal courts" (Meeker and Pontell 1985: 119 and 121). When adults are accused of a crime and are processed through the system to the point where they may either exercise their right to a jury trial or enter a guilty plea, chances are they will opt for the latter. Seventy to 95 percent of all adult defendants in criminal cases will plead guilty; many will have negotiated those pleas (Whitebread et al. 1980: 407; Halberstam 1982: 2; Kaplan and Skolnick 1982: 444; Farr 1984: 291; LaFree 1985: 289). The process of adult plea bargaining has taken on several forms, but commonly it involves an agreement between the prosecutor and the defense attorney whereby the accused is "convinced" to plead guilty to a lesser or reduced charge than that which would have been pressed had the case gone to trial. These lesser or reduced charge bargains usually mean that the defendant will face a lower maximum sentence or will not have to face the possibility of having consecutive sentences imposed. There are other forms of plea agreements that do not involve negotiating over less serious or reduced charges,

Source: Dougherty, Joyce. "Negotiating Justice in the Juvenile System: A Comparison of Adult Plea Bargining and Juvenile Intake." *Federal Probation*, Vol. 52 (June) 1988:72-80. Reprinted by permission of Federal Probation.

however. As Remington et al. note: "[a] defendant may plead guilty to a charge that accurately describes his [or her] conduct in return for the prosecutor's agreement to recommend leniency or for a specific recommendation of probation or of a lesser sentence than would probably be imposed if the defendant insisted on a trial" (Remington et al. 1982: 516). In this form of bargaining, the understanding is that the judge either passively or actively, becomes involved in the negotiation process.

As Newman points out, the [p]ermutations and combinations of plea agreements are almost endless" (Newman 1981: 170), but whatever form the final agreement takes, the bargaining process itself occurs behind closed doors, within the context of what Rosett and Cressey call a "private system" of justice (Rosette and Cressey,1976: 3). Although Federal Rule 11(e)(2) requires that counsel disclose any agreement at the time it is entered in open court, the negotiating itself is still shrouded in secrecy. When adult defendants forego their right to a public jury trial and enter into this closed system of "private justice," they find themselves embroiled in the complexities of behind-the-scenes "discretionary justice":

> The full courtroom trial is rigidly governed by rules of law stating what evidence may be received, how each of the officials shall act, and even specifying what the judge is permitted to say to the jury to help it determine the facts. In practice most official decisions are not strictly governed by a rule of law. Instead, the official is free to act as he sees fit. Less formal decisions are discretionary in the sense that the official who makes them can choose whether to act and often how to act in a given case. Such freedom of choice may arise from an explicit delegation of legal authority to the official—he is instructed to act as he thinks best, within broad limits. It also may exist because there is no rule concerning the action, or because the official asserts power to act despite a rule which should inhibit him.
>
> The behind-the-scenes courthouse visitor will find that cases are not processed by rules he had learned to expect . . . Cases are not tried or even decided; they are settled or compromised. The system . . . is designed primarily to convince defendants to plead guilty (Rosett and Cressey (1976: 4-5).

The plea bargaining system of private, discretionary justice "convinces" adult defendants that if they wish to avoid the possibility of harsher treatment and stiffer penalties, then they should forfeit their right to a trial and accept the deal that has been negotiated. In what is supposed to be a system of law strictly bound by democratic principles of justice, many find this situation objectionable. In the last 15-20 years, an enormous effort has been mounted to discover factors that influence plea bargaining negotiations in order to achieve a clearer understanding of how they work and of their impact on our democratic system of justice. Much of this research has been done within the framework of an exchange theory which, at one level, explains the negotiations in terms of a "trading of benefits" between the prosecution and the defense, and, at another level, explains them in terms of a balancing and incorporating of the administrative needs of the system and principles of justice (Farr 1984). There are, however, those who reject the exchange approach to plea bargaining, preferring to frame the negotiations within the structure of discourse. They maintain that "plea bargaining outcomes, including decisions on charges, sentences, continuances, and trial, can be related to specific patterns [of discourse] by which they are achieved" (Maynard 1984: 76).

Whichever factors one chooses to regard as influential, and whatever theoretical framework one chooses to adopt, there is no escaping, or it would appear resolving, the issues raised by plea bargaining. When one examines the process at the philosophical level of democratic ideals of social and criminal justice, one finds those who argue that "plea bargaining disrupts the proportionality between criminal actions and punishments . . . [and] renders justice a market value" (Jordon 1985: 51). In a system where crime and punishment, where justice, are reduced to matters of "dealing an settling," an "aura of disrespect" for the law is bound to emanate (Newman 1981: 178). Beyond that, there will always be the potential for the "corruption of ideology" in a system which allows too much room for the exercise of discretion. As Newman points out, "[t]here is always a thin line between the proper exercise of discretion and discrimination or even corruption . . . extending such broad discretionary powers to the prosecutor and to trial courts not only usurps legislative prerogative, but offers the opportunity for concealing discriminatory or corrupt practices under the guise of administrative discretion" (Newman 1981: 178).

The "private" nature of plea bargaining negotiations also can help to promote the possible distortion and corruption of democratic ideals of justice, but on a less abstract level it is this same quality which lies at the heart of a more practical issue of providing equal opportunity to negotiate—the issue of equal protection and due process. In a system where established bargaining practices are common, but always informally arranged, never formally institutionalized, negotiating equity may be in danger (Newman 1981: 177). With the "customary practices," the routine normative structure of plea bargaining remaining largely private—unrevealed—we find the potential for wide variations in practices among prosecutors and trial judges. As Remington et al. point out, this can "often cause bewilderment and a sense of injustice among defendants." More importantly, some actually "may be denied the opportunity to participate in the bargaining process and the benefits which may accrue because they or their counsel are unaware of the customary practices of plea negotiation" Remington et al. 1982: 517); the point being they may be denied their equal protection and due process rights.

One of the most troublesome issues raised by plea bargaining negotiations is the question of voluntariness; "the possibility that an innocent defendant may plead guilty because of the fear that he will be sentenced more harshly if he is convicted after trial or that he will be subjected to damaging publicity because of a repugnant charge" (Remington et al. 1982: 517). The private nature of plea negotiations can make it difficult to distinguish between when a defendant has been gently persuaded into accepting a deal voluntarily and when he or she has been coercively convinced to agree to it. By law, all guilty pleas must be "voluntary and intelligent, and [they] must be supported by a factual basis developed on the record" (Whitebread 1980: 409), and there are some procedural safeguards theoretically designed to help prevent innocent defendants from pleading guilty involuntarily. For instance, most judges will not accept a guilty plea until they have assured themselves of a defendant's guilt by questioning the defendant personally, and/or by hearing evidence to determine for certain that a plea is voluntary and intelligent (Whitebread 1980: 409; Remington 1982: 518). Beyond that, Rule 11(c) of the Federal Rules of Criminal Procedure and Standard

14-1.4 of the A.B.A. Standards for guilty pleas both provide that a defendant must be informed of and understand the following before a plea of guilty is accepted:

> (1) the nature of the charge to which the plea is offered; (2) the maximum possible penalty for the offense to which the plea is offered and the mandatory minimum penalty provided by law, if any; (3) the fact that he has a right to plead not guilty, or to persist in that plea if it had already been made; and (4) the fact that by pleading guilty he waives the right to trial (Whitebread 1980: 409).

The theoretical nature of these official safeguards for the voluntariness of guilty pleas, however, is highlighted when one examines the procedures within the context of what Casper describes in the following exerpt as a "cop-out ceremony":

> The peculiar and somewhat hypocritical nature of a system which is based upon the presumption of innocence, due process values, and the criminal trial, but which in practice is a game of plea-bargaining, is reinforced by what is known as the cop-out ceremony. After a defendant has agreed to plead guilty, he appears before a judge to enter his plea. He is asked a series of questions about whether he is pleading guilty because he is in fact guilty, about coercion or inducements to plead, about his satisfaction with the representation afforded him by his attorney . . . . Ostensibly, the questions are designed to make sure that defendants are not pleading guilty (as a result of coercion, extravagant promises, and so forth) to things they did not do.
>   . . . [T]he questioning of the defendant entering a guilty plea serves other latent functions. Some have called it a "successful degradation ceremony" in which a defendant is forced to shed publicly his identity as innocent citizen and accept the identity of "criminal."
>   . . . Thus, the defendant must appear before the judge and go through a ritual. The judge asks him questions, and he responds with lies; the judge knows they are lies and accepts his answer as true. Once more the defendant is placed in a position in which he must play out a game. Some of them have a good idea what the game is about . . . Others don't understand its purpose at all: when asked why they thought they had to answer the questions they responded with confusion; it was just something you had to do, and probably 'they' (the judges, the prosecutor, the state) had a reason for it, but the reason wasn't clear (Casper 1972: 81-82 &85).

When one reflects upon the issues that are raised by plea bargaining, one begins to understand it more clearly as a process of negotiation that can transform the ideal of democratic justice into a market principle and breed contempt for the law and cynicism for a private system of discretionary justice that not only fails to guarantee equal protection and due process rights but also promotes ritualistic ceremonies to create the illusion of voluntariness. There are, however, those who defend these negotiations of justice by stressing how they can be used to serve the needs of all of the participants in the process (Heumann 1984: 153) or by arguing that they are the only way to "bring the individualization of justice into our [adult] court system" (Newman 1981: 178). Even the United States Supreme Court has defended plea bargaining by consistently rejecting challenges to its constitutionality in every case that has come before it (Halberstam 1982: 3). In the final analysis there is one unavoidable fact: plea bargaining in the adult criminal justice system is wrought with controversy.

There are those who are committed to the idea that plea bargaining undermines the very principles of justice upon which our democratic system of law is based. They argue that if it is not discontinued, then, at the very least, it ought to be practiced "reluctantly and with grave misgivings" (Jordon 1985: 51). These are serious warnings, not to be taken lightly, and yet the impact of these warnings reaches beyond the realm of the adult criminal justice system. At the heart of the juvenile justice system lie negotiations which, when examined closely, can be seen as the qualitative equivalent of adult plea bargaining negotiations.

BENEVOLENT PROTECTION OR DISCRETIONARY JUSTICE?

At first one might be reluctant to accept the idea that any aspect of the juvenile justice system could be regarded as qualitatively equivalent to a process in the adult criminal justice system. After all, the two systems are, by design, very different. One tends not even to associate the term "plea bargaining" with any phase of the juvenile justice system; it is a process more readily associated with the adult system. There are those, including the juvenile litigants in *McKeiver v. Pennsylvania* (403 U.S. 528 (1971)), who argue "that counsel and the prosecution [in juvenile court] engage in plea bargaining," (McKeiver) and that "if a [juvenile] court does not have a prosecutor, plea bargaining can take place between defense counsel and the probation officer" (Simonsen and Gordon 1979: 178). However, those who acknowledge the possibility of "plea bargaining" in the juvenile system generally qualify themselves by noting that because of the unique character of the juvenile system there is "little necessity for plea bargaining" (Simonsen and Gordon 1979: 178), or it "has less value for juveniles than adults" (Guggenheim and Sussman 1985: 41). The implication seems to be that "plea bargaining" *per se* does not play a significant part in the juvenile justice system because of its unique design, the design which distinguishes it from the adult criminal justice system. However, when one examines the juvenile justice system closely, one discovers that it is the very nature of this unique design that necessitates a reliance upon the same kinds of negotiations, the same kind of discretionary justice, that lie at the heart of adult plea bargaining.

Since its inception in the latter part of the 19th century, the juvenile justice system in the United States has been shaped by the principles underlying the doctrine of "parens patriae," basic principles which have served to distinguish it from the adult system. Under this doctrine, a delinquent juvenile is treated as a "ward of the state" (Simonsen and Gordon 1979: 30), and the juvenile court is seen as his or her "benevolent protector" (Bortner 1982: 1). The original idea was to create an individualized system of justice with a unique organizational structure that would ensure the humanitarian treatment of juveniles. In order to achieve this ideal, however, there would have to be a shift in emphasis away from the punishment and toward the treatment of children. The essence of this shift was articulated well by the Supreme Court of Pennsylvania in 1905. In *Commonwealth v. Fisher*, the Pennsylvania Court argued that "the state was 'legitimate guardian and protector of children,' [and] that the goal of juvenile processing was not the 'punishment of offenders but . . . the salvation of children'" (Binder 1984: 358). The attitudinal transition from "punishment" to "salvation" in the processing of juveniles meant that, unlike in unnegotiated adult criminal court proceedings, the determination of guilt or innocence would become secondary (Blumberg 1979; Somonsen and Gordon 1979; Bortner 1982; Marshall and Marshall 1983). The "paramount questions" raised by the juvenile system would "concern the character and background of the accused, his needs and problems—questions which in traditional due process were not supposed to be raised, at least until guilt had been determined" (Blumberg 1979: 292). By focusing on a child's "needs" rather than on his or her "deeds," the system implicitly would relieve children of all criminal responsibility (Bortner 1982: 4).

Under the auspices of the parens patriae doctrine, reformers essentially "decriminalized" juvenile justice, transforming it into a nonadversarial system quite distinct in character from the adversarial adult criminal justice system. There would be no "sides" in the juvenile justice system; everyone involved in the process would be working toward an end which would, at least in theory, serve the best interest of the child. To this end, all proceedings would be closed to the public, and the extensive involvement of the state in the system would be characterized not by rigid formality, but rather by flexible informality. There would be a "paternalistic" attitude toward the rights of children. As the 1905 Pennsylvania Supreme Court argued, no constitutional rights could be violated by a process "designed to give protection, care, and training to children, as a needed substitute for parental authority and performance of parental duty" (Binder 1984: 358). Ultimately, what all of this meant was the establishment of a private system of individualized justice for children based on the unbounded exercise of discretion by agents of the state with little or no regard for the constitutional rights of the children.

Beginning in the mid-1960's, the United States Supreme Court handed down a series of decisions which "attempted to curb alleged abuse of discretion" in the juvenile justice system by establishing certain due process rights for children (Marshall and Marshall 1983: 197). The 1967 Gault decision (387 U.S. 1) had a "profound impact" on the juvenile justice system by mandating that certain traditionally adversarial procedures had to be followed when processing children who faced the loss of their liberty (i.e., right to counsel, privilege against self-incrimination, fair notice of allegations, and right to confront the cross-examine witnesses.) At the time, many believed that Gault represented a "new direction" in attitudes toward the rights of juveniles and some held out the hope "that juvenile delinquency and some held out the hope "that juvenile delinquency procedure was evolving into a new model of justice [with] juveniles . . . [as] legal actors who possessed increased power resources relative to those of the state" (Block 1985: 536). However, these hopes were shortlived. In 1971, the United States Supreme Court vehemently defended the traditional ideals underlying the doctrine of parens patriae. In *McKeiver v. Pennsylvania* (403 U.S. 528), the majority opinion of the Court held that there is no constitutional right to a trial by jury in juvenile court and went on to state the following:

> The juvenile [court] concept held high promise. We are reluctant to say that, despite disappointments of grave dimensions, it still does not hold promise, and we are particularly reluctant to say . . . that the system cannot accomplish its rehabilitative goals . . .

The arguments [in this case] necessarily equate the juvenile proceeding . . . with the [adult] criminal trial. Whether they should be so equated is our issue. Concern about the inapplicability of exclusionary and other rules of evidence, about the juvenile court judge's possible awareness of the juvenile's prior record an of the contents of the social file; about repeated appearances of the same familiar witnesses in persons of juvenile and probation officers and social workers—all to the effect that this will create the likelihood of prejudgment—chooses to ignore it seems to us, every aspect of fairness of concern, of sympathy, and of paternal attention that the juvenile court system contemplates.

If the formalities of the criminal adjudicative process are to be superimposed upon the juvenile court system, there is little need for its separate existence. Perhaps that ultimate disillusionment will come one day, but for the moment we are disinclined to give impetus to it. (McKeiver)

Today, the juvenile justice system remains a system of individualized, discretionary justice controlled by agents of the state who, in theory if not always in practice, have only the best interest of the child in mind. It is a system which at its heart relies upon the same kinds of informal negotiations of justice which have generated so much criticism of adult plea bargaining.

INTAKE: THE NEGOTIATIONS OF JUVENILE JUSTICE

At no point in the juvenile system is the parallel between adult plea bargaining and the negotiation of juvenile justice more clear than it is at intake. In and of itself, this is a disturbing fact since "the decisions made at intake may be the most significant ones in the whole process for an allegedly delinquent youth" (Wadlington et al. 1983: 338). During intake, negotiations take place which will determine whether or not a juvenile will have a delinquency petition filed against him or her and, if the decision to file is made, for what offense the petition will be filed. Given the fact that some state legislatures are not adopting sentencing guidelines which mandate that any record of delinquency adjudication be taken into account when sentencing an adult, the decision to file a delinquency petition at intake can carry with it serious implications that may follow a juvenile into his or her adult life. However, just as few adult cases ever make it to trial, few juvenile cases ever end up being formally adjudicated. In some jurisdictions, as high as 80 percent of juvenile cases never make it to a formal hearing (Miller et al. 1985: 243). It is the process which occurs at this critical intake stage of the juvenile justice system, a process of negotiation which ultimately determines the fate of the juveniles, that makes it so strikingly similar to adult plea bargaining.

In its most basic form, one might argue that juvenile intake appears to be quite distinct from adult plea bargaining. Most adult plea bargains involve private negotiations between the prosecutor and defense attorney. Occasionally one may find judges either passively or actively involved in the process. Traditionally defendants themselves rarely take an active part in the actual negotiations. On the other hand, intake negotiations, while not open to the public, can involve a much wider range of players. In most jurisdictions, the "hearings" (or, as they are often referred to in an effort to communicate the informality of the proceeding, interviews or conferences) are presided over by a probation officer who either has been permanently assigned the task of intake or assumes the responsibility on a rotating basis. In what are perceived by the intake probation officer to be less serious cases, the negotiations will usually only involve the child and his or her parent(s) or legal guardian(s). When the case is perceived to be more serious, for instance there are charges involving a violent offense, the "hearing" will tend to be more formal, in an effort to incorporate as much factual information into the negotiations as possible. In these more formal "hearings," along with the child and his or her parent(s) or legal guardian(s), police, victims or complainants, and witnesses may all be asked to appear and give their sides of the story (Arnold and Brungardt 1983: 300). Even in these more formal "hearings," defense attorney participation is rare. As Rubin points out, "waivers of rights tend to be finessed and the norm is for the parents to encourage the child to discuss his or her participation in the alleged offense with the intake officer" (Rubin 1980: 304).

Unlike adult plea bargaining which is routinely based on informally structured private negotiations, the structure of the juvenile intake process tends to be defined quite specifically by statutes, official standards, and/or procedural manuals. When one examines the options open to those who negotiate adult plea bargains and those open to juvenile intake officers, once again, rather than "striking similarities" one is struck by the apparent differences. Adult plea bargaining agreements can involve "permutations and combinations" which seem "endless," and yet the options available at intake seem quite limited. There are only two categories of options or dispositional alternatives available to juvenile intake officers: informal or nonjudicial, and formal or judicial (Silberman 1978: 449-451; Arnold and Brungardt 1983: 300-302; Miller et al. 1985: 239-242). The informal or nonjudicial options include outright or unconditional dismissal of the case, when "the charges are not seen as being serious enough to warrant further court action" (Arnold and Brungardt 1983: 300), and what is referred to as CWR, or counseled and warned and then released (Silberman 1978L 449), which also may be referred to as "conditional dismissal of a compliant" (Miller et al. 1985: 240). Another nonjudicial disposition is informal (or nonjudicial) probation which involves "the supervision by juvenile intake or probation personnel of a juvenile who is the subject of a complaint, for a period of time during which the juvenile may be required to comply with certain restrictive conditions with respect to his or her conduct and activities" (Miller et al. 1985: 239). Similar to this is what is called the "provision of intake services" which involves "the direct provision of services by juvenile intake and probation personnel on a continuing basis" (Miller et al. 1985: 240). The final nonjudicial option is referral or "diversion" to "an agency or program in the community or to a court sponsored program" (Arnold and Brungardt 1983: 300). Conditional dismissals also can include these kinds of agency referrals. Formal or judicial dispositional options at intake include the filing of a petition for an adjudicatory hearing of the case and a constant decree which "is a court order authorizing supervision of a juvenile for a specified period of time during which the juvenile may be required to fulfill certain conditions or some other disposition of the complaint" (Miller et al. 1985: 241). The decree usually is accomplished after the filing of a petition but before the entry of an adjudication order. In most jurisdictions, if the conditions of the consent decree are not met by the juvenile, the court automatically proceeds to the adjudicatory hearing on the original petition as if the decree had never been entered (Commonwealth of Pennsylvania J.C.J.C. 1984: 43 and 45). One other formal, judicial alternative is the transferring, waiving, or certifying of a juvenile case to adult criminal court. Usually done after a petition has been filed but before an adjudication hearing has been conducted, this alternative necessitates a special hearing and involves only youths suspected of having committed serious offenses who are over the minimum transfer age set by state law (Arnold and Brungardt 1983: 301; Commonwealth of PA J.C.J.C. 1984: 40).

One final area which seems to highlight the differences rather than the similarities between adult plea bargaining and juvenile intake is the perceived function of the two processes. As indicated previously, the function of adult plea bargaining is a subject open to a great deal of debate. In an effort to explain its function, many researchers have tried to determine which factors exert the most influence over the negotiations, and many theorists have tried to provide an appropriate conceptual framework within which the negotiations can be understood fully. There is little consensus among researchers or theorists who search for an answer to the question, "what is the function of plea bargaining?" On the other hand, pinpointing the function of juvenile intake seems to pose little difficulty. As the "Standards Relating to the Juvenile Probation Function" make clear, the central function of intake is to screen cases, legally and socially, for possible nonjudicial handling (Wadlington et al. 1983: 339). Intake negotiations do not function to assess or determine the guilt or innocence of a juvenile, but rather they serve to help provide understanding of the juvenile's situation and to select the most appropriate nonjudicial remedy whenever possible (Silberman 1978: 448). As the "Standards" point out, this strategy "allows the exercise of some control over the provision of services to a delinquent juvenile without the detrimental consequences of judicial processing, which labels the juvenile as a delinquent and by so doing stigmatizes the juvenile" (Wadlington et a. 1983: 339).

Thus far what is striking about the comparison between adult plea bargaining and juvenile intake is not how similar the two processes are, but rather how different they appear to be. One must look more closely at what actually occurs during juvenile intake if one is going to begin to appreciate fully the similarities between it and the impression that there are very few active players in plea bargaining negotiations; they are private negotiations of justice between tow adversarial parties. On the other hand, while they are not open to the public, intake negotiations seem to have the potential to involve a much wider range of people, and therefore they at least appear to be more open than the adult negotiations. When one talks to intake probation officers, however, one quickly learns that the norm is to have only the child and one parent (or legal guardian) show up for the "hearing." Victims or complaintants and witnesses, while they may be asked to attend, may not show up and the presence of the police tends to be determined by each separate police department's administrative attitude toward the importance of their attendance at such informal juvenile "hearings." In reality then, juvenile intake, like adult plea bargaining, routinely involves very few active players. Beyond that, while the theory underlying the juvenile justice system defines the relationships among these players as nonadversarial, it is not difficult to see how a child and his or her parent(s) or legal guardian(s) might see intake negotiations differently, as, for instance, a probation officer, without regard for the determination of the child's guilt or innocence, imposes an informal alternative to filing a petition of delinquency which for all intents and purposes places the child under conditions of formal probation for 3 to 6 months.

When one compares the structures of the two processes, the implication seems to be that there is a degree of formality and consistent consideration and or protection of rights for juveniles at intake that one does not find in the noninstitutionalized, informal structure of adult plea bargaining. However, underlying the pretense of official standards and guidelines what one finds at intake is one very basic fact: "Almost no procedural due process protections are afforded juveniles at intake" (Wadlington 1983: 340). Intake is regarded as an informal process, and as such, the courts, including the United States Supreme Court, have not recognized the need to have due process rights consistently enforced or safeguarded by Federal law (Binder and Binder 1982: 17-20; Wadlington et al. 1983: 339-340). For instance, while it is mandatory in many states, there is no constitutional right to an intake interview prior to a formal adjudication hearing when a complaint is lodged against a juvenile (Guggenheim and Sussman 1985: 37). The right to remain silent (or not participate at all) has been extended to intake "hearing" (Guggenheim and Sussman 1985: 37) but the cost of exercising that right inevitably will result in the filing of a petition of delinquency. Statements made during intake usually are not used against a juvenile in adjudication proceedings, but "statements made during intake interviews are often used against a child at dispositional hearings" (Guggenheim and Sussman 1985: 37). And finally, because intake is considered to be more of an informal, personalized conference, and not a formal hearing to determine guilt or innocence, "a child's request for counsel is almost always denied" (Guggenheim and Sussman 1985: 38), if not discouraged. Juveniles and their parent(s) or guardian(s) are told that they can have an attorney present, but then it is not unusual to find that they are told that the presence of a lawyer may jeopardize the chance for an informal (i.e., more lenient) resolution of the case. According to official standards, juveniles have certain rights at intake, but clearly there is a heavy price to pay if they choose to exercise those rights. So on the one hand we have an officially informal process for adults which, in theory at least, is structurally bound by constitutional provisions but not by official guidelines, and on the other hand we have an officially informal process for juveniles which, in theory at least, is structurally bound by official guidelines but not consistently by constitutional provisions. While their structures may appear to be different at one level, at another they are the same: both adult plea bargaining negotiations and juvenile intake negotiations are structured in ways which result in questionable equal protection and due process practices.

When one compares the alternatives available to the negotiators at juvenile intake and at adult plea bargaining, once again, the differences, not the similarities, are what stand out. Plea bargaining can involve an almost unlimited possibility of alternatives, while juvenile intake appears to be restricted to a few nonjudicial and judicial options. However, there is one factor which essentially negates this difference, and that is the factor of discretion. Whenever there are choices to be made, whenever there are decisions to be negotiated in an informal setting that is not bound by rigid guidelines, discretion will be exercised. One might think that because adult plea bargaining offers more alternatives than juvenile intake, the degree of discretion exercised must be greater. However, this is not necessarily the case. Few states or counties have adopted written guidelines for determining appropriate intake decisions (Guggenheim and Sussman 1985: 37), and as the "Standards Relating to the Juvenile Probation Function" point out, "intake officers generally have virtually unlimited discretion in making intake decisions" (Wadlington et al. 1983: 339). In any system where the boundaries of discretionary power are unclear, as they are in both adult plea bargaining negotiations and juvenile intake negotiations, the possibility of arbitrary, discriminatory, unequal treatment increases; problems which we have seen are only compounded by the mutual informality of their respective structures..

For years, researchers have been searching for factors which influence adult plea bargaining negotiations n an effort to determine if discriminatory behavior really exists. However, only recently has a similar interest in juvenile intake negotiations emerged, and as C.R. Fenwich notes in his 1982 article, "Juvenile Court Intake Decision Making: The Importance of Daily Affiliation," "much work remains to be done" (Fenwick 1982: 444). Beyond helping to pinpoint sources of possible discriminatory practices that have been routinized into the informal structure of both adult plea bargaining negotiations and juvenile intake negotiations, this kind of research also may be useful in deciphering the latent functions of these processes and developing theories to explain those functions. Such has been the case with research on plea bargaining, but, as yet, not with research on intake. This may help to explain why the functions of plea bargaining negotiations remain subject to debate, while those of juvenile intake negotiations are not. Beyond that, while descriptions of the function of juvenile intake appear to be clear-cut (i.e., screening cases legally and socially for possible nonjudicial handling), one of the rationales used to justify that manifest function hints at a latent function which directly links it to an exchange theory explanation of the functioning of plea bargaining. One rationale maintains that "non-judicial handling" is a better "way to provide social services and impose social controls without invoking the formal court process"; it is "more effective than judicial processing in 'rehabilitating' the juvenile" (Silberman 1978: 448; Wadlington et al. 1983: 339). This is clearly consistent with the conceptual framework provided by the doctrine of parens patriae. However, it is another rationale for the manifest screening function of juvenile intake which links it to plea bargaining: the handling of cases informally at intake, just as the bargaining of cases before trial, helps to keep court dockets at a manageable level (Silberman 1978: 448; Wadlington et al. 1983: 339).

The fact is that both adult plea bargaining and juvenile intake function to negotiate discretionary justice. They both create formal settings, where individuals who are, for all intents and purposes, presumed to be guilty are "convinced" to agree "voluntarily" to the officials' resolution of their cases or face the potentially harsher consequences of formal processing. Individual rights are at best ignored, or at worst denied. One might argue that the only true beneficiaries of these negotiations are the judges who are relieved of the burden of having to preside over the majority of cases that enter the adult and juvenile justice systems.

PARALLEL DILEMMA

More telling than the structural parallels between adult plea bargaining and juvenile intake are the similarities between the issues they raise. In both processes, questions over the degree to which equal protection and due process rights are violated are an ever-present concern. Any official process, whether it occurs within the context of the adult system or the juvenile system, which relies upon the informal negotiations of discretionary justice is bound to raise this issue. For sometime now, a great deal of attention has been focused on the problem of how far to extend the constitutional rights of adults accused of a crime and of juveniles in general. However, there are other issues raised by the two negotiating processes that are just as critical as the equal protection—due process issue, but which, for some reason, have failed to attract as much attention, especially within the realm of juvenile justice system.

The question of the voluntariness of the two processes has inspired much debate among observers of adult plea bargaining, but little among observers of juvenile intake, and yet one easily can see how both are structurally compatible with the coercion of admissions of guilt. In both cases, there is a situation where an individual accused of an offense if being told, directly or indirectly, by an official of the state that he or she can either admit guilt and be treated with whatever degree of leniency that has been negotiated, or, if he or she does not cooperate (i.e., insists upon his or her innocence), face the wrath of a formal system of justice that will look upon him or her as uncooperative or untreatable. It seems absurd to argue that admission of guilt under these circumstances could be anything other than coerced. In adult plea bargaining, we have seen there are theoretical safeguards to ensure the voluntariness of guilty pleas, and yet we also have seen how these safeguards in practice have been reduced to the hypocrisy of the "cop-out ceremony." In juvenile intake, there are no such safeguards, and so one might ask hopefully, there must be no such hypocrisy? Unfortunately, the hypocrisy we find a juvenile intake reaches far beyond the boundaries of a single informal process. Hypocrisy is an attitude—a condition—which has become an inherent part of the entire system of juvenile justice. Juvenile justice has become a system which patronizes or "finesses" the waiving of the rights of juveniles, while it tells the juveniles it only wants to help them—it is only doing what is best for them. It is a system which pretends to be sympathetic to the juveniles' plight, and yet it is a system which does not seem to want to hear denials of guilt. It is a system which insists that it is there to rehabilitate and not punish, and yet it is a system which forces juveniles into foster homes and institutions where they are abused, raped, and even murdered. Admissions of guilt at intake and the hypocrisy underlying the manner in which these admissions are accepted as voluntary are manifestations of an issue which impacts on the entire system of juvenile justice; and yet one which, when compared to adult plea bargaining, attracts relatively little attention.

Finally, the issue of corrupting the ideals of democracy impacts on both adult plea bargaining and juvenile intake. We have seen it pointed out in the study of adult plea bargaining that in a system where justice is reduced to matters of "dealing and settling" among officials of the state who are permitted to exercise their discretion indiscriminately; an "aura of disrespect" for the law is bound to emanate and the democratic ideals of fair and equal justice are bound to be corrupted. We have seen that a similar situation exists when we examine juvenile intake. During intake, discretionary justice is negotiated. Justice for all juveniles is reduced to matters of dealing and settling by officials of the state who are permitted to exercise their discretion indiscriminately. What is most disturbing about this is that it teaches our children a tainted, corrupted vision of what law and justice are in a democracy. It is a cynical lesson not easily learned, but one never forgotten, and yet it is a problem that has drawn little attention.

Much more research needs to be done in the area of juvenile intake. It is an empirically and theoretically fascinating process that reveals much about the realities of juvenile justice in this country, and these realities are what need to be understood if reform of the system is ever going to succeed.

BIBLIOGRAPHY

Alschuler, A. W. (1968) "The Prosecutor's Role in Plea Bargaining." *University of Chicago Law Review* 36 (Autumn): 50-112

Arnold, W. (1983) *Juvenile Misconduct and Delinquency*. Boston: Houghton Mifflin.

Binder, A. (1984) "The Juvenile Court, the U.S. Constitution and When the Twain Meet." *Journal of Criminal Justice* 12 (August): 355-366.

Binder, A. (1982) "Juvenile Diversion and the Constitution." *Journal of Criminal Justice* 10 (March): 1-24.

Block, K. J. (1985) "Balancing Power Through Law: The State v. the Juvenile in Delinquency Proceedings." *Justice Quarterly* 2 (December): 535-551.

Blumberg, A. S. (1979) *Criminal Justice: Issues and Ironies*. New York: New Viewpoints.

Bortner, M. S. (1982) *Inside a Juvenile Court: The Tarnished Ideal of Individualized Justice*. New York: New York University Press.

Brereton, D. (1981-82) "Does It Pay to Plead Guilty? Differential Sentencing and the Functioning of Criminal Courts." *Law and Society Review* 16 (Fall): 45-70.

Casper, J. D. (1972) *American Criminal Justice: The Defendant's Perspective*. Englewood Cliffs, NJ: Prentice-Hall.

Chambliss, W. J. (1971) Law, *Order and Power*. Reading, MA: Addison-Wesley.

Commonwealth of Pennsylvania Juvenile Court Judges' Commission. (1984) *Handbook for Juvenile Probation Officers: Introduction to the Juvenile Justice System in Pennsylvania*. Official Publication by the J.C.J.C.

Farr, K. A. (1984) "Administration and Justice: Maintaining Balance Through an Institutional Plea Negotiation Process." *Criminology* 22 (August): 291-319.

Fenwick, C. R. (1982) "Juvenile Court Intake Decision Making: The Importance of Family Affiliation." *Journal of Criminal Justice* 10 (August): 443-453.

Friedman, L. M. (1979) "Plea Bargaining in Historical Perspective." *Law and Society Review* 13 (Winter): 247-259.

Geraghty, J. A. (1979) "Cost and the Plea Bargaining Process: Reducing the Price of Justice to the Nonindigent Defendant." *The Yale Law Journal* 89 (December): 331-352.

Guggenheim M. (1985). *The Rights of Young People*. New York: Bantam Books.

Halberstam, M. (1982) "Towards Neutral Principles in the Administration of Criminal Justice: A Critique of Supreme Court Decisions Sanctioning the Plea Bargaining Process. "*Journal of Criminal Law and Criminology* 73 (Spring): 1-49.

Heumann, M. (1975) "A Note on Plea Bargaining and Caseload Pressure." *Law and Society Review* 9 (Summer): 515-528.

———. (1978) *Plea Bargaining: The Experiences of Prosecutors, Judges and Defense Attorneys*. Chicago: University of Chicago Press.

———. (1984) "Adopting to Plea Bargaining: Prosecutors." In G.F. Cole (ed.), *Criminal Justice: Law and Politics*. Monterey, CA: Brooks/Cole.

Jordon, S.M. (1985) "Two Thoughts of Plea Bargaining. "In S.M. Talarico (ed.), *Courts and Criminal Justice: Emerging Issues*. Beverly Hills, CA: Sage, pp. 35-51.

Kaplan, J. (1982) *Criminal Justice: Introductory Cases and Materials*. Mineola, NY: Foundation Press.

LaFree, G. D. (1985) "Adversarial and Nonadversarial Justice: A Comparison of Guilty Pleas and Trials." *Criminology* 23 (May): 289-312.

Marshall, C. E. (1983) "The Implementing of Formal Procedures in Juvenile Court Processing of Status Offenders." *Journal of Criminal Justice* 11 (July) 195-211.

Mather, L. M. (1974) "The Outsider in the Courtroom: An Alternative Role for the Defense." In H. Jacob (ed.), *The Potential for Reform of Criminal Justice*. Beverly Hills, CA: Sage, pp. 263-289.

Maynard, D. W. (1984) "The Structure of Discourse in Misdemeanor Plea Bargaining," *Law and Society Review* 18 (Fall): 75-104.

McCarthy, B. R. (1985) "Certainty of Punishment and Sentence Mitigation in Plea Behavior." *Justice Quarterly* 2 (September): 363-383.

McDonald, W. F. (1979) "The Prosecutor's Plea Bargaining Decisions." In W.F. McDonald (ed.), *The Prosecutor*. Beverly Hills, CA: Sage, pp. 151-197.

Meeker, J. W. (1985) "Court Caseloads, Plea Bargains, and Criminal Sanctions: The Effects of Section 17 P.C. in California." *Criminology* 23 (February): 119-143.

Miller, F. W. (1985) *The Juvenile Justice Process*. Mineola, NY: Foundation Press.

Nardulli, P. F. (1978) *The Courtroom Elite: An Organization Perspective on Criminal Justice*. Cambridge, MA: Ballinger.

———. (1979) "The Caseload Controversy and the Study of Criminal Courts." *Journal of Criminal Law and Criminology* 70 (Spring): 89-101.

Neubauer, D. W. (1974) *Criminal Justice in Middle America*. Morristown, NJ: General Learning Press.

Newman, D. J. (1966) *Conviction: The Determination of Guilt or Innocence Without Trial*. Boston: Little, Brown.

———. (1981) "Plea Bargaining." In R. G. Culbertson and M. R. Tezak (eds.), *Order Under Law*. Prospect Heights, IL: Waveland Press, 166-179.

Petersilia, J. (1981) "Juvenile Record Use in Adult Court Proceedings: A Survey of Prosecutors." *Journal of Criminal Law and Criminology* 72 (Winter): 1746-1771.

Remington, F. J. (1982) *Criminal Justice Administration*. Charlottesville, VA: Michie.

Rosett, A. (1976) *Justice by Consent: Plea Bargains in the American Courthouse*. Philadelphia: J. P. Lippincott.

Rubin, H. T. (1980) "The Emerging Prosecutor Dominance of Juvenile Court Intake Process." *Crime and Delinquency* 26 (July): 299-318.

Silberman, C. E. (1978) *Criminal Violence and Criminal Justice*. New York: Vintage.

Simonsen, C. E. (1979) *Juvenile Justice in America*. Encino, CA: Glencoe.

Wadlington, W. (1983) *Children in the Legal System*. Mineola, NY: Foundation Press.

Whitebread, C. H. (1980) *Criminal Procedure: An Analysis of Constitutional Cases and Concepts*. Mineola, NY: Foundation Press.

ARTICLE 35

Girls in Jail

MEDA CHESNEY-LIND

*Evidence drawn from a variety of sources is used to construct a profile
of girls held in adult jails and lockups in the United States. The data
indicate that girls are more likely than boys to be held in these facilities
for status offenses and minor crimes. Girls are also likely to be younger
than their male counterparts and, despite their less serious offenses,
they may be held almost as long as boys. The conditions of girls'
confinement, and the possible consequences of these situations, are
then reviewed. Chief among these problems is isolation that may result
in self-destructive behavior and the possibility of sexual assault by
male staff.*

DESPITE OVER A DECADE of federal efforts to remove youth from adult jails and lockups,
large numbers of adolescents continue to be held in these facilities. And, though girls
are arrested for far less serious offenses than boys, many of the youths in adult jails and
lockups are female. In 1984, for example, the Annual Survey of Jails revealed that there
were 95,580 juvenile admissions to the nation's jails; 16.7% of these were girls
(15,963). In 1983, according to a different census, girls made up 17.6% of all jail
admissions (Bureau of Justice Statistics, 1986, p. 2). To put these figures in context,
adult women during 1984 were 9.5% of all jail admissions (Bureau of Justice Statistics,
1986, p. 2). During roughly the same period (1982), girls constituted 20.7% of
detention center admissions (Schwartz et al., 1987, p. 227).

    The same year that girls were 16.7% of juvenile admissions to adult jails, girls'
arrests accounted for 22.2% of all juvenile arrests (Federal Bureau of Investigation,
1985, p. 167). Since the bulk of girls' arrests are for extremely trivial offenses, the
similarity of these figures is disturbing. To be specific, since 1975 nearly half of all

    Source: Chesney-Lind, Meda. "Girls in Jail." *Crime and Delinquency* , Vol. 34 (April) 1988: 150-
168. Reprinted by permission of Sage Publications, Inc.

girls' arrests have been for two offenses, larceny theft (which, for girls, is overwhelmingly likely to be shoplifting) and running away from home. In 1984, for example, these two offenses accounted for 46% of girls' arrests. Only about 2% of the girls' arrests are for serious violent offenses (Federal Bureau of Investigation, 1985, p. 167). Boys, by contrast, are more likely to be arrested for a wider variety of offenses as well as for more serious offenses.

Unfortunately, national data on the characteristics of girls held in jails, including reasons for admission, are sketchy, and those that are available may not be complete. For example, as this article will demonstrate, many youth spend less than 6 hours in jail, yet some of the monitoring reports do not count these youth (Steinhart and Krisberg, 1987). One description of the national picture, however, noted that "an estimated 30% of juvenile jail inmates are being housed for juvenile authorities. These inmates included runaways and juveniles awaiting transfer to juvenile facilities" (Bureau of Justice Statistics, 1986, p. 2). An additional 20% were "adjudicated or convicted" and the remainder were "awaiting adjudication or trial" (Bureau of Justice Statistics, 1986, p. 2). Another estimate was that 20% of the youth housed in adult jails were jailed for status offenses, that 4% had not been charged with an offense, and that only 10% of the youth held in adult jails were charged with "serious offenses" (Community Research Center, 1985, p. 1).

Since girls were a majority (58%) of those arrested for running away in 1983 (Federal Bureau of Investigation, 1985, p. 171), it is likely that many of the youth jailed for this as well as other status offenses were girls. Indeed, this article will provide considerable evidence to suggest that many of the girls held in jails across America are status offenders. Given the relatively minor role played by noncriminal status offenses in their misbehavior, one question seems unavoidable. Why do so many girls end up in adult jails? To answer this question requires a brief review of the special problems that girls have traditionally encountered in the juvenile justice system.

PATERNALISTIC JUSTICE

Girls have, since the inception of a separate system of justice for youth, been the recipients of a special, and discriminatory, form of justice (Chesney-Lind, 1973; Schlossman and Wallach, 1987; Shelden, 1981; Gordon, 1986). The bias against girls is largely a product of "status" offenses, whose vague language permits differential treatment of adolescents who come into the system. These offenses allow the arrest of youth for a wide range of behaviors that are not crimes but rather violations of parental authority: "running away from home," "being a person in need of supervision," "minor in need of supervision," being "incorrigible,." "beyond control," truant, in need of "care and protection," and so on.

An examination of official court populations in the United States and elsewhere (Hancock, 1981; Smith, 1978; Geller, 1981; Castro, 1981, p. 222) shows that a large proportion of young women arrested and/or referred to court are charged with status offenses. In the United States, for example, the most recent data (1982) show that 30%

of the girls in courts, but only 10% of the boys, are charged with these offenses. This means that girls constituted 46% of the status offenders in court populations, while males constituted around 80% of the other types of offenders (National Center for Juvenile Justice, 1985, p. 21).

For many years statistics showing large numbers of girls arrested and referred for status offenses were taken to be representative of the different types of male and female delinquency. However, self-report studies of male and female delinquency do not reflect the dramatic differences in misbehavior found in official statistics. Specifically, it appears that girls charged with these noncriminal status offenses have been and continue to be significantly overrepresented in court populations.

The National Youth Survey, for example, examined male and female delinquency offense patterns over time and found that there was no behavior in which girls were significantly more involved than boys—even in offenses traditionally ascribed to girls such as prostitution or running away from home (Canter, 1982). Teilmann and Landry (1981) compared girls' contribution to arrests for runaway and incorrigibility with girls' self-reports of these two activities, and found a 10.4% overrepresentation of females among those arrested for runaway and a 30.9% overrepresentation in arrests for incorrigibility. From these data they concluded that girls are "arrested for status offenses at a higher rate than boys, when contrasted to their self-report delinquency rates" (Teilmann and Landry, 1981, pp. 74-75). These findings were confirmed in another self-report study. Figueira-McDonough (1985) analyzed the delinquent conduct of 2,000 youths and found "no evidence of greater involvement of females in status offenses" (Figueira-McDonough, 1985, p. 277).

The most persuasive argument for such differences between unofficial and official rates of female delinquency is that the juvenile justice system's commitment to the notion of the state as parent has encouraged abuse of the status offense category. Essentially, the vague language of these offense categories has encouraged everyone in the juvenile justice system to become involved in monitoring behavior in girls, particularly sexual behavior, that they would ignore or even condone in boys.

Girls are also disadvantaged in juvenile processing, in part, because of parental bias. Parents have long had two standards of behavior for their adolescent children and have tended to involve the juvenile justice system in their disputes with their daughters (Andrews and Cohn, 1974; Sussman, 1977). Parental initiation of complaint either to the police or directly to the court plays a major role in status offense referrals. Ketcham (1978, p. 37), for example, reports that 72% of status offenders are turned in by relatives. Pope and Feyerherm (1982, p. 6) found, in their California study, that girls were "substantially more likely to be referred by sources other than law enforcement"; their figures showed that 7% of all girls referred to court, but only about 2% of boys, were referred by their parents.

While the possibility that the juvenile justice system is enforcing a "double standard" of juvenile justice is troubling, another possible and far more disturbing explanation for girls' problems with their parents also deserves attention. There is a growing awareness among those who work with female status offenders that a substantial number are the victims of both physical and sexual abuse.

A sample survey of 192 female youth in the juvenile justice system in Wisconsin (Phelps et al., 1982) revealed that 79% of the young women (most of whom were in the system for petty larceny and status offenses) had been subjected to physical abuse that resulted in some form of injury. The extent of the injury ranged from such things as bruises, welts, and severe pain, to "being knocked unconscious" (21%) or having a broken bone (12%). Additionally, 32% had been sexually abused by parents or other persons who were closely connected to their families, and 50% had been sexually assaulted ("raped" or forced to participate in sexual acts)(Phelps et al., 1982, p. 66).

Even higher figures were reported by McCormack, Janus, and Burgess (1986) in their study of youth in a runaway shelter in Toronto. They found that 73% of the females and 38% of the males had been sexually abused. Similar figures have been reported by other studies on the backgrounds of young prostitutes and drug offenders (Silbert and Pines, 1981).

These young women ran away from homes that bear little resemblance to the stereotypical "intact" family, and once on the streets they are often forced further into crime in order to survive. The Wisconsin study found that 54% of the girls who ran away found it necessary to steal money, food, and clothing in order to survive. A few exchanged sexual contact for money, food, and/or shelter (Phelps, 1982, p. 67; see also Chesney-Lind and Rodriguez, 1983).

The juvenile justice system and its officers have been extremely slow to recognize that youth might have legitimate reasons to be at odds with their parents. Instead, police, probation officers and judges have often embraced the parental role themselves (Chesney-Lind, 1973; Hancock, 1981; Gelsthorpe, 1986). There are two clear indications of this continued official commitment to judicial paternalism: studies that find that status offenders continue to be treated harshly once in the juvenile justice system and administrative actions taken by juvenile justice officials aimed at resisting or slowing the deinstitutionalization of status offenders.

Several studies of police behavior, for example, find that status offenders are more likely to be referred to court and to be detained than youth suspected of criminal offenses (Teilmann and Landry, 1981; Krohn, Curry, and Nelson-Kilger, 1983). Most relevant for this discussion are studies that suggest evidence of police and court bias in the detention decisions (see Chesney-Lind, 1987, for a review of these studies). Frazier and Cochran, for example, examined the detention decisions for all delinquency cases referred to intake in Florida between 1977 and 1979. In a regression analysis that examined the effects of seven legal and demographic variables, they found that gender was related to the detention decision in an "unexpected way" (Frazier and Cochran, 1986a, p. 295). Despite having less serious offenses and less likelihood of recidivism, girls were significantly more likely to be detained (Frazier and Cochran, 1986a). Recent reanalysis of the data collected by Teilmann and Landry on detention decisions in California also found evidence of bias against female status offenders (Curtis, 1987).

While it is not possible to draw a direct parallel between police or court decisions to detain a youth in a detention facility and those to house a girl in an adult jail, it is clear that the few cases that have resulted in litigation that many of the same biases may be present. It has also become apparent that current juvenile justice personnel are still deeply committed to the doctrine of the court as parent and moral guardian (*ParensPatriae*). Family court judges, for example, resented the limits placed on their power over status offenders and lobbied successfully for significant changes in federal policy during the 1980 hearings to reauthorize the Juvenile Justice and Delinquency Prevention Act (U.S. Senate, Committee on the Judiciary, 1981; U.S. Statutes at Large, 1981; see also Office of Juvenile Justice and Delinquency Prevention, 1985.

The resistance of juvenile court judges and other juvenile justice personnel to federal initiates that placed limitations on their ability to detain and otherwise punish youth charged with these offenses has also been identified as major impediments to the deinstitutionalization movement (General Accounting Office, 1978; Frazier and Cochran, 1986b).

More to the point, these orientations may explain why even determined federal efforts to remove youth from adult jails have met with such mixed success. Indications are, for example, that twenty-two of the fifty-two states and territories currently receiving "formula" grants from the federal Office of Juvenile Justice and Delinquency Prevention stand to lose these monies because they have failed to meet the "jail removal" mandate. This provision requires that states make demonstrable progress toward removing juveniles from adult jails, which is measured as a 75% reduction since 1980 and an "unequivocal commitment" to jail removal ("21 States Considered at Risk," 1987, p. 4). The absence of a strong commitment is certainly also apparent when the data on the characteristics of girls being held in adult jails are reviewed.

PROFILE OF GIRLS IN JAIL

As was mentioned earlier, national data on the offense characteristics of girls in jail are extremely sketchy. Juveniles constitute only about 1% of jail populations at any given time (Bureau of Justice Statistics, 1986, p. 2), and often studies of jail populations require that inmates be incarcerated for a considerable length of time for inclusion in research efforts. One example of this sort of research is a national survey of inmates of local jails, which was conducted in 1983 (Bureau of Justice Statistics, 1985).

Because the study design necessitated selection of specific respondents for interview purposes, very few juveniles were included and those who were interviewed were likely to be among the most serious offenders. Analysis of these data reveal that out of a sample of 5,785, there were 76 youth aged 17 and under identified for interviews. Of these, 21 were females (since the study oversampled for females this figure should not be assumed to be an accurate reflection of the proportion of girls in adult jails). Offense information was available for only 14 of the 21 girls and 35 of the 55 boys.

These data present a relatively serious portrait of the offenses committed by juveniles in jail. Two of the girls (14%) were in jail for murder or assault with intent to commit murder, two for robbery, and two for aggravated assault. In this sample, half the girls were in jail for violent offenses. The comparable male figure was essentially the same, 51.4%. More males were involved in property offenses than females (40% compared to 28.6%), and one of the girls was jailed for a juvenile offense (an offense for which no males were incarcerated). Finally, two of the girls were jailed for "other offenses." Two boys were also jailed for drug and traffic offenses.

TABLE 35.1 Percentage of male and female juveniles incarcerated in Minnesota in 1985 by type of offense

Offense	Females	Males
Part I Violent	1.6	3.7
Part I Property	26.7	35.8
Part II (except below)	10.1	17.6
Status offenses	35.3	13.8
Public order offenses	11.4	9.3
Contempt of court	1.9	1.2
Parole/probation violation	7.2	9.6
Other	5.7	8.8
Totals	100	100
	(745)	(2,975)

Source: Adapted from Schwartz, Harris, and Levi, 1987, p.11.

This profile is, however, markedly different from that which emerges from other data available on the characteristics of girls in adult jails. All of these indicate a far less serious pattern of offenses for which the youth are being held. Take, for example, a review of youth incarcerated in jails in Minnesota, which was conducted in 1985. Girls represented 20% of those jailed in that year, down from 26.2% the year before (Schwartz, Harris, and Levi, 1987, p. 5). And, despite statutory provisions that prohibit the incarceration of status offenders in that state, over a third of these girls, 35.3%, were jailed for status offenses (compared to 13.8% of the males). By contrast, only 1.6% were incarcerated for Part I violent offenses (compared to 3.7% of the males). Most males were incarcerated for Part I property offenses (35.8%)(see Table 35.1).

The Minnesota data also show substantial declines in both the number and rate of juvenile jailings. Since 1969, for example, there has been a 43% decline in juvenile admissions to adult jails in that state though the decline has leveled off a bit in the 1980s (Schwartz, Harris, and Levi, 1987, p. 4). Trends seen in Minnesota are important since they suggest that as states move to comply with the guidelines attached to the Juvenile Justice and Delinquency Prevention Act Program, the numbers of girls in jail (and the number of status offenders) may begin to drop more steeply than the male figures since girls' offenses are generally so trivial. This has certainly been the pattern in the juvenile incarceration arena where, as a result of deinstitutionalization efforts, detention of girls dropped dramatically (Krisberg et al., 1986).

Data on the jailing of youth in California are particularly important. The indications are that roughly 20% of the youth held in adult jails are confined in that state while California accounts for only 10% of the nation's youth (U.S. Senate, Committee on the Judiciary, 1983, p. 11). The California Youth Authority prepares reports on youth held over six hours in "secure confinement" (Department of the Youth Authority, 1985, 1986). These reports indicate that status offense jailings of longer than six hours have declined from 974 in 1984 (8.7% of all jailings) to 570 (5.7% of all jailings) in 1986. No data are presented on the overall percentage of confinements that are female in these reports, but in 1979 girls were approximately 20% of those jailed. This figure was, however, generated without the 6-hour requirement (U.S. Senate, Committee on the Judiciary, 1983, p. 42). These earlier figures showed girls to be about 10% of those held over 24 hours in 1979.

Of those youth held over 24 hours in 1985, 13% were female in 1985 (Department of the Youth Authority, 1986, p. 15). This figure is up considerably from 1982 when the figure was 8.1%, but down from 1983 when girls were 16.5% of the population (Department of the Youth Authority, 1983, p. 11; Department of the Youth Authority, 1984, p. 7). The percentage of youth charged with status offenses held over twenty-four hours in California declined very slightly from 2.1% in 1982 to 1% in 1986 (Department of the Youth Authority, 1983, 1986).

Analysis of data collected by the Public Justice Foundation and the Youth law Center on the jailing of youth in California provides a different picture of the dimensions of this problem in that state. The data also suggest that the 6-hour standard considerably reduces the number of youth, and particularly the number of girls, counted. In one Los Angeles jail examined, for example, 38.9% of the youth jailed stayed six hours or less in 1985.

Documents obtained by legal action on the characteristics youth held in the Long Beach Jail in 1983 reveal that girls accounted for 28% of the 4,511 youth held in that facility. Not surprisingly, the data revealed that a high percentage of status offenders were confined in the facility (16%). The data also showed that a large number of youth held in the jail were dependent youth (21%). Finally, a majority of the youth confined in this facility were minority group members (62%); jailings of black youth were, for example, 34% of the total.

Analysis of the data obtained by the Public Justice Foundation and the Youth Law Center on administrations to the Lennox jail in Los Angeles revealed a different pattern for the year 1985. This jail has a policy of not jailing status offenders, but it does hold youth who are dependent or neglected. Girls constituted 17.8% of youthful jail admissions, and 11% of the youth placed in cells. These data are important since the Youth Authority indicates that confinements in Los Angeles account for 89% of the state's jailing of youth (Department of the Youth Authority, 1986, p. 12). Data from both these jails indicate that the holding of girls in California continues to be a substantial problem, and that the jailing of status offenders, at least in some jurisdictions, persists as does the holding of abused and neglected youth.

More detailed, but earlier, information comes from Kentucky, where girls were 19.31% of the 290 youth admitted to Oldham County Jail during 1982 (these data were drawn from a suit filed by the Youth Law Center) (*Rita Horn et al. v. Oldham County, Kentucky,* 1983). Only about 2% of the girls, but 15.4% of the boys, were incarcerated for felonies; by contrast, nearly 20% of the girls, but less than 1% of the boys were incarcerated for status offenses. Girls also tended to be younger than boys; only 25% of the girls were 17 years of age compared to half of the boys. In fact, nearly a quarter of the girls (23.2%) were 13 and 14 years of age. The data also showed that girls stayed in Kentucky jails about the same length of time as did boys despite their less serious offense profile; 44.9% of the boys and 37.5% of the girls stayed only 1 day.

TABLE 35.2 Percentage of male and female juveniles incarcerated in Kentucky in January-June 1980 by type of offenses

Type of Charge	Females	Males
Status Offense, Runaway, Truant, Incorrigible	22.63	5.06
Public Offense: Misdemeanor	20.86	8.55
Public Offense: Felony	4.22	14.50
Public Offense: Violation	1.35	1.00
Public Offense: Traffic	4.81	15.08
Public Offense: No Degree	5.48	3.79
Theft: No Degree	0.16	13.74
Delinquency Petition, 208.020	17.56	6.49
Alcohol	11.48	22.15
Drugs	2.61	4.14
Offense: Abuse, Neglect, Mentally ill	0.03	0.10
All Other: Fugitive Safekeeping, Emergency Detention, Court Order, Contempt, Unassigned, Parole Violation, Other	8.44	5.33
Totals	100 (4,267)	100 (1,121)

Source: Adapted from Roche and Richart, 1981, p. 16.

Earlier research on the jailing of girls in Kentucky (Roche and Richart, 1981) took a detailed look at differences between the incarceration of male and female juveniles in that state during the late 1970s and early 1980s. The report notes a dramatic decline in the number of status offenders incarcerated in Kentucky jails (50% between 1977 and 1979). Despite these successes, the study found that over a thousand girls were jailed in Kentucky during the first six months of 1980 (20.8% of all jail admissions).

The study found that girls were more likely than boys to be incarcerated for status offenses; 22.6% of the girls jailed were held for status offenses compared to only 5.1% of the boys (Roche and Richart, 1981, p. 16). Girls were also more likely than boys to be jailed for misdemeanors (20.7% compared to 8.5%). Males, by contrast, were most likely to be jailed for felonies or other less serious criminal offenses (particularly traffic or alcohol-related offenses) (see Table 35.2).

This study also found that girls jailed tended to be younger than their male counterparts. The mean age for girls was 14.4 compared to 16.1 for boys (Roche and Richart, 1981, p.13). Finally, despite their less serious offenses, girls were far less likely than boys to stay one day or less; only slightly over a third of the girls but two-thirds of the boys were released after one day or less in jail. Boys were, however, more likely to be among those held over three days so that the average length of stay for boys was 3.4 days, and for girls it was 3.1 days (Roche and Richart, 1981, p. 18). Female status offenders were held an average of one day longer than females charged with alcohol and drug offenses (2.9 compared to 2.1) and about as long as those girls charged with misdemeanors (2.7); girls charged with felonies tended to stay much longer (6.17 days). Male status offenders, by contrast, had the shortest stay (2.76), while males charged with criminal offenses stayed longer than girls with similar charges.

A slightly different pattern is observed in Curry County Jail in New Mexico during 1981. Data gathered as part of a suit filed by the Youth Law Center (*Johnnie K. et al. v. the County of Curry, New Mexico,* 1982) showed that only 7 of the 54 youth held in this jail in that year were girls (13%). And, as might be expected, fewer status offenders were being jailed. Only 14% of the girls were held on status offenses, though 3 were "held" for violations of court orders; 10.6% of the males were held for status offenses. Most youth held in this jail were confined for criminal offenses, which suggests that as the number of status offenders declines in a jail population, the number of females declines as well. Finally, the New Mexico data provide information on the ethnic backgrounds of the youth jailed; these indicate that all of the females jailed were Caucasian compared to on 44.7% of the males.

Data from a suit filed regarding the Lawrence County Jail in Ohio (for the year 1980) confirm many of the patterns found in the Kentucky data *(Deborah Doe et al. v. Lloyd W. Burwell et al.,* 1981) Of the 165 youth held in that jail, 26.1% were female. These girls were considerably more likely than males to be charged with status offenses (41.9% compared to 15.6%). Males were most likely held for criminal offenses (77.9% compared to 46.5% of the girls). Again, girls were also more likely to be younger than their male counterparts; nearly half (44.4%) of the girls were 15 years old or less at the time of their jailing compared to 37.2% of the boys.

Data available from other states tend to be less specific, but these also indicate that as the number of status offenders jailed increases, so does the percentage of girls. In North Dakota, girls were 30% of those detained in 1985, and those charged with status offenses accounted for 30.7% of detentions. Girls were considerably younger (30.7% of the girls were under the age of 15 compared to only 12.7% of the boys), and they stayed for shorter periods of time. Girls stayed an average of 52 hours in jail compared to 65 for boys (Community Research Associates, 1986, p.3; Arnts, 1986). In Idaho, during that same year, girls were 20% of the detainers, and children charged with status offenses accounted for 9% of detentions (Commission for Children and Youth, 1986, pp. 12-13).

In general, these state-by-state accounts suggest large numbers of girls continue to be held in adult jails. It also seems fairly clear that these girls are charged with far less serious offenses than their male counterparts, and, in many states, they are being held in adult facilities for status offenses. Girls are on the average younger than their male counterparts. They may stay as long as boys despite their less serious offense backgrounds. Finally, it appears that as restrictions are placed on the jailing of youth, the number of girls held in these adult facilities may drop sharply.

CONDITIONS OF GIRLS IN JAIL

It has long been recognized that women in jail are housed under tighter security and more restrictive conditions than their male counterparts. This is largely due to the limited facilities available for incarcerated females. Many women are simply housed in a "women's unit" within a male facility. Because of this, they are rarely granted equal access to recreation and exercise, education and work release programs within the jail (Mann, 1984; Shaw, 1982) and, not infrequently, spend most, if not all, of their days in their cells—sometimes even eating in their cells (National Coalition for Jail Reform, n.d.). If conditions in jail are restrictive and harsh for adult women, that is doubly true for girls in adult jails. In attempting to protect youth from contact and abuse from adult inmates, girls, particularly those housed in sexually integrated facilities, are often held in what amounts to solitary confinement (Community Research Center, 1985, p.3).

A chilling example of what can happen to girls placed, for even a few days, in an adult jail graphically illustrates the problem with the holding of girls in such isolation. On August 25th, 1984 at 12:30 in the morning, 15-year-old Kathy Robbins was arrested for being a runaway. She was handcuffed and taken to the 54-year-old Glen County Jail. There she was refused permission to phone her mother. After being strip searched and dressed in a jail-issue jumpsuit, she was placed in a cell that measured twelve feet by twelve feet and nine feet, eight inches in height. It had a solid steel door with a small mesh window that measured 3 1/2 X 5 3/4 inches. It was the male juvenile cell, and she was held there, in virtual isolation, until Wednesday, August 29th, when she was taken to a detention hearing.

At the hearing, her probation officer recommended that she be held in custody until September 7th. The court ordered that the matter be continued until a later date and that Kathy remain incarcerated at the jail. That afternoon, Kathy was found unconscious and hanging in a kneeling position from the guard rail of the top bunk bed with a sheet wrapped around her neck. She was pronounced dead a few hours later.

Kathy had physical evidence of previous suicide attempts at the time of her jailing; jailers had denied her all but one short visit with her mother, and they had refused to provide her with reading material brought to the jail by her mother. They had also refused to take her phone message from her mother. Finally, at the time Kathy was incarcerated, there was space available at a nearby group home, but she was not taken there (*Lillian Robbins v. County of Glenn, California et al.*, 1985).

Kathy Robbin's suicide grimly highlights both the terrible consequences that can attend the jailing of youth as well as some of the special problems confronted by girls in jail in America. Chief among these problems is the isolation and lack of supervision that often accompanies adolescents' experiences in adult jails. Such conditions are particularly dangerous for girls whose backgrounds of sexual and physical abuse make them more vulnerable to depression and self-destructive behavior (Browne and Finkelhor, 1986). The suicide rate for youth in jail is 4.6 times higher than the youth suicide rate in the general population, and, remarkably, it is 7.7 times the rate found for youth incarcerated in detention centers (Community Research Center, 1983, p.2). This latter figure is particularly striking since youth tend to stay an average of 17 days in detention centers and only 7 days in adult jails. This difference was attributed by the researchers to the greater supervision available in the detention centers.

The Robbins case highlights one problem with isolation of youth in adult facilities—that of suicide. Another problem, that of girls' vulnerability to sexual assault, is also made possible by the isolation that accompanies girls' incarceration in sexually integrated jails. This problem was graphically illustrated by a different case. In this instance, a 15 year-old girl ran away from home with a friend in Ironton, Ohio, in 1981. Eventually the girls ran out of money and called her parents. After they were safely home, a juvenile court judge, over their parents' objections, decided to "teach them a lesson" by ordering them into the county jail for five days. On the fourth night, one of the girls was sexually assaulted by a male jailer (Soler, 1983, p.26).

This was not the only example of sexual abuse. Some ten years earlier, a 14-year-old runaway being held in the Wayne County Jail in Honesdale, Pennsylvania, was raped, not only by the deputy sheriff but also by two inmates—one an admitted murderer awaiting sentencing—whom the sheriff had released from their cells to participate in the rape (Wooden, 1976, p. 123).

The problem of sexual abuse by other female inmates has also surfaced in those facilities where youth are incarcerated with older offenders. In one case, a 15-year-old girl mistakenly held in an adult jail after having been arrested for breaking and entering, reported being sexually and physically abused by a group of women (Children's Defense Fund, 1976, p. 17). Contact with adult inmates is apparently unavoidable in many facilities. The Kentucky study reported that 56% of the jails holding youth did not have sight/sound separation (Roche and Richart, 1981, pp. 19-20). Such problems are also mentioned in the suits brought by the Youth Law Center against jails in California (*Robbins et al. v. Glenn County et al.*, 1985), New Mexico (*Johnnie K. et al. v. the County of Curry, New Mexico, et. al.*, 1982), and Ohio (*Deborah Doe et al. v. Lloyd W. Burwell et al.*, 1981).

Another earlier description of the section in a county jail in a "medium size town" where girls are held provides a graphic illustration of the physical conditions of these cells. The Children's Defense Fund team noted that:

> the section for girls is in the basement adjacent to the furnace and a storage room. It is dark, dirty and so far removed from the other sections of the jail that no one is within shouting distance of the girls held there, except on rare occasions. The dirty walls of the section were covered by layers of juvenile graffiti. A twin metal bed frame held two dirty, uncovered mattresses. Stacks of old magazines lay scattered on an old table and the floor. No light fixture could be seen [Children's Defense Fund, 1976, p. 28].

The report goes on to say that despite the fact that the sheriff had been expressing his concern about incarcerated youth, when he got to the girls section, "he opened the door without warning and walked in. No matron was present" (Children's Defense Fund, 1976, p. 28).

Medical care for women in most jails has also been a longstanding concern (Shaw, 1982; Mann, 1984). It is a problem that is sometimes exacerbated by the lack of adequate supervision, idleness, lack of exercise, and deteriorated conditions in which girls are held. In New Mexico, for example, youth are confined to their cellblocks "for the entire period of their confinement without access to exercise, recreation or reading materials" (*Johnie K. et al. v. the County of Curry, New Mexico,* 1982, p.2).

For girls, the problems involved in the jail experience revolve around their doubly disadvantaged status—as both females and juveniles. Jails have historically developed to house adult males and, as a consequence, are woefully ill-equipped to house juvenile females. Often, this situation results in the girls being locked in solitary confinement. The isolation and lack of supervision that can characterize girls' experience of jail is particularly risky given the history of sexual and physical abuse of many of the girls who are drawn into the juvenile justice system.

CONCLUSION

Despite ten years of federal pressure, girls continue to be detained in adult jails and lockups. Such detentions are troubling for a number of reasons. First, there is considerable evidence that girls held in such facilities are far less likely than their male counterparts to have committed serious offenses. Indeed, the evidence points to the fact that girls are more likely to be held for status offenses or minor property offenses rather than violent crimes. Girls are also, on the average, younger than the boys in jail.

While in jail, girls may be more vulnerable than boys to the kinds of problems that generally accompany the jailing of youth. Like boys in adult jails, they are likely to spend time in isolation and to be denied exercise and adequate health care. Such isolation, though, brings with it special problems for girls, many of whom have histories of abuse that may predispose them to self-destructive behavior. Like boys, girls are also vulnerable to physical and sexual abuse by other inmates, but girls are also vulnerable to sexual assault by staff while being held in facilities.

The delinquent behavior that brings most girls to the attention of authorities poses no threat to the safety and security of their communities. Indeed, a good number of these girls may be victims rather than offenders. Even if this were not the case, it is unlikely that males engaged in similar behaviors would be jailed. Given both the historic pattern of discrimination against girls in the juvenile justice system and the serious problems that attend the holding of girls in adult jails, it seems clear that a major effort should be directed to develop alternative community-based programming for girls so that such incarcerations are eliminated.

REFERENCES

Andrews, R. Hale and Andrew H. Cohn. (1974) "Ungovernability: The Unjustifiable Jurisdiction. "*Yale Law Journal* 83:1383-1409.

Arnts, Douglas. (1986). *Detention of Juveniles in Local Jail Facilities.* Report prepared by Office of the Attorney General, State of Idaho.

Browne, Angela and David Finkelhor. 1986 "Impact of Child Sexual Abuse; A Review of the Literature." "*Child Abuse and Neglect* 99:66-77.

Bureau of Justice Statistics. U.S. Department of Justice, 1985. *Survey of Inmates of Local Jails,* (1983) (1st ICPSR ed.). Ann Arbor: Inter-University Consortium for Political and Social Research.

——1986, *Jail Inmates* (1984). Washington, DC: Author.

Canter, Rachelle. (1982). "Sex Differences in Self-Reported Delinquency." *Criminology* 20:373-393.

Castro, L. Aniyar. (1981). "Venezuelan Female Criminality." *In The Incidence of Female Criminality in the Contempory World,* edited by Freda Adler. New York: New York University Press.

Chesney-Lind, Meda. (1973). "Judicial Enforcement of the Female Sex Role." *Issues in Criminology* 8:51-70.

—— (1987). "Girls and De-Institutionalization." *Journal of Criminal Justice Abstracts.*

—— and Noelie Rodriguez. (1983). "Women Under Lock and Key." *Prison Journal* 63:47-65.

Children's Defense Fund. (1976). *Children in Adult Jails.* Washington, DC: Author.

Commission for Children and Youth. (1986). *1985 Idaho Juvenile Jail Monitoring Report.* Idaho: Office of the Governor.

Community Research Associates. (1986). *Juvenile Jailings in North Dakota: Findings from a Statewide Needs Assessment.* Draft report. Illinois: Author.

Community Research Center. (1983). *Juvenile Suicides in Adult Jails: Findings from a National Survey of Juveniles in Secure Detention Facilities.* Washington, DC: U.S. Department of Justice, Bureau of Justice Statistics, No. 92639.

—— (1985). *Juveniles in Adult Jails and Lock-ups: It's Your Move.* Washington, DC: U.S. Department of Justice, Bureau of Justice Statistics, No. 98212.

Curtis, Craig. (1987). "Gender Bias in Discretionary Decision-Making in the Criminal Justice System: An Application of a New Model." Paper presented at the Western Society of Criminology Meetings, Las Vegas, NV.

Deborah Doe et al. v. Lloyd W. Burwell et al. (1981.) Plaintiffs' Memorandum in Support of Motion for Class Certification. Filed in U.S. District Court for Southern District of Ohio. Civil Action No. C.1-81-415.

Department of the Youth Authority. (1983). *The 1982 Jail Report: Minors Detained in California Jails and Lockups in 1982.* State of California.

—— (1984). *The 1983 Jail Report: Minors Detained in California Jails and Lockups in 1983.* State of California.

—— (1985). *The 1984 Jail Report: Minors Detained in California Jails and Lockups in 1984.* State of California.

—— (1986). *The 1985 Jail Report: Minors Detained in California Jails and Lockups in 1985* (Rev. October 1986). State of California.

Federal Bureau of Investigation. 1985. *Uniform Crime Reports, Crime in the U.S. 1984.* Washington, DC: Government Printing Office.

Figueira-McDonough, Josephina. (1985). "Are Girls Different? Gender Discrepancies Between Delinquent Behavior and Control." *Child Welfare* 64:273-289.

Frazier, Charles E. and John C. Cochran. (1986a). "Detention of Juveniles: Its Effects on Subsequent Juvenile Court Processing Decisions." *Youth and Society* 17:286-305.

—— (1986b). "Official Intervention, Diversion from the Juvenile Justice System, and Dynamics of Human Services Work: Effects of a Reform Goal Based on Labeling Theory." *Crime & Delinquency* 32:157-176.

Geller, Gloria. (1981). "Streaming of Males and Females in the Juvenile Justice System." Paper presented at the Canadian Psychological Association, Toronto, Ontario, June.

Geisthorpe, Loraine. (1986). "Towards a Skeptical Look at Sexism." *International Journal of the Sociology of Law* 14:125-152.

General Accounting Office. (1978). *Removing Status Offenders from Secure Facilities: Federal Leadership and Guidance are Needed.* Washington, DC: Government Printing Office.

Gordon, Linda (1986). "Incest and Resistance: Patterns of Father-Daughter Incest. 1880-1930." *Social Problems* 33:253-267.

Hancock, Linda. (1981). "The Myth that Females are Treated More Leniently than Males in the Juvenile Justice System." *Australian and New Zealand Journal of Sociology* 16:4-14.

Johnnie K. et al. v. the County of Curry, New Mexico, et al. (1982). Plaintiffs' Memorandum in Support of Motion for Class Certification. Filed in the U.S. District Court for the District of New Mexico. No. CIV 81 0914 M.

Ketchem, Orman. (1978). "Why Jurisdiction over Status Offenders Should be Eliminated from Juvenile Courts." *In Status Offenders and the Juvenile Justice System: An Anthology,* edited by Richard Allison. Hackensack: *National Council on Crime and Delinquency.*

Krisberg, Barry and Ira Schwartz. (1983). "Re-Thinking Juvenile Justice." *Crime & Delinquency* 29:381-397.

———Paul Litsky, and James Austin. (1986). "The Watershed of Juvenile Justice Reform." *Crime & Delinquency* 32:5-38.

Krohn, Marvin D., James P. Curry, and Shirley Nelson-Kilger. (1983.) "Is Chivalry Dead?" *Criminology* 21:417-439.

Lillian Robbins v. County of Glenn, California, et al. (1985). Amended Civil Rights Complaint for Damages. Filed in the U.S. District Court for the Eastern District of California. September. No. CIVS-85-0675 RAR.

Mahoney, Anne R. and Carol Fenster. (1982). "Female Delinquents in a Suburban Court." In *Judge, Lawyer, Victim, Thief,* edited by Nicole Rafter and Elizabeth Stanko. Boston: *Northeastern University Press.*

Mann, Coramae. (1984). *Female Crime and Delinquency.* Alabama: University of *Alabama Press.*

McCormack, Arlene, Mark-David Janus, and Ann Wolprt Burgess. (1986.) "Runaway Youths and Sexual Victimization: Gender Differences in an Adolescent Runaway Population." *Child Abuse and Neglect* 10:387-395.

National Center for Juvenile Justice. (1985). *Delinquency,* 1982. Pittsburgh: *National Center for Juvenile Justice.*

National Coalition for Jail Reform. n.d. Women in Jail: Special Problems, Different Needs. Washington, DC: National Coalition for Jail Reform.

Office of Juvenile Justice and Delinquency Prevention, 1985. *Runaway Children and the Juvenile Justice and Delinquency Prevention Act: What is the Impact?* Washington, DC: *Juvenile Justice Bulletin.*

Phelps, R.J. et al. (1982). Wisconsin *Juvenile Female Offender Project.* Wisconsin: Youth Policy and Law Center, *Wisconsin Council on Juvenile Justice.*

Pope, Carl and William H. Feyerherm. (1982). "Gender Bias in Juvenile Court Dispositions." *Journal of Social Service Review* 6:1-16.

Rita Horn et al. v. Oldham County, Kentucky, et al. (1983). Motion for Class Certification. Filed in the U.S. District Court for the Western District of Kentucky, Civil Action No. C-83-0208-LB.

Roche, Susan E. and David Richart. (1981). *A Comparative Study of Young Women and Men in Kentucky Jails: Fourth 1981 Interim Report.* Louisville: Kentucky Youth Advocates.

Schlossman, Steven and Stephanie Wallach. (1987). "The Crime of Precocious Sexuality:

Female Juvenile Delinquency in the Progressive Era." *Harvard Educational Review* 48:65-94.

Schwartz, Ira M., Gideon Fishman, RaDene R. Hatfield, Barry A. Krisberg, and Zvi Eisikovits. (1987). "Juvenile Detention: The Hidden Closets Revisited." *Justice Quarterly* 4:219-235.

Schwartz, Ira, Linda Harris, and Laurie Levi. (1987). *The Jailing of Juveniles in Minnesota*. Minnesota: Hubert Humphrey Institute.

Shaw, Nancy Stoller. (1982). "Female Patients and the Medical Profession in Jails and Prisons: A Case of Quintuple Jeopardy." In *Judge, Lawyer, Victim, Thief,* edited by Nicole Hahn Rafter and Elizabeth Stanko.Boston: *Northeastern.*

Shelden, Randall G. (1981). "Sex Discrimination in the Juvenile Justice System: Memphis, Tennessee, 1900-1917." *In Comparing Female and Male Offenders,* edited by Marguerite Q. Warren. Beverly Hills, CA: *Sage.*

Silbert, Mimi and Ayala M. Pines. (1981). "Sexual Child Abuse as a Antecedent to Prostitution." *Child Abuse and Neglect* 5:407-411.

Smith, Leslie. (1978). "Sexist Assumptions and Female Delinquency." In *Women, Sexuality and Social Control,* edited by Carol Smart and Barry Smart. London: Routledge, Kegan Paul.

Soler, Mark. (1983). *Prepared Statement.* Hearing to Inquire into the Continued Detention of Juveniles in Adult Jails and Lock-ups. Hearing before the Subcommittee on Juvenile Justice. Committee on the Judiciary, U.S. Senate.

Steinhart, David and Barry Krisberg. (1987). "Children in Jail." *State Legislatures* (March): 12-16.

Sussman, Alan. (1977). "Sex-Based Discrimination and the PINS Jurisdiction. "In *Beyond Control: Status Offenders in the Juvenile Court,* edited by Lee H. Teitelbaum and Aidan R. Gough. Cambridge: Ballinger.

Teilmann, Katherine S. and Pierre H. Landry, Jr. (1981). "Gender Bias in Juvenile Justice." *Journal of Research in Crime and Delinquency* 18:47-80.

"21 States Considered at Risk of Losing OJJDP Formula Grants." (1987). *Criminal Justice Newsletter* (August 17):4.

U.S. House of Representatives, Committee on Education and Labor. (1980). *Juvenile Justice Amendments of 1980.* Washington, DC: Government Printing Office.

U.S. Senate, Committee on the Judiciary. (1981). *Reauthorization of the Juvenile Justice and Delinquency Prevention Act of 1974.* Washington, DC: Government Printing Office.

———Subcommittee on Juvenile Justice. (1983). Hearing to *Inquire into the Continued Detention of Juveniles in Adult Jails and Lock-Ups.* Washington, DC: Government Printing Office.

U.S. Statutes at Large. (1981). *Ninety-Sixth Congress* (2nd Session). Public Law 96-509—(December 8, 1980). Washington, DC: Government Printing Office.

Wooden, Kenneth. (1976). *Weeping in the Playtime of Others.* New York: McGraw-Hill.

ARTICLE 36

Fulfilling Juvenile Restitution Requirements in Community Correctional Programs

H. TED RUBIN*

A REQUIREMENT for juvenile offenders to pay back their victims for losses or damages occasioned has become a frequent sanction in American juvenile courts. An alternative sanction, to require juvenile offenders to perform community work service hours to pay back the community for injuries sustained to its human or physical environment from delinquent offenses is also a commonly invoked penalty. Community work service may be compelled with victimless crimes or as an added sanction to financial restitution and victim reimbursement mandates. The concept of restitution that is used here encompasses these several forms of requirements, although in some jurisdictions, at present, the term restitution applies to financial requirements only.

Both forms of juvenile restitution are used by certain police agencies in approving diversion from further penetration is not the juvenile justice system (Rubin,

Source: Rubin, H. Ted. "Fulfilling Juvenile Restitution Requirements of Community Correctional Programs." *Federal Probation,* Vol. 52 (September) 1988: 32-42. Reprinted by permission of Federal Probation.

* H. Ted Rubin is senior associate, Juvenile and Criminal Justice, Institute for Court Management of the National Center for States Courts, Denver, Colorado.

Funding for this research was provided by the Office of Juvenile Justice and Delinquency Prevention. The views and opinions expressed here are those of the author and do not necessarily express the opinions or policies of the U. S. Department of Justice. The author wishes to acknowledge the cooperation of juvenile justice official in Denver, Sonoma County, California, the Erie, Pennsylvania, where site visits were conducted, and others, elsewhere, who responded to telephone-administered questionnaires.

1987). They are used at the intake stage of juvenile court processing in conjunction with diversion or informal probation determinations (Ariz. Rev. Stat. Ann § 8-230-01; Tex. Fam. Code Ann § 53.03). They are most commonly applied at the juvenile court dispositional stage, typically as a condition of probation but also as a sole sanction (Schneider and Bazemore, 1985; Juvenile Restitution Program, 1987). Restitution may be ordered by a juvenile parole authority, for example, when a juvenile on aftercare status reoffends and this offense is handled not through a court system but as a revocation or as the basis of additional requirements in retaining the aftercare status (Utah Code Ann. § 55-11b-23; Tex. Hum. REs. Code § 61.081).

This article focuses on the carryover of judicially ordered restitution requirements is not community correctional settings. These settings include day treatment programs, non-secure residential programs both public and private, drug and alcohol treatment settings, and local or regional secure pretrial detention facilities following a disposition or sentence of confinement.

Several approaches to restitution are followed with these placements. One is to order financial restitution for the offense that prompts placement but to avoid consideration of payment for this and any prior restitution requirements until the youth completes the program and returns home on regular probation status. A second rejects adding community work service hours to the placement disposition, reasoning that the placement is a sufficient sanction and the court should not enter mandates which may interfere with the facility's program of correctional treatment. Consistent with this approach, community work service hours ordered with prior offenses also go on hold during the placement period.

There are other models which better fit the accountability precept of restitution. Financial and community work service restitution are ordered in conjunction with the offense that leads to placement; placement agency administrators have designed their program opportunities for juveniles to earn money to pay back victims and perform unpaid work tasks that assist their agency or other non-profit or governmental agencies nearby. It is the author's contention that this latter approach is more beneficial to the victim, the community, and the juvenile, and that each juvenile court system should close any gaps in its continuum of restitution expectations and enhance its collaboration with placement settings to maximize restitution compliance.

The following sections present program models of these different types of placement resources and then discuss a range of issues related to implementing restitution in these settings.

DAY TREATMENT SETTINGS

The programs consist of all day or much of the day alternative education and psychologically oriented treatment. They may include recreation, cultural enrichment, and job skills orientation. An example is New Pride, Inc. in Denver, Colorado, that serves 12- to 18-year-old delinquent youths referred by the court as an alternative to residential or institutional placement. The program includes a learning center designed to remediate educational deficiencies and develop basic academic skills leading to a G.E.D., a high school diploma, or entry in vocational training. It is also in partnership with Midtown Services, a for-profit small business spinoff that trains and employs New Pride clients in property maintenance and business services jobs. The former includes janitorial work, building maintenance, snow shoveling, landscaping, and the setting up of and cleaning up after community events. The latter involves a variety of tasks in conjunction with bulk mailings. Virtually all juveniles enrolled in New Pride come with financial restitution requirements. Community work service hours are not assigned to these juveniles. All juveniles have significant records of law violations. The juveniles are paid for Both training and work during the 4-month job component of the overall 6-month New Pride program. Enrollment in the overall 6-month New Pride program. Enrollment in the learning center is a requisite for enrollment in the job component. Midtown Services provides an 80-hour pre-work vocational training program, knowing that an investment in training will achieve better contract performance with the business and organizations it serves. Juveniles begin at $3.35 an hour. They typically work 20 hours a week and must make restitution payment from their weekly pay. Restitution fulfillment is central to the New Pride accountability philosophy.

RESIDENTIAL SETTINGS

The Sonoma County Probation Camp, Healdsburg, California, serves 20 delinquent juveniles ages 16 through 18 years. Most are repetitive property offenders. All juveniles are under court commitment and remain at the camp 7 to 8 months. A school program consists of one-half day academic education and one-half day industrial education. The latter features welding, carpentry, cooking, gardening and landscaping, and janitorial training. Through contracts with the state parks department, residents make picnic tables, food lockers, outdoor toilets, road and parking barricades, garbage cans, and picnic camp stoves that must meed quality control standards. Income generated through contracts is used to improve vocational equipment and tools, enable recreational and wilderness experiences, and, in special cases, assist in the independent living of a camp graduate when no parental support is available. On weekends or on an afternoon in lieu of industrial education, camp residents have done landscaping at boys' clubs, constructed and installed a sand table and storage shed at a school for developmentally disabled children, land painted nursery school buildings.

Approximately 75 percent of camp residents bring financial restitution requirements with them; community work service hours are not part of the judicial order, possibly, the camp superintendent says, because the court knows that residents perform community service projects as part of the camp's program.

The camp has a written rule that each juvenile ordered to pay restitution, fines, or court costs must earn $50 a month for payment. To implement the rule, the camp's administration takes responsibility for creating earning opportunities for these youths. At the time of the author's site visit, the earning opportunity enabled juveniles to place kiln dried walnut wood scraps in a duffel bag for sale to the public. The wood is obtained at no cost from a company whose personnel manager sits on the 24-member camp advisory committee. County employees and the public are notified they can pick up the kindling wood for $1 a bag at the camp. The juveniles are paid 75 cents per bag, the sack costing 25 cents. With effort, residents can earn $7.50 an hour for restitution payment. Other restitution earning projects have been to make concrete foundation blocks, engineer's stakes that were sold to lumber yards for resale, and metal crossing signs of a goose or a chicken that were sold to the public. During fiscal year 1987, residents paid back $2,372 to victims.

The administration has the flexibility, if it is unable to come up with similar restitution-earning jobs, of converting certain of its contract wood and metal products efforts in a post-school hours or weekend time shift and then to stipend the juveniles from the contract income to make restitution payments. Camp staff members also serve as aftercare counselors; the same monthly restitution requirement is mandated following release, when there is a balance. A pre-release job-obtainment skills program facilitates community employment achievement.

Harborcreek Youth Services, Erie, Pennsylvania, is a multidimensional agency that serves 50 delinquent and dependent juveniles in its residence that has a school on the grounds; it provides a day treatment program that is also on the grounds and maintains specialized foster homes and six group homes at different locations in the area.

The residential facility includes a structured Work Experience Program for juveniles, 15 through 17 years, who are not seen as capable of completing high school. The program begins with aptitude and occupational interest testing, shifts into a 2-week orientation to the world or work, and then progresses to a 5-month evaluated work experience.

The work includes building maintenance, food and laundry service, vehicle maintenance, serving as aids to health, clerical, and educational staff, and other on-grounds tasks. The three steps in this phase move from observation to responsibilities without pay to responsibilities with pay. A successful evaluation leads to off-campus jobs doing maintenance, pressure cleaning, and truck cleaning at a bakery, washing cars at the nearby state police barracks, and work for other off-campus businesses. Classes at a nearby technical school may be arranged. Youths from other Harborcreek components may participate in the Work Experience Program. Over time, pay can increase to the minimum wage. The Harborcreek administration is committed to juvenile payment of financial restitution and any court fines or costs during a juvenile's residence. During the first 10 months of 1987, $7,243 was paid back for these purposes, mostly for financial restitution. Reportedly, approximately 80 percent of juveniles clear up financial restitution requirements while in residence.

Community work service orders are rarely included in an order of placement, although they do accompany children placed by the court into an agency foster home. Residential staff are not particularly attentive to any community work service requirements.

Perseus House, Inc., Erie, Pennsylvania, maintains four group residences for delinquent and dependent youths placed in its care by the local juvenile court. In 1981, it added an employment preparation program when it opened a gasoline service station. The agency's commitment to financial restitution requirements is clear. The juveniles may earn these funds in the summer time through participation in Job Training Partnership Act employment or year round at the gas station. Perseus House emphasizes that the objective of the gas station experience is that juveniles will go on to jobs and not only to gas station jobs. Further, the method used is training and not work. This training program requires from 5 and 8 months. It is for 16- and 17-year-olds, mostly boys, is an alternative educational setting, and supplements the residential program. Youths are at the station from 3 to 5 days a week.

There are five stages to the training that is based on the development of a productive work ethic, a "proper employment attitude," and the application of "performance aptitudes as well as verbal skills." There is an initial orientation phase where youngsters are instructed in an employment manual and in how to serve customers at the gasoline dispensing islands. In the second phase, they move more into an employee position, are paid, are given their own key to the cash register, pump gas regularly, are introduced to the tire changing machine and limited mechanics' duties, and receive further instruction on work habits and employers' expectations. In the third stage, youths both pump gas and work under instruction at mechanics' chores such as tune ups and engine and transmission repairs. Phase four includes limited gasoline pumping, major work in the auto repair shop, and instruction on how to look for jobs. In the final phase, juveniles prepare resumes, obtain references, and go out for job interviews. They continue to work at the station until they secure employment.

The youths are paid for pumping gas, working up to the minimum wage over a 9-week period. Typically, they work 20 hours a week at the station. They are not paid for garage repair work which is seen as strictly educational. G.E.D. training, provided concurrently with the gas station training experience, normally is completed about the time a youth seeks employment. An estimated $4,500 is paid in restitution through juveniles' gas station earnings annually; 80 percent of these youths pay their requirements that juveniles bring to placement. The work is performed at such local nonprofit agencies as the Boys' Club, the Florence Crittenon Home, the YMCA, and at nursing homes.

There are other examples of fulfillment of restitution requirements while in placement. Northwest Passages, Webster, Wisconsin, is a 20-bed facility for delinquent boys located in a town of 600 population within a county of 14,000 residents. Its director acknowledges, "because we always facilitate restitution achievement, the system expects it from us." The agency provides earning opportunities and unpaid community work service on the grounds of this facility. Work is done after school and when one is not otherwise engaged in an agency program. The work includes cutting and stacking firewood, cutting the lawn, painting, putting in shrubs, and assisting the maintenance man with minor construction jobs. Approximately 10 percent of youngsters come to the residential program with a restitution requirement. During later stages of their stay, juveniles, restitution-owing or not, may obtain jobs in the community work service through placement with the county road maintenance agency.

The Sanctuary, Mercer, Pennsylvania, is a 12-bed group home for delinquent boys 13 through 18 years of age. During the first month of residence, a treatment plan is developed with the juvenile, his parents, probation officer, and the staff. Any outstanding financial or community work service restitution obligation is routinely included in the treatment plan. More than 80 percent of the boys owe restitution or court fines or costs; 50 percent owe just financial restitution.

The Sanctuary emphasizes a youth's fulfillment of his responsibilities, believing this increases one's feeling of self worth. All residents undertake a job orientation workshop geared to finding an off-grounds job. Those owing financial restitution must make installment payments from their earnings. Community work service requirements are performed at the group home, at nearby nursing homes, or with Meals on Wheels where juveniles prepare and deliver food preparations to senior citizens. On grounds. juveniles in their free time perform work service hours by helping repair the group home, remodeling a garage into a storage facility, and other projects in which staff members work with the youngsters on planning and supervising the tasks.

The Idaho Boys Ranch, Boise, Idaho, also a nonprofit organization, serves 36 boys at its main campus facility and operates a 12-bed group home in another community and a 9-bed independent living unit in Boise. Approximately 15 percent of boys come with an outstanding financial or community work service restitution obligation. During the average 9-month ranch experience, all residents have paid job opportunities: table waiting, dishwashing, and yard crew work. They earn allowances based on performance in the overall program which can also be allocated to financial restitution requirements; some participate in summer Job Training Partnership Act jobs and make restitution payments from these earnings. Several boys have completed financial restitution through participation in a 4-H program. The ranch provides the boy with a calf. The boys raises the calf, grooms the calf, and then shows it at the county fair. The animal is sold at the fair's 4-H auction. The ranch takes 50 percent of the proceeds to pay for the original cost of the calf and feed while the remaining 50 percent goes to the juvenile. Several boys have paid off restitution of $500-$600 from their share of the proceeds.

Juveniles perform community work service at the ranch by digging and raking weeds, washing cars, and accomplishing other menial tasks. The agency also maintains thrift stores in four Idaho communities. Ranch and group home juveniles can complete their hours in various tasks at a store. The thrift stores are also community work service sites for juvenile probationers in the four communities.

The Lucas County Juvenile Court, Toledo, Ohio, utilizes approximately $90,000 of its state subsidy program money to pay restitution-owing juveniles to perform community work service for repayment to victims. Work crews are used, rather than individualized agency placements. Juveniles placed by the court at Circle C group homes, 20 miles away, and at the Timberville Boys' Ranch, 30 miles way, perform their paid community work service on the grounds of the residential agency rather than coming to Toledo for the work crew experience. The directors of these agencies regularly advise the director of the Lucas County Juvenile Restitution Program of the number of hours worked; funds are then released to victims.

Despite these constructive forms of restitution fulfillment during residential placement, the author's inquiries have found numerous respondents who indicated that restitution compliance was not a consideration with residential placement. Apparently, the carryover of restitution requirements in drug and alcohol treatment facilities carries still fewer expectations.

DRUG AND ALCOHOL TREATMENT PROGRAMS

Abraxas II, Erie, Pennsylvania, is a community-based residential program for drug and alcohol dependent persons 16 to 25 years of age, male and female. The main Abraxas facility is at Marienville, Pennsylvania, and involves a 6- to 9-month residential stay. Re-entry houses are maintained in Erie, Pittsburgh, and Philadelphia, where the stay averages 3 to 6 months. Residents move from the Marienville site to one of these three Re-entry residences. The third and final phase of the program takes place in each of these three communities and is an Out-Client program that helps participants through the early weeks of independent living and seeks to assure continuance of a chemical-free lifestyle. There is also a three-phase shorter program, Assist, that is provided in Erie, Pittsburgh, and Philadelphia for juveniles whose drug dependency is less severe and whose families will participate actively in counseling. Abraxas, Erie, then, has in residence Both Re-entry and Assist juveniles.

During the Re-entry phase, juveniles phase back into school or find employment in the community. There is educational and vocational guidance, individual treatment planning, individual and group counseling, and family counseling. There is job orientation training and a life management skills course. Resident juveniles who become employed are required to contribute to a restitution requirement with the second and subsequent paychecks. This continues during the third Out-Client program when clients return to their homes or move into an independent living arrangement. During these two phases, Abraxas' juvenile clients who owe restitution may participate in the Erie Earn-It Janitorial Services, Inc., the non-profit affiliate of the juvenile probation department that has a contract to clean up the courthouse each night and also performs janitorial services at a public library and public social services agency.

Obstacles to fulfilling restitution requirements for residents of drug and alcohol facilities can be overcome. Similarly, earning restitution monies can become a focus of re-entry and out-client phases of specialized residential programs for juvenile sex offenders. Community work services requirements can be completed during residential phases of drug and alcohol or sex offender programs. Restitution opportunities can also be developed when courts confine juveniles to secure detention facilities as a sanction.

SENTENCES TO DETENTION

California and approximately 13 other states authorize juvenile court judges to use a sentence to a pretrial secure detention facility as a dispositional option. The confinement period may be for several weekends, up to 45 days or 3 months, or longer. Often, sentenced juveniles are mixed with pretrial juveniles in the same facility, and there is no specialized program, restitution-wise or otherwise, for sentenced youngsters. This is true in the juvenile detention center in Chicago where 10 percent of its 390-400 residents have been sentenced for from 3 days to 60 days. It is true in Denver an other communities. There are more positive program models.

Sonoma County, California, maintains a Juvenile Correctional Program for up to 12 delinquent youths at its Juvenile Hall in Santa Rose. This minimum 6-month program is located in the sprawling detention center complex certified for a 118-bed capacity, but which averages 65 juveniles including those sentenced to the program. More typically, it takes from 8 to 10 months to earn release from the program. Residents frequently have a significant offense history. Some residents had earlier run away from the Sonoma County Probation Camp or otherwise failed that program. Other juveniles may be sentenced briefly to the facility but not into the Juvenile Correctional Program. These dispositions tend to be for 2 to 5 days.

Program participants attend school on the grounds and may prepare for a G.E.D. examination. They are engaged in individual and group counseling sessions and also participate in a work program. They are graded weekly on a series of requirements. Specified grade scores are necessary to move through the various steps of the program and to move toward furloughs and ultimate release. The work component, which emphasized work attitudes, habits, and skills, allows for restitution payments.

Program juveniles attend school each morning. They work 2 hours daily, one evening, and 8 hours each Saturday and Sunday on one of four projects. One is a furniture refinishing program that began with county employee clients but has spread to the community. A second project is bicycle repair and sales. The program obtains unclaimed bicycles from the police department, fixes them up, and sells them at flea markets or to county employees through a newsletter notice. A third is picture framing, and a fourth is an animal husbandry project that raises pigs and sells them. From the earnings, a maximum of $300 may be paid to a juvenile's restitution account.

Program juveniles not owing restitution do not share in the earnings unless, on a case-by-case basis, funds are seen as necessary for a youth to enter into independent living. Also, when close to graduation from the program, juveniles may obtain jobs in the community. From their earnings, money is diverted to victim payments when there is an unfulfilled restitution requirement. The court attaches financial restitution but not community work service requirements with this disposition. However, the program makes community contributions in the form of building or refinishing county furniture at no cost, constructing storage boxes for a battered women's shelter, and raising and providing fresh vegetables for the detention facility and a senior citizens' center.

In Washington State, under its justice model juvenile code, juvenile court judges may sentence juveniles to secure detention facilities for up to 6 months and even longer. The duration of stay is related to one's age, present offense and offense history, and elapsed time between offenses. State funding subsidized long-term detention sentences. Here, too, the sentence is to a program and not just to a facility. In Spokane County, a 6-month sentence is divided into three phases. The first 2 months involve school in the facility, life skills and social skills training, and job orientation. During the next 2 months, juveniles are furloughed on work or school release, returning to the facility at night. Those who obtain jobs must, if they owe restitution, make payments to victims from their earnings. Payments are also made during the final 2 months where juveniles live at home, attend school, or are employed, and come into a detention center for one overnight stay per week. Earlier that evening, the parents and juvenile meet with probation and detention staff members to review progress and problems.

A similar approach is taken in Pierce County (Tacoma) Washington. The center's director noted that there is no difficulty obtaining jobs for juveniles during phases two and three through the assistance of the state employment service, since program juveniles qualify for this service. Also, here, juveniles sentenced to the program who carry community work service requirements from past orders must perform their hours on their own time, working on maintenance and related tasks on center grounds. The court does not order community work service requirements with juveniles sentenced to longer terms for an offense that prompted this disposition. Additionally, about 10 juveniles are sentenced annually for about 5 days each for failure to fulfill restitution obligations in the community. The number of days served in these cases is prorated to the amount of money unpaid or number of hours not performed. These youths do not perform special work tasks at the center to accomplish the original order. The detention sentence is a substitute, then, for the original order.

Judges in Orange County, California, utilize community work service as an alternative to a short detention sentence. This may be invoked with a willful failure to comply with a financial restitution or with a less severe repeat offense. These juveniles may work four weekends with a probation department work crew instead of spending four weekends of "dead time" in the detention center.

The fulfillment or restitution requirements is not a prominent consideration with lengthier detention sentences in this jurisdiction. But a small number of these juveniles may be released on work furlough, toward the end of their stay, to a former job if they had one or to a new job if a probation officer can help them find one. Partial earnings, if restitution is owed, are directed to victims.

New Jersey statutes authorize sentences to detention not to exceed 60 continuous days, but the physical and program standards of the local detention facility must meet Department of Corrections requirements. The department specifies the capacity of the facility for sentenced juveniles, which may not exceed 50 percent of the maximum capacity. Between 30 and 40 juveniles are sentenced annually to the Ocean County Juvenile Detention Center at Toms River, some for non-compliance with restitution requirements. A typical sentence is 30 days, and a youth can earn up to 5 days of good time performing additional work assignments, during free time, at the center. Sentenced juveniles with unperformed work hours can perform these at the facility painting walls, cutting lawns, maintaining outside gardens, and doing general clean up, all on their own time. During good weather months, an arrangement with the local buildings and grounds department results in juveniles doing lawn maintenance, raking leaves, and assisting a carpenter. These youths are picked up daily at the center following the work experience. Financial restitution obligations cannot be earned at the center, but juveniles who had employment when sentenced may be work-furloughed to their former position, with certain earnings directed to victim payment. The center also arranges jobs for these juveniles at a local cinema, in other private sector settings, and in conjunction with the Job Training Partnership Act.

Through a different legal procedure, a deferred plea, juveniles are held in a detention facility at Clarksboro, New Jersey, for failure to comply with restitutional requirements. A juvenile may be driven by a staff social worker to a paid job that was held prior to confinement so that victim payments may be reinitiated. Juveniles failing to comply with community work service requirements may complete their hours by working at the center or be taken back and forth by the staff social worker to a probation department work site to complete their hours.

The fulfillment of restitution requirements in community correctional settings requires resolution of a series of policy and implementation issues.

THE NEED FOR REVIEW AND CLARIFICATION OF COURT POLICY REGARDING THE CARRYOVER OF RESTITUTION ORDERS INTO COMMUNITY PLACEMENT

Community agencies receiving court juveniles look to the court's policies, requirements, and the messages it communicates. Any number of juveniles courts, in general, assess financial restitution without high expectations of full payment and lack a program to facilitate earnings and compliance. In effect, these courts have not been accountable to victims. Even outstanding restitution programs have not always clearly assessed, thought through, and implemented a consistent policy regarding carryover of restitution requirements to community placements.

The preceding review indicates that financial restitution is typically ordered by the courts in conjunction with an offense that prompts placement, but that community work services hours are often avoided with such a placement, even though when a juvenile previously has been before the court with a lesser offense, community work service may have been ordered. There is also evidence that a court's practices may be to wait until a juvenile leaves placement to begin pressuring for collection of financial restitution. Yet the program models cited earlier suggest that ways can be found to implement both financial and community work service restitution during placement or, at least, in the latter stages of placement.

It would seem advisable for all courts and their restitution components to treat a placement-prompting offense no differently than any other offense as to restitution requirements and to expect their fulfillment during placement unless the facility's program is able to convince the court that fulfillment is fundamentally incongruous with the constraints of its program.

The restitution policy of the Court of Common Pleas, Juvenile Section, Allegheny County (Pittsburgh), Pennsylvania (1986, p. 142), is a useful reference with financial restitution carryover:

> At the initial institutional contact when treatment goals and objectives are reviewed, the issue of restitution is to be incorporated. The probation officer should encourage the development of a restitution payment schedule while the child is in placement. At all review hearings the probation officer will address efforts made to satisfy the restitution order . . .

The mission statement of a juvenile court or restitution agency is another policy foundation. For example, the mission statement of the Santa Clara County (San Jose), California, Probation Department (1987, p. 4) states that "offenders will be held responsible to the community and to themselves through personal accountability and restitution as a part of any sanction whether or not it involves custody."

THE NEED FOR COMMUNITY PLACEMENT AGENCIES TO INCORPORATE FULFILLMENT OF RESTITUTION REQUIREMENTS INTO THEIR PROGRAM PURPOSES

Many community agencies that work with juvenile court youths may prefer not to accept responsibility for assisting with the fulfillment of restitution requirements during placement. They have developed their own program design and treatment methods and usually have structured the time of these juveniles quite extensively. Some will contend that their treatment regimens or facility limitations provide no opportunity for restitution fulfillment. Yet, an accountability precept is consistent with how these agencies usually approach a juvenile's errant past and behavioral present. They use levels or steps, allow privileges to be earned or withdrawn, and through various means require juveniles to accept responsibility for their actions. Further, these agencies are dependent on the court and probation department for many of their referrals.

The program models described earlier, indicate that such agencies can and often enthusiastically do, incorporate restitution requirements into their programs, on grounds and off grounds. In other communities this issue may be ignored.

Communities work service hours appear to be relatively easy to arrange on grounds. Further, some placement agencies are able to build payments for work performed by juveniles owing restitution into their fee schedule or educational budget. Others can innovate earning opportunities with the assistance of governmental and private sector organizations and interested citizens. Placement agencies should recognize that it is instructive for other juveniles in the program, not required to perform such work or earn restitution, to observe their peers fulfilling their requirements during nonprogram time.

It is largely an educational and negotiation process that bridges this gap. Juvenile courts and probation agencies should take the initiative in working out clear expectations but flexible approaches for placement agencies in this regard. In some cases, they may need to assist these agencies by helping arrange in-the-community job earning and community work service opportunities for those who can be related from their settings.

THE NEED FOR PLACEMENT AGENCY AWARENESS OF RESTITUTION REQUIREMENTS

Harborcreek Youth Services serves juveniles from a number of Pennsylvania counties in its residential program. The agency reports that placement orders received from some counties do not always specify restitution requirements, though restitution may have been ordered. Further, some of these directives fail to clarify whether restitution payments should be made to the county, the clerk or court, or the victim. It is likely that private placement agencies have more difficulty receiving full information on restitution obligations than do court-related governmental organizations.

The statewide Utah Juvenile Court and the Utah Division of Corrections share a computerized information system that enables the division to obtain an instant printout of factual information, including restitution requirements, when a court commits a youth to the custody of the division for either community correctional or state institutional placement. A division case manager who works with juveniles in proctor homes or contract residential facilities has the information to communicate to the youth and the residential staff the amount of money or work service hours that need to be paid or performed. State institutional staff also have this information. Utah statutes provide that parents must pay toward the costs of their children's out-of-home placements and specify this money is to be used to pay division juveniles to perform paid community work service, with payments directed to victims.

Other public facilities, the secure detention center in Tacoma, Washington, and the probation camp in Sonoma County, California, reported that court orders accompany commitments to their programs, and the orders specify restitution requirements.

It is incumbent upon court and probation officials to inform placement agencies speedily and fully as to outstanding restitution obligations concerning juveniles placed in their care.

THE NEED FOR APPROPRIATE RESTITUTION REQUIREMENTS, CONSISTENTLY ADMINISTERED, TO ASSIST PLACEMENT AGENCIES' COLLABORATION WITH FULFILLMENT

"Before ordering monetary restitution, the court must determine that a youth has a present ability to pay, or is likely in the near future to obtain the ability to pay" (Feinman, 1985). This is the law in most states, but the law is not always meticulously adhered to by judges. Instead, some judges may order whatever the victim claims and place the burden on the juvenile, at a contempt or revocation of probation proceeding, to demonstrate that a failure to comply with the order was not willful. A related defect involves juvenile court orders of community work service hours. A number of juvenile courts still set these hours on an individualized basis determined by perceptions of a juvenile's offense, offense record, and attitude without regard to consistency in the requirement of the number of hours among offenders. Different probation officers may recommend differently, and different judges may enter disparate orders with juveniles who have similar offenses or offense histories. Alternatively, a court approved grid or matrix guideline better assures equal and proportional justice among offenders (Rubin, 1986).

Placement agencies must deal with the consequences of incorrect, excessive, and inconsistent requirements. Several agencies have complained that their juveniles talk with other juveniles about restitution requirements and feel their orders were set unfairly in comparison with others. Further, excessive orders, some reaching $6,000-$7,000, are unable to be complied with even by motivated juveniles and constitute a negative factor in the rehabilitation efforts of placement agencies.

Harborcreek Youth Services reports that some judges order juveniles to repay insurance companies over and above monies they are ordered to pay for the cost of an insurance deductible. Judges from other courts limit the requirement to the cost of the insurance company's deductible. It is desirable that a common policy as to monetary restitution provisions be mandated statewide.

Denver's New Pride agency reported that juvenile court youths it places in paid jobs with it employment affiliate. Midtown Services, work side-by-side with committed juveniles, on parole status, placed with Midtown Services for job training and paid employment by the Colorado Division of Youth Services. The court requires victim restitution payments from monies earned by its juveniles; the state agency discourages the payment of restitution requirements, wanting its youths to use earnings toward independent living costs.

A restitution objective is to reimburse victims as fully and as speedily as possible. When a placement agency has designed a program to facilitate financial restitution and a juvenile is targeted for this program, the court can, within the law, set a higher rather than lower amount since there is a likelihood of obtaining the ability to pay. Also, when a placement agency has designed a program to facilitate community work service restitution and a juvenile is targeted for this program, the court can order work service hours knowing they can be fulfilled.

PLACEMENT AGENCIES NEED TO REVIEW THEIR INSURANCE COVERAGE FOR JUVENILES FULFILLING RESTITUTION REQUIREMENTS

There are three types of insurance coverage for community work service that are desirable and also superior to the practice that obtains from a juvenile and the parents a waiver of liability that, as has often been said, may not be worth the paper it is written on:

- for juveniles who may become injured while performing paid or unpaid community work service.
- for juveniles who may injure the person or property of others while performing paid or unpaid community work service.
- for staff members who make work arrangements for juveniles that lead to injury or liability.

A state may, by statute, cover court youths for community work service injuries through workmen's compensation (Fle. Stat. Amm. §39.04) or may expressly provide that juveniles are not covered by these provisions (Colo. Rev. Stat. § 19-2-706). An agency, nontheless, may buy this coverage or buy private insurance for the first of these coverages or all three.

Juveniles who obtain paid jobs in the private sector are employees, like other employees, protected by an employer's workmen's compensation coverage. Juveniles who obtain paid jobs with governmental agencies are employees, like other employees, and protected by workmen's compensation or a governmental self-insurance program. Juveniles who perform community work service hours at non-profit or governmental agencies may be protected under these organizations' policies or self insurance programs.

The insurance concern is one that private agencies need to deal with more than governmental placement agencies. Their present policies may or may not cover juveniles working on the grounds or staff members who place juveniles in inappropriate work settings or tasks that may lead to injury. The liability issue is one that has been successfully handled by hundreds of restitution programs. It should not forestall restitution implementation, but it requires review and resolution by all placement agencies, private and public. The reality has been that liability claims are few.

Some agencies require juveniles to contribute a small sum to insurance coverage costs from their earnings. Conditions of an insurance policy such as prohibiting payment for injuries due to power tool use, need to regulate the work youths may or may not perform. Further, child labor laws need to be observed. Comprehensive insurance coverage may be a significant budget item, and placement agencies may want to build these costs into their rate structures.

PLACEMENT AGENCIES NEED TO REVIEW WHAT DEDUCTIONS MAY BE REQUIRED TO BE MADE FROM RESTITUTION EARNINGS

Deduction practices vary considerably among placement agencies that provide payments to juveniles for work that is performed in order to pay victim restitution. Some deduct Federal and state withholding taxes and social security. One agency also deducts a worker's compensation contribution. Several deduct only the social security tax and contend that the earnings are too low to require withholding tax deductions. Others deduct nothing and consider payment to be some form of stipend that does not merit any deductions. Some, where 100 percent of earnings are paid over to victims, also take a view that this procedure requires no deductions.

While some agencies may be very cautious in their reading of legal deduction requirements, more typically the agencies slant toward minimizing deductions. It is desirable that placement agencies seek informed opinions to guide them on this issue.

PLACEMENT AGENCIES NEED TO HAVE PROCEDURES FOR OBTAINING RESTITUTION MONIES FROM JUVENILES' EARNINGS

Three approaches to this issue have been discerned:

1.   Where placement agencies control job earnings, they make payments to the court or restitution program for the juveniles' victim accounts. If the policy provides that 100 percent of earnings shall be paid to victims, no partial payment is made to the juvenile. By policy or negotiated agreement, placement agencies may pay a percentage of earnings to a juvenile as a work or compliance incentive or to cover transportation and other expenses incidental to the work. The agency control of job earnings or public subsidy funds is the simplest and most efficient procedure.

2.   An agency may control job earnings but make full payment to a juvenile expecting the juvenile to cash the check and return an agreed upon percentage of payment to the placement agency for remission to a victim account. Underpinning this approach is the viewpoint that juveniles should be given responsibility to cash their

checks and pay their bills. Through a life skills training course, juveniles have been taught the rudiments of a bank account. Staff members have helped them open their account. Reportedly, occasional difficulties arise when a juvenile cashes the check but expends his earnings for other purposes and fails to honor the restitution requirement. A placement agency may have a staff person accompany the juvenile to the bank, oversee the cashing of the check, and then accompany the youth to the court to witness payment to the officially designated recipient. Alternatively, juveniles may be provided with envelopes and encouraged to write their own checks and mail them to their victim accounts. This overall approach has clear merit, but is far from foolproof and makes it more difficult for the placement agency to be certain that payments are made and to obtain accurate figures on how much victims restitution is facilitated during a year's period.

3. The final method involves obtaining restitution payments from juveniles whose jobs are in the community and job earnings are controlled by an employer who makes direct compensation to the youth. A common control approach used by placement agencies is to require that pay stubs be submitted to staff members for review each pay period, along with evidence that restitution has been paid by way of a money order or cashier's check receipts.

One placement agency commented that in facilitating jobs for juveniles in a Job Training Partnership Act program, it did not believe it had authority to pick up the juvenile's check, go with the youth to the bank, have the youth cash the check, and then have the youth pay over the restitution percentage for transmission. Instead, the agency would inform the probation department of the job and of scheduled pay days and ask that the probation officer meet with the youth to ensure payments were made to the restitution account. Regretfully, probation officers were not responsive to these requests and restitution payments were not made.

It is important that placement agencies have procedures that prioritize restitution payments from earnings that these expectations and procedures are presented directly and up front to juveniles, that controls are in place so that restitution payments are, in fact, made, and that reinforcement is provided by the official restitution agency.

PLACEMENT AGENCIES NEED A POLICY CONCERNING A JUVENILE'S RETENTION OF A PERCENTAGE OF EARNINGS

There are various rationales with this issue. The rationales depend, at least in part, on whether the earnings utilize public subsidy funds, whether the agency facilitates an on-grounds or off-grounds agency-related earning capability, or whether a juvenile obtains employment in the community. Modifying circumstances include whether a court has ordered a percentage payment, a placement. a placement agency's viewpoint regarding partial payments to juveniles as incentive and motivator, transportation costs to the job, and the needs of juveniles to have money for necessities or general spending purposes. Agency policies vary significantly as to juveniles' retention of partial earnings.

In Utah community correctional programs, 100 percent of paid community service goes to the victim. This is true, also, with the juvenile restitution program in Waterloo, Iowa, where limited state subsidy funds are available. The rationale there is that transmission of 100 percent of earnings enables more juveniles to perform work and complete restitution payments. However, when youths find employment in the community, they are permitted to retain from 15 to 50 percent of earnings. The Sonoma County Probation Camp receives all payments from the sale of residents' products and transmits 100 percent of this income to victims. Harborcreek Youth Services turns over 90 percent of juveniles' earnings from on-grounds and off-grounds employment. Northwest Passages, Webster, Wisconsin, allows juveniles to retain a small part of their earnings if they "do a good job"; otherwise, 100 percent is paid for restitution. Juveniles in residential programs who participate in the Erie Earn-It Janitorial Services Program retain 25 percent of earnings. The Perseus House program in Erie authorizes juveniles to utilize their entire first paycheck for clothing and other needs and directs juveniles to pay 75 percent of future earnings for restitution. Further, staff members strongly encourage juveniles to set aside portions of retained earnings to prepare for independent living. The Sanctuary Group Home, Mercer, Pennsylvania, allows juveniles to retain 50 percent of their earnings from jobs they secure in the community. New Pride, Denver, requires enrollees to pay from 25 to 50 percent of earnings, most juveniles in this day treatment program being indigent. Some enrolled juveniles who earlier had failed to make restitution payments have been ordered by the court to pay 50 percent of earnings for restitution. The residential work release program, Ventura, California, authorizes juvenile retention of 20 percent of earnings. The detention center in Tacoma, Washington, authorizes juveniles on work release during phase two of their detention sentence to retain 50 percent of earnings from community jobs.

A placement agency policy will need to consider factors such as those described above.

PLACEMENT AGENCIES NEED TO HAVE PROCEDURES TO SANCTION RESTITUTION NON-COMPLIANCE

Placement agencies, like probation departments and community restitution programs, experience restitution non-compliance. A written restitution contract and clear communication of requirements tend to reduce the need for sanctions. The Ultimate sanction involves a return to court and judicial determination of a new disposition. Placement agency control of earnings, as is obvious, reduces non-compliance.

Placement agencies report little difficulty in obtaining compliance with restitution requirements when this is a purpose of their program and earning opportunities are in place. They report few examples of non-compliance that prompt a court hearing for this factor alone. They use sanctioning procedures such as not moving a juvenile up to a new level of privilege that would have brought program graduation at an earlier date. A consequence, also, may be a dropping of a level or requiring additional unpaid work.

Agencies need to anticipate that non-compliance may occur develop strategies that enhance compliance, and implement reasonable sanctions that are administered consistently.

SUMMARY

The primary forms of restitution financial and community work service, have become frequently used sanctions in juvenile courts. It is likely that this approach to accountability on the part of juvenile offenders will continue its expansion and become a regularized requirement. Programs to assist with restitution requirements must supplement judicial orders if courts and communities are to be accountable to victims through high rates of compliance. Courts that place juveniles in day treatment and community-based residential programs should include restitution requirements in their orders and expect that these requirements will be fulfilled during the course of placement. A number of placement agencies have successfully incorporated restitution projects and compliance opportunities into their programs. Others should.

The court and its restitution arm should place the burden on a placement agency to show why restitution compliance cannot be fulfilled during placement. A series of policy issues that require resolution has been presented. Some are directed to the courts; others are directed to the placement agencies. None are impossible. Victim payments need not be deferred and reasonable community work service sanctions need not be passed by or overlooked when placement occurs. Present practices should be evaluated for gaps; remedies should be designed. Re-thinking juvenile restitution can result in many payoffs.

REFERENCES

Court of Common Pleas, Family Division, Juvenile Section, Allegheny County, Pittsburgh, PA. *Policies and Procedures Manual,* 1986, p. 142.

Feinman, Howard. "Legal Issues in the Operations of Juvenile Restitution Programs." In Anne L. Schneider (ed.), *Guide to Juvenile Restitution.* Washington, DC: U.S. Government Printing Office, 1985, p. 148.

Juvenile Restitution Program, Lucas County Court, Toledo, OH. *Annual Report,* 1987, p.8.

Rubin, H. Ted. "Community Service Restitution by Juveniles: Also in Need of Guidance." *Juvenile and Family Court Journal* 37, 1986, pp. 1-8.

————. *Police Administration of Juvenile Restitution,* manuscript submitted to Office of Juvenile Justice and Delinquency Prevention, U.S. Department of Justice, 1987.

Santa Clara County Probation Department, San Jose, CA. *Annual Report,* 1987. p. 4.

Schneider, Peter R. and Gordon Bazemore. "Research on Restitution: A Guide to Rational Decisionmaking." In Anne L. Schneider (ed.), *Guide to Juvenile Restitution.* Washington, DC: U.S. Government Printing Office, 1985, pp. 139, 141-142.

STATUTES

Ariz. Rev. Stat. Ann § 230.01.
Colo. Rev. Stat. § 19-2 706.
Fla. Stat. Ann. § 39.04
Tex. Fam. Code Ann. §53.03.
Tex. Hum. Res. Code § 61.081.
Utah Code Ann. § 55-11b-23.

Delinquency Prevention
Legislation, Financing, and Law Enforcement are Not Enough

WILLIAM C. KVARACEUS

Despite current efforts to rewrite legislation, finance delinquency prevention programs, and bolster law enforcement agencies, the growing delinquency and crime rates have not been reduced. A number of basic conditions or prerequisites of delinquency prevention and control go beyond the necessary but insufficient legislative-fiscal-enforcement approaches. Among the contingencies are the following: the public's willingness to relinquish delinquency, better definition of and differentiation among delinquents, the development of a positive and helpful attitude in the community and in supporting agencies, the use of knowledge and facts in planning the involvement of youth in the solution of youth problems, and the recognition of positive aspects of delinquency.

CURRENT EFFORTS to prevent and control juvenile delinquency are preoccupied with trying to attain improved legislation, a more adequate base of financial support, and stronger law enforcement and police protection, reflecting the myth that the panacea for reducing crime and delinquency rates is better laws, more money, and better trained police—three *necessary but insufficient* means for solving the problem. Certain underlying contingencies or conditions must exist if the combined law-fiscal-

Source: Kvaraceus, William C. "Delinquency Prevention: Legislation, Financing, and Law Enforcement are Not Enough." *Crime and Delinquency* Vol. 15 (October) 1969: 463-470. Reprinted by permission of Sage Publications, Inc.

555

police approaches are to achieve their goals of prevention and control. These goals will be realized more effectively and readily (1) *if* the public is willing to "give up" delinquency (2) *if* the delinquent targets are better defined and differentiated, (3) *if* the community attitude is positive and not exclusive, (4) *if* planning proceeds from a base of knowledge and facts, (5) *if* youth are involved in the solution of youth problems, (6) *if* early identification of future delinquents can be followed by systematic referral for help, (7) *if* agency aims are clearly enunciated and their activities are continuously evaluated, (8) *if* local resources can be effectively coordinated, and (9) *if* the positive aspects of delinquency are not ignored.

IF PUBLIC IS WILLING TO "GIVE-UP" DELINQUENCY

The average citizen, beset with his own problems of daily life, seldom reacts to episodes and reports of delinquency with any degree of objectivity or understanding; often he becomes emotionally involved. An informed and disinterested citizenry is a prerequisite to effective social planning. It is the rare community that can achieve this.

Most middle-class citizens live staid and settled lives devoid of excitement or adventure other than what they can purchase through vicarious experience in the sports arena, in a book, or on the screen. Reports and accounts of juvenile "sex orgies," vandalism, mugging, unwed mothers, and drinking bouts can be titillating. It is no accident that the newspapers and other mass media—like the swarm of camera men in *La Dolce Vita*—record for the adult consumer the vivid details of youth's more sensational violations of the community's norms. The adult provides a good market for such accounts—although he may complain, sometimes ruefully and sometimes bitterly, of the goings-on of today's youth. You can almost hear him smack his lips. On catching himself in this act, he reacts guilty and frequently turns his wrath on the young rascals who were responsible in the first place for stirring in him these feelings of forbidden delights.

Nor are adults beyond direct exploitation of the delinquency phenomenon. Both political parties have been known to vie for the sponsorship of federal, state, and local conferences and programs aimed at preventing and controlling juvenile delinquency. And, of course, Hollywood has been quick to exploit the "west side story," the "rebels without a cause," and "the wild ones." Even the professional workers in the field are suspect. Note how frequently community fund drives for support of family welfare and youth services are spearheaded by the threat of increased delinquency and maladjustment if contribution goals are not reached.

The pornographic outlets, the crime-comic publishing houses, the prostitution rackets, and the drug channels are not controlled by teenage monsters; they are run by adults.[1] Coming to grips with delinquency prevention will mean confronting the "responsible" and "respectable" adults who find in the social inadaptation of youth a

---

[1] See "Peep Shows Have New Nude Look," *New York Times,* June 9, 1969, p. 58.

profitable—even pleasurable—business. It will also mean broadening and intensifying efforts in informing the public of the meaning and implications of norm violation among youth.

IF THE DELINQUENT TARGETS ARE BETTER DEFINED AND DIFFERENTIATED

The term *juvenile delinquent* is a nontechnical and pejorative label; it refers not to a specific diagnostic category but to a potpourri of many kinds of youthful offenders. Few communities bother to define delinquency or to distinguish one kind of delinquent from another. In fact, we do not yet know how many different types of offenders are to be found in the delinquency spectrum. Pure types do not exist, and there are many variants along the norm-violating continuum.

In planning preventive programs, the police and courts must differentiate more adequately among the varieties of delinquent youth. For example, they will have to spot the emotionally disturbed or sick offender for whom child guidance clinic treatment is indicated. They will have to identify the culturally determined offender for whom the delinquent act may represent sportive—even acceptable—behavior when viewed in the light of the value system of the gang or neighborhood. For example these youngsters community programs are needed which will change and improve the way of life that is reflected by the norms and values of their subgroups. And of course they will have to be aware of the largest group, a strong mixture of pathologically and culturally determined delinquents for whom a dual treatment program must be envisioned. The boy who steals a car to prove his manhood to his gang and the boy who steals a car to strike back at his parents operate different motivations, which should be distinguished. Currently, most juvenile courts are prone to place most or all of their delinquents in the child guidance clinic basket.

IF THE COMMUNITY ATTITUDE IS POSITIVE AND NOT EXCLUSIVE

Apart from the conscious and unconscious exploitation of delinquents, one can sense in the climate of any community five moods or attitudes—Messianic-sentimental, punitive-retaliatory, positive-humanistic, diagnostic-therapeutic, and cultural-reconstructionist—expressed by citizens who are concerned with delinquency prevention. The delinquency prevention and control programs that are "sold and sponsored" will vary considerably according to the point of view that dominates the power structure of city and state. In many state institutions and agencies, the prevailing mood swings back and forth uneasily from retaliation to rehabilitation and accounts for much friction and conflict concerning the most promising approach to solving the problems of youth. Let us take a closer look at these five positions.

The *Messianic-sentimentalist* believes there is no such thing as a "bad boy" (until he meets up with two on the same day and thereafter tends to avoid them) and clings optimistically to the notion that all would be well if the youngster could only "be reached" somehow. There aren't many Messianic-sentimentalists left these days.

On the other extreme, we have perhaps the most popular stance taken in dealing with delinquents, the *punitive-retaliatory* orientation—the "hard line" or "get tough" school of thought. Today many state officials and a large segment of the citizenry, fed up with the mounting rate of serious offenses and frustrated by the ineffectiveness of "scientific approaches," revert to "sterner measures." including the night stick, the curfew, and the extended sentence to institutional confinement. (This is the official FBI line.) The underlying reasoning is that the offending youngster and his family should not be tolerated or mollycoddled; rather, they should be made to suffer for the error of their ways. Having suffered, the delinquent will have learned his lesson and will sin no more. Although it is true that the delinquent often is hostile and vengeful he also must face a hostile and vengeful community. Caught up in this mood, the state agencies find themselves playing cops-and robbers games on a two-way street of hate and hostility.

In contrast to the punitive back-of-the-hand, the *positive-humanist* extends a helping hand. Believing that "there is no problem children, merely children with severe problems," he looks for causes but often confuses them with cures. Noting, for example, the kinds of leisure-time habits that are characteristic of young offenders, the positive humanist would hasten to provide more playground space or would use recreation like a flit gun to eradicate the problem. In the meantime, the gang merely shifts its crap game to the lot behind the billboard.

If the school counselor joins with the positive humanist, the mood may swing in another direction. Plans for prevention and control would now recommend the services of the clinical team—psychiatrist, psychologist, and social worker—found in the child guidance centers. This *diagnostic-therapeutic* stance assumes that the delinquent or his parents are emotionally disturbed and require the services of the clinical team. True, some delinquents are sick (to estimate-exactly what proportion is difficult) and need medical help within mental health centers, but what proportion of the delinquents seen in the juvenile courts should or could receive the services of these specialists needs to be studied carefully.

However, as indicated earlier, many delinquents are not emotionally disturbed; rather, delinquency is regarded as a normal way of life in their subculture, often representing a route to status and prestige within the youngsters' primary reference group or gang. The *cultural -reconstructionist* views the neighborhood or the peer group with its value system as "the patient" to be studied and helped. In this approach, the agency or institution—school, public housing, recreation department, church, Boys' Club, Boy Scout troop, YMCA—is considered a powerful means of cultural change and renewal. In this sense, the agency sees itself as both a creation and an instrument of the culture. The cultural-reconstructionist stance is perhaps the most promising and the most neglected one at the local level.

Depending on the nature of the youthful offender, a case can be made for each of these moods, The danger is that the public and professional worker often ride only one hobby horse, and different ones at that. There is little doubt that the popular citizen attitude leans in the direction of the punitive and retaliatory, whereas the professional power structure in state departments (mental health, welfare, education, division of youth services) leans toward the therapeutic mood. The law-enforcement agencies, police and courts, are frequently caught between two moods and leap from one to another depending on the pressure from newspaper headlines and letters to the editors. The concerned citizen should not place all his bets on one horse—there are many different kinds of delinquents, and we need different approaches. Even the punitive approach, via consequences attached to certain behavior, can help to prevent certain kinds of delinquency. What is needed is a broad program of public education using mass media (television, radio, press) to inform the citizenry of the relative merits of the various approaches. And at all times, both eyes must be focused on what the research says about the relative effectiveness of different approaches with different kinds of offenders.

IF PLANNING PROCEEDS FROM A BASE OF KNOWLEDGE AND FACTS

A community or state agency that makes a commitment "to do something about delinquency" will succeed beyond merely scratching the surface only to the extent to which it becomes knowledgeable at three levels. First at the level of theory, the worker must conceptualize and integrate a frame of reference of personality and behavior as a form of adjustment to our culture and subcultures. Second, the agency must know the local neighborhood and community situation in which youth live, go to school, play, and work. Third, the agency must come to know, via case study methodology, the individual offender whom it is trying to help. One of the main reasons for the singular lack of success in community or agency approaches in working with delinquent and predelinquent youth can be found in the lack of knowledge at any one or all of these three levels. If the planned activities aimed at delinquency prevention and control are to be effective, they must always be relevant to the antecedents of the delinquent act. Without adequate information on any of these three levels—theory, community, and individual—workers engaged in prevention and control will run the heavy risk of program irrelevancy.

IF YOUTH ARE INVOLVED IN THE SOLUTION OF YOUTH PROBLEMS

Youth can be mined as a rich community resource, but in most communities they are a surplus commodity on a glutted market. Juvenile delinquency is a youth problem and only youth can solve it. It cannot be solved by professionals working on their own.

Agencies in which adults are the subject of the verb *serve* and youth the direct object will be limited in their attempts to prevent or control norm-violating behavior. Youth must become the subject of *serve*, for only when they begin to serve themselves and the community can we expect to stem the rising rate of juvenile delinquency.

Generally, youths are kept powerless in adult society. They have no vote; they are locked out of significant jobs; they are kept dependent through prolonged education; they are unorganized. Organized power movements on college campuses and some student political groups can be viewed as youthful organizations seeking a voice in decision making. Youth must be organized into a corporate structure in order to communicate and work with other corporate structures in American Society, such as schools and colleges, police, labor, unions, court systems, health and welfare agencies, churches, etc.

Youth involvement in the containment of delinquency is based on the following assumptions:

1. Every youth meeds to feel that there is a significant place for him as an adolescent is his immediate social world.

2. Every youth needs to be able to exercise his intelligence initiative, and growing maturity in solving problems of real concern to him and to the adult world.

3. Every youth needs to be given an opportunity to learn that his own life situation is not the only one there is.

4. Youth need to be incorporated in order to communicate and deal with the corporate structures maintained by adults in the urbanized, bureaucratic, anonymous society.

5. The emergence of an adolescent subculture characterized by self-directing community participation is not likely to occur without specific and special adult leadership. According to one study,[2] adult leadership will be helpful only as it (a) gives supportive guidance—i.e., is responsive to adolescent problems, needs, and interests; (b) is positive and symbolic—i.e., in its behavior encourages identification with relevant values, (c) practices appropriate process manipulations—i.e., is sensitive and effective in both intervention and withdrawal tactics designed to maximize self-direction and community participation.

Youth involvement in community action programs that aim to prevent and control delinquency will be guided by the following working postulates:

1. Self-direction and initiative of youth will be maximized.

---

[2] Irving Lukoff, Franklin K. Patterson, and Charles Winick, "Is Society the Patient? Research and Action Implications," *Journal of Educational Sociology,* October 1956. pp. 106-07.

2. Participation in vital and significant community activities and operations will be encouraged.

3. The adult role will be supporting and nondirective. The adult theme will be: "You can be free and significant. Go ahead and try; you can count on us to help."

4. The first and major emphasis will be on the development of local units; later development will call for regional and state organizations.

All youths up to voting age should be eligible for participation. This may call for two major (but overlapping) groups—the younger membership, ages thirteen to eighteen and the older segment, ages eighteen to twenty-one.

Effort must be made to ensure two-way communication so that the youths will not lose linkage and identification with their own primary reference group—i.e., to avoid the fink slur.

Participants may be elected, appointed by the governor or the governor's council, the mayor, or other authority (selectman, police chief, superintendent of schools), or designated as representatives by youth organizations. Various approaches should be tied out in different situations to ensure the most representative and active leadership among neighborhood youth. For example, Boston Mayor Kevin White's promising proposal to establish decentralized city halls through a "network of neighborhood service centers" in an attempt to involve more citizens in discussion and participation in the study and solution of community problems can provide a parallel for participation of the junior citizen in the same important participatory processes. To omit the junior citizen would be to overlook a vital source of energy, imagination, and brain power.

IF EARLY IDENTIFICATION OF FUTURE DELINQUENTS CAN BE FOLLOWED BY SYSTEMATIC REFERRAL FOR HELP

Delinquency is not a 24-hour malady; it does not develop overnight, but builds over a long period of time. The future delinquent may often give many hints of his coming explosion. Why can't the cities, working through such agencies as the schools, look for early indication of future delinquency and systematically screen out for study and treatment all those youngsters who are prone, susceptible, vulnerable, or exposed to delinquent patterns of adjustment? A number of researchers,[3] have developed some techniques for prediction, but most of these are still in the experimental stage and require further validation.

[3] William C. Kvaraceus, *Anxious Youth: Dynamics of Delinquency* (Columbus, Ohio: Charles E. Merrill, 1966), pp. 89-115. See also William C. Kvaraceus, Walter Miller, *et. al., Delinquent Behavior:*

IF AGENCY AIMS ARE CLEARLY ENUNCIATED
AND THEIR ACTIVITIES ARE CONTINUOUSLY EVALUATED

Many public and private community agencies and institutions, in their sincere concern for troubled youth and in their zeal to help, have tended to deflect from their special aims and unique functions. Out of this confusion of roles has emerged a never-never urban world in which parents act like their youngsters' peers, police in juvenile details are acting like probation officers or recreation leaders, probation officers conduct informal hearings as though they were judges, and juvenile court judges act in adjudication process like psychiatrists. Other community workers, such as those in public schools, are taking on omnibus functions, trying to be everything to every pupil. Unless agencies and institutions stop and define or redefine their unique goals and functions and begin to gather housekeeping statistics with which to evaluate their efforts, the result will be seen in a community suffering from institutional schizophrenia. The incipient stages are already visible in many metropolitan centers.

IF LOCAL RESOURCES CAN BE EFFECTIVELY COORDINATED

Implicit in any discussion of local prevention and control programs is the concept of coordination of all community resources so that any child or family requiring help can get the kind of services needed at the strategic moment of need. This assumes that public and private agencies know one another's resources and that they have developed liaison relationships and effective lines of communication, Here is where the big cities with their multiple agencies and institutions—more than 250 in the city of Boston, for example—fail most clearly.

Effective coordination will remain a vain hope or a professional fantasy until the city has established an overall community organization representing all child and family agencies, public and private, with full-time executive personnel trained to plan, coordinate, and steer the activities of this umbrella organization. It is this apparatus that should conduct local surveys and research, do local planning, and supervise continuous review of community needs and results. Youth and lay citizenry should form the core of such coordinating machinery.

IF THE POSITIVE ASPECTS OF DELINQUENCY ARE NOT IGNORED

The communication channels between the adolescent subculture and adults are seldom open and clear. Many youth subconsciously say to the adult world via their norm-violating behavior that "something is wrong" within the adolescent subculture or in the individual personal make-up. A delinquent act may serve as an SOS that the adult community cannot afford to ignore.

Delinquent behavior may also represent the youth's method of coming to grips with reality and with his problems in the best-way, even the only way, he knows. The delinquent youngster often is putting up a good but losing fight against great odds. T.C. Gibbons, the British psychiatrist, in an official report to the United Nations, dared to raise the question, "Is juvenile delinquency necessary?" Even if it were possible to eliminate juvenile delinquency, we must face the question, "Is it desirable to do so?"

> There is much to indicate that delinquency, is a disorder with a comparatively good prognosis and may represent a valuable safety valve...
> From the wider aspect of mental health, it is arguable whether the elimination of delinquency in the present state of society would not generator more interactable disorders... Where the mental hospital population is large, the prison population is small and vice versa.[4]

The alternative to juvenile delinquency may be too awesome to contemplate. However, with the lessons that can be learned from the lives of juvenile delinquents, society can do much toake the community a safer place in which to grow to maturity.

IN SUMMARY

Two major myths concerning delinquency prevention pemeate the American scene—first, that "nothing can be done about it," and second, that "somewhere there is a neat and simple cure for the problem. "The average citizen frequently finds himslef floundering between the two extremes. However, if legislation, financial support, and law enforcement are surrounded and supported by the conditions outlined in this paper, we may have the best prognosis for reducing the steadily increasing rates of serious norm violations among the nation's youth.

[4] T.C. Gibbens, *Trends in Juvenile Delinquency*, Public Health Paper No. 5 (Geneva: World Health Organization, 1961), p. 21.

ARTICLE 38

The Prevention
of Juvenile Delinquency

VIRGINIA M. BURNS AND
LEONARD W. STERN*

INTRODUCTION

Any study of the prevention of crime and delinquency faces a dilemma of scope. The grave problems it is addressing are associated, to a large degree, with conditions producing other social problems. Thus strategies aimed at intervention must converge

* The authors wish to acknowledge the editorial assistance of Eleanor Rubin Charwat.

Source: Virginia M. Burns and Leonard W. Stern: Excerpted from *Task Force Report: Juvenile Delinquency and Youth Crime.* Washington, D.C.: U.S. Government Printing Office, 1967:353-355; 361-362. Reprinted by permission.

Virginia M. Burns, A.B., 1946. M.S.S.S., 1951, Boston University, Miss. Burns is Special Assistant to the Assistant Secretary for Individual and Family Services of the United States Department of Health Education and Welfare. When this report was written, she was Chief of the Training Section of the Office of Juvenile Delinquency and Youth Development in HEW; before that she was a training specialist with the Children's Bureau, also in HEW. Among her other previous positions are Associate Executive Secretary of the Group Work Council, a Community planning agency in the Cleveland Welfare Administration; group work consultant; and instructor in social work. Her published articles include "The Practice of Social Group Work With Handicapped and Disturbed Children in a Summer Camp" (with Ralph Kolodny); "Problems of Adolescent Girls"; and "Contributions of the Federal Delinquency Program to Training Manpower for Juvenile Delinquency Programs."

Leonard W. Stern, A.B.: 1951, Temple University; M.S.W., 1953, University of Pennsylvania. Mr. Stern is Deputy Assistant Director for Program Development and Evaluation in the Model Cities Administration of the United States Department of Housing and Urban Development. At the time, he collaborated in this report, he was Chief of Demonstration Programs for the Office of Juvenile Delinquency and Youth Development in the United States Department of Health, Education, and Welfare. He came to the office of Juvenile Delinquency from Philadelphia, where he was Chief of Community Services for the Division of Youth Conservation Services in the Department of Public Welfare.

with other programs directed at related problems. The dilemma is complicated by the fact that delinquency prevention touches all young people living among others in a free society, including those who may not have committed any delinquent act, or those who may not have been lawfully adjudicated in a manner which warrants official intrusion into their lives on the basis of their delinquency

Limitations and Preventions

It might be best, therefore, to note briefly at the outset of this discussion, a number of questions and considerations which should guide and caution us as we establish the proper parameters of delinquency prevention efforts:

- Which young people are appropriate subjects for preventive efforts? While certain illegal acts can clearly help to identify those for whom treatment, rehabilitation, correction, or control is proper, the means for identifying those in need of preventive services are not so precise. Attempts to develop techniques to identify potential delinquents predict only the probability of delinquency; a number of those identified as potentially delinquent do not fulfill the prediction.

Since our ability to predict delinquent careers for specific individuals is imperfect, we must exercise caution on two levels. First, resources should not be wasted on self-fulfilling phrophecies of success by developing "delinquency prevention" programs for those who, in all likelihood, would not have become delinquent anyway. Second, and perhaps more important the nonadjudicated individual's civil liberties and right to due process should be protected from trespass, even if the motivation for intervention is to help him and protect him from delinquency. The need for caution is this area is extended by the potentially invidious effects of labeling an individual as a possible delinquent.

The proper balance between individual rights and the protection of society is always a legitimate concern in matters of law enforcement and correction: in prevention programs, where a crime or delinquency may not have been established, even greater care is required.

- Knowledge and practice in the field of delinquency prevention are not as fully developed as we should like. In addition to our inability to know with much certainty which individual is likely to become delinquent and which is not, there is little in the way of research or evaluation to back claims of success for any programs designed specifically to prevent delinquency.

- While there is a paucity of supportive evidence for the effectiveness of programs which have been implemented, there is no shortage of those who claim to have the solution. The abundance of proposed solutions reflects the depth of the national concern; from it can emerge fresh new ideas, for no profession or group has a monopoly on potentially useful approaches.

But the conventional wisdom also perpetuates mythology and exaggerated confidence in simple approaches: exhortation and moralizing; censorship of television and literature; recreation to keep youth off the streets; harsh sanctions to set examples for others; counseling the family. And community agencies sometimes out of conviction and sometimes in exploitation of public concern, find it easier to obtain financial support for youth programs if they purport to prevent delinquency.

It is important to break the barriers of vested interest so that ineffective programs in delinquency prevention, even those with long tradition and powerful support, give way to approaches holding greater promise. Many of these may continue to warrant support as legitimate youth programs, but they should not promise something they cannot deliver.

• The line between acceptable deviance from preferred behavior and intolerable, dangerous delinquency is not always easy to find, and it shifts with changing times. While some forms of delinquency are always properly the subject for official concern, a certain amount of deviance which we call delinquency is a necessary concomitant of a free society. For we cannot value individualism, initiative, imagination and nonconformity without expecting some of it to be manifested in ways which we do not like. And some special understanding is required when those without opportunity to implement those qualities, through legitimate channels open to others, choose alternate means available to them.

Particularly with youth, it is important to use discretion in determining the difference between behavior which is dangerous enough to require action and that which is not harmful, even though it may be different from the norm which adults hold for youth. Such behavior can be stifled only at the expense of creativity, liberty, and individual initiative. Delinquency prevention cannot be a cover for the undue enforcement of conformity.

• It is sometimes difficult to distinguish among the desire to punish offenders, the need to protect society and the wish to rehabilitate or correct those who violate the law. Unfortunately, this motivation to punish is sometimes operative in situations where it is not clear that a crime has been committed. While punishment may be a legitimate response to illegal activity, it should not be allowed to creep into programs aimed at keeping the nondelinquent out of trouble.

We must guard then, against overzealousness in our efforts to prevent crime and delinquency, setting realistic limits on the extent to which we seek out and intervene in the lives of potential delinquents. Probably we should begin with the assumption that it is impossible to have a crime-free America. This will enable us to set goals which are possible to attain, and seek preventive measures which are consistent with our national ideals.

The Need For Preventive Efforts

In spite of these limitations and cautions, the Nation cannot afford the cynical luxury of focusing only upon controlling crime and correcting offenders. A humanitarian and productive nation concerned with the well-being of its members must vigorously address those factors which produce delinquency in an effort to reduce its occurrence.

In 20th century America, it is part of our national style to prevent as well as to correct, as is evident when we look at other problems which jeopardize the health and well-being of our population. In areas of physical environmental and mental health, human safety and the protection of property, we are committed to prevention. Certainly our effort should not be less in the field of crime. The arguments for a maximum effort to prevent delinquency among young people are overwhelming:

• The evidence suggests that, in terms of cost effectiveness alone, corrective measures are highly expensive. The average cost of maintaining a youngster in a public training school is $3,020 per year[1]. In private institutions for delinquents, costs are considerably higher. In California, it is estimated that an average combined juvenile and adult criminal career costs the governmental system $10,000. By 1975 this State is expected to spend almost $900 million per year on its police functions, adjudication functions, probation, incarceration, and parole functions directly related to crime and delinquency. This does not include the costs of crime itself measured in "value of property" lost or destroyed, or intangible emotional or psychological losses.[2]

• Further, much of the money spent for such correctional programs seems ineffective. Recidivism among young people who have been institutionalized is exceedingly high; considerable numbers of young people placed on probation commit further offenses. And few programs have been evaluated to determine whether it was the corrective service which was responsible in the case of the nonrepeater, or whether the youngster might not have avoided further delinquency, even without the corrective or rehabilitative service. In the face of such meager success, it seems appropriate to prevent young people from those beginning encounters with police and courts which frequently herald the beginning of delinquent and criminal careers, rather than the end.

• In addition to the actual cost of apprehending, adjudicating, and rehabilitating juveniles, there are other costs to the Nation in terms of wasted human resources when lives become enmeshed in delinquent careers. The earning power and contribution to the economy of persons who enter our process of juvenile and criminal justice and corrections is considerably reduced.

• It is clear that the delinquent or criminal label, even if the individual does not continue in delinquent paths, imposes upon him a stigma which is difficult to erase, and blocks him from access to the full resources of society. Consequently, every effort should be made to prevent marking young people with this indelible stamp.

• The case for the early implementation of improved preventive programs, whether they are treatment-oriented or part of the general upgrading of basic education, services, opportunities and living conditions, is bolstered by our psychological insights into the importance of the earlier years as a period when personalities and behavior patterns are more likely to be affected than in the later years when they are more firmly fixed.

[1] "Statistics on Public Institutions for Delinquent Children: 1964." U.S. Dept. HEW, Welfare Administration, Children's Bureau, 1965.
[2] "Prevention and Control of Crime and Delinquency," prepared for youth and adult corrections agency, State of California, by Space-General Corp., July 29, 1965.

• A disproportionate amount of illegal activity occurs in later adolescence and early adulthood. The "Uniform Crime Reports for 1964" noted that nearly one-fifth of all persons arrested by police in that year were between 16 and 21. The youth population of the Nation is growing proportionately and will continue to increase. The 1960 census indicated that 30 million people, or 16.8 percent of the population, were between the ages of 10 and 19. By 1975, young people within this age range are expected to number 42 million or 18,1 percent of the population. It seems clear that, even without an increase in the rates, we can predict a larger amount of delinquency and crime, unless something is done to impede its rise.

• Preventive programs are frequently similar to those required to correct other social imbalances. Successful prevention programs, many of which will not be specifically against crime, will have multiple payoffs, providing visible benefits in other areas as well. Not only will they reduce the cost of correctional and rehabilitative programs; they will equip individuals for more effective social and economic performance and they will upgrade the capacity of many of our Nation's most significant institutions to deliver a share in the Great Society to all young people.

Even though we have relatively little concrete evidence to substantiate the effectiveness of particular preventive approaches, we are not without knowledge. More research and more effective evaluation may be necessary, but action need not await the findings of such studies. The insights we now have into individual behavior, the culture of youth, the nature of delinquent patterns, and the functioning of community institutions can be utilized as a basis for action which holds promise for the prevention of a significant portion of delinquency. . . .

A NATIONAL PROGRAM OF YOUTH DEVELOPMENT AND DELINQUENCY PREVENTION: GENERAL STRATEGIES

From the web of interconnected factors which shape youthful behavior, two major themes appear again and again to guide national efforts to prevent delinquency. They are: (a) The need to involve young people with greater meaning, respect, and responsibility in those affairs of society which affect them, and (b) the need for our institutions to produce better education, strengthen family life, improve opportunities for employment, and make the activities of law enforcement and individual and social services more relevant and more accessible to those who need them most.

It becomes apparent that the multifaceted problem of delinquency will not be prevented through small or simple programs. What we need is a comprehensive effort to make changes in the system which produces juvenile delinquency and other forms of antisocial behavior. If this suggests that delivering the fruits of the Great Society to all with equal opportunity is indispensable for the reduction of delinquency, then let us accept that fact.

One cannot isolate the treatment and prevention of a social problem which has its roots in the conditions and other problems of society. Thus a variety of programs are important to the prevention of delinquency.

The increasing urbanization and the disproportionate share of crime and delinquency in crowded innercity areas where delinquency exists side by side with problems of poverty, inferior education, poor housing, bad health, and high unemployment, suggests that the Nation's effort to eliminate poverty, rebuild the slums, and achieve maximum employment are all crucial as a base for efforts to decrease crime. The heavier crime rate among minority groups crowded into the innercities and facing the deprivations of these areas emphasizes the importance of efforts to wipe out discrimination. While we are not content to make general recommendations about sweeping reforms in the living conditions of our society—we believe such reforms are not only essential to the prevention of crime and delinquency, but can be justified in their own right—neither can we, in good conscience, recommend only narrower programs of enforcement, control, and reform which focus on those who are already treading delinquent paths. It would be foolhardy to tout such a program as truly preventive.

In actuality, what is required is more than a program of delinquency prevention, for such a program parades under a banner with a negative slogan. America's goal for it's youth should extend beyond stopping antisocial activities, and its programs for youth should not require the justification of predicted delinquency.

We, therefore, recommend a national youth development program which subsumes the goal of delinquency prevention, and aims to fulfill the maximum potential of young people for productive participation in society and for lives of self-actualization. Such an effort will seek increased commitment on the part of youth to a society which they can perceive as responsive, relevant, and just; a society in which meaningful opportunities are available to them: a society in which they have a significant share and stake.

Such a proposal returns us to the dilemma of scope with which we began. How can a national youth development program maintain the broad vision mandated by necessity and implied in its title, while remaining practical, feasible, and goal-directed?

Such a program must reflect our insights into the personalities and subculture of youth. It must set some priorities so that its strategies for intervention are directed at the areas most likely to have impact on the most vulnerable youth. It must be flexible enough to encompass divergent strategies. In relatively affluent and stable areas, for example, approaches to individual psychological factors may be more important, though such approaches would be insufficient where social disorganization abounds.

Problems of individuals and their interpersonal relationships must be addressed, to be sure, but a national effort must hold promise to affect, large numbers of potentially delinquent youth; it cannot be dependent upon a case-by-case approach, particularly when our ability to detect those cases needing preventive services is so underdeveloped. And to focus upon individuals and groups alone can lead one down a never-ending path of offering preventive services to person after person, while an increasing number of potential delinquents is propelled by society into the waiting line.

Since the individual's aspirations, directions, and achievements are profoundly influenced by the choices provided by the institutions in his community, major emphasis on institutional changes is probably the best and most lasting way of preventing large numbers of youth from entering delinquent careers. . .

ARTICLE 39

Juvenile Delinquency
Can Social Science Find a Cure?

DON C. GIBBONS

*In the first half of this century, criminologists voiced a good deal of op-
timism regarding the search for the causes of crime and delinquency.
Further, they exhibited a good deal of enthusiasm for correctional
intervention based upon scientific knowledge. However, although
criminological knowledge has grown impressively in the past two or
three decades, criminologists have produced many specific findings
and conditional propositions but few unequivocal scientific generalizations. In addition, pessimism about treatment has replaced optimism,
following the discovery that "nothing works." This article takes stock
of the current state of affairs and offers suggestions regarding directions to be pursued.*

THE TASK BEFORE ME in presenting this address is not an easy one. The problem at which
I hint is that theorizing and research activities by American criminologists on the
causes of youthful misbehavior or on its cure or prevention have been confined almost
entirely to American delinquency.[1] Accordingly, the question might be asked: What
can American criminology contribute to the understanding or treatment of delinquency in other countries? More specifically, do American criminologists have
anything to say that might be useful in the Asian-Pacific region of the world?

This article is a revised version of the keynote speech delivered at the Fourth Asian-Pacific
Conference on Juvenile Delinquency, Tokyo, Japan, November 12, 1985. I would like to thank Joseph F.
Jones, Peter Garabedian, and Barry Krisberg for constructive comments on an earlier version of this article.
Source: Gibbons, Don C. "Juvenile Delinquency: Can Social Science Find a Cure?" *Crime and
Delinquency* Vol. 32 (April) 1986: 186-204. Reprinted by permission of Sage Publications, Inc.

I believe that participants in an Asian-Pacific conference can benefit from an examination of American experiences regarding delinquency and attempts to understand and/or control it. Accordingly, I want to comment upon the implications of American social scientific accomplishments in the study of delinquency. But let me hasten to add that many of these remarks have to do more with the limitations of existing knowledge than with a celebration of the discoveries from criminological inquiry.

THE RISE OF MODERN CRIMINOLOGY

When did scientific criminology arise? What are the major directions criminological inquiry on the causes and control of crime and delinquency have taken over the past decades? How much has been learned about the etiology and treatment of lawbreaking? How much remains to be probed by scientific investigation? These are large questions; a full answer to each would require much more time than I have available in this brief address. Regarding the origins of American criminology, suffice it to say that they can be traced to the writings of Parmelee, Gillin, Sutherland, and a few other pioneering figures in the early 1900s (Gibbons, 1979). Juvenile delinquency received a good deal of attention from sociologists Clifford Shaw, Henry D. McKay, and a few other investigators in the 1930s and 1940s, but it was not until after World War II that research and theorizing on juvenile delinquency became a "growth industry."

The two decades following World War II saw the dramatic expansion of the discipline of sociology. Much optimism was voiced, both about the prospects for scientific sociology generally and for one of its subfields, criminology, more specifically. Most persons educated in this period assumed that once we harnessed the powerful tools of science in the service of social inquiry, we would quickly discover the major causes of lawbreaking and find effective cures for misbehavior and lawbreaking.

One can point to a number of other developments during the 1950s and 1960s, such as the invention of self-report techniques for studying delinquency. Additionally, this period was one in which much optimism for correctional intervention was voiced by criminologists. Many took it as an article of faith that correctional treatment was both desirable and capable of achievement. This faith in the efficacy of treatment seemed to be supported by the results of experiments such as the Highfields project in New Jersey, various experimental treatment ventures conducted by the California Youth Authority, and kindred evidence. My book, *Changing the Lawbreaker* (Gibbons, 1965), was a case in point from this period in which the "rehabilitative ideal" held the allegiance of most American criminologists. That book put forth a detailed version of the "differential treatment" or "different strokes for different folks" argument, in which forms of treatment specific to different offender types were identified.

Criminology has continued to flourish in the United States, as indicated by the growth of organizations such as the American Society of Criminology, which currently has over 1,000 members. It seems fair to say that criminological knowledge has advanced by rather giant strides in the past two or three decades. But on the other hand, criminologists have also come to see that the real world is markedly more complex than they supposed it to be in the 1940s and 1950s. Scientific efforts have not produced unequivocal propositions about the causes of delinquency or about its treatment; rather, we have discovered that few bold and unconditional assertions are warranted from the data at hand. In short, criminologists have become less sanguine and more guarded about the scientific potential of criminological knowledge.

TAKING STOCK OF CRIMINOLOGICAL KNOWLEDGE

Let me begin with some observations on the current state of knowledge regarding the etiology of criminality or delinquency, drawn out of a perusal of textbook contents. Consider first the case of Sutherland's *Criminology*, first published in 1924 and now in its tenth edition, coauthored with Donald Cressey (1978). It is clear from a quick glance at these different editions that criminological theory has grown markedly in sociological sophistication and that the stockpile of research findings has increased at an exponential rate. The same claim can be made about the contents of my general criminology text, first published in 1968, and due to appear in a fifth edition next year, for they also demonstrate the growing explanatory prowess of criminology. Finally, much the same argument can be made regarding delinquency textbooks. My delinquency book first appeared in 1970, with the fourth edition having just been published (Gibbons and Krohn, 1986). The successive editions of it indicate that much has been learned about youthful lawbreaking during the past 15 or 20 years.

However, these remarks about the growth of criminological wisdom need to be qualified. It is unfortunately true that some of our most notable accomplishments in recent decades have involved disconfirmation of hypotheses about lawbreaking and lawbreakers. For example, research findings from the 1960s and 1970s have indicated that most of the claims that were made about gang delinquency by Cohen, Miller, and Cloward and Ohlin are incorrect. Along the same line, we now have a large body of evidence that indicates that the vast majority of juvenile offenders are persons who are free from psychological disturbances, psychiatric opinion notwithstanding, but we are less clear on the question of whether more benign psychological differences contribute to youthful lawbreaking.

I do not mean to suggest that criminological progress has been restricted solely to the accumulation of data that demonstrate that various hypotheses and theories are without foundation in fact. To the contrary, current textbooks and other repositories of knowledge reveal that much has been discovered about factors that play a causal role in lawbreaking. At the same time, these collections of criminological wisdom indicate that our knowledge is incomplete, conditional, and also that many of the tentative conclusions reached by some investigators have been challenged by others. Then, too, ours is a kind of "black box" situation in that although we have identified some of the important factors or influences that are implicated in lawbreaking, there clearly are a host of other causal variables that remain undiscovered and unidentified. Consider the case of predatory crime. The evidence at hand seems to indicate that, in the United States at least, variations in income inequality across American cities have some causal connection to observed levels of predatory criminality. At the same time, this relationship is a relatively weak one that is apparently conditioned by a number of other variables that have yet to be specified. To put the matter in the language of the statistically inclined, the etiological variables that we have uncovered to date separately and jointly explain only a modest portion of the variance in delinquency/ nondelinquency.

Let me draw attention to an important recent example that illustrates the limits of criminological science, namely, James Q. Wilson and Richard J. Herrnstein's (1985) *Crime and Human Nature*. This book, authored by two prominent Harvard University scholars, is filled with myriad "facts" about criminality, along with proposals for public policies toward the control of crime. It seems destined to be one of the most influential works on crime and delinquency produced in the 1980s.

Opinions are likely to be divided about this book. On the one hand, its dust jacket contains a number of highly laudatory remarks by other criminological scholars and it has already received very positive reviews in the mass media. On the other hand, some might question the chutzpah or audacity of the authors in their choice of a title for this tome, given that most of the evidence they have examined has to do with criminality in the United States rather than among humans everywhere in the world. Additionally, although Wilson and Herrnstein repeatedly claimed that their intent was to articulate a theory of crime and to review the evidence supporting that theory, they also deliberately restricted their attention to "predatory street crime" and to individuals who engage in "aggressive, violent, or larcenous behavior" or who "hit, rape, murder, steal, or threaten" (Wilson and Herrnstein, 1985:22). Almost entirely missing from their analysis are persons who engage in white-collar crime, mundane lawbreaking, or a number of other varieties of criminality.

Although Wilson and Herrnstein are free to focus their attention on one segment of the crime problem to the exclusion of other portions, they were not justified in redefining the scope of criminology in such a way that large numbers of real-life lawbreakers disappear from criminological scrutiny. Crime is what the criminal law says it is, not what Wilson and Herrnstein chose to single out for attention. Stated another way, Wilson and Herrnstein have engaged in product mislabeling, for their book and their theory did not address crime in its many forms. It was silent on the question of whether their theory applies to patterns of criminality additional to assaults, homicides, rapes, and larcenous acts, but it seems unlikely that Wilson and Herrnstein would contend that physicians who have been involved in Medicare fraud, pharmaceutical manufacturers who have engaged in violation of Food and Drug Administration statutes, and other criminals of that ilk can be accounted for by the theory they set forth in their book.

Leaving aside these larger conceptual issues regarding the Wilson and Herrnstein volume, what can be said about the causal generalizations about predatory street criminals that they have drawn out of the research literature? How convincing is their theory of crime and human nature? Reduced to barest details, their argument is that these persons are uncommonly mesomorphic in bodily build, they exhibit low normal or borderline intelligence, and display atypical personality patterns in the direction of psychopathy, all of which are indicators to Wilson and Herrnstein of constitution factors in criminality. Further, offenders are from homes characterized by defect' "under the roof culture" and are persons who in later life perform poorly in school and in the world of work.

These authors are not entirely wrongheaded. Indeed, their contention that the last word has not been heard on the question of constitutional and biological factors in crime is a point with which many criminologists would concur. Also, I agree that individual psychological differences probably do play a part in lawbreaking and in lawabiding conduct. At the same time, I am less persuaded by the evidence they cite from two studies and research on adopted children; moreover, it is likely that a considerable number of other criminologists will also cavil with their conclusions about constitutional factors, based on this evidence. Along the same line, my reading of the literature on psychopathy and on other alleged indicators of personality problems among offenders has led me to conclusions different from those of Wilson and Herrnstein. For example, they noted with favor the Interpersonal Maturity levels theory of Marguerite Q. Warren (1976) involving a scale of delinquent types and detailed recommendations for differential treatment of juvenile offenders that are related to these types. Although this differential treatment "model" provided the guiding theory behind the Community Treatment Project in California and has also been adopted for use in at least one jurisdiction in Australia as well as a number of places in the United States, a number of criminologists have raised questions both about the claims made about juvenile offenders and about the treatment recommendations for them (Beker and Heyman, 1972; Gibbons, 1970).

Another quarrel with Wilson and Herrnstein that many will share concerns their conclusions about the role of schools in the genesis of delinquency as well as the part played by unemployment in both juvenile and adult crime. I do not have time here to develop a full critique of this book, but enough has been said to indicate that considerably less than complete criminological consensus exists regarding the "facts" that these authors discussed.

What accounts for these disagreements between Wilson and Herrnstein and other criminologists regarding the causes of crime? The answer is that although marked growth has occurred in criminology in recent decades, it is still an infant science attempting to grapple with the details of a complicated collection of social phenomena that are caused by a multitude of factors or variables that are intertwined in a number of complex ways. The research studies that have been carried out to date are too few in number, conducted in too few places, and many of them are plagued with methodological deficiencies, all of which results in equivocal findings.

Let me add a few more remarks about the causes of delinquency, before moving on to some observations about treatment or prevention of juvenile lawbreaking.[2] First, it seems doubtful that any single explanatory or causal statement, however complex, accounting for delinquency, can be drawn out of the research evidence. "Delinquency," in American studies, is not a uniformly defined phenomenon that has been investigated by different researchers. One fact that has not always been acknowledged by those who speak of delinquency is that this topic has been "trivialized" by sociologists over the past several decades. Where delinquency once referred, in the work of Shaw and McKay and others, to inner-city neighborhood gangs and delinquent groups who were involved in persistent and serious acts of lawbreaking, more recent investigators, using self-report techniques, have often identified as delinquent, youngsters who have confessed to involvement in one or another relatively innocuous or petty act of misconduct within the past year or so. But it seems doubtful that the Philadelphia youths who appear as delinquents in the cohort studies of Wolfgang et al. (1972) are closely similar to the "delinquents" who turn up in the pages of Hirschi's (1969) study in Richmond, California, or in other self-report investigations.

The picture of fuzzy criminological knowledge I have drawn about adult criminality applies to delinquency as well; that is, causal generalizations about juvenile lawbreaking cannot be stated in precise or equivocal terms, nor is there much reason to suppose that all criminologists would be in agreement even on those conditional propositions that can be stated from the research evidence. Consider the 50-odd "propositions" that appear in *Delinquent Behavior*. Among these claims are the following three (Gibbons and Krohn, 1986: 274):

• Strain, as measured by perceptions that occupational and other long-term opportunities are limited, does not appear to be an important factor in producing delinquent conduct. However, the perception of limited opportunities relative to the more immediate concerns of adolescents is related to delinquent behavior.

• Although social bond and its constituent elements are related to the probability of delinquent behavior, other factors must also be taken into account to explain delinquent conduct adequately. For one, those youths who show low levels of social bond are also more likely to associate with others who have committed delinquent acts. In turn, association with delinquent others is strongly related to delinquent behavior, with the result that elements of the social bond are related both directly and indirectly to delinquent behavior.

• Overly aggressive offenders are the product of situations of parental rejection, with the most severe forms of aggression stemming from conditions of early and marked rejection and milder patterns from less marked instances of parental rejection.

The last of these propositions has been drawn out of a large quantity of research evidence; hence there is relatively little disagreement among criminologists about its accuracy. Further, we know a good bit about treatment programs that might be employed in order to reduce "unsocialized aggression" on the part of children and youths. Unfortunately, however, this knowledge does not apply to many delinquents, for the majority of them do not fit the category of overly aggressive child.

The first claim in the preceding list will be recognized as a revised version of theories such as those associated with Cohen and Cloward and Ohlin; however, there is more emphasis upon the discrepancies perceived by youths between their aspirations for good marks in school and the like and their relatively immediate expectations that they are not going to get these good grades, than on expectations that the goals they project for themselves in adulthood are going to be frustrated. The second proposition combines social bonding or control theory, particularly that version created by Hirschi, and hypotheses about the added impact of delinquent associates upon juveniles.

As with the generalization about aggression, there is some research support for the two contentions that, taken together, claim that "strain," control, and association patterns all contribute in some degree to delinquent conduct. However, these relati ships have not yet been so clearly documented that broad consensus exists among criminologists concerning these claims. On the one hand, Hirschi (1979) has argued that little or no explanatory power is gained by attempts to merge variables from other theoretical perspectives such as the learning or strain ones with bond theory. On the other hand, a number of studies, the most recent and impressive of which is by Elliott et al. (1985), seem to show that an integrated theory of this kind is able to account for more of the variance in delinquency and drug use than is bond theory alone.

The causal significance of bond theory has been rendered more muddied by two other studies published in 1985, one by Agnew and the other by Liska and Reed. The first, involving longitudinal data, indicated that bond or control variables only explained about 2% of the variance in delinquency measured at a later point in the lives of the youths studied; the Liska and Reed investigation, involving a non-recursive causal model, reported that involvement in delinquency affected subsequent levels of bonding, as well as the other way around.

RESULTS OF INTERVENTION WITH DELINQUENTS

There is much more that could be included in the commentary upon unsettled issues and unresolved questions in delinquency causation. However, let us move on to examine the status of knowledge regarding efforts to deal with juvenile lawbreaking.

It might be useful to begin with a few brief comments about recent trends in the processing of juvenile offenders in the United States. The National Council on Crime and Delinquency has recently prepared a detailed examination of various kinds of statistical data on delinquency and the processing of youthful lawbreakers, which indicates the following (National Council on Crime and Delinquency, 1984:5):

1. The "at risk" youth population is declining.
2. Juvenile arrests are declining.
3. Juvenile detention populations are increasing.
4. Juvenile training school populations are increasing.
5. In general, fewer youths are entering public facilities but the average length of stay is increasing.
6. Expenditures are increasing.
7. The proportion of incarcerated youth who are Blacks and Hispanics is increasing whereas the White incarcerated youth population is decreasing.

These conclusions, and the statistics behind them, are reflections of a variety of processes and changes going on in the United States, including the following: movement to divert petty offenders and status offenders in particular out of the official machinery; "get tough" policies in some states such as Washington, where a 1977 Juvenile Justice Act mandated the incarceration of serious offenders in training schools; deinstitutionalization programs that have occurred in Massachusetts, Utah, and some other states; and a number of other developments.

What have the results been from programs of deterrence, incapacitation, prevention, treatment, or control of lawbreaking? These are very large questions, each of which could be discussed at great length. The data that are required in order to answer these queries are not entirely adequate, indeed, data that would answer questions about the impact of some of the recent developments to which I have alluded are nonexistent.

Take the matter of correctional treatment. Although there is a large body of evidence indicating that treatment ventures have not usually reduced recidivism or produced other positive results, some persons continue to find some encouraging signs of treatment success in the data (Jenkins, 1985; Palmer, 1971; Shireman et al., 1978). Nonetheless, there are some general propositions and conclusions about these matters that are in order.

First, most of the evidence on the results of deliberate, planned efforts to increase the impact of correctional treatment or other intervention upon offenders has indicated that these have not been successful (Bailey, 1966; Robison and Smith, 1971; Greenberg, 1977b; Sechrest et al, 1979). The mass of existing studies indicate that few of the treatment programs that have been directed at juvenile or adult offenders have achieved more than very modest results, at best.

The record of treatment failures in juvenile corrections is extensive (Lerman, 1968; Gibbons and Krohn, 1986: 223-268). For example, we know that detached worker or street worker programs designed to wean gang members away from lawbreaking were unsuccessful. Similarly, a number of large-scale efforts to revamp community life, increase opportunity structures for delinquents, and the like, including Mobilization for Youth, the Chicago Area Projects, the Mid-City Project, and a work opportunities program in Seattle, all produced mixed results, at best (Schlossman et al., 1984; Miller, 1962; Brager and Purcell, 1967; Hackler, 1966). Then, too, a number of efforts have been made to create therapeutic milieus in correctional institutions, but to no avail (Jesness, 1965). The record of various and sundry counseling-oriented ventures in the juvenile justice system is a dismal one. Finally, most of the evidence on one of the newest approaches, diversion, indicates that (a) many of these programs have had little or no impact upon youths diverted to them, and (b) many of them have resulted in "net widening," which is the opposite of what was intended by the architects of such ventures (Binder and Geis, 1984; Polk, 1984; Decker, 1985; Frazier, 1983).

This kind of bad news continues to come in, as illustrated by a recent report on a controlled experiment in California (Jackson, 1983) involving parole supervision as opposed to outright release of juvenile wards. The results indicated that the dischargees and parolees had similar recidivism rates. However, the offenses committed by the parolees were more serious than those of the dischargees. Also, parolees who recidivated received harsher sentences than did dischargee recidivists.

As an example of frustrated hopes, consider the case of the Community Treatment Project, conducted over a seven-year period by the California Youth Authority (Palmer, 1974; Lerman, 1975). The central hypothesis of that program was that delinquents who normally are shunted off to training schools could be successfully treated in the community if they were first assigned to Interpersonal Maturity Level diagnostic types and then provided with intervention programs geared to th particular needs. This was an elaborate social experiment involving random ass ment of juveniles either to the community program or to conventional institutional commitment, with the community treatment portion of it representing a highly developed version of the "different strokes for different folks" perspective.

The initial results of this experimental program in the form of parole performance and parole violation rates seemed to favor community treatment. However, subsequent analyses by Lerman (1975) of the Youth Authority's own data on the experiment turned up quite different findings. The differential parole performance by the community-treated youths was produced by lenient parole revocation policies on the part of parole officers rather than representing improved parole behavior on the part of the wards. Further, the community-treated youths actually spent more time in custody in juvenile halls than they did in treatment in the community. Finally, because of the small caseloads in the community portion of this experiment, community treatment actually cost more per treated youth than did institutional commitment.

I do not mean to suggest that the evidence is now crystal clear that correctional intervention efforts of one kind or another have all failed to have any impact upon juvenile lawbreaking. Instead, the picture is parallel to the one regarding etiological knowledge presented at the beginning of these remarks. There is some evidence upon which one can draw that seems to suggest that some kinds of treatment or preventive activities may have a payoff. However, these studies are too few in number, as well as often being plagued with methodological problems, to provide the basis for bold and dramatic policy recommendations.

Pursuing this comment a bit further, some criminologists have found some encouragement in the quasi-experimental research study by Murray and Cox (1979), which seemed to indicate that commitment to Illinois state training schools, or alternatively, to a number of other correctional placements outside of institutions, all produced a suppression effect. The youngsters who went through these programs tended to commit fewer delinquent acts in the posttreatment period, even though they did not discontinue lawbreaking entirely. At the same time, some criminologists have found reasons to be somewhat skeptical of the conclusions by Murray and Cox, arguing that desistance from delinquency may have been due to a maturation effect rather than to anything contained in the programs (Lundman, 1984:198-214). In other words, these boys may have passed through the age period of peak incidence of delinquency during the time they were under supervision.

Advocates of treatment can perhaps find some comfort also in a recent experimental group treatment project in St. Louis (Feldman et al., 1983) that focused upon a variety of kinds of "antisocial" juveniles, some of whom were involved in delinquency. The authors of the report on this study indicate that some antisocial youths were assigned to groups composed of other misbehaving youths; others were put in groups of mixed composition, involving both antisocial and nondelinquent boys; and a control group of nondelinquent boys was also involved. Experienced group counselors apparently managed to bring about behavioral changes on the part of the members of their groups, whereas inexperienced counselors did not produce those results. However, this study contained no evidence on the posttreatment delinquent behavior of the subjects.

These gaps and uncertainties in our knowledge about the impact of intervention upon offenders have not prevented some criminologists from offering strong recommendations for public policy. For example, in a recent volume on public policy and the crime-delinquency problem, Hirschi (1983) set out a blueprint that closely parallels American folk advice: "Spare the rod and spoil the child." According to Hirschi (1983:55), a parent-centered strategy of preventing delinquency is called for in which parents must (a) monitor the child's behavior; (2) recognize deviant behavior when it occurs; and (3) punish such behavior. In this same volume, Jackson Toby (1983) articulated a set of policy recommendations for the control of school violence and school-related delinquency, centering around lowering the age of compulsory school attendance to 15 and relaxation of minimum wage laws so that those who drop out (or are pushed out) of school would have a source of employment, albeit at a very low wage. It is perhaps true, as Toby argued, that the school violence problem would be reduced if large numbers of youths were encouraged to leave school and obtain low-paying jobs in fast food restaurants and the like, but what is less clear is whether such policies would increase the army of young adults who are chronically underemployed or unemployed and who make up the disadvantaged part of the split labor market. Further, it is at least plausible that the policies advocated by Toby would eventually exacerbate the problem of predatory street crime in the United States. For reasons of this kind, a number of criminologists would find much to quarrel with in these "hard-nosed" recommendations.

WHERE DO WE GO FROM HERE?

Richard Lundman (1984) has recently provided a detailed critique of a variety of delinquency control ventures, including efforts to identify predelinquents and engage in preventive intervention with them, diversion projects, postadjudication treatment programs, deterrence-oriented ventures, community treatment efforts, and institutionalization of offenders. His policy recommendations, drawn out of that review and critique, are as follows (Lundman, 1984:221-238):

1. It is recommended that traditional delinquency prevention efforts be abandoned.
2. It is recommended that diversion be the first response of the juvenile justice system to status and minor offenders.
3. It is recommended that routine probation be retained as the first and most frequent sentencing option of juvenile court judges.
4. It is recommended that efforts to scare juveniles straight be abandoned.
5. It is recommended that community treatment programs be expanded to accommodate nearly all chronic offenders.
6. It is recommended that institutionalization continue to be used as a last resort reserved primarily for chronic offenders adjudicated delinquent for index crimes against persons.

The accumulated evidence about delinquency that fills the pages of delinquency textbooks, as well as the more specific material considered by Lundman in his book provides considerable underlying support for these broad recommendations. F example, although research has often failed to discover evidence that community treatment ventures are markedly more effective than institutionalization of offenders, the other side of the coin is that the former have generally been shown to be at least as effective as incarceration and at considerably less cost. Accordingly, the recommendation to establish programs such as the National Institute of Justice-sponsored "New Pride" venture (Regnery, 1985) makes a good deal of sense. Project New Pride is a nonresidential, community-based program for juvenile offenders that provides a blend of counseling, alternative schooling, correction of learning disabilities, vocational training, job placement, recreation, and cultural activities.

In my opinion, the most significant recent attempt to rescue rehabilitation and intervention of delinquents is the small book, *One More Chance*, by Greenwood and Zimring (1985). Greenwood and Zimring began with the reasonable argument that those surveys of treatment evaluation studies that have concluded that "nothing works" have failed to look for differences in impact within intervention program types—such as milieu treatment or group counseling. Perhaps some specific efforts have worked while others have been unsuccessful, depending upon whether they were headed by a charismatic, vigorous director and staffed by dedicated workers or contained other positive program elements.

Greenwood and Zimring constructed an eclectic picture of delinquency causation and argued that we need multifaceted treatment approaches that will address these varied causal factors. They then went on to examine a number of specific programs that seem, more on the basis of educated guesswork than hard evidence, to hold particular promise. Certain of these are addressed to chronic or serious offenders and include a number of efforts that are operated by private organizations rather than local or state governments. Other promising intervention efforts were identified for predelinquents or less serious lawbreakers, including programs that strive to teach parenting skills to offenders' parents, intensified schooling programs, and the like.

I am not entirely persuaded by all of the arguments made by Greenwood and Zimring. For example, privately operated programs are difficult to monitor and have sometimes subjected delinquents to highly questionable experiences carried out in the name of treatment. This small volume should not be viewed as a collection of firmly based recipes for treatment of juveniles, nor did the authors make such a claim for it. But there is much food for thought in it for those who are concerned about treatment of offenders.

CONCLUDING REMARKS

It should be apparent that the thesis of this essay is not that the search for causes and cures for delinquency should be abandoned because current evidence on these matters is incomplete, controversial, or unclear. To begin with, it would be incorrect to describe our current situation as one of criminological nihilism, in which each person's assertions about causal factors or effective intervention policies carry equal weight. Rather, the evidence at hand is sufficient to demonstrate that some criminological claims are in error whereas others are buttressed by some measure of empirical support. For example, the weight of the evidence is clearly not consistent with Samenow's (1984) contentions about an alleged "criminal personality." In short, Samenow is simply wrong. Contrariwise, there is considerable research support that indicates that social control or social bond variables play some role in delinquency, even though the precise extent to which they do so is not entirely clear. In much the same way, it can be argued that some intervention tactics have been shown to be ineffective whereas research evidence suggests that some other programs hold considerable more promise.

However, we need to refrain from naive scientism. Criminologists should not promise more than can be delivered and policymakers should not look to criminologists for panaceas or other miracle cures for delinquency.

We have little choice but to pursue our efforts to learn more about delinquency through the methods of science and to inform our intervention efforts with the available knowledge. In the years ahead, those who labor at prevention or treatment will need to continue to look to social scientists for guidance on the causes or control of delinquency, while in turn, academically based theorists and researchers ought to redouble their efforts to improve upon the knowledge base employed by justice system workers. Steady, incremental progress in the way of more effective tactics of coping with delinquency will result, it is hoped, as we go about developing intervention programs based on criminological knowledge and conducting careful research evaluations of these programs. But it seems unlikely that we will move ahead by great leaps forward, rather, our progress is likely to be measured in small but significant steps.

NOTES

1. In the dozen or so delinquency textbooks currently in print, the phenomena they discuss concern almost entirely youthful misconduct in the United States. My own text (Gibbons and Krohn, 1986) is the only one of these books with an entire chapter given over to an examination of juvenile misconduct around the world. Even so, that chapter is relatively limited in that most of it is devoted to delinquency in England and some other western European countries. A few studies of delinquency in Russia, Argentina, and Taiwan are also mentioned, along with some remarks about juvenile lawbreaking in Ghana, Nigeria, Iraq, and India.

2. This discussion is restricted to mainstream delinquency theories and research, along with treatment and intervention proposals that flow out of that work. Radical-Marxist theorizing has not been included here. Some of the important radical writings are by Greenberg (1977a), Colvin and Pauly (1983), and Schwendinger and Schwendinger (1979). Those essays locate the main sources of delinquency in structural flaws in the social and economic order of capitalist societies. Prescriptions for the control and amelioration of delinquency have not usually been offered by radical-Marxist theorists, except for the implicit proposal that massive alterations that would create social and economic opportunities for youths are required in the structure of capitalist societies. However, the Schwendingers have articulated a number of recommendations for dealing with delinquency in the United States; most of these, however, seem little different from various liberal proposals, some of which have been noted in this article. Their policy recommendations are considerably less radical than is their analysis of the sources delinquency.

REFERENCES

Agnew, R. (1985). "Social control theory and delinquency: a longitudinal test." *Criminology* 23 (February): 47-61.

Bailey, W.C. (1966). "An evaluation of 100 studies of correctional outcome." J. of Criminal Law, *Criminology, and Police Sci.* (June): 153-160.

Beker, J. and D.S. Heyman (1972). "A critical appraisal of the California differential treatment typology of adolescent offenders." *Criminology* (May): 3-59.

Binder, A. and G. Geis (1984). "*Ad populum* argumentation in criminology: juvenile diversion as rhetoric." *Crime & Delinquency* (October): 624-647.

Brager, G.A. and F.P. Purcell (eds.) (1967). Community Action Against Poverty, New Haven, CT: *College and Universities Press.*

Colvin, M. and J. Pauly (1983). "A critique of criminology: toward an integrated structural-Marxist theory of delinquency production." *Amer. J. of Sociology* 89 (November): 513-551.

Decker, S.H. (1985). "A systematic analysis of diversion: net widening and beyond." *J. of Criminal Justice* 3: 207-216.

Elliott, D.S., D. Huizinga, and S.S. Ageton (1985). Explaining Delinquency and Drug Use. Beverly Hills, CA: *Sage.*

Feldman, R.A., T.E. Caplinger, and J.S. Wodarski (1983). The St. Louis Conundrum. Englewood Cliffs, NJ: *Prentice-Hall.*

Frazier, C.E. (1983). "Evaluation of youth services programs: problems and prospects from a case study." *Youth & Society* (March): 335-362.

Gibbons, D.C. (1965). Changing the Lawbreaker. Englewood Cliffs, NJ: *Prentice-Hall.*
——— (1968). Society, Crime, and Criminal Careers. Englewood Cliffs, NJ: *Prentice-Hall.*
——— (1970). "Differential treatment of delinquents and interpersonal maturity levels theory: a critique." Social Service Rev. 44 (March): 22-33.
——— (1979). The Criminological Enterprise. Englewood Cliffs, NJ: *Prentice-Hall.*

Gibbons, D.C. and M.D. Krohn (1986). Delinquent Behavior. Englewood Cliffs, MJ: *Prentice-Hall.*

Greenberg, D.F. (1977a). "Delinquency and the age structure of society." *Contemporary Crises* 1 (April): 189-224.
——— (1977b). "The correctional effects of corrections," pp. 111-138 in D.F. Greenberg (ed.) Corrections and Punishment. Beverly Hills, CA: *Sage.*

Greenwood, P.W. and F.E. Zimring (1985). One More Chance. Santa Monica, CA: *Rand.*

Hackler, J.C. (1966). "Boys, blisters, and behavior: the impact of a work program in an urban central area." J. of Research in Crime and Delinquency 3 (July): 155-164.

Hirschi, T. (1969). Causes of Delinquency. Berkeley: Univ. of California Press.
——— (1979). "Separate and unequal is better." J. of Research in Crime and Delinquency 16: 34-38.
——— (1983). "Crime and the family," pp. 53-68 in J.Q. Wilson (ed.) Crime and Public Policy. San Francisco: Institute for Contemporary Studies.

Jackson, P.G. (1983). The Paradox of Control. New York: Praeger.

Jenkins, R.L. (1985). No Single Cause. College Park, MD: American Correctional Association.

Jesness, C.V. (1965). The Fricot Ranch Study. Sacramento: Department of the Youth Authority.

Lerman, P. (1968). "Evaluative studies of institutions for delinquents: implications for research and social policy." Social Work (July): 55-64.
——— (1975). Community Treatment and Social Control. Chicago: Univ. of Chicago Press.

Liska, A.E. and M.D. Reed (1985). "Ties to conventional institutions and delinquency: estimating reciprocal effects." *Amer. Soc. Rev.* 50 (August): 547-560.

Lundman, R.J. (1984). *Prevention and Control of Juvenile Delinquency.* New York: Oxford.

Miller, W.B. (1962). "The impact of a 'total community' delinquency control project." *Social Problems* (Fall): 168-191.

Murray, C.A. and L.A. Cox, Jr. (1979). Beyond Probation. Beverly Hills, CA: *Sage.*

National Council on Crime and Delinquency (1984). *Rethinking Juvenile Justice*: National Statistical Trends. Minneapolis: University of Minnesota.

Palmer, T. (1971). "Martinson revisited." *J. of Research in Crime and Delinquency* (January): 67-80.

(1974). "The youth authority's community treatment project." Federal Probation (March): 3-14.

Polk, K. (1984). "Juvenile diversion: a look at the record." *Crime & Delinquency* (October): 648-659.

Regnery, A.S. (1985). "Introducing new pride." *NIJ Reports* (September): 9-12.

Robinson, J. and G. Smith (1971). "The effectiveness of correctional programs." *Crime & Delinquency* (January): 67-80.

Samenow, S. (1984). The Criminal Mind. New York: *Times Books.*

Schlossman, S., G. Zellman, R. Shavelson, M. Sedlak, and J. Cobb (1984). Delinquency Prevention in Chicago: A Fifty-Year Assessment of the Chicago Area Project. Santa Monica, CA: *Rand.*

Schwendinger, H. and J. Schwendinger (1979). "Delinquency and social reform: a radical perspective," pp. 245-287 in L.T. Empey (ed.) Juvenile Justice: The Progressive Legacy and Current Reforms. Charlottesville, VA: *Univ. Press of Virginia.*

Sechrest, L., S.O. White, and E.D. Brown (eds.) (1979). *The Rehabilitation of Criminal Offenders*. Washington, DC: National Academy of Sciences.

Shireman, C.H., K.B. Mann, C. Larsen, and T. Young (1978). "Findings from experiments in treatment in correctional settings." *Social Service Rev.* (March): 38-59.

Sutherland, E.H. and D.R. Cressey (1978). *Criminology*, Philadelphia: Lippincott.

Toby, J. (1983). "Crime in the schools," pp. 69-88 in J.Q. Wilson (ed.) *Crime and Public Policy*. San Francisco: Institute for Contemporary Problems.

Warren, M.Q. (1976). "Intervention with juvenile delinquents," pp. 176-204 in M.K. Rosenheim (ed.) Pursuing Justice for the Child. Chicago: *Univ. of Chicago Press.*

Wilson, J.Q. and R.J. Herrnstein (1985). *Crime and Human Nature*. New York: Simon & Schuster.

Wolfgang, M.E., R.M. Figlio, and T. Sellin (1972). Delinquency in a Birth Cohort. Chicago: *Univ. of Chicago Press.*

ARTICLE 40

Rethinking Juvenile Justice

BARRY KRISBERG
IRA SCHWARTZ*

*Data on juvenile arrests, court processing, and admissions to juvenile
correctional facilities offer important information to help rethink
juvenile justice policy directions of the last decade. Most striking is the
progress in reducing the involvement of status offenders within the
juvenile justice system between 1974-1979. Less encouraging is that
similar progress was not achieved in the case of delinquent offenders.
Moreover, the primary consequence of the removal of status offenders
from the juvenile justice system is the large decline in female admissions to public correctional facilities whereas male admissions were
either stable or actually increased from 1974-1979. Also interesting is
the levelling off of rates of Part 1 juvenile arrests from 1974-1979: this
directly contradicts public perceptions of a steady and alarming
increase in serious youth crime.*

    *Preliminary analysis of state trends in rates of admissions to
detention and training schools revealed a complex pattern of increases
and decreases. This pattern was largely unrelated to the distribution of
OJJDP funds. Indeed juvenile correctional admissions are highly
concentrated in a few states. An exploratory attempt to explain the
large variations in state rates of correctional admissions suggested
that most of the variation in detention admissions can be explained by
the number of detention beds per 100,000 youth population. For
training school admission rates, the number of beds per 100,000 youth*

* With the assistance of Paul Litsky, Research Associate, NCCD, and Dan Haugen, Research Assistant,
Hubert Humphrey Institute for Public Affairs.

    Source: Krisberg, Barry and Ira Schwartz. "Rethinking Juvenile Justice." *Crime and Delinquency*
Vol. 29 (3) 1983: 333-364. Reprinted by permission of Sage Publications, Inc.

*population is also the most powerful explanatory variable but nearly
two-thirds of the variation in state training school admissions is not
explained by bed availability, rates of juvenile arrests for serious
crimes, or youth unemployment. Future research should analyze the
determinants of the wide disparities between states in rates of detention
and training school admissions. Other important areas for further
policy investigation are the detaining of juveniles in adult jails and the
enormous growth in private residential placements for troubled youth.*

*"The moral test of government is how it treats those who are in
the dawn of life, the children; those who are in the shadows of life, the
sick, the needy, and the handicapped."*

—Hubert H. Humphrey

INTRODUCTION

This is one of the most important periods in our nation's history. Bold proposals have
been put forth calling for fundamental changes in our economic and domestic policies
and in the relationship and distribution of power between the states and the federal
government. Social reforms and programs, some of which had their beginnings nearly
a generation ago, are being questioned and re-examined. While the outcomes of this
process remain uncertain, few would argue the fact that major changes are underway.

Beginning with the creation of the Children's Bureau in 1912, the federal
government has played an increasingly more active role in juvenile delinquency. Now,
within the context of broader economic and domestic policy debates, it has been
suggested by some that the federal government cease its activities in this area. This
proposal has polarized discussion and has served as a barrier to thoughtful assessment.

Nearly a decade ago, after more than five years of exhaustive study on the part
of the Senate Subcommittee to Investigate Juvenile Delinquency, Congress concluded
". . . that our present system of juvenile justice is failing miserably." (U.S. Senate
Committee on the Judiciary, 1975:3) Congress found large numbers of status offenders
and non-offenders locked up in adult jails, detention centers, and training schools. They
found overcrowded and understaffed juvenile courts and evidence of abusive practices.
They found a critical shortage of alternatives to formal court processing and institutionalization.

Congress responded by enacting the Juvenile Justice and Delinquency Prevention Act of 1974. This legislation was to represent the federal government's ". . .
commitment to provide leadership." (U. S. Senate Committee on the Judiciary, 1975:4)
It was to serve as a ". . . framework. . ." and catalyst for better mobilizing the resources
of our country" . . . to deal more effectively with juvenile crime and delinquency
prevention." (U. S. Senate Committee on the Judiciary, 1975:4) "The Act . . . [wa'

. . . specifically designed to prevent young people from entering our failing juvenile justice system, and to assist communities in developing more sensible and economical alternatives for youngsters already in the juvenile justice system." (U.S. Senate Committee on the Judiciary, 1975:2)

In drafting the Juvenile Justice and Delinquency Prevention Act, its authors recognized that "some youthful offenders must be removed from their communities for society's sake as well as their own." (U.S. Senate Committee on the Judiciary, 1975:2) They felt, however, that the number of such offenders were relatively small, and that ". . .incarceration should be reserved for those youth that cannot be handled by other alternatives." (U.S. Senate Committee on the Judiciary, 1975:2) It was hoped that the Act would ". . .discourage the use of secure incarceration and detention. . . " (U.S. Senate Committee on the Judiciary, 1975:XXII) and encourage the development and use of ". . . community based alternatives to juvenile detention and correctional facilities." (U.S. Senate Committee on the Judiciary, 1975:XXI)

Clearly, Congress as well as the juvenile justice reformers of the early 1970s, recognized the excessive use and undesirable consequences of institutionalizing youth. It was felt that the Act should mandate the de-institutionalization of all but the most serious offenders as a condition of voluntary participation on the part of states wishing to receive federal funding. But, as with any piece of controversial legislation, compromises had to be made in order to secure its enactment. Consequently, the de-institutionalization mandates were restricted to status offenders and non-offenders. The Act did, however, strongly encourage the development of alternatives for delinquent youth.

This study is primarily concerned with taking stock and reflecting on the de-institutionalization movement within the juvenile justice system. We wish to explore what policy implications have surfaced as a result of this movement. To examine this issue, we assembled and reviewed data from all pertinent national criminal and juvenile justice information systems.

While the data contained in this report are fairly comprehensive and help to further our understanding there are a number of important gaps in our information. For example, there are no reliable data on admissions to detention centers and training schools by race. Also, data on admissions to facilities by offense types are generally unavailable. Staff from the OJJDP and the U.S. Census Bureau have been concerned about these shortcomings and have moved to rectify them by modifying the survey instruments used in the biennial "Children in Custody" survey. These modifications will allow a more comprehensive analysis of the significance of race in juvenile justice decision making.

Another major gap is the absence of data on juveniles admitted to adult jails. These data are needed to get a complete picture of the numbers of incarcerated youth. Data have been collected regarding the number of juveniles held in adult jails and prisons of a particular day, but comprehensive data on admissions of juveniles to adult correctional facilities are unavailable.

Finally, while there are significant problems with all of the various criminal and juvenile justice information systems, once assembled, we were impressed by what data were available and by the implications these data hold for policy makers. Unfortunately, much of the information that could be helpful has not always been fully accessible in forms either easily understood or usable. These national data sources are important tools for juvenile justice reformers and policy makers. They reveal a sobering picture of the limited achievement of the last decade's reforms. Further, these national data provide a useful array of indicators to stimulate policy evaluations at state and local levels. Such local assessments of juvenile justice reform may encourage a rethinking of juvenile justice and, perhaps, encourage more effective reform strategies.

SOURCES OF DATA

Comprehensive national data about youth crime and its control do not exist. At best, policy analysts can examine only a few independent national data bases to asses national trends. Only a few states such as Utah, Pennsylvania, and Florida have detailed information systems reporting on the flow of youth from arrest to juvenile court disposition. Even these state data bases are relatively new and not easily adapted for research purposes. At present there are only two national data sets from which one can reasonably examine trends to respond to specific policy questions. While these can still produce useful policy data and cues for strategic research opportunities, the analyst must proceed with a healthy respect for the real limitations of available data.

Data On Delinquent Behavior

A first area of concern involves the nature and extent of delinquent behavior both reported and unreported to law enforcement agencies. This is essentially an unknown area. Only crimes which involve the arrest of a juvenile are recorded at this time. Thus, we may know the number of crimes reported to the police (as reported by the FBI) or the number of reported victimizations (reported in the National Crime Survey), but the proportion of these offenses attributable to youth has not been documented. Official police data do not record crimes by age until a person is taken into custody. Attempts to use the victimization studies such as the National Crime Survey (NCS) to estimate youth crime are limited to: (1) offenses in which the victim actually witnesses the offender, and (2) victim *perceptions* of the offender's age. (McDermott and Hindelang, 1981) These methodological shortcomings cast doubt on the ability of the NCS to yield stable estimates of crime committed by youth.

Still another potential source of national data on the extent of delinquent behavior is the National Youth Survey (NYS) which administers a self-report delinquency questionnaire to a national probability sample of youth. (Elliot, Ageton, and Huizinga, 1980) The NYS was not originally designed to yield national estimates of youth crime but rather to measure the attrition of youth involved in delinquency over a three year period. While it can be adapted to yield national figures on youth crime, the NYS application will require considerable further testing and development of the self report technique. It can yield reliable national data on the extent of youthful criminal behavior.

Arrest Data

Data on the number of youth arrested by police are compiled by the FBI's Uniform Crime Reports (UCR) from approximately 12,000 local and state police agencies across the nation. (Federal Bureau of Investigation, 1980) The UCR classifies offenses into 29 categories. These crime categories are further collapsed into two major categories: Part 1 offenses[1] which are considered to be most serious crimes and the most likely to be reported to police, and Part 2 offenses, which include all other offenses. The UCR also report arrests for juvenile status offenses such as truancy, runaways, ungovernability, etc. Critics of the UCR have pointed out that some Part 2 offenses such as arson may be more serious than Part 1 crimes. Further, there exists variability in the number of police agencies that annually provide data to the UCR. While the reporting of Part 1 arrests is reasonably uniform, local practices on reporting Part 2 and status arrests are somewhat less consistent.

Juvenile Court Processing

Juvenile court statistics are gathered by the National Center for Juvenile Justice (NCJJ). (National Center for Juvenile Justice, 1981) Aggregate data are collected from over 80 percent of the nation's juvenile court jurisdictions on: (1) the total number of cases handled, (2) the sex of the youth, and (3) the method of handling (with or without a formal petition). In addition, individual case-based data are collected from states and large jurisdictions supplied juvenile court data from 830 (or 26 percent) of the 3,143 counties in the United States. After a lengthy process of editing to standardize the data elements, the data were analyzed to estimate the rate and characteristics of cases passing through the nation's juvenile court process. While the aggregate data had been collected since 1926, the detailed case-based data were first collected in 1975 with support from OJJDP. The NCJJ case-based data do not report figures for each participating state; only national level statistics are produced. These analyses also include estimates of the nation's use of detention and court dispositions resulting in correctional facility placements. NCJJ's procedures for constructing national estimates based on 26 percent of the nation's juvenile courts are extremely innovative; however, NCJJ warns that the size of sampling errors may be large for more refined data analysis tasks. Thus, small numerical trends must be reviewed with extreme caution.

Juvenile Corrections

The primary national source of data on juvenile corrections is the biennial census on children in public juvenile correctional facilities—known popularly as Children in

---

[1] Part 1 offenses include criminal homicide, forcible rape, robbery, aggravated assault, burglary, larceny, and auto theft.

Custody (CIC). (U.S. Bureau of Census, 1978) Begun in 1971, this series consists of six biennial national surveys administered by the U.S. Census Bureau to all known public juvenile correctional facilities. A special CIC survey was conducted in 1974 to coincide with the implementation of the Juvenile Justice and Delinquency Prevention Act of 1974. In 1979, the survey response rate was 100 percent (1,136 facilities). The response rate has never been lower than 96 percent in any year.

The CIC survey requests data from facility administrators on the number of youth admitted to the facilities, their demographic characteristics, a one-day count of inmates, as well as various budgetary and programmatic facts about each facility. Starting in 1974, survey data were also collected on private juvenile correctional facilities. A major omission of CIC is the number of juveniles held in adult jails. These data, however, are reported as part of the National Census of Jails conducted in 1970 and 1978, and data on juveniles in adult prisons are available for 1978 as part of Abt's monumental study of American prisons and jails. (Abt Associates,1981)[2]

The CIC series contain a rich source of data about juvenile correctional facilities across the 50 states and the District of Columbia. In most county-by-county level within states. The high response rate as well as preliminary tests of data reliability suggest that CIC holds great potential for future juvenile justice policy research.

How CIC and NCJJ Data Systems Differ

Since the CIC and NCJJ both collect data on detention and placements in correctional facilities, it is useful to examine how these two systems differ from each other. In general, CIC reports a larger universe of activities (i.e., total admissions to a facility per year) and includes admissions caused by agencies in addition to the juvenile court which are not documented through the NCJJ system. Detentions reported by NCJJ include only cases detained while undergoing court processing. Detentions admissions in CIC include court-ordered detention, police and other pre-adjudicatory detention, as well as temporary detentions initiated by probation, parole, or other agencies which may not appear in the NCJJ. In 1979, CIC reported 496,526 admissions to detention nationwide, whereas NCJJ reported 249,700 detentions via the court process.

It is important to note that both data systems yield valuable but dramatically different estimates about the use of detention by courts and by other components of the juvenile justice system. Data from NCJJ on court dispositions involving placements in public correctional agencies will differ from CIC statistics on admissions to post-adjudication correctional facilities. CIC juvenile admissions data (for training schools and other commitment facilities) will include initial court commitments, probation and parole violators, inter-facility transfers, and returned AWOLS. Both systems will involve "double-counting" in the sense that individual youths may account for many juvenile court cases or admissions in a year.

---

[2] A National Census of Jails was completed in 1982 but the sampling approach yields nationwide estimates of juveniles held in adult jails but not state-by-state figures.

Probation and Parole

National data exist for a one day count of the number of juveniles on probation and parole on September 1, 1976. (U.S. Bureau of Census, 1978) This survey documented 328,854 juveniles on probation and 53,347 on parole. No data in this survey are presented on the volume of juvenile admissions to community supervision. Data on client characteristics, on the conditions of supervision, and on the nature of supervising agencies are extremely limited. This lack of data is a significant omission because many studies show that informal and formal probation are the most frequent juvenile justice dispositions. (Krisberg and Austin, 1978) Without more current and comprehensive data on community supervision for juveniles, a major dimension of the juvenile corrections system remains obscured.

Summary

This brief review of available national juvenile justice data sources makes clear the urgent need for better and more reliable data. There are many significant gaps in existing information, and analyses across these data systems must be performed with great care. Our grasp of the statistical contours of juvenile justice in America is not likely to improve greatly in the near future because of the enormous resource investment required to develop more comprehensive data. Plus, the highly decentralized nature of juvenile justice makes centralized and uniform national data collection highly problematic. National juvenile justice data that are already available can, however, be employed to guide policy discussions if they are analyzed carefully and cautiously. In the next section, we discuss the key juvenile justice trends reflected in each of the national data sources.

NATIONAL JUVENILE JUSTICE TRENDS

Juvenile Arrest Trends

During the period 1971-1979 the number of youth in age groups under the jurisdiction of the juvenile court declined from 30 million to 28.7 million (a drop of 4.2 percent). In 1971 there were 1.6 million juvenile arrests; by 1974 (the date of the Federal Juvenile Justice and Delinquency Prevention Act), this number had increased 15.7 percent to 1.9 million arrests. From 1974 to 1979, however, total juvenile arrests declined by 3.2 percent to 1.8 million arrests. When considered in proportion to the overall decline in the youth's population, and juvenile arrest rate per 100,000 youth rose by 17.5 percent from 1971 to 1974 but remained unchanged (a decrease of 0.5 percent) from 1974 to 1979.

Arrests for violent offenses also climbed sharply from 1971-1974, levelling off

TABLE 40.1 Juvenile arrests by sex 1971, 1974, 1979

	1971			1974			1979		
	Total Arrests	Arrests Per 100,000	Percent Change 71–74*	Total Arrests	Arrests Per 100,000	Percent Change 74–79*	Total Arrests	Arrests Per 100,000	Percent Change 71–79*
Total Arrests	1,624,310	5414	17.5	1,879,387	6363	−0.5	1,819,673	6329	16.9
Male	1,252,396	4174	18.7	1,463,910	4957	−0.1	1,424,534	4954	18.7
Female	371,914	1240	13.4	415,407	1406	−2.3	395,139	1374	10.8
Part I Arrests	591,909	1973	32.3	771,608	2613	0.2	753,428	2620	32.8
Male	491,076	1637	30.2	630,090	2135	0.3	615,653	2141	30.8
Female	100,833	336	42.4	141,518	479	0	137,775	479	42.5
Status Offense	536,266	1787	7.8	569,481	1928	−15.8	466,885	1624	−9.1
Male	350,966	1170	9.2	377,400	1278	−14.8	313,086	1089	−6.9
Female	185,300	618	5.2	192,081	650	−17.7	153,799	535	−13.4
Violent Arrests	55,093	184	36.4	74,012	251	3.6	74,850	260	41.3
Male	49,214	164	36.0	65,950	223	4.4	66,893	233	42.1
Female	5,879	20	35.0	8,062	27	0	7,957	27	35.0
Eligible Youth Population	30,003,141	—	−1.5	29,534,292	—	−2.6	28,752,877	—	−4.2

*Percent Change denotes change in the juvenile arrest rate per 100,000 youth age 10 to upper age of juvenile court jurisdiction.
Source: Uniform Crime Reports, 1971, 1974, 1979.

again towards the end of the decade.[3] The rate of violent arrests for 100,000 youth population[4] increased by 36.4 percent from 1971-1974, but grew by only 3.6 percent from 1974-1979. Similarly, the rate of Part 1 arrests rose by one-third in the first part of the 1970s, but increased by a more 0.2 percent in the second half of the decade. The largest declines in arrest figures were for status offenses; with the rate of status arrests dropping by 15.8 percent after 1974. The decline in status offense arrests followed a national effort to reduce the processing of these cases by the juvenile justice system.

Although males are disproportionately represented in all types of juvenile arrests, juvenile arrest rates for males and females were quite similar during the 1970s, mirroring the pattern of sharp increases from 1971-1974 and levelling off from 1974-1979. As described in Table 40.1, changes in female arrest rates for Part 1 offenses and violent crimes closely paralleled those for males. For example, the female violent arrest rate increased by 35.0 percent over the entire decade; the male violent arrest rate increased by 42.1 percent. From 1974-1979, the rate of female status arrests declined by 13.4 percent, while the male status arrest rate declined by 6.9 percent.

Juvenile Court Trends

As noted earlier, detailed national juvenile court data were first available in 1975 through the NCJJ data base. (See Table 40.2) In 1975, slightly over 1.4 million cases were disposed of by the nation's juvenile courts. Of this total, 660,867 or 47.0 percent were handled with formal delinquency petitions. From 1975-1979, the rate per 100,000 youth referred to the juvenile court declined by 5.0 percent. In 1979, the proportion of cases handled by petitions was 45.7 percent—virtually identical to the 1975 figure. The rate of cases involving property crimes[5] increased by 17.0 percent from 1975-1979. During this same period, the rate of cases involving crimes against persons[6] was stable (+0.8 percent). By contrast, the rate of status offense cases declined sharply (21.1 percent), a decrease consistent with the decline in arrests for status offenses. Overall, however, both the stability in rates of juvenile court processing and the use of formal petitions do not confirm the hopes of reformers that significant numbers of youth were diverted from formal court processing to other more voluntary community agencies.

Another goal of juvenile justice reformers was to reduce the court's use of detention, partly as a result of the incentives provided by the federal juvenile justice legislation to divert and deinstitutionalize young offenders. Indeed, the rate of detentions per 100,000 youth did decline by 26.9 percent and the female detention rate decreased by 44.4 percent.

Interestingly, NCJJ reported that the rate of detaining status offenders declined by 68.0 percent from 1975-1979. This dramatic decline may well be a direct result of

[3] Violent arrests include homicide, rape, robbery, and aggravated assault.
[4] Rates are computed for those youth ages 10 to the maximum age of original juvenile court jurisdiction in each state. Adjustments were made if states changed their ages of juvenile court jurisdictions.
[5] Property offenses include burglary, auto theft, larceny, vandalism, arson and trespassing.
[6] NCJJ defines crime against persons as the UCR violent offenses plus simple assault.

TABLE **40.2** National juvenile court statistics 1975 and 1979

	1975			1979	
	Total Cases	Cases Per 100,000	Percent Change 75-79*	Total Cases	Cases Per 100,000
Cases Disposed Of:	1,406,100	4786	–5.0	1,307,000	4546
With Petition	660,867	2250	–7.7	597,000	2076
Without Petition *	745,233	2537	–2.7	709,800	2569
Status Offense Cases	335,600	1142	-21.1	259,000	901
Property Offense Cases	588,400	2003	17.0	674,200	2345
Person Offense Cases	145,100	494	0.8	143,200	498
Detentions:	349,000	1188	–26.9	249,700	868
Male	245,800	837	–19.5	193,700	674
Female	103,200	351	–44.4	56,000	195
Status Offense Cases	143,000	487	–68.0	44,807	156
Property Offense Cases	108,000	368	4.9	111,100	386
Person Offense Cases	38,200	130	7.7	40,239	140
Eligible Youth Population	29,378,014	—	–2.1	28,752,877	—

*Percent Change denotes change in the juvenile processing rates for 100,000 youth. Population figures are taken from U.S. Census Bureau data for 1970 and 1980.

federal policies implemented by OJJDP and its state affiliates. In sharp contrast to the large drop in the status offense detentions however, the detention rates for youth charged with property crimes and person crimes increased during 1975-1979 by 4.9 percent and 7.7 percent, respectively.

Trends In Juvenile Corrections

ADMISSIONS TO DETENTION. In 1971 there were 496,526 admissions to detention facilities in the United States. By 1974, total detention admissions increased by 6.5 percent to 529,075 and then declined by 14.6 percent to 451,810 in 1979. Thus, overall, from 1971-1979 the detention admissions rate per 100,000 youth declined by 5.1 percent, with the most dramatic decline occurring from 1974-1979 (12.3 percent). This 1974-1979 decline is principally accounted for by a drop in admissions of females to detention. Of the 77,265 fewer detention admissions in 1979 compared with 1974, 62,207 or 80.5 percent were females. The drop in the female detention admissions rate was 37.6 percent compared with a 1.4 percent decline in the male detention admissions rate between 1974-1979. Recalling the 15.8 percent drop in the status offense arrest rate from 1974-1979 and the 21.1 percent decline in status offense cases disposed of by juvenile courts from 1975-1979, the sizeable decrease in female detention admissions most likely reflects the policies to divert status offenders from the juvenile justice

TABLE 40.3 Public juvenile detention and training school admissions and expenditures 1971, 1974, 1979

	1971			1974			1979		
	Total Admissions	Admissions Per 100,000	Percent Change 71–74*	Total Admissions	Admissions Per 100,000	Percent Change 74–79*	Total Admissions	Admissions Per 100,000	Percent Change 71–79*
Total Admission To Detention	496,526	1655	8.2	529,075	1791	−12.3	451,810	1571	−5.1
Male Admissions	349,407	1165	7.9	371,225	1257	−1.4	356,167	1239	6.4
Female Admissions	147,119	490	9.0	157,850	534	−37.6	95,643	333	−32.0
Total Admissions To Training Schools	67,775	226	0.9	67,406	228	0	65,416	228	0.9
Male Admissions	53,089	177	2.8	53,737	182	8.8	56,972	198	11.9
Female Admissions	14,686	49	−6.1	13,669	46	−37.0	8,444	29	−40.8
Detention Expenditures	$92,110,196	—	41.4	$130,274,470**	—	75.7	$228,848,730	—	148.5
Training School Expenditures	$248,759,346	—	16.9	$290,933,166**	—	37.3	$399,485,111	—	60.6
Eligible Youth Population	30,003,141	—	−1.6	29,534,292	—	−2.6	28,752,877	—	−4.2

* Percent Change denotes change in admissions rate per 100,000 youth.
** 1974 Expenditures figures are the average of 1973 and 1975 data.
Source: U. S. Census Bureau, *Children in Custody.*

TABLE 40.4 National juvenile court statistics 1975 and 1979

	1975			1979	
	Total Admissions	Admissions Per 100,000	Percent Change 75-79*	Total Admissions	Admissions Per 100,000
Admissions To					
Private Facilities	42,005	142	20.4	49,298	171
Males	27,215	92	13.0	29,771	104
Females	14,790	50	36.0	19,527	68
Admission To					
Public Facilities	641,857	2,173	−11.0	556,172	1,934
Males	463,247	1,568	−0.8	447,428	1,556
Females	178,610	605	−37.5	108,744	378
Eligible Youth -					
Population	29,534,292	—	−2.6	28,752,877	—

system. Although in general, males are arrested more frequently than females for status offenses, females are more often detained and sent to juvenile correctional facilities for these behaviors. (Chesney-Lind, 1977)

JUVENILES ADMITTED TO TRAINING SCHOOLS. As shown in Table 40.3, rates of admissions to training schools were largely unchanged throughout the decade of the 1970s. There were 67,775 training school admissions in 1971; and by 1974, the number of admissions was 67, 406. In 1979 there were 65,416 admissions to training schools nationwide—a decline of only 2.9 percent from the admissions reported in 1974. This pattern of stability in national admissions to training schools actually masks a dramatic decline in the rate of female admissions to training schools. From 1974-1979, the female admissions rate dropped by 37.0 percent, paralleling the decline in female detention admissions. By contrast, the male training school admissions rate *increased* by 8.8 percent. These data lend further support to the view that the accomplishments of the deinstitutionalization movement were largely confined to female status offenders.

ADMISSIONS TO PRIVATE CORRECTIONAL FACILITIES. In addition to data on admissions to public juvenile correctional facilities, the CIC collected data on admissions to private correctional facilities beginning in 1974.[7] As shown in Table 40.4, these figures reveal 42,005 admissions to private facilities in 1974 compared with 49,298 admissions in 1979—an increase of 17.4 percent in total admissions. The rate of male private admissions changed only by 13.0 percent between 1974-1979 compared to a signifi-

[7] Data were also collected on admissions to private shelter facilities but these are excluded from our analysis because these facilities mostly house dependent and neglected youth as well as some status offenders.

cant increase of 36.0 percent for females, suggesting that females have been transferred from the public correctional system of privately operated facilities. Whether youth are better treated in these private facilities is an issue that demands further investigation.

CORRECTIONAL EXPENDITURES. National Data sources on juvenile correctional expenditures only report on the operating costs of institutions. They do not report on parole and probation expenditures. Further, since the CIC census of juvenile corrections asks only about operating expenses of facilities; capital improvement, new construction, centralized research, and administrative expenditures are excluded from this analysis. Given these omissions, the following figures on juvenile correctional costs must be viewed as extremely conservative.

In 1971, over $92.1 million were spent on juvenile detention facilities; by 1979, this amount had grown by 148.5 percent to over $228.8 million. Even as detention admissions were declining (by 12.3 percent) between 1974-1979, expenditures for detention rose by 75.7 percent during that same period.

Training school budgets in the United States totalled $248.8 million in 1971, rising to $399.5 million in 1979—an increase of 60.6 percent. Between 1974-1979, when training school admissions remained unchanged, expenditures increased by 37.3 percent. Costs associated with admissions to private correctional facilities are currently not available from national data sources.

Individual State Trends In Juvenile Corrections

While the national-level data on arrests, court processing, and corrections are extremely interesting, they consolidate and therefore mask a broad variety of state and local juvenile justice experiences. For example, forty-four states, voluntarily participation in the 1974 Juvenile Justice Act, received funds: (1) to remove status offenders from secure custody, (2) to separate adults and juveniles in correctional facilities, and (3) to implement certain "advanced techniques" to reduce unnecessary penetration of youth into the juvenile justice system. How these changes impacted specific states and localities is a major public policy question. More complete analyses of inter-jurisdictional juvenile justice data trends may yield better clues to successful strategies for reducing unnecessary youthful incarceration. While it is beyond the scope of this paper fully to examine juvenile justice trends for 51 states[8] or for over 3000 local juvenile court jurisdictions, let us review some examples of this diversity.

STATE TRENDS IN DETENTION AND TRAINING SCHOOL ADMISSIONS. From 1974-1979, 30 states reported decreases in rates of detention admissions. Fourteen states experienced increased rates of detention admissions, and another seven states[9] did not report detention admissions to CIC because in these jurisdictions, youth are detained in adult jails or other facilities. Wisconsin reported a 66.4 percent decline in its detention

---

[8] For this analysis the District of Columbia is treated as a state.
[9] Idaho, Maine, Montana, New Hampshire, Rhode Island, Vermont, and Wyoming.

TABLE 40.5 Changes in rates of admissions to detention by state—1974 and 1979

State	1974 to 1979 Percent• Change	1974 Total Admissions	1974 Admissions Per 100,000	1979 Total Admissions	1979 Admissions Per 100,000
States With Decreasing Detention Rates:					
Wisconsin	-66.4	7,844	1,104	2,499	371
Massachusetts	-51.8	7,928	1,091	3,581	526
Kentucky	-51.0	7,947	1,529	3,841	750
Utah	-42.4	8,698	4,382	5,126	2,525
Alaska	-39.7	309	580	196	350
District of Columbia	-38.3	48,887	5,487	2,545	3,384
Louisiana	-36.6	6,144	1,105	3,793	700
Delaware	-30.4	1,788	2,033	1,192	1,415
Oklahoma	-29.4	3,085	909	2,461	642
Alabama	-27.9	5,348	1.096	4,273	790
Illinois	-25.9	17,262	1,176	11,817	871
Florida	-25.6	33,279	3,331	28,258	2,480
Mississippi	-23.1	3,476	892	2,618	686
Connecticut	-22.4	3,293	960	2,376	745
South Carolina	-22.2	1,287	328	992	256
Georgia	-20.3	17,467	2,607	14,076	2,078
California	-18.9	165,521	5,415	133,285	4,393
Colorado	-18.2	11,628	3,145	9,709	2,572
New Jersey	-17.6	12,996	1,215	10,288	1,001
New York	-16.8	10,468	547	7,981	455
New Mexico	-16.8	4,527	2,366	3,792	1,969
Washington	-16.3	22,279	4,085	18,413	3,420
Michigan	-15.2	19,443	1,528	15,264	1,295
Tennessee	-10.8	14,681	2,353	13,081	2,100
North Carolina	-8.8	3,718	610	3,287	556
Minnesota	-8.1	6,833	1,110	5,876	1,019
Kansas	-7.4	4,338	1,296	3,658	1,199
Arizona	-6.6	9,811	3,026	10,173	2,826
Indiana	-5.2	10,238	1,249	9,180	1,184
Oregon	-3.8	4,431	2,200	7,111	2,116
States With Increasing Detention Rates:					
Pennsylvania	2.6	15,605	901	14,775	925
Iowa	3.0	1,320	304	1,253	313
Texas	10.4	19,129	1,152	21,511	1.271
Missouri	13.5	9,404	1,534	9,905	1,741
Nevada	14.9	3,973	4,948	4,894	5,685
Virginia	15.2	10,373	1,412	11,832	1,626
Hawaii	20.1	1,881	1,513	2,266	1,816
Ohio	22.1	27,538	1,670	30,850	2,039

TABLE 40.5 (Continued) Changes in rates of admissions to detention by state—1974 and 1979

State	1974 to 1979	1974		1979	
	Percent• *Change*	*Total* *Admissions*	*Admissions* *Per 100,000*	*Total* *Admissions*	*Admissions* *Per 100,000*
States With Increasing Detention Rates:					
West Virginia	26.7	1,025	373	1,246	473
Nebraska	50.0	1,152	509	1,599	763
Arkansas	105.0	1,806	578	3,733	1,186
Maryland	179.0	1,207	194	3,282	542
North Dakota	197.3	185	201	609	598
South Dakota	201.8	453	418	1,217	1,260

*Percent change denotes change in rate of admissions per 100,000 youth aged 10 to upper age of Juvenile Court Jurisdiction. Idaho, Maine, Montana, New Hampshire, Rhode Island, Vermont and Wyoming did not report detention admissions one or both years.
Source: U.S. Bureau of Census, *Children in Custody.*

admissions rate. Massachusetts and Kentucky experienced drops in detention admissions rate of 51.8 percent and 51.0 percent, respectively. By contrast, Arkansas, Maryland, North Dakota, and South Dakota all showed detention rates that 105.0 percent to 201.8 percent between 1974-1979. Table 40.5 summarizes these trends by state.

For training school admissions, the states are evenly split. Twenty-five states reported declining rates of training school admissions between 1974-1979 and 25 states reported increases.[10] Vermont experienced a 100 percent decline in its training school admissions rate, while New Mexico, New York, and Texas all reported significant declines in rates of training school admissions during this same period. States reporting sharp increases in training school admission rates include Kentucky, Oregon, Washington, Delaware, and Indiana. Table 40.6 reports on changes in training school admissions rates for each state.

TRENDS IN CORRECTIONAL ADMISSIONS AND FEDERAL JUVENILE JUSTICE POLICIES. A brief examination of individual state trends in rates of admissions to detention centers and training schools yields no obvious patterns. At best these data focus attention on questions for further investigation. One obvious question is the relationship of state trends during 1974-1979 to the amount of funds received from the OJJDP. Combining both special emphasis and formula grant funds awarded states from 1975 through 1979, one finds no statistical relationship between OJJDP funds received and progress in reducing rates of detention and training school admissions. The correlations of OJJDP funds with changing detention and training school rates are -.08 and -12, neither of

[10] Massachusets failed to report training school admissions in 1973 and 1974 but began reporting these again in 1975.

TABLE 40.6 Changes in rates of admissions to detention by state—1974 and 1979

State	1974 to 1979 Percent* Change	1974 Total Admissions	1974 Admissions Per 100,000	1979 Total Admissions	1979 Admissions Per 100,000
States With Decreasing Training School Rates:					
Vermont	100.0	346	648	0	0
New Mexico	-64.5	933	488	333	173
New York	-58.2	1,725	90	661	38
Texas	-56.9	3,700	223	1,624	96
North Carolina	-47.0	2,740	450	1,408	238
Michigan	-41.5	1,163	91	630	53
Oklahoma	-37.2	843	249	598	156
Florida	-27.5	3,324	333	2,747	241
Colorado	-26.4	560	151	421	112
Illinois	-26.3	2,270	155	1,546	114
South Dakota	-26.0	170	157	112	116
Ohio	-25.0	3,690	224	2,538	168
Rhode Island	-22.4	821	618	605	480
Mississippi	-21.3	861	221	663	174
Minnesota	-18.4	2,404	390	1,837	319
Maryland	-17.0	5,106	822	4,131	682
Tennessee	-16.6	1,962	314	1,633	262
Louisiana	-15.4	1,780	320	1,467	271
New Jersey	-12.9	723	68	605	59
Wisconsin	-10.0	1,269	179	1,082	161
New Hampshire	-9.0	953	854	970	776
Montana	-6.9	416	355	360	331
Connecticut	-6.8	490	143	425	133
Pennsylvania	-2.6	1,446	83	1,300	81
Georgia	-0.7	1,671	249	1,677	248
North Dakota	1.3	165	179	185	182
Idaho	5.8	215	168	231	178
South Carolina	5.8	812	207	851	219
Missouri	11.3	1,192	194	1,231	216
California	12.1	12,201	399	13,573	447
Hawaii	14.7	219	176	252	202
Nevada	15.9	285	355	354	411
Alabama	16.7	517	106	669	124
Maine	24.0	536	362	704	449
Alaska	26.0	993	1,865	1,315	2,249
Virginia	26.5	1,205	164	1,510	208
Arkansas	30.7	659	211	868	276
Utah	31.8	290	146	391	193
Nebraska	44.2	407	180	543	259
West Virginia	58.5	553	201	841	319
Kansas	78.6	526	157	856	281
Arizona	80.8	853	261	1,700	472
Iowa	82.4	662	152	1,112	278
Wyoming	88.1	173	275	358	518
District of Columbia	89.7	959	1,077	1,536	2,043
Indiana	100.2	1,152	140	2,181	281
Delaware	123.8	238	271	510	605
Washington	131.8	378	69	865	161
Oregon	176.3	651	193	1,789	532
Kentucky	717.4	199	38	1,603	313

*Percent change denotes change in rate of admissions per 100,000 youth aged 10 to upper age of Juvenile Court Jurisdiction
**Massachusetts missing data for 1974.

which are statistically significant. Of course, these low correlations cannot be interpreted as measuring the impact of the federal juvenile justice involvement during this period since the only specific de-institutionalization objective of the 1974 Act involves status offenders and data presented earlier strongly suggest significant progress in removing status offenders from several stages of the juvenile justice system. Yet the null finding (i.e., of no statistical relationship) itself suggests further analyses of the CIC data. For example, the CIC survey reports that public juvenile correctional costs totalled over $842 million in 1979. OJJDP special emphasis and formula grant funds were approximately $75.9 million during that same year. Thus, funds intended to reduce unnecessary incarceration of youth, as well as a number of other congressional goals, represented less than 10 percent of the most conservative estimates of juvenile correctional facility operational costs. The CIC data also point to the lack of fit between the actual distribution of rates of detention and training school admissions and the block grant funding approach of the Juvenile Justice and Delinquency Prevention Act of 1974.

A block grant funding approach assumes that the distribution of targeted funds is roughly distributed as is the youth population. But examination of individual state variations in rates of admissions to detention and training schools reveals that most admissions are concentrated in a few states, and that often, the less populated jurisdictions have the highest admission rates. For example, in 1979, 29.5 percent of all national detention admissions occurred in California—a state with 10.5 percent of the age—eligible youth population. The top five states in volume of detention admissions (California, Ohio, Florida, Texas, and Washington) accounted for over half the national total volume of detention admissions in 1979. These states, however, received only 24.9 percent of the OJJDP special emphasis and formula grant funds. The same pattern holds true for training school admissions in 1979: the top five states— California, Maryland, Florida, Ohio, and Indiana—accounted for 38.4 percent of all admissions but received only 21.9 percent of the OJJDP funds (See Table 40.7.)

If one considers the highest rates of admissions to detention and training schools, the discrepancy between high rate jurisdictions and block grant allocations is even more pronounced. In 1979, states with the top 15 rates of admissions but receive 33.6 percent of the funds. The top fifteen states in training school admission rates reported 46.5 percent of all training school admissions in 1979 but accounted for only 18.8 percent of OJJDP grant funds in that same year. (See Tables 40.8A and 40.8B.) Potential policy implications of these findings will be discussed later.

STATE VARIATIONS IN DETENTION AND TRAINING SCHOOL ADMISSIONS RATES. The analysis of admission rates ad OJJDP funds allocations surfaced an even more profound research and policy question: What accounts for the large differences between states in rates of admissions to detention and training schools? Tables 9A and 9B report the top ten states in rates of detention and training school admissions for 1971, 1974, and 1979. These data show that, with few exceptions, the top states in admissions have been consistent across the decade. Indeed, the rank ordering of state rates of detention and training schools admissions were essentially stable over the period 1971-1979.

Data gathered in the 1979 CIC survey also permit a view of the diversity of uses

TABLE 40.7 Top 5 states in volume of admissions to detention and training schools with OJJDP special emphasis and formula grants, 1979

State	Admissions				OJJDP Grants			
	Total	Percent Of All Admissions	Cumulative Total	Cumulative Percent Of All Admissions	Total $	Percent Of All $	Cumulative Total $	Cumulative Percent Of All $
Admissions to Detention:								
California	133,285	29.5	133,285	29.5%	$6,699,075	8.8	$6,699,075	8.8
Ohio	30,850	6.8	164,135	36.3	3,961,750	5.2	10,660,824	14.0
Florida	28,252	6.3	192,387	42.6	3,180,418	4.2	13,841,242	18.2
Texas	21,511	4.8	213,898	47.4	3,797,000	5.0	17,638,242	23.2
Washington	18,413	4.1	232,311	51.5	1,295,000	1.7	18,933,242	24.9
Admissions to Detention, 51 States	—	—	451,810	100	—	—	75,933,261	100
Admissions to Training Schools:								
California	13,573	20.7	13,573	20.7	$6,699,075	8.8	$6,699,075	8.8
Maryland	4,131	6.3	17,704	27.0	1,192,000	1.6	7,891,074	10.4
Florida	2,747	4.2	20,451	31.2	3,180,418	4.2	11,071,492	14.6
Ohio	2,538	3.9	22,989	35.1	3,961,750	5.2	15,033,242	19.8
Indiana	2,181	3.3	25,170	38.4	1,578,000	2.1	16,611,242	21.9
Admissions to Training Schools, 51 States	—	—	65,416	100	—	—	75,933,261	100

Source: U. S. Bureau of Census, *Children in Custody Series*

TABLE 40.8A   Top 15 states in rate of admissions to detention with OJJDP special emphasis and formula grants, 1979

State		Admissions				OJJDP Grants			
	Rate Per 100,000	Total	Percent Of All Admissions	Cumulative Total	Cumulative Percent	Total Grants	Percent Of Total	Cumulative Total	Cumulative Percent
Detention Admissions:									
Nevada	5685	4,894	1.1	4,894	1.1	$686,998	0.9	$686,998	0.9
California	4393	133,285	29.5	138,179	30.6	6,699,074	8.8	7,386,072	9.7
Washington	3420	18,413	4.1	156,592	34.7	1,295,000	1.7	8,681,072	11.4
District of Columbia	3384	2,545	0.6	159,137	35.3	225,000	0.3	8,906,072	11.7
Arizona	2825	10,173	2.3	169,310	37.6	855,880	1.1	9,761,952	12.8
Colorado	2572	9,709	2.1	179,019	39.7	1,519,345	2.0	11,281,297	14.8
Utah	2525	5,126	1.1	184,145	40.8	430,000	0.6	11,711,297	15.4
Florida	2480	28,252	6.3	212,397	47.1	3,180,418	4.2	14,891,715	19.6
Oregon	2116	7,111	1.6	219,508	48.7	644,000	0.8	15,535,715	20.4
Tennessee	2100	13,081	2.9	232,589	51.6	1,204,000	1.6	16,739,715	22.0
Georgia	2078	14,076	3.1	246,665	54.7	2,239,798	2.9	18,979,513	24.9
Ohio	2039	30,850	6.8	277,515	61.5	3,916,750	5.2	22,941,263	30.1
New Mexico	1969	3,792	0.8	281,307	62.3	386,000	0.5	23,327,263	30.6
Hawaii	1816	2,266	0.5	283,573	62.8	268,000	0.4	23,595,263	31.0
Missouri	1741	9,905	2.2	293,478	65.0	1,948,850	2.6	25,544,113	33.6
Detention Admissions 51 States	1571	—	100	451,810	100	—	100	75,933,261	100

Source: U. S. Bureau of Census, *Children in Custody Series*

TABLE 40.8B Top 15 states in rate of admissions to training schools with OJJDP special emphasis and formula grants, 1979

State	Admissions					OJJDP Grants			
	Rate Per 100,000	Total	Percent Of All Admissions	Cumulative Total	Cumulative Percent	Total Grants	Percent Of Total	Cumulative Total	Cumulative Percent
Training Schools:									
Alaska	2349	1,315	2.0	1,315	2.0	$225,000	0.3	$225,000	0.3
District Of Columbia	2043	1,536	2.3	2,851	4.3	225,000	0.3	450,000	0.6
New Hampshire	777	970	1.5	3,821	5.8	525,000	0.7	975,000	1.3
Maryland	682	4,131	6.3	7,952	12.1	1,192,000	1.6	2,167,000	2.9
Delaware	605	510	0.8	8,462	12.9	225,000	0.3	2,392,000	3.2
Oregon	532	1,789	2.7	10,251	15.6	644,000	0.8	3,036,000	4.0
Wyoming	518	358	0.5	10,609	16.1	0	0	3,036,000	4.0
Rhode Island	480	605	0.9	11,214	17.0	252,000	0.3	3,288,000	4.3
Arizona	472	1,700	2.6	12,914	19.6	855,880	1.1	4,143,880	5.4
Maine	449	704	1.1	13,618	20.7	313,000	0.4	6,456,880	5.8
California	447	13,573	20.7	27,191	41.4	6,699,074	8.8	11,155,954	14.6
Nevada	411	354	0.5	27,545	41.9	686,998	0.9	11,842,952	15.5
Montana	331	360	0.5	27,905	42.4	227,000	0.3	12,069,952	15.8
West Virginia	319	841	1.3	28,746	43.7	513,000	0.7	12,582,952	16.5
Minnesota	319	1,837	2.8	30,583	46.5	1,736,716	2.3	14,319,668	18.8
Training Admissions 51 States	228	—	100	65,416	100	—	100	75,933,261	100

Source: U. S. Bureau of Census, *Children in Custody Series*

TABLE 40.9A Top 10 states in rate of admissions to detention: 1971, 1974, 1979

1971		1974		1979	
State	Rate Per 100,000	State	Rate Per 100,000	State	Rate Per 100,000
1. Nevada	6611	District Of Columbia	5487	Nevada	5685
2. District Of Columbia	5626	California	5415	California	4393
3. California	5114	Nevada	4948	Washington	3420
4. Florida	3330	Utah	4382	District Of Columbia	3384
5. Washington	3013	Washington	4085	Arizona	2826
6. Arizona	2935	Florida	3331	Colorado	2572
7. Georgia	2574	Colorado	3145	Utah	2525
8. Oregon	2496	Arizona	3026	Florida	2480
9. Colorado	2275	Georgia	2607	Oregon	2116
10. Delaware	2200	New Mexico	2366	Tennessee	2100

Source: U.S. Department of Census, *Children In Custody Series*

TABLE 40.9B Top 10 states in rate of admissions training schools 1971, 1974, 1979

1971		1974		1979	
State	Rate Per 100,000	State	Rate Per 100,000	State	Rate Per 100,000
1. District Of Columbia	2313	Alaska	1865	Alaska	2349
2. Alaska	1980	District Of Columbia	1077	District Of Columbia	2043
3. New Hampshire	736	New Hampshire	854	New Hampshire	777
4. Delaware	666	Maryland	822	Maryland	682
5. Vermont	645	Vermont	648	Delaware	605
6. Nevada	510	Rhode Island	618	Oregon	532
7. Rhode Island	499	New Mexico	488	Wyoming	518
8. Wisconsin	434	North Carolina	450	Rhode Island	480
9. North Carolina	402	California	399	Arizona	472
10. Florida	364	Minesota	390	Maine	449

Source: U.S. Department of Census, *Children In Custody Series*

TABLE 40.10 Top 15 States in rates of admission to detention and training schools in 1979. Commitments to detention excluded. Training school detainees added to detention

State	Rate Per 100,000 Youth	Total Admissions
Detention Admissions:		
District Of Columbia	4,875	3,666
Nevada	4,846	4,896
California	4,058	123,143
Washington	3,408	18,348
Arizona	2,826	10,163
Alaska	2,539	1,421
Utah	2,525	5,126
Florida	2,480	28,252
Colorado	2,419	9,133
Oregon	2,116	7,111
Tennessee	2,100	13,081
Georgia	2,063	13,997
Ohio	2,030	30,720
New Mexico	1,969	3,793
Hawaii	1,838	2,266
All States	1,552	446,057
Training School Admissions:		
Delaware	605	510
District Of Columbia	552	415
Oregon	532	1,789
Wyoming	518	358
Arizona	473	1,700
California	447	13,573
Nevada	351	354
Montana	331	360
Kentucky	287	1,472
New Hampshire	283	353
Arkansas	276	1,700
Louisiana	271	1,467
Minnesota	268	1,542
Tennessee	262	1,633
Georgia	248	1,677
All States	196	56,347

to which corrections facilities are put. For example, we found that 16 states detained 9,069 youth in training schools in 1979. Likewise, 14 states reported 13,323 admissions to detention centers on a commitment status. In California alone, 10,142 admissions or 7.6 percent of all detention admissions were for purposes of a post-adjudication commitment rather than temporary custody during court processing. These findings allowed us in Table 40.10 to recompute those 1979 state detention and training school admission rates that reflect a policy of using detention centers as temporary holding facilities and training schools as post-adjudication placement facilities.

Next, we attempted a very tentative exploration of factors that might account for variation in state rates of detention and training school admissions using 1979 CIC data. Multiple regression techniques were employed using such independent variables as violent arrest rates, Part 1 property arrest rates, the bed capacity of each state, and teenage unemployment rates. For rates of detention admissions, these four independent variables explain 81.4 percent of the variation among the states, The number of detention beds per 100,000 youth population explains 76.8 percent of the variation in detention admission rates, with the rate of Part 1 property arrests adding only another 4.1 percent in explanatory power. Neither the violent arrest rate nor teenage unemployment rates explain much variation in state detention admissions rates.

For training school admission rates, on the other hand, the same independent variables account for only 32.9 percent of the state variations. Roughly, two-thirds of the variation among the states in training school admissions rates is not explained by serious youth crime, youth unemployment, or the availability of beds. Of these factors, the number of training school beds per 100,000 youth population accounts for 27.0 percent of the variation in rates of training school admissions or 82.1 percent of all the variation that is explained by the selected independent variables. Part 1 property arrest rates separately explain 4.5 percent of the variation among the states in training school admission rates. Neither teenage employment nor violent arrest rates significantly boost our explanatory ability.

Summary Of Juvenile Justice Trends

Data on juvenile arrests, court processing, and admissions to juvenile correctional facilities offer important information to assess juvenile justice policy directions of the last decade. Most striking is the progress in reducing the involvement of status offenders within the juvenile justice system between 1974-1979. Less encouraging is that similar progress was not achieved in the case of delinquent offenders. Moreover, the primary consequence of removing status offenders from the juvenile justice system was the large decline in female admissions to public correctional facilities while male admissions either remained stable or actually increased from 1974-1979. Also of importance is the leveling off of rates of Part 1 juvenile arrests from 1974-1979: This directly contradicts public perceptions of a steady and alarming increase in serious youth crime.

Preliminary analysis of state trends in rates of admissions to detention and training schools revealed a complex pattern of increases and decreases largely unrelated to the distribution of OJJDP funds. Indeed, juvenile correctional admissions are highly concentrated in a few states. An exploratory attempt to explain the large variations in state rates of correctional admissions suggested that most of the variation in detention admissions could be explained by the number of detention beds per 100,000 youth population. For training school admission rates, the number of beds per 100,000 youth population is also the most powerful explanatory variable; but nearly two-thirds of the variation in state training school admissions is not explained by bed availability, rates of juvenile arrests for serious crimes, or youth unemployment. Future research should analyze the determinants of the wide disparities between states in rates of detention and training school admissions. Other macro-level variables should be examined and more in-depth micro-level studies should be conducted to understand better the link between availability of beds and admissions to detention centers and training schools.

POLICY CONSIDERATIONS

The data presented in this paper permit a starting point for a thorough and systematic rethinking of juvenile justice. Yet even this first level of analysis suggests a number of immediate policy issues. In our opinion, policy considerations requiring urgent attention are as follows:

1. The removal of status offenders and non-offenders from secure institutions has been one of the more successful juvenile justice policy thrusts of the 1970s. Reports from state juvenile justice advisory committees, testimony delivered before Congressional Committees, and the findings of various studies attest to the success of this initiative. Kobrin and Klein, for example, in their national study of status offender programs, reported significant reductions in status offender admissions to detention centers and training schools. (Kobrin and Klein, 1982) The United States Census Bureau reported a sharp reduction of the number of status offenders held in secure facilities on a particular day in 1979 as compared to the same day in 1977. (U.S. Department of Justice, 1980) The findings of this study are consistent with those of others. There has, for instance, been a substantial decline in the number and rate of female admissions to detention centers and training schools. Because females made up the vast majority of the status offenders and non-offenders admitted to secure facilities, the decline in female admissions provides additional documentation for what has been achieved. Now, steps must be taken to ensure that the progress that has been made will not be reversed.

2. While the policy thrust to remove status offenders and non-offenders from secure institutions has proven to be a major success, the overall results with respect to de-institutionalization have been far less than what reformers had hoped for. As noted earlier, the decline in the rate of admissions to detention centers from 1971 to 1979 was a modest 5.1 percent. The decline in detention admission rates from 1974 to 1979 was 12.3 percent. Considering the fact that upwards of 40 percent of all youth detained in

the early 1970s were status offenders and non-offenders, and considering that large numbers of youth accused of minor and petty delinquent offenses were also detained, the reductions are, at best, disappointing. (U.S. House of Representatives, 1981)

The rate of admissions to training schools has remained relatively constant throughout the decade. There were substantial reductions in the rates of female admissions while rates of male admissions increased. The decline in the rates of female admissions were essentially offset by the increases for males.

As stated earlier, one of the major purposes of the Juvenile Justice and Delinquency Prevention Act was to provide states and localities with leadership and resources for the development of programs" . . . to divert juveniles from traditional juvenile justice systems and to provide critically needed alternatives to institutionalization." (Gough, 1976) Implicit in this policy was the assumption that the availability of alternatives would result in reducing input into the system.

Unfortunately, with few exceptions, this has proven not to be the case. Diversion and alternative programs have mushroomed while detention admission rates declined only slightly and training school admission rates not at all. In fact, many leading juvenile justice researchers and practitioners maintain that one of the unanticipated consequences of the proliferation of alternative programs has been a widening and strengthening act of the "net of social control." (Haugen, 1982)

This study has reported a statistical relationship between correctional admission rates and the number of detention and training school beds per 100,000 youth population. Significantly, admissions rates are relatively unaffected by juvenile arrests and teenage unemployment rates. If detention and training school beds are being used for purposes other than public safety and treatment, this creates a tremendous and perhaps unnecessary expense for taxpayers. This finding is strikingly similar to that of Poulin and his colleagues. (Poulin et al., 1980)

In light of these results, states and localities should adopt and aggressively pursue policies seeking to limit the use of detention and training school placements including, in some instances, closing down such facilities. The potential waste of limited public funds to be spent on the unnecessary confinement of youth becomes even more apparent when considered in light of projected declines in the eligible youth population as well as current fiscal realities.

3. There is a pressing need to develop strategies both to inform and educate the public about the realities of the juvenile crime problem. At present, a huge gap separates the trends in juvenile crime from the public's perception of the problem. The best available evidence suggests that the rate of serious juvenile crime, and violent youth crime in particular, has been relatively stable since the mid 1970s. In contrast, the public perceives that serious juvenile crime has been increasing as a steady and alarming rate. One can hardly expect the development of sound policies with respect to preventing and controlling youth crime unless and until the public's perception is brought more into line with the reality of the situation.

4. Enormous variation exists between the states in their rates of admissions to detention centers and training schools. These variations have persisted over time and are largely unexplained arrest factors. Needless to say, this disparity raises serious legal and public policy questions regarding due process, equal protection, and the exercise of discretion in the juvenile justice system.

More immediately, the large disparities between the states suggest a need to exert greater monitoring and regulation over discretionary decision making. They further suggest a need to develop mechanisms for the implementation of such things as national standards, dispositional guidelines, and legislative reform.

The problems in juvenile justice are so deep-seated and national in scope that the federal government must continue to play an active role in providing assistance to state and local units of government and public and private agencies and organizations. Accordingly, the federal government should continue:

a. To promote, encourage, and support juvenile justice research. Most importantly, the federal government can play an important role in assisting states and localities in the application of research findings to policy development, in the upgrading of practices, and in program development.

b. To collect, analyze, and disseminate data on the juvenile justice system.

c. To serve as an information clearing house and disseminate pertinent data, information, and studies to individuals and organizations throughout the country.

d. To provide technical assistance and consultation.

5. The primary method for distributing funds under the Juvenile Justice and Delinquency Prevention Act is through the formula grant program. This method is essentially a block grant program to states with funds distributed on a per capita youth population basis. The funds can be used in a flexible manner for the development of "... more effective education, training, research, prevention, diversion, treatment, and rehabilitation programs in the area of juvenile justice and programs to improve the juvenile justice system." (U.S. Senate Committee on the Judiciary, 1975)

The distribution of funds on a per capita youth population basis is an equitable and politically acceptable method for allocating resources. However, this approach has major deficiencies with respect to furthering the goals of de-institutionalization.

Under the block grant system, the states with the largest youth populations receive the bulk of the funds. But with a few notable exceptions, the larger states are not the ones with the highest rates of admissions to detention centers and training schools. In other words, if the goal is to reduce incarceration of youths, the block grant approach does not target resources to where the needs are greatest.

Also, it is clear that the excessive use of detention on the part of a few states is "... an enduring phenomenon resistant to change." (Poulin et al., 1980) For example, the states with the highest rates in 1979, were, by and large, the states with the highest rates in 1974 and in 1971.

These findings suggest that the use of the block grant strategy as a means of promoting de-institutionalization should be carefully re-examined. Such an assessment should consider the following:

• Can federal fiscal funding incentives be used to bring about substantial changes in state and local policies and practices with respect to de-institution-alization?

• Can resources be targeted to where the needs are greatest? If resources can be targeted, it must be done in such a way as not to appear to serve as an incentive or reward to states with higher rates of incarceration.

6. De-institutionalization policies must be broadened to take into account the interrelatedness of the juvenile justice, child welfare, mental health, and the newly emerging chemical dependency and private youth residential systems. Paul Lerman was one of the first to point out in a systematic way that one gets a distorted view of the impact of de-institutionalization policies by focusing solely on the juvenile system. It seems that ". . . there has emerged, in an unplanned fashion, a new youth-in-trouble system that includes old and new institutions from . . . juvenile correction, child welfare, . . . mental health" (Lerman, 1980:282) and chemical dependency. Lerman suggested that gains made in de-institutionalizing juveniles in the justice system could well be offset by corresponding increases in these other systems. While an assessment of the juvenile institutional trends in the child welfare, mental health, and chemical dependency systems is well beyond the scope and resources of this study, some data supporting Lerman's insights were collected. As reported earlier, there has been a significant increase in female admissions to private correctional settings.

In the state of Minnesota, which ranked 15th in the rate of admissions to training schools in 1979, data were collected at the state and local levels with respect to placements in all of the various youth-caring systems. While it appears that Minnesota's youth-caring systems are plagued with some of the same record keeping and information system problems commonly found elsewhere, the data show a tremendous growth in the numbers of youth placed in residential treatment settings, particularly on a "voluntary" basis. Specifically,

a. In 1976, there were 1,123 juveniles admitted to in-patient psychiatric settings in private hospitals in the Minneapolis/St. Paul Metropolitan Area. They accounted for 46,718 patient days. By 1980 the number of admissions had grown to 1,775 and they accounted for 74,201 patient days. (Mental Health Data Appendix, 1980)

b. In 1980, there were an estimated 3000 to 4000 juveniles admitted to in-patient chemical dependency treatment programs. Although it is unknown how many juveniles were admitted to such programs in the early 1970s, it is generally assumed that the numbers were substantially less because there were few chemical dependency residential treatment facilities at that time.[11]

---

[11] Letter from Cynthia Turner, Ph,D., Director, Planning, Research and Evaluation, State of Minnesota, Department of Public Welfare, Chemical Dependency Program Division, November 6, 1981.

c. Between fiscal years 1973 and 1981, the Minnesota Department of Public Welfare reported a substantial increase in the number of juveniles placed in group homes and residential treatment centers for the emotionally disturbed.[12]

In Minnesota, the growth in the number of out of home placements, the reasons and methods of referral, and the ultimate impact of these placements on youth raise significant policy questions. One can hypothesize that a "hidden" or private juvenile correctional system has rapidly evolved for disruptive or "acting out" youth who are no longer processed by the public juvenile justice control agencies. Moreover this second system may be vastly expanding the net of youth experiencing some kind of institutional control. The dimensions and nature of this second system of juvenile control should be a major component of future research agendas at both state and federal levels.

7. Any examination of the interrelationship between the various youth-caring systems should take into account the various public and private methods of financing services. In addition to the traditional public and quasi-public funding sources, consideration should be given to the role and impact of funds emanating from the private health care system.

The private sector has been assuming an increasingly larger role in paying for costs of residential care. Because payments are made through third party reimbursement as a part of health insurance coverage, little is known about the nature and extent of services provided and the total dollar amounts involved.

The area of chemical dependency can serve as an example of the potential implications of the role of the private sector. At present, there are 27 states with legislation mandating that private health care insurance provide reimbursement for the cost of chemical dependency treatment as part of their programs. There are some who feel that such requirements serve as strong incentives for promoting the use of in-patient care. They also feel that they are important factors contributing to the escalating costs of health care generally.

8. There is a need to collect comprehensive and reliable data on an ongoing basis concerning juveniles admitted to adult jails and local lock-ups. Rosemary Sarri, in 1974, noted that "an accurate account of the extent of juvenile jailing in the United States does not exist." (Sarri, 1974:4) That statement is just as true today as it was then. Hopefully, the collection of such data could be made part of an existing national criminal or juvenile justice data gathering system. Efforts must also be undertaken to collect data on the "hidden" juvenile justice system.

[12] The Department of Public Welfare classifies admissions to non-correctional facilities by facility type and by funding category. Funding categories represent more conservative indices of placement trends. Counts within one funding category, emotionally disturbed children, generally include placements in group homes and residential treatment centers, although some similar placements are made under other funding categories. Nevertheless data for the emotionally disturbed category indicate that in fiscal year 1973, 464 placements were funded. In fiscal year 1981, 1959 placements were funded.

CONCLUSION

Rethinking juvenile justice involves a process of posing policy questions and reviewing the best available data to formulate answers. It also requires a candid confrontation with both the successes and failures of past reform efforts. But this reassessment may produce new guidelines for more effective reform strategies.

We have learned that available data sources contain important findings that can be used by policymakers and reformers. But there are many other juvenile justice policy concerns not readily answered by available national data. For example, our review of juvenile justice information sources illustrated how little is known about the personal characteristics of the nearly half million children who are annually confined in public juvenile correctional facilities. Not much more is known about youth confined in adult prisons and jails. We lack even basic information about the consequences of juvenile incarceration in terms of public safety. Much more should be known about the impacts of these incarceration experiences on young lives.

The goal of rethinking juvenile justice is to help sustain the reform thrust of the 1970s. Both the goals and strategies of that movement must be carefully reexamined and re-evaluated. Likewise, more analysis should be given to the extreme resistance of the juvenile justice system to constructive reform approaches. This rethinking is not a mere intellectual exercise, it is critical to achieving the unfinished agenda of juvenile justice reform.

Acknowledgements: Extensive data retrieval, literature searches, and computational services were provided by Paul Litsky, Theresa Costello, and Dan Haugen. Data for this report were generously provided by staff of the Uniform Crime Reports, National Center for Juvenile Justice, and U.S. Census Bureau. In several instances special data requests for previously unpublished data were provided on short notice. We would especially like to commend Paul Zolbe of the FBI, Rick, Meyer, Jim Stephens of the Census Bureau and Howard Snyder of NCJJ.

Helpful suggestions about the strengths and limitations of the data were provided by Charles Lauer and Buddy Howell of OJJDP and Hunter Jurst of NCJJ. Valuable advice for data analysis and interpretation came form Ken Polk, Jim Austin, Solomon Krobrin, Lloyd Ohlin, Robert Coates, Rosemary Sarri, Delbert Elliott, Brad Smith, Paul Demuro, Jack Calhoun, Robert Figlio, Nancy Anderson, John Korbelick, Jerome Beker, Tom Dewar, Barbara Knudson, Barry Feld, and David Hollister.

Typing and production of graphs were performed by Christy Lord, Jan Casteel, and Dawn Saito.

Financial support for the research was provided by the Northwest Area Foundation. The Spring Hill Center, the Dayton-Hudson Foundation and the Northwest Area Foundation provided support for sharing and making the study findings available.

REFERENCES

ABT Associates (1981). *American Prisons and Jails.* National Institute of Justice, Washington, D.C.

Chesney-Lind, M. (1977). "Judicial Paternalism and the Female Status Offender: Training Women to Know Their Place." *Crime and Delinquency,* April: 121-30.

Elliot, D.S., S.S. Ageton, and D. Huizinga (1989). *The National Youth Survey*. Behavioral Research Institute, Boulder, Colorado.

Federal Bureau of Investigation (1980).*Uniform Crime Reports* 1979. U.S. Government Printing Office, Washington, D.C.

Gough, A.R. (1976). *Beyond Control: Status Offenders in the Juvenile Court*. Ballinger, Boston, Massachusetts.

Haugen, D. (1982) *"Decriminalization."* University of Minnesota, Minneapolis, Minnesota, unpublished.

Kobrin, S and M. W. Klein (1982). *National Evaluation of the Deinstitutionalization of Status Offenders Programs—Executive Summary*. Social Science Research Institute, University of Southern California, Los Angeles, California.

Krisberg, B. and J. Austin (1978).*The Children of Ishmael*. Mayfield, Palo Alto, California.

Lerman, P. (1980). "Trends and Issues in Deinstitutionalization of Youths in Trouble."*Crime and Delinquency*, July: 282

McDermott, J. M. and M. J. Hindelang (1981).*Juvenile Criminal Behavior in the United States: Its Trends and Patterns*. Office of Juvenile Justice and Delinquency Prevention, Washington, D.C.

Metropolitan Health Board (1980). *Mental Health Index*. Minneapolis, Minnesota.

National Center For Juvenile Justice (1981). *Delinquency 1978: United States Estimates of Cases Processed by Courts with Juvenile Court Jurisdiction*. Pittsburgh, Pennsylvania.

Poulin, J.E. et al. (1980). "Juveniles in Detention Centers and Jails: An Analysis of State Violations during the Mid 1970's." *Reports of National Juvenile Justice Assessment Centers,* U.S. Government Printing Office, Washington D.C.

Sarri, R. (1974). *Under Lock and Key*: Juveniles in Jails and Detention. National Association of Juvenile Corrections, Ann Arbor, Michigan.

United States Bureau of The Census (1978). *Children in Custody*. U.S. Government Printing Office, Washington, D.C.

United States Bureau of Census (1978). *State and Local Probation and Parole Systems*. U.S. Government Printing Office, Washington D.C.

United States Department of Justice (1980). *Children in Custody: Advance Report on the 1979 Census of Public Juvenile Facilities*. Office of Juvenile Justice and Delinquency Prevention, U.S. Government Printing Office, Washington, D.C.

United States House of Representatives, Committee on Education and Labor (1981). *Compilation of the Juvenile Justice Act*. U.S. Government Printing Office, Washington, D.C.

United States Senate Committee on the Judiciary (1975). *Ford Administration Stifles Juvenile Justice Policy*. U.S. Government Printing Office, Washington, D.C.

Summary and Discussion

THE ARTICLES in Part Five have focused on the social control of juvenile delinquency. A common theme throughout all of the articles is the idea that if delinquency is to be controlled meaningfully in the future, society must seriously rethink current laws, policies, programs, and societal attitudes regarding juvenile delinquency.

Part Five begins with a synopsis of Edwin Schur's classic book *Radical Non-Intervention: Rethinking the Delinquency Problem*. Utilizing the labeling perspective, Schur contends that many of society's efforts to control and prevent juvenile delinquency are unsuccessful, and in fact, rather than reducing the problem of delinquency, may exacerbate it. Radical non-intervention as a social policy requires that society clearly and uniformly define those behaviors which society cannot and will not tolerate from youths. Other behaviors which can and sometimes are tolerated such as truancy, smoking, running away from home, and other status offenses (acts that are illegal only because of the offender's status as a juvenile) should not be processed through the legal system. In many cases, he insists, the best way to treat minor forms of youthful norm violation would be to simply ignore them. This expansion of society's range of tolerance for adolescent behavior would eliminate the stigma experienced by many youths who are labeled delinquent by the juvenile justice system for committing acts that would be legal if they were adults. From Schur's perspective this delinquent label and subsequent stigma only leads to further norm violation and internalization of the delinquent role by youths.

The first three articles in Part Five take a critical look at the juvenile justice system. Joyce Dougherty's "Negotiating Justice in the Juvenile System . . ." compares and contrasts the negotiation which often occurs during the intake phase of the juvenile court with adult criminal plea bargaining. The similarities discussed are striking, but she points out that the differences are significant. Most importantly, according to Dougherty, is the coercion experienced by juveniles under the guise of benevolence and protection. Although certain due process rights (such as the right to remain silent) are legally extended to juveniles during intake, Dougherty points out that exercising those rights is likely to be costly to the youth. She indicates that whereas approximately 80 percent of juvenile cases are handled through intake negotiations which does not lead to official adjudication, when youths fail to cooperate, admit their guilt, and otherwise forfeit some of their basic rights, they are extremely likely to be adjudicated delinquent. Dougherty's article concludes with a call for more research into juvenile intake negotiations and suggests that this phase of the juvenile justice system needs to be carefully rethought.

"Girls in Jail" by Meda Chesney-Lind looks at an even more controversial aspect of juvenile corrections. For decades the federal government has first urged, and finally required the removal of juveniles from adult jails. As incidents of youths being beaten, raped, and killed have come to public attention, serious efforts have been made to find alternatives to placing juveniles in jail. Yet, as Chesney-Lind points out, juveniles are jailed by the thousands annually. Further, she indicates that girls are more likely to be jailed for relatively trivial offenses and may spend a longer time in jail than their male counterparts who committed more serious crimes. Interestingly, Chesney-Lind provides evidence that many of the girls held in jails committed status offenses—those acts which Edwin Schur argued would be better ignored! The problems of harassment, neglect, physical abuse, and rape suffered by juvenile females is unconscionable regardless of their offense. Yet, it is even more shocking to learn that they may suffer this abuse as a result of having committed acts that would have been legal if they were adults.

The article "Fulfilling Juvenile Restitution Requirements in Community Correctional Programs" written by former juvenile court judge H. Ted Rubin indicates that there are viable alternatives to placing delinquent youths in jails. His article discusses some specific Day Treatment and Residential Settings as well as some drug and alcohol treatment programs for youths. He also discusses juvenile restitution programs. Rubin points out however, that rarely has juvenile corrections successfully implemented a program to combine the two alternatives (community corrections and restitution). He emphasizes the need for community placement agencies to be aware of the restitution requirements mandated by the court and to incorporate methods for fulfilling those requirements into their programs. His suggestions would demand the serious rethinking of current juvenile correctional practices.

Similarly, William Kvraceus' article "Delinquency Prevention" also demands the rethinking of the juvenile justice system, and insists that "legislation, financing, and law enforcement are not enough." Kvraceus contends that the social problem of juvenile delinquency can be meaningfully addressed only if nine issues are addressed: (1) the public must be willing to "give up" delinquency (2) delinquency must be better defined (3) community attitudes must be positive (4) knowledge and facts must precede planning and policies (5) youths must be involved in the solutions (6) early identification and referral must take place (7) goals and activities of agencies must be clearly stated and continuously evaluated (8) local resources must be coordinated, and (9) the positive aspects of delinquency must be ignored.

The first five and the last three points made by Kvraceus are quite consistent with the policy of radical non-intervention espoused by Schur. However, a clear point of departure can be found in the sixth suggestion by Kvraceus, where he calls for the early identification and referral of "future delinquents." This early identification and referral could lead to the labeling and stigmatization against which Schur warns. Nevertheless, both Schur and Kvraceus are insisting that the problem of delinquency must be redefined and reassessed. Also, both call for a reevaluation of the norms regarding delinquency.

Virginia Burns and Leonard Stern also address the limitations of delinquency prevention programs and stress the need for new preventive efforts. Their article was part of the prestigious *Task Force Report on Juvenile Delinquency* which began this anthology as the classic work in Part One. Like Kvraceus, Burns and Stern warn that simply pumping new money into old efforts will not prove successful in controlling and preventing juvenile delinquency. Their article, like Schur's book and the article by Kvraceus, call for a more clearly enunciated definition of delinquency. Similarly they warn that predicting delinquency is a very inexact process, and that all programs of prevention should avoid encapsulating individuals who in all probability would not have actually become delinquent if left alone.

Consistent with the argument propounded by Schur, Burns and Stern assert that "The line between acceptable deviance from preferred behavior and intolerable, dangerous delinquency is not always easy to find . . ." and that definitions of tolerable and intolerable behavior are socially determined. They too call for a rethinking of the definition of delinquency and a broadening of the range of tolerance regarding youthful behavior. Those activities which are not dangerous enough to require official action are probably best left alone.

Don Gibbons reviews major criminological theories regarding the etiology of delinquent behavior in his article "Juvenile Delinquency: Can Social Science Find a Cure?" After summarizing major developments in criminological theories, Gibbons summarizes that attitudes toward delinquency treatment and prevention have grown very pessimistic. Gibbons' brief summary of various delinquency treatment and prevention programs confirms why much of the pessimism may be deserved.

On the other hand, Gibbons points out that it is not clear that all correctional efforts have been totally ineffectual and unsuccessful. Rather, he concludes that there is evidence which suggests that some kinds of treatment and prevention efforts may have positive effects. Gibbons asserts that the search for causal theories and effective delinquency treatment and prevention strategies has not been in vain, nor should it be ended. Rather, it should be recognized that some theories and some strategies have been much more productive than others. He ends his article with a call for new and continued scientific research in the areas of delinquency causation and treatment.

The final article "Rethinking Juvenile Justice" by Barry Krisberg and Ira Schwartz examines some of the major policy changes in the handling of juvenile delinquents that resulted from the Juvenile Justice and Delinquency Prevention Act of 1974. Their primary focus is on the impact of the deinstitutionalization movement in the handling of delinquents.

After presenting a variety of data on juvenile delinquency (and discussing some of the problems and inconsistencies in those data), Krisberg and Schwartz suggest eight major policy issues regarding juvenile delinquency. Similar to Gibbon's contention, they indicate that the removal of status offenders and nonoffenders from secure institutions has been a success. However, they also point out that while deinstitution-alization has been a success, there is evidence that alternatives have not diverted large numbers of juveniles from the juvenile justice system as intended. Krisberg and

Schwartz contend that there must be aggressive policies at the state and local level to limit the use of detention and training school facilities, perhaps closing many of them down entirely.

Krisberg and Schwartz also address the problem of the general public's misconception about the realities of juvenile crime. Sounding a theme quite close to that of Gibbons', they indicate that serious juvenile crime has not been increasing at the alarming rate perceived by most people. Rather, data indicate that serious juvenile crime has leveled off. Like Gibbons, Krisberg and Schwartz call for more research on juvenile delinquency, and contend that the federal government should pay a significant role in financing that research. Krisberg and Schwartz conclude by reemphasizing a theme found throughout all of the articles in Part Five—and in many ways, suggested by all of the articles in this entire book—the need to rethink juvenile justice and the problem of delinquency. They insist, and we concur, that this "rethinking" must not be simply an intellectual exercise.

Questions for Review and Discussion

1. Explain Edwin Schur's policy of "radical non-intervention." Do you agree with his assessment that much of what is considered delinquent today would be better ignored? If so, to what types of delinquency should society apply Schur's suggestion of "leaving the kids alone?" What types of delinquency cannot be ignored?

2. What are the similarities between juvenile intake and adult plea bargaining as outlined by Joyce Dougherty? What are the differences? What does she see as the most serious problem with juvenile intake?

3. In her article "Girls in Jail'" Meda Chesney-Lind contends that female delinquents are discriminated against in the juvenile justice system in a number of ways. What are some of these? How does Chesney-Lind explain this discrimination? What does she recommend be done to solve the problem?

4. How does Ted Rubin contend that juvenile restitution requirements should be filled in community correctional programs?

5. William Kvraceus contends that youths must be involved in the solutions to delinquency. Do you agree with this assessment? If so, in what ways can youths become actively involved? If not, why not?

6. Virginia Burns and Leonard Stern note a number of "questions and concerns which should guide and caution us as we establish the proper parameters of delinquency prevention efforts." What are these questions and concerns? Do Burns and Stern believe that an effective delinquency prevention program is possible? If so, what would be the key elements of such a program?

7. Don Gibbons asks the question regarding delinquency "Can social science find a cure?" What is his answer? Do you agree or disagree with his final assessment?

8. How do Barry Krisberg and Ira Schwartz assess the overall results of deinstitutionalization efforts in the United States since passage of the Juvenile Justice and Delinquency Prevention Act of 1974? Summarize some of their major suggestions for changes if the problem of juvenile delinquency is to be adequately addressed in the future.

9. Based upon the articles in Part Five, outline the major ideas that you view as an essential part of a program for juvenile delinquency control, treatment, and prevention.